Economics and Public Policy in

WATER RESOURCE DEVELOPMENT

edited by | **STEPHEN C. SMITH**

EMERY N. CASTLE

IOWA STATE UNIVERSITY PRESS

Ames, IOWA, U.S.A.

Second printing, 1965
Third printing, 1966

LITHOPRINTED IN THE UNITED STATES OF AMERICA BY
CUSHING - MALLOY, INC., ANN ARBOR, MICHIGAN, 1966

Preface

THE GENESIS of this book was in the deliberations of the Committee on the Economics of Water Resources Development. The fruits of these deliberations are incorporated in a series of 12 annual reports. This committee, appointed by the Western Agricultural Economics Research Council, is composed of representatives from the departments of Agricultural Economics in the 11 western states. Meetings of these representatives along with invited participants from water resources agencies were arranged for the purpose of making initial explorations into problem areas. On the basis of this examination, formal research projects have been initiated and carried out through the western land-grant universities. These projects have taken the form of regional projects as well as individual investigations.

The demand for the Committee's reports has exceeded the quantity available. Therefore, we decided to select a group of papers as a nucleus around which to build a more complete treatment of water resources development problems. Thus 12 papers were initially selected from among those originally presented to the committee. These papers appear in this volume as Chapters 2, 5, 7, 8, 9, 10, 12, 14, 16, 18, 19 and 22. To this selection other papers were added which complement the initial group.

The editors want to acknowledge their appreciation to the authors for their efforts in revising their papers. Some have been revised to reflect current situations, while we have felt it desirable for others to remain in the original form. In this way the date of original presentation will be given emphasis and the stream of economic thought will be clearer.

Special acknowledgment must be given to The Farm Foundation, Chicago, Illinois, for their continued financial support. The Committee on the Economics of Water Resources Development has received support throughout the years from The Farm Foundation through a grant to the Western Agricultural Economics Research Council. Further, The Farm Foundation supported the publication of this volume as a separate undertaking. Therefore both Committee members and other participants in the annual meetings are indebted to The Foundation.

OWEN L. BROUGH
Washington State University

Contents

CONTENTS

STEPHEN C. SMITH is Professor of Economics at Colorado State University. He has been on the staff of Civil Functions, Office of the Secretary of the Army; the University of California, Berkeley; and the Tennessee Valley Authority. His research and writing in natural resource economics have dealt mainly with questions of organization.

EMERY N. CASTLE is Professor of Agricultural Economics at Oregon State University. He has developed a productive water resources research program and has served on the staff of Purdue University, Kansas State University, The Federal Reserve Bank at Kansas City, and the Bureau of Land Management, U.S. Department of the Interior.

Chapter 1

STEPHEN C. SMITH
EMERY N. CASTLE

Introduction

W ATER RESOURCES DEVELOPMENT has been an issue in public policy at local, state and national levels of government for over a century. In fact, more than 60 years have elapsed since the basic reclamation legislation was enacted. During this period the application of formal economics to issues in water policy has been meager, with a few thoughts in this direction being expressed in the 1920's but with the real impetus coming in the 1930-40 period. But it was not until the latter part of the 40's and early 50's that the serious thinking of the preceding decade was published. This early literature is mentioned in the chapters which follow. Two of these papers, prepared for the Committee on the Economics of Water Resources Development, are published as Chapters 2 and 12.

Agricultural economists and governmental agency economists played a dominant role in this early work, and in the 1960's probably the largest group of economists working in the area are from these groups. By the latter part of the 1950's and the 1960's a wider professional concern with public investment grew, and articles and books have continued to appear. The proceedings of the Committee have been a part of this literature, although circulated only to a limited audience. Continued professional demand for the points of view expressed through this series of reports led to the planning of this volume.

1

APPROACH TO WATER POLICY

The approach to policy has been rather pragmatic, for this is the nature of public action. To understand it and to be useful in its development, a point of view which does not attempt to look at the whole problem nor integrate the many facets yields results which are lacking in relevance. Anyone who studies water policy — the resolution of conflicts over water resources use — is impressed by the multiplicity of interest groups and the variety of objectives. No one academic discipline has within it constructs which can handle all of the policy issues. Man, as an analyst, must exercise care or he may leave the impression that he can do more than he is really equipped to do. Policy change, in fact, is incremental.

Although the Committee and the editors never formally agreed to the above position, it is believed their activities have been consistent with it. Thus this point of view has served as a guide in selecting papers. Most of the following chapters were originally prepared for the Committee with other sources serving to round out the discussion. Because of this many-sided character of water policy, the economist, lawyer, political scientist and engineer each have a voice and must be heard in order to understand economics in water policy.

The desire has been to let the authors speak rather than intersperse with editorial comments. We do not find "lack-of-fit" in style to be jarring but useful to emphasize that the central concern is water policy and its nature. By taking this perspective, the traditional orientation upon the economics of the firm and the market is not the central theme, albeit it is important and not neglected as an underlying institution of our economy. In fact, a focal point of policy analysis is with the institutions which yield the policy result, for these are not given and fixed and cannot be handled as if they were, without realizing the fictional character of "as if."

Three basic categories of policy serve as organizing ideas — economic evaluation, financing and organization — and are distributed among five sections. Economic evaluation issues are divided into two parts, with the chapters emphasizing quantification grouped in one section. Likewise with questions of organization, the chapters mainly dealing with issues of law are grouped together. But in both cases, the distinction is one of convenience rather than conceptual presentation. Within each section it will become evident that the authors have not lost sight of the other sections.

The problem of economic evaluation of public expenditures for water development has been thorny and persistent with a political clamor "to do it." This clamor has resulted in the publication of several basic documents by the federal government. These include the following:

(a) U.S. Federal Inter-Agency River Basin Committee, Subcommittee on Benefits and Costs, "Proposed Practices for Economic Analysis of River Basin Projects," (Government Printing Office, Washington, 1950) 85pp.

(b) Clark, J. M., E. L. Grant, and M. M. Kelso, "Secondary or Indirect Benefits of Water-Use Projects," Report of a Panel of Consultants to M. W. Straus, Commissioner, Bureau of Reclamation, June 26, 1952.

(c) U.S. Federal Inter-Agency Committee on Water Resources, Subcommittee on Evaluation Standards, "Proposed Practices for Economic Analysis of River Basin Projects," (Government Printing Office, Washington, 1958) 56pp.

(d) U.S., the President's Water Resources Council, "Policies, Standards, and Procedures in the Formulation, Evaluation, and Review of Plans for Use and Development of Water and Related Land Resources," (Government Printing Office, Washington, 1962) U.S. Senate Document No. 97, 87th Congress, 2nd Session, 13pp.

These documents are not reviewed in detail but are mentioned several times in the text.

Benefit-Cost Analysis

Chapters 2 and 3 deal with theoretical and practical issues of benefit-cost analysis and present an interesting comparison with particular reference to their conclusions. One was written in 1954 and the other almost a decade later in 1961. During the intervening years the literature elaborated on the earlier structure and began to adapt activity and other forms of analysis as noted in Chapter 11. But the formalities of benefit-cost analysis are set in a governmental structure which allocates water development funds through a public budgetary process. This fact has been handled differently, and as a side issue, by many contributors to the literature. Chapters 4 and 5 directly consider the question of budget allocation as it relates to investment in water resources development.

These investment decisions are made by our political processes, but of all of the professions, engineering has played a central role at all decision levels. Consequently, a prominent economist, following his association with a water development program, was asked for his view of the relationship between economics and engineering, while a prominent water engineer was asked to address the same subject. Chapters 6 and 7 yield insight into interfield relationships calling for a greater degree of integration.

The chapters in Part II deal with various aspects of quantification in the analysis of public investment in water resources economics. For the most part the desire was to handle issues of quantification directly rather than just "talk about them." The day-to-day problems of quantifying direct benefits from western irrigation development are examined critically in Chapter 8. In similar detail, but in an eastern setting, the problem of obtaining quantitative information on flood protection benefits is the issue in Chapter 10. As is well illustrated, quantification is more than wanting a particular number. It must encompass the design of the organizational system through which it is obtained. These "details" are important if we consider the size of the federal

and other budgets, the number of people engaged in this one activity and
the influence of the resulting decision on the day-to-day activities of
people throughout the nation.

Other quantitative techniques than "typical" benefit-cost type analysis are important and are being used to an increasing extent. Aggregate production function analysis is applied in the instance of Chapter 9
to the question of irrigation. Another approach — activity analysis — is
discussed in Chapter 11. Its application to "small" problems has been
particularly helpful. Interest in developing the technique has been high
and is appraised from a background of having tested its use.

Evaluation has been separated from financing because their purposes are different, yet they must be considered hand-in-hand. The
struggle over who pays, and how much, is often decisive in the issue of
whether a water development project is approved. Cost allocation is
the central theme of these issues, and Chapter 12 represents the foundation for much of the subsequent literature during the following decade. But the problem of dividing costs among cooperating agencies
must also be considered as shown in Chapter 13. In fact, the frequency
with which different agencies have grouped themselves together to develop a water project has been increasing and has been an issue in international river basins such as the Columbia. Questions of pricing,
cost allocation and cost sharing are separate yet interwoven within the
financing web. The functions of "water price" and the "pricing complex" and to what extent these have been and can be separated from
costs are discussed in Chapter 14.

Background of Water Rights

The analyses in the chapters mentioned have been directed mainly
to public projects; yet the most prevalent means of obtaining water is
for the user to capture it according to rules of property. Even the
large projects cannot be operated devoid of these rules. Consequently,
an understanding of these rights themselves and their economic meaning is imperative. The four chapters in Part IV contribute to this understanding. Chapter 15 pioneers into an examination of the economic
underpinnings of water rights and the role of economic analysis in
dealing with this type of subject matter. If fact, as one reads this
chapter and ponders some of the earlier discussion, the meaning and
usefulness of the concept of a "scientific fiction" should become clearer.

The beneficial-use concept as applied to surface water is examined
in Chapter 16. A better understanding of its content will help overcome
one of the stumbling blocks inhibiting lawyers and economists from
communicating with each other. Groundwater is also significant in the
United States and particularly in the 17 western states. Rights to this
water have developed along different lines as discussed by a leading
water rights scholar in Chapter 17. Not only do individuals and water
development organizations come into conflict with each other over the
rights to use water, but also the relationships between state and federal

governments have been a focal point of disagreement. The background of these differences is the subject of Chapter 18.

At mid-twentieth century more is required to bring water to beneficial use than a system of water rights, although it provides a basis for further action. The organization of groups of people is necessary whether the problem is one of supplying water to a community or working between nations to agree to the development of large basins. On the community level, the public district or other form of public corporation has been used. It has been adaptable to many situations, and the problems found in integrating the management of surface and groundwater (Chapter 19) are also prevalent in other localities. An organization which may fit a situation at a particular time and place may not be suitable to another. Both the law and organizations have to adapt to the dynamic conditions of our economy. One of the biggest changes which has come about is the increased urbanization of our economy. It is this shift as it relates to water organizations and water rights that is discussed in Chapter 20.

For many years water resources development has received special attention at the highest national levels, yet the critics remain unsatisfied in terms of administrative and political action. Chapters 21 and 22 delve into some of the basic issues of this problem as a question of political decision making as well as administrative organization. Water resources development is not just a question of internal national concern, particularly to a world whose citizenry is striving for greater economic and political development. International streams now become significant resources for national economic development. The old question of the right to use water is raised on a new level (Chapter 23), and the answer can make a significant contribution toward the development of the world's economy and peace.

PART I

Economic Evaluation, Concepts

S. V. CIRIACY-WANTRUP is Professor of Agricultural Economics at the University of California, Berkeley. His significant contributions to the field of natural resource economics have earned him a national and international reputation.

Chapter 2

S. V. CIRIACY-WANTRUP

Benefit-Cost Analysis And Public Resource Development*

DECISIONS BY THE GOVERNMENT regarding resource development are essentially political rather than economic. This holds for their substance, for the social process by which they are reached, and for the institutions through which they are implemented. This in itself is merely a commonplace observation of reality, neutral in terms of value judgments. But in connection with my topic it gives rise to a crucial question.

There is fairly general agreement that benefit-cost analysis is subject to many weaknesses. There is also recognition that benefit-cost analysis can be and has been distorted and abused.[1] We may ask then: Is it worthwhile investing considerable effort and expense in benefit-cost analysis if the risk of misleading results is great and — even though this risk is avoided — if the results are of relatively minor significance as compared with political factors in actually affecting public resource development?

*Giannini Foundation Paper No. 146. An earlier version of this paper was presented before the Annual Meeting, American Association for the Advancement of Science, Joint Session, Sections K (Economics) and M (Engineering), Dec. 27, 1954; and published in Rept. No. 3 of the Committee on the Economics of Water Resources Development; also in the *Jour. Farm Econ.*, Vol. 37, No. 4, 1955, pp. 676-89.

This question has been answered in the negative by individuals and groups with quite different attitudes toward public resource development. Some regard benefit-cost analysis as merely a waste. Others feel that economic measurement — being allegedly "static" — understates the "induced" benefits. Benefit-cost analysis thus tends to hold public resource development at a lower level than is desirable. Therefore, instead of benefit-cost analysis, some feel that the political process should be relied upon. Still others fear that inflated benefit-cost ratios may be a pretext for the government to propose projects that are economically unsound, to be undertaken mainly for empire building of a particular agency or to satisfy a pressure group. Alternatively, if the projects are economically sound, they should be paid for by beneficiaries. Thus, instead of benefit-cost analysis, many feel that "willingness to repay" a portion of the costs should be made the criterion for public resource development.

I should like to submit — and at this point of my chapter, it is meant merely as a proposition — that this question can be answered clearly in the affirmative. This means that benefit-cost analysis by the government appears worthwhile *in spite* of its weaknesses, its risks and its relatively small, direct influence upon the actual course of events.

ABUSE OF BENEFIT-COST ANALYSIS

The first point mentioned in support of this proposition relates to distortion and abuse of benefit-cost analysis. We must keep in mind that economic and pseudoeconomic arguments are by far the most important weapons in the arsenal of opposed regional, industrial and occupational interests contending in the political arena for or against a public project. Hence, distortion and abuse of benefit-cost analysis would not disappear if the government were to stay out of it. Quite the contrary. There would then be no calculation in which the general public could have confidence and that could be used as a standard to measure various claims. Furthermore, there would be no calculation easily open to public scrutiny in every detail. Such a standard can be provided only by a government. Even if this standard is not simon-pure compared with an ideal standard conceived through economic theory, it still serves a worthwhile purpose *to restrain the abuse of economic arguments in the political process.*

We may admit that abuse of government benefit-cost analysis is more dangerous in its consequences than abuse of private calculations because of the greater confidence placed in the government by the general public. In the United States, however, abuse of the government standard is made more difficult by the variety of government institutions.

In benefit-cost analysis, as in other fields, the U.S. government is not a monolithic structure. Besides the federal government, state governments are highly important in resource development. In all these governments there is division between the executive and the legislative branches. In the federal government alone, the agencies engaged in benefit-cost analysis comprise at least four major executive departments (some of them with several fairly independent bureaus), the Federal Power Commission and, of course, the Bureau of the Budget. Many of these government agencies have their own traditions and objectives in benefit-cost analysis. Some of them compete directly or indirectly for public funds and therefore take a lively interest in each other's calculations. The rivalries and duplications among various agencies are well known. From the standpoint of benefit-cost analysis, however, the results have not been all bad. Inconsistencies and conflicts are brought into the open. Mutual review and criticism encourage improvements.

QUANTIFYING IN BENEFIT-COST ANALYSIS

Benefit-cost analysis requires quantification both in physical and economic terms. Quantifying in economic terms involves evaluating on the basis of a common denominator or weight. In practice this means money, although other denominators are conceivable and are used in economic theory.

The necessity of quantifying in terms of money is frequently pointed out as a weakness of benefit-cost analysis. We may wonder whether this necessity does have a positive side. Economics and the social sciences in general do not stand alone in dealing with important problem areas in which quantifying is difficult or irrelevant. On the other hand, an attempt to overcome these difficulties and to determine the relevance of quantification is an important stimulus of scientific progress. In economics, particularly, an attempt at evaluation compels the student to face and take into account his own preferences, to scrutinize whether or not he has considered all relevant variables and to get some idea of the relations among the variables and the institutional restrictions in economic measurement.

An attempt to quantify in one science frequently has stimulating effects upon others. This holds for benefit-cost analysis. Engineers, hydrologists, ecologists and other physical scientists who furnish the necessary basic data for benefit-cost analysis have sometimes regarded the social scientist as an irritant, if not as a nuisance. But would they deny that his persistent quest for additional quantitative information has stimulated research in the physical problems of flood control, reclamation and land management?

It may be argued, therefore, that the mere necessity of quantifying makes benefit-cost analysis worthwhile *because of its stimulating effects in expanding scientific understanding of the physical as well as social problems involved in public resource development.* This role of benefit-cost analysis, like the preceding one of restraining the abuse of economic arguments in the political process, exists even if some weaknesses could not be overcome and if direct influences upon policy decisions should remain relatively minor.

After dealing with the two most frequent general objections against benefit-cost analysis, let us now attempt to appraise some of its weaknesses and to consider potentialities for reducing them. If these potentialities could be realized, the influence of benefit-cost analysis would be greater.

EXTRAMARKET BENEFITS AND COSTS

When the necessity of quantifying is cited as a weakness of benefit-cost analysis, two types of benefits and costs are usually mentioned or implied: "intangible" and "indirect" or "secondary." The evaluation problems posed are theoretically intriguing and of considerable practical significance. Next to problems of cost allocation,[2] such evaluation raises the most controversial problems of benefit-cost analysis among students and government agencies.

I should like to focus on these two problems in this chapter. The problem of "intangibles" is considered first because its discussion touches upon the more basic weaknesses of benefit-cost analysis.

At first glance, one portion of benefits and costs appears rather obvious and simple to evaluate. Such items are usually called "tangible." Examples are the value of cotton produced by an irrigation project and the costs of cotton, the dam and the productive agricultural areas flooded by the reservoir. On the other hand, if the project water is to be used to rehabilitate wintering grounds for waterfowl (such as the "grasslands" in the western San Joaquin Valley), if the dam interferes with anadromous fisheries (as in most rivers of the Pacific Slope) and if a reservoir floods a canyon — a "product" of which is impressive scenery as in the Upper Colorado Storage Project — these benefits and costs are usually called "intangible."

The price of cotton, of course, is reported every morning in the newspapers. Similarly, the current prices of raw materials, the wages and the interest rates used in computing the costs of the cotton and of the dam can be ascertained easily. The same holds for the price of an acre of agricultural land that is flooded. However, if such unit values yielded directly by the market are to be used in public resource development, such use is by no means obvious and simple. At this point I do not refer to the problems connected with elasticities of demand and supply, with economic fluctuations, with changes over time of preferences and technology and with the uncertainties attaching to all these estimates. Solution of these problems is not simple, but practical approximations can be found. More basic difficulties are created by the fact that the functioning and results of the price system itself are profoundly affected by aggregate income, income distribution and market form. These in turn are affected by a host of social institutions having an important and highly complex status in individual preference systems.

For some purposes it makes sense in economic analysis to regard properly defined institutional conditions as dependent or independent

variables. For example, relations among the systems of tenure, taxation and credit on one side and resource development on the other may
be discussed usefully in this way. Similarly, the effects of changes in
particular statutes or government organization can be studied.[3] On the
other hand, for purposes of benefit-cost analysis, which comprises only
a small part of economic analysis, most social institutions can only be
brought into the calculation as logical restrictions (constraints). This
means that benefit-cost analysis has relevance for an economic criterion of public resource development only under "given" institutional
conditions. The investigator should be clear about this even if he does
not state the significant institutional conditions explicitly.

    Institutional restrictions on the validity and relevance of values di-
rectly yielded by the market are far more severe than the additional
restrictive assumptions that become necessary if evaluation is extended
to those benefits and costs not evaluated directly in the market place.
We may wonder whether or not economists are justified in placing
great confidence in the validity and relevance of the price of cotton, for
example, in evaluating water resource development and rejecting the
evaluation of recreational opportunities as belonging to the field of
meta-economics.

    The implied conclusion is not that benefit-cost analysis of "tangi-
bles" should be abandoned. Rather, in accordance with the over-all
role of benefit-cost analysis suggested above, evaluation procedures
should be tightened but not necessarily confined to goods whose values
are directly yielded by the market. The semantics of "tangible" and
"intangible" reflect and strengthen confusion and emotional attitudes in
matters of evaluation. Various evaluation procedures range from those
that use market values directly to those that use market values with
considerable adjustments, or only indirectly.

    In public resource development in the United States, recreational
opportunities in a broad sense — including fish and game, wilderness
areas and national and state parks — are some of the items among extramarket values that may well be considered in benefit-cost analysis.
Whether the economist likes it or not, evaluation of these items (and
also dismissal of such evaluation) is already a part of the political
process. Reports of fish and game departments and other public agencies illustrate many attempts to evaluate these resources. We may
have professional doubts about some of the procedures used. Still,
these attempts should be encouraged. Otherwise the arguments of
well-organized groups interested in market values alone, who dismiss
these resources as "intangible," might receive disproportionate attention in policy decisions.[4]

    This is not to suggest that *all* benefits of recreational resources
could be evaluated. In connection with many such resources, however,
market values can be used indirectly — for example, through analyzing
data on fees, leases and real estate transactions. In other cases,
measurement in terms of physical units of use — for example, man-
days — can be accomplished fairly easily. Values of additional units of

use can be approached through questionnaires and the study of behavior in other experimental choice situations. Even such crude and partial measurement is more useful than disregarding these values altogether or substituting for them some figure based on the expenditures of users for transportation, room and board, guns, fishing tackle and similar items.

PRIMARY (DIRECT) AND SECONDARY (INDIRECT) BENEFITS AND COSTS

Let us turn to the problem of indirect benefits and costs. Although this problem is sometimes confused with that of "intangibles" — "indirect" and "intangible" are even used interchangeably — there is little relation between the two. Most indirect benefits and costs considered in benefit-cost analysis are evaluated in the market place. But this is not the issue. The issue is whether or not, and for what purpose, indirect benefits and costs should be considered and added to direct ones.

First, what is the meaning of direct and indirect benefits and costs? We may adopt the definition and terminology of the Subcommittee on Benefits and Costs of the Federal Inter-Agency River Basin Committee.[5] According to this definition, direct costs are the value of the goods and services needed for the establishment, maintenance and operation of the project and to make the immediate products of the project available for use or sale.[6] Direct benefits are the value of the immediate products and services for which the direct costs were incurred. Indirect benefits are the values added to the direct benefits as a result of activities "stemming from or induced by" the project. Indirect costs are the costs of further processing and any other costs (above the direct costs) "stemming from or induced by" the project. The subcommittee prefers "primary" and "secondary" instead of "direct" and "indirect," presumably because in the economics of flood control, "indirect" or "incidental" have for some time been used in connection with products (other than the prevention of direct flood damage) which, in the terminology of the subcommittee, must be regarded as "immediate."

Three problem areas are as important in appraisal of secondary benefits and costs as in discussion of cost allocation.[7] The first problem area is the selection of the "best" project; the second is the repayment by beneficiaries to the government; the third is the pricing of those immediate products of a project that are sold. These problem areas are connected in benefit-cost analysis through economic concepts, some common basic data and existing statutory provisions. But the potentialities and limitations of benefit-cost analysis differ among these three areas, the concepts and basic data needed are not all the same and the statutory provisions that connect them are neither precise nor unchangeable. This chapter is concerned mainly with the two problem areas of project selection and repayment. The problem area of pricing is excluded because of space limits, not because it is less important.

For purposes of project selection, benefits or costs that constitute transfer items among regions, among industrial or occupational groups and among individuals should not be considered. Whether or not such transfers are desirable is a separate issue in public policy. Considerations concerning income distribution will appear in clearer focus if they are separated from the problems of increasing real national income. An account in which transfer items are not considered may be called a national account.

On the other hand, repayment of net benefits to certain regions, to industrial or occupational groups and to individuals may well be considered even if they are transfer items. Such repayment accounts will generally be on the basis of regional, industrial or occupational groupings. For that reason they may be called regional or industry accounts. The significance of differentiating among these various accounts will appear presently.

Secondary Benefits "Stemming from" a Public Project

The many kinds of secondary benefits (and costs) considered in the literature[8] and practice of benefit-cost analysis may be divided into two major classes. The first comprises those alleged to accrue in connection with the processing of the immediate products; this class is referred to as "stemming from." The second class comprises those benefits (and costs) alleged to accrue because expenditures by the producers of the immediate products stimulate other economic activities; this class is referred to as "induced by."

Let us start with secondary benefits from processing.[9] Under competitive markets, net benefits arising from processing (above all corresponding costs of processing) quickly find expression in the demand by processors for the immediate products of a project. In connection with public resource development, a demand function may be identified with a marginal benefit function. An estimate of the demand function for the immediate products of a public project is, therefore, the most essential basic step in considering primary benefits.[10] Hence, if by some more or less arbitrary accounting procedure secondary net benefits from processing are determined and added to the primary net benefits, a portion of primary benefits is counted twice.[11]

If abnormal profits would be derived from processing the products of a public project under monopsonistic or monopolistic markets, there are several possibilities. This situation sometimes can be avoided by expanding the project. Processing facilities — for example, for transporting power — may be included as a part of public resource development. In other cases, competition may be encouraged by appropriate public policies. Many opportunities for such action exist because the government either is the producer or has considerable influence with the producers to set up processing facilities on a cooperative basis.

If this approach is not chosen, correction for these market conditions may be made in benefit-cost analysis. If the problem area is project selection, such correction should be made through the demand function used as the basis for computing primary benefits. In such a computation quantities and values are used "as if" markets for the immediate products were competitive. To construct such a demand function, data are required on revenues and costs in processing. But such data are also required for identifying "secondary benefits" from processing.

If the problem area is repayment, net income in processing industries "stemming from" the public project may be identified as secondary benefits in regional or industry accounts. However, benefit items in these accounts should not be added to benefit items in the national account.

Identification of secondary net benefits in industry or regional accounts stimulates a better understanding of regional effects of public resource development. Such identification has practical significance as a preliminary step toward broadening the repayment base — which is sometimes rather narrow if confined to primary benefits — toward obtaining dependable repayment contracts from groups of beneficiaries and toward making special taxes socially more acceptable. The term "preliminary" is used because the problem area of repayment is dominated by social institutions. Benefit-cost analysis in itself can only call attention to economic aspects and thereby facilitate changes.

Sometimes it is argued[12] that secondary net benefits from processing arise from the fact that the goods produced by a public project may lower market prices. Since the immediate products are available to processors at lower prices, the project then should receive a credit for secondary net benefits equal to the price differentials times the quantities produced. Some question may be raised about this argument.

The quantities produced by a public project may be large enough, of course, to have effects upon prices; but such a situation in itself does not indicate additional profits from processing. At best, such additional profits are short-lived. The quantities produced by the project should be evaluated with the prices at which these quantities can be absorbed.

On the other hand, the project should not be debited with the effects of price decreases of intramarginal quantities — that is, of quantities that would be produced without the project. Such price effects of a project, both through products supplied and services demanded, are transfer items among producers and consumers that should not be considered in benefit-cost analysis for purposes of project selection. For purposes of repayment, on the other hand, net income resulting from such effects may be considered as secondary benefits in industry or regional accounts.

Secondary Benefits "Induced by" a Public Project

Next let us consider the other major class of secondary benefits — those from an expansion of economic activity "induced by" the public project. This is a more complex and more important problem than the preceding one.

The argument for including this class of secondary benefits is supported on the academic level through analyses based on Keynesian economics. In the practice of benefit-cost analysis, however, this class of benefits is computed regardless of underemployment among productive services in the course of general fluctuations of investment, saving and income. First, therefore, it is advisable to deal with this class under the assumption that there is no cyclical underemployment.

This assumption does not mean that there is no unused capacity. In reality an economy is in constant change even if aggregate investment, saving and income are assumed constant. In such an economy there is always unused capacity, not only in industries in a state of stagnation or decay but also in those in a state of growth, because growth rates are different in interrelated activities. Furthermore, such "structural" underemployment is generally concentrated in particular industries and regions. Public resource development, under some conditions, can help make use of such underemployed services.

The most logical and practical way to take such effects into account for benefit-cost analysis is through evaluation of primary costs — not through secondary benefits. Under competitive markets the fact that productive services are underemployed is reflected in the prices at which they are available — *in situ* or including costs of movement — to the public project. Under monopolistic markets this may not be true. In such cases appropriate corrections can still be made through the supply functions of productive services used as a basis for computing the primary costs. If data are not sufficient to estimate prices of productive services "as if" their markets were competitive, an "offset" to primary costs may be calculated in connection with cyclical underemployment. This procedure is indicated for the problem area of project selection.

For the problem area of repayment such effects may be identified as secondary benefits through income statistics. But again care should be taken that such benefits are not counted twice, both on the cost and on the benefit side. Besides income statistics, some new techniques of economic analysis — for example, Leontief's input-output model — may become helpful in the *ex ante* identification of such induced secondary benefits.

Economists frequently argue that secondary benefits are induced regardless of underemployment of productive services, cyclical or otherwise. Public resource development — e.g., irrigation development in an arid region — may certainly induce many new economic activities. Under the assumptions of no underemployment and no change in technology and preferences, one may doubt that this increase is "net" for the national account. In other words such increases are offset by decreases elsewhere in the economy. Hence the increases may be considered for repayment but not for project selection.

On the other hand, public resource development may, over time, induce economic change in a broader sense. That is, it may change technology and preferences and thereby induce shifts of supply and demand

schedules for the immediate products of a project. Some argue that
such changes should be taken into account in benefit-cost analysis
through secondary benefits (or costs) and that otherwise such analysis
would remain static.

Admittedly, the instantaneous supply and demand schedules used as
basis for benefit-cost analysis involve highly restrictive assumptions
with respect to future economic change. Far too little is known about
the conditions of economic change to trace in practice a continuous path
over time in terms of expected benefits and costs functionally related
to public resource development. On the other hand, benefit-cost analysis may well be undertaken within discrete consecutive time periods —
each involving different but interrelated assumptions. I have shown
elsewhere that such time-period analysis and explicit consideration of
the future are basic issues in resource economics.[13] "Pay-out schedules" commonly used in benefit-cost analysis may well be refined with
respect to expected shifts in supply and demand for the immediate
products of a project.

Only a part of the change in these assumptions from period to period will be related to the effects of public resource development itself.
In the United States especially the effects of other forces are far more
important. There are practical limits on the number and extent of periods and assumptions considered. Still, the fact remains that long periods of gestation — at least ten and usually closer to twenty years from
the time of project selection — make emphasis on future rather than
past conditions of supply and demand a necessity in public resource development. Improvements in the direction of a period analysis of primary benefits and costs would seem more meaningful than an attempt
to make benefit-cost analysis dynamic through a more or less arbitrary addition of secondary benefits and costs — which are static in the
same sense as alleged for primary ones.

Finally, there is fairly general agreement that public resource development can have secondary beneficial effects under the assumption
of cyclical underemployment and should be considered from the standpoint of integration with other more direct and more effective anticycli-
cal policies. The possibilities and difficulties of such integration need
not be considered here.[14] In connection with the present topic the issue
is: How much weight should these beneficial effects be given in benefit-
cost analysis?

As in the case of structural underemployment discussed above, the
most logical and practical way to consider such effects is through evaluation of primary costs — especially construction costs — not through
secondary benefits. Public resource development is most effective in
reducing cyclical underemployment during the construction period. By
taking the state of employment into account in the evaluation of construction costs, public projects will appear economically more attractive during depressions and less attractive during booms. This is because no corresponding adjustment should be made in benefits. As just
emphasized, benefits from a public project start to flow only after a

long period of gestation. Even if this start does not coincide with the next boom phase, it can be assumed that the flow continues over several cycles.

Under competitive markets cyclical underemployment of productive services is reflected in the prices of such services. Under monopolistic (monopsonistic) markets this is not likely. Still, adjustments can often be made in the computation of construction costs by using prices for productive services "as if" their markets were competitive. Alternatively, a sliding-scale "offset" to primary costs may be calculated.

The Panel of Consultants of the U.S. Bureau of Reclamation suggested that such an offset be added to construction costs. This offset is calculated by multiplying construction costs with a plus (full employment) or minus (unemployment) factor, which is "the percentage of the resources used in construction of this project which is estimated will be drawn from unemployment rather than diverted from other uses." [15]

Although this method seems in need of clarification, there is no conflict in logic between it — if properly used — and the method that tries to take underemployment into account directly through prices of productive services used in the evaluation of construction costs. The method suggested by the Panel may be regarded as a first approximation to the other method. Care should be taken, however, that underemployment is not counted twice — that is, through prices used in evaluating construction costs *and* through the offset factor. Because of this danger, I prefer the more direct method. Also, practical advantages in obtaining basic data are probably in favor of this method, except in the case of labor costs.

CONCLUSIONS

When we try to draw conclusions from this analysis of secondary benefits and costs, we are forced to suggest that all classes of secondary net benefits be dropped from consideration if the problem area is project selection. This is the most important problem area in which benefit-cost analysis is presently used.

This suggestion may seem to reflect an overly conservative if not negative attitude toward public resource development. This is not at all the case. But the effort presently invested in justifying the inclusion of secondary benefits and costs in the national account should be employed to greater advantage in a more careful evaluation of primary benefits and costs.

This advantage would accrue to the twofold over-all role of benefit-cost analysis indicated above, especially the first one of restraining the abuse of economic arguments in the political process. Secondary benefits and costs have for some time been suspected by legislative bodies as facilitating double counting and other forms of padding benefits. [16] If the foregoing analysis is correct, these suspicions are not unfounded. Elimination of secondary benefits and costs in the national account

would make benefit-cost analysis more straightforward, not only for
the professional economist but also for the layman. The influence of
benefit-cost analysis with legislative bodies and the public at large may
thereby be increased.

Beyond that, advantages may accrue to the second over-all role of
benefit-cost analysis, that of stimulus to scientific understanding.
There are few issues in benefit-cost analysis that force the student to
ask more searching questions regarding public resource development
than a critical appraisal of secondary benefits and costs in their relation to primary ones.

Another conclusion to be drawn is the need for a clear differentiation among problem areas, or purposes, of benefit-cost analysis. Some
items that should not be considered for project selection may well be
considered for repayment. For other items the reverse may be true.
For example, recreational benefits should be considered for project
selection, but as a matter of policy or practical expediency they may
be omitted for repayment.

The twofold over-all role of benefit-cost analysis appears no less
important for repayment than for project selection. Most of the economic arguments by interested regional, industrial and occupational
groups are concerned with repayment. A government standard in the
above sense is especially needed in this problem area.

Establishing regional and industry accounts, as discussed for
benefit-cost analysis of repayment, stimulates research in the regional
effects of public resource development, in the factors affecting the economic growth and location of industries and in the social institutions —
as variables and as restrictions — that dominate the criteria, the form
and the assessment of repayment.

Practical influences of benefit-cost analysis — in broadening the repayment base, in obtaining dependable repayment contracts and in making public districts and special taxes more acceptable — exist insofar
as appropriate changes of social institutions are facilitated. The latter
influences are largely educational and must operate through the political process.

Such indirect and modest influences may seem to give support to
the proposal mentioned in the beginning — to adopt "willingness to repay" as a more direct and effective substitute for benefit-cost analysis.
If this willingness were affected primarily by economic factors, ascertaining it would require an effort similar to that for benefit-cost analysis. But willingness to repay is more akin to "requirement to repay"
as determined by statutory provisions, precedent and political influence
of beneficiaries. It makes little sense to employ or even to define willingness to repay as an economic criterion. Through benefit-cost analysis, on the other hand, an economic upper limit of willingness to repay
can be determined. Furthermore, through benefit-cost analysis the political lower limit of willingness to repay may be raised through the indirect and modest influences suggested above.

We conclude that there is no substitute for benefit-cost analysis in
public resource development. Its role in the actual course of affairs

may be unspectacular, but properly used the effort is worthwhile. Furthermore, there are potentialities for improvement that may render the practical influence of benefit-cost analysis considerably more potent.

FOOTNOTES

[1] Luna B. Leopold and Thomas Maddock, Jr., The Flood Control Controversy; Big Dams, Little Dams, and Land Management, Ronald Press, New York, 1954; also Raymond Moley, What Price Federal Reclamation? American Enterprise Association, New York, 1955, Series "National Economic Problems" No. 455.

[2] S. V. Ciriacy-Wantrup, "Cost allocation in relation to western water policies," *Jour. Farm Econ.*, Vol. 36, No. 1, 1954. Chap. 12 of this volume.

[3] These and other examples are discussed in greater detail in S. V. Ciriacy-Wantrup, Resource Conservation, Economics and Policies, 2d rev. ed. Univ. of California Div. Agr. Sciences, 1963.

[4] In order not to be indicated of subjective bias in favor of recreational resources, an attempt to evaluate another still more problematical but related item, namely, leisure — may be cited: Simon Kuznets, "Long-term changes in the national income of the United States of America since 1870," Income and Wealth of the United States, Trends and Structure, Income on Wealth, Series II, Bowes & Bowes, Cambridge, 1952, esp. pp. 63-69.

[5] U.S. Federal Inter-Agency River Basin Committee, Subcommittee on Benefits and Costs, Proposed Practices for Economic Analysis of River Basin Projects, U.S. Govt. Print. Off., May, 1950, pp. 8-9.

[6] The latter costs are called "associated costs," but this differentiation is not material for our present purpose.

[7] Ciriacy-Wantrup, "Cost allocation in relation to western water policies," *op. cit.*

[8] U.S. Federal Inter-Agency River Basin Committee, Subcommittee on Benefits and Costs, Proposed Practices ..., *op. cit.*

U.S. Bureau of Reclamation, Secondary or Indirect Benefits of Water-Use Projects, Washington, June 26, 1952, 63pp. Report of Panel of Consultants to Michael W. Straus, Commissioner, Bureau of Reclamation.

U.S. Congress, Economic Evaluation of Federal Water Resource Development Projects, U.S. Govt. Print. Off., Dec. 5, 1952, 55pp., 82nd Cong., 2nd sess., Rept. to the Comm. on Public Works by the Subcomm. to study Civil Works.

Executive Office of the President, U.S. Bureau of the Budget, Reports and Budget Estimates, Relating to Federal Programs and Projects for Conservation, Development or Use of Water and Related Land Resources, U.S. Govt. Print. Off., December 31, 1952, 20pp. (Circ. A-47.)

M. M. Kelso, "Evaluation of secondary benefits of water use projects," Water Resources and Economic Development of the West: Research Needs and Problems, Berkeley, Calif., March, 1953, pp. 49-62. Rept. No. 1, Conference Proceedings of the Committee on the Economics of Water Resources Development.

[9] In the case of power, these benefits are sometimes subdivided further under the terms "savings benefits," "extended benefits" and "utilization benefits." See U.S. Congress, Trinity River Basin, Central Valley Project, Calif., U.S. Govt. Print. Off., 1953, pp. 73-75, 83rd Cong., 1st sess. 4. Doc. 53.

[10] For more details on this point, see Ciriacy-Wantrup, Resource Conservation, Economics and Policies, *op. cit.*, Chap. 17.

[11] In arriving at secondary benefits, it has become customary to apply standard percentages to the primary benefits. These percentages are derived from the statistics of average values added in processing. Thus, for cotton and other industrial raw materials produced by a public irrigation development the percentages are high (80 percent and more), and smaller for livestock products.

[12] For example, U.S. Federal Inter-Agency River Basin Committee, Subcommittee on Benefits and Costs, Proposed Practices ..., *op. cit.*, pp. 10, 40.

[13] Ciriacy-Wantrup, Resource Conservation, Economics and Policies, *op. cit.*, Chaps. 3, 4.

[14] *Ibid.*, Chap. 15.

[15] Kelso, *op. cit.*, p. 56. A similar statement and illustrative graph appear in the Panel report itself (Secondary or Indirect Benefits ..., *op. cit.*, pp. 31, 32). However, these statements do not clarify how a positive factor is calculated.

[16] For example, see U.S. Congress, Economic Evaluation of Federal Water ..., *op. cit.*

JOHN V. KRUTILLA is an economist with Resources for the Future, Inc. His writings have made original applications of economics to the water resources field. He was formerly on the staff of the Tennessee Valley Authority.

Chapter 3

JOHN V. KRUTILLA

Welfare Aspects of Benefit-Cost Analysis *

T HERE IS SUBSTANTIAL INTEREST in developing decision rules for public expenditures under a variety of conditions. To a large extent in the literature dealing with governmental expenditures in the United States the interest has been confined to the field of resource development and the activity known in general as benefit-cost analysis.

Benefit-cost analysis can be characterized as the collection and organization of data relevant by some conceptually meaningful criteria to determining the relative preferredness of alternatives (24, Parts II, III). As is typical of much of economic analysis, the objective is to attempt by analysis to indicate how a particular desideratum can be maximized — accomplished by comparing the differences in the relevant costs and benefits associated with alternatives among which choices are to be made. This activity, of course, does not differ in kind from the economic analysis employed in reaching decisions with respect to

*Reprinted with the permission of Univ. of Chicago Press. From the *Jour. of Political Econ.*, 1961, Vol. 69, No. 3, pp. 226-35.

Acknowledgments are due to Robert Dorfman, Otto Eckstein, Francesco Forte, George Hall, Orris Herfindahl and Vernon Ruttan for helpful comments on an earlier draft of this chapter. The substance of this chapter was presented as a lecture in a series given in the training program sponsored by the United Nations Economic Commission for Latin America at the University of Mexico in the summer of 1960.

production or other policies of the firm. Nevertheless, while the analytic activity does not differ in *nature,* the desideratum and the choice variables on which it depends will differ.

Essentially, a private cost-gains calculus is employed in deciding private firms' policies; externalities and other divergences between private and social product are neglected. Benefit-cost analysis, on the other hand, seeks to take account of such divergences as a basis for guiding public action either when market prices do not accurately reflect social value or when, by virtue of the indivisible nature of collective goods, no market exists from which to observe directly objective evidence of the community's valuation of the social marginal product. Speaking loosely, while the decision rules of the theory of the firm aim at profit maximization, the decision rules of benefit-cost analysis seek to maximize "public benefits" or "general welfare" within the area of responsibility (29, p. 3).

In this connection the normative nature of the analysis needs to be emphasized. Unlike the assumption of profit maximization, which is a descriptive hypothesis having explanatory value (but cf. 28, 38), benefit-cost analysis is intended to be prescriptive. Underlying the analysis is the value judgment that, if governmental intervention is justified in part[1] by virtue of the market's failure to achieve an efficient allocation of resources (1, 3, 16, 22, 23, 26, 34), public officials ought to apply decision rules which tend to *improve* the allocation. That is, the *general* welfare should be improved rather than their personal or specially interested clientele's welfare.[2]

I. INITIAL CONDITIONS AND SIDE EFFECTS

While intervention is required to correct divergences between private and social product and cost, both the initial conditions and the associated side effects of intervention are of relevance in assessing the welfare implications of supramarket allocations of resources. Public intervention to redirect the use of resources involves costs. Assuming that the gross benefit achieved exceeds associated opportunity costs if, in addition: (a) opportunity costs are borne by beneficiaries in such wise as to retain the initial income distribution, (b) the initial income distribution is in some sense "best" and (c) the marginal social rates of transformation between any two commodities are everywhere equal to their corresponding rates of substitution except for the area(s) justifying the intervention in question, then welfare can be improved by such intervention. And, to the extent that the objective is pursued to the point where the social marginal rates of transformation between commodities in this area and other sectors are likewise equal to the rates of substitution for correspondingly paired commodities, welfare is maximized.

However, since condition (a) is only partially feasible in the majority of cases dealt with by benefit-cost analysis, the likelihood of condition (b) has been subject to considerable question, and in the world of reality condition (c) is improbable, consideration of these stringent conditions is necessary to assess in pragmatic terms the welfare implications of supramarket allocation of resources suggested by benefit-cost comparisons.

II. IMPLICATION OF REDISTRIBUTIVE EFFECTS FOR THE MEASUREMENT OF WELFARE

Considering condition (a), we may recognize the practical possibility of multipart pricing or corresponding special assessments as limited; and thus we must retreat to weaker positions. This retreat will require, at best, that the analyst rely on interpersonal comparisons of utility before he can hazard any judgment with respect to welfare, *plus* a degree of faith that the redistributional consequences for the measurement of welfare are of the second order of significance. Or (at worst) the analyst can abstain from saying anything about the magnitude or even the direction of the change in either wealth or welfare, that is, about the change in the size of the national real income or its welfare implications.

To claim that welfare has increased, when the *ex ante* distribution is not automatically preserved by the mechanism of intervention, requires that those who gain are able to *and do* compensate those who lose, and still have something remaining. However, if we are uncertain about the "goodness" of the original distribution of income (condition b), we cannot contend that failure to compensate would not result in a greater gain in welfare. Such failure means only that the issue cannot be resolved without making interpersonal comparisons (31).

If we are content to attach no greater normative significance to the result of "maximizing" decision rules, however, than to aver that national income has been increased, taking the distribution as given, we can envisage a broader application of benefit-cost decision rules. We are then content to accept the "production-distribution" or the "efficiency-ethics" dichotomy of the Kaldor-Hicks-Scitovsky line of development (9, 10, 15, 36, 37). We say that if those who benefit by virtue of the increase in production can overcompensate those who suffer losses (but do not actually make the compensating payments), the "aggregate real income" has been increased irrespective of its distribution and, accordingly, of its welfare implications.[3]

Kaldor's production-distribution dichotomy and the resulting test of an increase in real income appear supportable for the more or less marginal adjustments for which benefit-cost criteria were originally developed and typically applied in the United States. This remains true, I believe, despite Samuelson's and De Graaff's criticism of the proposition in general (33, pp. 10-11; 8, p. 90 ff.). At the most fundamental level is De Graaff's criticism; if we wish to base our economics on an individualistic rather than on an organic conception of the community and its welfare, and if there is more than one commodity, then the "aggregate real income" cannot be evaluated without weighting components, which in turn is not independent of the income distribution. We may resort to the "size-distribution" dichotomy, but it has no operational significance, for "we do not know the size unless we know the distribution" (8, p. 92).

De Graaff's concern with the distributional implications for aggregate real income corresponds to Scitovsky's concern with the *re*distributional consequences for measuring the *change* in real income. Consideration of only the latter and lesser question will suffice for our immediate purpose. Scitovsky's critical point can be summarized somewhat as follows: An indicated net increase in real income when valued in terms of prevailing prices may not prove so when valued in terms of prices reflecting the attendant income redistribution. Admittedly, for a structural reorganization of the magnitude implicit in the repeal of the corn laws, the effect of the income redistribution on the constellation of relative prices cannot be ignored. On the other hand, the relative magnitude of the redistribution associated with investment decisions for which benefit-cost expenditure criteria have been traditionally employed will be of the second order of smalls in terms of its implication for measuring the change and, for practical purposes, can be ignored (16, p. 50).[4]

Thus, while the absolute size of the national income may not be independent of its distribution, a relatively small change in its size, for practical purposes, can be considered independently of its redistributional consequences in determining the magnitude and direction of the change. The distinction for benefit-cost analysis, of course, is significant, as it provides the theoretical basis for benefit-cost practices. For if the more simple criteria of Kaldor and Hicks had to be supplemented even by Scitovsky's extension alone — not to mention Samuelson's all-possible distributions test (33) — no *ex ante* judgment with respect to the anticipated change in economic efficiency resulting from a contemplated supramarket allocation could be supported by benefit-cost analysis. This follows because the analyst does not have the power to manipulate the distribution of income experimentally before rendering a judgment; nor does there exist sufficient information regarding individual preference maps to simulate results from hypothetical distributions.

Samuelson's requirement that an improvement in efficiency must be tested not only against the *ex ante* and *ex post* income distributions but against all possible hypothetical distributions stems from two partially distinct considerations. The first involves the degree to which an implicit value judgment has been made in either Kaldor's and Hicks's criterion or Scitovsky's double criterion in spite of the intended preoccupation solely with production or efficiency. That is, to take the *ex ante* distribution (or in the case of Scitovsky the *ex post* as well as the *ex ante*) as a datum confers too significant a normative status on these particular distributions. For, as Fisher has observed:

The refusal to make a value judgment ... is in itself a value judgment, not only in the sense that one is saying that one ought to abstain from making value judgments, but also in the sense that the results obtained are those that would result from glorifying the present distribution (7, p. 394).

The second consideration underlying Samuelson's position seems to be concerned with the distinction between the "utility possibility frontier" and the "utility feasibility frontier," that is, between potential and feasible welfare. Here, while the utility-possibility function may be shifted outward uniformly or welfare potentially increased by a policy prescription, the implementation of the policy may cause such distortion of marginal conditions and "undesirable" income redistribution that the utility-feasibility frontier twists inward (33, pp. 18-21).

The first of these observations is related directly to condition (b), whereas the second bears obliquely on condition (c).

III. THE WELFARE STATUS OF THE STATUS QUO

Considering condition (b), I believe it fair to say that the redistributive consequences of small changes of the sort encountered in benefit-cost analysis in the United States are negligible. But, as Fisher points out, this does not mean that benefit-cost analysis is free of distributional value judgments. Equating incremental benefits and costs in the designing of projects and "scoping" of programs relies on price data, which in turn are dependent on the prevailing distribution. Accordingly, if for no other reason than this, a judgment is implied regarding the normative status of the existing distribution.

A proper question to raise at this junction, however, is: Can the prevailing distribution indicate, as a pragmatic approximation, the socially sanctioned one in a democratically organized society? There are at least three ways in which to answer this question. We can reply with a qualified yes, following a line of reasoning to be sketched below. We can maintain that it is really not possible to know, but that the answer may not be too important, given the level and distribution of income approached in the United States. Finally we might argue, as does Little, that the prevailing distribution of income does not enjoy a social sanction, so that any judgment with respect to efficiency must be in the nature of a second-best solution contingent also on a value judgment that the resulting income distribution is "good."

It can be argued that the prevailing distribution of income is approved by the community, since in a democracy the community has the means of changing it. Little discounts this rationale, apparently on the basis of the observed historical tendency toward persistent reduction of inequalities in income in modern industrial nations (19, p. 114). Yet the degree of income equality sought by a community may not be unrelated to the level of per capita income, and the reduction of inequality over time may be only a function of technological advances and the increase in efficiency of economic organization.

Differential rewards of income appear to be compatible with a Jeffersonian concept of democracy which accommodates an aristocracy of ability. Indirect evidence that the community sanctions some inequality of income has been reflected perceptively in the writings of Perlman (27, pp. 164 ff.). In a wholly different fashion Anthony Downs provides an interesting rationale for the existence of income inequality in a po-litical democracy (4, pp. 199-200, but also cf. p. 94).[5] If I interpret Downs correctly, it seems probable that the income distribution resulting from the explicit redistributive activities of the government is a reasonable approximation to the socially sanctioned distribution, assuming that the incidental redistributive consequences of other governmental activities are noncumulative.[6]

Related to the first is a second possible argument that, although there may be reasons for rejecting the prevailing distribution as in some sense "best" reflecting a social welfare function, at the present level of income distributional (and redistributional) questions are not dominant considerations.[7] This does not imply that all members of society have their nonfrivolous needs met equally amply, but only that the associated dead-weight losses of moving toward greater equality would be judged to exceed the compensating distributional gains.

A third possible argument is advanced by Little. He abandons interest in a welfare maximum, regarding such an aspiration as utopian. Considering the existing distribution as nonoptimal,[8] he focuses on conditions *sufficient for an improvement* in welfare rather than on conditions *necessary for a welfare maximum* (19, pp. 115-16). To render an improvement in efficiency desirable — that is, for it to improve welfare — the attendant redistribution of income must be acceptable. To pursue the matter to its ultimate conclusion, we could accept the frankly ascientific approach made by Meade (25, Chaps. v, vii) and assign distributional weights based on interpersonal comparisons of welfare in order to incorporate redistributional aspects into a multidimensional objective function. In a similar, if more restricted, sense there is the possibility, consistent with Little's position, of maximizing a one-dimensional benefit function subject to an income-redistribution constraint.[9]

IV. WELFARE IMPLICATIONS
OF NONOPTIMAL INITIAL CONDITIONS
OF PRODUCTION AND EXCHANGE

The third possibility noted immediately above touches on maximization problems best treated in connection with an evaluation of general condition (c), problems associated with the nonexistence of the necessary conditions for a Pareto optimum. Here it must be acknowledged that, by reason of market imperfections and distortion of marginal conditions owing to government activities (both explicit redistribution and the financing of supramarket allocations), the Pareto-optimum conditions (c) are at best only approximated in practice and at worst are

universally breached so that the slopes of Samuelson's feasibility fron-
tiers have little relation to prices and marginal costs (33, p. 18). The
significant problem then remains one of evaluating the welfare implications of benefit-maximizing criteria under real world conditions.

Of the major participants in the postwar discussion of welfare economics, only Little (later joined by Meade) attempts to come to grips
with problems of this nature. These problems appear to be at least as
great in practical importance as is the issue of interpersonal comparisons and income distribution; and they are, if anything, less susceptible
to an intellectually satisfying solution. This is brought home decisively
by the pessimistic conclusions of the statement by Lipsey and Lancaster of the general theory of the second best (18). They have demonstrated that, if any one of the conditions for a Pareto optimum is not
attainable, it is in general not desirable to achieve any of the remainder
(18, pp. 11, 26-27). The following quotation reflects the flavor of their
nihilistic conclusions:

> The problem of sufficient conditions for an increase in welfare, as compared
> to necessary conditions for a welfare maximum, is obviously important if policy
> recommendations are to be made in the real world. Piecemeal welfare eco-
> nomics is often based on the belief that a study of the *necessary* conditions for a
> Paretian welfare optimum may lead to the discovery of *sufficient* conditions for
> an increase in welfare. In his *Critique of Welfare Economics*, I. M. D. Little...
> says, "...necessary conditions are not very interesting. It is *sufficient* condi-
> tions for improvement that we really want." But the theory of second best leads
> to the conclusion that there are in general no such sufficient conditions for an in-
> crease in welfare. There are necessary conditions for a Paretian optimum. In a
> simple situation there may exist a condition that is necessary and sufficient. But
> in a general equilibrium situation, there will be no conditions which in general
> are sufficient for an increase in welfare without also being necessary for a wel-
> fare maximum (18, p. 17).

And, to erode further the faith of the innocent, they conclude that in
general there is no proof of the existence of a second-best solution (18,
pp. 27-28).[10]

Nonexistence of a second-best solution in a technical sense, however, does not mean that if an additional constraint is imposed on the
welfare function there is no actual relative maximum. Intuitively, we
perceive that some adjustments in response to the given constraints
will be better than others and that there must be an actual peak whether
or not we can stipulate what conditions must obtain at the margin for
all permutations. But the question remains whether or not supramarket
allocations, guided by marginal equalities rather than the unknown appropriate inequalities, will tend to move the economy further away from
such an actual relative maximum when similar marginal equalities are
absent elsewhere in the economy.

While it follows that, in general, supramarket allocations guided by
marginal equalities will prevent the economy from achieving the constrained maximum, it does not follow that abstention from intervention
would permit the economy to remain closer to the constrained maximum.

The possibility always exists that an observed inefficient situation is dominated by an attainable more efficient situation (12, p. 98; 13, p. 208). An example drawn from the field of resources may illustrate this point. Three alternative plans of development were proposed for the Hell's Canyon reach of the Snake River, the third of which was a privately advanced plan of development. For the three plans of development the following conditions hold:

$$O_1 > O_2 > O_3$$

and

$$I_1 > I_3 > I_2 \, ,$$

where O and I refer respectively to physical output and inputs, and the subscripts to the respective plans of development (16, Chap. v). As between the second and third alternatives, it is obvious that the efficiency of the former dominates the latter. Hence, we can argue by dominance that — subject to an economic demand for the output — appropriate public intervention is a sufficient condition for an improvement without regard to necessary conditions for a welfare maximum.

On the other hand, since the first alternative requires more inputs to achieve the greater output than does either the second or the third, and the value of the difference in output is greater than, equal to or less than the opportunity costs of the inputs depending on a critical factor price, we cannot make a decision without recourse to prices. Now, if prices are not exact measures of opportunity costs — a condition implicit in the negative theorem of the general theory of the second best — they do not provide an unambiguous criterion.

Three partially distinct positions can be discerned in the approaches adopted by benefit-cost analysts in such cases. McKean takes the following position:

> Those conditions (Pareto optimum) are not completely realized and moving toward the achievement of *one* alone is not necessarily a step in the right direction. However, if a frequency distribution of the possibilities is imagined, it seems likely that increased production where price exceeds cost would usually be a step toward efficiency, even though the other conditions are only partially fulfilled. The conclusion here is that prices and costs show how to "maximize production" (24, pp. 130-31).

Eckstein (5, p. 29), following Little (20, pp. vii-xiv), approaches the problem in the following manner:

> Insofar as there are monopoly elements, prices will exceed marginal costs, but from a quantitative point of view, these deviations are both widely — also perhaps evenly — diffused and relatively small, particularly in the range of markets most relevant to water resource development. Projects in these fields produce outputs which in largest part are producer goods, such as raw materials, electric energy and transportation services. In these areas, advertising, consumer loyalty and asymmetric market power concentrated on the side of the seller are less prevalent than in markets for consumer goods. Thus while prices do not serve their function perfectly, we hold that they are generally adequate for the range of policy decisions with which we are concerned. At the same time, in any appli-

cation of the methods of this study, we must keep in mind the assumptions which validate the use of prices, and we must not hesitate, in certain situations, to reject them in favor of other measures of social benefit and cost.[11]

A third position supporting the use of prices (adjusted for obvious divergences) as measures of opportunity costs, and of criteria based mainly on the presumption of the existence of marginal equalities, is the following (16, p. 73, n. 32). While the benefit-cost analyst must recognize that he does not institute utopian reforms simply by an act of analysis, he must also recognize that his criteria, in the dynamic context of the real world, should be consistent with the higher-level aims which dominate the work of those public servants responsible for policing monopoly, improving market performance and otherwise monitoring the economy with the objective of increasing the efficiency of its operation. And, while he must recognize the prevalence of departures from ideal conditions, he should not feed such departures systematically back into the optimizing calculations. For, in contrast to the static situation to which the negative theorem of Lipsey and Lancaster applies, such feedbacks can have a cumulative effect, resulting in progressive divergences from conditions of optimum production and exchange.

The choices in which one alternative clearly dominates another (or all others), while they may be numerous absolutely, must still represent a small proportion of the total of choices which face the economic decision makers. And the positions advanced above to deal with the more representative situation can neither rest on formal proofs nor claim much by way of an intellectually satisfying status. Also, while the analyst must be sensitive to "higher-level aims," by virtue of the nature of his problems and analysis he must work largely in a suboptimizing or partial-equilibrium context (24, pp. 30 ff.). Conclusions reached by analysis at this level of generality need not hold in more general cases and may require substantial reconsideration (see, for example, 21, 30, 32). The application of criteria for improving welfare therefore cannot be a mechanical or a compellingly logical activity. Rather, it requires perhaps more intimate knowledge of the economy, experience and highly developed intuitive sense than analysts commonly possess — which suggests the quality of results and degree of precision to be anticipated.

V. CONCLUSIONS FOR PRACTICAL CHOICES
IN THE PUBLIC INTEREST

Does the array of positions advanced previously provide an adequate rationale for attempts to evaluate the benefits and costs of resource-development alternatives? Or are the comments herein transparent rationalizations which leave little conviction that analysis of benefits and cost and of their distribution can help improve welfare significantly through public intervention? One's view, of course, will differ depending on the nature of his experience, temperament and perhaps also his personal situation. The academic theorist without responsibility for policy can afford to be puritanical (and probably should) without regard to whether or not this is immediately constructive.

On the other hand, the practicing economist in government, charged with responsibility to act under constraints of time and information, will often be grateful for perhaps even a perforated rationale to justify recommendations "in the public interest." Since the alternative is not to retire to inactivity but rather to reach decisions in the absence of analysis, we may take some comfort from the belief that thinking systematically about problems and basing decisions on such analysis likely will produce consequences superior to those that would result from purely random behavior. Nonetheless, the utility and welfare effects of benefit-cost analysis are likely to be viewed differently, depending on the end of the telescope through which the affected party is privileged to look.

FOOTNOTES

[1] That part of governmental intervention characterized by Musgrave's "allocation branch" (26).

[2] See Downs (4) for a positive theory of political behavior which may more accurately mirror actual rather than "desirable" behavior of public officials.

[3] Of course it is not to be inferred that Hicks ignores the welfare issue, since he attempted a defense of such an interpretation of the rise in social income. Among others, Hotelling (14) preceded and Ciriacy-Wantrup (2) followed Hicks in providing a defense of such welfare implications.

[4] This does not necessarily imply that the redistributive implications for welfare (discussed in the following section) can be similarly ignored. Such welfare effects might be important, especially if redistributive effects from expenditures for development of resources were cumulative. But cumulation hardly seems likely in the area of such expenditures. Additional annual expenditures of the Bureau of Reclamation, for example, do not benefit individuals previously favored because such additional expenditures represent predominantly extension of the program to new areas and, accordingly, to different individuals.

[5] See Lampman (17) for a comprehensive survey of thoughts on egalitarianism which, though exhaustive, is not conclusive.

[6] Musgrave, in his discussion of voting methods (26, Chap. 6), observes the numerous difficulties of implementing an unadulterated social ethic and concludes that perhaps majority voting in a democracy comes as close to achieving the desired end as the mechanics of social organization will permit.

[7] Of course, while such an argument can be advanced following, or perhaps interpreting liberally, Fisher's argument (7, pp. 407-8), at such levels of income considerations of efficiency may also be of the second order of significance. That is, freedom from extension of governmental intervention may be purchased at the expense of some relative reduction in potential national income. On the other hand, maximum efficiency may be viewed as a possible good in its own right irrespective of the level of opulence if the welfare function depends on the relative rate of growth vis-à-vis some ideologically competitive society.

[8] Although Little rejects the notion that the prevailing distribution of income is sanctioned, his willingness to rely on prices as indicators of value suggests that its departure from optimality is not sufficient to affect relative prices — or else that individuals' preferences are sufficiently similar that redistributions will not affect the constellation of relative prices appreciably.

[9] To implement these suggestions, however, the benefit-cost practitioner would require supplemental legislation suspending the congressional directive in the Flood Control Act of 1936 to the effect that dollar democracy is to prevail.

[10] Professor Dorfman, in private correspondence, has taken exception to this conclusion. In his opinion a second-best optimum exists under the same conditions that a Pareto optimum does, but in general the familiar Pareto-marginal equalities will not hold at a second-best optimum. Therefore, under the second-best conditions an allocation of resources that satisfies some of the Pareto-marginal equalities is not necessarily preferable to an allocation that satisfies none of them. Nevertheless there does exist a second-best optimum which is an allocation of resources that satisfies the distorting constraints that make "second-besting" necessary and that is socially preferable to any other allocation that satisfies those constraints.

[11] Consistently with the latter part of the statement, Eckstein has done much original work in developing benefit-maximizing criteria subject to a variety of constraints in addition to the resource-technology constraint (5, 6). This effort has been extended and generalized by Steiner (39), Marglin and other members of the Harvard Water Resources Seminar.

REFERENCES

1. Baumol, William J. Welfare Economics and the Theory of the State, Harvard Univ. Press, Cambridge, Mass., 1952.
2. Ciriacy-Wantrup, S. V. "Concepts used as economic criteria for a system of water rights," *Jour. Land Econ.*, 32:295-312, 1956 (Chap. 15 of this volume).
3. Colm, Gerhard. "Comments on Samuelson's theory of public finance," *Rev. Econ. and Stat.*, 38:408-12, 1956.
4. Downs, Anthony. An Economic Theory of Democracy, Harpers, 1957.
5. Eckstein, Otto. Water Resource Development: The Economics of Project Evaluation, Harvard Univ. Press, Cambridge, Mass., 1958.
6. _____. "A survey of the theory of public expenditure criteria," paper read at Universities-National Bureau Conference on Public Finance, Univ. of Va., Charlottesville, April, 1959.
7. Fisher, Franklin M. "Income distribution, value judgments and welfare," *Quart. Jour. Econ.*, 70:380-424, 1956.
8. Graaff, J. de V. Theoretical Welfare Economics, Cambridge Univ. Press, Cambridge, 1957.
9. Hicks, J. R. "Foundations of welfare economics," *Econ. Jour.*, 49:696-712, 1939.
10. _____. "The valuation of social income," *Economica*, N.S., 7:105-24, 1940.
11. _____. "The rehabilitation of consumer's surplus," *Rev. Econ. Studies*, 8:108-16, 1941.
12. Hitch, Charles. "Suboptimization in operations problems," *Jour. of the Operations Research Society of America*, 1:87-99, May, 1953.
13. _____. "Economics and military operations research," in "Economics and Operations Research: A Symposium," *Rev. Econ. and Stat.*, 40:199-209, 1958.
14. Hotelling, Harold. "The general welfare in relation to problems of taxation and of railway utility rates," *Econometrica*, 6:242-69, 1938.
15. Kaldor, Nicholas. "Welfare propositions of economics and interpersonal comparisons of utility," *Econ. Jour.*, 49:549-52, 1939.
16. Krutilla, John V., and Eckstein, Otto. Multiple Purpose River Development: Studies in Applied Economic Analysis, Johns Hopkins Press, Baltimore, 1958.
17. Lampman, Robert J. "Recent thoughts on egalitarianism," *Quart. Jour. Econ.*, 71:234-66, 1957.
18. Lipsey, R. G., and Lancaster, Kelvin. "The general theory of the second best," *Rev. Econ. Studies*, 24:11-32, 1956-57.
19. Little, I. M. D. A Critique of Welfare Economics, Clarendon Press, Oxford, 1950.
20. _____. The Price of Fuel, Clarendon Press, Oxford, 1953.
21. _____. "Direct vs. indirect taxes," *Econ. Jour.*, 61:577-84, 1951.
22. Margolis, Julius. "A comment on the pure theory of expenditures," *Rev. Econ. and Stat.*, 37:347-49, 1955.

23. _____. "Secondary benefits, external economies and the justification of public investment," *Rev. Econ. and Stat.*, 39:284-91, 1957.
24. McKean, Roland. Efficiency in Government through Systems Analysis, with Emphasis on Water Resource Development, Wiley & Sons, 1958.
25. Meade, J. E. The Theory of International Economic Policy, Vol. II: Trade and Welfare, Oxford Univ. Press, New York, 1954.
26. Musgrave, Richard A. The Theory of Public Finance, McGraw-Hill, 1959.
27. Perlman, Selig. A Theory of the Labor Movement, Macmillan, 1928.
28. Reder, M. W. "A reconsideration of the marginal productivity theory," *Jour. Polit. Econ.*, 60:450-58, 1947.
29. Regan, Mark, and Timmons, John F. "Benefit-cost analysis," paper presented before a joint session of the Economics and Engineering Section of the American Association for the Advancement of Science, Berkeley, Calif., December 27, 1954. Reproduced by the Committee on the Economics of Water Resources Development of the Western Agricultural Economics Research Council, Rept. No. 3.
30. Rolph, Earl, and Break, George. "The welfare aspects of excise taxes," *Jour. Polit. Econ.*, 62:46-54, 1949.
31. Ruggles, Nancy. "The welfare basis of the marginal cost pricing principle," *Rev. Econ. Studies*, Vol. 17, No. 2, pp. 29-46, 1949-50.
32. _____. "Recent development in the theory of marginal cost pricing," *Rev. Econ. Studies*, Vol. 17, No. 3, pp. 107-26, 1949-50.
33. Samuelson, P. A. "Evaluation of real national income," Oxford Economic Papers, N.S., II (Jan., 1950), 1-29.
34. _____. "The pure theory of public expenditures," *Rev. Econ. and Stat.*, 36: 387-89, 1954.
35. _____. "Aspects of public expenditure theories," *Rev. Econ. and Stat.*, 40: 332-38, 1958.
36. Scitovsky, Tibor. "A note on welfare propositions in economics," *Rev. Econ. Studies*, 9:77-88, 1941.
37. _____. "A reconsideration of the theory of tariffs," *Rev. Econ. Studies*, 9:89-110, 1942. Reprinted in Readings in the Theory of International Trade, Howard S. Ellis and Lloyd A. Metzler, eds., Blakiston Co., Philadelphia, pp. 358-89, 1949.
38. Simon, Herbert. "A behavioral model of rational choice," *Quart. Jour. Econ.*, 69:99-118, 1955.
39. Steiner, Peter O. "Choosing among alternative public investments," *Amer. Econ. Rev.*, 49:893-916, 1959.

PETER O. STEINER is Professor of Economics at the University of Wisconsin. He has applied his interest in problems of public investment to the water resources field.

Chapter 4

PETER O. STEINER

Choosing Among Alternative Public Investments in the Water Resource Field *

S HOULD THE FEDERAL GOVERNMENT have permitted the Idaho Power Company to develop Hells Canyon or should it instead have developed a public project? If the latter, should it have built one high dam, two intermediate-sized dams or three smaller ones? Questions like these, involving the amount and form of public investments, require criteria for evaluating the investments and operational guides for applying the criteria. In this chapter attention will be focused on the problem of choosing among alternative public expenditures with particular reference to water resource development.[1]

As a classical problem in efficient resource allocation, there is a solution that is both simple and well known. In an efficiency-oriented mold where there are no barriers to the flows of funds or resources,

*Reprinted with the permission of *The Amer. Econ. Rev.*, Vol. 49, No. 5, 1959, pp. 894-916.

The author gratefully acknowledges the assistance of the Social Science Research Council whose faculty research fellowship made this research possible. The Water Resources Planning and Development Project of the Graduate School of Public Administration, Harvard University, provided stimulus, assistance and a forum for discussing the ideas with a wide assortment of experts. Too many people have read and commented on earlier drafts of this chapter to be individually named, but my thanks to them all. Robert Dorfman, Otto Eckstein, Stephen Marglin and Roger Miller have been particularly helpful.

where "benefits" and "costs" are correctly determinable, it is evident that appropriate policy is to build every project for which benefits exceed costs and to develop every project to the point where marginal benefits equal marginal costs.[2]

There are several reasons why this solution is not satisfactory.

1. The pure efficiency criterion is not dominant in determining the volume of public expenditures. Other sensible dimensions of public welfare such as cyclical stability, economic growth, income distribution and the size of government are (and should be) significant determinants of the volume of public expenditures. For this reason there may be effective budget constraints on the expenditure possibilities. Efficiency has a role but it is within limits established by these constraints. Such constraints imply opportunity costs:

(a) When budgetary constraints leave the marginal benefit-cost ratio different in the public and private sectors, there is an opportunity cost of transferring dollars from one sector to another.[3] Evidently the size of this opportunity cost will vary according to the way in which funds are transferred and the level of resource use in the sector from which transferred.

(b) So far as budgets are constraining, otherwise meritorious projects will not be undertaken. There is thus an opportunity cost of foregone public alternatives. Specifically this will imply development of projects to a point short of the level where marginal benefits equal marginal costs.[4]

2. Because of the pre-emptive right of government in certain areas, a positive decision with respect to some public project may preclude (I shall subsequently use the word *displace*) an alternative private development. The significance of such displacement is that it involves loss of those public benefits that would arise through private endeavor. But the opportunity cost of such displacement is not usually the whole of the benefits from private development, since displaced funds may be employed elsewhere. It is only the "superior attractiveness" (which I will call *supramarginality*) of the specific displaced project over *its* marginal alternative that is a proper opportunity cost of displacement. Because of pre-emption, these private opportunities may be exceptionally attractive. The extent to which private marginal alternatives have relevance will depend upon the level of employment of resources.[5]

3. A specific public program will consist of some selection of individual projects (e.g., dams of specified heights as specified locations) from among a larger number of possible projects. Not only are the benefits and costs of particular projects interdependent (and thus the value of a specific dam depends upon what other dams are built) but some projects will be mutually incompatible. This incompatibility may be of two kinds: it may be purely technological (it is not possible to build two dams on the same site, or to use a given increment of a specified dam for two conflicting purposes at the same time); it may be purely economic (a specified community requiring X units of electric power may have a choice among any of a series of hydro sites and also

a series of possible steam-generating plants; but if every such project is capable of producing the required X units, any two such projects will be economically incompatible). The significance of this is to complicate enormously the choice among alternative projects.

4. Discreteness of individual projects is essential for an operational solution to the problem. Not only is discreteness sometimes required for technological reasons, but estimation of the magnitudes of benefits and costs on the basis of potentially available data requires comparison of discrete alternatives.

All of these considerations taken together make choice of the "best possible program," given the restraints, a complex one which no simple marginal equivalence can handle. It is the primary purpose of this chapter to provide an *operational* framework for choosing efficient programs (and thus also program elements, or projects) subject to appropriate budget restraints, incompatibility restraints and discrete restraints while recognizing (or approximating) the full range of opportunity costs of any action.

The next sections develop a model which will suggest how to assign a numerical value to every potential project so that it may be compared directly with every other potential project; and thus the program (combination of projects) may be chosen that will maximize the appropriate welfare criteria subject to all appropriate restraints. The essential features of this model are: (1) its recognition of the general equilibrium character of the consequences of a specified public investment decision that result from both the source(s) of funds and the displacements (if any) that occur; a central conviction of the model is that second- and even third-round effects may not be negligible; (2) its framing of decision rules in such a form that data for their application are likely to be available and that can be applied by modern techniques of numerical analysis; (3) its generality, which embraces a whole series of potentially relevant special cases.

This model, by focusing on the choice problem, neglects other important problems. Specifically, it takes as given (a) the identification of the feasible components of a program,[6] and (b) the determination of the net benefits that accrue from using these components singly or in specified combinations. These "givens" represent difficult and important elements in the over-all problem of water resource development, and there is no intention of minimizing their importance.

An initial oversimplified example may serve to illustrate the central difference between the present approach and conventional benefit-cost analysis. Suppose a choice must be made between two public projects, A and B, for which the relevant basic data are shown in the table which follows. Notwithstanding the identical benefits and costs, the two projects are not identical in their effect. Project A if undertaken will use $20 less of the scarce public budget, but will leave $20 less in taxpayers' hands; additionally, Project A will displace a supramarginal private investment. Project A will be preferred if, but only if, the net benefits produced by the additional $20 within the public budget exceed

	Project A	Project B
Net benefits (net of all costs, appropriately discounted)	100	100
Cost to government	70	70
Source of government funds:		
from existing budget	50	70
from increased taxes	20	0
Displaced private project:	yes	no
Net benefits	40	0
Private investment	30	0

the combined net benefits foregone by the transfer of funds through taxation and by foregoing of the supramarginal investment opportunity.

THE MODEL

The Function To Be Maximized

Recognizing the general equilibrium nature of a public investment decision, the objective function is the present value of the difference between total benefits and total costs *in all sectors of the economy.*[7] While measurement of benefits and costs is not discussed in this chapter, what is meant in principle is the market values (actual or imputed) of the stream of goods and services produced and of the resources used. Present values are the time streams of anticipated benefits and costs discounted by an appropriate rate of discount. This objective function comprehends the indirect as well as the direct effects of a public expenditure.

The role of the rate of discount in this analysis is to permit the evaluation at a point of time of streams of benefits and costs that occur over time; it is a metric for comparing unlike time profiles. It is the opportunity cost of deferred consumption (some would call it "social time preference"), and should not be confused with a number of other interest rates that may be appropriate in other connections.[8] It will be designated as π.

In choosing to maximize a concept embodying net benefits, it is evident that attention is being directed toward an efficiency objective. Are we making this the overriding criterion for decision? Were this an unconstrained maximum, the answer would be yes; for a constrained maximum, the answer is no. The size of the budgets that are restraining leaves economic efficiency in a relatively secondary role. Within the limits imposed, efficiency seems the sensible criterion.

Sectors of the Economy

While the objective function comprehends the general equilibrium effects in the entire economy, it is evident that it is necessary to consider only those sectors on which a public expenditure (of the kind herein considered) will have an impact. Our sectors may, therefore, comprehend less than the entire economy. If, as seems likely, a specific governmental decision in the water resources field will not affect the size of the defense budget, that budget need not be included. In a truly general equilibrium sense, of course, everything affects everything else. But the imposed constraints in the form of budgets may in fact provide significant insulation against many kinds of effects. For the present, consider four sectors (two public and two private) as defined in the following paragraphs. Some expansion of this number may be necessary, as is noted subsequently.

The Public Sectors (S1 and S3). Sector 1 is defined to include the set of projects among which direct choice is to be made. It might include all water resources projects everywhere in the nation under the jurisdiction of the agencies selecting projects and allocating budgeted funds.[9] It might be defined more broadly to include all public works projects, or it might be defined much more narrowly. What is controlling is (a) the jurisdiction of the budget that is controlling, and (b) the range of alternatives that are to be specifically considered for inclusion. The more broadly it is defined, the greater the scope given to the "efficiency" criterion in choosing outlets for public expenditure.[10] Specific projects in Sector 1 are designated by the subscript ij.[11]

But while the appropriate budget comprehends all projects in this sector, it is not so limited. Not all the possible public projects for which benefits exceed costs are explicitly considered. Since both project design and benefit and cost estimation are expensive activities, it is neither feasible nor sensible to develop plans for them if they have a low probability of being built because of the limited budget. Sector 3 is viewed as the reservoir of such inchoate projects. If, because of a lack of meritorious projects in Sector 1, or because of the lumpiness of discrete projects in Sector 1 there are extra funds, funds become available for expenditure in Sector 3. Consideration of Sector 3 thus serves two purposes: first, it requires that the yield of any project from Sector 1 included in the final program exceed the yield of any project not specifically considered, and second, it provides recognition of the fact that unutilized funds have some productive value.

Sector 3 thus plays a role analogous to "slack activities" in linear programming and results in making the total expenditure from the restrained budget in the two public sectors *definitionally* equal to the amount of that budget. In what follows we assume, for simplicity, that the yield (to be defined) per dollar in Sector 3 is an estimable magnitude that can be represented by a constant, a_3.

The Private Sectors (S2 and S4). Sector 2 consists of the relevant private projects that are alternative to the projects included in Sector 1 and that will thus be displaced if the public projects are undertaken. The jth project is the private alternative to the one or more public projects for providing the jth service.[12] If there is more than one private alternative for each public project, the one included in Sector 2 is the one (or the set of compatible ones) that will actually be undertaken. This may be a matter that the government can specify (via licensing, for example) or it may be the one most attractive to private investors.

It must be made clear that the projects in this sector are actual alternatives, not idealized "private alternatives." As such, the quantity and/or quality of the private service may differ from that comprehended in the public alternative.[13] If there is no alternative that would be undertaken, it is convenient to imagine a dummy alternative whose costs and benefits are both zero. By this definition, Sector 2 consists of a set of $j*$ elements.

Evidently we are assuming that public authorities have first choice: by building a specific project *(ij)* they preclude the *j*th private project; by failing to provide the *j*th service by one of the *ij* public projects they (in effect) have left it to be provided by the *j*th private project.

Sector 4 consists of what may be called the pool of marginal private investment opportunities. Need for this sector is due to the fact that the real opportunity cost of displacing a private project is the supramarginality of that project, not its total net benefits. For simplicity it is assumed that this sector consists of a homogeneous stock of investment opportunities whose yield per dollar can be represented by a constant, a_4.[14]

If there is no alternative investment, that is, if funds displaced remain wholly idle, we regard a dummy alternative for which $a_4 = 0$. In this way it is appropriate to regard the sum of the private investment in sectors 2 and 4 as a constant, unless because of the adoption of some project or program there is a transfer of funds from the private to the public sector (for example, via taxation). Put differently, if the public development occurs wholly within the preassigned budget limit, we assume it can affect the productivity of private investments (by displacing supramarginal investment opportunities) but not the volume of that investment.

If adoption of a specific public program causes a net increase in the size of the restraining budget, it will imply a transfer of funds into the public sectors, and the opportunities thus foregone must also be considered.

Forms of the Objective Function

The function to be maximized (subject to subsequently enumerated restraints) can be written as follows:

$$(1) \qquad N = \sum_{s1} x_{ij} G_{ij} \; - \; \sum_{s2} x_j G_j \; + \; \sum_{s3} x_p G_p \; + \; \sum_{s4} x_p G_p$$

where the G's are the "gains," i.e., the present values of the benefits over all costs, and the x's represent the level of specific projects and p is a running subscript. For our discrete case, each project has a level of either zero (it is not undertaken) or one (it is undertaken). In this form, the objective function does not help solve anything. But as shown in the appendix, it is equivalent to find the maximum (subject to the same restraints) of the following function:

$$(2) \qquad\qquad\qquad Z = \sum_{S1} x_{ij} y_{ij}$$

where

$$(3) \qquad\qquad y_{ij} = (G_{ij} - a_3 k_{ij}) - (G_j - a_4 l_j) - a_2 m_{ij}$$

and where:

a_3 and a_4 have the meanings previously assigned.

a_2 is opportunity cost per dollar of funds transferred from the private sectors to the public sector.

k_{ij} is the drain of the ijth project on the limiting budget.

l_j is the capital cost of the jth private project.

m_{ij} is the number of dollars transferred to the public sector as a result of the adoption of the ijth public project.

$\bar{k}_{ij} = k_{ij} + m_{ij}$.

Each y_{ij} is a number. Equation (2) tells us that if we choose a program of projects in such a way as to maximize the sum of the y_{ij}, we will have maximized the basic objective function specified in equation (1).

The several terms in equation (3) have been arranged to facilitate interpretation. The first parenthesis consists of difference between the present value of net benefits of the ijth project and the present value that the scarce funds it takes from the limited budget would produce if applied outside of Sector 1.[15] It is thus the gain of the specific project over other public use of the limited public funds. The main function of this term is to permit direct comparison of alternative public projects of very different size, a problem that has worried many people and led to some foolish solutions.[16]

The second parenthesis represents the supramarginality of the private project displaced. It is only the supramarginality of any displacement that is truly an opportunity cost of that displacement.

The final term measures the opportunity cost of transferring m dollars from the private sector to the public sector *in addition* to the previous budget. There is some disagreement about how frequent such transfers are. Probably for most specific projects considered, funds come entirely from within the previously assigned budget limits, but it is not impossible that in specific cases authorization of specific projects is accompanied by willingness to provide some increase in taxes and thus an increase in the total federal budget.

In sum, the y's represent net gains of three separate kinds of opportunity costs: (1) the cost of using scarce public funds, (2) the cost of displacing a supramarginal private project and (3) the cost of the net transfer of funds from the private to the public sector specifically attributable to the adoption of the project. It should be noted that the y's are relative, not absolute, measures of net benefits over all opportunity cost.[17]

Restraints.

Were it not for incompatibilities among projects and for budget limitations, choosing all projects for which y is positive would assure a maximum. Given a budget restraint but neglecting incompatibilities, it would be sufficient to rank projects according to the size of the y's and move down the list until the budget was exhausted. But the combined existence of both budget restraints and incompatibilities are central *practical* features of the problem of choosing an optimal expenditure program. We hope to specify the restraints in such a way as to be consistent with techniques of solution of the choice problem.

Budget Restraint.

(a)
$$\sum_{S1} x_{ij} k_{ij} \leq K$$

where K is the restrained budget.

What is the appropriate definition of K? Should it be the total budget for capital expenditure, total expenditure, total expenditure not reimbursable, or (as Eckstein [3] suggests) the present value of total expenditures? There are interesting issues here, which space precludes discussing at this time. In terms of the model, any one can be implemented. Indeed, only slight modification is required to substitute a series of budget restraints which differentiate according to type and timing of expenditures.

Discreteness.

(b)
$$x_{ij}, x_j = 0, 1; \quad \text{all } ij, j.$$

Assume discreteness is essentially a matter of definition. Suppose we imagine a dam at a given location which can be built alternatively at three different heights. This is most conveniently handled by defining the dam as three discrete (and mutually incompatible) projects, one corresponding to each of the feasible heights. Of course the height of a dam may be truly continuous, at least within limits; the procedure suggested is to choose (either by sampling techniques or by judgment) discrete levels for analysis.[18]

Incompatibility Restraints.

(c)
$$\sum_i x_{ij} + x_j = 1; \quad \text{all } j.$$

(d)
$$\sum_j x_{ij} \leq 1; \quad \text{all } i.$$

The first of these restraints recognizes that, of all the included public projects that could provide the jth service, not more than one can be chosen. Considering also the private alternative (which may be a dummy alternative), one and only one is always chosen.

The second restraint recognizes that the same facility (e.g., dam site) can be used only once. This does not mean it can be used to provide only a single function. If, for example, a given dam *(i)* can be used alternatively (a) for flood control, (b) for hydropower and (c) for some lesser amount of hydropower plus some flood control, we envisage three *j*'s, one corresponding to each of the uses.

Evidently the coding of projects (defining i and j) is critical. The fundamental purpose of this coding is to recognize the incompatibilities. In the absence of complementarities of uses and of benefits, this coding occasions few problems. Complementarities do exist, and they complicate matters. For example, if two compatible projects used together provide benefits different from the sum of the benefits received if they are used alone (because they are operated in series and outflows from one become inflows into the other), we must multiply the number of projects. For example, if two projects (1, 2) can be used in combination in three different ways *(a, b, c)* as well as separately, we must identify five different projects $(1; 2; 1 + 2, a; 1 + 2, b; 1 + 2, c)$, which are mutually incompatible. In general all problems of coding, including the problems of complementarity, are solved by increasing the number of "projects" defined. Since the selection among projects is to be made by mechanical means, the extent to which feasibility is impaired depends upon the power (and cost) of computational techniques.

PROBLEMS OF SOLUTION

Any attack on the water resource problem involves estimation of the benefits and costs of individual projects. This formidable task presumably provides the G's of the present model, and is taken as given. The significant additional data required in this model are the values for the a's, the opportunity costs not reflected in factor prices.

Each of the parameters, a_3, a_4, a_2, involves the public valuation of the net benefits of a dollar of expenditure outside Sector 1 (the subscripts referring to the sector in which spent). To understand the factors determining the magnitudes of these parameters, consider the following simplified problem:

Suppose that for an initial expenditure of v dollars, a net benefit stream of B dollars per year for T years is generated. Let $D(i)$ be the present value of B dollars per year for T years, discounted at the rate i.

$$D(i) = B \int_0^T e^{-iT} \, dt = B \frac{(1 - e^{-iT})}{i} .$$

Let $G(i) = D(i) - v$, the excess of present value over initial expenditure. Our parameters, a, are of the form:

$$a = \frac{G(\pi)}{v} = \frac{D(\pi)}{v} - 1$$

where π is the public rate of discount. It is probable, in view of scarce budgets, that the $G(\pi)$, and thus a, are positive. For any project it is possible to find an internal rate of return, r, which will make $G(r)$ exactly zero, i.e.:

$$D(r) - v = 0,$$

$$D(r) = v$$

whence,

$$a = \frac{D(\pi)}{D(r)} - 1 = \frac{r}{\pi} \frac{(1 - e^{-\pi T})}{(1 - e^{-rT})} - 1$$

and thus the value of a depends upon π, r, and T. Table 4.1 shows values of a for selected values of π, r and T:

Table 4.1. Values of a

r	T = 25			T = 50			T = 100		
	$\pi = .02$	$\pi = .04$	$\pi = .06$	$\pi = .02$	$\pi = .04$	$\pi = .06$	$\pi = .02$	$\pi = .04$	$\pi = .06$
.02	0.0	− .20	− .34	0.0	− .33	− .50	0.0	− .43	− .62
.04	.24	0.0	− .18	.46	0.0	− .27	.76	0.0	− .32
.06	.52	.22	0.0	1.0	.36	0.0	1.6	.48	0.0
.08	.82	.46	.20	1.6	.76	.29	2.5	.96	.33
.10	1.1	.72	.41	2.2	1.1	.60	3.3	1.5	.67
.15	2.0	1.4	.99	3.7	2.2	1.4	5.5	2.7	1.5

It is evident that when $\pi = r$, $a = 0$. This situation would necessarily pertain in, say, a purely competitive model in which (if there is more than one sector) funds would flow between sectors until the yield of the marginal projects in each sector was the same, and, further, equal to π, the rate of discount. That this need not be the case is due to the imposition of budgets that impede such free flow of funds, and further to the pre-emptive reservation of certain types of projects to the public sector. If such impediments exist, attention to differences in marginal alternatives must be recognized. The values of a serve this purpose.

The Relevance and Size of a_3

The constant a_3 represents the opportunity cost of using one dollar of the restrained budget within the list of projects in Sector 1 rather than in Sector 3. It is thus the "shadow price" of the scarce budget. Its relevance occurs within the maximization procedure because of the discreteness and unequal size of individual projects. Suppose, for example, that within an over-all budget limit of $500, program A (consisting of one group of projects) produces net gains of $100 for an expenditure of $500, while program B provides net gains of $90 for an expenditure of $400. Which is the preferred program? Evidently the answer depends upon the use to which the saved $100 might be put. In this case, if $a_3 = .1$, the two programs are identical in merit.[19]

The appropriate size of a_3 is fundamentally an empirical question to which I do not have the answer. It cannot be negative: if the internal rate of return (call it r_3) of projects in Sector 3 is less than π, the projects have no merit whatever. Beyond this, a_3 is probably relatively small; one would expect the strongly supramarginal projects to be included in Sector 1. Evidently the size of a_3 is crucially affected by the ratio r_3 /π which in turn will depend upon how binding is the budgetary limit.

The Relevance and Size of a_4

This constant, while formally symmetrical with a_3, is both more important and has more conceptual difficulties. Its purpose is to permit comparison of a specific private project displaced with its (marginal) private alternative. Difficulties are of two sorts:

First, supposing there is a homogeneous class of private investment opportunities that are marginal as privately measured, we require an evaluation of these private investments discounted at the public rate, π. This causes difficulty because two projects whose present value is equal if evaluated at r_4 (as we will designate the internal rate of return of marginal private projects) may be unequal if evaluated at π. Indeed, project A may be superior to project B if evaluated at r_4 and inferior if evaluated at π, because of differences in the time periods over which benefits are received, or in the time profiles, or both. The practical solution would appear to require making some estimate of the average time paths and time durations for classes of marginal projects, although something more sophisticated than simple averaging is probably desirable [1].

The second difficulty is that marginal private investment opportunities are probably not homogeneous in view of the variety of organizations that we include in the private sector. For example, large private manufacturing firms require a higher rate of return than do privately owned public utilities, and municipal governments doubtless would apply still a third rate. At the limit this would involve the tedious task of identifying the specific marginal alternative to every displacement; more likely it will be possible to simplify by considering a few subclasses of alternatives to public expenditure and estimating separate values of r_4 (and thus a_4) for each.[20] In any case, given high marginal cut-off rates of return in at least some private sectors, the numerical value of a_4 may be substantially greater than zero, as reference to Table 4.1 will suggest.[21]

The Relevance and Size of a_2

The opportunity costs of transferring funds from the private to the public sectors will depend ultimately upon which groups in the private sector furnish the funds. Krutilla and Eckstein [5, Chap. 4] consider the effect of two types of tax reduction: the first, reducing income taxes in a manner most advantageous to low-income families, and also reducing sales taxes; the second, reducing income taxes with special emphasis on upper-income brackets, and also reducing corporate income taxes. In each case they find that the "appropriate" weighted average "interest rate" is between 5 and 6 percent. This interest rate is analogous to the internal rates of return with which we have been dealing and may be designated r_2. Reference to Table 4.1 will show the magnitude of a_2 for various values of T and π.[22]

How important the transfer of funds is depends upon the budgetary facts of life. Given an economy with a persistent tendency toward inflation, and given the large size of defense and related expenditures, the size of the public works budget would seem to be confined within rather narrow limits by over-all political and economic considerations. So far as budgets are rigid, no attention need be paid to the cost of transfer of funds. The term $a_2 m_{ij}$ is included in the metric chiefly to permit flexibility in its application. At present the m_{ij} seem likely to be small; so far as they are, the magnitude of the constant a_2 loses importance.

AN APPLICATION OF THE MODEL

A simplified application may serve to clarify the model and to illuminate the role of the various opportunity costs in the special cases. Table 4.2 presents data for a public decision between two alternative public projects and the private alternative thereto.[23] In treating this

Table 4.2. Simplified Case (millions of dollars)

Public project S1	Code ij	$\pi = .025$		$\pi = .055$	
		Present value of net benefits G_{ij}	Investment k_{ij}	G_{ij}	k_{ij}
High dam	11	1000	400	250	430
2 lower dams	21	800	200	300	220
Private alternative S2	j	G_j	l_j	G_j	l_j
3 low dams	1	550	200	150	200

Private interest rate = 5%.

example, we assume that investment funds are the limiting resource, that the budget is at least $430 million, and that choice is limited to the specific alternatives listed. The problem is then simply to maximize.

$\sum_{s_1} x_{ij} y_{ij}$ subject to x_{11}, x_{21}, $x_1 = 0$, 1 and $x_{11} + x_{21} + x_1 = 1$.

We analyze three cases according to the source of the investment funds: Case 1 in which they come entirely from the existing public budget ($k_{ij} = \bar{k}_{ij}$); Case 2 in which they come entirely from the private sector ($m_{ij} = \bar{k}_{ij}$); and Case 3 in which half comes from each source ($m_{ij} = k_{ij} = .5\bar{k}_{ij}$). Each case assumes a discount rate, π, equal in turn to .025 and .055.

Consider Case 1 for $\pi = .025$. We can immediately write:

$$y_{11} = 1000 - 400a_3 - (550 - 200a_4)$$

$$y_{21} = 800 - 200a_3 - (550 - 200a_4)$$

We will prefer project 11 to project 21 if $y_{11} > y_{21}$. We will prefer it to the private alternative if $y_{11} > 0$. These conditions and the condition that $a_3 \geq 0$ immediately yield the condition for choosing $x_{11} = 1$ as:

$$0 \leq a_3 < \min. \begin{Bmatrix} 1.0 \\ 1.12 + .5a_4 \end{Bmatrix}$$

Similarly we will choose project 21 (i.e., let $x_{21} = 1$) if $y_{21} > y_{11}$ and $y_{21} > 0$, which yield the condition:

$$1.0 < a_3 < 1.25 + a_4.$$

Finally, we will choose the private alternative if both y_{11} and y_{22} are negative which yield the condition for $x_1 = 1$:

$$a_3 > \max. \begin{Bmatrix} 1.12 + .5a_4 \\ 1.25 + a_4 \end{Bmatrix}$$

For a specific value of a_4 (which depends, given π, on r_4, the marginal private rate of return) the decision rule becomes a simple function of a_3. That is, for $r_4 = .05$, $a = .85$, the rule is (we arbitrarily assign the borderline cases):

$$\text{choose } x_{11} = 1 \quad if \quad 0 \leq a_3 \leq 1.0$$

$$x_{21} = 1 \quad if \quad 1.0 < a_3 \leq 2.1$$

$$x_1 = 1 \quad if \quad 2.1 < a_3$$

Analysis of the other cases is equally straightforward. Table 4.3 summarizes the decision rules in terms of the values of the a's. Table 4.4 gives them for the assumed values $r_4 = .05$ and $r_2 = .055$.[24]

The main point worth noting is that the decision in general does not rest solely upon the value of the public discount rate (π), since the value of π affects not only the benefits but also the several values of the a's.

This illustration is of course extraordinarily oversimplified in that it involves a choice between only two alternatives, each of which has

Table 4.3. Decision Rules for Choice of Project

	Public: high dam	Public: 2 lower dams	Private: 3 low dams
$\pi = .025$			
Case 1	$0 \leq a_3 \leq \min \begin{Bmatrix} 1.0 \\ 1.12 + .5a_4 \end{Bmatrix}$	$1.0 < a_3 \leq 1.25 + a_4$	$\max \begin{Bmatrix} 1.12 + .5a_4 \\ 1.25 + a_4 \end{Bmatrix} < a_3$
Case 2	$a_2 \leq \begin{Bmatrix} 1.0 \\ 1.12 + .5a_4 \end{Bmatrix}$	$1.0 < a_2 \leq 1.25 + a_4$	$\max \begin{Bmatrix} 1.12 + .5a_4 \\ 1.25 + a_4 \end{Bmatrix} < a_2$
Case 3	$0 \leq a_3 \leq \min \begin{Bmatrix} 2 - a_2 \\ 2.25 - a_2 + a_4 \end{Bmatrix}$	$2 - a_2 < a_3 \leq 2.5 + 2a_4 - a_2$	$\max \begin{Bmatrix} 2.25 - a_2 + a_4 \\ 2.50 - a_2 + 2a_4 \end{Bmatrix} < a_3$
$\pi = .055$			
Case 1	—	$0 \leq a_3 \leq .75 + 1.1a_4$	$\max \begin{Bmatrix} .75 + 1.1a_4 \\ .23 + .47a_4 \end{Bmatrix} < a_3$
Case 2	$a_2 \leq \min \begin{Bmatrix} -.24 \\ .23 + .47a_4 \end{Bmatrix}$	$-.24 < a_2 \leq .75 + 1.1a_4$	$\max \begin{Bmatrix} .75 + 1.1a_4 \\ .23 + .47a_4 \end{Bmatrix} < a_2$
Case 3	$0 \leq a_3 \leq \min \begin{Bmatrix} -.48 - a_2 \\ .47 + .93a_4 - a_2 \end{Bmatrix}$	$-.48 - a_2 < a_3 \leq 1.37 + 1.82a_4 - a_2$	$\max \begin{Bmatrix} .47 + .93a_4 - a_2 \\ 1.37 + 1.82a_4 - a_2 \end{Bmatrix} < a_3$

Table 4.4. Decision Rules if $r_4 = .05$, $r_2 = .055$

	Public: high dam	Public: 2 lower dams	Private: 3 low dams
$\pi = .025 \begin{Bmatrix} a_4 = .85 \\ a_2 = .93 \end{Bmatrix}$			
Case 1	$0 \leq a_3 \leq 1.0$	$1.0 \leq a_3 \leq 2.1$	$2.1 < a_3$
Case 2	all a_3	—	—
Case 3	$0 \leq a_3 \leq 1.07$	$1.07 < a_3 \leq 3.27$	$3.27 < a_3$
$\pi = .055 \begin{Bmatrix} a_4 = -.09 \\ a_2 = 0 \end{Bmatrix}$			
Case 1	—	$0 \leq a_3 \leq .65$	$.65 < a_3$
Case 2	—	all a_3	—
Case 3	—	$0 \leq a_3 \leq 1.99$	$1.99 < a_3$

the same private alternative, in that the budget restraint is not binding, and in other ways. More complicated problems can be most effectively handled by machines.

METHODS OF SOLUTION

Choosing the levels of the choice variables (the x_{ij}) in such a way as to maximize equation (2) subject to the restraints can, in principle, be done in at least two ways. The most general is a problem in linear programming; indeed, since the x_{ij} are all either zero or one, it is the simplest form of linear programming — the so-called transportation problem.[25] In essence, the standard (simplex) method of solution is iterative, proceeding from an arbitrary feasible solution to an optimal one.

An alternative algorithmic procedure based upon enumeration of feasible combinations is available and may prove less expensive for problems of moderate size. Because of the particularly simple form of the objective function and of the restraints, this procedure, easily adapted to machine computation, is as follows:

Step 1: Identify the combinations that are feasible with respect to
the incompatibility restraints.

Consider a case in which there are N projects identified. N is by
definition the number of ij's identified, and cannot be greater than $i*$
times $j*$ (where * indicates the largest value assigned), and is most
likely smaller, because not all facilities can be used for all purposes.
For instance, a dam site below a city cannot be used to provide flood
control protection to the city. Since the problem is to assign each such
project a level of either zero or one, there are 2^N total combinations of
projects — a truly fearsome number for even moderate sizes of N (e.g.,
if $N = 30$, 2^N exceeds 1 billion). Fortunately, not all must be considered, for any program containing more than the smaller of $i*$ or $j*$
projects will necessarily violate one of the incompatibility restraints
on the x_{ij}. Thus, letting $n = \min (i*, j*)$ it is necessary to consider
only

$$\sum_{\alpha=0}^{n} \binom{N}{\alpha} \text{ combinations,}$$

which is a very much smaller number (e.g., if $N = 30$, $n = 4$, the number is about 32,000; if $N = 30$, $n = 5$, the number is about 174,000).[26]
Many of these combinations violate the incompatibility restraints
(c) and (d) which in effect require that programs be taken from an
$(i* + 1) \times j*$ matrix in such a way that not more than one project be included from any row or column. Those programs that do not violate
this condition become a set of addresses for future reference.

Step 2: Compute for each feasible combination identified in Step 1
the $\sum_{ij} x_{ij} k_{ij}$ and eliminate all that violate the budget restraint.

Since the combinations remaining after the first step consist of a
series of programs having some elements with $x_{ij} = 1$, and the rest
equal to zero, all that is required is summation of the k_{ij} of the nonzero components of each program. Those programs that do not violate
this restraint are retained as addresses for the third step.

Step 3: For the addresses identified in Step 2, the $\sum_{ij} x_{ij} y_{ij}$ is
computed, and the program with the largest value is the
best of the feasible programs.

Once again the computation involved is a simple sum of the values
of y_{ij} for each of the projects with nonzero values of x_{ij} in each remaining program.[27] Instead of simply choosing the maximum, it is of
course possible to rank programs in decreasing order, thus leaving the
way open to evaluate the differential merit of alternative programs and

permitting the introduction of such other (nonefficiency) considerations as may be desired. (For example, the second-best program may be very nearly as good as the best and yet provide a politically better geographical distribution of expenditures.)

The choice between the alternative methods of solution will depend upon the relative cost of computation. Either in principle can solve the problem in a straightforward manner.

CONCLUSION

The basic equation (3) of the present model,

$$y_{ij} = (G_{ij} - a_3 k_{ij}) - (G_j - a_4 l_j) - a_2 m_{ij}$$

represents a *general* form of a sensible objective function. It encompasses therefore a variety of special cases which rest implicitly upon certain limiting assumptions. A number of these special cases have been advocated as the correct solution; the present section attempts to place them in context. Special cases can be generated in a number of ways by choice of limiting assumptions concerning the sources of funds, the existence of supramarginal private alternatives and the level of employment.

If federal budgets are regarded as fully flexible, then all marginal funds come from the private sector and the term $a_3 k_{ij}$ vanishes. If private alternatives either do not exist or are merely marginal, the term $(G_j - a_4 l_j)$ also vanishes, and all that remains is $G_{ij} - a_2 m_{ij}$.[28]

Given the heavy defense and related demands upon the federal budget, given full employment of resources and heavy taxes, a different view is that public works budgets are virtually rigid — in which case the term $a_2 m_{ij}$ vanishes. Given also supramarginal private alternatives, this suggests that the relevant terms are $(G_{ij} - a_3 k_{ij}) - (G_j - a_4 l_j)$. These are reasonably realistic assumptions for the bulk of the postwar period.

In an economy characterized by heavy underutilization of resources, one might expect few or no marginally attractive investment opportunities, and the value of a_4 would become zero (since $r_4 = 0$). Similarly, one might visualize a mechanism for transferring funds from private to public sectors that tapped idle resources. Thus the value of a_2 would approach zero, and a larger public works program would be justifiable on efficiency as well as on stability grounds, since some of the indirect opportunity costs would vanish.

That the nature of the choices made will vary according to the general budgetary and economic situation is of course not an exclusive feature of the present model. Transfer costs or internal rates of return also reflect these considerations. The chief advantages of the model are: (1) its flexibility in allowing for changes in the relevance and magnitude of the *different* classes of opportunity costs, (2) its flexibility in defining the appropriate restraint or restraints, (3) its handling of the displacement problem and (4) its ability to handle choice among incompatible alternatives. [29]

MATHEMATICAL APPENDIX

The purpose of this appendix is to show the derivation of equation (2) (p. 40), which maximizes over Sector 1 only, from equation (1), which concerns the maximum over all sectors, and to make clear the role played by the particular assumptions and definitions.

Definitions — Let:

Sectors, $S1$, $S2$, $S3$, $S4$ be defined as in text;

p be a general running subscript ($p=ij$ in $S1$; $p=j$ in $S2$);

π be a discount rate;

G_p be the present value of the pth project over capital and operating costs, evaluated using π;

x_p be the level of the pth project;

$\bar{k}_{ij}$ be cost in units of the scarce budget, $\bar{k}_{ij} = k_{ij} + m_{ij}$, where k_{ij} is the drain on the existing budget, m_{ij} is the net increase in the budget which adoption of the ijth project will cause; m_{ij} represents the amount of funds transferred from the private sector (by taxation or borrowing);

K be the existing budget restraint for $S1$ and $S3$;

l_p be the capital cost of the pth private project;

A be the amount of private investment if no funds transferred;

$\alpha \sum_{S1} x_{ij} m_{ij}$ be the change in private investment owing to the transfer of

$\sum_{S1} x_{ij} m_{ij}$ dollars from private to public sectors;

$$
\left.
\begin{aligned}
a_3 &= \frac{G_p}{k_p} \text{ for } S3 \\[2mm]
a_4 &= \frac{G_p}{l_p} \text{ for } S4
\end{aligned}
\right\} \quad \text{assumed constant,} \quad a_3 \geq 0;
$$

$$a_2 = \alpha a_4.$$

Objective Function:

$$(1) \qquad N = \sum_{S1} x_{ij} G_{ij} + \sum_{S2} x_j G_j + \sum_{S3} x_p G_p + \sum_{S4} x_p G_p.$$

Restraints:

$$\sum_{S1} x_{ij}k_{ij} \le K \text{ (budget restraint).}$$

$$x_p = 0, 1, \text{ all } p \text{ (discreteness restraint).}$$

$$\sum_i x_{ij} + x_j = 1 \text{ (incompatibility of } j\text{'s).}$$

$$\sum_j x_{ij} \le 1 \text{ (incompatibility of } i\text{'s).}$$

Since the direct choice variables are the x_{ij}, it is convenient to reformulate the objective function in a form relying only on these variables.

From the definitions, we note that:

(i) $$\sum_{S1} x_{ij}k_{ij} + \sum_{S3} x_p k_p = K;$$

(ii) $$\sum_{S2} x_j l_j + \sum_{S4} x_p l_p = A - \alpha \sum_{S1} x_{ij}m_{ij};$$

(iii) $$G_p = a_3 k_p, \text{ for } S3;$$

(iv) $$G_p = a_4 l_p, \text{ for } S4.$$

Thus, we can write:

$$\sum_{S3} x_p G_p = a_3 \sum_{S3} x_p k_p = a_3 \left(K - \sum_{S1} x_{ij}k_{ij} \right),$$

$$\sum_{S4} x_p G_p = a_4 \sum_{S4} x_p l_p = a_4 \left(A - \alpha \sum_{S1} x_{ij}m_{ij} - \sum_{S2} x_j l_j \right).$$

Substituting, in eq. (1):

$$N = \sum_{S1} x_{ij}G_{ij} + a_3 K - a_3 \sum_{S1} x_{ij}k_{ij} + \sum_{S2} x_j G_j + a_4 A$$
$$- a_4 \alpha \sum_{S1} x_{ij}m_{ij} - a_4 \sum_{S2} x_j l_j.$$

(1.1) $$N = \sum_{S1} (G_{ij} - a_3 k_{ij} - a_2 m_{ij})x_{ij} + \sum_{S2} (G_j - a_4 l_j)x_j + a_3 K + a_4 A.$$

Let $w_{ij} = G_{ij} - a_3 k_{ij} - a_2 m_{ij},$

$w_j = G_j - a_4 l_j,$

$y_{ij} = w_{ij} - w_j.$

We can rewrite eq. (1.1):

$$N = \sum_{S1} w_{ij}x_{ij} + \sum_{S2} w_j x_j + a_3 K + a_4 A.$$

From the restraints we know that $x_j = 1 - \sum_i x_{ij}$, and thus:

$$N = \sum_{S1} w_{ij}x_{ij} + \sum_{S2} w_j - \sum_{S2} w_j \sum_i x_{ij} + a_3K + a_4A$$

$$= \sum_{S1} (w_{ij} - w_j)x_{ij} + \sum_{S2} w_j + a_3K + a_4A.$$

Since the last three terms are constant, they will not affect the maximum, and we can maximize instead:

$$(2) \qquad\qquad Z = \sum_{S1} y_{ij}x_{ij}$$

where, to expand,

$$(3) \qquad\qquad y_{ij} = (G_{ij} - a_3k_{ij}) - (G_j - a_4l_j) - a_2m_{ij}.$$

FOOTNOTES

[1] While the focus is on water resources, I believe the analysis can be readily extended to other aspects of the applied theory of public expenditure. Water resource development is particularly suitable for analysis for several reasons: (1) it involves the critical border between public and private expenditures, which are often truly alternatives; (2) it presents enormously complicated practical problems of choice among alternatives that can serve to illustrate merits (and limitations) of the analysis; and (3) it has received a remarkable wave of attention in recent years from professional economists. See, most recently: O. Eckstein (3), J. V. Krutilla and O. Eckstein (5), R. N. McKean (6). Margolis' able review article of these three books (7) notes with exceptional clarity certain of the fundamental difficulties that the solutions offered in these contributions encounter.

The parent discussion of the federal government (4) is known, and hereafter cited, as the "Green Book."

[2] Eckstein (3, pp. 47-73) provides a nice derivation from classical welfare economics.

[3] Krutilla and Eckstein (5, Chap. 4) provide a "special case" solution designed to recognize this. I will refer to modifications that recognize one (but not all) of the crucial complications as special cases, in contrast to the more general case developed in this chapter.

[4] This special case is recognized by Eckstein (3), where he suggests using a marginal benefit-cost cut-off ratio of $1 + \nu$, where ν is so chosen that the list of all projects so designed for which total benefits exceed costs just exhausts the scarce budget. For similar reasons the Green Book (4) rejects maximizing benefits minus costs as a criterion since it favors large projects over small ones. McKean (6) also addresses this problem. His procedure is to choose the rate of discount in such a way that building all projects for which marginal benefits equal marginal costs will just exhaust the budget.

[5] Stephen Marglin has called my attention to the fact that displacements may be negative as well as positive — that a public project may *create* supramarginal private investment opportunities. That this possibility (of what are often called secondary benefits) can be handled within the framework of the model developed in the following section is neglected in the subsequent exposition.

[6] Feasible, as used here, does not mean compatible. If, say, a dam can be built at three different sites, at five different heights at each site there will be 15 feasible component projects. The choice technique developed can easily handle incompatibility restraints.

[7] The use of *net* benefits may be questioned. Why should we be concerned with costs at all — why not maximize the discounted value of *gross* benefits subject to a whole series of resource restraints, one for each resource used? In principle this procedure seems superior, but it would require inclusion of the benefits of deferred use of scarce resources in the value of the discounted benefit stream. Use of net benefits assumes that the market-determined factor prices (which lead to costs) attach the appropriate reservation values to resources not currently used, and thus saves a totally impossible burden of estimation. Every restraint used implies a shadow "factor price" for the restrained resource; we use

such restraints (and hence such shadow prices) only for the key constraining budget or budgets.

[8] Among them: the government borrowing rate; the private borrowing rate; the opportunity cost of transferring funds from the private sector to the public sector; the internal rates of return of marginal projects in any sector; a risk or uncertainty premium; the rate of discount used in the private capital market to evaluate unequal time streams. As we have need for any of these perfectly sensible measures they will be introduced. But they are not necessarily equal to the opportunity cost of deferred consumption of net benefits. Some of these (e.g., interest actually paid) are included in the costs subject to discounting. Under some institutional circumstances some or all of these rates may coincide, but there is no necessary reason why they must.

[9] Whether state and municipal projects are included here or treated in a private sector depends upon how decisions are in fact to be made. If an integrated intergovernmental agency is allocating pooled funds over pooled opportunities, the entire pool is in Sector 1; if state and municipal funds are independently administered, they are not included in Sector 1. Hereafter we assume the latter.

[10] The sensible definition must avoid triviality or unusability. If the budget is defined overnarrowly — e.g., to apply to a specific dam at a specific location — the consideration of the value of that dam vis-à-vis other possible projects is lost. If defined too broadly — e.g., to cover all federal expenditures — it must become nonoperational. But whether it should cover specific river basins, or comprehend all water projects, I leave to others.

[11] The double subscript is designed to recognize that a project involves use of a certain facility ($i = 1, 2, \ldots i^*$) for a certain purpose ($j = 1, 2, \ldots j^*$). The coding of projects plays an important role in recognizing incompatibilities, as will be discussed below.

[12] We here assume that it is the jth public *service* that displaces a private project providing a substitute source of that service. The assumption may be wrong. Facilities as well as services can displace. For example: a specific public flood-control dam not only may displace a private flood-control project but, by pre-empting a location, may displace (say) a private power plant as well. The appropriate procedure is to regard the projects in Sector 2 as the private projects actually displaced by the ij public projects — for whatever reason. This causes no difficulties unless there are internal incompatibilities *within* Sector 2.

Such incompatibilities, while unlikely because of the definition of projects in Sector 2 as actual (rather than fictional) alternatives, can occur. If they do, they must be recognized by additional incompatibility constraints, and they complicate somewhat the techniques of solution discussed. In no case will they prevent solution.

[13] For example, a series of public projects for providing respectively 90, 150 and 200 units of hydro power may all potentially displace the same 100-unit private steam-generating plant.

[14] The value of a_4, as subsequently shown, depends upon the internal rate of return of marginal investment opportunities that are the alternatives to private investment in specific, displaceable alternatives to public projects. The homogeneity of these is in fact doubtful — public utilities, municipal governments and large private corporations surely have different "cut-off" rates of return. For this reason it would probably be appropriate to use a few broad subclasses of "marginal private investment" with separate values of a_4 for each. This creates no difficulties in the analysis, but would complicate the exposition considerably.

[15] Notice that we do not compare the gain of this project with that of another project in Sector 1 which may ultimately not be built for lack of funds. *That* opportunity cost comes in selection of the group of projects that maximize equation (2) subject to the budget restraints. We here compare the considered project with alternatives that are not specifically considered. This has a tremendous advantage over the procedure described in footnote 4; we do not have to predict before we start which projects will not be built — we do not have to assume the answer to our problem in order to arrive at it. It is perhaps possible that some iterative procedure could be used in that (other) approach, but I have not been able to find one that converged on the correct solution. The relevance of this in a practical sense is to the problem of suboptimization. I find no solution unless one can take subbudgets as being predetermined and acceptable.

[16] For example, attempting to maximize the ratio of benefits to costs.

[17] Equation (2) is equivalent to equation (1) for finding a maximum, but it is not identical. A number of constant terms, that affect the value of the function but not the location of its maximum, have been dropped. See appendix.

[18] Benefit and cost functions, if they are presented continuously, usually result from fit-

ting a function to discrete observations in any case. For many other cases data are estimable only for discrete levels. It is of course quite possible that the optimal height may be missed by this procedure, but if assumed discrete observation points are chosen so that the continuous function is monotonic between them, an iterative procedure is available with which to move from an approximate solution to a final optimal solution.

[19] Why should the two programs be unequal — why is not program B expanded to exhaust the budget? It may not be possible because of the discreteness of the included projects to find an increment that will (a) increase the gains and not violate the restraints, budgetary or other, and (b) will have a marginal benefit greater than projects in Sector 3.

[20] In effect this means replacing sectors 2 and 4 by several subsectors in the analysis. This causes no difficulty, but expands the number of terms in the *generalized* valuation metric. For a specific project with a specific private alternative the problem remains the same, but one must choose the "right" value of a_4. The algebraic extension of the argument to subsectors is omitted, but it is straightforward.

[21] To appreciate the real significance of this fact, recall that the constant occurs in the expression $(G_j - a_4 l_j)$ whose two terms are dimensionally equivalent. The higher the value of a_4, the less is the supramarginality of a given G_j. For example, the cost of displacing a steel mill (say by flooding its proposed site) is only the difference between the value of that site and some other site to which the steel investment will probably be directed. Obviously if displaced projects are marginal they can be ignored; that they may well not be marginal is due to the governmental rights of pre-emption. But if supramarginal, only the supramarginality is significant. This fact has plagued the attempts to recognize displacement through limiting benefits to "alternative cost," and it has similarly given the use of secondary benefits (which are negative displacements) such a shady reputation.

[22] It should be noted that I am giving the transfer of funds a very different role than that assumed by Krutilla and Eckstein (5, Chap. 4). They assume that the alternative to every (small) expenditure is a tax cut (of the appropriate form) of equal amount within a successful governmental stabilization policy. Thus this computed interest rate is the *sole* opportunity cost they consider. In my view this not only neglects displacements but also neglects the fact that the real alternative may be another public project. To the extent that this is so, specific investment decisions do not imply transfers of funds from private to public sectors. It is possible, however, that *part* of the funds required will represent an addition to the federal budget, and for this part the type of weighed average interest rate that they compute is relevant.

[23] The data are based upon the Krutilla and Eckstein (5, Chap. 5) analysis of the Hell's Canyon alternatives. Since a detailed explanation of the derivation of these rounded data from the underlying data requires more space than the example justifies, this had best be regarded as a quasi-hypothetical example. Annual benefits and costs are discounted at π over 100 years in each case. An expanded development of this case is in mimeographed form.

[24] These values appear to be the ones Krutilla and Eckstein imply. Since they make the assumptions of Case 2, the decision appears to be a unique function of the rate of discount, and since they further argue that the correct rate of discount is $\pi = r_2$, their solution is to have the public build the two lower dams.

[25] There are a number of expositions of the method. See for one, (2, Chap. 5). Markowitz and Manne (8) developed a technique for solution that is appropriate for discrete values of the choice variables even if not restricted to zero and one. A more recent (unpublished) work by R. E. Gomory ("An Algorithm for Integer Solutions to Linear Programs," Princeton-I.B.M. Math. Res. Project Tech. Rept. No. 1, Nov. 17, 1958) has developed a solution to the discrete programming problem that is better suited to machine computation.

[26] This maximum number of combinations that the machine must consider in the first step of the analysis can be evaluated directly using binomial tables, or can be approximated for all but very small values of N using areas under the normal curve:

$$\sum_{\alpha=0}^{n} \binom{N}{\alpha} = 2^N \sum_{\alpha=0}^{n} \binom{N}{\alpha}\left(\frac{1}{2}\right)^N \approx 2^N \int_{-\infty}^{t} g(t)dt$$

where $g(t)$ is a normal curve of zero mean and unit standard deviation, and t, the normal deviate.

$$t = \frac{2n + 1 - N}{\sqrt{N}}$$

[27] The three-step procedure here suggested is designed to economize computational time. In principle it would be possible to combine the last two, or even all three steps. For example, it would be possible to compute both $\Sigma x_{ij} k_{ij}$ and $\Sigma x_{ij} y_{ij}$ for all the addresses found in step one, thus combining steps two and three. But to do so would be to calculate the $\Sigma x_{ij} y_{ij}$ for many programs which are of no interest since they violate the budget restraint, and therefore to multiply the number of machine operations required.

An alternative procedure is available if it is desired to leave the budget limit unspecified until the last step.

[28] If, in addition, one follows Krutilla and Eckstein (5) and regards the appropriate $\pi = r_2$, a_2 is zero and the criterion is simply to maximize G_{ij} evaluated at this "transfer-cost" interest rate.

[29] With respect to (1) above, I believe that most of the case studies of 1950-58 made in Krutilla and Eckstein (5) and McKean (6) require re-evaluation in terms of the assumptions appropriate to the period. With respect to (2) above, both Eckstein (3) and Krutilla and Eckstein (5) assume that the appropriate restraint is the present value of total cost; McKean (6) assumes capital cost is the scarce resource. With respect to (3) above, the problem is usually assumed away by supposing all private alternatives are marginal, or by assuming $a_4 = 0$. With respect to (4) above, it is standard practice to ignore incompatibilities — apparently the assumption is made that choice is limited to mutually compatible alternatives. But this ducks a major part of the problem: choosing the efficient compatible sets.

REFERENCES

1. Blyth, C. A. "The theory of capital and its time-measures," Econometrica, 24:467-79, 1956.
2. Dorfman, R., Samuelson, P. A., and Solow, R. M. Linear Programming and Economic Analysis, McGraw-Hill, New York, 1958.
3. Eckstein, O. Water Resource Development: the Economics of Project Evaluation, Harvard Univ. Press, Cambridge, Mass., 1958.
4. Federal Inter-Agency River Basin Committee, Subcommittee on Benefits and Costs, Proposed Practices for Economic Analysis of River Basin Projects, Washington, 1950.
5. Krutilla, J. V., and Eckstein, O. Multiple Purpose River Development: Studies in Applied Economic Analysis, Johns Hopkins Press, Baltimore, 1958.
6. McKean, R. N. Efficiency in Government Through Systems Analysis with Emphasis on Water Resource Development, Wiley & Sons, New York, 1958.
7. Margolis, J. "The economic evaluation of federal water resource development," Amer. Econ. Rev., 49:96-111, 1959.
8. Markowitz, H. M., and Manne, A. S. "On the solution of discrete programming problems," Econometrica, 25:84-110, 1957.

M. M. KELSO is Professor of Agricultural Economics at the University of Arizona. He has made many professional contributions to the natural resources economics literature as well as holding administrative posts at Montana State College and the U.S. Department of Agriculture.

Chapter 5

M. M. KELSO

Economic Analysis
In the Allocation
Of the Federal Budget
To Resource Development

FOR MORE THAN A CENTURY before 1936 the federal government had engaged in programs to develop America's water resources. During this long period, requests for appropriations for such purposes were presented to Congress by the relevant federal agencies. The presentations followed no prescribed formulae to show "worthwhileness." Each recommending agency presented supporting documentation of its case; inevitably, such documentation embraced economic together with broader benefit-and-cost comparisons. These were prepared with terminology and procedures formulated *ad hoc* by each agency — no doubt with an eye to the presentation that would make the most favorable impression on the higher decision makers. To quote Otto Eckstein (1, p. 15):

"The number of resource development projects which local interest and the federal agencies might desire to build in any period will always exceed the number for which funds can actually be made available. Competing claims for money within the federal budget and the difficulty of increasing the general level of taxation impose a limit on the total funds available for water-resource development. Thus choices among projects are unavoidable. To some extent, politics will determine what projects will be undertaken, but there must also be general standards by which projects can be appraised and compared, for political bargaining is no more than one facet of the decision process."

In 1936 a change occurred that instigated empirical and theoretical introspection by federal agencies and by outside analysts leading to the present rash of "stock taking." The change was the adoption by Congress, in the Flood Control Act approved June 22, 1936, of a welfare-economic criterion for appraisal of flood control projects which states that the federal government should sponsor and finance such projects " ... if the benefits to whomsoever they may accrue are in excess of the estimated costs, and if the lives and social security of people are otherwise adversely affected." The economic-feasibility and social welfare criteria embodied in this act have since been extended to almost all federal water and watershed development proposals by combinations of congressional and agency practice.

Prior to 1950, attempts to develop operationally appropriate yet theoretically correct concepts and measurements were largely the product of analyses by Congress and by each separate agency, modified by the debates such disjointed developments inevitably engendered. In 1950 the federal government published the first definitive prescription for the acceptable benefit-cost appraisal of proposed federal water development projects — the "Green Book" (18). In 1952 the first group of economic analysts from outside the federal government was brought in to appraise the conceptual and operational adequacy of the Green Book's prescription for the proper treatment of secondary benefits (19). The Green Book's statement of the acceptable benefit-cost analysis and report, and the inter-agency and agency-congressional debates it stimulated, led to the participation — partly by request, partly volunteer — of technical minds from outside the government. Their aim was to improve the technical respectability of evaluations required of the recommending agencies in support of their competing requests for federal funds.

Several volumes (1, 2, 3) and their reviews (4, 5, 6, 7, 8), together with numerous other papers (see bibliography accompanying this chapter) mark the status of theoretical and empirical development of the economic evaluation of proposed federal resource development undertakings. It is my purpose to examine the stage of development we have reached in defining and organizing the needed concepts and measurements.

IS ECONOMIC EVALUATION A WILL-O-THE-WISP?

Before turning to the mechanics of economic evaluation, let us question whether it is possible to make meaningful evaluations. If relevant economic evaluations of federal resource developments are impossible to attain, or are not significant if attained, we can dispense with a lot of time, effort, money and worry by going about more profitable business. There is respectable opinion that *does* question it. (See 28.)

No one denies the desirability of better decision making in federal budget allocation among competing choices of alternative resource development projects and of other uses of federal moneys. Natural resource development is only one. The point at issue is whether one can analyze objective data in the light of accepted values and determine which decisions would be "sinful" and which "righteous" — a challenge of quite a different order.

The peak criterion that directs decision making in resource development embraces many second-order criteria — economic, social, political and others. It cannot be questioned that many (maybe most, perhaps even all) of these second-order criteria are beyond the pale of cardinality and that if any subcriterion remains noncardinal, the peak criterion remains noncardinal also. Nevertheless, many individuals believe that *economic* second-order criteria can be cardinally ordered as among projects and programs and that, though this leaves the peak criterion imperfect and incomplete, it is worthwhile to determine the economic magnitudes in spite of the rather considerable expense entailed.

Negative attitudes toward this judgment rest on two general grounds: (1) relevant values, constraints and functions, even within the economic second-order criteria, are far too complex for finite and fumbling mortal minds to grasp and manipulate; further, third-order criteria (within economic second-order criteria) of any income equity redistribution generated by resource development cannot be assigned a cardinal measure of preferredness free of value judgments — thus restricting economic second-order criteria to efficiency consequences only. Therefore, all such attempts at economic evaluation turn out to be partial and simplified so that results must be extensively modified by decision-makers to account for excluded items — noneconomic and economic alike — in making the hard choices of reality. (2) The outcome of such a process, limited though it might be to an economic efficiency outcome, will be seriously if not disastrously restricted because many of the relevant economic magnitudes are not market priced.

Both grounds for criticism are valid and relevant. Nevertheless, such second-order, suboptimal evaluations may be useful though noncardinal and imperfect (11). On what grounds does such limited economic evaluation have sufficient usefulness in federal budget allocation to warrant spending scarce resources on it?[1]

Complex decision making such as that involved in setting the federal budget "is molded by limitations on human problem-solving capacities not taken account of in the conventional picture of rational choice." Attempts at a comprehensive overview of choice alternatives in the federal budget run into man's limited intellectual ability, that is, his limited ability to grasp, calculate and remember; and his limited information. "With few exceptions the formal theory of decision making has not faced up to the possibility that complexity can outstrip limited intellectual capacity". (20, pp. 300-304)

Lindblom (20) suggests that policy making and choosing are in reality attained by the incremental method which involves ignoring all elements in the problem not here and now varying (hence without causative significance in the immediate situation), restricting the variables under analysis to the more important few in order to keep the analysis within the bounds of ponderability, determining only what changes will result from small additions and deletions at the margin of events and choosing on the basis of values pertinent to the evaluation of these marginal outcomes relative to the marginal costs.[2]

Lindblom and others writing in the same vein have ignored or have not made clear that setting the federal budget is more than a congressional act. The congressional act is the apogee of the process, the attention-centering act, the point where peak policy decisions as to revenues and expenditures, as to broad programs and, frequently, as to individual projects (sometimes even individual purposes) are made. But the budget is built up by a hierarchy of decisions from project to program to department to Budget Bureau to Congress (usually operating under broad prescriptions laid down from Budget Bureau to department to program to project). Following congressional final action on it, the appropriated amounts are allocated within whatever leeways Congress has left open among departments, programs, projects and purposes again by hierarchical decision making. Thus, decision making relative to the federal budget is colored by more than the complexity of the problem and the limited intellectual capacity of man at the congressional level. The very process by which the budget is built and allocated outside of Congress is an attempt to simplify, to bring the innate complexities closer to the intellectual capacities of man and thus, through the processes of incremental decision making in the budget-building and allocating process — as well as in the congressional policy-deciding process as described by Lindblom — to enhance the role of rationality in the process.

Economic analysis in resource development projects plays its role in the several acts that compose the whole play and not in the final act only. It serves as an aid to rational decision makers at all levels of government in building, setting and allocating the federal budget. Just as no single decision maker in government can encompass the rational totality of norms and functions involved in any single decision situation and because hierarchial choosing by the governmental group at all levels may come closer to doing so (see Lindblom, *loc. cit.*), so it is that no single economic analysis of any single project or of any separate program can embrace all the norms and functions involved. But economic analysis of resource development projects supplies some additional ordinal and cardinal quantitative bases to which such hierarchical group decision making can moor itself while considering other factors of choice. There are few who presume that evaluations in economic analyses are the voice of the absolute speaking through its mortal mouthpieces, that they are the gospel to be ignored at peril, or that government decision makers are going to stand in awe before the revelatory brilliance of their pronouncements.

Economic analyses provide one fund of fact and analysis to aid the government practitioners of the incremental method of decision making to act more wisely. (See esp. 23, p. 445; and 2, pp. 29 ff.) They deal with only limited sets of choice alternatives; they analyze only those aspects of resource development projects with respect to which the developed resources differ from the undeveloped; they treat the marginal values of objectives under constraints; and they are a mixture of empirical analysis and evaluation and treat only a small number of all the important relevant values.

Resource development projects will be evaluated against the background value judgments which vary among project analysts at all levels and among the final political and administrative decision makers. But this observation does not foretell a random hodgepodge of evaluational outcomes. To begin with, much agreement emerges simply because the practitioners share a common culture which disposes them to some important degree of consensus on moral values and for valuations in which moral values are minimal. Agreement is further engendered through use of limitations or constraints on choices which minimize the choice problem and encourage agreement, because the more the constraints the fewer the points of disagreement. Furthermore, a heritage of successive incremental choices which have been the foci of past evaluations and choices gives analysts and choosers a commonly shared background of experience. Also, factual and value analyses are closely intertwined, and factual propositions can be verified and agreed upon through observation and experiment; hence, agreement on factual propositions in evaluations pulls analysts and decision makers toward agreement on values. (Paraphrased from 21, p. 176; see also 22, Chap. XXI.)

It follows from the foregoing propositions that evaluational judgments on resource development projects may differ, but that the differences resulting from value differences will be incremental relative to the areas of agreement. Furthermore, though disagreements will exist because of differences over values, it is the very function of the political decision-making process to weigh and aggregate such differences and to decide among the diverse values represented. Neither individual analysts nor individual decision makers can possibly take into account all the relevant values or even all the relevant economic values that enter into the project or program evaluation. Under such conditions, "political processes may achieve a consideration of a wider variety of values than can possibly be grasped and weighted by any one analyst or policy maker. It is this accomplishment at the political level that makes agreement among analysts less necessary" (21, p. 178). That decision making in this context is rough is obvious; but that it is any poorer than would be achieved if individual analysts tried to take all relevant values into account in their evaluational efforts (or if they took no values, economic or otherwise, into account at all) is not at all obvious (21, p. 176).

It is also pertinent to recall that economic analysis of governmental investment was unheard of not many years ago. As recently as 1936, the only way known to government to choose even between undertaking

A and B in the same field was the method of hearing and debate at the peak decision level. The growing role of and demand for economic rationality that increasingly characterizes decision making in all sectors is both result and cause of a growing understanding of the relevant economic processes. It parallels similar changes for similar reasons in decision making on matters of public health, military requirements, the incidence and impact of taxation, etc. The growing understanding of the economic processes involved in resource development leads to growing possibility of and demand for decision tools in government as in private firms. That they are less definitive in the context of public choosing or that the processes to be measured are more complex and that the choice criteria are more qualitative does not deny the usefulness of economic analysis. Counseling perfection in economic analysis before placing any reliance on its usefulness would have denied the workability of capitalism and would question the worth of economic analysis in private economic decision making even in the 1960's.

These considerations lead to an affirmative answer to the question of whether economic evaluations of resource development projects or programs have sufficient usefulness in allocating the federal budget to warrant spending scarce resources on them (assuming, of course, they are technically and analytically as sound as the state of our analytical knowledge can make them). Because universal inclusion of all relevant values and functional relations bearing on evaluation of resource projects is beyond the scope of finite and fumbling human minds, the total problem must be fragmented into ponderable parts to be evaluated incrementally. The final coordination of choice must be achieved by partisan mutual adjustment. It follows that project (or policy) evaluations executed to the best level of attainment permitted by the state of our analytical and empirical knowledge will provide a range of objective, rational measurements that will sharpen the efficiency of the partisan-adjustment process of final decision making (11 and 20).

What Constitutes Technically Sound Economic Evaluations?

If the worthwhileness of such analyses is accepted, what constitutes evaluations that are technically and analytically as sound as experience and knowledge will permit? This question can be broken into two parts — first, the general question of economic efficiency versus economic welfare criteria and, second, an examination of the evaluational process itself.

Must Economic Evaluation Encompass Welfare As Well As Efficiency Criteria?

We might begin by considering what we mean by "welfare" and "welfare maximization." The concept of welfare seems to imply, as a synonym, the concept of health or happiness or prosperity. It makes little difference which term we use, for each is equally clear, equally vague, equally value-loaded, equally nonoperational. To be operational a concept must be capable of measurement by observation even if only in relative magnitudes. These terms are not operational as they stand in this sense; hence if, in some sense, enhancement of welfare is to be a criterion in resource project evaluation, some way must be uncovered to order the concept in magnitude among alternatives of project or policy content.

The "new" welfare economics has spun out elaborate structures of thought attempting to specify the conditions, concepts and principles of *economic* welfare maximization. The ultimate test of any theory lies in its ability to specify operations which, if carried out in the real world, will lead to tests of its workability (i.e., its validity, or warrantability). Unless means can be found to clothe welfare with measurable attributes or to replace it with a measurable indicator, the usefulness of welfare maximization as a criterion for project selection remains questionable.

A commonly accepted criterion of a social change that leads to increase of economic welfare is the Pareto criterion "that a change that makes at least one individual better off and leaves no individual worse off" represents an increase of welfare. This criterion is usually interpreted to mean that welfare is increased by a change rendering it possible to make at least one person better off and leave no individual worse off by compensating the losers. An increase in national income resulting from a resource development project or policy is sufficiently close (though not coterminous) with the Pareto criterion "with compensation." An increase of national income (13, pp. 307 and 310)

may be regarded as a practical, first approximation, to the [Pareto "with" criterion], provided that the policy under consideration does not appreciably increase inequality of income distribution; and provided further that there are other policies in operation which work independently and continually in the direction of greater equality of income distribution.

Increases in national income resulting from increases in economic efficiency can be taken as indicators of increases in economic welfare if certain restrictive assumptions are accepted and if the resulting distribution of income is not materially altered toward inequality.[3]

The concepts "materially" in my statement and "not appreciably" in the quotation from Ciriacy-Wantrup somewhat beg the question, for how big is materially? The answer, of course, is a value judgment and must be left to the analyst, the analyst's administrative superiors and political decision-makers in the spirit of Lindblom's incremental method, fragmentation and partisan mutual adjustment (20). The absolutist position that the efficiency results of project or policy are valid only when income distribution consequences are *absolutely* unaltered or are altered toward equality is unacceptable because a little increase in inequality may fall far short of offsetting the benefits of a much bigger increase in aggregate income. This declaration obviously derives from a relativistic rather than from an absolutist philosophy.

But this contrast demonstrates the philosophical value judgment implicit in the issue. Resolution of the value judgment in governmental deciding can occur only as a "partisan adjustment" process of group decision making. If the staff analyst and his hierarchial superiors should be required to hold rigidly to the absolutist faith on this issue, those projects or policies deviating minutely from the faith would not even be placed before the final decision makers for consideration.

Under these circumstances the analysts and their superiors would be "legislating" negatively for the group. Project and policy evaluations looked upon favorably by decision makers at any level, because they show an appropriate increase of economic efficiency and a resulting increase of national income, should be evaluated and described by the decision makers successively concerned and placed before the final decision makers for judgment, even though they may show some degree of increase in inequality of income distribution. Consequently the criterion "not appreciable" is proper though not scientifically and philosophically tidy — as real life never is.

There is need, however, to spell out quite clearly, as separate questions, the efficiency considerations involved in each resource development project and its income redistributive consequences. With reference to neither criterion can the economic analyst say which is best, because doing so involves value judgments as much if the criterion is "most efficient" as when it is "most equalitarian." But, for the efficiency criterion he can determine a cardinal measure of preferredness, subject to restrictive assumptions, whereas for the income redistributive consequence he can do no more than describe it. Both are, however, equally the proper domain of economic analysis. More will be said on the meanings and limitations of these concepts later.

It would seem, then, that projects and programs leading to more or most *enhancement* of national income, together with marginal notes on each concerning its income redistributive consequences, are operational goals for resource project evaluations. Even this criterion — enhancement of national income — can be applied only with restrictive assumptions that eliminate any possibility for an optimal *maximum* of national income to be determined. However, approximations of comparative increases in income as between each pair of visualized alternatives and hence of most increase as among all the alternatives thus compared are within reach — although "only under restrictive assumptions with respect to institutions, preferences, technology and time periods" (13, p. 310).[4]

The conclusion is that (1) for any attempt to determine a *welfare* maximum among alternative projects (policies of limited scope) even the Pareto criterion "with compensation" is unattainable, although the impact of each alternative project on income distribution may be describable and, if so, should be so described; (2) the ordering of alternative projects is attainable by way of the criterion "enhancement of national income"; (3) enhancement of national income is, though with restrictive assumptions, an outcome of enhancement of economic efficiency; and (4) maximum enhancement of economic efficiency is determinable cardinally among alternative projects in the sense of the most income gain among those examined.

THE ENHANCEMENT OF NATIONAL INCOME

By enhancement of national income I mean the *additions* to aggregate wages and salaries, rents, interest incomes and profits received by the aggregate of households in the United States by virtue of having the project as compared to not having it, everything else remaining constant. The maximization of this enhancement is the formal test of preferredness; it is not the optimal maximization of national income "in the sense of a useful scientific fiction" (12, p. 214). By maximizing its enhancement, the national income is maximized *insofar as that particular kind and amount of resource development at that particular time and place* can accomplish this desired end.[5]

It is evident that the concept "national income," as defined above and as measured by the Department of Commerce, is of only formal usefulness as a criterion for resource development budgeting. A single resource development project or any set of such projects likely to be undertaken in a single time period will register such small effects upon the total national income of the United States as to be immeasurable with available measurement techniques; their effects will be lost among changes in national income brought about by inaccuracies of measurement and by changes in a host of other causative influences. We cannot, then, use the concept and measurement techniques employed by national income accountants; we will, however, want a measure as near akin to the formal concept as we can find and yet have it be adequately operational for our purposes. Using McKean's terminology, we are seeking a "proximate" criterion to enhancement of national income (as formally defined) which is, itself, a proximate criterion of enhancement of economic welfare.[6]

The proximate criterion generally agreed upon is some form of maximized present dollar value among alternative streams of net dollar gains generated by alternative federal project expenditures after appropriate allowances have been made for all opportunity costs connected with expenditure of these funds in these projects rather than in other available federal, public or private alternatives. The gains, gross or any of several levels of net, are generally referred to as *benefits* following federal terminology; the offsetting charges against these benefits resulting in the several possible levels of netting are commonly called *costs* — again honoring federal terminology.

The procedure is to: (1) examine alternative arrays of project purposes, (2) select sets of purposes which we call projects, and sets of projects we call programs, (3) calculate the benefits less costs (including opportunity costs) or net benefits generated by each project and program, (4) examine a sufficient number of alternative sets of purposes and projects to insure that the array of net benefits generated by the several alternatives surrounds the probable theoretical maximum.

The balance of this chapter will be devoted to consideration of the use of these criteria in project and program selection and some of the unsettled issues involved in their definition and measurement.

AN OPERATIONAL MODEL OF THE CRITERIA

An appropriate model to serve the needs of the described criteria must include the following elements:[7]

1. The present worth of the stream of net gains generated in all sectors of the economy by the federal investment; the net gains are the stream of market values (actual or imputed) of goods and services produced (benefits) less the stream of market values (actual or imputed) of resources committed to their production (costs) and less the opportunity costs of nonfederal inputs to their (nonfederal) suppliers; hereafter this concept will be referred to as the "net prime benefits" (equivalent to Steiner's [24] "gain"); this value may be calculated for any definable segment of a federal resource development undertaking such as a single facility, a combination of facilities composing a project or a combination of projects composing a program.

2. The appropriate restraints on the federal funds.

3. The opportunity costs of federal funds that arise because of budget restraints and the pre-emptive power of government; such costs are measured by opportunities foregone to use federal funds or their equivalents in their next best income-producing alternatives which may be other federal, nonfederal public or private pursuits.

4. As final outcome of the model, a cardinal number representing the present dollar value of the stream of net prime benefits further debited with the relevant opportunity costs and subject to relevant restraints; this value, herein called the "pure benefits," may be determined for each potential federal investment undertaking so that each may be compared to every other; the combination of compatible and complementary undertakings that maximizes this value is the combination that maximizes enhancement of national income, the proximate criterion of economic welfare.

Element (4) in the model — the final value measure of the alternatives — specifies the final, pure addition to national income generated by the specified federal investment in excess of the addition that would be made by investment of these same funds or their equivalents in available alternatives *outside* the restraining budget. In more familiar terms, it measures the net benefits *with* the project in relation to net benefits *without* the project — the familiar "with the project: without the project" comparison. This explains the use of the term pure benefits for this measure as the net prime benefits have been refined of their opportunity debits. Determining the pure benefits for each of several alternative undertakings *within* a restraining budget specifies the range of additions to national income that might be generated by the array of alternatives examined *within* that budget. Choosing that one which generates the maximum of pure benefits from among an array of alternative combinations of purposes and facilities within a particular budget for a specified site designates the project from within that budget at that site which, the model forecasts, will maximize enhancement of national income so far as that site and that budget are concerned. Choosing a program of projects from among the array of alternative projects at each site and over a number of sites so as to maximize the sum of these predicted project pure benefits reveals the program of expenditures from the restraining budget that will maximize enhancement of national income.

Specifying the array of facility and project alternatives and evaluating their pure benefits must be done with due regard to any incompatibilities and complementarities that may exist among them, both as between alternative facilities for a single site and as between projects at different sites. To facilitate this demand, two of the relevant restraints should be (1) a discreteness restraint specifying that each alternative facility and project so defined can be chosen to be either in or out but not partly in; and (2) an incompatibility restraint specifying that each alternative facility and project be assigned a coded designation such that one and only one of each of the same coded designation can be chosen in a single project or program (24, pp. 902-3).

To many persons, specification of a model as above (and as Steiner's) is questionable either for reasons of inoperability or over-specificity of elements. (For example, see (28) and (16, Rept. No. 5, pp. 105 and 115) and (12) Sections 3 and 5 and (13) Sections V and VI.) Models are not representations of reality but are isolates of a few simple aspects of the real world to give the imponderable complexities of reality that degree of simplification prerequisite for investigation. The usefulness of a model lies in its prescription as to facts that must be observed, functional relations that must be measured, constraints that must be imposed (9, p. 13). An operational model such as that specified above is a recipe for evaluating the economic efficiency outcomes of alternative uses of federal funds in resource development. It has no greater meaning than this, and more should not be read into it. It is not a scientific law in the sense of an explanation of reality; it is a guide — and an incomplete one — to human action in deciding between doing this or doing that.

The degree of its completeness is measured by the extent to which all facets of reality find symbols to represent them in the model in appropriate functional relation to one another. To castigate models on principle, then, is to castigate acting with reflective thought rather than by headlong plunges into impulsive choices. To criticize models in order to remove error or to add additional relevant variables and relationships is to bring them closer to full reflection of reality. The model of the criterion (enhancement of national income) advanced above to guide federal resource investing is offered in this setting and in this setting only, as a useful guidebook for the analyst through the complexities of reality but is a guidebook not guaranteed to satisfy the traveller's quest for certainty that he be led to the one right destination.

The Several Elements in the Model

The present value of the stream of net prime benefits. Each purpose (i.e., facility) and combination of facilities (project) and combination of projects (program) generates a flow of outputs through time at the expense of both an initial investment of resource assets and a time flow of resource inputs. The value of the flow of outputs less the value of the flow of inputs including the opportunity value of the nonfederal inputs (with or without the subtraction also of the initial federal investment)[8] is the stream of net prime benefits.

Because time is endless and because the future is not worth as much as is the present (because the future is discounted), this stream must be converted to a single value by a process that aggregates the discounted values of the annual nets.

There are many questions implicit in this process, some of which will be discussed on following pages. A more elaborate discussion of these questions and others will be found especially in (1), (2) and (3). Because of space limitations, it must suffice to say that I mean by the present value of the stream of net prime benefits: (1) each output through time accruing to private and nonfederal public agents priced at the point in time when it will appear, (2) each input (including investments) committed through time by private and nonfederal public agents to the production of the above stream of outputs priced at the point in time when they will appear, and with due regard to their opportunity price to the agent who will commit them, (3) the input (including investment) committed through time by the federal government to the production of the above stream of outputs, priced at the point in time when they will appear and (4) a rate of discount reflecting the opportunity cost of deferred consumption (or of social time preference) to be applied to annual values over time and their summation and differencing to a present net value.

Calling this concept "net prime benefit" follows from its definition as the net gain of market-valued outputs over market-valued inputs (plus opportunity prices of inputs acquired *outside* the *restraining* budget) *before* opportunity costs of the federally committed funds are debited. It is the initial measure of net social gain before subtraction of opportunity gains of the federal funds committed.

This prescription for calculation of the present worth of the net prime benefit for each individual facility and project appears to be a simple and straightforward empirical task of technological planning using market prices (actual or imputed) to determine values of the outputs and inputs. But it is deceptively simple and straightforward. It is no easy and routine task. There are several baffling problems in this individual facility and project evaluation of net prime benefits that belie its straightforward and simple appearance.

Among the most baffling problems to be discussed herein are these: (1) use of market prices, whether actual or imputed; (2) imputing prices for nonmarket outputs and inputs; (3) uncertainty relative to future technologies, preferences and institutions; (4) defining and measuring outputs and inputs generated beyond the immediate confines of the federal project by outputs and inputs generated directly by it; and (5) the rate of discount used in arriving at the present value of the time streams.

Market prices and the measurement of benefits and costs. It is generally accepted that market prices of outputs so far as the private economy is concerned are acceptable measures of the value of those outputs to the whole economy. Market prices of inputs are similarly acceptable as measures of the values of alternative products which those inputs could produce or, in other words, as adequate measures of the nonfederal opportunity costs of the outputs (2, p. 103). This presumption rests on an implicit assumption that the allocation of resources and the structure of prices in the economy are approximately close to those which would rule if the economy were perfectly competitive. Within the structure of welfare economic theory, if the economy is perfectly competitive, market prices reflect the "true" value of outputs and inputs to the economy.

The validity of this presumption must be severely questioned (19, Part IV, Section Al, p. 39) (4, p. 100) when, for example, we contemplate evaluation of agricultural benefits flowing from an irrigation purpose. Are market prices of cotton, or of wheat, or of milk, or of any major agricultural output for that matter, true measures of the value of those outputs to the whole economy? It is obvious, in this age of government price supports and market interference in agriculture, that market prices do not fit the competitive restraint in the welfare model.

What is needed is a stand-in competitive price for such noncompetitive prices. It is necessary for an imputed price to be imagined as the market price that would prevail in the absence of noncompetitive elements in its market; such an imputation implies existence of a demand function over the relevant range for the products in question. But distortions of market prices of agricultural outputs from the competitive restraint of the welfare model are not the only shortcomings in the use of market prices. To what degree are *all* prices in our contemporary economy freed, some more, some less, from restraints of the competitive model? Must we impute a stand-in price for all project *inputs* also? And if we must, our model falls far short of reality at one of its critical points. Accepting this stricture eliminates the easy out of market prices as the opportunity cost measure of outputs and inputs. Yet, until someone comes up with a better device, I fear that evaluation of benefits and costs is going to rest heavily on market prices, though the more obviously and more grossly affected of such prices, such as many agricultural outputs, must be doctored to reflect the "as if" of competitive conditions. But, as McKean (2, p. 176) points out in another connection, highly refined price estimates might have the effect of concealing the uncertainty that attaches to cost-benefit estimates by giving a false impression of great precision.... For these reasons ..., by and large, new efforts could better be used to improve other aspects of present procedures. This is not to say that the pricing of project outputs can be neglected. It deserves plenty of attention. But this should be mainly an effort to get these prices "in the right ball-park" not to introduce subtle variations....

Another knotty question concerning output prices is whether prices of additional outputs to be created by the federal investment are to be those that will prevail for the last additional unit (the marginal unit) produced or whether the price for each additional unit of output, assuming each in turn to be the marginal one, shall prevail. In other words, shall competitive or discriminatory (monopoly) pricing be presumed? McKean and Krutilla-Eckstein (2, 3) agree that the additional output should be valued as if each additional unit were produced separately and priced at the maximum amount that would be paid for it. The value of additional outputs might be found by using price discrimination, that is, by valuing each unit of output at the highest amount that would be paid for it (2, p. 170). According to Krutilla and Eckstein (3, p. 74):

The aggregate value of the increment in supply [of output] is represented by the amount which could be collected if each unit of the block of new output could be offered separately for sale at the price it could command. Accordingly, neither the price which would prevail in the absence of the project, nor the price which would be necessary to clear the last unit from the market, would directly indicate the value of each unit of output.

The clear implication is that the value of the outputs — the gross benefits — is the area under the demand curve of the output. Both authors, in implicit recognition of the vague knowledge of demand functions for the many different outputs that might arise in federal resource projects, refer favorably to the assumption that such functions are linear; hence, "the value of the total increase in supply could be approximated by using an average price midway between the price which would prevail with the project supply and without it" (3, p. 74). But this is strangely at variance with McKean's earlier assertion that since "market prices of outputs are accepted ... as measures of the value of those outputs to the whole economy ... it does make sense to look at cost-benefit estimates in which prices that would apply in the private sector of the economy are extensively used" (2, pp. 103 and 107). Then, he refers with favor to the procedures which "apply to the new output a price that is probably *in between* the amount for which the first extra units could be sold and the amount for which the last units could be sold." (2, p. 175, italics in the original).

It is evident there is conflicting advice here. Probably for single projects the impact of project outputs and inputs on *national* market prices will be negligible because the quantities will be small relative to the whole of the market. (Their impact may not be negligible on local or regional market prices.) But for whole programs, this may not be the case. In any event, it is evident that here lies a theoretical and conceptual issue to be resolved. So far studies have not done so.

This issue can be extended to include the problem of pricing privately produced output that may be alternative to the federal project under evaluation. If discriminatory pricing is attached to the publicly produced project output, it must also be attached to the privately produced alternative. If consumer's surplus is a benefit on the "with the federal project" side of the comparison, it is equally a benefit on the "with the private alternative" side.

For the several reasons discussed — viz., the presence of noncompetitive elements in market prices and the use of discriminatory pricing in valuing prime benefits of government output — market prices are not the only proper measure of project outputs and inputs. Except where the foregoing limitations clearly enter in, market prices will continue to be the most feasible and most generally used measure of benefits and costs for estimating the economic welfare consequences of federal investment in resource development projects. But much theoretical and empirical work needs to be done by economic analysts on the improvement of value measurements of government resource development outputs and inputs.

Imputed values of nonmarket outputs and inputs. Many project outputs are not sold through the market, and hence do not carry market prices. Some inputs may not be acquired in any market. The opportunity prices to be assigned to nonfederal inputs are not directly market determined. For all these cases, prices will require imputation. Much theoretical and empirical work on this problem in both fundamental and applied terms is required of economic analysts to improve value measurements of government project outputs and inputs not sold or bought through the market and hence which do not carry market-determined price tags. For an excellent beginning on fundamental study of the problem see (10, pp. 85 and 238-49) and (27, pp. 191-96) and for applied analysis see Clawson (25).

The problem of uncertainty. The future is uncertain as to changes in technologies, changes in consumer preferences as between outputs and time periods and changes in institutional arrangements. Yet the essence of resource development planning is the identification and measurement of time streams of outputs and inputs in this dimly seen context of changes. This is the least satisfactorily resolved problem of all those in the tangle which constitutes the economic evaluation of resource development. No models of the evaluation process yet proposed have incorporated uncertainty functions. The unsatisfactory state of uncertainty analysis, as much as any one thing, underlies the questioning of benefit-cost analysis in decision making, at least insofar as determining optima or maxima is concerned. The questioning is pertinent. But until better handling of uncertainty is worked out in our economic laws, we will not be able to improve our models of economic evaluation of resource projects and will continue to project within an array of assumptions about uncertainty parameters.

For a full discussion of the status of the matter, see Eckstein (23, pp. 468-478) in which he concludes as follows:

I am sure that enough has been said to indicate that this particular problem is far from a solution. In the meantime, judgment methods must be used, whether verbal or formal, with the identification of the major contingencies and some provision being made against them constituting a minimum program for the design of reasonable decision procedures in the face of uncertainty. [9]

Defining and measuring superinduced outputs and inputs. This problem has probably elicited more debate than any other single problem in the whole benefit-cost procedure. (Only the interest rate competes with it for attention. See 18, pp. 9-11 and 34-36; 19.) It may be accepted that the federal undertaking will induce, directly, certain benefits at the expense of certain outlays such as electric power, flood damage reduction and agricultural products, to name a few. But the question is: Does the contribution of the undertaking to national income stop with the net market value assignable directly to the additional power or protection or produce? It is evident that these direct values induce in turn a long series of net values stemming from them as these products and their secondary, tertiary, quaternary and further derivatives fan out through the economy. This gives rise to the further question: Should the sum of these additional net values stemming from the immediate net values of the project output be added as an element in net prime benefits of the federal undertaking?

Net benefits have been defined herein as the additions to national income. It follows that the net values of superinduced activities are a component of net prime benefits *if* they are truly *net additions to* the national income. When put thusly, our attention is directed to an examination of the value of *outputs* stemming from the generating activity but also to the value of the *outlays* stemming from the same generating activity and to opportunity costs associated with these superinduced outlays. It is the latter element in the calculus about which controversy swirls.

It is agreed that the costs of producing cotton yarn, cloth and shirts should be deducted from the value of the shirts produced from additional cotton created by a federal investment in irrigation. But it should also be argued that the opportunity cost of the resources used in creating the shirts is the net value of alternative products *they* might be expected to produce in the absence, not of cotton in general, but of the project-induced cotton. Furthermore, because cotton from somewhere else than the project in question will be secured to produce the shirts and will in all likelihood be usable at no greater manufacturing cost, the only net prime benefit of the shirts produced *with* the project compared to what will be produced *without* it will be the net value of the project-induced cotton, plus whatever higher price, if any, may have to be paid for the alternative cotton supply. Following this line of reasoning, it is argued by many that there are no national (though there may be local) benefits beyond the immediate net benefits of direct project output (power, protection, produce) because alternative sources of supply or alternative opportunities for the committed resources may wipe out all superinduced net benefits (11) (19).

This tangled thread of argument is a prime candidate for unsnarling. The space limitations of this chapter do not permit doing so. It is necessary to leave the subject with these observations: (1) it is evident that the net additions to national income derived from superinduced net benefits of federal resource investments are much less than they often are pictured, but (2) they may be a positive magnitude in many situations (e.g., where federally produced water power may be sufficiently cheaper than alternative power to make possible the cheaper recovery of a valuable item "at home" in place of obtaining it from more expensive sources "abroad"); (3) the magnitude of such superinduced benefits differs with the geographic extent of the alternatives (opportunities) examined. That is, in the immediate vicinity of the federal investment, the superinduced benefits may be substantial whereas within the national economy they may be zero or even negative; (4) the problem of superinduced benefits from federal investment in resources is much more a problem of empirical classification and measurement than it is of conceptual refinement, if the evaluator is objectively honest in measuring the outcome of his subject project in terms of *net* addition to the national income.

The problem of the rate of discount. The measure of the relative desirability of federal investment undertakings first rests on the difference between the *present* value of the time stream of net prime benefits from each activity. These present values are the differences between the time streams of anticipated benefits and their associated resource costs reduced to an aggregate present value by an appropriate rate of discount. The rate of discount "is the opportunity cost of deferred consumption (some would call it 'social time preference'), and should not be confused with a number of other interest rates that may be appropriate in other connections." (24)

Nowhere have I come across an operational definition of the opportunity cost of deferred consumption — the social rate of time preference. Steiner (24) is clear that it is a different concept from the social opportunity cost of capital raised by federal taxes.[10] Krutilla-Eckstein (3, Chap. IV), by implication, identify the social opportunity cost of deferred consumption (the social rate of time preference) with the social opportunity cost of capital raised by taxation which is denoted by Steiner as "the opportunity cost of transferring funds from the private sector to the public sector" and is listed by him among the six incorrectly defined discount rates. Eckstein (23, pp. 461-463) agrees with Steiner's criticism of the Krutilla-Eckstein implication that the discount rate and the opportunity cost of capital expressed as a rate are equivalent:

Thus both opportunity cost and an interest rate must be specified for expenditure models ... in conventional benefit-cost analysis, a present value of benefits must be computed, using some interest rate. The rate at which costs result in present value of benefit, that is, the marginal benefit-cost ratio, must be compared with the rate at which present value is foregone elsewhere, i.e., the opportunity cost. ...It is because there are imperfections in the private economy, particularly in the capital market, that opportunity cost must be measured and utilized as a criterion in determining public budgets, and must be valued at a social rate of interest.

But what this interest (discount) rate is does not appear. Eckstein (23 pp. 453-460) discusses "the interest rate as a measure of value of outputs at different points in time." He explores, cursorily, a number of "elements that enter into the choice" of a discount rate and has "presented two models which derive elements of interest rates from empirical magnitudes .... But these must be combined with subjective judgments that cannot be value-free." He concludes "thus the choice of interest [discount] rates must remain a value judgment."

I agree with Margolis (4) that "clearly the treatment of time has not been resolved by these studies." But it has been advanced somewhat by Steiner (24) and Eckstein (23), for it is now clear that the discount rate and the opportunity cost of capital (expressed as a rate of return) are two different concepts, that there is no necessary reason why they will be the same magnitude, and both are required in the evaluation of net prime benefit from a federal investment in resource development.

The two different rate concepts and their magnitudes are required, because one of them defines and measures the stream of annual outputs attributable to the alternative investment of the federal funds in sectors alternative to the restraining budget and the other describes and measures the present value of this stream of opportunity output. The first of these concepts is the "annual internal rate of return," or annual return per dollar of initial investment, *within* the alternative sector and measures the opportunity cost of the federal funds transferred to the restraining budget from use in that alternative sector. The second concept is the "rate of discount" or "social rate of time preference" and measures the degree of preference for present over future returns or the present value of the stream of annual returns per dollar of initial investment (the stream of opportunity costs). Little light has been cast, philosophically or empirically, on the notion of the "social rate of time preference." How much more value attaches to a bird in the hand than to one in the bush? And whose time preference values should prevail — the present marginal consumer's? the present public decision maker's? the imagined preferences of the next generation? or whose?

Although these doubts beset us, we cannot simply go into suspended animation awaiting their resolution by intellectual analysts. Planners and decision makers require a discount rate. Because choosing such a rate involves value judgments, uniformity of decision making requires that, by order or agreement, all federal decision making as to the commitment of federal funds similarly transferred from nonfederal sectors shall use the same discount rate. This condition requires central determination of the rate.

The Restraints

Rarely is it possible to attain the best of all possible worlds. Counsels of perfection may be useful in lifting our eyes from the all too imperfect affairs of the world around us to higher goals and attainments. But in the hardheaded affair of allocating scarce resources to most efficient ends, it is neither wise nor practicable to get too far away from the limitation of reality. The limitations of reality, whatever they may be in each planning situation, are the *restraints* in the meaning of this section. They are the restrictions on the planner's freedom of choice. Their kind is infinite, for every condition that prevents a decision maker from doing as he pleases is a restraint. They range from gravity (that won't let water run uphill), diminishing returns, mortality and the barriers of time and distance to politics, social controls, interpersonal relations and the market. Although man cannot decide (plan) in the total absence of restraints, he can impose restraints so rigid and all pervasive as to restrict outcomes to only one possibility. The selection of restraints so pervasive and rigid becomes a spuriously objective way to reach a foregone conclusion.[11]

Restraints, then, may be of many sorts — physical, legal, administrative, financial, institutional, uncertainties and others. Some aspect of each of these is incorporated in benefit-cost analysis implicitly — diminishing returns, conditions of time and distance, the market, the law, etc. However, many other aspects of them become matters of specific choice — financial (budget) limitations, uncertainty limitations, limitations on the administrative scope and complexity of project undertaking, limitations on the extent to which market prices shall be restraining, limitation on the influence of time preference, on allocation of costs as between direct beneficiaries and the general society, on the recognition of external economies and diseconomies, etc. Some of these restraints have already been mentioned earlier in passing — discreteness restraints, compatibility (complementarity and competitive) restraints, time preference and discount, the role and limitations of market prices and uncertainty. Frequently, restraints imply opportunity costs; conversely, opportunity costs are the economic dimension of certain restraints. For example, the time preference restraint was described (supra p. 72) as the "opportunity cost of deferred consumption" and was measured by the "discount rate." In economic evaluation for public budget allocation the restraints incident to budget and financial limitations stand out so boldly as to demand especial consideration.

Financial and budget restraints. Generally, these restraints specify some limitation on the amount of federal money available for project (program) purposes. These will include limitations on the timing and form of its availability and limitations on the realization, timing and disposition of revenues flowing from the federal investments and operating inputs. Financial restraints are intimately related to the specification and measurement of opportunity costs.[12]

Financial and budgetary restraints are specifiable by the controlling decision makers and may be of the following kinds:

1. limitation on the total amount of federal money available as a planning ceiling or as an operating allocation; such allocation limitations may be set at each of the several hierarchical levels of administration in ever-widening (or narrowing) contexts;

2. specifying the degree to which federal investment must maximize net benefits above returns from specific displaced alternative sources of similar services and from alternative federal opportunities for use of the limited funds;

3. specifying the degree to which the time stream of net benefits shall be determined by the use of market prices and the rates of return from alternative uses of the federal funds; and

4. specifying to what degree the present value of the time stream of net benefits shall be determined by time preference, by discount rates and by time horizons.

This statement of financial constraints closely parallels the specification of opportunity costs. (See 23, pp. 452-453.) This is not coincidental. Financial restraints are, in large part, the statement of opportunity costs in the administrative language of financial policy or, put differently, opportunity costs are the operational specifications of financial policy.[13]

Consequently, the economic evaluation of net benefits commonly restricts itself to constraints such as those specified above and they enter into the calculations as opportunity costs. There are, however, numerous other constraints that demand consideration. In the fullness of decision making in the real world, many and maybe most of these other constraints will demand attention. But most of the other constraints are noneconomic, not because they have no economic consequences, but because they are exogenous parameters to the economic calculations. They are held constant by assumption during the economic evaluation. As other technicians or administrators convert these noneconomic parameters into functional variables in the system, they, too, will generate instructions for their conceptualization and measurement as is now so extensively attempted (as shown in preceding pages) for the economic efficiency variables. For the present, however, they will be laid aside. It follows that the discussion of financial and budgetary restraints herein will be couched in the decision-making language of opportunity costs.

The Opportunity Costs of the Federal Funds

The core of the decision model discussed herein is the present value of the stream of output less the cost of the resources committed to its production and is dubbed the net prime benefit. The net prime benefit is the capitalized value of the stream of additions to national income predicted to flow if the committed resources are used as specified by the planner. But the net prime benefits of each project or program do not provide a satisfactory criterion of choice as between projects or programs, despite the fact that the net prime benefit for each project has been and is the terminal evaluation in all federal programs.[14]

Individual projects, alike insofar as their net prime benefits are concerned, may differ significantly in the alternatives available to the federal funds to be committed to each and thus may differ significantly in their benefits net of opportunity costs. Put another way, the net prime benefit of a project or program tells us how much that activity will add to future national income implying that, if the contribution is positive, the activity is profitable, and hence desirable. But it does not tell how much more (or less) this activity will add to the national income than would be added if it were not undertaken; it does not tell us what income the nation must give up if the federal funds or their equivalents are not used in their alternative pursuits. Therefore, a complete decision model must include measures to account for these alternative opportunities for benefits from other uses to which the federal funds might be put. These measures are the social opportunity costs of the federal funds.

These social opportunity costs of the federal funds are the returns realizable by the use of these federal funds or their equivalent in alternative pursuits outside the restraining budget (1, Chap. III, Sec. 8). Such costs are of the following kinds:

1. the net prime benefit obtainable from the best alternative non-federal (probably private) means of supplying the same or a closely similar service displaced by the federal project net of the alternative's opportunity costs (24, p. 894);[15]

2. the marginal internal rate of return available to liquid capital in the general economy tapped by each different means the federal government may use to obtain the funds; and

3. the opportunity value of national defense, unemployment abatement, other resource developments, and any other federal noneconomic opportunity that can be put into a reasonable opportunity value to reflect its worth as a competitor for federal funds.

Space limitations do not permit full development of the meaning, measurement and use of these costs in benefit evaluation. Consequently, an extended discussion of each must be omitted, substituting a brief general discussion pertinent to this class of opportunity cost.

The central desideratum of an opportunity cost is that it is the foregone opportunity for income which might be realized by using the funds outside the restraining budget. Furthermore, as a cost, it is a deduction from the net prime benefits of the undertaking under analysis. In consequence, no bureaucratic administrative officer will relish taking such opportunity costs into account: (1) because the alternative uses lie outside the budget that restrains him, he will not be familiar with them and hence, very honestly, he will not feel competent to evaluate their opportunity benefit[16]; and (2) because the alternative gain foregone is a deduction from the net prime benefits of his proposal, the bureaucratic administrator is put in the paradoxical position of playing down the worth of his activity *vis-à-vis* that of his competitors.

Furthermore, comparability among competing plans for competing uses of federal funds even as between different resource development undertakings requires uniform treatment of those opportunity costs that are identical for all.[17] These very real (and human) considerations lead to serious question as to how these opportunity costs can be brought into the decision-making process. It is questionable indeed whether reliance or responsibility for them can be put on the bureaucratic agent.

This argument leads to the conclusion that opportunity costs of classes (2) and (3) above can be properly handled only at some single location in the hierarchical budget-building and allocating process. This clearly implies that responsibility for their definition and measurement and authority for their inclusion as costs in project evaluation be placed at or near the apex of the budget-building and approving process — Budget Bureau, Council of Economic Advisors or congressional committee. The desideratum is that the level of decision making where opportunity costs such as these are brought into the program should be at the level where concern for the taxpayer, for broad social and economic welfare rather than for more narrowly bureaucratic interests finds the greatest opportunity to express itself. There is no assurance, of course, that perfection in this regard will be attained even at these pinnacles, but it does point up the practical question of whether these opportunity costs can be objectively determined at any lower level.

The opportunity costs of class (1) above exhibit problems of a somewhat different character. The nonfederal alternatives to each federal plan are unique to that undertaking; hence, standard central determination of the appropriate cost deduction as for opportunity costs (2) and (3) is not possible. Yet, in the same way, the opportunities are in strange undertakings outside the planner's domain and they represent deductions from the apparent net benefit of his proposal. Here is a real conundrum so well exemplified by the Hell's Canyon conflict. The issues here embrace many broadly noneconomic values: the size of central government, the preference for the private or a local government way of doing things, etc.

But even relative to the more purely economic values involved, their evaluation can hardly be much more than crude estimation unless performed by the nonfederal agents directly concerned with the nonfederal alternatives. And the federal budget planner hardly can be expected to work with the nonfederal agent when the alternative being studied will be pre-empted by the federal undertaking if approved and the nonfederal agent thus thrown back upon *his* second-best opportunity — his opportunity cost. Possibly the only means at hand for handling this problem is the hearings system where this opportunity cost can be brought into consideration.[18]

Space limits this discussion of the opportunity costs attached to alternative uses of the federal funds. Much more should be said, but this is a topic for later elaboration. In leaving the subject, however, it should be noted again how the problem of opportunity costs of the federal funds turns out to be a problem of budget and financial restraints as they are expressed in federal resource policy.

FOOTNOTES

[1] Economic evaluations of public resource development projects may have sufficient usefulness to warrant their cost for purposes other than project selection (or budget allocation). "Evaluation of public investment in water resources projects, or for short, project selection, is only one of three important problem areas in which benefit-cost analysis may be useful in watershed policy. The other two areas comprise the broad problems of repayment of project costs, including problems of cost sharing and financing and the related problems of pricing those products of a project that are sold. . . . One may submit that the contribution of economics as an operationally significant policy science is potentially greater in the areas of repayment and pricing than in that of evaluation." (12, pp. 219-20.)

[2] "The incremental method is characterized by its practitioners' preoccupation with: (1) only that limited set of policy alternatives that are politically relevant, these typically being policies only incrementally different from existing policies; (2) analysis of only those aspects of policies with respect to which they differ; (3) a review of the policy choices as one in a succession of choices; (4) the *marginal* values of various social objectives and constraints; (5) an intermixture.of evaluation and empirical analysis rather than an empirical analysis of the consequences of policies for objectives independently determined; and (6) only a small number out of all the important relevant values." (Italics in the original.) (20, p. 306.)

[3] Increase in *national* income is the appropriate indicator when consideration of the *federal* budget is the subject. However, a more general description of the indicator would be that it is the increase in income generated within whatever institutional complex defines the decision-maker's area of liberty to act and choose. This formulation encompasses the nation at one extreme and the individual firm at the other with place for state, local and various private group forms in between.

[4] Also see Ciriacy-Wantrup, "For policy decisions of more limited scope — for example, evaluating individual watershed projects — incremental improvements in social welfare can be determined cardinally. This may be done by comparing hypothetical changes of aggregate national or regional income that can be attributed to alternative projects or parts of them." (12, p. 214.)

[5] For a more complete discussion of this point see (9) Section 3.

[6] "In practical problem solving, therefore, we have to look at some 'proximate' criterion which serves, we hope, to reflect what is happening to satisfaction, profits, or well-being. Actual criteria are the practicable substitutes for the maximization of whatever we would ultimately like to maximize." (2, p. 29.)

[7] The model I attempt to describe here is very similar to the model more formally described by Steiner (24). An appraisal of the strengths and shortcomings of Steiner's model will be found in M. M. Kelso, "Economic analysis in the allocation of the federal budget," published in Water Resources and Economic Development of the West, Proceedings of the Committee on the Economics of Water Resources Development of the Western Agricultural Economics Research Council, Rept. No. 8, Jan. 1960. (See Chap. 4 of this volume for the *Steiner* model.)

[8] The final measure being sought determines whether the initial investment cost is actually subtracted from outputs. If a benefit/cost ratio is sought, the net prime benefits before subtraction of the federal investment cost is the numerator and the latter is the denominator. (For discussions of how the costs should be divided between numerator and denominator in calculating a benefit/cost ratio, see (2) pp. 107-14 and (26) pp. 656-58.) If the benefits minus costs of all inputs is the answer sought, then the federal investment cost is also subtracted.

[9] Also, in this connection, see especially (2, Chap. 4) and (1, Chap. IV, Section 1).

[10] Steiner lists six interest rates, including this one. Most, and possibly all, of these rates have been named (incorrectly) by others as appropriate measures of the time preference discount rate.

[11] Like the college boy who sets up the following restraints on his decision making concerning his evening's activity by flipping a coin: if it comes up heads, to go to the show; tails, to go to the dance; if it stands on edge, to stay home and study.

[12] An excellent discussion of restraints in the theory of public expenditure criteria will be found in (23) Section 2, pp. 450-453.

[13] ". . . in a fundamental sense, the theory of constraints is at the heart of the theory of budgeting" (23, p. 452). ". . . there may be effective budget constraints on the expenditure possibilities . . . such constraints imply opportunity costs . . ." (24, p. 894).

[14] This statement is made in spite of the fact that some federal water program agencies have gone to elaborate lengths to evaluate secondary or indirect net benefits flowing from investment of federal funds in their programs. The statement is justified because, first, secondary net benefits are an element of justification in only a few of the federal bureaus; second, secondary net benefits, when included, are simply added as an extended form of direct net benefits distinguished only in that they impinge on secondary, tertiary, quaternary and successive factors; and third, secondary costs in the way of alternatives foregone by virtue of the federal investments have not been added to the calculus.

[15] Concepts and measurements pertinent to the evaluation of this class of opportunity cost deserve discussion herein because they are not self-evident. Consider the problem of taxes: Are they a cost against the private but not against the federal alternative? Consider the uncertainties of time: Are they or should they be treated as if they are the same cost in both alternatives? Consider the problem of defining an alternative: Is pre-emption of a dam site and power plant by the federal government thus eliminating a private opportunity to erect the dam and produce power of the same order of alternativeness as, say, the pre-emption of a market for power by virtue of a cheaper price for federal water power that eliminates an opportunity for privately produced steam power to supply that market? Space does not permit elaboration on these problems.

[16] Such alternatives may be such similar opportunities as privately constructed power dams versus the federal erection of such dams concerning which the federal bureau planner simply feels at a loss as to how to measure and treat the private alternative; at another extreme, the alternative use for the funds may be soil erosion prevention in the corn belt versus a western irrigation project. The planner of the latter project knows little about the former and is at a loss as to how to evaluate and treat it in his reclamation evaluation. As clearly apparent from the list of the three kinds of opportunity costs here under consideration, this problem could be so abstruse as the opportunity alternative between western reclamation and national defense, or aid to education.

[17] The marginal internal rate of return to capital in each sector of the general economy, tapped by each means used by the federal government to obtain the project funds, e.g., is common to all users of that federal fund and the opportunity costs of other federal uses, should also be the same as between any two of the uses under comparison.

[18] Handling the matter in this way seriously interferes with the operational feasibility of Steiner's neat and logical model (24).

REFERENCES

1. Eckstein, Otto. Water Resource Development: The Economics of Project Evaluation, Harvard Univ. Press, Cambridge, 1958.
2. McKean, Roland N. Efficiency in Government Through Systems Analysis with Emphasis on Water Resources Development, A RAND Corporation Research Study, Wiley & Sons, New York, 1958.
3. Krutilla, John V., and Eckstein, Otto. Multiple Purpose River Development: Studies in Applied Economic Analysis, Resources for the Future, Inc., Washington, D. C., published by the Johns Hopkins Press, Baltimore, 1958.
4. Margolis, Julius. "The economic evaluation of federal water resource development — a review article," Amer. Econ. Rev., Vol. 49, No. 1, 1959, pp. 96-111.
5. Tolley, G. S. "McKean on government efficiency," Rev. Econ. and Stat., Vol. 41, No. 4, 1959, p. 446.
6. Ostrom, Vincent. "Tools for decision-making in resource planning — a review article," Public Admin. Rev., Vol. 19, No. 2, 1959, p. 114.
7. Hammond, R. J. A Review of Krutilla and Eckstein, "Multiple purpose river development," Jour. Polit. Econ., Vol. 67, No. 3, 1959, p. 314.
8. Castle, E. N. A Review of Krutilla and Eckstein, "Multiple purpose river development," Jour. Farm Econ., Vol. 40, No. 4, 1958, p. 980.
9. Ciriacy-Wantrup, S. V. Conceptual Problems in Projecting the Demand for Land and Water, Giannini Foundation Paper No. 176. Univ. of Calif., Division Agr. Sci., Agr. Exp. Sta., Berkeley, May, 1959.

10. Ciriacy-Wantrup, S. V. Resource Conservation: Economics and Policies, Univ. of Calif. Press, Berkeley, 1952, esp. Parts IV and V.

11. _____. "Benefit-cost analysis and public resource development," *Jour Farm Econ.*, Vol. 37, No. 4, 1955, p. 676. (Chap. 2 of this volume.)

12. _____. "Philosophy and objectives of watershed development," *Land Econ.*, Vol. 35, No. 3, 1959, p. 211. And in G. S. Tolley and F. E. Riggs, Economics of Watershed Planning, The Iowa State Univ. Press, Ames, 1961, pp. 1-14.

13. _____. "Concepts used as economic criteria for a system of water rights," *Land Econ.*, Vol. 32, No. 4, 1956, p. 295. (Chap. 15 of this volume.)

14. Heady, E. O., and Timmons, J. F. "Economic framework for planning and legislating efficient use of water resources," Iowa's Water Resources, The Iowa State Univ. Press, Ames, 1956, Part II.

15. Holje, Helmer, Huffman, R. E., and Kraenzel, C. F. "Indirect benefits of irrigation development," Mont. Agr. Exp. Sta. Bul. 517, Mar., 1956.

16. Water Resources and Economic Development of the West, Proceedings of the Committee on the Economics of Water Resources Development of the Western Agricultural Economics Research Council, Berkeley.
    Rep. No. 0: Direct and Indirect Benefits. 1951.
    Rep. No. 1: Research Needs and Problems. 1953.
    Rep. No. 2: Institutions and Policies. 1954.
    Rep. No. 3: Benefit-Cost Analysis. 1954.
    Rep. No. 4: Impact and Measurement, Organizational Integration; Small Watershed Development; Desert Land Development. 1955.
    Rep. No. 5: Ground Water Economics and the Law. 1956.
    Rep. No. 6: Small Watershed Development. Rehabilitation and Reorganization of Irrigation Projects. 1957.
    Rep. No. 7: Rehabilitation and Reorganization of Irrigation Projects. Evaluation Methodology of the Upper Colorado River Development; Alternative Water Uses. 1958.

17. Renshaw, Edw. F. Toward Responsible Government: An Economic Appraisal of Federal Investment in Water Resource Programs, Idyia Press, Chicago, 1957.

18. Proposed Practices for Economic Analysis of River Basin Projects. Report to the Federal Inter-Agency River Basin Committee prepared by the Subcommittee on Benefits and Costs, Washington, D. C., May, 1950. (Revised May, 1958.)

19. Clark, J. M., Grant, E. L., and Kelso, M. M. Secondary or Indirect Benefits of Water-Use Projects. Report of a Panel of Consultants to M. W. Straus, Commissioner, Bureau of Reclamation, June 26, 1952.

20. Lindblom, Charles E. "Decision-Making in Taxation and Expenditures," Public Finance: Needs, Sources and Utilization, Nat. Bur. of Econ. Res., New York, 1961, pp. 295-336.

21. _____. "Handling of norms in policy analysis," from the Allocation of Economic Resources. Essays in Honor of Bernard Francis Haley. Abramovitz, Moses, and others. Stanford Univ. Press, Stanford, Calif., 1959.

22. Northrop, F. S. C. The Logic of the Sciences and the Humanities, Macmillan, 1947.

23. Eckstein, Otto. "A survey of the theory of public expenditure criteria," Public Finance Needs, Sources and Utilization, Nat. Bur. of Econ. Res., New York, Princeton Univ. Press, 1961, pp. 439-504.

24. Steiner, Peter O. "Choosing among alternative public investments in the water resource field," *Amer. Econ. Rev.*, Vol. 49, No. 5, 1959, p. 893. (Chap. 4 of this volume.)

25. Clawson, Marion. Methods of Measuring the Demand for and Value of Outdoor Recreation. Reprint No. 10, Feb., 1959. Resources for the Future, Inc., Washington, D. C.

26. Tolley, G. S. "Analytical techniques in relation to watershed development," *Jour. Farm Econ.*, Vol. 40, No. 3, 1958, p. 653.
27. Huffman, R. E. Irrigation Development and Public Water Policy, Ronald Press, New York, 1953.
28. Hammond, R. J. Benefit-Cost Analysis and Water-Pollution Control, Food Research Institute, Stanford University, Stanford, Calif., miscellaneous publ. 13, August, 1959.

KENNETH E. BOULDING is Professor of Economics at the University of Michigan. The subjects of his internationally known writings range over a broad area of economic theory and its application, including water resource economics.

The Economist And the Engineer: Economic Dynamics of Water Resource Development

IT CAN BE STATED almost as a political axiom that water resources are developed by engineers. Economists usually have very little to do or to say about it and perhaps in all decency they should keep silent. However, the engineer in general is not apt to be aware of the contributions the economist can make to this problem. It is perhaps these contributions which are the main justification of this chapter.

I may say I have no wish to be derogatory to engineers — indeed, some of my best friends are engineers. If I am going to live below a dam I would much rather have it built by an engineer than by an economist. Nevertheless, the economist comes into the picture perhaps by asking the awkward question as to whether the dam should have been built in the first place.

DIFFERING ATTITUDES

We can sum up the distinction between the economist's point of view and the engineer's by saying that, on the whole, the engineer is project oriented whereas the economist is system-oriented. In other words, the business of the engineer is concrete while the business of the

economist is abstract. The engineer is concerned with particular projects in particular places; the economist is concerned with the impact
not only of actual projects but of potential projects upon all of society.
It is this difference perhaps which makes criticism by the economist so
distasteful to the engineer. The economist is always concerned with
"might-have-been", the engineer is always concerned with "what will
be"; the engineer is concerned with plans, the economist with unreal-
ized alternatives. Hence, on the whole, the engineer is talking about
"what is" or "what shortly will be" — the economist is always talking
about "what is not" — giving the economist a certain disadvantage in the
argument. A big dam is a very solid argument compared with all the
things that might have been done if the dam had not been built, yet it is
precisely with these invisible alternatives that the economist is primarily concerned.

Project Versus Value

One is tempted to say also that the engineer thinks mainly in physical terms whereas the economist is interested primarily in values.
This is an overstatement, for many engineers and certainly all good
engineers are deeply concerned about the valuation of their projects
and do, in fact, evaluate these projects in highly economic language.
Nevertheless, the heart and soul of the engineer is in the project rather
than in the impalpable value which may attach to it. It is all the more
difficult for the engineer to think in terms of values, because the value
is something which is not inherent in the construction itself, but consists of alternative uses of resources. Value again is in the shadowy
realm of the might-have-beens.

There is a third and still more subtle distinction between the mode
of thinking of the economist and the engineer: the engineer tends to regard his activity as a kind of "war against nature"; the economist, on
the other hand, thinks of nature as a factor of production to be treated
gently in a cooperative manner. It may, of course, be a mere accident
that the care of our rivers and particularly of our floods has been given
to the army engineers. Again perhaps this is no accident. Perhaps
there is something very deep in our culture which regards the conquest
of nature somewhat in the same sense as the conquest of an enemy. I
shall suggest later that this seems to me a profoundly mistaken attitude
and one that can only lead to ultimate failure and frustration.

Price System: A Variable or a Constant?

Perhaps the greatest difference between the economist and the engineer lies in their respective attitudes towards the price system, interpreting this in a broad sense. The engineer on the whole takes the
price system for granted and tends to regard prices as cost. The economist, by contrast, regards the price system as essentially a variable
and is always interested in the question as to what would happen if

prices were different from what they are now. The engineer tends to regard the price system as a mere obstacle to the attainment of his engineering ideals — he would like to build wonderful dams, beautiful aqueducts and magnificent roads. But the nasty economist and accountant and financier stand behind him reprovingly, always preventing him for reasons which seem to have nothing to do with engineering.

Perhaps the classic expression of his attitude comes not from engineering at all but from a misguided economist, Thorstein Veblen, in his book *The Engineers and the Price System* (publisher B. W. Huebsch, New York, 1921). Veblen clearly regards the price system as simply a nuisance in the way of ever-expanding miracles of engineering. If only we could dispose of it, giving the engineers complete leeway, the world would soon be transformed into something like an engineer's paradise.

A special case of this difference in attitude toward the price system may be seen in the difference in attitude toward the rate of interest. For the engineer the rate of interest often is seen as an arbitrary obstacle to the attainment of his cherished projects. He tries to justify the building of a dam, shall we say, where the benefits are a long way in the future, and he finds that if they are discounted at a high rate of interest the project is clearly not financially feasible, whereas if they are discounted at a low rate of interest, the project is clearly justified. If I may quote one of my own verses:

> Around the mysteries of finance
> We must perform a ritual dance
> Because the long-term interest rate
> Determines any project's fate:
> At two percent the case is clear,
> At three, some sneaking doubts appear,
> At four, it draws its final breath
> While five percent is certain death.

It is hard to blame the engineer if he feels often that the rate of interest is merely an arbitrary obstacle to the attainment of his plans. For most economists (although I must confess there are exceptions to this) the rate of interest is a reflection of some basic conditions in the economy. If the high rate of interest is not merely the result of the country's political instability or mismanagement by the monetary authorities, this is an indication that in the society there is a certain unwillingness to sacrifice present enjoyments for future benefits. This means that projects from which the benefits are to be found a long way into the future will have to fight harder for their lives or will have to promise larger net benefits than those which will be realized in the near future. It must be confessed that the problem of the socially optimal rate of interest is one which economists have not solved, and until they have solved it they can hardly blame the engineer for a certain restiveness under the restriction imposed by high interest rates which seem to be arbitrary.

Engineer a "Politician"

Another distinction between the economist and the engineer — which perhaps does more credit to the engineer than to the economist — is that the engineer is by nature more of a politician. This is particularly true of the water engineer and the highway engineer. Funds for projects frequently come from public treasuries, and if he is to see his projects carried through, he must be sensitive to sources of political power and the strange forces which bring about political decisions. The economist, on the other hand, is inclined to stand aloof from society and to make judgments in terms of the abstract standpoint of social welfare, in which each man counts as one and one only. The engineer in a sense is more realistic. He knows that a small benefit which is clearly obvious and which goes to a politically powerful group is of much more weight politically than a larger benefit which is not visible and which is diffused over a large and politically inactive and impotent section of society. Consequently, it is hard to blame the engineer for keeping his ear to the political ground, and for designing his projects to appeal to those decision makers in whose hands the fate of the project ultimately lies.

Nevertheless, there is a certain virtue in the economist's point of view because he seeks a standard by which the actual performance of a society may roughly be judged and from which significant deviations may be properly denounced. It has always been a cherished function of the economist to point out that benefits to the few are obtained at the cost of much larger injuries to the many. This is what sometimes we call the "welfare criterion" of judgment upon political decisions. Even though it may be unrealistic in a narrow sense, the very fact that these judgments are made affects somehow the grounds upon which political decisions are taken. It is the business of the economist to see that special interests have a bad conscience.

I am inclined to think that engineers and economists unite somewhat against the accountant and the financier when it comes to assessing nonreimbursable benefits of various projects. In defense of this project the engineer is likely to bring together as many nonreimbursable benefits as he can. The economist, however, is quick to point out that financial returns alone are not sufficient justification for any human endeavor and that financial returns must be modified by many imponderable factors — not only those described as "human factors" but also what the economist calls "external economies and diseconomies." By this we mean the impact which expansion of a particular operation or industry in society will have upon other sectors of society which cannot, however, be financially chargeable to the operation which induces them. Engineers have not been slow to pick up this conception, particularly where it seemed to favor the expansion of their projects. They have naturally been slower to seize on those external diseconomies which likewise may follow from the expansion of particular industries or occupations.

PUBLIC VERSUS PRIVATE DEVELOPMENT

Let me now descend from the high altitude of generality and come down to the problem of water resources. One of the first things that strikes the economist as he looks at the water industry is the extraordinary extent to which water is not treated as a commodity. Again perhaps I may be forgiven if I quote my own verse:

> Water is far from a simple commodity,
> Water's a sociological oddity,
> Water's a pasture for science to forage in.
> Water's a mark of our dubious origin,
> Water's a link with a distant futurity,
> Water's a symbol of ritual purity,
> Water is politics, water's religion,
> Water is just about anyone's pigeon.
> Water is frightening, water's endearing,
> Water's a lot more than mere engineering.
> Water is tragical, water is comical,
> Water is far from the Pure Economical.
> So studies of water, though free from aridity,
> Are apt to produce a good deal of turbidity.

Of all the easily recognizable physical commodities, water seems the one we are least willing to leave in private hands, and even in the least socialized countries there is a strong tendency to socialize the "water industry." It is a useful exercise in nonpolitical economy to ask ourselves what would happen if in fact the state did nothing about water and if the provision of this estimable commodity were left entirely in private hands. It is clear that water would in general be supplied to people who wanted it and who are prepared to pay for it. There would be problems requiring political solution in the field of eminent domain, the transmission of pipelines and so on; but these presumably would be no more difficult than we face in the transmission of private gas or oil lines or electric power lines.

But when we ask this question it is by no means clear why water is so sharply differentiated politically from oil, gas and electricity and why the private water supply has become the exception. I suspect we may have to find the answer to this somewhere outside economics, perhaps even in the deeply symbolic nature of water in our society and in our almost neurotic fear of being without it. One even gets a feeling abroad that if the state or municipality did not supply water, nobody would! This clearly is absurd. Indeed, I think it can be argued quite seriously — although I do not have enough evidence to be sure that the argument is correct — that we would have been better off if the state had never intervened in the supply of water, or even if the municipality in general did not feel itself obliged to take on this enterprise but instead had provided legal framework for the use of private enterprise.

Irrigation

In the case of irrigation, the case is much clearer. In the early days of irrigation, private enterprise did most of the work. It is only as irrigation has moved, as it were, into the public and political domain, that it has become an enterprise so firmly concerned with government and the struggle for appropriations. It can be argued cogently that the first 10 million acres of irrigation in the West made so much sense that private enterprise would have done it and, for the most part, did do it. The second 10 million acres perhaps can be justified as a public enterprise in terms of external economies and the advantages derived from the building up of denser population. The third 10 million acres is of much more dubious value, and the fourth 10 million acres, on which we now seem to be embarking, is of very dubious value indeed and can only be explained in terms of the momentum of a large political organization designed to do a certain thing.

I am not, however, fanatical on the subject of private enterprise, and I have no prejudice against public enterprise, particularly in this kind of industry where there are substantial advantages in monopoly. I have no particular desire to turn municipal waterworks back to private companies, although I confess to having a certain itch to ask embarrassing questions about the Bureau of Reclamation.

It may well be that a lot of the difficulties in this field arise from the failure of people to recognize that under most circumstances water is a commodity and not a free good. We are so accustomed to thinking of rain as a free good that we confuse rain with water. Rain is no more water than grass is milk, and water supplied to a particular person in a particular place is just as much a commodity as oil. There seems no reason to suppose why, in the first place, it should not be supplied in the cheapest possible way and, in the second place, once it has been supplied it should not pay its full cost. Furthermore, the situation is often confused because of the failure to realize that water is not one but many commodities. Water supplied to the urban bathtub is not the same commodity as water supplied to the field, the factory or the recreational area.

ECONOMIC ISSUES IN WATER DEVELOPMENT

Let me now approach still closer to earth and ask what the main economic issues in water development are. I would argue that the first issue is the apparently simple one of *how much*. If we think of the water industry as an industry, we question if it is overexpanded or underexpanded. Are we putting too much into this particular occupation of resources or too little? My guess would be (and this may not be a very well-informed guess) that in urban water supplies on the whole we are doing about right; that in regard to irrigation we are doing far too much in the dry areas, and probably not enough in the moist ones; and in regard to flood control we are creating disasters for ourselves in the future and are living in a fool's paradise.

In the case of urban water supplies we have a commodity with a fairly elastic supply in most cases. Where adequate local government exists, not much of a problem tends to arise. There are some places, perhaps in the arid areas, where too little investment is going on. There are almost certainly other places, such as Los Angeles, where too much has gone on and is still going on. Los Angeles is going to run out of air long before it is going to run out of water. This is almost a classic example of economic presbyopia — farsightedness in the optical sense of the term. In Los Angeles water is not a commodity but a religion. There is a strong tendency for religions to expand their use of resources beyond the strict needs of their practitioners.

Flood Control

I have already suggested the possibility that the development of irrigation has gone far beyond the point of proper social returns and that social return to investment in a great deal of irrigation is now negative, especially in view of bounding agricultural surpluses. The real scandal, however, is flood control. Professor Gilbert White of the University of Chicago has suggested that after spending four billion dollars on flood control we are more in danger of flood damage, and indeed disaster, than we were before. This is largely because we have regarded flood control as a problem in engineering rather than in sociology. I suggested earlier that we invite trouble if we regard nature merely as an enemy to be conquered rather than as a friendly home. It may be perhaps accidental that army engineers have been responsible for flood control. The truth is that what we call "flood control" means the eradication of little disasters every 10 years or so at the cost of a really big disaster every 50 or 100 years in any given floodplain. No flood-control program is able to protect a floodplain against the 100-year flood. After all, that is why the floodplain is there!

When, however, we build dams and levees, we give people the illusion that the problem has been conquered whereas, in fact, it has merely changed from a benign to a very dangerous form. The danger of flood damage increases despite flood control because people have confidence in the works themselves, which leads them to build out over the floodplain. It is because flood control is *not* linked in any sense with social policy nor especially with the growth of urban areas that the more flood control we have the more damage we are likely to have from floods.

It is particularly striking to visit a city such as Sacramento in California, where the old houses have long stone stairs leading up to the first floors, where the ground floor is devoted merely to storage and life begins at 15 feet. In the old days when there was a flood the family went upstairs and waited till the flood went down. Now with dams and levees constructed, everybody builds low ranch-type houses on the floodplain. It may be next year or it may not be for 100 years or for 200 years, but one of these days the really big flood is going to come, the levees are going to break and the dead will be counted in tens of thousands, and the water will be several feet over the rooftops of most of the new housing developments. The same story could be repeated in floodplain cities all over the country.

It seems to me that we need an entirely new philosophy for flood control which may involve treating the river not as an enemy to be conquered but as a rather dangerous friend with whom one has to learn to live. It is perfectly possible to design cities on the floodplain to *accommodate* floods instead of taking on the impossible task of trying to prevent them. There is no reason, for instance, why we should not build our floodplain cities on stilts; there is much to be said for this architecturally and from the whole point of view of city design. It would provide parking spaces under the buildings and would enable a separation of levels of traffic.

Development and the Distribution of National Wealth

The other question an economist asks besides "how much," is "to whom." What is the impact of our resource development on the distribution of wealth and income? This is a difficult question to which we do not know the answer. Nevertheless, there are some fairly clear pitfalls which we may avoid. There has been a tendency, for instance, to justify a subsidy to irrigation on the grounds that this redistributes income away from the rich taxpayer towards the poor farmer. The fallacy of this proposition is the general fallacy of trying to do justice to a commodity or an industry rather than to individuals. It is true that some farmers are poor but some are rich; so when we subsidize *water* as such, we aid the rich more than we aid the poor because the rich use more. It is true that the Bureau of Reclamation has tried to avoid this dilemma by imposing a 160-acre limitation on subsidized water. In California, however, and I am sure in many other parts of the country, there are a good many ways of getting around this. I would be surprised if a careful study did not reveal that the impact of the subsidy is more favorable to the larger farmer than it is to the smaller. Even if we want to redistribute income from the rich to the poor, this is one of the worst ways in which to do it, for it encourages people to stay in an occupation that they should leave. It contributes to agricultural surpluses and to the general maldistribution of resources.

Price Structure of Water Industry

This brings us to the large and difficult question of the water industry's price structure and of the positive or negative subsidies which may be implied in it. It is surprisingly difficult to define what we really mean by a subsidy, particularly where we have a commodity which is only one of many joint products. This is usually the case with water.

There is always an arbitrary element in the allocation of fixed costs among a number of joint products, and under these circumstances it is often hard to say when a given price for a given use involves a subsidy or a tax. We must evaluate this whole question from the viewpoint of a sound philosophy of the whole price structure and particularly from a clear view of the functions of the price structure.

One of the great difficulties in price policy is that there are at least three functions of the price structure which may not be compatible one with another, and a good deal of the pulling and hauling in economic policy arises because we are trying to make the one institution of the price system perform three incompatible tasks.

Allocate resources. The first of these three tasks is the allocation of resources to different industries so that the structure, i.e., the relative proportions, of different commodity outputs is such that each output can be distributed without difficulty. The function of the price structure here is to prevent shortages and surpluses in the sense of unwanted accumulations or decumulations of storable commodities or in the sense of unsatisfied buyers or sellers of nonstorable commodities.

Distributor of income. The second function of the relative price system is that of the distributor of income. Given the distribution of property, the distribution of income is largely a function of the relative price system. If we raise the price of wheat, the income of wheat farmers will be raised at the expense of wheat consumers. If we make the price of water very low, as a result those who use a lot of water will be better off and those who use a little will be worse off than they otherwise would be. It is one of the great dilemmas of economic policy that the attempt to rectify what are regarded as socially undesirable distributions of income through use of the price system almost inevitably involves the misallocation of resources or the development of shortages and surpluses. Water is no exception to this. If we "subsidize" water — that is if we lower its price in some sense below the Marshallian normal — this means that from the standpoint of ideal resource allocation too much has been devoted to water and not enough to other things. Water will be produced in quantities too large and will be used wastefully.

Direct technical change. The third function of the price system is seldom mentioned in the textbooks, but in the long run it may be perhaps the most important. This is the function of directing the course of technical change and of the larger dynamics of the economy. Inexpensive products are not economized, and attention is not drawn towards their economization. On the other hand, the course of technical change always tends to work toward eliminating the costly and dear. This is a principle of great importance in the development of water resources. If we have a commodity which is fairly plentiful today, but which is likely to be much scarcer in the future with expanding population and perhaps increasingly costly sources of supply, the slogan of the water resource man should be "water should be dear and plentiful." It should be dear because only if it is dear will people bother to economize; only if it is dear will technical change move in the direction of water-saving improvements.

I came across a striking example of this in California. In the Los Angeles area where even agricultural water is quite expensive, there is a regular profession of water savers, men who teach farmers how to use as little water as possible in order to irrigate their fields. In the Central Valley where water costs little, thanks to the taxpayer and the public enterprise of the Bureau of Reclamation, no such occupation exists. The farmers use water as wastefully as they like and it is hard to blame them, for there is no incentive to economize and particularly no incentive to develop water-saving improvements.

The same principle applies to industrial water. In the steel mills in Fontana in the desert the water is used again and again. In the Great Lakes area it is used wastefully and quite rightly so. But if any substantial water-saving technology is to emerge from the steel industry, we would expect it from Fontana and not from Cleveland. There is therefore a strong social case for making water expensive in the hope that this will persuade technical change to go in the direction of water-saving improvements.

The easiest way to make water dear is to tax it. Water is an excellent commodity for tax. It has a fairly inelastic demand, so the yields of taxation should be high. The rich use a lot more than the poor, so the tax should not be unduly regressive. Moreover, when the overhead of the economy at the state level is nowhere being met on an adequate scale and where the balance between the public and the private sector, as Galbraith has suggested, is deficient on the public side, an almost unobjectionable object of taxation such as water should not be overlooked, especially as a source of state and local revenue.

It is not impossible that we are on the edge of large changes in water-saving technology. One of the crucial questions in the economic dynamics of the water industry is how such changes may both be foreseen and encouraged. It is possible, for instance, that one by-product of the enormous amount of resources in space research may be the development of the totally self-sufficient household in which water, along with other necessities of life, is continually processed through a closed circuit of human intake and output and purification. The results of sea water purification research have been disappointing to date, and it may be that the energy requirements are too great to make it cheap enough to get fresh water from the sea, even though the freshening of brackish water seems to have great possibilities. Nevertheless, we have scarcely begun to ask the right questions about the *use* of sea water. It does, after all, support a great deal of life and metabolism, and the payoff here may come through the biological approach and through developing better ways to take salt water directly into the human bio-economy. As far as the immense resource of the sea is concerned, we are still in the food collection stage and have not even domesticated any plants or animals, if we except the humble oyster. A marine equivalent of agriculture might make a lot of land irrigation unnecessary!

Another line of technical development which may have a great impact on water resource development is the cheapening of sea transport of liquids (or even granular solids) through the use of floating plastic bags. Rather than getting its water from the Feather River through immense and costly aqueducts, Los Angeles might well import it from Alaska by sea. Engineers, like the rest of us, like to do what they have been trained to do. In economic dynamics, however, it is frequently through doing what nobody has been trained to do that brings about the critical "entrepreneurial" breakthrough into a new technology.

It may well be that in the future it will be the skills of the biologist, the meteorologist (in weather control) and the mariner which will dominate the development of water resources rather than those of the hydraulic engineer. What is pretty certain, however, is that the skills of the economist will not have much impact and that the economist will continue to be a voice crying in the wilderness. If he cries loudly and long enough, however, somebody may listen to him out of sheer irritation. To that irritation this chapter is intended to be a small contribution.

RAY K. LINSLEY is Professor of Civil Engineering at Stanford University. He is a well-known hydrologist who has creatively combined economics and engineering in education and research.

Chapter 7

RAY K. LINSLEY | *Engineering and Economics In Project Planning*

E NGINEERING AND ECONOMICS are the essential features of project planning. They are not, however, independent. While some features of a project analysis can be done independently, for the most part the work in the two areas must be closely coordinated.

Engineering is not, as many suppose, the mere application of physical science to the design and construction of project works. A properly engineered project must satisfy the requirements of safety, efficiency, economy and esthetics. Safety requires that the structures withstand specified natural forces without serious damage. It is implicit that the probability of forces occurring beyond the capability of the structure during the life of the project is very low. However, permanence in the true sense of the word is not expected and some probability of failure within the period of useful life is accepted. The acceptable probabilities should be established on economic and social grounds.

Efficiency requires that the project perform its intended function in a proper fashion. The key words here are "intended function." Since the economic evaluation of the project is usually based on the assumption that the intended function will be achieved, anything less than 100 per cent efficiency leads to a corresponding overestimate of the benefits.

93

The requirement of economy means: (1) that project cost be a minimum consistent with the requirements of safety, efficiency and esthetics; (2) that if there are alternatives, the selected project represent the best of all possible alternatives and (3) that the project return benefits at least as great as its cost. Economy thus involves two distinct concepts — one of minimum cost, primarily an engineering problem, and one of evaluation, primarily an economic problem.

Esthetics requires that the project be pleasing in its external appearance. The words "pleasing appearance" can engender much argument, and further refinement will not be attempted here. However, cost can be greatly influenced by special esthetic requirements beyond the functional needs of the project.

The building of a project is not evidence that it was engineered. Any person of reasonable intelligence, given sufficient funds, could direct the building of most engineering projects and arrive at a finished product which at least approximately fulfills its goals. The project would very likely fail to satisfy the criteria of an engineered project. Evidence of this assertion is found in many quite incredible structures of the Old World. The cathedrals and canal systems of western Europe, the great mosques of the Near East and the pyramids of Egypt are examples. Men with little knowledge of science and no concern with economics succeeded in copying and enlarging earlier structures until some very large and imposing works resulted. There were, however, many failures during construction, and many of these structures are preserved only because of strengthening added subsequent to the original construction. It might be very interesting to study some of the ancient water projects to determine why they failed and whether we have learned anything from the mistakes of the past. But that is another story.

Much has been written about the techniques of engineering design and the application of economic principles to water-project planning. We face a period of great population growth which brings large water requirements. We have built those water projects which offered the most favorable balance between cost and benefits. We face the future with a need to develop new projects under conditions that are far from favorable. Technological improvements will overcome some of the handicap, but it will be necessary to be more skillful in planning than in the past.

The final form of a project is determined largely by the nature of its conception, by engineering decisions in the design process and by standards which govern certain aspects of design and construction. These aspects of planning get well mixed in the usual project and it is often difficult to separate them. However, I propose to discuss each aspect with emphasis on those problems which lead to uncertainty in the design process.

NEED FOR CREATIVE THINKING
IN PROJECT CONCEPTION

It is often difficult to say when and how the very first idea for a project originated. There is reason to suspect, however, that the conditions of conception play a far more important role in shaping the final project than is generally realized. The aim of project planning is to achieve the best possible project. The use of the superlative implies comparison of all possible alternatives until the best is isolated by elimination. The hazard in the conception phase is that the project plan is frozen before a comprehensive comparison of alternatives is made.

There are three basic patterns of project conception. The key words are *need, dream* and *master plan.* A pressing need for water may lead to the employment of engineers to find a solution. The thoroughness of the search will depend on the ability of the engineer and the time and money allotted to the study. Unless the engineer is capable of creative thinking, the more unusual alternatives may never be recognized. Our system of education tends to encourage the stereotyped rather than the original solution.

Between 1917 and 1955 several studies were made of possible new surface water supplies for Stanford University. Each time the cost was too great, primarily because of the cost of water purification. During this same period the university was plagued with leakage of water from Lake Lagunita. In 1957, under pressure from the State Supervisor of Dams, a firm of soils engineers was employed to solve the problem of the leaky embankment. They suggested a clay cutoff wall and blanket which were installed. Throughout all these studies no one noted that Lagunita could be a large filtration basin with collections wells around the periphery. This would eliminate the cost of water treatment, solve the problem of leakage and make the storage in Lagunita useful for the first time since Governor Stanford last watered stock there. Thus, for 40 years a highly desirable project went unrecognized.

The foregoing example not only emphasizes the need for creative thinking, but also points out that considerable time may be required for all alternatives to be recognized. If there is a pressing need for water, the engineer is usually given very little time to make his study. There is also a notable reluctance to pay for adequate engineering. This has reached its ultimate in the practice of contingent engineering. Here the engineer agrees to make the preliminary investigation without charge to the client with the understanding that if a feasible project is found, he will be employed for the final design. The hazards of this highly unethical practice are obvious, and a share of the blame must rest on the clients who are unwilling to pay for proper engineering.

Sometimes an individual will have a vision of a project long before a real need exists. John Powell's vision[1] of an irrigated West as a result of his explorations during the nineteenth century is an example. One nearer to us is the well-known Reber Plan for the construction of barriers in San Francisco Bay. Dreams rarely encompass alternatives, and dreams in the hands of a crusader are hard to supplant. The Reber Plan is so thoroughly embedded in the public mind that there still remains some pressure for its construction even though engineering recommendations are contrary.

Sometimes a systematic search for possible projects is instituted. The California Water Plan is an example. Such plans inevitably include projects originating on the basis of need and dreams. Often a broad-scale search becomes a sort of game in which projects are tucked into every possible location. In one way this is advantageous because it contributes to the search for all alternatives. However, if these projects are recorded in an official document, they become more than alternatives in the mind of the public. They become projects which should be built even though the evaluation of economic and engineering feasibility was quite cursory. I am continually startled by the way in which estimates and assumptions from a plan of this kind slowly become indistinguishable from fact. Many of the assertions now being made about the Feather River Project fall in this category.

Project Future Conditions

The visualization of a project requires a projection of future conditions — population, economic development, water requirements, etc. Techniques for such projections are very poor and many efforts are little more than an extrapolation of a past trend into the future. No change other than growth is anticipated, yet significant changes in social habits and economic development are possible. Does the California Water Plan consider possible changes which might occur in the California economy of the future? Will technological change diminish the importance of irrigated agriculture? Should water planning be directed toward the encouragement of such changes? Does project planning really plan for the future or does it simply help to regiment the future into the pattern of the past? This is an area in which much study is needed.

One last psychological factor which inevitably influences planning is size. Engineering structures are monuments to their builders, and there is much personal satisfaction in a completed project for even the least of the engineering staff. That engineers should be especially interested in large projects is only natural, and it seems likely that very large projects are particularly susceptible to premature fixation.

ENGINEERING DECISIONS

Throughout the design of a project the engineers must make numerous decisions. These decisions influence the safety and economy of the project and, hence, the cost and economic justification. Probably the most troublesome decisions are those involving estimates of future events. For the most part we must assume that the future will be statistically the same as the past. Hoyt and Langbein[2] give examples of the effect of the possible error in statistical analysis on flood control and power projects.

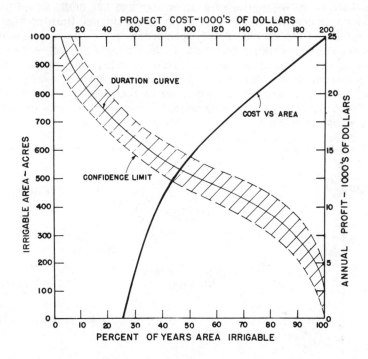

Fig. 7.1. Characteristics of a hypothetical project.

Figure 7.1 gives the characteristics of a hypothetical irrigation project. Assuming a constant duty of water, a duration curve showing the percentage of years in which it would be possible to irrigate various acreages is derived from the streamflow record. Assuming a fixed net profit per acre, the duration curve also indicates the percentage of years in which various profits will be equalled or exceeded. The other curve on the figure is a plot of the estimated cost of works to irrigate various acreages from zero to 1,000 acres. Any statistical curve may be in error, and a duration curve is no exception. Therefore confidence limits representing one standard deviation are shown; that is, there are two chances in three that the true duration curve lies within the indicated confidence band. Figure 7.1, less the confidence band, represents the sort of data usually used in project planning.

If we assume that all water available will be used for irrigation up to the limit set by the size of the project, the average annual return from any project size is the area under the duration curve up to the limiting area. If we use the mean duration curve for this estimate, there is a 50 per cent probability that the estimated profit is too great;

but if we use the lower confidence limit, there is only one chance in six of an overestimate. The location of the lower confidence limit is dependent on the length of record. Figure 7.2 shows the variation in return on investment as a function of project size and length of record based on the lower confidence limit. The lower confidence limit of Fig. 7.1 was estimated for various lengths of record and the areas under each of these curves computed to obtain the curves of Fig. 7.2. A project life of 50 years was assumed as a basis for calculating rate of return. If a minimum rate of return of 8 per cent is acceptable, a variation of 19 per cent in project size is indicated as record length varies from 5 to 100 years. This is a considerable degree of uncertainty to interject into a project analysis.

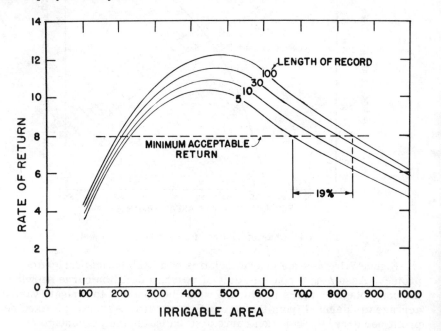

Fig. 7.2. Effect of record length on return.

Figure 7.2 is based on the assumption that the mean duration curve of Fig. 7.1 remains unchanged as length of record shifts and that only the confidence limits are altered. This brings up one of the most important unsolved problems in hydrology today — the question of climatic trend and its effect on future streamflow. Figure 7.3 is a frequency count of the number of times a particular year in any quartile of the record is followed by a year in any other quartile. Data are for the Kings River at Piedra, California. This distribution is evidently random. In fact, the chi-square test indicates that similar departures from randomness could be expected in about 7 out of 10 such trials by chance. The bulk of the evidence supports the conclusion of randomness

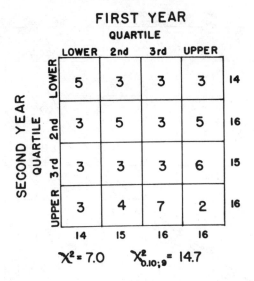

Fig. 7.3. Test of serial correlation, Kings River at Piedra.

for the data available to us. The few instances where slight trends are
indicated are clouded by the possibility that the trends are artificially
induced in the station record by man's activity.

The other side of the coin is the indisputable evidence of major climatic changes in geologic time. The magnitude of these changes is only
approximately known and the causes are yet to be discovered. They
are, however, evidence that trends do occur and lead to the suspicion
that our records are too short to disclose these trends. As we begin to
plan for a twofold population increase by 2000 A.D. and for the use of
the last increment of water from some local supplies, we may well be
concerned with the possibility that climatic trend may reduce the total
water available to us. It is, of course, equally likely that the trend, if
any, will be to increased supplies.

Random errors and trends are not the only problems with frequency
curves. Curve A of Fig. 7.4 shows the flood frequency curve used in
the analysis of a flood control project. Based on 18 years of record
(1931-41 and 1951-57) the figure shows the highest flood of the period
is assigned a return period of 18 years. Mean annual damage was calculated at $300,000 and the benefit-cost ratio of the project was taken
as 1.04. This is in accord with conventional practice, although it is
possible to argue that a straight line rather than a curve should have
been fitted to the data. It is quite certain, however, that no flood during
the period of missing record (1942-50) equalled the maximum recorded
flood. The period of record might be taken as 27 years and Curve B
constructed using the procedure suggested by Benson.[3] The mean annual damages become $214,000 and the benefit-cost ratio 0.74. It is
possible that one could go back as far as 1920 without finding a flood

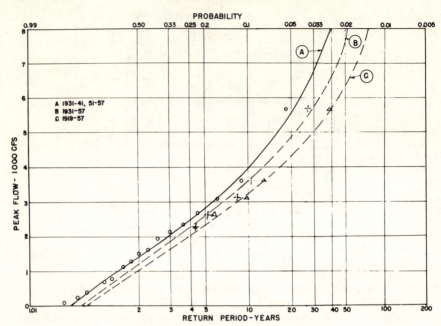

Fig. 7.4. Flood frequency curves.

exceeding the observed maximum. On this basis, Curve C results with mean annual damages of only $147,000 and a benefit-cost ratio of 0.51. It is not clear whether Curve A was deliberately adopted to make the project feasible or whether ignorance of the alternate interpretations was the controlling factor.

Another area of the design process which requires an assumption of future conditions is the operation study. An operation study is a paper simulation of the project operation for a period of time. Usually the actual record of past streamflow is assumed as project inflow, and out-flows are assumed to occur according to an established operation plan. It is then possible to compute the amount of water in storage at any time and the amount of spill which will occur. For a flood-control proj-ect, past floods are routed through the reservoir to determine the flow reduction to be expected.

On paper it is relatively simple to project the operation at the opti-mum level. In actual practice the operation is much more difficult. Many decisions must be made with incomplete information regarding the future. It would be instructive to compare an actual operation with that assumed in the operation study, but this is difficult since the pre-project conditions are never precisely duplicated in the post-project period. It seems probable, however, that actual project efficiency will be somewhat lower than that anticipated in the design conditions. Rut-ter,[4] in a study of three large floods in the Tennessee River, found that the TVA system actually effected about 50 per cent of the flood peak reduction which was theoretically possible. This is no reflection on the ability of TVA water control engineers. The numerous compromises necessary in multiple-purpose projects and the uncertainties of future weather make the theoretically perfect operation generally unattainable.

No point would be served by further detail of the many uncertainties of design which stem from ignorance or inadequate data. Our collective ignorance of many design problems makes it necessary to use approximate or empirical methods. Because of individual ignorance, the engineers on a given project may fail to use fully the knowledge that is available. Finally, inadequate or inaccurate data may cause the best engineer to reach wrong conclusions.

STANDARDS

Many aspects of project design are governed by standards set by policy decisions or by that vague arbiter known as "good engineering practice." Where standards govern, the design engineer follows the procedures of his agency or of good practice without any particular decision on his part. Therefore, standards can become a relief from the effort of thinking or a shield against errors. An engineer who departs from common practice and has a failure is open to severe censure. One who conforms to accepted procedure is relatively free from blame even though excess cost or a less efficient project results.

Construction standards cover the methods and materials of construction. They are embodied in the project specifications limiting height of pour, time between pours, method of placing fill, character of materials, etc. White[5] has suggested that the combined effect of unnecessary restrictions during the construction of Bull Shoals Dam increased the cost by seven million dollars or roughly 25 per cent. Giddings[6] points out many arbitrary and, to him, unnecessary restrictions enforced by inspectors on the construction of the Clark Hill powerhouse. It has been said many times that bid prices for a project will vary as much as 15 per cent, depending on the supervising agency. Certainly construction standards cannot be lowered below the level required for safety nor can contractors be allowed to perform unsatisfactory work. However, these standards are often arbitrary. Each echelon of supervision tends to be a bit more restrictive then the one below it in order to be "safe." This can easily lead to excessive restrictions. The capitalized values of a small current saving will pay for a considerable amount of future repairs.

In the design area much controversy exists regarding the standard of spillway design. Should a spillway be capable of discharging the 100-year, 1,000-year, or maximum probable flood? To what extent should low-cost emergency spillways or discharge over normally nonoverflow sections of the dam be tolerated to minimize spillway costs? The problem is that of defining the acceptable probability of spillway capacity exceedance. Because the economic cost of such an exceedance cannot be reliably predicted, the decision is usually based on policy grounds.

A similar problem is encountered in the decision on the project design flood for flood control. Absolute flood control — that is, control such that the probability of flooding in the protected area is zero — is virtually impossible. While it would seem to be possible to balance cost against benefits to find the optimum level of protection, so many intangible factors enter the decision that it ultimately becomes quite arbitrary.

Water supply projects are often governed by local standards for the acceptable level of watershed protection. One nearby water district is willing to spend more than 30 million dollars to avoid using a source from which its neighboring community obtains water. This decision is based entirely on the issue of water quality *not* involving public health. If the customers are willing to pay the difference in cost, one cannot criticize the decision very strongly. It is offered only as evidence of the dollar value which is built into some standards.

CONCLUSIONS

Substantial differences in project design are possible within the bounds of what is currently accepted as good practice. Indeed, a considerable gray zone bounds the band of good practice. These differences can lead to substantial differences in cost and benefits. It would be difficult and probably unwise to attempt to specify the magnitude of these differences except to say that they can be quite large. Equal uncertainties exist in the evaluation of the economic consequences of projects.

There should be an effort to analyze the principles of design in order to develop a systematic approach to project conception which will assure that all possible alternatives are considered.

There is need for continued effort to collect basic data on all aspects of water planning. In the 1960's we are spending less than half of 1 percent of the annual investment in water projects on hydrologic data. This 25 million dollars would hardly pay the cost of one space rocket flight. Data alone are not sufficient. We must learn to make better use of the data we have and will get. A program of research to make this possible is necessary. Concurrently, increased efforts to educate personnel in the use of new methodology are urgently needed.

It will be impossible to eliminate many of the sources of uncertainty in project planning, and project evaluation should include analysis of the probable effect of these uncertainties on the relation of benefit to cost. The final decision on feasibility could then be made with the knowledge of the probability that the decision might be wrong.

FOOTNOTES

[1] W. C. Darrah, Powell of the Colorado, Princeton Univ. Press, Princeton, 1951.

[2] W. B. Langbein, and W. G. Hoyt, Water Facts for the Nation's Future, Ronald Press, New York, 1959.

[3] M. A. Benson, "Use of historical data in flood frequency analysis," Trans-American Geophysical Union, 31:419-24, 1950.

[4] E. J. Rutter, "Flood-control operation of Tennessee Valley Authority reservoirs," Proceedings, American Society of Civil Engineers, Vol. 76, May 1950, separate 19, 33 pp.

[5] Ross White, "A contractor assays the specifications for Bull Shoals Dam," *Civil Engineering,* 21:638-39, 1951.

[6] W. A. Giddings, "A contractor reviews his headaches at Clark Hill Powerhouse," *Civil Engineering,* 24:158-60, 1954.

PART II | *Economic Evaluation,*
Quantification

CLYDE E. STEWART is with the Economic Research Service, U.S. Department of Agriculture. He is well known for his research on the economics of irrigation development.

Chapter 8

CLYDE E. STEWART

Economic Evaluation Of Public Irrigation Development

PRIMARY OR DIRECT agricultural benefits from irrigation must be quantified in analyzing many water development projects in the United States as well as throughout the world. Secondary or indirect benefits are discussed in this chapter only when relevant to the main theme. We use a specific application of methods — the investigations, 1956-62, of the U.S. Department of Agriculture in the Upper Colorado Basin — as an illustrative case for pointing up the needs and problems associated with quantification of direct agricultural benefits.

Senate Document No. 97, published May 29, 1962, "Policies, Standards, and Procedures in the Formulation, Evaluation, and Review of Plans for Use and Development of Water and Related Land Resources," and other policy and economic developments may have altered economic evaluations in the Upper Colorado River Basin if they had been in effect. The basic elements described in this chapter would likely remain unchanged except possibly for the discount rate applied to benefits. Price projections would probably be based more on normalized historical levels. Less emphasis may have been placed on production and more emphasis on stabilizing effects of irrigation development on the local economy, and on secondary and indirect benefits generally. Senate Document 97 emphasizes the need for comprehensive river basin plans as a framework for project evaluations; future efforts in river basin developments will include more emphasis on such plans than was feasible in the Upper Colorado work. Quantification problems relating to direct benefits have apparently not diminished and, in fact, may have become more complex.

ORIENTATION

Primary or direct agricultural benefits from public irrigation development have received less attention in recent years than have secondary or indirect benefits. This is largely because less question has been raised as to whether direct benefits should be recognized in project evaluation and selection, and because they are viewed as market-priced.

Problems of evaluating primary agricultural benefits take on significance for two reasons. (1) Serious problems prevail in expressing some resource costs in monetary values. (2) The magnitude of secondary and public benefits, according to procedures in the period under consideration, hinged on the magnitude and composition of the primary benefits. Secondary benefits often exceed primary benefits as a part of agricultural net benefits under existing procedures of analyzing the federal reclamation program.

The need for more thorough analyses and investigations regarding agricultural benefits is accented by an unresolved question as to the most adequate procedure for estimating benefits. Methods considered most frequently are the farm income budget method, a method based on market land values, and a landlord share approach. The farm budget approach is considered in this chapter.

Data and measurement problems are both economic and physical. The basic need for physical data, especially for a soil classification designed for evaluation purposes and for production functions under various soil and water situations, has not been met. Although it is recognized that economists have a responsibility to physical scientists to outline the physical data needed for economic evaluations, the scope of this chapter will not permit this undertaking.

Quantification aspects of economic evaluations are important from the standpoint of developing an adequate conceptual framework. Quantification gives meaning to many theories, meaning that is not apparent at the qualitative level, and may lead to the reformulation of certain concepts. Exclusive attention to these aspects may have led to a substantial slowing in the rate of breaking through the problem barriers of economic evaluation of water resources development.

PERSPECTIVE OF THE COLORADO SURVEY

In 1954 the President of the United States directed the departments of Agriculture and Interior to cooperate in an appraisal of direct

agricultural benefits on "a number of participating projects" of the
proposed Upper Colorado Basin development. Arrangements for carrying out these investigations were not completed until around the middle of 1956. In the meantime, on April 11, 1956, the Colorado River
Storage Project Act was approved which authorized the construction of
11 participating irrigation projects as well as four major storage dams
and reservoirs. In effect, this act specified the particular projects on
which cooperative investigations would be made. "Authorization" does
not mean that a construction budget is available; detailed feasibility
analyses are made following project authorization. This chapter draws
heavily upon the experiences of the author as a member of the USDA
Field Advisory Committee during four years of investigations under
these cooperative appraisals in the Upper Colorado River Basin.[1] The
measurement features are discussed mainly as they evolved from the
Upper Colorado Survey.

The Department of Agriculture broadened the scope of its activities
somewhat beyond an estimate of direct agricultural benefits; this enlarged scope was suggested by the directive from the President. The
assurance of a successful, stable agricultural economy became one of
the chief goals of its investigations. The economic analysis of irrigation projects was directed toward two main objectives: (1) An appraisal
of prospective farm incomes from representative sizes and types of
farms most likely to develop with the projects and (2) an appraisal of
direct agricultural benefits from project development.

Economists of the U.S. Department of Agriculture followed the
Inter-Agency Report, "Proposed Practices for Economic Analysis of
River Basin Project," revised May, 1958, in their appraisal of direct
agricultural benefits in the Upper Colorado River Basin. Measurement
aspects discussed will be within the general framework of the "Green
Book."

Direct agricultural benefits are defined as "the value of farm production estimated with project development in excess of farm production estimated without the project, less the value of additional farm inputs or associated costs." Obtaining agreement on this general definition does not seem to be difficult. But differences between agencies
and individuals arise in defining the terminology of the definition.

The cooperative work outlined above was restricted to primary agricultural benefits. However, the U.S. Bureau of Reclamation places a
heavy weight on "secondary" and "public" benefits in its evaluation
work. The magnitude of these latter benefits hinges greatly upon the
assumptions and procedures applied for the primary benefits. In terms
of public policy in the particular period, therefore, it is appropriate to
consider secondary benefits.

Another important aspect of these cooperative investigations was
the decision that the Department of Agriculture should not be concerned
with the scale of the project. Its investigations were based on an acceptance of the construction features, total water supply and land to be
irrigated with the project as determined by the Bureau of Reclamation.

This operational framework restricted contributions by these investigations. In some instances the joint economic investigations resulted in changes in the project — but these changes were incidental. Land was included in some projects when the analysis by the Department of Agriculture showed zero benefits and showed, in fact, that residual returns to water would not meet annual operation and maintenance expenses for irrigation. A case such as this suggests that net primary benefits would have been enlarged by decreasing the scale of the project. Both supplemental and full irrigation were considered.

The orientation was mainly to economic evaluation; in a sense, the goal was to estimate a net primary benefit for the total project. The same evaluation can be used for repayment and financial feasibility considerations. These analyses should contribute also to efficient use of water and other resources after a project has been constructed.

A basic assumption is that the national economy will operate at essentially full employment for the evaluation period. Based on this general assumption, alternative employment opportunities would exist in the national economy for resources used in the development and operation of irrigated farms, including the labor and management skills of farm operators. Also, the projected levels of farm prices received and paid exceeded those under a significant amount of unemployment. As we shall see, some exceptions regarding level of employment and pricing of resources and commodities were necessary.

Price Projections

Price projections developed by the U.S. Department of Agriculture have generally been used for evaluation work in the federal reclamation program. The main exception involved the projections issued in June of 1956 and slightly revised in September of 1957. These projections resulted in an index of 235 for prices received and an index of 265 for prices paid, with a parity ratio of 89. The Bureau of Reclamation did not accept the projection of prices received, and in the late 50's it was using indexes of 250 and 265, with a parity ratio of 94.

Even with acceptance of the national projections, the economist is confronted by several difficult problems and essential tasks: (1) Adaptation of the national demand projections to local conditions, (2) pricing for particular quality and grade of products and (3) estimation of the extent to which technological improvements and institutional influences should enter into specific prices, or the extent to which the national price projections include technological changes.

Practically, some improvement in technology over the present situation was usually included in the analyses. However, it is difficult to project the magnitude of these changes. In some instances, inputs and outputs used apparently differed little, if any, from current practices and results.

The pricing of products and resources for project evaluation can be implemented by research on the outlook for and the impact on agricultural production for local and regional areas. These studies provide basic information on the demand and supply of products expected to come from project areas.

Income Approach to Value of Water

The income or residual approach is currently used in evaluation of irrigation water on federal reclamation projects. To date, a more adequate method has not been devised. This procedure also has merit in its convenience for repayment purposes and in its usefulness for appraising the adequacy of the potential agricultural economy on a given project area.

This procedure involves income analyses by budgeting farm situations projected with and without project conditions. The residual income is assumed to measure the value of a specified quantity of irrigation water. A workable number of farm situations is selected that can be added together by weighting to estimate project benefits.

Some economic study of each project area seems to be essential as a basis for projections related to the local economy. Input-output data and local prices were collected from farmers and others. Data from studies in other areas were relied upon almost exclusively for new projects.

The critical and sensitive nature of some items is evident. An hour of labor per acre can affect benefits by $1.00 or more per acre. A tenth of a ton of alfalfa per acre at $20.00 per ton affects benefits to the extent of almost $2.00 per acre, or a $1.00 per ton difference in the price of alfalfa can affect net benefits by several dollars per acre.

The Green Book suggests that the evaluation of primary benefits should usually be made at that point where the product or services have an actual or estimated market value. An approach that has some overall merit first develops farm income budgets, including livestock enterprises as projected. These income budgets enable an appraisal of farm income prospects, one goal of the analysis by the Department of Agriculture. These same farm budgets also serve as the basis for an estimate of primary benefits, at the first point of product market value, by removing the livestock. For analytical purposes the farms become cash-crop farms, although cropping patterns and forage prices are estimated on the basis of livestock projected for the area and of off-farm markets for crops not fed to livestock. Conceptually, the crop-budget approach is the same as the complete income-budget approach, as the influence of livestock is maintained throughout in both sets of budgets.

The crop-budget approach is strictly a procedural technique applied in the budgetary process. Removal of livestock avoids some of the problems of allocating costs and returns to different levels of management and different qualities and quantities of other inputs and outputs associated with livestock. Capital, labor and management needed for livestock enterprises are especially difficult to measure and evaluate. The procedure[2] suggested here appears to be a more simplified and reliable alternative for estimating primary benefits than would be total farm income budgets.

Use of farm income budgets for estimating benefits requires the determination of weights or relative importance of various livestock enterprises and farm types and projection of aggregate farm incomes for the project. The partial budget does not avoid completely an income aggregation. This problem is greatly simplified, especially on some projects. For example, on one project in Wyoming projected cropping patterns were essentially the same among different farm types for given land and water situations. Thus the crop-budget approach permitted the use of a single budget for each land and water situation rather than working through several budgets for each situation to reflect the projected livestock economy.

The objective is to estimate the effects that the proposed water development will have on the economy. This estimate is a comparison of two projected economies. In the future, adjustments without the project as well as changes expected to relate to an increased water supply must be recognized.

Both projections must be oriented to "realistic" or "expected" situations. They should avoid maximization or optimum conditions. They must recognize institutional limitations to adjustments. In many irrigated areas of the West, adjustments have occurred slowly. Inadequate water supplies and associated income and capital limitations to adjustment have often been important reasons.

Evaluation Period and Discounting

Development period. Historically it has taken a number of years to achieve full development of farms on new irrigation projects. Thus a lag occurs before agricultural incomes and project benefits are at a level associated with an established economy. This lag is recognized by federal reclamation legislation which permits a development period of up to 10 years before repayment charges are levied. Public agencies have applied this period in project evaluation, although for some projects a 10-year span may not be adequate.

Benefits from the use of supplemental water begin to accrue on presently irrigated land as soon as the project is completed. Usually, however, several years elapse before adjustments are made and full benefits are achieved. New land intermixed with land now irrigated probably will also be developed rapidly. Blocks of new land on supplemental projects usually are developed at a slower rate.

On the basis of these general considerations these development periods were assumed: (1) 10 years on new projects, (2) 5 years for substantial areas of new land on supplemental projects and (3) 3 years on presently irrigated land to receive supplemental water.

Not only is the length of this development period critical to net primary benefits, but the rate at which the farm is developed within the period is important. Several diagrammed possibilities follow:

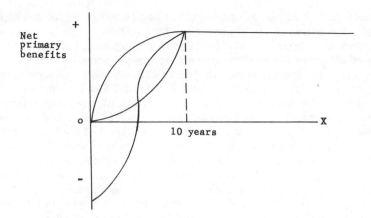

In lieu of specific data on which to determine the shape of the net benefit curve, the following curves were assumed for the three development periods described:

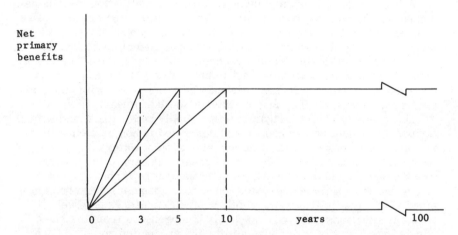

Evaluation Period. The economic life of the project is generally viewed as the maximum length of the period of analysis. The upper limit, considered to be 100 years, was used by agriculture in the Upper Colorado Basin. Some preferences were for 50 years; but the 100-year span was selected partly because of its use by the Bureau of Reclamation.

The choice between 50 and 100 years is not particularly important. With a 10-year development period, discounted average annual benefits differ about 2 percent between these two periods.

Discounting. Gross primary benefits are discounted to arrive at an average annual net benefit quantity that can be compared with average annual project costs. The discount factor is based on the development or waiting period necessary for full realization of the projected production and incomes on the project. The factor is a function of interest rate, the length of the evaluation period and the length and shape of the income and benefit curves during the development period. The magnitude of all three elements is critical to the net annual benefits.

At 5 percent interest and a 100-year evaluation period, the discount factors are .95271, .90844 and .80927 for 3-, 5-, and 10-year development periods respectively. The discount factor at 5 percent interest, a 10-year development period and a 50-year evaluation period is .793. On a new project if development could be accelerated so that farms were fully developed in 5 years instead of 10 years, net primary benefits would be enlarged by around 12 percent using the above procedure.

With a 10-year development period the discount factor is .88750 at the rate of 2 1/2 percent, which has been used by the Bureau of Reclamation. An interest rate of 2 1/2 percent gives net benefits that are about 10 percent larger than net benefits at a 5 percent rate.

Classification of Soil and Water Resources

A basic need in economic evaluation is a classification of soils designed for the purpose of evaluation. The classification of physical resources should be oriented to a potential or developed situation, recognizing the costs necessary to achieve the specified state of development. The classification should recognize the major soil situations in terms of homogeneity with respect to productivity, crop adaptability and production costs. These areas may be synonymous with contiguous geographic areas, or they may be intermixed land areas.

Major variations in irrigation water supply both without and with the project should be recognized and described in conjunction with the major delineations of soils. The classification of water supply has been seriously handicapped by lack of measurements of the present water supply, including the efficiency of use on the farm.

Inventories of soils and water, once done adequately, can be combined with climatic features and other physical resources to set up physical situations that are reasonably homogeneous from the standpoint of productivity, crop adaptability and production costs. These homogeneous situations constitute what have been variously called land classes and other terms. In the Colorado Survey the Department of Agriculture applied the term "evaluation areas."

A next step in the analysis involves the estimation of economically feasible farm development work — land leveling, clearing, farm ditches and drainage. This problem is now in the initial stages of solution. However, inadequate as the data are, cost estimates must be made of achieving the state of development that can reasonably be expected in the area and to associate it with the appropriate levels of production.

The establishment of yields and cropping patterns by evaluation areas with the given physical resources and state of development requires input-output relationships for each soil and water situation. These relationships are very difficult to obtain either from experiments or from farm surveys because of the many variables involved. An additional reason for this difficulty is the failure to establish homogeneous soil and water situations in terms of productivity. Variations in management are an additional complicating factor.

In practice, homogeneity of physical resources was assumed within farms and within evaluation areas. In fact, variations in quality of physical resources often occur both within farms and within evaluation areas.

Returns to Resources Other than Water

Projected market prices are commonly accepted as the basis for allocation of returns to farm resources in the income or residual approach. The market system has at least two basic limitations in this respect: (1) Market prices are not always equivalent to the contribution to income for given resources on particular projects and under given farm situations, and (2) several important farm resources are not priced directly in the market. Resources not priced in the market or those for which market prices may deviate widely from monetary returns are operator and family management and labor, machinery and buildings, land and irrigation water.

Labor and other resources were valued on an opportunity cost basis — the value of benefits foregone in some other productive use by their use on the project. An adjustment was required for labor employed on the project farms because of lack of mobility. Problems also were encountered in the determination of a charge for farm capital. A third problem related to land charges or land returns in the absence of irrigation water.

On new projects the assumption was made that resources needed to develop and operate project farms would be fully employed elsewhere in the economy. These resources, including operator and family labor, were priced on the basis of full employment.

On supplemental water projects, assumptions of resource mobility hinged on specific conditions in the local area. Variations from full employment assumptions related mainly to labor and management of the operator and his family.

Operator and family labor and management. When alternative employment opportunities for labor and management were limited without the project, an assumption was made of some unemployment during the initial years of the evaluation period. The amount of time needed for adjustment to full employment was estimated on the basis of institutional and economic conditions projected for the area. An arbitrary maximum period of 25 years was set, assuming that unemployment will diminish to zero within that length of time. The cost of additional labor and management needed to utilize irrigation water developed by the project was discounted during the initial years of the evaluation period, depending upon the extent of employment both on and off the farm which is projected for the without-project situation. When opportunities for

full employment were projected without the project, the cost of operator and family labor was valued in terms of market prices. As noted
earlier, this consideration related only to supplemental water projects.

Pricing of the management of the operator was somewhat arbitrary
as little empirical basis existed for its evaluation. The analysis was
oriented to a concept of "average" management. The assumption was
made also that utilization of water provided by the project occurs without a basic change in managerial ability. Additional water facilitates
and encourages new practices and enlarged inputs of capital and other
resources. Improved income and capital positions of farmers permit
them to apply profitably greater quantities of certain inputs. These adjustments may be interpreted erroneously by some persons as changes
in basic management ability. In fact, arguments are presented by some
persons that these improvements should be attributed as a benefit to
water.

Use of the partial or cash-crop budget described earlier removes
the problem of pricing labor used for livestock. This approach seems
somewhat simpler as labor on irrigated crops is concentrated within a
shorter time period and is of a somewhat more uniform quality. In estimating benefits, the charge for additional operator and family labor
and management was based upon the hourly farm wage rate that pre-
vailed in the area. This rate should be appropriate to the summer or
crop production season.

On new projects the hourly rate for hired labor was applied to family and operator labor. A charge was required also for management.
In practice, the Department of Agriculture somewhat arbitrarily used
an amount equivalent to 15 percent of the hired wage rate. On projects
where a management charge was applied, total operator and family labor were weighted, for example 75 and 25 percent respectively, to get
a weighted hourly rate.

On supplemental projects where operators would be fully employed
without the project, including work off the farm, operator and family
labor and management were evaluated in the same way as on new projects. If significant amounts of underemployment of operator and family labor were estimated without the project, the hourly rate was adjusted to reflect the underemployment. No charge was made for management where unemployment was projected.

Under the 1957 price projections of the U.S. Department of Agriculture the summer farm wage rate in the Upper Colorado Basin was about
$1.00 per hour. The projected wage rate index was 510, or about the
average in 1952-56. This projection is viewed by many as too low. An
index proposed and used in some projective analyses is 625, or 122
percent of the 1957 projection. On new projects a rate of $1.11 per
hour at the 1957 projections would be increased to $1.35 per hour.

The effect of application of a 625 projection for farm wage rates
can be illustrated for a project in Wyoming. In 1958 the U.S. Department of Agriculture estimated net primary benefits of about $495,000
for this project. A labor and management rate increase to $1.35 per

hour would reduce this net benefit to about $380,000, or 77 percent of the original estimate.

Capital charge. The rate of interest that should be charged for farm capital and used in discounting benefits has given rise to controversy and considerable attention. The general framework set down by the Inter-Agency Committee and applied by the Department of Agriculture in the Upper Colorado River Basin was based on the opportunity cost of capital — the value in the use to which the capital would have been put if not used on project farms.

Within this framework consensus seems to be that this rate should be around 5 or 6 percent. The Department of Agriculture used 5 percent as return on farm capital and as a discount rate. Implications of this interest rate are illustrated later.

Land. As a working procedure the income or residual approach attaches a value to land that is equivalent to its price in its nonirrigated use plus capital investment (clearing, leveling, drainage, farm irrigation system) necessary to achieve under irrigation the crop yields assumed for the evaluation analysis. The land investment was amortized over a 100-year period at 5 percent interest (factor .05038), and the farm irrigation system was amortized over a 50-year period at 5 percent interest (factor .05478).

The valuation of land was of primary concern on new projects and on new land on supplemental projects. The evaluation problem was one of estimating the effects of additional water so that the problem of evaluating the income contribution of presently irrigated land was not involved. The over-all problem was difficult because market prices of land in western irrigated areas and especially in the Upper Colorado Basin were generally recognized as exceeding the prices warranted strictly on the basis of historical or expected incomes to land and water.

INCOME ALLOCATIONS AND LAND AND WATER VALUES

The procedures and assumptions described here make it possible to place a value on land. When this value is compared with market prices apparent inconsistencies sometimes appear. This result is expected because market prices for agricultural land usually are not consistent with monetary incomes from the land in its agricultural use. So the apparent inconsistency may not exist. The procedure does not have the same result when applied to irrigation water for full and supplemental supplies. This section explores several aspects of these two problems. Capitalization of net primary benefits tends to overvalue because it includes investment incentives.

Net direct benefits (USDA) on the Seedskadee Project in Wyoming were estimated at $8.31 per acre. Deduction of $3.00 for annual operation and maintenance left an annual return to water (4.06 acre-feet) of $5.31 per acre or $1.31 per acre-foot. Capitalization at 5 percent gave a value of water of $106 per acre. The estimated land purchase price and land development was $60 per acre, giving an irrigated land price of about $165 per acre. This price does not seem unreasonable for the project area as climate and location are unfavorable to agricultural production.

The Vernal Unit of the Central Utah Project is a more favorable agricultural area than the Seedskadee Project area, although both areas are based on forage-livestock production. At the time the water supply in the Vernal area was substantially less adequate than that proposed for Seedskadee, but average yields were somewhat greater with the poor water supply. In 1959 farmers reported the average market value of irrigated land and water, without buildings, in the Vernal area at around $270 per acre.[3] This price is about $100 more than the price derived above for Seedskadee. The $270 undoubtedly reflects higher production and better location both agriculturally and with respect to other elements of the economy.

The Smith Fork Project is also based on livestock and production of feed crops. Mainly because of differences in the growing season, projected yields were substantially higher than on Seedskadee (Table 8.1). However, two evaluation areas — C for Smith Fork and A for Seedskadee — each had projected yields of 3.0 tons of alfalfa per acre.

Table 8.1. Selected Data for Seedskadee and Smith Fork Projects,
Upper Colorado River Basin

Item	Unit	Seedskadee	Smith Fork
Alfalfa yield – Project	Ton	2.5	3.2
Alfalfa yield –			
Evaluation Area C	do.	–	3.0
Evaluation Area A	do.	3.0	–
Additional water from project	Acre-foot	3.5	1.0
Total water needed	do.	3.5	3.78
Net primary benefits-total[a]	Dollars per acre	8.14	7.12[c]
Net primary benefits per acre-foot[b]	do.	2.32	7.12[c]

[a] Excluding operation and maintenance costs.
[b] For project water.
[c] One acre-foot per acre of supplemental water supply.

Additional water supplies from the project would be 1.0 acre-foot for Smith Fork and 3.5 acre-feet per acre for Seedskadee for the two evaluation areas. Net primary benefits would be $7.12 and $8.14 per acre, or $7.12 and $2.32 per acre=foot. If similar production functions for alfalfa prevail for the two evaluation areas, the net benefit computed for the last acre-foot on the Smith Fork project is markedly greater than the net benefit for the Seedskadee project. Conversely, if the last acre-foot yielded about the same net benefits in the two instances, the net benefit per acre would be only $1.00 for the first 2.75 acre-feet on the Seedskadee project.

These two projects suggest a problem in the applicability of methods described earlier or in the adequacy of projections and data for the projects. For a new project, particularly, one can argue that farm resources ought to return the rates suggested before the public is warranted in investing in the project. However, application of an opportunity-cost approach may encounter difficulty when applied rigidly to irrigated farms of the sizes and types found in areas of the Mountain West. Many farmers in these areas may not receive the rates of return, especially on capital and labor suggested above. This may be characteristic of many segments of the economy and of many agricultural areas under full employment conditions.[4]

Thus the residual approach may show a relatively low total net return to water. But this does not mean that irrigation water has little or no value in these instances; it may mean that other resources, such as capital and family and operator labor, are not receiving a 5 percent return and current hired wage rates for the inputs assumed. While the procedure may be sound from the standpoint of public investment decisions, the estimated value of water may not, in fact, represent the actual return to water. This estimated value may have limitations for other purposes such as value comparisons in alternative uses.

On the supplemental irrigation projects, the net return to total water supply may be less relevant from the standpoint of public investment. These areas are established agriculturally except that the water supply is inadequate to maximize returns from water and other farm resources. The evaluation problem now becomes one of estimating the extent to which the economy will be improved with additional water, as measured in terms of primary agricultural benefits. The difference between the without-with situations may be large for an increment of irrigation water. In the Smith Fork example (Area C) the income to family labor, land and water was increased $1,844 per farm by changes attributable to an additional acre-foot of water per acre. The increased farm size from adding new land to the farm and the increased production from supplemental water gave a net benefit increase over the without situation of $7.12 for one acre-foot (Table 8.1). The effect in this evaluation area also was considerably less than on much of the project that had more productive soils.

These problems and others closely related have suggested to some economists the use of land and water market prices for evaluation purposes. However, land and water market prices contain so many nonmonetary and nonagricultural values that to date most investigators have concluded that this approach has more basic problems than the income approach. Personal preferences and other factors lead to acceptance of low rates of return on land and water resources in many areas. In effect this lowers the discount rate and results in prices of land and water that are high in terms of incomes from these resources.

Land Tenure and Farm Size

Customarily in economic evaluation an assumption of owner-operatorship has been applied. Apparently this assumption is

satisfactory unless acreage limitations result in unrealistically sized
farming units.

Farm incomes, primary agricultural benefits and financial feasibility will be reflected in subsequent years through farm operating units,
not through ownership units. An assumption of owner-operatorship
units that differs markedly from projected operating units does not
seem defensible. The Bureau of Reclamation makes the latter assumption, apparently because of its interpretation of reclamation law and its
definition of total benefits from irrigation development.

Ordinarily if all resources are priced at a market value, increased
size will result in larger total net agricultural benefits within the size
ranges of a large part of the irrigated areas of the West. More efficient use of resources apparently occurs with larger sizes. Although
part of the increased profit is allocable to resources other than water,
inadequate data may lead to attributing residual profit to water that
should be allocated to other resources. The analytical problem is also
inherent in the use of market prices and the residual approach. For
example, additional water may make it profitable for a farmer to apply
more commercial fertilizer. But the residual approach usually allocates returns to fertilizer that are equivalent only to the market price
of fertilizer and the "profit" from the added fertilizer will accrue to
irrigation water.

Critical adjustment problems arise both in projecting farm sizes
without and with the project and projecting adjustments in cropping patterns. Adjustments in the cropping pattern plus increased production
with more water are critical elements in estimating direct benefits.
Consideration should also be given to the feasible profitable adjustments that farmers might make with present or limited water supplies.
These adjustments may influence greatly the without-project farm incomes.

It is likely that adjustments in a given economy will differ between
poor and adequate irrigation water supplies. Cropping patterns, livestock enterprises and farm sizes may all be different in the two situations. The most difficult problem analytically is a projection of these
two sets of farm sizes. It is often hard to support an argument for
larger farm acreages without the project, although this adjustment usually seems to be a logical expectation. It is also easy to negate the
value of water by adjustments in farm size without the project. In most
instances the same number of acres per farm have been assumed in
both conditions.

Acceptance of the 160-acre ownership limit in federal reclamation
law as a restriction of upper limit on size of operating unit can pose an
analytical problem for the economist. On supplemental projects this
assumption can mean that the with-project size of farm would be less
than the present size. Even though size of farm is forced legally in irrigated areas of small farms, it seems unlikely that the operating units
would reduce substantially, if at all.

Several procedures are available for estimating the without income situation where the land is nonirrigated before the project. From the standpoint of primary benefits, it seems adequate to estimate net income without the project as an interest return on the value of the land in its nonirrigated use.

Methods of Aggregating Project Benefits

One end product of economic evaluations of public resource projects is an estimate of total net project benefits that can be compared with total project costs. However, the process by which this total is derived can also be useful for other purposes. In federal reclamation the same basic analysis has been used for both evaluation and repayment or financial feasibility. The income analysis provides an estimate of income potentials on the project for various sizes and types of farms and for a general appraisal of the prospective agricultural economy. The analysis can also serve as a guide to development of the project and farms and to the use of the irrigation water.

Farm operating units seem to be the most adequate unit of analysis for estimating primary benefits and they are an essential basis for the accomplishment of the other purposes listed. Identification of the firm should be carried throughout the analysis so that the final summary and weighting are applied to net benefits for specific farm units. An alternative that seems less adequate is to develop a per-acre net benefit for various crop enterprises; these per-acre benefits are applied to project acreages for various crops. The firm loses identity early in this latter approach. The farm unit is used only as a means of deriving per-unit values that can be applied as averages to specific crop enterprises and total acreages.

The farm-operating-unit approach seems more adequate than the crop-enterprise approach for maintaining balance in the cropping pattern, as it reflects prospective adjustments in farm size and considers farm overhead costs. It also recognizes more adequately other organizational and adjustment elements as they may occur in farm operating units throughout the evaluation period.

New Land on Supplemental Projects

Most of the participating irrigation projects in the Colorado River Storage Act include some new land. This land is intermixed with presently irrigated land or occurs as substantial blocks in other instances; usually the land is part of an irrigated farm. Assumptions as to organization and use of this land under irrigation are highly important to estimated benefits from the projects. The net primary benefits usually are substantially greater when acreage of new land is added to an existing farm than when new farms are assumed. The addition of land to existing farms also poses again the question of farm size without the project; that is, will the project result in a net addition of farm size equivalent to the new land brought under irrigation?

As a general operating rule, the Department of Agriculture used location and size of the nonirrigated land tracts as the guide for determining whether new farms will be assumed. Small tracts interspersed with presently irrigated land were included as a part of existing farm units. Substantial blocks of nonirrigated land were assumed to be developed into newly irrigated farms. For example, one project in Colorado would provide supplemental irrigation water for 13,720 acres of land and irrigation water for 5,730 acres of nonirrigated land. The assumption was made that 2,380 acres would be added to existing farms and that the remaining new land (3,350 acres) would be used to establish new farm units.

The effectiveness of this procedure in handling new land on supplemental projects can be illustrated by one of the farm situations in Evaluation Area A_1 on the project discussed previously; land in this area is among the most productive on the project (Table 8.2).

If water is added to presently irrigated land (situation A) to provide an adequate supply on a 160-acre farm, the net primary benefits are $7.60 per acre-foot of supplemental supply. If new farms are created (situation B), the net benefits in this instance are $6.47 per acre-foot.

One possibility in this project is to assume that farm size is enlarged by adding newly irrigated land to presently irrigated farms (situation C) (Table 8.2). In this case the net benefit is $9.00 per acre-foot.

Table 8.2. Effects of Various Uses of Water on Nonirrigated and Presently Irrigated Land on a Project in Colorado[a]

Item	Area	Additional Water Per Acre	Net Discounted Benefits Per Acre-Foot
	Acres	Acre-Foot	Dollars
A. All presently irrigated	160	.77	7.60
B. All newly irrigated	160	2.19	6.47
C. Partly irrigated	146	.77	–
Partly new land	14	2.19	–
Farm	160	.89	9.00
D. Presently irrigated farms	160	.77	–
Nonirrigated new farms	160	2.19	–
Weighted average	160	.89	7.36

[a] Evaluation Area A_1.

The other possible line of action is to assume that presently irrigated farms receive enough additional water for an adequate supply and that new farms are organized out of the nonirrigated land (situation D). From an evaluation area standpoint the net benefits would be $7.36 per acre-foot.

The effect of adding about 9 percent of new land to an irrigated farm in the case above can now be compared with the assumption that new farms are developed on all of the new land. If the new land goes into new farms, the net benefit to water is $14.17 ($6.47 x 2.19) per acre. If the new land is added to existing farms, the effective net increases in benefits attributable to 14 acres in the 160-acre farm is $30.97 per acre.

The Bureau of Reclamation assumed that all new land on supplemental projects was used to develop new farms. The illustration above suggests the effects of this procedure in diminishing direct benefits, especially as compared with the procedure used by the Department of Agriculture.

OPPORTUNITY COSTS AND PRESENT POLICY RELATING TO INDIRECT AND PUBLIC BENEFITS

The federal reclamation program now includes indirect and public benefits from irrigation as part of total benefits, a fact generally known. Direct benefits often constitute only about half the total estimated annual benefits from irrigation projects; the rest are indirect and public benefits. Only one of the 11 irrigation projects in the Colorado River Storage Project had a benefit-cost ratio with respect to direct benefits (including power, flood control and recreation) greater than one. [5] The average for all projects of costs to direct benefits was 1.0 to 0.8.

The intent is not to consider specific aspects of secondary benefits; details of procedures in federal reclamation can be found in several books and publications. Rather, several items are noted in which the procedures and measurements for calculations are related to primary benefits and are also important to secondary and public benefits as viewed under federal reclamation. In addition, some implications of secondary and public benefits to direct benefits are considered.

Obviously the partial- or crop-budget approach is not suitable for estimating secondary benefits by the method currently applied, as livestock become highly important sources of these benefits. In this connection wool is a particularly good source of secondary benefits. One category of indirect benefits is a proportion of farm production expenses so that complete farm budgets are essential also.

The indirect benefits estimated for federal reclamation projects, though derived from farm budgets used for estimating direct benefits, are designed to reflect the impact of the project on the economy generally. They are benefits stemming from or induced by the project.

"Public" benefits in present evaluations can arise from several sources. Probably the leading source is an increase in settlement opportunities from establishment of new farms. Even on supplemental projects, public benefits relate closely to the acreage of new land on the project. Their magnitude depends upon the number of new farms developed. Public benefits will vary according to whether new land on supplemental projects is assumed as an addition to existing farms or as new farms. Some question exists as to which procedure gives the largest total benefits as direct benefits are reduced if public benefits are increased.

Public benefits from new farm opportunities have varied over the years. In the Upper Colorado Basin they were estimated at about $1,250 per farm. The amount was identical with the alternative earnings placed on family and operator labor as a cost in deriving primary benefits. In effect, the procedure results in a zero opportunity cost for family and operator labor. The opportunity cost at the farm level is balanced by the public benefit for settlement opportunities, the net result being that no charge is made for family labor.

The Bureau of Reclamation, operating within a framework of maximizing farm numbers (public benefits) and of indirect benefits, estimated a total benefit from irrigation development comprised of three components — direct, indirect and public. The Department of Agriculture identified only one benefit from irrigation — direct or primary. The concepts and practices applied on federal reclamation projects have developed from new projects on public land where settlement and development controls can be exercised. The Colorado River Storage Project includes one reasonably large irrigation project of this nature.

Since the public benefit allowance seems to remain rather constant on a per farm basis, total benefits are enhanced by maximizing farm numbers. Procedures premised on an interpretation of reclamation law (maximizing farm numbers), rather than on a "realistic" approach in terms of prospective sizes, enhance public benefits as explained in this instance.

Maximization of public benefits as defined by U.S. Bureau of Reclamation may decrease direct agricultural benefits. Setting farm size to meet a minimum income standard usually leads to smaller, less efficient farm operations and, in turn, fewer direct benefits. But increased numbers of farms leads to more public benefits as defined above. Total benefits also are enhanced by this process through larger indirect benefits. It seems that more, less efficient farms also results in greater indirect benefits through the "factor" process applied.

Maximizing total benefits as described, through enlarged secondary and public benefits, conflicts with maximizing direct agricultural benefits from irrigation projects. Analyses and projections based on minimum standards of farm incomes with emphasis on "public" benefits usually differ substantially from apparently prospective economies in terms of income potentials, primary benefits and financial feasibility of the projects. This result seems especially evident on projects where sizes projected for analytical purposes are substantially smaller than present farm sizes.

CONCLUSIONS

A basic quantification problem still prevails with respect to description and measurement of physical resources for evaluation purposes.

A soils classification oriented to productivity and to evaluation needs has not yet been fully developed. Measurements of water supplies and efficiencies under farming conditions are not always available. Adequate production functions for various land and water situations have not been determined. These inadequacies place severe initial restrictions on evaluation of water resource development and use.

The evaluation procedures applied by the U.S. Department of Agriculture in the Upper Colorado River Basin were an attempt to adhere to an opportunity-cost basis, using the farm-income-residual approach for arriving at a value of water for irrigation. The production of food and stabilization of agricultural incomes were the main accomplishment for consideration from an agricultural point of view. It is apparent that decisions by Congress have not been made solely on this basis; in fact, direct primary benefits have been somewhat "secondary" in arriving at decisions for public investments.

Several conflicts arise in connection with rigid application of market prices and an opportunity-cost point of view in pricing resources used by the farmer in connection with irrigation water. Although this general framework seems more defensible, the question as to whether modifications should be made in terms of specific values and prices may be suggested.

A frequent argument for government participation in water resource development is recognition that the market and pricing system is inadequate for this purpose. Is it then appropriate to hold rigidly to market prices in evaluating nonmarket activities? Historically, also, public policy has recognized goals other than food production as paramount in public resource investments. Acceptance in their entirety of market prices may hinge, then, on the aim or goals of government activity; these goals are not yet clearly stated.

Two other aspects may be noted in connection with evaluation of farm resources: (1) Are costs the amounts that must be paid to attract resources to the project? (2) Is the appropriate estimate of direct benefits the value of irrigation water to the farmers? If these questions are answered affirmatively, a rigid application of the opportunity-cost framework may not be appropriate, at least in the Upper Colorado Basin. As pointed out earlier in this chapter, these questions relate mainly to capital, operator and family labor and management.

At 5 percent interest on farm capital and a labor and management rate in excess of the seasonal summer wage rate for hired labor, is the residual value of irrigation water a correct measurement of return to this resource? Are these rates of return to capital and labor based on larger, more efficient farm operations than those prevailing in many irrigated areas? If farmers accept less than these rates, does their application in a residual method yield the correct value for irrigation water? Or would a more accurate estimate of the value of water be achieved by (1) increasing farm size for analytical purposes above the projected size or (2) applying lower rates of return for labor or capital, rates that apparently would be more consistent with actual returns?

Procedures and analytical techniques applied by agencies evolve from legislation and administration oriented to specific agency programs and public goals reflected in legislation. Selection and justification of projects are made within this framework. Returns on public investments have been compared only in a general manner at the national level for such programs as flood control and irrigation. Only general comparisons have been made also of alternative means of achieving a particular goal or product.

Legislation for a given program may actually be in conflict with over-all decision making in terms of resource investments. Or goals specified for a program — for example, settlement opportunities in irrigation development — may not seem relevant to a rigid opportunity-cost view of resource alternatives. The values may differ widely. Regional versus national economies enter as important factors. Group interests may lead to entirely different criteria for decisions.

It is apparent that quantification for evaluation purposes is modified by purposes and goals. Procedures and data needed differ so long as the products or goals of resource developments differ. Evaluations of alternative water developments for production of food will likely differ from evaluations of water development to create settlement opportunities.

In spite of the weaknesses in resource evaluation analysis, it still serves a useful purpose. Many strong features are apparent. These analyses are used effectively for screening projects and for financial feasibility and repayment purposes. They formalize careful scrutiny of various project features and lead to improved projects. Improvements in procedures are being made continually. Basically, it is a necessary element in making decisions, and this kind of analysis will likely become increasingly effective in public policy.

FOOTNOTES

[1] Details of procedures and assumption applied by the USDA during this period may be found in a paper by Clyde E. Stewart and Carl B. Smith, "The evaluation of direct agricultural benefits from participating irrigation projects, Colorado River Storage Project, U.S. Department of Agriculture," Water resources and economic development of the West; evaluation methodology of the Upper Colorado River development, Denver, Nov. 17-19, 1958, pp. 73-84, Rept. No. 7, Conference Proceedings of the Committee on the Economics of Water Resources Development, and in USDA, Guide for Reappraisal of Direct Agricultural Benefits and Project Relationships, Salt Lake City, July 1959, p. 66.

[2] Details of this procedure can be examined in USDA, Guide for Reappraisal..., *op. cit.*, and in reports on individual participating projects of the Colorado River Storage project.

[3] Unpublished survey data, ARS, USDA.

[4] Other studies show similar results. For example, see "Farm costs and returns," ERS-USDA, Agr. Inf. Bul. 230, June 1960. This study showed that as a residual, operator and family labor received less than 50¢ per hour for 14 of 29 commercial type farms in the United States in 1959 and that the return on only 8 of 29 farms was greater than $1.00 per hour. These farms were large specialized crop and livestock farms.

[5] U.S. Bureau of Reclamation, Financial and Economic Analysis: Colorado River Storage Project and Participating Projects, Salt Lake City, Feb. 1958, processed.

J. C. HEADLEY is Assistant Professor of Agricultural Economics at the University of Illinois. He developed his interest in water resources economics while on the staffs of the University of California and Purdue University.

VERNON W. RUTTAN is Agricultural Economist on the staff of The International Rice Research Institute, Los Banos, Philippines. He is on leave from Purdue University and has served on the staffs of the President's Council of Economic Advisors, the University of California, Berkeley, and the Tennessee Valley Authority. His numerous writings have contributed to the analyses of the role of resource development to economic growth.

Chapter 9

J. C. HEADLEY
V. W. RUTTAN

Regional Differences
In the Impact of Irrigation
On Farm Output*

I NFORMATION ON THE RELATIONSHIPS between irrigation inputs, other inputs and output can be useful at a number of levels.

First, such information can make an important contribution to decisions regarding the allocation of water or irrigated land among different uses and over time within an individual production unit such as a farm or an industrial firm. This problem has two dimensions: (1) There is a short-run problem of factor utilization under given technical conditions of production. (2) There is also the longer-run *adjustment planning problem* where the objective of the firm is to change the combination of inputs, the product mix or production practices and technology.

Second, information on the relationships between factor inputs and output can make an important contribution to the problem of allocating

*Purdue *Agr. Exp. Sta. Jour.* Paper 1570. V. W. Ruttan was formerly professor of agricultural economics, Purdue University.

The authors wish to express their appreciation to E. W. Kehrberg, G. E. Schuh, D. W. Thomas and H. O. Carter for helpful comment and criticism on an earlier draft of this paper, and to Christoph Beringer, I. M. Lee, Stephen C. Smith and S. V. Ciriacy-Wantrup for counsel during the project formulation stages of the study.

factors among individual production units, industries or geographic areas. Two dimensions of this problem can also be identified.

(a) There is the problem of *allocating existing factor supplies among individual firms, industries or areas*. Social and political-economic relationships play a more important role, relative to technical input-output and production response relationships, than in allocation decisions at the intrafirm level. Two reasons account for this shift in emphasis. (1) Technical and equity considerations frequently conflict with each other until modifications in either technology or in institutional arrangements can be developed to reduce or eliminate such conflicts. (2) Interactions between economic units are sufficiently complex that they can be understood only by resorting to a rather high degree of abstraction. Thus it becomes necessary to deal with "aggregate production functions," highly simplified "activities" or aggregate cost-benefit budgeting procedures which reflect the interaction of both technical and institutional factors rather than primary input-output or production response relationships. At this level the primary contribution of economic analysis is to clarify the effects on resource utilization and on income distribution of conflicts between equity and technical considerations and of policies designed to deal with such conflicts.

(b) The problem of *planning for additional water resource development also is pertinent*. Failure of the incidence and time sequence of costs and returns to coincide results in social- and political-economic considerations becoming even more important relative to technical-economic considerations. Here the primary contribution of economic analysis is to clarify the effects on resource utilization and income distribution over time of alternative resource development policies and programs.

This chapter represents a preliminary report on an attempt to use "aggregate" production functions to construct estimates of regional differences in the productivity of irrigated cropland. The report is presented in three parts: (1) discussion of the "aggregate" production function model and its limitations; (2) presentation of the regional production elasticity and marginal productivity estimates; and finally (3) two illustrations of how the results can be used to assess the impact of irrigation development on the growth of farm output.

THE AGGREGATE PRODUCTION FUNCTION MODEL

Economic theory assumes that the micro-production process can be described by a functional relationship between factors and products. It can also be argued that macro-production processes can be described by such relationships.[1] In this study, aggregate regional production functions are estimated for 13 major farming regions. The resulting resource productivity coefficients are employed to compute marginal productivity estimates for irrigated cropland and other inputs.

The Function

A function of the Cobb-Douglas form $(X_0 = A \overset{\pi}{\underset{i=1}{\Sigma}} X_i a_i)$ was used. X_0 represents output, A is a constant, X_i is the quantity of the ith input and a_i is the exponent of the ith input.

The Cobb-Douglas function has a number of advantages and several disadvantages as a device for explaining the production process.[2]

The Model

An economic model is a construct which is based upon economic theory and which specifies a relationship or set of relationships concerning a particular segment of the economy. It is useful in tracing the impact of specified changes upon the set of relationships. When cast in certain statistical forms, quantification is possible.

The working model specified for this study was:

$$ log\ X_0 = log\ A + \overset{n}{\underset{i=1}{\Sigma}}\ a_i\ log\ X_i $$

fitted statistically by least-squares regression. This is a statement in logarithmic form of the Cobb-Douglas function described above.

Estimates of the marginal productivities of inputs are computed by the general formula $a_i \frac{X_0}{X_i}$ where X_0 and X_i are the quantities of output and input respectively.

The estimated marginal rate of substitution of input i for input j is given by $\frac{a_j X_i}{a_i X_j}$ where X_i and X_j are the quantities of inputs i and j respectively.

This model, then, is a statistical statement of the regional production relation which was used for quantitative estimation.

The original hypothesis was that the regional production functions included the following variables:

Output — X_0 - value of all farm products sold (\$)
Labor   — X_1 - total farm employment — family and hired (number of persons)
Capital — X_2 - machinery investment (number of tractors)
          X_3 - livestock investment (\$)
Land   — X_4 - irrigated cropland harvested (acres)
          X_5 - irrigated pasture (acres)
          X_6 - nonirrigated cropland (acres)
          X_7 - nonirrigated pasture (acres)

Operating
expenses   — X_8 - Output increasing current operating expenses —
              fertilizer, livestock, feed ($)[3]
              X_9 - Machine operating expenses — expenditures for
              petroleum, repairs and machine hire ($)

The data used in the estimates of the regional production functions were obtained from the *Census of Agriculture 1954*. The county was the unit of observation. All counties in each region were enumerated with the exception of those having fewer than 10 acres of irrigated land in 1954. These counties were excluded because the acreage of irrigated land was too small to show the effect of irrigation on the agricultural output of the county as a whole.

Limitations of the Model

The statistically fitted Cobb-Douglas production function is subject to several limitations in addition to the limitations of the function with respect to the theory of production.

All relevant inputs cannot be quantified and thus lead to specification bias.[4]

High intercorrelation of inputs leads to absurd estimates.[5] Exclusion of one of a pair of intercorrelated inputs to correct for intercorrelation biases the remaining coefficients if the input excluded was relevant. The nature of the bias depends upon whether the excluded input was positively or negatively correlated with the remaining inputs.[6]

Often negative coefficients appear which, within the realm of production theory, appear to be meaningless.[7] It is difficult to conceive of output declining due to increases in inputs with the exception perhaps of extremely high levels of water and chemicals. One phenomenon which may be responsible for such behavior is the use of data from a series of units to estimate the behavior of the average unit. These units may be firms, counties or states. If there is a lack of homogeneity between units so that efficient units may use less of a resource than less efficient units, then an average relationship of the two may have a negative slope since the observations are only for a point on each unit's production function.

Aggregation bias may result from lack of correspondence between county and farm firm coefficients. Ideally the county coefficients would be an arithmetic average of the individual farm coefficients. However, the coefficients of the individual farms require weighting in order to compensate for differences in the levels of output from farm to farm. Consequently, if these structural coefficients are not known, the simple aggregation of individual farms within a county may result in bias in the derived coefficients.[8]

If there is intercorrelation between the random error terms of the system of equations of which the production function is a member, then the use of a single-equation least-squares procedure may result in bias in the coefficients.[9] The possibility of such bias in agricultural production functions is small since most inputs are predetermined due to the long production period.

Some economists have expressed serious doubt as to the exact meaning of the statistically fitted production function. When output is measured in value terms, then marginal productivities of resources in different regions may reflect only differences in markets for output and inputs and hence may not be a true estimate of the contribution of the input at the margin.[10]

Recognition of the preceding limitations is necessary for the proper interpretation of the results yielded by the model. Because of the complexity of "aggregate" production problems, approximation and subjective interpretation are necessary regardless of the particular method of empirical investigation.

REGIONAL PRODUCTION ELASTICITIES AND MARGINAL PRODUCTIVITIES

Five *major* regional groupings were identified from the 13 regions included in the analysis: (1) the North, including the Northwest, lake states and Corn Belt regions; (2) the South, including the Appalachian, Southeast, Florida and Delta regions; (3) the Plains, including the major and limited irrigation counties of the northern and southern plains; (4) the northern and southern mountain regions; and (5) the Pacific, including the Northwest and the major and limited irrigation counties of California (Figure 9.1).

Fig. 9.1. Type of farming regions and sub-regions.

Table 9.1. Factor Marginal Productivity Estimates in Humid and Arid Regions, 1954 (Calculated at Arithmetic Means)

Region	Equation	All Farm Workers X_1 ($/year)	Machinery Investment X_2 ($/tractor)	Irrigated Cropland X_4 ($/acre)	Nonirrigated Cropland X_6 ($/acre)	Current Operating Expenses X_8 ($/$ spent)
North						
Northeast	I (a)	1,117		1,130	− 3.91	1.13
Lake States	I (a)	508		428	21.66	2.48
Corn Belt	I (a)	1,051		801	38.88	1.88
South						
Appalachian	I	551	1,266	884	12.38	1.46
Southeast	I	238	838	608	12.62	1.53
Florida	I	527	1,449	213	19.06	2.83
Delta	I	655	490	103	1.62	1.24
Plains						
Northern						
All irrigation counties	I (a)	879		66	11.59	2.47
Major irrigation counties	I (a)	1,554		46	12.24	2.13
Limited irrigation counties	I (a)	472		1,003	12.92	2.68
Southern						
All irrigation counties	I (a)	588		91	8.81	1.75
Major irrigation counties	I (a)	971		77	10.00	2.21
Limited irrigation counties	I (a)	122		1,072	10.87	1.58
Mountain						
Northern	I (a)	3,025		17	11.72	1.38
Southern	I (a)	1,999		29	3.60	2.36
Pacific						
Northwest	I (a)	1,640		98	44.64	1.58
California						
All irrigation counties	I (a)	1,379		83	34.17	2.92
Major irrigation counties	II (a)			134		3.10
Limited irrigation counties	I (a)	861		87	50.01	2.05

With but two exceptions the relationship between inputs and output in each major region appears to be described adequately by the function:

$$X_0 = f(X_1, X_4, X_6, X_8) \qquad \text{I (a)}$$

In the South the function

$$X_0 = f(X_1, X_2, X_4, X_6, X_8) \qquad \text{I}$$

was employed while the function

$$X_0 = f(X_4, X_8) \qquad \text{II (a)}$$

was used for California's major irrigation counties.

The marginal productivity estimates, calculated at the arithmetic mean, are presented in Table 9.1.[11] Except for irrigated cropland, the marginal productivity estimates are typically quite similar at both the arithmetic and geometric means. The sharp differences in the marginal productivity estimates for irrigated cropland at the arithmetic and geometric means occurred mainly in regions where irrigation has developed to only a limited extent and reflects the highly skewed distribution of irrigated cropland among counties in these regions. For this reason, discussion of marginal productivity estimates is based mainly on those estimated at the arithmetic means which are presented in Table 9.1.

Interpretation of the Marginal Productivity Estimates

In interpreting the marginal productivity estimates the following factors should be emphasized.

1. The Southeast is the only region in which the aggregate production function indicates substantial cross-sectional substitution between machinery investment and farm employment. The typical pattern seems to be one of complementarity rather than substitution. In most regions machinery investment was highly correlated with labor inputs with the result that (a) high regression coefficients for machinery investment were typically accompanied by low or even negative coefficients for labor, and (b) high regression coefficients for labor were typically accompanied by low coefficients for machinery investment.

2. Calculation of separate production functions for major irrigation counties (1,000 acres or more of irrigated cropland) and for limited irrigation counties (10-999 acres of irrigated cropland) in the northern and southern Plains indicated sharp productivity differences between these two groups of counties. The marginal productivity of labor was substantially higher in the major irrigation counties than in the limited irrigation counties. The marginal productivity of irrigated cropland, on the other hand, was higher in the limited irrigation counties than in the major irrigation counties.

In both the northern and southern Plains, the productivity coefficients and marginal productivity estimates for all irrigation counties are, with but one exception, bracketed by the estimates for the major and limited irrigation counties. This suggests that the estimates for all irrigation counties are not subject to serious aggregation bias in these regions.

3. In California, where an alternative definition of major (50,000 or

more acres of irrigated cropland) and limited (under 50,000 acres of irrigated cropland) irrigation counties was employed, the aggregation problem is apparently more severe. The productivity coefficients and marginal productivity estimates for farm employment are greater for all counties than for either the limited or major irrigation counties. This bias probably results from the extremely wide variation in irrigated acreage and in quality of irrigated cropland among California counties. The problem of variation in the quality of land irrigated is particularly acute with the 26 limited irrigation counties which are located primarily in northern California or in the mountain regions.

4. The California results would seem to imply the desirability of analyzing the major and limited irrigation counties separately in the Northwest and in the mountain regions as well as in California and in the northern and southern Plains. This point is reinforced by the relative instability of the productivity coefficients in these two areas (Appendix Table 9.4).

Exceptionally severe water shortages in 1953-54 resulted in a decline in acres irrigated in 1954 throughout much of the southern Mountain region and in parts of the northern Mountain region to below the 1949 level. In both the northern and southern Mountains the number of water applications was restricted in 1954.

5. The marginal productivity estimates for irrigated cropland seem fairly reasonable in Florida, the Delta, the major irrigation counties of the northern and southern Plains, the major irrigation counties of California and in the Pacific Northwest. They seem exceptionally high in the three northern regions, two southern regions — the Appalachian and the Southeast — and in the limited irrigation counties of the northern and southern Plains.[12]

The high marginal productivity estimates for irrigated cropland in these regions appear to reflect the operation of two factors: (1) irrigation of limited acreage of high-value crops and/or crops which are highly complementary to other enterprises and (2) under-reporting of irrigated cropland in areas where irrigation has been adopted to only a limited extent.

Under-reporting, if evenly distributed, would have the effect of increasing the marginal productivity estimates. It is believed that acreage could have been 100 percent under-reported in the Corn Belt in 1954.

6. The marginal productivity estimates for nonirrigated cropland seem reasonable in 10 of the 13 regions studied. The estimates appear too low in the Northeast and in the Delta and too high in the Northwest and in the limited irrigation counties of California.

7. The marginal productivity estimates for current operating expenses also appear reasonable in most regions. Ibach and Lindberg[13] have estimated the marginal productivity of fertilizer at $2.93 for the United States as a whole in 1954. Their calculations for major crop groups show marginal productivities of $3.40 for all intertilled crops and $1.96 for close-growing grain crops. Our estimates, which include

expenditures for purchased livestock feed and lime as well as fertilizer, are somewhat lower than the Ibach and Lindberg estimates of the marginal productivity of fertilizer.

General Evaluation of Productivity Estimates

In spite of the limitations of the method and data, it is our judgment that the procedure employed in the study has provided reasonable productivity coefficients in most of the regions studied. The major exceptions are the northern and southern Mountain regions where unfavorable weather was probably an important factor. In several other regions, possible bias is recognized in one of the coefficients (nonirrigated cropland in the Northeast, the Delta, the Northwest and the limited irrigation counties of California). In several regions in the North and South, irrigated cropland acreage probably should be adjusted upward to compensate for under-reporting to produce meaningful marginal productivity estimates.[14]

REGIONAL PRODUCTIVITY DIFFERENCES AND FUTURE IRRIGATION DEVELOPMENT

We now present two illustrations of how the production functions in appendix tables 9.1 through 9.5 can be utilized to evaluate the potential impact of future irrigation development on farm output. In the first illustration, the potential contribution of additional irrigation and additional use of current operating expenses to output growth are shown for the major irrigation counties of California. The second example is an attempt to project the levels of irrigation development in the humid region.

Irrigation and Output Growth in California's Major Irrigation Counties

The California Department of Water Resources has projected an "ultimate" net irrigated area (excluding lands having rights in and to the water of the Colorado River) of approximately 16.7 million acres.[15] This is more than a 100 percent increase over the Department of Water Resources estimates of approximately 6.9 million acres in the early 1950's[16] and Census of Agriculture estimates of slightly above 7.0 million acres in 1954. No firm estimates for 1980 are available, although a figure of 13.75 million acres has been suggested.[17]

An estimate of the distribution of this total between the major and limited irrigation counties and between irrigated cropland and irrigated pasture based on data presented in the California State Water Resources Board Bulletin No. 2 is presented in Table 9.2. Lands identified as requiring supplemental water to replace recently depleted groundwater supplies were included in Development Stage 1. The Central Valley

Table 9.2. A Schedule for Irrigation Development in California Showing the Distribution of Irrigated Land Between Major and Limited Irrigation Counties and Between Irrigated Cropland and Pasture

	All Counties			Major Irrigation Counties			Limited Irrigation Counties		
	Irrigated Land (000 of acres)	Irrigated Cropland (000 of acres)	Irrigated Pasture (000 of acres)	Irrigated Land (000 of acres)	Irrigated Cropland (000 of acres)	Irrigated Pasture (000 of acres)	Irrigated Land (000 of acres)	Irrigated Cropland (000 of acres)	Irrigated Pasture (000 of acres)
Irrigated acreage in 1949-50 [a]	6,875	5,818	1,057	5,952	5,161	791	923	658	265
Stage 1. Initial water deliveries to stop potential loss of irrigated land in San Joaquin–Tulare Lake Basin due to overdraft	1,000	830	170	1,000	830	170	--	--	--
Stage 2. Add New Valley Units in Central Valley (Sacramento, San Joaquin and Tulare Lake Basins)	4,870	4,835	35	4,870	4,853	35	--	--	--
Projected Level at Completion of Stage 2	11,745	10,653	1,092	10,822	9,996	826	923	658	265
Stage 3. Add Valley Mountain Units, High Desert and other acres to reach projected ultimate development	4,972	3,015	1,927	2,055	890	1,165	2,917	2,155	762
Projected Ultimate Irrigated Acreage [a]	16,717	13,698	3,019	12,877	10,886	1,991	3,840	2,813	1,027

[a] Including land having rights in and to waters of the Colorado River at present levels.

Source: Estimated from material presented in Calif. Water Resources Board, "Water utilization and requirements of California," Vol. 1, Calif. Water Resources Board, Bul. No. 2, Sacramento, June 1955.

mountain land and high desert lands of southern California which are
less productive or which cost more to develop were included in Stage 3.
In order for irrigation development to reach the level of 13.75 million
acres, all of the land included in Stages 1 and 2 plus slightly more than
2.0 million acres of land identified under Stage 3 will need to be developed.

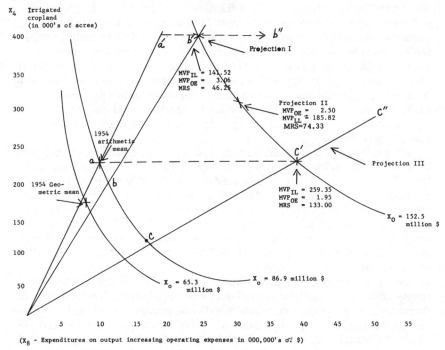

Fig. 9.2. Iso-product curves for irrigated cropland and output increasing
operating expenses in "typical" major irrigation county.

In Projection I in Figure 9.2, production function II (a) was employed
to estimate the farm output which would result by 1980 in a hypothetical
"typical" major irrigation county if (1) irrigated cropland rose to the
level projected at the completion of Stage 2 (Table 9.2) and (2) current
operating expenses continued to rise by the same average amount per
year, adjusted for price changes, as during the 1939-54 period. The
estimated farm output resulting from these input changes in a "typical"
major irrigation county is 75.6 percent higher than in 1954 (estimated
with inputs at arithmetic mean values). This is a somewhat smaller
increase than occurred in California between 1925 and 1960 (110 percent) and somewhat higher than the estimated increase in national farm
output between 1954 and 1980 (55 to 65 percent). The input combination
used to produce the increased output implies somewhat higher marginal
productivity for irrigated cropland (MVP_{IL}) and somewhat lower

marginal productivity of current operating expenses (MVP$_{OE}$) than if the expansion were projected along the scale line aa'. Projection along aa' would, of course, hold the marginal rate of substitution unchanged.

In Projection III an attempt was made to determine the quantity of current operating expenses that would be required to produce the same increase in farm output as in Model I if irrigation development is limited to the level of Stage I. This implies that irrigation development proceeds only fast enough to prevent land now being irrigated from groundwater sources from going out of irrigation due to further lowering of groundwater levels. This result can be achieved by approximately tripling the input of current operating expenses in the major irrigation counties. In spite of these large increases, the marginal productivity of current operating expenses would remain relatively high — $1.95 per dollar of expenditure. With irrigation development restricted to this level, the marginal productivity of irrigated cropland shifts sharply upward.

Projections of the actual output level or input combination that will be used in the major irrigation counties in 1980 are not possible with the information available in this study. But if 400,000 acres can be taken as the upper limit and 218,000 acres (the 1954 arithmetic mean) as the lower limit, then any output level and input combination in the area c"c'aa'bb" should be feasible. At any point in this area, the marginal rate of substitution between current operating expenses and irrigated cropland will be at least as high as the value calculated for 1954 at the arithmetic mean -43.01.

One point should be emphasized. The analysis assumes that the input-output relationships described by the production function for California's major irrigation counties will not be affected by technological change during the projection period. Also, factor price ratios are assumed to remain approximately unchanged. In addition to the rigidity of the price and technology assumptions, the use of the Cobb-Douglas function for projecting either output or marginal productivity when inputs depart sharply from geometric mean values may be criticized.[18]

A defense can be offered, however, against both criticisms. (1) The coefficients for irrigated cropland and output increasing operating expenses in Equation II (a) did not change significantly (at the 5 percent level) between 1939 and 1954 in the California major irrigation counties. This was a period of very rapid irrigation development in California. (2) The projections for the "typical" irrigation county do not exceed the range actually observed among major irrigation counties in 1954.

Potential Expansion of Irrigated Acreage
in the Humid Area

No attempt was made in the previous analysis to introduce technological change explicitly. The constant term in the production function and the productivity coefficients for current operating expenses and irrigated cropland was assumed to remain unchanged. Increased efficiency could be introduced only by moving closer to equating marginal productivity and price ratios. In projecting potential levels of irrigation development in the humid regions, technological change has been introduced explicitly with the analysis.

Projections for the humid region were made in three steps. The *first step* was the construction of three Uniform Regional Output Growth models in which output was assumed to expand in each of the seven humid area regions to an index of 160 by 1980. As in the case of the projections for the major irrigation counties of California, attention was centered on changes in irrigated cropland and current operating expenses. Declines in labor inputs and growth of capital inputs were assumed to offset each other approximately and were not treated explicitly. In Model I the marginal rate of substitution between irrigated cropland and current operating expenses was assumed to remain at the 1954 level. In Model II irrigated acreage was assumed to expand sufficiently for the marginal productivity of irrigated cropland in each region to fall to the same level projected for the major irrigation counties of California — $141 per acre. In Model III irrigated acreage was projected assuming a continuation of the 1949-54 trend in irrigated acreage (except in the Delta where an average of the 1944-49 and 1949-54 trend was employed).

The *second step* was to construct three Differential Regional Output Growth models. This was achieved by adjusting current operating expenses up or down to produce more uniform marginal productivity estimates among regions. By imposing convergence in this manner, the marginal productivity estimates for current operating expenses were forced to relatively low levels — typically in the neighborhood of $1.00 per dollar spent. From past experience farmers are unlikely to increase their use of current operating expenses to the point where marginal productivity falls much below $1.25 to $1.50 per dollar spent.

The *third step* was to construct three Technological Change Models. Using these models, an attempt was made to answer the question: If technological change, operating through the constant term of the production function, tended to shift productivity upward at the same rate during 1954-80 as during 1925-27 to 1953-55,[19] would the marginal productivity of operating expenses rise to levels that seem reasonable in terms of past experiences? The results of the three-step procedure are shown in Table 9.3.

Introduction of differential regional output growth and technological change rates resulted in productivity estimates for current operating expenses that are somewhat higher and also more uniform among regions than in 1954. The projected marginal productivity estimates can be discounted considerably without implying a limitation on the profitability of output expansion due to declining marginal productivity of irrigated cropland.

The Model I_B projections approximate for the humid region as a whole the Model III_B (trend) projections, although the regional

Table 9.3. Irrigated Cropland Projections and Marginal Value Productivities of Irrigated Cropland and Current Operating Expenses, 1980: Technological Change Models, by Region

Region	1980 Output Index 1954=100	Model I$_B$			Model II$_B$			Model III$_B$		
		Acreage Thousand Acres	MVP Irrigated Land $/A	MVP COE $/$	Acreage Thousand Acres	MVP Irrigated Land $/A	MVP COE $/$	Acreage Thousand Acres	MVP Irrigated Land $/A	MVP COE $/$
Northeast	140	491	625	2.17	2,176	141	3.08	640	489	2.31
Lake States	160	139	523	2.91	564	141	3.37	150	486	3.07
Corn Belt	160	191	436	2.58	591	141	3.14	330	254	2.72
Appalachian	150	260	424	2.58	783	141	2.97	460	243	2.78
Southeast	160	149	418	2.16	441	141	2.60	300	195	2.52
Florida	170	750	220	4.86	1,173	141	5.66	680	250	4.82
Delta	140	3,151	97	3.92	2,170	141	3.06	3,150	97	3.92
Humid Area		5,131			7,898			5,710		

distribution of irrigated acreage is somewhat different among the several regions. In Model II$_B$ projected irrigation development is expanded to the point where the marginal productivity of irrigated cropland in humid area regions declines to the level projected for the major irrigation counties of California. As a consequence, the possibility is suggested that the rate of irrigation development in most humid area regions will exceed even the rapid rates achieved during 1949-54.

The projections in Table 9.3, ranging from 5 to 8 million acres, are regarded as somewhat conservative although consistent with the projection made by other researchers. The exact amount of expansion of irrigated acreage in the humid area will depend upon changes in the relative costs of irrigation development, shifts in the demand for farm products and changes in public policy with respect to irrigation development and agricultural prices. Changes in these variables can have important effects on the regional distribution of irrigation development in the humid area as well as on the growth of total farm output in each region.

SUMMARY AND CONCLUSIONS

In this chapter we have presented statistical estimates of the productivity of irrigation for *major* agricultural regions of the United States. In spite of limitations, it is believed the results of the analysis provide reliable quantitative estimates of the factor productivity coefficients and marginal productivity estimates in most of the regions studied.

The estimated productivity coefficients were used along with certain other "reasonable" output growth rate assumptions to illustrate how the estimated production functions could be used as an aid in evaluating the impact of irrigation development on the growth of farm output.

The material presented deals entirely with the direct irrigation benefits. No conclusion with respect to the profitability or feasibility of irrigation development in the area studied can be made without thorough analysis of the cost aspects of such development and the assessment of the indirect irrigation benefits to the area.

Incremental increases of irrigation inputs add more to total output in certain regions than in others. The humid area has largely been ignored with regard to public policy in irrigation development. However, the prospects for future irrigation development appear better than in the arid area, assuming nearly equal marginal costs of development in both areas.

The analysis emphasizes broad possibilities of substitution among aggregate input categories to achieve given output levels in each region. In other words, the problem of future irrigation development cannot be cast meaningfully in terms of land and water requirement. This is true even in California where a major share of the farm output is produced on irrigated land. Set in this framework, public investment in irrigation can be viewed in terms of an investment alternative rather than as an essential element in a region's economic growth.

Appendix Table 9.1. Alternative Factor Productivity Coefficients for Northern Humid Region Counties, 1954

Region	Constant Term (in $\log_e$) a_0	All Farm Workers X_1	Machinery Investment X_2	Irrigated Cropland X_4	Nonirrigated Cropland X_6	Current Operating Expense X_8	Sum of Coefficients	Coefficients of Determination R^2	Standard Error of Estimate (in $\log_e$) $\bar{S}$
NORTH									
Northeast									
I	1.8840	.4098	.0618	.0909	-.0563	.3934	.8996	.9068	.2660
		(.0761)	(.0895)	(.0143)	(.0414)	(.0342)	-	-	-
I (a)	1.6836	.4472	-	.0921	-.0340	.3977	.9030	.9066	.2958
		(.0404)		(.0028)	(.0092)	(.0164)	-	-	-
I (b)	2.4158	-	.3998	.0990	-.1165	.4336	.8159	.8938	.2875
			(.0550)	(.0028)	(.0217)	(.0152)	-	-	-
II	2.2369	-	-	.1249	.1007	.5813	.8067	.8754	.3105
				(.0026)	(.0055)	(.0096)	-	-	-
Lake States									
I	.8731	-.0464	.4450	.0288	.2522	.2846	1.0644	.9088	.2839
		(.1257)	(.1619)	(.0217)	(.0828)	(.0682)	-	-	-
I (a)	.4965	.2086	-	.0137	.3754	.4781	1.0759	.9041	.2694
		(.0852)		(.0052)	(.0578)	(.0417)	-	-	-
I (b)	.8147	-	.4007	.0249	.2560	.3874	1.0692	.9087	.2888
			(.1087)	(.0191)	(.0819)	(.0676)	-	-	-
II	1.9855	-	-	.0365	.4590	.5417	1.0372	.9004	.3066
				(.0042)	(.0412)	(.0338)	-	-	-
Corn Belt									
I	.2047	-.2134	.9153	.0313	.3327	.1866	1.2526	.8901	.2464
		(.0601)	(.0577)	(.0132)	(.0474)	(.0445)	-	-	-
I (a)	-.9026	.3113	-	.0186	.6056	.4317	1.3673	.7833	.3493
		(.0427)		(.0118)	(.0192)	(.0426)	-	-	-
I (b)	-.1658	-	.8094	.0147	.3204	.1860	1.3305	.8851	.2543
			(.0491)	(.0125)	(.0492)	(.0454)	-	-	-
II	-.4083	-	-	.0496	.6950	.4908	1.2354	.7684	.3604
				(.0024)	(.0295)	(.0265)	-	-	-

Appendix Table 9.2. Alternative Productivity Coefficients for Southern Humid Area Regions, 1954

Region	Constant Term (in Log e) a_0	All Farm Workers X_1	Machinery Investment X_2	Irrigated Cropland X_4	Nonirrigated Cropland X_6	Current Operating Expense X_8	Sum of Coefficients	Coefficients of Determination R^2	Standard Error of Estimate (in Log e) $\bar{S}$
Appalachian									
I	.4734	.3765 (.0427)	.2504 (.0570)	.0437 (.0171)	.1631 (.0457)	.3536 (.0446)	1.1873	.8422	.3350
II	.5152	-	-	.0736 (.0024)	.4661 (.0096)	.6303 (.0092)	1.1700	.7875	.3911
Southeast									
I	.6911	.1890 (.0427)	.1674 (.0570)	.0435 (.0171)	.2214 (.0457)	.4645 (.0446)	1.0856	.8562	.2766
II	.6553	-	-	.0668 (.0036)	.4154 (.0111)	.5652 (.0144)	1.0474	.8348	.2993
Florida									
I	1.4742	.1201 (.1224)	.1049 (.1233)	.1947 (.0264)	.0932 (.0464)	.6045 (.0801)	1.1200	.9471	.2937
II	1.1407	-	-	.1999 (.0073)	.1600 (.0169)	.7364 (.0428)	1.0963	.9415	.3199
Delta									
I	.9245	.5638 (.0588)	.0824 (.0533)	.1463 (.0146)	.0228 (.0807)	.2226 (.0501)	1.0380	.8743	.3475
II	.5379	-	-	.1663 (.0015)	.6028 (.0251)	.2930 (.0194)	1.0621	.7998	.4432

Region	Constant Term (in Log_e) a_0	All Farm Workers X_1	Livestock Investment X_3	Irrigated Cropland X_4	Nonirrigated Cropland X_6	Current Operating Expense X_8	Sum of Coefficients	Coefficients of Determination R^2	Standard Error of Estimate (in Log_e) $\bar{S}$
SOUTHERN PLAINS									
All irrigation counties									
I	.6254	.2912 (.0356)	.1971 (.0720)	.2033 (.0101)	.1232 (.0150)	.1786 (.0552)	.9934	.7936	.4065
I (a)	.8779	.2726 (.0076)	-	.2049 (.0062)	.1911 (.0013)	.2881 (.0087)	.8967	.7886	.4107
II	.9112	-	-	.2228 (.0109)	.1855 (.0142)	.4550 (.0346)	.8633	.7475	.4481
Major irrigation counties									
I	.4922	.3349 (.0441)	.1048 (.0800)	.2932 (.0199)	.1157 (.0146)	.1546 (.0650)	1.0032	.8020	.3197
I (a)	.6640	.3157 (.0169)	-	.2890 (.0038)	.1162 (.0021)	.2193 (.0174)	.9402	.8000	.3203
II	.7388	-	-	.3488 (.0207)	.1432 (.0163)	.3894 (.0412)	.8814	.7330	.3690
Limited irrigation counties									
I	-.1077	.0993 (.0580)	.6159 (.1223)	.1059 (.0258)	.1729 (.0295)	.1172 (.0813)	1.1112	.8013	.4219
I (a)	.6034	.0805 (.0188)	-	.1230 (.0037)	.2124 (.0045)	.4061 (.0188)	.8220	.7626	.4594
II	.5568	-	-	.1194 (.0277)	.2395 (.0225)	.4482 (.0535)	.8071	.7330	.3690

NORTHERN PLAINS

All irrigation
counties

I	.0201	.2300 (.0448)	-.0285 (.0408)	.0404 (.0070)	.3680 (.0369)	.3422 (.0246)	.9521	.8579	.2376
I (a)	.0081	.2265 (.0350)	-	.0408 (.0009)	.3614 (.0226)	.3362 (.0094)	.9649	.8576	-.2369
II	-.5261	-	-	.0367 (.0072)	.4891 (.0265)	.4268 (.0153)	.9526	.8435	-.2485

Major irrigation
counties

I	.2252	.3890 (.0813)	-.1122 (.0575)	.0763 (.0175)	.3233 (.0496)	.3062 (.0466)	.9826	.8662	.2225
I (a)	.0939	.3394 (.1206)	-	.0756 (.0062)	.3177 (.0494)	.2790 (.0400)	1.0117	.8571	-.2254
II	-.2911	-	-	.0795 (.0191)	.4276 (.0467)	.4418 (.0270)	.9488	.8316	-.2436

Limited irrigation
counties

I	-.3754	.1291 (.0603)	-.0250 (.0700)	.0322 (.0169)	.4531 (.0601)	.3768 (.0326)	.9662	.8652	.2422
I (a)	-.3646	.1325 (.0035)	-	.0319 (.0003)	.4423 (.0027)	.3714 (.0082)	.8781	.8651	-.2407
II	-.7750	-	-	.0248 (.0167)	.5338 (.0322)	.4212 (.0184)	.9799	.8606	-.2446

Appendix Table 9.4. Alternative Factor Productivity Coefficient for Mountain Region Counties, 1954

Region	Constant Term (in Log e) a_0	All Farm Workers X_1	Livestock Investment X_3	Irrigated Cropland X_4	Nonirrigated Cropland X_6	Current Operating Expense X_8	Sum of Coefficients	Coefficients of Determination R^2	Standard Error of Estimate (in Log e) S
MOUNTAIN									
Northern Mountain									
I	.5093	.7077	.3271	.0430	.1018	-.0116	1.1681	.8224	.3512
	-	(.0872)	(.0662)	(.0378)	(.0254)	(.0771)	-	-	-
I (a)	.8782	.6758	-	.0924	.1404	.1237	1.0324	.7819	.4927
	-	(.0296)	-	(.0223)	(.0047)	(.0420)	-	-	-
II	.8074	-	-	.1608	.2397	.5514	.9519	.6816	.4659
	-	-	-	(.0469)	(.0272)	(.0617)	-	-	-
Southern Mountain									
I	.7567	.5317	.2097	.1056	.0075	.2834	1.1378	.8939	.4331
	-	(.0546)	(.0789)	(.0420)	(.0159)	(.0584)	-	-	-
I (a)	1.0235	.5369	-	.1288	.0154	.3596	1.0407	.8884	.4425
	-	(.0159)	-	(.0090)	(.0013)	(.0138)	-	-	-
II	.9379	-	-	.2554	.0200	.6953	.9707	.8135	.5701
	-	-	-	(.0514)	(.0205)	(.0498)	-	-	-

... Estimated Factor Productivity Coefficients for Pacific Region Counties, 1954

Region	Constant Term (in Log_e) a_0	All Farm Workers X_1	Livestock Investment X_3	Irrigated Cropland X_4	Nonirrigated Cropland X_6	Current Operating Expense X_8	Sum of Coefficients	Coefficients of Determination R^2	Standard Error of Estimate (in Log_e) S
PACIFIC (Northwest)									
I	.2225	.4346 (.0876)	-.1865 (.0967)	.2353 (.0468)	.3316 (.0418)	.2035 (.0827)	1.0186	.7852	.4130
II (a)	.1704	.4374 (.0207)	-	.1849 (.0192)	.3143 (.0098)	.1623 (.0374)	1.0989	.7712	.4225
II	.4919	-	-	.2250 (.0457)	.3039 (.0491)	.4568 (.0648)	.9557	.6776	.4974
California major irrigation counties									
I	2.0592	.0911 (.1158)	-.1132 (.0780)	.3882 (.0759)	.0085 (.0105)	.4933 (.0832)	.8680	.9296	.1859
I (a)	1.7886	.0968 (.1189)	-	.3485 (.0726)	.0093 (.0190)	.4521 (.0803)	.9067	.9218	.1910
II	1.7368	-	-	.3833 (.0583)	.0138 (.0180)	.5059 (.0452)	.9031	.9192	.1894
II (a)	2.0641	-	-	.3710 (.0556)	-	.5021 (.0445)	.8731	.9169	.1876
California limited irrigation counties									
I	.6873	.2465 (.1410)	.0171 (.1606)	.1431 (.0771)	.1456 (.0732)	.4871 (.1270)	1.0394	.9375	.3269
I (a)	.7581	.2404 (.1258)	-	.1467 (.0678)	.1486 (.0660)	.4954 (.0976)	1.0311	.9374	.3191
II	.7127	-	-	.1984 (.0643)	.1852 (.0654)	.6413 (.0628)	1.0249	.9286	.3304
California- All counties									
I	.3241	.2620 (.0896)	.1735 (.0895)	.2667 (.0347)	.0279 (.0206)	.3813 (.0699)	1.1114	.9724	.2594
I (a)	-	.2648 (.0990)	-	.2200 (.0481)	.0360 (.0227)	.5017 (.0699)	1.0225	.9119	.2886
II	.8909	-	-	.3335 (.0357)	.0538 (.0227)	.6426 (.0370)	1.0299	.9613	.3034

FOOTNOTES

[1] L. R. Klein, "Macro-economics and the theory of rational behavior," *Econometrica,* Vol. 14, No. 2, 1946, pp. 93-108.

[2] See Cecil Haver, "Economic interpretation of production function estimates," in Earl O. Heady, Glenn L. Johnson and Lowell S. Hardin, eds., Resource Productivity, Returns to Scale and Farm Size, Iowa State University Press, Ames, 1956, p. 146.

[3] Hereafter we shall shorten the designation of X_8 to current operating expenses (or COE).

[4] A problem may arise due to the fact that the "econometric production function" is only at best an approximation of the true "economic production function." This may result in estimated parameters which differ widely from the true parameters of the economic model. These may be statistically unbiased estimates in relation to the data used. That is, the expected value of the statistical estimate is the population coefficient. This estimate, however, may not be an estimate of the parameter in the economic model which it was intended to represent.

[5] Ragnar Frisch, Statistical Confluence Analysis by Means of Complete Regression Systems, Universitetes Økonomiske Institutt, Oslo, 1934, p. 6.

[6] Zvi Griliches, "Specification bias in estimates of production functions," *Jour. Farm Econ.,* Vol. 39, No. 1, 1957, pp. 8-20.

[7] G. Tintner and O. H. Brownlee, "Production functions derived from farm records," *Jour. Farm Econ.,* Vol. 26, No. 3, 1944, p. 568.

[8] See H. Theil, Linear Aggregation of Economic Relations, North-Holland, 1954.

[9] Irving Hoch, "Simultaneous equation bias in the context of the Cobb-Douglas production function," *Econometrica,* Oct. 1958, pp. 566-78.

[10] E. H. P. Brown, "The meaning of the fitted Cobb-Douglas function," *Quart. Jour. Econ.,* Vol. 71, No. 4, 1957, pp. 546-60.

[11] Appendix Tables 9.1 to 9.5 (at end of chapter) give the regression coefficients. Certain measures of "goodness of fit" are also presented. Coefficients of determination (R^2) range from .68 to .97 for the 44 functions used for the five major regional groupings.

[12] There are very little data available on the marginal productivity of irrigated cropland at the micro-level. Cost data are more generally available. Our review of the literature indicates that in the humid regions a marginal productivity of between $100 to $150 per acre is typically sufficient to cover costs. In the northern and southern Plains, northern Mountains and Pacific Northwest a range of $75 to $125 is indicated. In California and the southern Mountains a $125 to $175 range appears reasonable. Since the marginal productivity estimates have to be interpreted as the marginal productivity of an acre of irrigated land and associated inputs, the relevant cost estimates must include a return on land and irrigation equipment plus depreciation and direct operating costs of irrigation equipment.

[13] D. B. Ibach and R. C. Lindberg, "The economic position of fertilizer use in the United States," USDA, Agr. Inf. Bul. No. 202, 1958, pp. 7-8.

[14] Suggestions for improving the results obtained by using the procedure employed in this study center on three points: (1) Counties in each region should be classified into two or more sub-categories based on criteria such as the number of acres irrigated or the type of commodity irrigated. This suggestion is supported by the results obtained in the northern and southern Plains. (2) The data should be set up in a manner that permits the combining of complementary inputs into a single-input categories rather than letting one member of a complementary group of inputs stand as a "proxy" for the excluded inputs. (3) The production function should be computed for a series of census periods to determine if the productivity coefficients are stable over time or if they respond in a consistent pattern to technological change and weather variations. Functions were constructed for the major and limited irrigation counties of California for 1939, 1949 and 1954. In the major irrigation counties the coefficients for irrigated cropland and output increasing operating expenses did not change significantly between 1939 and 1954.

[15] Calif. Water Resources Board, "Water utilization and requirements of California," Vol. 1, Calif. Water Resources Board Bul. No. 2, Sacramento, June 1955, p. 223.

[16] *Ibid.,* p. 223.

[17] Calif. Water Resources Board, "Water utilization and requirements of California," Vol. II, Calif. Water Resources Board Bul. No. 2, Appendices and Plates, Sacramento, June 1955, p. 242.

[18] For other examples see Earl R. Swanson, "Determining optimum size of business

from production functions," in Earl O. Heady, Glenn L. Johnson and Lowell S. Hardin, eds., Resource Productivity, Returns to Scale and Farm Size, Iowa State University Press, Ames, 1956; Vernon W. Ruttan, "The contribution of technological change to farm output; 1950-75," Rev. Econ. and Stat., Vol. 37, No. 1, 1956, pp. 61-69.

[19]The regional productivity estimates are adapted from Thomas T. Stout and V. W. Ruttan, "Regional patterns of technological change in American agriculture," Jour. Farm Econ., Vol. 40, No. 2, 1958, pp. 196-207.

RALPH E. FREUND, JR., is in the Marketing Structure and Costs Branch of the Economic Research Service of the U.S. Department of Agriculture. He was formerly with the Niagara Chemical Company of New York. He received a B.S. degree at Colorado State University and an M.S. degree from North Carolina State University.

GEORGE S. TOLLEY is Professor of Agricultural Economics at North Carolina State University. His research and writing have dealt with many public policy questions important to the land and water resource field.

Chapter 10

R. A. FREUND, JR.
G. S. TOLLEY

Operational Procedures For Evaluating Flood Protection Benefits*

THE INDIVIDUALS who determine the fate of water resources projects are dependent to a great extent upon reports of the various action agencies. The reliability of the physical and economic assumptions underlying the reports as well as the method of reporting technical information is important if the reports are to be used most advantageously.

In earlier work it was found that benefit estimates are particularly sensitive to future economic conditions and that these cannot be predicted with a great deal of reliability.[1] This finding suggests a need to improve the data and to modify evaluation methods in view of the data variability that must inevitably remain. This chapter attempts to meet this need by: (1) suggesting modifications in the presentation of information about the flood-protected areas and (2) presenting the results of an investigation of less laborious methods of estimating benefits.

With respect to (1), a project write-up is presented that provides a description of alternative possible lines of development in floodplain agriculture. A main source of uncertainty about project outcomes

*Approval by the Director of Research of the North Carolina Agr. Exp. Sta. as Paper No. 1223 of the journal series. Thanks are due to Lacy Coats and C. V. Lyle for help in obtaining information and for criticisms. The authors are solely responsible for the contents.

150

pertains to future economic trends that are not susceptible to quantification. It is believed the suggested write-up will permit readers of project reports to obtain a better grasp of the situation in the area. In view of the amount of time currently being expended by economists on computation of flood control benefits, any saving in time would permit reduction of planning costs and/or improvement of ingredient data.

This chapter is oriented to small watershed projects of the Soil Conservation Service. Because planning problems for small watersheds are similar to those for larger projects, the study should be relevant to other water resource programs.

BRIEF DESCRIPTION OF PLANNING

The Soil Conservation Service develops plans for watersheds ranging up to 250,000 acres. A variety of water development purposes may be included, but so far over 90 percent of the estimated benefits have come from flood control.

Details of planning procedures vary somewhat by regions. The description that will be given in this section is based on experience in the Southeast.

Each state has a watershed planning work party consisting of a party leader, engineer, geologist, hydrologist and economist. A work party may typically complete plans for about three projects a year. The economist divides his time roughly as follows: The first month is spent making preliminary checks on the feasibility of the project and negotiating with local sponsoring groups. In the second month he gathers data to be used in evaluating the project. These data come from interviews with farmers in the floodplain and anyone else having knowledge of the flood damages. The rest of the time is devoted to computations. The most time-consuming part of the computations is the estimation of flood damages to crops being grown in the floodplain. The floodplain is divided into relatively homogeneous segments, called reaches, and each requires approximately a week's computation.

The first step in estimating benefits from reduction in flood damages is to record the proportions of the different crops in the floodplain and, for every month, the loss that would be incurred per acre of a crop if it were totally destroyed. Based on the farmer interviews, tables are made for the percent of damage to crops from flooding at one-foot depth intervals for each month. From this information the damage to an average or composite floodplain acre is found for depths of flooding and months.

The hydrologist prepares a table showing the number of acres flooded to different depths by floods of various heights or stages. From these tables the stage-damage tables are made. These show the total crop damage from floods of different stages for each month. The hydrologist first determines the number and stage of the floods for the previous 20 years and next what the stage would have been if the project had been installed.[2] From the 20-year series of floods and the stage-damage tables the total damage for the 20 years is found and then what the damage would have been if the project had been installed. The difference divided by 20 is the average annual flood damage reduction benefit.

TWO SHORTENED METHODS OF ESTIMATING AGRICULTURAL FLOOD DAMAGES

With the evaluation procedures being used in the Southeast, estimation of floodwater damages to crops accounts for about two-thirds of the party economist's computational activities. If part of the time now devoted to calculations of the current method were spent in obtaining better data and modifying the workplan as suggested later, the resulting evaluation of benefits might be more reliable. Toward this end, two shortened methods of estimating floodwater damage to agriculture are compared with the present procedure.

The first shortened method approaches the problem from an income standpoint, thus being considerably different from the current method (which was described in the opening section of this chapter). Farmer estimates of average yields with and without flood damage are compared; whereas the current method starts with flood-free yields and adjusts them on the basis of percent-damage tables. Furthermore, the first shortened method relies on percent of reduction in average area inundated in the hope that damages are closely related to the area flooded and not very dependent upon depth of flooding. In contrast, the present method allows for increasing damage by depth.

The second method is more similar to the current one. With the current method, total damages are estimated by developing stage-damage tables and then finding the damage caused by each flood in a 20-year series. The second method follows the same procedure but uses data on a *quarter* basis instead of on a *monthly* basis. Another source of shortening is to make an average adjustment for sequent floods (floods within the same year) instead of adjusting each sequent flood separately as does the current method.

The first shortened method may require only 2 or 3 hours to prepare the data and make the analysis for a reach. The second method requires about a 3-hour preparation of damageable values and percent-damage tables. With other tables furnished by the hydrologist, flood damages for a reach could be estimated in less than a day. This compares favorably in length and complexity with the current method. Using current procedures, the complete evaluation of a reach takes nearer to five days, with three spent in estimating flood damages. The second shortened method would reduce time devoted to analysis by perhaps 50 percent.

Short Method I Described

The first method measures floodwater damages to crops grown in the floodplain by first finding what the net income would be if present cropping practices were followed but no flooding occurred. Next, net income with flood damages is determined. The difference between these is the total damage to crops. The hydrologist calculates the percentage of reduction in average area flooded annually as a result of the project. This percentage times the total damage gives the project benefits from reduced floodwater damage to crops. A worksheet using this method for a reach of a watershed is presented in Table 10.1.

Table 10.1. First Short Method: Income With and Without Flood Damage

Net income using present cropping practices, if no flood damage

Crop	(Acres)	(Yield x Price - Cost/Acre)	= Net Return
Corn	(282)	(61 bu. x $1.39 - $42.62)	= $11,891.94
Soybeans	(34)	(20 bu. x $2.21 - $25.92)	= 621.52
Unimproved pasture	(414)	(4 AUM x $4.00 - 0)	= 6,624.00
		Total	$19,137.46

Net income at present

Crop	(Acres)	(Yield x Price - Cost/Acre)	= Net Income
Corn	(282)	(38 x $1.39 - $44.14)	= $ 2,447.76
Soybeans	(34)	(10 x $2.21 - $25.92)	= -129.88
Unimproved pasture	(414)	(2 x $4.00 - 0)	= 3,312.00
		Total	$ 5,629.88

After net income without flood damage and present net income are found, the second is subtracted from the first to get total flood damages to crops:

$19,137.46 minus $5,629.88 equals $13,507.58.

To determine the amount that the project will reduce flood damages to crops the total damage is multiplied by the percentage of reduction in average area flooded annually:

$13,508 times 52.3 percent equals $7,065.

The project benefits from reduction of damage to crops is $7,065.

The data are obtained from interviews with farmers who have land in the floodplain. Prices are long-run projections furnished by the U.S. Department of Agriculture. It can be seen that the only changes in the data in the two calculations of income are in yields and the cost of production. Replanting of corn because of flood damage is done one year out of eight, which increases average annual costs per acre by $1.52. The farmers' estimates of average yields for the last 10 years are used.

Short Method II Described

The second method utilizes a table giving the number of floods in a 20-year period by stages for each quarter of the year. This is illustrated in Table 10.2. The hydrologist furnishes Table 10.3, which shows the number of acres flooded at different depths for varying stages of flooding. From the foregoing two tables is derived the number of acres flooded to various depths by quarters for the 20 years, as shown in Table 10.4.

Table 10.2. Second Short Method: Frequency of Floods by Quarters

Stage in Feet	Quarters			
	1	2	3	4
8	1		4	1
9	1	2	3	
10		3	2	
11		2	2	
12			1	
13			3	
14			2	
15				1

Table 10.3. Second Short Method: Acres Inundated by One-Foot Depth-Inundation Intervals

Stage in Feet	Acres inundated to depths of:				
	1 ft.	2 ft.	3 ft.	4 ft.	5 ft.
7.2	0	0			
8.0	135	11			
9.0	149	147	0		
10.0	155	142	124	0	
11.0	157	142	177	73	0
12.0	142	154	136	154	64
13.0	76	152	152	129	193
14.0	66	95	153	140	311
14.6	82	78	125	153	390

Table 10.4. Second Short Method: Acres Flooded by Depths and Quarters

Depth	Quarters			
	1	2	3	4
1	284	1077	2113	217
2	158	1004	1853	89
3	0	726	1500	125
4	0	146	967	153
5	0	0	1265	390

Table 10.5. Second Short Method: Average Percent of Damage
by Depths of Inundation and Quarters

Depth	Quarters			
	1	2	3	4
Corn				
1	15	22	12	0
2	25	47	20	10
3	50	83	37	20
4	75	97	83	75
5	75	97	100	100
Soybeans				
1	0	22	18	10
2	0	42	43	50
3	0	83	97	100
4	0	92	100	100
5	0	92	100	100
Pasture				
1	15	17	20	25
2	25	27	30	42
3	35	37	42	62
4	50	53	62	88
5	50	60	73	100

Next, Table 10.5 is prepared which tells the percent of damage for
each quarter to crops which are flooded at different depths. This information is obtained from interviews with farmers on the floodplain.

Tables 10.4 and 10.5 are used to compute the number of acres of
each crop which it might be said would be completely destroyed if the
floodplain were entirely in that crop. This is entered in Table 10.6 under the column "Acres."

In the next column of Table 10.6 the "composite-acre" concept is
used to adjust for the proportion of each crop in the floodplain. A "composite acre" contains the same proportions of crops as found in the entire reach. Thus, to obtain "Damageable Value per Composite Acre"
the average value of an acre of the crop is multiplied by the percentage
of that crop in the reach. The use of the composite acre makes the assumption that the damageable value of the lower part of the floodplain
is the same as that of the upper part. In most of the small watersheds
this assumption is realistic because the floodplain is so narrow that approximately the same land use occurs from the stream to the outer edge
of the floodplain.

Table 10.6. Second Short Method: Damage by Crops and Quarters

	Quarter	Acres	Damageable Value for Composite Acre			Damages
Corn						
	1	82	x	.27	=	22.14
	2	1453	x	14.93	=	21,693.29
	3	3247	x	25.47	=	82,701.09
	4	539	x	6.37	=	3,433.43
Soybeans						
	2	1396	x	.44	=	614.24
	3	4864	x	1.39	=	6,760.96
	4	734	x	.47	=	344.98
Pasture						
	2	800	x	1.05	=	840.00
	3	3131	x	.70	=	2,191.70
	4	694	x	.35	=	242.90
	1	82	x	.23	=	18.86
	Total Unadjusted Damage				=	118,863.59
	Times: Sequent Flooding Adjustment Factor					x .90
	Equals: Total Adjusted Damage				=	$106,977.23

The final column in Table 10.6 shows how the damage to each crop in each quarter is obtained through multiplication.[3] These damages are summed to obtain the total damage to crops for 20 years. The total damage divided by 20 gives the average annual unadjusted damage.

The estimate is reduced 10 percent to allow for sequent flooding. When one flood follows closely behind another, the calculated damages of the second flood must be adjusted to allow for the reduction in damageable value caused by the first flood. Reaches were examined from four watersheds in North Carolina and the average reduction to allow for sequent flooding was found to be approximately 10 percent. The sequent flooding adjustment will probably change for different sections of the country, but the use of a general figure for areas of similar climate and topographical characteristics may be sufficiently accurate. It saves considerable computing time.

To obtain an estimate of flood damage reduction due to a project, the process that has been described must be gone through twice. First, a 20-year sequence is used assuming no project. Second, a sequence is used adjusted by the hydrologist to reflect flooding if the project measures were installed. The difference between flood damages computed the first time and the second time is the estimate of flood damage reduction benefits.

Comparison of Results

To check the accuracy of the two shortened methods, they were
tested on two reaches on each of three watersheds, making a total of
six reaches tested. The three watersheds are located in North Carolina, one in a mountainous area in the western part of the state, one in
the Piedmont and the other in the Coastal Plain. The results are compared to the answer computed by the Soil Conservation Service economist using the current detailed method. In applying the second shortened method exactly the same data were used as in the current method,
but for the first method it was necessary to revisit the watersheds to
obtain new data on yields.

The results of the tests were as follows:

Method		Watershed #1		Watershed #2		Watershed #3	
Current		$4,068.00		$17,245.00		$ 6,347.00	
First	Reach #1	$7,065.00	+74%	$ 8,686.00	-50%	$23,324.00	+267%
Second		$3,598.00	-12%	$19,145.00	+11%	$ 7,067.00	+11%
Current		$1,598.00		$ 1,318.00		$18,693.00	
First	Reach #2	$5,896.00	+269%	$ 1,779.00	+35%	$88,955.00	+376%
Second		$1,280.00	-20%	$ 1,324.00	$+\frac{1}{2}\%$	$21,198.00	+13%

In the preceding table the first figure in a box is the benefit estimate
using the current method. The next figure is the estimate using short
method number one and the final figure is the estimate using short
method number two. On the assumption that the current detailed method
gives a correct estimate, the percent of error of each short method is
shown. The average of the absolute percentage errors for method number one is 178 percent and for method number two it is 11.2 percent.

Reliability of Short Method I

Three possible sources may be noted for the large error in method
number one. The first is that the use of the percent of reduction in average acres flooded annually is not an accurate way to measure flood
damage reduction benefits. A second possible source is that the data
used do not correspond to those in the present method. Yields with
flood damage were not available from the old data, so the watersheds
had to be revisited to obtain them. Since a different person did the interviewing as long as three years after the first data were collected, it
is likely that different assumptions entered the analysis. The third
possibility as to the source of the error is that the "error" lies in the
present method instead of in the first method. Since we do not know the
true flood damage reduction benefits, we cannot be sure that the detailed
method is a reliable standard of measurement.

After examining the data and worksheets of the first method, it appears that the first two sources of error are present. There is little way of knowing about the third. In the reach where benefits were underestimated by the first method, the percent of reduction in average area inundated annually was very small. Where a floodplain is level, the percent of reduction in average area inundated annually will be small but benefits will still accrue from the reduction in depth of flooding. The first method does not recognize this and thereby fails to pick up the benefits.

The biggest error probably came from the second source. The revisited farmers were asked for their yields with present flood damage and for what their yields would be if they kept present cropping practices and had no flood damage. There usually seemed to be a consensus of opinion about yield levels in an area. When asked about their yields, they replied without much deliberation. When asked about what yields would be if they kept present cropping practices but did not have flood damage, the farmers' estimates varied greatly within a reach of a watershed. One popular response was that yields would be doubled.

Farmers have a rough idea of their yields but appear unable to make reliable distinctions requiring averaging in their heads for yields over a number of years with and without flood damage.

Reliability of Short Method II

While results for the first method are clearly not reliable by ordinary statistical standards, the error of the second method is small enough to merit testing.

From a frequency distribution derived in an earlier paper, the coefficient of variation of estimated benefits caused by data variability was found to be 62 percent.[4] A comparable coefficient of variation associated with the second method is 13.7 percent. To obtain this latter coefficient, the damage estimate for results by the second method on each of the six reaches was divided by the estimate using the present procedure. The six resulting observations, giving the number of dollars of damages the second method estimates for each dollar estimated under the present method, are thus adjusted for the widely varying size of the reaches in the sample and present an idea of the variability that the second method might introduce on a reach of given size. The much larger coefficient of variation found in the earlier paper to be associated with data variability suggests that over-all accuracy might be improved by using the second method so as to be able to improve data accuracy.

A t-test was run to check any bias in the second method. The sample described above of results for the second method was tested to see if its mean differed significantly from the mean of the present method. The null hypothesis that the two methods have the same mean could *not* be rejected even at an alpha level of 80 percent. An alpha level of 5 or 10 percent is usually used as a rejectance criterion. Thus the difference between the means would have to be much larger than observed before one could conclude that the second method gives significantly different results from the present method.

SUGGESTIONS FOR WATERSHED WORKPLANS

After the project is planned and the evaluation computed, a descriptive workplan is prepared. The workplan is sent to higher Soil Conservation offices, to the Bureau of the Budget and finally to Congress where action is taken by appropriate committees. A main purpose of the workplan is to define benefits of the project so that an informed opinion can be made as to its desirability.

The workplan contains a description of the engineering, hydrologic, geologic and economic features of the watershed and of the measures to be installed. While economic information is only one of the four types of information included, it is perhaps the most important from the standpoint of determining whether funds should be spent on the project.

It appears more feasible to put most of the economic information into one section instead of scattering it in bits throughout the workplan. This would save the reader time in assessing the reliability of benefit estimates, and it would help those who have never been at the site to form a picture of what the watershed is like.

In addition to putting most of the economic information in one place, it may be desirable to include more economic information than is contained in present workplans. Table 10.7 presents an outline of contents for the present workplan, and Table 10.8 presents an outline for a modified workplan. The letters (A), (B), (C) and so forth by the headings of the present plan are put by the headings of the suggested plan to indicate the rearrangements.

The suggested outline of contents in Table 10.8 aims at a workplan that makes sure to answer the following three questions. First: *What are the main features of the agricultural economy of the watershed, and what are trends that may affect its future?* The answer to this question requires information on sources of income and on organization of typical farms in the watershed. The generalized type-of-farming area needs to be noted, and differences between the economy of the watershed and the surrounding area should be described. It would be desirable to include information on off-farm work availability and its importance as an income source. The watershed farms should be grouped into the most important modal types, and for each type figures could be presented on typical farm enterprises, net family income, age and education of operator, family size, total farm investment and net worth. Information on yields and cultural practices could be given to impart an idea about management levels. This helps demonstrate whether farmers are progressive. If so, they may be more likely to take advantage of opportunities for more productive use of protected land provided by flood control.

Table 10.7. Table of Contents for Present Workplans

(A) SUMMARY OF PLAN

DESCRIPTION OF THE WATERSHED

(B)   Physical Data

(C)   Economic Data

WATERSHED PROBLEMS

(D)   Floodwater Damage
(E)   Sediment Damage
(F)   Erosion Damage
(G)   Problems Relating to Water Management

(H) EXISTING OR PROPOSED WORKS OF IMPROVEMENT

(I) WORKS OF IMPROVEMENT TO BE INSTALLED

Land Treatment Measures for Watershed Protection
Land Treatment Measures Primarily for Flood Prevention
Structural Measures for Flood Prevention

(J) BENEFITS FROM WORKS OF IMPROVEMENT

(K) COMPARISON OF BENEFITS AND COSTS

(L) ACCOMPLISHING THE PLAN

(M) PROVISIONS FOR OPERATION AND MAINTENANCE

(N) COST-SHARING

(O) CONFORMANCE OF PLAN TO FEDERAL LAWS AND REGULATIONS

Table 10.8. Suggested Table of Contents for Workplans

SUMMARY OF PLAN (A)

PHYSICAL DESCRIPTION OF PROJECT (B, G, H, I)

Physical Characteristic of the Watershed
Nonproject Watershed Improvements
Works of Improvement To Be Installed

ECONOMIC EVALUATION (C, D, E, F, J, K, plus additional information)

The Economy of the Watershed
    Type of Farming Area
    Characteristics of Watershed Farms
    Economic Trends Affecting the Watershed
Floodplain Use in Relation to the Project
    Present Role of Floodplain
    Estimated Effects of the Project on the Floodplain
Information on Purposes Other Than Flood Prevention
Comparison of Benefits and Costs
    Types of Benefits Claimed and Data Used
    Benefit Estimates

ACCOMPLISHING THE PLAN (L, M, N, O)

Installation of Measures
Operation and Maintenance
Cost-Sharing
Compliance to Federal Requirements

The description of trends affecting the watershed should present the assumptions used for the numerical benefit estimates. At the same time it should be made clear that these assumptions are only the most likely ones and that the future cannot be predicted with certainty. The discussion should give a feel of the probabilities of a more pessimistic and more optimistic turn of events. The factors to be considered include the outlook for the demand for farm products of the watershed and the likely future competitive advantage of the watershed area in producing the products. Effects of government programs, the possibilities of future mechanization and other factors that affect farm size may need to be considered.

A second question is: *What is the role of the floodplain in farm operations?* If the floodplain is a major source of income, such as providing a fertile source of feed for a cattle herd, the project may be likely to have pronounced benefits. Valuable crops in the floodplain mean there are high damage-reduction benefits to be captured. Even more productive use may be made of the floodplain after protection is provided. On the other hand, suppose the floodplain is a minor source of income accounting for only a small portion of the land of any one farm. Then there may be little possibility for flood damage reduction and little prospect for more productive use after protection is provided. Knowing how the floodplain fits into total farming operations can help verify the reasonableness of farmers' answers on how they will use the floodplain.

The watershed planning economist almost automatically acquires most of this information about the floodplain in the course of his present activities. The suggestion is that it be included in the workplan write-up in order to edify readers who have never been in the watershed.

The two questions that have been considered indicate need for a significant expansion in the economics section of the workplan. To answer the third question requires clarity more than inclusion of much new data: *Does the workplan explain the benefits in nontechnical language?* In addition to breaking down the benefits into various types (for example, flood damage reduction, changed land use, sediment damage reduction, prevention of infertile deposition), the assumptions about time streams of benefits and the relation of benefits to each other should be made clear. This would help avoid the double-counting charge often levelled at benefit estimates. Some of the information might be repetitious from workplan to workplan. The cost of the repetition seems small in view of the gain of ensuring that the workplan is an understandable and self-contained document.

To further spell out the foregoing suggestions, a model economics section of a workplan will be presented. This corresponds to the section entitled "Economic Evaluation" in Table 10.8. The watershed situation is hypothetical:

ECONOMIC EVALUATION

The Economy of the Watershed

Type-of-Farming-Area. The watershed is located in a tobacco farming area in the coastal plain of North Carolina. Tobacco is the primary income producer but corn, cotton, soybeans, small grains, hogs and cattle also figure in the area's economy.

Two types of farms are predominant in the watershed. In 1959 single-family farms averaged 62 acres in size. There were 126 of these farms, and they occupied just over half the watershed area. The other main type of farm, averaging 247 acres, has sharecropper tenants. Though only 14 in number, these large farms utilize 27 percent of the land area of the watershed. The remainder of the area is held predominantly by paper and other industrial companies in unfarmed tracts.

Based on a budgeting analysis to estimate typical income for different crops, approximately two-thirds of farm income is from tobacco. Characteristics of watershed farms, as contrasted to averages for the surrounding seven-county area, are given in Figure 10.1.

Compared to the rest of the North Carolina coastal plain, the watershed has relatively more tobacco, and yields on the tobacco are about 10 percent higher. There is relatively less cotton in the watershed but more corn and cattle.

Eighty-one percent of the farms have land in the floodplain. There is little discernible difference in size and enterprise combinations among farms that have and do not have land in the floodplain.

The only large industry within 20 miles of the watershed area is a synthetic fiber plant employing about 1,200 persons. A nearby Air Force base and five surrounding towns of less than 10,000 population each offer some employment opportunities, but agriculture is the preponderant source of income in the area.

Characteristics of Watershed Farms

Of the two general types of farms in the watershed, one ranges from 50 to 75 acres in size and is operated by one family. The other type ranges in size from 200 to 250 acres and is farmed by two or more tenant families and the owner. Usually the tenants raise tobacco, cotton and corn on a share-rental basis. The owner almost always lives on the farm and operates crop and livestock enterprises.

Farms of the first type have a total investment of 15 to 20 thousand dollars, depending upon the tobacco allotment. An acre of tobacco land with an allotment is worth approximately $4,000, and the farms of the first type usually have about four acres. From 50 to 60 percent of these farms have a tractor, but there is little other farm machinery. Based on a budgeting analysis for different enterprises, these farms appear to have a net income of about $3,000 per year, of which 50 percent may be from tobacco. Corn is the second most important crop from an income standpoint. On the average, 15 percent of the income is from off-farm employment. The farm family has four to five members, providing a two-man equivalent labor force. The operator has an average of nine years of school and an average age of 41 years.

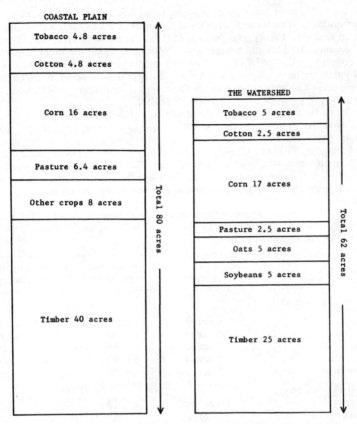

Fig. 10.1. Land use on single-unit 50-acre farms in the watershed compared to the same units for the entire coastal plain.

Income sources for a typical 50-acre family farm in the watershed are as follows:

Enterprise	Acreages	Net Income Per Acre	Total Income for the Enterprise
28 acres of cropland:			
Tobacco	4 acres	$360	$1440
Corn	14 acres	50	700
Cotton	2 acres	60	120
Oats	4 acres	28	112
Soybeans	4 acres	26	104
Other income sources:			
Timber	20 acres	10	200
Pasture	2 acres	15	30
Off-farm employment	-	-	450
		Total net income	$3156

The second type of farm (multiple-unit type) has a total investment of 60 to 75 thousand dollars. The tobacco allotment is about 14 acres, some of which is farmed by tenants. Eighty-one percent of these farms have tractors. There are minor amounts of additional machinery. Tobacco is again the most important income producer, followed by corn. The larger farms often have a livestock operation of cattle or hogs. Income from these enterprises is about 10 thousand dollars per year. The average age of the farm owner-managers is 48 years, and 78 percent of these persons have 12 years of school.

The large farms have an average of two tenant families living on them. These families have six to seven members who, it seems reasonable to suppose, furnish three man-equivalents of labor. A typical tenant family may take care of about 5 acres of tobacco, 15 acres of corn and 3 acres of cotton. This farming is usually done with mules and with hand labor methods. The land is rented on a one-half share basis — half the income to the landlord and the tenant keeping half. Most expenses are divided equally, also. Income to the tenant family is about $1500 per year.

Estimates of income sources for a typical multiple-unit farm of 200 acres are presented below. Out of the total income of $10,206, approximately $3,000 will go to the two tenant families.

Enterprise	Acreages	Net Income Per Acre	Total Income for the Enterprise
100 acres of cropland			
Tobacco	14 acres	$360	$ 5,040
Corn	60 acres	50	3,000
Cotton	8 acres	60	480
Oats	9 acres	28	252
Soybeans	9 acres	26	234
Other income sources			
Timber	60 acres	10	600
Pasture	40 acres	15	600
		Total net income	$10,206

In this case the 40 acres of pasture is grazed by a beef herd, but sometimes part of the pasture land is put into corn for a hog enterprise, instead.

Management in the watershed appears above average for the coastal plain. Yields on tobacco in the watershed are 1,800 pounds as compared to a coastal plain average of 1,650 pounds. The higher yields may be associated with heavy fertilization and close planting. Yields on other crops are about the same as coastal plain averages.

The average length of ownership of the watershed farms is 15 years. Only 10 percent of the watershed land is rented. Persons in the area indicate that when an occasional farm is offered for sale it is usually purchased within several months by an adjoining farm owner.

Economic Trends Affecting the Watershed

The economy of the watershed is closely tied to developments in tobacco, which is controlled under the federal price-support program. During the years 1955 to 1957, allotments were decreased 29 percent, which had important effects on the area's economy.

There are several factors responsible for the cutback in the tobacco acreage.

The supply of tobacco increased as a result of higher yields while demand failed to follow suit. A process was developed which reconstitutes the tobacco leaf allowing more cigarettes to be made from less tobacco. Also, foreign tobacco growers have increased their production and are able to sell to European markets at low prices, thereby restricting the export market. Also, restraining demand has been publicity about studies purporting to relate tobacco and cancer.

The reduction in tobacco allotments is partly responsible for the outmigration from the coastal plain. From 1955 to 1957 there was a 21 percent reduction in the number of families farming tobacco on a sharecrop basis and a 15 percent reduction in the total number of farm families. On many of the farms where a tenant farmed some of the tobacco, the owner took over the entire tobacco acreage, causing the tenant to move elsewhere.

For the longer run, a further decline in the tobacco acreage might cause more outmigration and a decrease in the intensity of land use in the watershed. In this event tobacco might go out and with it other crops. With less agriculture, project benefits would be less than estimated in the present workplan.

However, another possibility is that while the tenant labor is mobile, the farm owners would adjust to a reduced tobacco acreage by shifting to other crop enterprises. Since tobacco is an extremely labor-intensive crop, the increase in the acres of other crops would be much greater than the decrease in the tobacco acreage. This would cause land now in woods or pasture to be put into intensive, mechanized crop production. Floodplain land would probably be involved in these conversions and, if so, project benefits from flood protection would be increased.

Another possibility is that even if there were further tobacco acreage declines, the coastal plain has a sufficient comparative advantage that it would stay in tobacco production with other more marginal areas going out. This would be favorable to the assumption of continued present type-of-agriculture for the watershed that underlies the benefit estimates of this report.

A trend that has not yet materialized is mechanization of tobacco production. No effective mechanical substitute has been found for the large amounts of labor connected with harvesting. Experts feel this will be accomplished eventually. If so, there would be far-reaching effects for tobacco farming. With less labor, farm size and cropping patterns could be expected to change. Among other things, floodplain land use would be affected, and thereby flood-protection benefits of the proposed project would alter. No attempt is made in this workplan to estimate what the direction of these effects might be.

Two facts are important in assessing how future trends will affect the project: (1) tobacco is not grown in the floodplain and (2) floodplain land is therefore not now a major source of income. For these reasons trends affecting other crops may be relevant, but at the same time farmers relying predominantly on tobacco may not develop their floodplain possibilities as much as they might if this land were involved in the major enterprise. A continuation of this situation implies that optimism about land-use conversions in response to flood protection may need to be tempered.

On the other hand, grain production has been on a long-time increase in the coastal plain. Further increases may make for more grains in floodplains — a relatively intensive use — in which case there would then be greater flood protection benefits from the project.

These alternative trends discussed are an indication of the degree of uncertainty surrounding the project. Every investment for the future is characterized by uncertainty. The most likely assumption adopted in the workplan is that in the absence of the project there would be continuation of present type-of-agriculture in the watershed. While some of the trends discussed in this section would make project benefits higher and some would make them lower, numerical estimates associated with these uncertain trends have not been attempted.

Floodplain Land Use in Relation to the Project

Present Role of the Floodplain. For the farms bordering the creek, the typical division of land between floodplain and upland is one-third floodplain and two-thirds upland. At present about 12 percent of the income from these farms comes from the floodplain. This is because the tobacco and most of the other higher value crops are grown on the upland.

Older residents of the watershed estimate that in the 1930's, 85 percent of the floodplain was used in the production of crops and improved pasture. Because of stream channel clogging and sediment damage, now only 35 percent of the floodplain remains in crops and improved pasture.

Areas where sediment damage and swamping are especially severe have gone into scrub bush and timber. This now comprises one-third of the floodplain.

The largest floodplain use is native and improved pasture. Forty percent, or about 1,700 acres, is devoted to this. There are two dairies in the watershed which graze cows on the floodplain. The multiple-unit farms often have small beef herds to graze the floodplain pasture. There are approximately eight beef herds of 40 cows each.

Twenty-seven percent of the floodplain is in cultivation. Primarily corn is grown. It is on the smaller farms that most of the cultivation of the floodplain occurs, since they seldom have cattle for pasture grazing. A small farm with 15 acres of corn will have 5 acres in the floodplain, plus a few acres of soybeans. The total amount of corn in the floodplain is 1,012 acres.

Farmers and government agricultural workers in the area think that the floodplain would be some of the most valuable land in the watershed if flood prevention measures were taken. For instance, corn yields in the floodplain when there is no flood damage are 54 bushels per acre in comparison to yields of 38 bushels on the upland.

Estimated Effects of the Project on the Floodplain. As a result of the project, the frequency of flooding will decrease from 1.8 times per year to 0.8 times per year, and the average area flooded annually will decrease by 59 percent. The average area damaged annually by deposits of infertile material during flooding will decrease from 286 acres to 63 acres, and the average annual rate of swamping will decrease from 10 to 3 acres.

The above physical effects will reduce floodwater damage to crops and farm improvements by $12,715 or $3.01 per acre of floodplain. The reduction in sediment damage will be $4,450 or $1.06 per acre of floodplain.

From interviews with farmers in the floodplain, main changed land-use benefits as a result of the project were estimated to be from additional land being put into corn and improved pasture. It is anticipated that there will be 238 more acres of corn and 842 more acres of improved pasture with a corresponding decrease primarily in idle and brush land and unimproved pasture. Total changed land-use benefits are $20,618, or $4.89 per acre of floodplain.

Total monetary benefits from the project to floodplain land are expected to be $37,783. This amounts to an increase in annual income of $8.96 per acre of floodplain. Since income per acre of floodplain now appears to be about $18.00, the estimate is for a 50 percent increase in net income from the floodplain.

Information on Purposes Other Than Flood Prevention

(This section is omitted in the present study dealing only with flood protection.)

Comparison of Benefits and Costs

<u>Types of Benefits Claimed and Data.</u> The benefits occurring to the floodplain can be portrayed as follows:

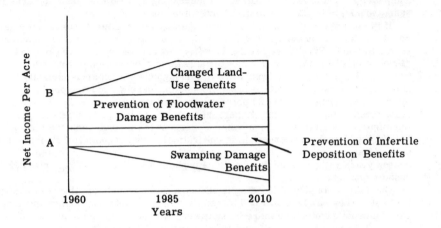

Model Workplan Table A. Benefits From Changed Land Use

Land Use	Present Condition			Future Condition With Project		
	Acres	Yield Per Acre	Net Value	Acres	Yield Per Acre	Net Value
Corn	864	54 bu.	30,576	1,102	58 bu.	42,741
Soybeans	105	23 bu.	2,463	111	23 bu.	2,628
Unimproved pasture	1,050	4 AUM	14,700	208	4 AUM	2,912
Improved pasture	398	6 AUM	8,358	1,240	8 AUM	45,549
Idle	151			81		
Brush	169			38		
Woods	863			820		
Total	3,600		56,097	3,600		93,830

Calculations:

Increased net value (93,830 - 56,097) $37,733

Less associated costs (drainage, development,
fencing, etc.) 14,808

Less added flood damage (due to increased
damageable value) 516

Total changed land-use benefit 22,409

Less restoration benefit creditable to land treatment
measures for watershed protection 1,791

Changed land use benefits creditable to structural
measures and land treatment measures for
flood prevention $20,618

Point "A" is the present net income from an acre of floodplain land. Due to swamping, the income will decline unless flood prevention measures are taken. The area labeled "Swamping Damage Benefits" illustrates this source of benefits and how they increase through time. Swamping is present on approximately 1,475 acres, causing 500 acres to remain idle and 975 acres to be suitable only for hay and pasture. The swamping damage is increasing at a rate of about 10 acres per year, causing more land to go out of intensive use.

If the project is installed, floodwater damage and sediment damage to existing crops and farm improvements will be reduced so that income will be immediately raised to point "B". These are the benefits represented by the area labeled "Prevention of Floodwater Damage Benefits" and "Prevention of Infertile Deposition Benefits." Infertile deposits are occurring annually on approximately 286 acres of crop and pasture land in the floodplain, thereby reducing production on the damaged areas by about 20 percent. Present land use in the floodplain was determined to be as follows: 40 percent is in fair to low quality pasture yielding from four to six animal-unit-months; 33 percent is in scrub bush and medium to low quality timber; 27 percent is in cultivation; corn accounts for 88 percent of the cultivated land and soybeans the rest. The yield for corn in average growing season years without flood damage is 54 bushels per acre. Soybeans yield 23 bushels per acre.

Once the frequency of flooding is reduced, farmers indicate they will change land use. They say land will be cleared, idle land put into use, higher income-earning crops planted and more intensive cultural practices maintained. These are the "Changed Land-Use Benefits" illustrated in the graph. This is the most important source of benefits estimated for the project. Of the 4,218 acres of floodplain, 3,600 will be involved in changed use. Table A shows the changes by crops and indicates the calculations leading to the benefit estimate.

Model Workplan Table B. Benefit Summary

	Average Annual Benefits	
Item	Total	Per Acre of Floodplain
Floodwater damage		
To crops and pasture	$11,820	$2.80
To farm improvement	895	.21
Changed land use	20,618	4.89
Sediment damage		
Swamping	3,777	.90
Infertile deposition	673	.16
Indirect damage	1,716	–
On-site conservation	1,292	–
Total	$40,791	$8.96

"Swamping Damage Benefits" and "Changed Land-Use Benefits" both change through time, and so they are computed by using the present value of an increasing annuity. All benefits after 50 years are not counted. Although required maintenance should make the project permanent, to count the benefit after 50 years would make only a small difference to the estimate of benefits.

In addition to the benefits shown, which accrue inside the floodplain, there are also benefits outside the floodplain. One of these is "Indirect Benefits" which include the saving of such costs as rerouting traffic, relief, rehabilitation and care and protection of property. Indirect damage is not computed in a detailed fashion for each watershed. Instead a rule of thumb is used. Indirect damage is estimated to be 10 percent of floodwater damage, infertile deposition and swamping damage benefits.

"Conservation On-Site Benefits" are claimed when land treatment for flood prevention will restore critically damaged areas above the floodplain to a productive use or prevent damages above the floodplain. Reduced maintenance on 18 miles of road gives benefits of $320. Production from 50 acres given stabilization measures is valued at $885 per year and 51 acres of trees were planted giving a value of $87 per year.

Benefit Estimates. Total average annual benefits for the project are $40,791 as compared to $14,421 for average annual costs, giving a benefit-cost ratio of 2.8 to 1. All land treatment and structural measures have a benefit-cost ratio of greater than 1. A breakdown of benefits is given in Table B.

The discussion of the workplan in this chapter has concerned only Part I of the workplan. Part II contains supporting data and information about the methods used in the investigation. The suggestions that have been made would result in transferring some of the material of Part II to Part I. We will not discuss Part II further, except to note that additional data might then be put in Part II such as percent of damage tables, land use and yields by reaches, detail on price assumptions and changed land use by reaches.

There would be greater burdens on the Soil Conservation Service field economist if the type of model economics section presented above were adopted. Information about economic conditions in the watershed would have to be collected more systematically, and more effort would be required in writing his part of the workplan. He would have to make decisions about alternative future trends and how these would affect benefits.

The added responsibilities of the economist would make even more desirable less tedious methods of estimating the flood-reduction benefits.

SHOULD THE PROCEDURES CONSIDERED
IN THIS CHAPTER BE ADOPTED?

A case can be made for adopting as a package the modified workplan and the second shortened evaluation method. This would shift the emphasis of the party economist's activities, leaving his total commitments roughly the same.

The expanded economic content of the workplan would recognize explicitly that benefits cannot be predicted with certainty. Alternative possible outcomes would be described. It might be argued that this opens the door on pressures for overoptimism, with pessimistic possibilities played down. To guard against such bias, the workplan could be circulated for more thorough review by outsiders than at present. The modified workplan would be a self-contained document and therefore could be reviewed more easily.

The second shortened evaluation method would release the economist's time for more effort on the workplan. It employed the same methodology as the present lengthy method but is less refined in the details of application. The accuracy of the second shortened method is great enough so that it would lead to doubt about whether benefits exceed costs only for marginal projects.

The less encouraging results obtained with the first shortened evaluation method do not rule out its use altogether. In conjunction with judgment on the part of the planning party, the method may be helpful in preliminary stages, e.g. in choosing which watersheds deserve further planning effort. The method has been so used in the Southeast. The present study indicates that unusual care is needed in interviewing and interpreting results to be sure to obtain estimates that are of a correct order of magnitude. For final evaluation a method is needed whose reasonableness can be judged on the basis of information presented in the workplan. The first shortened method does not pass this test because it would have to rely too heavily on judgments whose reasonableness an outsider cannot check.

This chapter has not questioned the total amount of watershed planning effort. If more were to be expended on planning, consideration might be given to enlarging the regional planning units. If persons in these offices could develop estimates of damages caused by inundation (preferably through controlled studies instead of interviews), evaluation would be less subject to the caprice of farmers' answers. Project evaluations would be more comparable among states. If a special responsibility of economists in these offices were to keep cognizant of trends affecting the region's agriculture, they could help in filling in the parts of the modified workplan requiring this information. A centralized service for doing the sheerly computational work in estimating flood damages would be inexpensive in relation to total planning costs and might eliminate the need for any shortening at all of evaluation procedures.

FOOTNOTES

[1] G. S. Tolley and R. A. Freund, "Does the state of the data suggest a program for modifying planning and evaluation procedures," Economics of Watershed Planning, Iowa State University Press, Ames, 1960.

[2] In situations where floods occur as often as once a year, the use of a historical flood sequence appears to give results that are similar to a probability or "frequency" method for determining the expectation of annual damages. In sections of the country where damage is principally from large, less frequent floods, the frequency approach is needed.

[3] If the percentage of crop in the reach had been multiplied by the "Acres" column (to obtain total acres of the crop destroyed) instead of by value per acre of the crop, the procedure would be intuitively more straightforward. Then we would have acres of corn destroyed times the value of an acre of corn, giving total corn loss. The procedure of Table 10.6, which gives the same result, is a computational convenience.

[4] Tolley and Freund, *op. cit.*

EMERY N. CASTLE is Professor of Agricultural Economics at Oregon State University. He has developed a productive water resources research program and has served on the staff of Purdue University, Kansas State University, The Federal Reserve Bank at Kansas City, and the Bureau of Land Management, U.S. Department of the Interior.

Chapter 11

EMERY N. CASTLE

Activity Analysis
In Water Planning*

A N EVALUATION of quantitative techniques can proceed in at least two directions. One approach would view the techniques largely as ends in themselves with only indirect reference to application. The main focus would be on forging new tools or adding interesting wrinkles to those that exist. The other would lead into areas of application with emphasis on possible usefulness in decision-making situations. This chapter takes the latter approach, although there are interesting and useful things to discover in the other direction.

In the traditional view a hierarchy is presupposed in which policy objectives establish the appropriate economic model which in turn indicates the most efficient quantitative technique. Yet there is reason to believe that this view is much oversimplified. There is danger that our economic models or our techniques of measurement in fact may specify ends or objectives without determination of the relevancy of these ends or objectives. Instead of society's having a list of clearly stated, consistent and operational policy objectives, there are individuals and groups within society that have objectives more or less clearly stated, often inconsistent and usually not oriented directly to our usual techniques of theory and measurement.

---

*Technical Paper 1653, Oreg. Agr. Exp. Sta.

In the case of water development and allocation, decisions are made at many levels of government as well as in the private sector of the economy. At each level of decision making, more than one objective usually exists. These objectives may be both economic and noneconomic in character. Of the economic objectives, economic efficiency is one, but only one. Other economic objectives may be greater equality of income distribution, economic growth of the nation or of a geographic area within the nation and/or stabilization of economic activity. Of these, the economist's framework for measuring economic efficiency[1] is probably more highly developed than for the others. Furthermore, most of his quantitative techniques have been designed to fit efficiency models. If the economist selects one objective — economic efficiency — and pursues it to its logical conclusion, he may not properly take into account other, but perhaps equally valid, objectives. Other objectives may be included, yet if the primary emphasis is on efficiency, other objectives may get "short suit" because of the way the problem is structured.

Numerous assumptions are implicit in the measurement of economic efficiency. The whole social order is usually assumed as given. For example, different distributions of income will yield different results in terms of economic efficiency. While it is legitimate to assume a given distribution of income and analyze the efficiency aspects of a project, the analyst is mistaken if he believes he has isolated a social optimum simply by determining if a project should be built on grounds of a restricted criterion which in turn is based on numerous implicit assumptions.[2] Even if the researcher recognizes this, the user of his research may not, unless what is usually implicit is made explicit. As quantitative techniques become more formal and complex it becomes increasingly difficult for the layman to understand the process by which answers are obtained. The criterion or choice indicator, which must be incorporated in the model if it is to function, should be clearly stated. The results which are obtained should also be related to the problem that gave rise to the investigation. Correct interpretation requires a rigorous statement of objectives, alternatives and restrictions. Yet the view taken in this chapter is that quantitative techniques have a contribution to make and that the effort needed for proper use is worthwhile.

The economist working in the water field may either be independent of or intimately associated with a particular interest group. If he is independent, he may be free to choose the objectives he believes are relevant or the ones his training and background suggest society "ought" to have and tailor his research accordingly. Such freedom entails both danger and responsibility. Sight may be lost of the fact that policy problems arise because of conflicts in objectives. Quantitative work aids in the resolution of policy conflicts by clarifying questions of fact. At the most general level of policy formulation the usefulness of such work may be limited. There is danger that the assumed ends of an investigation may be accepted as *the* policy ends and the results accepted as "solutions." This may be due to the apparent precision of the results or because the presuppositions, assumptions and rather complex procedures are not clearly understood.

SYSTEMS ANALYSIS

Quantitative work in the economics of water resources development is of many kinds. Considerable attention has been given to the use of systems analysis as an aid to planning. The problems treated have varied from a nationwide system for the ranking and selection of projects to the detailed treatment of a particular problem within a specific water development project. The principal quantitative tool in most of this work has been linear programming or activity analysis. The remainder of this chapter is an evaluation of this work with particular reference to the decision-making framework within which it must be applied.[3]

Macro-analysis of Water Resources Projects

Benefit-cost analysis has been used traditionally to test the economic feasibility of watershed structures. A budgeting type of procedure that permits the systematic organization of benefits and costs is used. Recent writings have placed increased emphasis on economic evaluation and more rigorous application of benefit-cost analysis has been attempted. Efforts have been made to standardize procedures and select a criterion that would permit a ranking of projects.[4] Attention has also been given to the establishment of a framework that would permit the productivity of investment in water resources projects to be compared with the productivity of investment in other public projects as well as in the private sector.[5]

In view of the discussion of the Steiner model elsewhere in this volume, only brief comment will be made here. The Steiner model is both interesting and imaginative. Its contribution, however, is not reduced by raising two points relative to the environment in which it might be used.

We may wonder whether the political environment in the foreseeable future is likely to be modified in such a way that the returns from all alternative public investments will be compared and evaluated as decisions are made. It is inappropriate in this chapter to enter into an extensive discussion of this point. However, the question must be raised if we are to form a judgment as to the eventual impact of such a model on the allocation of public funds in the water resources field.

Such an approach implicitly assumes a substantial role for economic efficiency. Should some measure of economic efficiency be used as a necessary condition for the building of a project or should it be both the necessary and the sufficient condition? Under the present system it is treated as a necessary condition. If it becomes a sufficient condition, a project would not be built unless it can be shown that it has no superior alternative on an efficiency basis. Projects have varying effects on national or area growth, income distribution and extramarket benefits. Unless and until all of the possible policy objectives can be integrated and weighted, it does not seem proper that the whole problem should be removed from the political arena.

Basin and Watershed Studies

The heart of many watershed and basin planning problems involves the simultaneous solution of a number of functional relationships. Examples of these variables are the possible capacities of a number of dam sites with different uses to which water can be put with each use having different seasonal water requirements. It is apparent that traditional budgeting procedures become quite laborious if all of the alternatives are to be considered. Systems analysis undoubtedly has potential in watershed or basin planning from the computational standpoint. It may also aid in conceptualizing problems as it makes the various relationships explicit. No theoretically complete system has existed by which all of the many variables involved in project planning can be related.

The most comprehensive treatment of this problem is to be found in a book authored by a Harvard University group interested in water resources.[6] This book is the result of several years of interdisciplinary work. These economists have applied their work to actual river basin problems and several action agencies have used such tools in planning. There appears to be little question that these techniques have considerable impact on river basin planning. A sufficient number of studies show that the method can be used and that fewer arbitrary assumptions need be made.[7]

To illustrate some of the problems and potentialities of systems analysis in watershed planning, an irrigation problem is analyzed in some detail.[8] Green Valley, typical of many of the intermountain valleys of the West, has more irrigable land than there is water for irrigation. The stream from which water is obtained is a typical snow-melt stream. Its peak runoff coincides with the snow-melt period (March-May). By June 1 normal stream flow is inadequate to provide a full irrigation supply unless supplemented by storage. By July 1 the stream flow is negligible.

The net acreage irrigated is 5,100 acres. Green Valley reservoir, with a usable capacity of 12,650 acre-feet, was built to store excess spring flows. The total water supply — stream flow and storage — is 18,000 acre-feet. Normally, with the cropping pattern and system and farm irrigation efficiencies prevailing, reservoir drawdown starts in June since the stream flow in June is limited on the average to about 4,183 acre-feet. After July 1 the entire irrigation supplement comes from storage.

The canal system from the reservoir to the irrigated land loses an average of 40 percent of the amount diverted. The farm irrigation efficiency is 45 percent, which gives an over-all irrigation efficiency figure of 27 percent (.60 x .45 = .27).

It is possible to make the following changes which might make more efficient use of the limited water supply.

1. Rehabilitate the canal system to provide 90 percent instead of the existing 60 percent efficiency.

2. Improve farm irrigation system efficiencies from 45 to 60 percent.

3. Maintain the present cropping pattern but increase the amount of water applied to each crop.

4. Change the cropping system to make a more profitable use of the limited water supply.

5. Any combination of the above.

The project limitations as determined by the Soil Conservation Service are:

1. Soil and topographic conditions require that land be in soil conserving crops (hay or pasture) 50 percent of the time.

2. 3,700 tons of alfalfa must be produced for winter feed.

3. Not over 510 acres of wheat may be grown because of acreage limitations.

4. No additional water is available.

5. Potato acreage cannot exceed one-fourth of the acreage in soil conserving crops.

The questions to be answered are:

1. Is the present water usage the most profitable, assuming the existing cropping pattern and irrigation system efficiencies?

2. Is the present cropping pattern optimum, given the existing efficiencies?

3. What benefits would be forthcoming from improvements in (a) the canal system and (b) farm irrigation efficiency?

Systems analysis can be used to answer these questions. The alternative crops (seven in this situation) can be treated as processes. Restrictions are water supply in May and June and after July 1, conservation requirements, acreage restrictions and hay requirements. Water requirements by months for each crop are necessary to construct the matrix. Additional processes are needed to permit stored water to be transferred from one period to another if that becomes necessary to maximize profits.

The interpretation of the results illustrates some of the problems associated with programming in that they bring out some of the basic assumptions relative to the decision-making situation. Income could be improved by 27 percent simply by applying more water per acre and leaving the cropping system unchanged. This would mean that some land would be left idle. With an optimum cropping pattern and with increased water application on a per-acre basis, income could be increased by about 93 percent. This means that considerable improvement could be made in income with existing irrigation efficiency. Why are these improvements not made? There are various economic and noneconomic reasons underlying the present pattern. Increasing water usage while preserving the existing cropping pattern would result in a reduction of acreage irrigated. Changing the cropping pattern and increasing water application would cause two drastic adjustments. Acreage would be reduced by about 12 percent. This might mean the acreage irrigated on some farms would decline severely. The other change would be in the direction of greater specialization in crop production. Farmers might believe that this specialization would be associated with greater income variability.

If an investment in the improvement of irrigation efficiency is being evaluated, can the assumption be made that farmers will use the increased supply of water more effectively? The results make it possible to compare points on the "high" level of management (Table 11.1). Moving to the "high" level of management involves the assumption of the perfect economic man. Should plans 3 and 4 be compared or should the prevailing level of technology be used in evaluating investment possibilities? The probable productivity of the investment would be somewhere between these two extremes. The investment undoubtedly would open up opportunities to the farmers; therefore, it is doubtful that the existing level of technology would be appropriate. It is also doubtful that optimum cropping combinations and optimum water application levels would be appropriate.

This brings into the open one of the fundamental problems associated with activity analysis. If we assume for a group of people an objective and then maximize this objective, is this a reasonable approximation of the way they will act? The evidence available indicates a substantial gap between predicted and actual performance. This suggests it is hazardous to evaluate investment opportunities which depend on individual action when the assumption is made that every decision-making unit within the group will perform "as if" they had complete information and were maximizing profits. Before widespread use is made of the technique, more attention to this problem appears appropriate.[9]

In the preceding examples the programming models are oriented to the efficiency criterion. Uses and structures are evaluated on the basis of their contribution to maximizing benefits over costs. To the extent that other objectives are important, they need to be specified before being built into formal programming models. There are two ways in which this might be done. One would be to change the choice indicator from net benefits to some other criterion. Another might be to build into the restrictions other objectives. For example, if a particular level of flood control is desired, independent of any economic efficiency criterion, it would be possible to specify the amount of needed storage and solve for the least-cost system of structures. Such techniques do not really get at the basic problem unless the other objectives can be quantified.

Table 11.1. Acreage Irrigated, Income and Value of Water for Various Use Plans

Use Plan[a]	Acreage Irrigated	Benefits	Value of Water per Acre-Foot[b]	Benefits as a Percentage of Use Plan 1	Efficiency
		(dollars)	(dollars)		
1	5,100	204,656	11.37	100	.27
2	4,851	261,127	14.51	127	.27
3	4,533	395,303	21.96	193	.27
4	6,799	454,990	25.28	222	.36
5	6,898	603,097	33.50	295	.405
6	9,248	808,498	44.92	395	.54

[a] The following use plans were evaluated:

1. Present use of water, existing cropping pattern and efficiency of 27 percent. (.60 x .45)
2. Full use of water (recommended rates), existing cropping pattern and efficiency of 27 percent. (.60 x .45)
3. Full use of water, optimum cropping pattern and efficiency of 27 percent. (.60 x .45)
4. Full use of water, optimum cropping pattern and efficiency of 36 percent. (.60 x .60)
5. Full use of water, optimum cropping pattern and efficiency of 40.5 percent. (.45 x .90)
6. Full use of water, optimum cropping pattern and efficiency of 54 percent. (.60 x .90)

[b] This is a gross value figure in that it is a return to the limiting factors.

As the geographic area in question becomes larger it becomes increasingly difficult to incorporate objectives other than economic efficiency. If a river basin were to be planned using a simultaneous technique such as the one described, growth and income characteristics would appear quite important, given the objectives of various special interest groups. Regional input-output models may be a more appropriate analytical device here than linear programming based entirely on efficiency criteria. By "more appropriate" it is meant that this technique might bring out more of the variables that are relevant from the political point of view. Regional input-output models might predict the effect of different allocations of water on payrolls, retail sales, population and the tax base. Even when benefit-cost analysis is used to test for economic feasibility from a national point of view, local objectives may not be consistent with national objectives and different analytical techniques may be needed.

This becomes even more important when local cost sharing is involved. It does not appear the analytical problem would be any more difficult than for benefit-cost analysis, but the data collection problem would be substantial. The construction of realistic models would involve a considerable number of interindustry studies, but perhaps the chief obstacle is of an institutional nature. Geographical areas are not necessarily decision-making units. Instead, there are various groups within a geographical area which are interested in specific ends.

Support and acceptance of such comprehensive investigations may not be forthcoming when there is no single agency or group that has a comprehensive viewpoint.

An additional limitation of activity analysis must be noted with reference to river basin or watershed planning. This relates to the absence of multiple-purpose planning agencies in the federal branch of government. The various agencies have particular purposes for which they have been given responsibility in the law. In numerous instances this lack of comprehensive planning failed to take account of all relevant alternatives. An analyst faces the alternative either of adopting the viewpoint of a particular agency and working within this framework or taking a comprehensive viewpoint and running the risk of having little impact in view of the political environment. The development and use of inter-agency river basin study committees has attempted a partial answer to this problem. It is doubtful, however, that such groups really will be sufficiently well coordinated to consider all possible alternatives. For example, it has been difficult to convince agencies they should insist on nonstructural alternatives as floodplain zoning when it is the most economic alternative.

Planning at the State Level

States must not be overlooked as decision-making units in water use. Although traditionally dependent on the federal government for development funds, states do a great deal in influencing the direction of development. They decide on the allocation of unappropriated water and establish the rules by which disputes over appropriated water are settled.[10]

Many states have over-all planning authorities that are under instructions from the legislature to consider multiple use of water resources. To the extent these bodies really do this, they take a more comprehensive viewpoint than many federal action agencies. For example, in some respects the Oregon Water Resources Board has taken a more comprehensive view of the Middle Snake than any other single group. On the other hand, state governments are generally interested in the development of the resources of their state. They may pursue policies designed to maximize the flow of federal dollars into development of resources in the state. Because this must be done by working through the federal government agencies, economic efficiency may not have the highest priority.

For those states that use prior appropriation with beneficial use as their system of water law, quantitative analysis oriented toward efficiency criteria may have application. A need arises for precise definition and measurement of beneficial use under two circumstances. In the case of unappropriated water, state authorities may have to choose among two or more uses. If water shortages develop, rationing all uses or a choice among uses may be necessary. There is some evidence that greater emphasis is being placed on beneficial uses relative to prior rights,[11] although Hutchins[12] has indicated that prior rights have tended to be impregnable despite statutory and legislative declarations that one use shall be preferred to another in times of shortages. Generally speaking, prior rights have been protected either absolutely or by payment of compensation. Even if compensation is paid, definition and measurement are still needed relative to use preferences in time of shortages. The legal meaning of beneficial use is closely related to the economic concept of opportunity cost. "Highest and best" use can be defined in economic terms, with a possible exception in the case of recreation.

Activity analysis may have value in defining and measuring beneficial use. Water may be entered in a programming model as a restriction. Uses or users may be entered as processes. Such a procedure will result in water being allocated to its most economic use, given the assumptions of the model. Perhaps the more significant result is the value which is placed on the limiting factors in the process of solving the allocation problem. These "marginal values" are not identical with the marginal values of traditional economic theory because of the assumptions of the programming model. They represent what an entrepreneur would pay for one more unit of the limiting factor.[13] As a result, these marginal values for a particular use may be taken to represent the opportunity cost of the water if it is diverted to another use.

Examples of water law questions that these marginal value estimates can be expected to help resolve are:

1. In the event of a water shortage, what would be the effect of reducing the use of water by all appropriators, regardless of prior right, by an equal amount as contrasted to discontinuing junior rights in favor of senior rights? A within-use study on the adjustment of firms to varying quantities of water would measure the relative marginal productivities. Such an analysis may also be used to recommend adjustment of water users to varying water supplies. Whether the studies should be made on a within- or between-use basis would depend on the problem at hand.

2. In the case of unappropriated water the marginal values might be helpful in deciding which of two uses, equal in time, should have priority.

3. In the case of unappropriated water, a user, representing a low value productivity, may make application for a right. Users representing the "higher" use may not be on the scene for one reason or another. A state agency then faces the problem of whether to reserve water for the higher use in the expectation that water will be filed for at a later date or to grant the right to the lower use. If the magnitude of the difference of the two uses is known, it is possible to estimate the amount of time that would need to elapse for the lower appropriator to recover his investment. If the decision maker believed that this is likely to be the case, the right could be granted with the expectation that compensation could be paid later and the right transferred to another use. If it

were considered likely that application for the higher right would be made before this much time had passed, the right could be denied or granted subject to withdrawal.

The preceding discussion suggests that a degree of quantitative precision should be introduced into groundwater doctrine that thus far has been lacking. It also suggests rather heavy reliance on economic efficiency as a criterion, although the law historically has placed considerable emphasis on equity. Equity and efficiency are not necessarily in conflict if compensation is made a necessary condition for the transference of water rights. Transferring a water right to a higher economic use should provide a return sufficient to compensate the one who is currently putting water to a lower economic use. It is doubtful that such quantitative work will ever serve as an exact blueprint for decision makers. Much more than static economic efficiency is involved. But when a decision is to be made such work does provide a systematic method of relating relevant variables and may permit a more accurate appraisal of the existing situation.

RECREATION

If benefit-cost and systems analyses are to have general application, methods of bringing extramarket goods into the analysis must be found. Flood control is, in general, an extramarket good; but it is common practice to assign benefits and costs to flood control. Examples of extramarket goods that are not routinely valued are recreation and pollution control. However, instructions to operating agencies direct them to assign values to these extramarket goods whenever possible.[14] Even so, the methodology for doing this is not well accepted. It is appropriate, therefore, to comment on this problem.

Some people argue that recreational benefits are so intangible that it is impossible to assign an economic value to recreation. Yet, in fact, if it is decided that public investment is required to meet the crisis in outdoor recreation, the judgment is made that the benefits (market or nonmarket) exceed the costs.[15] These benefits may not be so intangible as they first appear and can be brought within the framework of benefit-cost analysis.

When the necessity of quantifying is cited as a weakness of benefit-cost analysis, two types of benefits and costs are usually referred to: "intangible" and "indirect" or "secondary." The evaluation problems posed by these two types are theoretically intriguing and of considerable practical significance. Next to that of cost-allocation, they are also the most controversial problems of benefit-cost analysis among students and government agencies.[16]

Outdoor enthusiasts may deny that money can really measure the satisfaction from observing the unspoiled beauty of a unique natural area. But consider the satisfaction that comes to some as they listen to an outstanding singer or watch a star basketball or baseball player. No one knows the "consumer surplus" from such an experience, but

price does serve as a rationing device in many instances. This means
the individual consumer "measured" the value of the experience when
he decided to allocate his budget among competing uses. This is not to
argue against public subsidy of either outdoor or indoor recreation but
to point to the fact that the price system does "value" many kinds of
recreation.[17]

Sufficient analytical work has been done to encourage empirical
work on the problem.[18] Such work would indicate more precisely the
problems of measuring relevant variables; it would permit the answers
obtained to be subjected to the test of reasonableness; and it would undoubtedly result in an improvement in the theoretical formulations.
The empirical work that has received the greatest attention has been
concerned mainly with the impact of recreation on a local area or region rather than an attempt to measure primary benefits. Yet the measurement of primary benefits is necessary if recreation is to be put on
equal footing with other water uses in project evaluation.

There may be good reason for this state of affairs. Utilizing gross
expenditure data permits a more impressive picture of the importance
of recreation. It also avoids attempting to value something of such a
subjective nature as the recreation experience – a bothersome problem
to many. Yet it is doubtful that this attitude can be maintained very
long in view of the great demands being placed on public agencies which
influence water usage by recreationists. Searching questions are being
asked and they deserve appropriate answers.

Transfer Costs

The analytical work done thus far centers around an examination of
expenditures made in order to enjoy a recreational facility. Clawson[19]
believes that such data can be used to isolate a demand function. The
assumption is made that "cost per visit" as a function of distance from
the recreational facility serves the same rationing purpose as does
price. We encounter here expenditures which have not received extensive treatment in economics. This group of expenditures might be classified as transfer costs.[20] Transfer costs are those that must be borne
either by the buyer or the seller when goods are exchanged but which
are not normally included in the price. Under most situations, of
course, they are borne by the buyer or they will be included in the
price. Examples of transfer costs are transportation to or from a
market or the installation cost of a piece of equipment when such costs
are not included in the price.

It is possible that a careful analysis of transfer costs, as Clawson
has indicated, will throw considerable light on the demand for recreation. Clawson has assumed that the only difference among "consumers"
of national park facilities is the distance they must travel. It is probable that a somewhat more sophisticated analysis would be fruitful. As
distance increases it seems likely that the possibility of substitution
would also increase. Variables permitting substitution effects to be

taken into account may be needed for a satisfactory analysis. In any case, careful analysis of the role of transfer costs in valuing recreation may be of considerable value.

It appears that when transfer costs are borne by the buyer they should be analyzed on the demand side of the market as Clawson has done. James H. Crutchfield[21] has argued that if a demand curve can be isolated on the basis of transfer costs the facility might be valued at that price which, if a price were charged, would maximize revenue. Still another possibility is to view the user of the recreational facility as being both the "supplying" as well as the "demanding" unit. In this case transfer costs might be viewed as rising as additional users make use of the facility. At that point where the marginal transfer cost equals the marginal utility of the recreational experience, an equilibrium is reached. If such an approach were to be used, simultaneous equations would be needed for a solution. Variables such as leisure time, alternative recreational possibilities and income would need to be entered on the "demand" side. In any case, the outlook that recreation will be brought within the framework of benefit-cost analysis is promising.

Other work of a rather fundamental nature would be the substitution possibilities between indoor and outdoor recreation as well as among types of outdoor recreation. As outdoor recreational sites become relatively more scarce and expensive, the extent to which substitution can take place acquires relevance. A related question pertains to the limited use of wilderness or near-wilderness areas as contrasted to the intensive use of such areas if developed into park-type facilities and with access provided for the general public. Such a question necessarily involves interpersonal utility comparisons, but insight will be gained if monetary estimates can be placed on the primary benefits of recreation. Quantitative work on the economics of recreation will not be simple nor can the results be accepted as being absolutely accurate. Yet neither simplicity nor absolute accuracy characterizes the determination of flood control, navigation or irrigation benefits. Until the benefits from recreation can be valued in monetary terms, evaluation techniques will lack completeness and quantitative methods cannot make their full contribution to multiple-purpose planning.

IMPLICATIONS AND EVALUATION

The purpose of this chapter has been to explore possible application of a particular quantitative technique in the evaluation of water resources development at various levels of decision making. It has been argued that economic evaluation, as commonly practiced, mainly involves the measurement of economic efficiency, even though there may be other economic and noneconomic objectives in the investment of public funds in water resources development.

At lower levels in the decision-making process formal quantitative techniques may have greater application. To be sure, objectives other than efficiency are present here also, but it may be possible to build these into the formal analysis in the form of restrictions. Even so, the lack of a multiple-purpose viewpoint on the part of decision-making units makes planning difficult when multiple purposes should be considered as alternatives. Given the political realities, the efficiency framework may not be appropriate.

At the state level, the efficiency framework with accompanying quantitative techniques may have considerable usefulness. Two studies were cited that have had an impact on decision making. Even here, a major objective may be to maximize the growth of a particular geographic region.

The conclusion is reached that formal quantitative techniques are in no sense a panacea that will remove from the political arena large areas of controversy and place technicians in control. It is doubtful if those who exercise political power would relinquish it readily. Technicians have not yet learned how to incorporate into their analysis all of the legitimate objectives of society, both economic and noneconomic. Too, the existing institutional structure is responsive to a considerable degree to changing forces in our society. [22] This institutional structure does take into account various economic and noneconomic objectives. Even so, work of the nature suggested in this chapter should be encouraged for at least three reasons.

1. There are numerous problems where objectives other than economic efficiency are not particularly important. It is possible that activity analysis can lead to improvement over traditional planning procedures.

2. On a more mundane level, more systematic evaluation procedures should lead to an improvement in data. Since the data must be collected and organized prior to evaluation, the newer techniques vividly highlight any inadequacies which exist. Because the funds for data collection are also dependent upon political processes, it may be that this is a rather dim hope. However, data which are collected may be more relevant and pertain to more alternatives than would be the case if traditional procedures continue to be used. In the short run the interest in formal maximizing or minimizing models may have directed researchers' attention away from data collection with the result that workers have become temporarily oriented to technique rather than to data or to problems. It has now become apparent even to these people that the difficulties in obtaining adequate data are indeed formidable and deserve real attention.

3. Another benefit from the application of such procedures is more idealistic in nature. Marshall has said that if congressmen wish to build pyramids in Nevada, they are not necessarily irrational if they know all of the costs, both of a direct and of an opportunity nature. [23] If studies can show the loss in efficiency resulting from existing political arrangements, presumably citizens can decide if they wish to pay this cost. This is not to deny the importance of other objectives but simply holds that if the efficiency aspects are known, a better evaluation of the

other objectives is permitted. The main danger here is not that the analysis is partial in the sense that only efficiency is included, but that other values creep in without being recognized. If it can be shown in a number of watersheds or basins that incomplete planning leads to inefficient utilization and either under- or overdevelopment, this should provide some basis for more rational decisions regarding the appropriate political structure.

FOOTNOTES

[1] Efficiency is used here in the economic sense. It is recognized that the term has different meanings in other fields.

[2] Gunnar Myrdal, The Political Element in the Development of Economic Theory, Harvard University Press, Cambridge, Mass., 1954.

[3] The linear programming technique is well developed in: R. Dorfman, P. Samuelson and R. Solow, Linear Programming and Economic Analysis, McGraw-Hill, 1958; also E. O. Heady and W. Candler, Linear Programming Methods, Iowa State University Press, Ames, 1958.

[4] Foremost among such works are: Otto Eckstein, Water Resources Development, Harvard University Press, Cambridge, Mass., 1958. J. Krutilla and Otto Eckstein, Multiple Purpose River Development, John Hopkins University Press, Baltimore, 1958. R. N. McKean, Efficiency in Government through Systems Analysis, Wiley, 1958.
For a discussion of some fundamental questions raised by these publications see: S. V. Ciriacy-Wantrup, "Philosophy and objectives of watershed development," Land Econ., Vol. 35, No. 3, 1959; G. S. Tolley and F. E. Riggs, Economics of Watershed Planning, Iowa State University Press, Ames, 1961, pp. 1-12.

[5] Peter O. Steiner, Chap. 4 of this volume. For a discussion of the Steiner model see M. M. Kelso, Chap. 5 of this volume.

[6] Arthur Maass, et al., Design of Water-Resource Systems, Harvard University Press, Cambridge, Mass., 1962.

[7] E. N. Castle, "Programming watershed structures," Economics of Watershed Planning, op. cit., Chap. 12.

[8] E. N. Castle, "Evaluating investment in supplemental irrigation," Jour. Soil and Water Conservation, Vol. 17, No. 3, 1962.

[9] For an interesting example of the use of activity analysis on a similar problem see George H. Pavelis and John F. Timmons, "Programming small watershed development," Jour. Farm Econ., Vol. 42, No. 2, 1960.

[10] Some states do not depend entirely on the federal government for public investment. California is an example of a state that is making a tremendous investment of its own funds in water resources development.

[11] Douglas Strong, "Profitable farm adjustments to limited water supplies through increased irrigation efficiency of water use," Rept. No. 8, Proceedings of the Committee on Economics of Water Resources Development, 1960, pp. 141-52.

[12] Wells A. Hutchins, "The concept of reasonable beneficial use in the development of ground water law in the West," Rept. No. 5, Proceedings of the Committee on Economics of Water Resources Development, 1956, pp. 1-20. (Chap. 17 of this volume.)

[13] For examples of studies where these marginal productivity values have been determined for within-use situations, see Strong, op. cit.; E. N. Castle and Karl Lindeborg, "The economics of ground water allocation: a case study," Jour. Farm Econ., Vol. 42, No. 1, 1960.

[14] "Policies, standards, and procedures in the formulation, evaluation and review of plans for use and development of water and related resources," Senate Document 97, 87th Cong., 2nd Sess.

[15] Marion Clawson, The Crisis in Outdoor Recreation, Reprint No. 13, Resources for the Future, Inc., 1959.

[16] S. V. Ciriacy-Wantrup, "The role of benefit-cost analysis in public resource development," Rept. No. 3, Committee on the Economics of Water Resources Development, Dec. 1954. (Chap. 2 of this volume.)

[17] Marion Clawson, "Methods of measuring the demand for and value of outdoor recreation," Reprint No. 10, Resources for the Future, Inc., 1959, p. 3.

[18] Andrew H. Trice and Samuel E. Wood, "Measurement of recreation benefits," *Land Econ.*, Vol. 34, No. 3, 1958. "The economics of public recreation," Land and Recreational Planning Division, National Park Service, Washington, D. C.

[19] Clawson, see footnote 17.

[20] Clifford Hildreth has called this to my attention. I am indebted to both Dr. Hildreth and W. G. Brown for the material in this section.

[21] James A. Crutchfield, "Valuation of a fishery resource," *Land Econ.*, Vol. 38, No. 2, 1962, pp. 145-54.

[22] Stephen Smith, Chap. 20 of this volume.

[23] Chap. 22 of this volume.

PART III

Financial Responsibility

S. V. CIRIACY-WANTRUP is Professor of Agricultural Economics at the University of California, Berkeley. His significant contributions to the field of natural resource economics have earned him a national and international reputation.

Chapter 12

S. V. CIRIACY-WANTRUP

Cost Allocation
in Relation to
Western Water Policies *

COST ALLOCATION in the sense of apportioning joint costs of multiple-purpose projects to individual products (purposes) has been of considerable significance for western water policies.[1] It will become of even greater significance in the future: an increasing proportion of water resources development is taking place in the form of large, public, multiple-purpose projects. There has been an intimate connection between cost allocation and several basic and vital policy issues. These issues will be called here "economic feasibility," "repayment," "rate making," "yardstick" and "form of contract." It appears fitting that the spotlight of economic analysis be thrown on these issues.

Focusing on the connection between these issues and cost allocation entails some unavoidable sacrifices. These should be made clear at the outset in order not to arouse in the reader expectations which cannot be fulfilled.

First, not *all* important aspects of the above policy issues can be

*An earlier version of this chapter was presented before the Committee on the Economics of Water Resources Development, March 2-3, 1953, Berkeley, Calif., under the title "Economic analysis of water resources policies." The present version was published as Giannini Foundation Paper No. 136 in the *Jour. Farm Econ.*, Vol. 36, No. 1, 1954, pp. 108-29.

considered here. For example, the issue of "economic feasibility" has
several crucial aspects — such as the definition and quantitative determination of so-called "secondary" or "indirect" benefits and costs —
which have no necessary connection with cost allocation. These other
aspects are analyzed in some detail in a paper republished as Chapter 2
of this book.[2]

A second sacrifice follows from the first. Since we cannot possibly
analyze all important aspects of the issues mentioned, we cannot attempt
to devise a detailed blueprint which would provide precise substitute
procedures for those which are in use by public agencies operating in
this field. For example, concerning the policy issue of "repayment,"
detailed proposals as to how payments under various conditions may be
computed, assessed and collected are beyond the scope of this study.
However, we can clearly indicate the connection between repayment and
cost allocation and draw conclusions with respect to certain broad but
important changes in present procedures.

Third, the connection of cost allocation with water policies touches
upon some knotty problems of economic theory. This is not a chapter
on the economic theory of joint production but an economic analysis of
policy issues closely related to each other through their connection with
cost allocation in procedures in use. It is unavoidable, therefore, that
some conclusions based on the economic theory of joint production are
supported by references to other publications which supplement this
analysis. Otherwise the focus would be blurred.

EXPERIENCE WITH COST ALLOCATION

The problems of cost allocation have been discussed in numerous
committees and commissions. There is a voluminous literature on the
subject written by engineers, lawyers, accountants and economists.
After lengthy arguments — sometimes reminiscent of medieval dialec-
tics on ecclesiastical dogma — the conclusion invariably is reached that
cost allocation must be more or less arbitrary.

As a consequence, total joint costs of a multiple-purpose project
are allocated among the various products in such a way as to afford an
acceptable compromise of the divergent interests of federal, state and
local governments and of municipal and private users of water, power,
navigation, recreation (including fish and waterfowl) and other products.[3]
Because of the connection between cost allocation and the important
policy issues mentioned, these divergent interests are strong and sensitive. Reference is always made to existing laws, precedents, engineering data and economic concepts. The initiated, however, will probably agree that "rationalization" is not too strong a word for the kind of
economic reasoning used to justify cost allocations recommended to
Congress or other bodies which make the final decisions on authorization and appropriation.

It may be submitted that this state of affairs will not change until those who analyze, recommend and authorize projects clearly recognized the problems of economic feasibility, repayment, rate making, yardstick and form of contract as quite different economic issues. They require different approaches and different sets of tools for their solution. These approaches and tools, in turn, have little relation to past and present practices of cost allocation.

After stating the main theme in these negative terms, let us see what can be said positively to clarify the issues of economic feasibility, repayment, rate making, yardstick and form of contract without falling into the semantic traps of cost allocation.

COST ALLOCATION AND ECONOMIC FEASIBILITY

Determination of economic feasibility in federal multiple-purpose projects is connected with cost allocation through statute — for example, through the important sections 9 (a) and 9 (b) of the Reclamation Act of 1939.[4] Statutes differentiate between reimbursable and nonreimbursable costs and stipulate different proportions between these two kinds of costs for different purposes, such as irrigation, power, municipal water, navigation and flood control.

As interpreted by the most important public agency operating in this field, there are two standards for determining economic feasibility. Both standards must be met by a project. They may be stated in the words of Commissioner Michael W. Straus in his testimony before Congress:[5]

The first, required by reclamation law, consists of an allocation of project costs among the purposes served and a showing that the anticipated project revenues will return all reimbursable costs. The second, although not required by reclamation law, is the showing of estimated benefits and costs, and is made as a matter of Bureau policy. Thus, a reclamation project must meet two standards of economic feasibility: The estimated benefits must exceed the estimated costs and the anticipated project revenues must provide for return of all reimbursable costs.

The first standard mentioned by Commissioner Straus is a standard for the possibility of repayment under the requirements of relevant laws. Sometimes this standard is referred to as "financial feasibility." In the statutory sense it is a necessary condition for feasibility. In the economic sense it is neither a necessary nor a sufficient condition for feasibility because, in multiple-purpose projects reimbursable costs include only a portion of total costs and project revenues only a portion of total benefits. Moreover, which portion of costs is designated as reimbursable and which portion of benefits has to be repaid as project revenues are not determined on the basis of a functional relation between costs and benefits.

The second standard does not involve cost allocation. It is a necessary condition for economic feasibility, provided that benefits and costs are properly evaluated.[6] It is a sufficient condition for economic feasibility under three restrictive assumptions: (1) that the benefit-cost ratio of the project considered cannot be improved further, (2) that there are no alternative projects with a higher benefit-cost ratio on which available public funds could be spent and (3) that it is desirable to make public funds available.

In order to determine economic feasibility — that is, to make a recommendation on economic grounds whether a public project should be undertaken and when — one must ascertain in the planning stage the optimum proportion of products for various time intervals and the optimum quantities of products at that proportion. In more technical language, we want to determine the direction and the length of an optimum product vector extending over time. In order to avoid a term that has been little used by economists, this vector will be called the "optimum product combination."

Neither the proportion of different products yielded by a multiple-purpose project nor the quantities of these products at given proportions are fixed and constant over time on the basis of engineering or other technological data. For example, the Central Valley Project in California can be planned, constructed and managed to yield water, power and flood control — to mention only the three most important products — in various proportions and in various quantities for each proportion. Construction can be delayed or speeded up, and the yield of products can be varied over time. Decisions in this sphere do not merely concern the consumers of these products but also affect deeply the relations between federal, state and local governments.

In focusing on these decisions, three broader aspects of economic feasibility already mentioned are left out of consideration. This omission happens to be in accord with the political realities which determine authorization and appropriation. These aspects are the following — in increasing order of broadness.

First, there is the question whether a similar product combination could not be obtained more economically by alternative projects in different geographic locations — for example, by supplemental irrigation, drainage, clearing and fertilizing projects in the humid portions of the United States.[7]

Second, there is the question whether alternative public projects with an entirely different product combination may not be preferable. For instance, public investment in the conservation of natural resources may compete with public investment in slum clearance, schools, hospitals and the like.

Third, there is the question to what extent funds should be withdrawn from the private sector of the economy and invested in public projects. An answer to this question depends on the type of project and on the phase of economic fluctuations; beyond that, problems of taxation, public credit and the effectiveness of the whole system of private enterprise need to be considered.[8] To some extent the answer to this question can be arrived at through appropriate practices in evaluating benefits and costs. This is not possible with the first two questions.

Economic analysis can make a contribution in clarifying these three aspects of economic feasibility. But joint-cost allocation is not immediately involved.

It is not necessary to treat the economic theory of joint production in detail at this time.[9] Cost allocation in the sense of obtaining the total costs of a project first and then apportioning them to individual products is meaningless for obtaining the optimum product combination. The approach is different. The optimum product combination yields the total costs, which need not be allocated for determining economic feasibility. What is needed are the marginal benefits and costs of various products in the sense of partial derivatives of total benefit-and-cost functions. The independent variables of these functions are the rates of production of various purposes planned for various time intervals.

Theoretically such partial derivatives can be determined. This possibility, however, has little practical relevance. In actuality, approximations must be used. It is practical to calculate the present value of the expected flow of total benefits and costs from a small number of alternative (dated) product combinations. For each of these alternatives, in turn, benefits and costs may be calculated for various assumptions with respect to evaluation — for example, for various interest rates and prices of products and cost factors. Superior product combinations can be selected on the basis of benefit-cost ratios.

Usually, economic feasibility of only one product combination constant over time and based on only one set of assumptions with respect to interest and prices is calculated and submitted to Congress. By the time the political decision about construction is made, prices (including interest) may have changed, e.g., in the course of economic fluctuations. Mistakes can be reduced if the submitting agency has thoroughly considered alternative product combinations and price assumptions and if the decision-making political body has a clear idea of what such changes mean in terms of benefits and costs.

State and local governments, universities and private groups of potential beneficiaries should participate in — or at least should have an opportunity to scrutinize — the determination of the optimum product combination. The Columbia Basin Joint Investigations and the Central Valley Project Studies have pointed the way. However, these studies were started too late and were not concerned with *ex ante* economic feasibility. Such studies should be completed *before* a project is recommended. Differing opinions of state and local governments and of potential beneficiaries, together with appropriate material to substantiate such opinions, should be submitted to Congress with the report of the agency responsible for recommending.[10]

In determining economic feasibility no consideration should be given to direct and indirect subsidies. Such subsidies are given — for example in the form of interest-free funds to individual purposes (irrigation). If comparison is made between taxed and tax-free value flows, an appropriate correction for this difference becomes necessary. Likewise, no consideration should be given in determining economic feasibility to whether costs are reimbursable or nonreimbursable. The extent to which subsidies and tax exemptions are granted and costs are regarded as reimbursable creates important policy decisions for determining repayment but not for determining economic feasibility (see section on Cost Allocation and Repayment on following pages).

More Liberal Standards of Feasibility?

As noted, determination of economic feasibility must be understood as a critical appraisal of whether a project should be undertaken at all, when, and with what product combination. The objective of such determination is *not* to find an economic justification for a project which appears desirable to an agency or to a pressure group. There is a tendency to focus on such a justification and on attempts to liberalize standards for appraisal. These attempts are not helpful in eliminating existing weaknesses of benefit-cost analysis.

Besides constituting a retrogression in analytical method, these attempts have undesirable practical effects. Usually, water development for municipal and industrial uses and for power has high benefit-cost ratios as compared with irrigation use. Attempts to liberalize standards of economic and financial feasibility are concerned with irrigation use. Thus if competitive relations exist between municipal and industrial uses and power on one side and irrigation use on the other, liberalization of feasibility standards leads to a change in the optimum product combination to the disadvantage of the former. In other words, multiple-purpose projects in which irrigation is the dominant use of water will be undertaken in preference to those in which municipal and industrial uses of water are more significant. From the standpoint of *future* water needs, such a development is especially questionable. In most western states, water needs for municipal and industrial uses are increasing rapidly.

The most extreme attempt to liberalize standards of economic and financial feasibility is the suggestion to replace economic analysis simply by objectives imputed to the reclamation laws; namely, "to settle the arid lands of the West and further the economic development of the nation." [11] It is claimed for these objectives that "the policy implications are clear." [12]

Even if one accepts these objectives, should no priority be given to economically feasible projects? In many parts of the West, projects and purposes compete not merely for public funds but, more importantly, for scarce water resources. The dispute over the water of the Colorado River is an outstanding example. Granted that such disputes are finally decided in the political arena — that is, in this case, through court decisions, compacts and treaties — is it in the public interest to eliminate costs in the consideration of benefits? Can economic evaluation be discarded as a tool for taking into account the welfare of *all* groups and regions? Can the decision about what priorities and what product combinations are to be recommended to Congress be left entirely to subjective judgment? Or do those who use the above argument contend that there are no economically feasible projects in western water resources development and that there is no objective basis for making selections between alternative product combinations?

COST ALLOCATION AND REPAYMENT

Let us turn to the problems of repayment. Recommendations of multiple-purpose projects and studies like those mentioned for the Columbia Basin and the Central Valley have given a great deal of attention to cost allocation in connection with repayment. Statutes, executive orders and traditions have made the allocation of total construction costs to various project purposes the basis of repayment. According to these same social institutions, costs allocated to some purposes need not be repaid at all; some purposes need not pay the interest portion; other purposes must repay all costs allocated to them including interest; for still other purposes, allocated costs include costs which other purposes cannot repay. [13]

This institutional situation would lead to strong and sensitive interest in cost allocation even if no connection between repayment and rate making existed. Beneficiaries who must repay allocated costs are interested that the largest possible proportion of total costs is allocated to purposes the cost of which need not be repaid. Navigation, flood control, recreation (wildlife) and national defense, for example, are often burdened with higher cost allocations than are warranted by their relation to costs and to benefits received. Generally, the Department of the Interior has been in favor of such shifting of cost allocations while the Corps of Army Engineers and the Federal Power Commission have been more conservative. [14]

Among beneficiaries, such shifting of cost allocations is favored mainly by users of water and power. Cost allocations to water and to power, on the other hand, are influenced by a more complex grouping of interests. Frequently, irrigation interests are in favor of high cost allocations to municipal water and to power. With respect to cost allocations to power, this tendency is supported by private power interests because of the connection between cost allocation and rate making. This connection will be discussed presently.

If irrigation is based to a considerable extent on groundwater and, therefore, on electric power, pressures exercised by beneficiaries become even more complex. The positions taken in these matters by California farm organizations and the political alliances formed are interesting for the student of western water policies.

To summarize: Cost allocation for purposes of repayment has been a much broader institutional problem than the term would seem to indicate. From the standpoint of future water policy it would be desirable to recognize this situation frankly and to separate problems of repayment entirely from any reference to construction costs and their allocation. What, then, could be the basis for repayment?

It appears economically justified and politically equitable that beneficiaries from public resource development pay for the benefits received
— provided such benefits are practically assessable and provided that
enough incentive is left for beneficiaries to participate in resource development. Payments under these provisions are the best guarantee
that the determination of economic feasibility will receive the most
thorough scrutiny by state and local governments and by private groups
of beneficiaries. As suggested previously, such scrutiny appears necessary if all aspects of economic feasibility are to be considered in the
planning stage.

For some projects the principle just suggested — that assessable
benefits and not costs are to be repaid — may mean that more is paid
by beneficiaries than the total costs of a project. For other projects
the principle may mean that only a small portion of total costs is repaid. For still other projects it may mean that payments are about
equal to total costs. Payments may go to a reclamation fund or, preferably, to the general treasury fund.

It may be noted that the principle suggested here is not identical
with the various "benefit methods" used in cost allocation.[15] The principle has broader implications. It does not solve *all* problems of "speculation" and of "unearned" increments of income and capital caused by
public projects. But it goes far enough in this direction to offer a more
effective and economically more acceptable alternative to policies designed to reduce speculation and unearned increments — for example
the so-called "160-acre limitation."[16] This is especially true if the
water furnished by public projects is supplemental to other waters in already developed irrigation areas, as in the Central Valley of California.

As a matter of public policy it may be desirable not to assess certain benefits even if it is practical to do so. Recreational benefits may
fall into this class. Some benefits are not practically assessable to
natural or legal persons. Benefits to national defense are an example.

As a corollary of this policy it may become an important part of
federal policy to induce state, local and private agencies to plan and
build their projects with full consideration of benefits to recreation and
national defense. Various forms of "inducements" appear practical and
have been used in other connections.[17] Besides making repayments for
such benefits, the federal government may stipulate consideration of
such benefits when the use of federal waters and land is involved. Under some conditions tax incentives may also be used.

One important point regarding repayment needs to be mentioned at
this time, although a more detailed discussion must be deferred until
later: The assessment of benefits for repayment should not determine
unit prices of products sold — that is, for example, water and power
rates. On the other hand, assessment for repayment is usually dependent on such prices. The form of repayment may be directly connected
with such prices (power and water revenues) or may be made in the
form of various types of taxes and fees. Not only power and water users
but as many other beneficiaries as can practically be assessed should
participate in payments.

Evaluation for determining repayment is not necessarily identical with evaluation for determining economic feasibility. To illustrate, some localized benefits which may be assessed for repayment may be offset in the determination of economic feasibility by costs elsewhere in the economy. On the other hand, as already mentioned, in the determination of repayment some benefits — for example to recreation (wildlife) and national defense — which are important in the determination of economic feasibility may not be assessed for reasons of policy or practical expediency.

Determination of economic feasibility is strictly *ex ante*. Determination of repayment is partly *ex post*. That means repayment is subject to revision if actual benefits should prove different from expected ones. However, repayment is facilitated if methods of assessment, form of repayment and expected quantities and values (rates, taxes, fees) are clear to all parties concerned at the time when economic feasibility is determined. For instance, beneficiaries of power can enter into purchase agreements with the federal government with the understanding that rates will be set according to principles discussed in the next section. If payments are to be made by beneficiaries in the form of taxes and fees to local and state governments, agreements on methods of assessment can be formulated.

Such an early arrangement for repayment has two advantages: first, the determination of economic feasibility will be taken seriously by all parties concerned; and second, less difficulty will arise in disposing of products and in repayment after the commitment for the project has already been made. Such difficulty has arisen in the Central Valley Project. In other words the federal government — and the taxpayers — will not be left holding the bag.

COST ALLOCATION AND RATE MAKING

As suggested in the beginning, determination of water and power rates is an economic issue quite different from that of repayment. Problems involved in the determination of water and power rates may be considered next.

Cost allocation is directly connected with rate making in the Bonneville Project Act of 1937.[18] In other legislation the connection between cost allocation and rate making is indirect but nevertheless effective. Two factors are mainly responsible. First, net revenues obtained from the sale of water and power are by far the most important — and thus far usually have been the only — financial source of repayment. Second, in view of the statutory differentiation between reimbursable and nonreimbursable costs, all reports on public multiple-purpose projects contain implications or direct suggestions about rates "necessary" to support cost allocations to water and power or to make these purposes "self supporting."

This connection between cost allocation and rate making is recognized by all federal departments involved.

General Lewis A. Pick, Chief of Army Engineers, stated in his testimony before Congress:[19]

Rates for sale of this power [that is, power produced by projects built by Army Engineers] are established by the marketing agency upon approval by the Federal Power Commission, and according to the law should return the cost of producing the power. Power rates are thus affected by the cost allocations made by the Corps of Engineers.

Secretary of Agriculture Charles F. Brannan stated before the same congressional committee:[20]

The allocation of costs of multiple-purpose reservoir projects is important to agriculture insofar as it affects the charges to farmers for electric power and the reclamation of land by irrigation, drainage, and flood control.

Undersecretary of Interior Richard Searles had this to say as a witness:[21]

Reasonable allocations are of the greatest importance because repayment requirements, which in turn govern power rates, are as dependent upon the allocations to reimbursable purposes as they are upon the actual construction costs.

Private power companies have taken a lively interest in this issue. This is explained by the frequent attempts to employ rates charged for public power as a "yardstick" for rates charged by private companies. So long as cost allocations in public multiple-purpose projects influence rate making, such allocations are indeed of concern to private power companies. On the other hand, if this connection between cost allocation and rate making did not exist, one important reason for private power companies to oppose public projects would disappear.

Before we can analyze the economic soundness of the yardstick idea, we must inquire about the principles on which rate making may be based and about the significance, in terms of these principles, of past costs of physical plant.

Theoretically the problem of setting rates for water or power can be approached with tools similar to those used in determining the optimum product combination.[22] A demand and supply function for water and power must be constructed. From the standpoint of social economics a demand function can be interpreted as a marginal benefit function, and a supply function as a marginal cost function. On this basis an optimum (dated) product combination can be determined.

The physical plant for public projects can be adjusted to yield the optimum product combination without regard to price incentives. Rates can be set in such a way that supply and demand in each time interval are in equilibrium. Rates for private industry must be set in a way, first, that the optimum product combination results and, second, that supply and demand are in equilibrium in each time interval. To obtain these two results, rate making may have to be supplemented by tax incentives — for example by provisions regarding depreciation allowances.

Such theoretical rates are not necessarily equal to short-run or long-run marginal costs of instantaneous economics. Rates set must make allowance for maintenance and discontinuous changes of physical plant in accordance with changes of demand and of technological conditions. Determination of such rates is possible only in economic theory. In the present case, as in the preceding one, practical approximations to theoretical solutions must be found. A proposal for such an approximation will be considered next.

Rate Making and Public Utility Commissions

The potentially most useful approximation to a theoretical determination of rates for public water or power may be based on the procedures developed by public utility commissions. In regulating rates, some of the more progressive commissions attempt to take into account expected changes of demand, the physical plant needed to satisfy such demand, the costs of such plant, "normal" efficiency of management and "normal" profits to give an incentive to provide such plant.[23]

It may be admitted that many (possibly most) public utility commissions still look more toward the past than the future in appraising demand and "allowable" cost of physical plant. However, the various proposals for incremental cost pricing have started some healthy discussion.[24] For our purposes the direction of change in public utility regulations and the possibilities of further improvement are more interesting than past and present shortcomings. On the other hand it would be naive to forget that in a field so exposed to political pressures — like the field of rate making — considerations based on economic theory will be only one (decidedly minor) factor in political decision making for some time to come.

Besides the realities of political pressures, another factor which limits the immediate relevance of theoretical considerations must be mentioned. In order to have the desired effects upon future supply, rates regulated by public utility commissions must be realistic in terms of cost accounting and budgeting practices used by private utility companies in planning maintenance and changes of physical plant. These practices differ from the techniques employed in the theoretical determination of the optimum product combination. Likewise, the practical definition of "normal" efficiency and profits poses some knotty problems. However, through give-and-take between public utility commissions and private utility companies over many years, cost accounting and budgeting practices have been developed which are reasonably well suited as a basis for regulation.

Such practices are becoming required standards for private companies of the regulated industry. There is a tendency for these standards to become more uniform for jurisdictions of different utility commissions. There is also a tendency for these standards to improve. Modern cost accounting has become a highly skilled profession. Since World War II, cost accounting as a means of controlling prices and profits has been used on a large scale in negotiating defense contracts. A great deal of experience has been gained in this field.

Rate Making for Public Water and Power

Rates regulated by public utility commissions in a way that takes account of supply and demand functions extending over time and a wealth of cost data in the regulated private industry can be used for approximating a solution of our problem: setting rates for water and power produced by public multiple-purpose projects — for short, "public" water and power. Such rate making can be divorced entirely from the problem of cost allocation.

In the western part of the United States, conditions of demand and supply are such that any reasonably projected addition — through public projects — to otherwise existing supplies of water and power can be absorbed without substantial reduction in rates. For demand, changes point strongly upward. Increases of supply have to come from greater distances, poorer sites or steam plants. The latter have lower costs only under revolutionary changes of energy inputs, e.g., fusion energy.

Under these conditions, water and power produced by public multiple-purpose projects can be sold at rates corresponding with or only slightly below the rate structure as regulated by public utility commissions.

Such a price policy is opposed, not only by preference customers of public water and power (see footnote 25), but also by many public-spirited citizens because of "indirect" and "intangible" benefits of lower public rates — regardless of supply and demand conditions. However, in social economics the effects of lower rates upon public revenues need to be considered, as well as the possibility that such rates, in combination with rationing, may change consumption patterns to the disadvantage of those "higher" social uses which could compete successfully for available water and power at higher rates. Moreover, increases in the total volume of water and power available from public *and* private sources are no less important in social economics than decreases in rates. In other words, effects of price on future supply cannot be neglected.

It should be emphasized that we are talking about rates at the points of production — that is, at or near the multiple-purpose dams. Generally, these rates will be wholesale rates. Appropriate correspondence between wholesale and retail rates can be found on the basis of cost data available to public utility commissions. Obviously, the seasonal distribution or "firmness" of the quantities available for sale must be considered. Under western conditions, water and power available at different seasons are, economically speaking, quite different commodities. Differences in firmness and in load factor are generally taken into account in the existing rate structure.

There are some geographic differences in the relevance of rates set by public utility commissions from the standpoint of rate making for public water and power. Rates regulated by public utility commissions are relevant in those regions where new public resources development is to be integrated into a large, already existing private development. This is the case in California. In other regions of the country — for

example in the Missouri Basin — public development of water and power
is so important relative to the private development that the rate structure of public projects is more relevant for private projects than the
reverse.

If no regulated rates are geographically relevant for a public project, or if there are potential customers of a public project who are
willing to pay higher than the regulated rates, preference in the sale of
public power and water may be given to the highest bidder.[25] Price discrimination in the sale of large blocks of power and water is frequently
possible. In the case of public projects, such price discrimination is
not necessarily objectionable.

The principle of highest bidder must be qualified with respect to
imperfections in the capital market when transmission lines and distribution facilities are not available. For most projects, some major
transmission lines must be constructed in any event in order to connect
the project with existing systems and to serve other project purposes,
such as pumping plants. Such transmission lines are an integral part
of the project. In some cases public credit may be given to groups of
customers who want to construct their own distribution facilities. For
instance, more than two billion dollars has been lent through the REA
to rural cooperatives. These and other means to overcome imperfections in the capital market are outside our immediate field of inquiry.

Cost Allocation and the Yardstick Idea

In the reasoning about the absence of any necessary connection between cost allocation and rate making presented in the preceding sections, it has already been implied that rates set for water and power
produced by public multiple-purpose projects cannot be used as a yardstick to measure whether the rates charged by private utility companies
are too high. Even if it is assumed that rate making for public water
and power is not based on the principles just discussed but on allocated
costs, such costs would not be comparable with those of private companies. The latter are generally not favored by the economies of joint
production and tax exemptions.

Rejecting the yardstick idea does not mean that rates charged by
private utility companies are always justified. Economic possibilities
for rate reduction exist largely with respect to retail rates. As already
stated, we are concerned mainly with wholesale rates. The spread between the two types of rates is great — especially for power. Costs of
transmission and distribution represent by far the greatest portion —
around 80 percent and more — of total power costs at points of consumption.

If, in a given situation, rates charged by private power companies
lead to monopoly profits, the most direct relief is brought not by using
cost allocation as a means to justify lower rates for public water and
power but by making public utility commissions more effective in their
highly important regulatory functions. There are several practical

possibilities of doing this. Public utility commissions fall short of fulfilling the important role assigned to them here. However, they are an
institutional device, developed by a democratic society, which gives
promise of further development.

Cost Allocation and Form of Contract

By separating repayment and rate making entirely from cost allocation — as advocated in the preceding sections — another problem of water
policy can be clarified. This problem is the form of the contract entered into between the government agency responsible for construction
and marketing — particularly the Bureau of Reclamation — and the water
users, particularly the irrigation districts.

The two principal forms of contract have become known as the 9(d)
and 9(e) contracts in reference to the relevant subsections on the Reclamation Act of 1939. The 9(d) contract is a repayment contract; it
provides for repayment of allocated reimbursable costs within time periods specified in the act. The 9(e) contract is a service contract; it
does not provide for repayment but merely for water service over a
number of years (40) under conditions also specified in the act.

Construction costs of water distribution systems are covered by
9(d) contracts. Construction costs of the main project works, on.the
other hand, can no longer be treated in the same way. At least that is
claimed by the Bureau of Reclamation, because the resulting payments
would exceed the financial ability of the districts. The 9(e) contract,
therefore, has become more and more common since it became available through the 1939 act and is frequently employed in large, multiple-
purpose projects. For example, in the Central Valley Project all contracts concluded in the period considered are 9(e) contracts, and
according to announcements by the Bureau of Reclamation this situation
will not be changed.

Although the 9(e) contract is financially more attractive than the
9(d) contract, it creates problems which are not presented by the latter.
Without going into detail about the somewhat controversial and legally
complex nature of these problems, we may summarize with respect to
the most important point — the security of water rights.

A repayment contract leads to a definite transfer of administration
and operation of physical works — and, therefore, of permanent control
over water deliveries — to the water users themselves. [26] Under a service contract, by contrast, the Bureau of Reclamation retains control
over administration and operation indefinitely. The Bureau claims it is
legally free to make changes in water deliveries from one group of
users to another after the time period (40 years) specified in the contract has expired. No provision for renewal is contained in the contract
nor in federal law.

It can be argued that changes in water deliveries would create so
much opposition in Congress that the attempt would not be made. However, Congress is usually divided in such matters. Security of water

rights is so important in irrigation farming that the weak substitute for a renewal clause is not sufficient.[27] This is especially true of the Central Valley Project in view of the large expenditures by the irrigation districts in constructing distribution systems. It may be submitted that the rights of users of water produced by federal multiple-purpose projects should not be less secure than other water rights established and protected by the laws of each state.

There is no need to argue here the question of state law versus federal law so often referred to in this connection. For the purposes of this chapter the issue is primarily an economic one: an optimum development of irrigation farming in an institutional system based on private initiative cannot be expected if the security of water rights is uncertain. For the economist such uncertainty would be relevant even if it were merely subjective. Subjective uncertainty influences the economic decisions of water users.[28]

Security of water rights under state laws does not mean that such rights cannot be transferred from one user to another. As real property, water rights are bought and sold — with land if they are "appurtenant" or without land if they are not — in all western states. By and large, such transfer of water rights through an open market gives sufficient flexibility for adapting to changing economic conditions. In some cases water rights can be transferred through loss, forfeiture, condemnation and in other ways also defined under state laws.

Likewise, security of water rights under state laws does not mean that service contracts for water are undesirable. Many western farmers obtain their water from water companies on a contract basis. However, these water companies are public utilities operating and regulated under state laws. Such utilities are not free to shift water service to other customers.

Although insecurity of water rights is the most important problem raised by 9(e) contracts, it is not the only one. Perpetuation of direct controls by a federal agency over the affairs of public districts organized and operating under state laws and supervised by state agencies has led to difficulties.

Here, again, there is no need to argue whether local, state or federal control is preferable in water resources development. Neither federal, state nor local governments are inherently superior with respect to the competence and integrity of their civil servants and with respect to freedom from corruption and rule by pressure groups.

On the other hand, too much concentration of economic power in any single agency — federal, state or local, public or private — appears undesirable. Although it can be argued that economic power can be controlled by political power, in the end a system of countervailing economic powers appears safer. On the basis of this value judgment, federal, state and local governments, together with private agencies, may well participate in water resources development. Some duplication and conflict may result from such multiplicity. As discussed elsewhere,[29] there are several practical possibilities to reduce these results through better coordination. The irreducible minimum of inefficiency caused by the multiplicity of participating agencies is the price paid for avoiding too much concentration of economic power.[30]

Regardless of one's attitude toward the over-all issue of federal versus state and public versus private control, it may be submitted that the scrambling of federal, state and local law and government as brought about by the 9(e) contract is unnecessary and undesirable. The internal economic affairs of irrigation districts are intrastate. The 9(e) contract contains provisions which are irritating, to say the least, to local and state governments. For example, the final decision in interpreting many important clauses is left entirely to the "contracting officer," that is, to the Federal Commissioner of Reclamation or his representative. Institutional machinery for consultation and arbitration would be more appropriate.

Let us assume that use of water facilities created by a federal project is entirely intrastate. If repayment of benefits is arranged between federal, state and local governments, water rights vested in the federal government and control over administration and operation of water facilities may well be transferred to the state and, under appropriate agreements, to the water users soon after the project is put into operation. If costs have no connection with repayment, as explained in the preceding sections, individual parts of projects are independent from each other with respect to repayment. The problems created by joint costs, by the gradual completion of large projects — like the Central Valley Project — and by the financial inability of districts to repay allocated construction costs, would no longer prevent transfer of control. Such transfer would overcome objections against a water service contract that are based on insecurity of water rights and on federal control over affairs which can be safely left to the control of state and local governments.

There is no implication in the foregoing statement that control *must* be transferred. There are several intrastate projects in operation in which irrigation districts have preferred that the constructing federal agency remain in control.

Likewise there is no implication that control over *other* features of an intrastate multiple-purpose project — for example over power or flood control — should be transferred to water users. Such control *may* be transferred under adequate agreements protecting federal and state interests if that is desired by the water and power users and other beneficiaries.

With respect to federal projects which have important interstate or international implications the situation is different. It is difficult to see how control of such projects could be turned over to state or local governments. Most large multiple-purpose projects have interstate or international implications. Thus the federal government should remain an important factor not only in the development but also in the administrative control of water resources. This is in accord with the position taken above concerning the principle of division of economic power.

How far the states can actively and harmoniously cooperate with the federal government in the administrative control of such projects — for example through federal-state compacts — needs to be explored further.

Although the federal government should remain important in the administrative control over interstate projects, secure water rights still may be acquired by the water users of each state. If use of water facilities is interstate, state allotments will have to be made in any event by state compact, international treaty or supreme court decision, or by a combination of these. Water users may acquire water rights in these allotments according to the laws of each state. If a service contract for water is used, regulations of each state can be applied to its allotment. ment.

THEORETICAL ANALYSIS VERSUS PRACTICAL APPLICATION

It may be considered that an economic analysis of water resources policies has the dry taste of theory and cannot be applied to the political and legal facts of life. Economists restrict their own usefulness severely if they consider water policies only within the framework of existing statutes. In many cases it is relevant to view laws as tools or obstacles of policy, and economists should make proposals for relevant changes.

Reclamation laws are not entirely antagonistic to the principles suggested here. With respect to the determination of economic feasibility and the processes of rate making, existing laws are not specific. In any event, only broad principles for the solution of these two problems could be stated by law. Detailed practices must be worked out by professional staffs and through agreement between agencies and governments.

The 1939 Reclamation Act is more specific with respect to repayment through water and power sales. I have tried to show elsewhere[31] that each paragraph of the relevant Section 9(a) is capable of an interpretation which is not in conflict with the principles suggested here. Obviously it would be much better if economic reasoning were clearly expressed in the act rather than read into it. A suitable interpretation is possible only because the economic terminology that appears in the act is rather vague.

With respect to repayment in other form than through water and power sales, the practice of regarding national defense and recreation as nonreimbursable may be continued. But benefits from flood control, salinity control and navigation can be assessed in part at least for repayment. As already implied, this has the advantage that these benefits would receive closer scrutiny in determining economic feasibility. Further, in some cases political opposition to desirable projects would be reduced. For example, the benefits of the Central Valley Project through flood control, salinity control and navigation are geographically concentrated in the Central Valley. Taxpayers in other parts of the state, such as southern California, receive only small benefits, if any, from these purposes. In other regions of the country a similar differentiation exists between upstream and downstream interests in a big watershed such as the Missouri and Mississippi valleys. A more equitable participation of different groups of taxpayers in the financial burden of a project might facilitate authorization by Congress.

The most practical way of assessing the benefits from flood control, salinity control and navigation would be through public districts, equipped with taxing power, formed for that purpose under state law. In the case of navigation benefits there are economic arguments in favor of tolls. The United States has revived this principle for some important freeways. But the tradition of toll-free navigation is strong, and there are also economic arguments in favor of paying for navigation (and road) benefits other than through tolls.

All western states have had experience with public districts in the field of irrigation. Most states, especially California, have a variety of laws under which districts concerned with water resources development other than irrigation can be organized and operated. Likewise, it is a well-established practice that public districts enter into repayment contracts with the federal government.

Considerable literature exists on assessment practices in irrigation districts. Several studies undertaken in the Columbia Basin and the Central Valley have a bearing on assessment practices in districts other than irrigation. Further studies in this direction are desirable, but there is little doubt that practical means to repay benefits in the way suggested can be found.

By and large, changes in repayment as suggested here would mean a simplification of laws. Most students and interested parties are in agreement that amendment of reclamation laws is sorely needed. A codification of reclamation laws by the House Judiciary Committee has been in progress.[32]

FOOTNOTES

[1] The term "joint costs" as employed here is a shorthand for "costs in joint production." The logical corollary is "separate costs." In multiple-purpose projects it is advisable to differentiate between production and distribution. The distribution of products — for example, of water and power — can generally be regarded as separate processes. However, in some cases a part of distribution must be included in joint production.

The term "separable costs" is avoided here. This term is employed in practices of cost allocation. It is defined as follows: "the separable cost for each project purpose is the difference between the cost of the multiple-purpose project and the cost of the project with the purpose omitted." In connection with these same practices, "joint costs" are defined as "the difference between the cost of the multiple-purpose project as a whole and the total of the separable costs for all project purposes." U.S. Federal Inter-Agency River Basin Committee, Subcommittee on Benefits and Costs, Proposed Practices for Economic Analyses of River Basin Projects, U.S. Govt. Print. Off., May, 1950, p. 54.

[2] Striking differences sometimes occur in the benefit-cost analysis of different federal agencies for the same project. For example, in the recent Trinity River report, the Bureau of Reclamation calculates a benefit-cost ratio of 3.26:1 and the Federal Power Commission, a benefit-cost ratio of 1.5:1. U.S. Congress, House, Trinity River Basin, Central Valley Project, California, U.S. Govt. Print. Off., Jan. 9, 1953, 197 pp. (83 Cong., 1st Sess., H. Doc. 53).

The Corps of Army Engineers does not use indirect benefits in the same sense as the Bureau of Reclamation. The Federal Power Commission has gone on record that "reliance should be placed upon the more direct or primary types of benefits and costs susceptible of being evaluated." Survey reports on upstream flood control by agencies of the Department of Agriculture show an increasingly critical attitude in matters of evaluation. Reports on Bureau of Reclamation projects, on the other hand, sometimes show "indirect" benefits equal to or exceeding "direct" ones. The Federal Inter-Agency River Basin Committee is experiencing difficulties in resolving these differences among the agencies in the field of evaluation.

[3] The various methods of cost allocation that have been used or considered need not be discussed here. The most important methods are reviewed in a congressional report. U.S. Congress, House, Subcommittee To Study Civil Works, Committee on Public Works, The Allocation of Costs of Federal Water Resource Development Projects, U.S. Govt. Print. Off., Dec. 5, 1952 (82nd Cong. 2nd Sess., House Committee Print No. 23). This report will be cited henceforth as Allocation Report.

[4] Act of Aug. 4, 1939, Ch. 418, 53 St. 1187, 43 U.S.C. 485.

[5] Allocation Report, op. cit., p. 11.

[6] As stated previously, it is not possible at this time to go into the important problem of evaluating benefits and costs (including the use of interest and uncertainty allowance). This problem is not peculiar to multiple-purpose projects. The principles involved in obtaining market and extramarket values have been discussed elsewhere. (S. V. Ciriacy-Wantrup, Resource Conservation, Economics and Policies, rev. ed., Univ. of Calif. Div. of Agr. Sci., 1963.) Some of the procedures have been critically reviewed in a congressional report. U.S. Congress, House, Subcommittee To Study Civil Works, Committee on Public Works, Economic Evaluation of Federal Water Resource Development Projects, U.S. Govt. Print. Off., Dec. 5, 1952 (82nd Cong., 2nd Sess., House Committee Print No. 24). This report will be cited henceforth as Evaluation Report.

[7] For an interesting, although controversial, beginning toward a quantitative analysis of "western" and "eastern" alternatives see Rudolph Ulrich, "Relative costs and benefits of land reclamation in the humid Southeast and the semiarid West," Jour. Farm Econ., Vol. 35, No. 1, 1953, pp. 62-73.

[8] On these points see S. V. Ciriacy-Wantrup, "Taxation and the conservation of resources," Quart. Jour. Econ., 58:157-95, 1953; also S. V. Ciriacy-Wantrup, "Resource conservation and economic instability," Quart. Jour. Econ., Vol. 60, pp. 412-52, 1946.

[9] For a detailed treatment see S. V. Ciriacy-Wantrup, "Economics of joint costs in agriculture," Jour. Farm Econ., Vol. 23, No. 4, 1941, pp. 771-818. An application of this theory to problems of "time jointness" is offered in Ciriacy-Wantrup, Resource Conservation, Economics and Policies, op. cit.

[10] In some legislation — in the Flood Control Act of 1944 and the River and Harbor Act of 1946 — it is stipulated that individual projects planned by federal agencies must be submitted to the states for review and that the latters' comments must accompany requests for appropriations. (Sections 1 (a) and 1 (c) of Flood Control Act, 1944. Public Law 534, 78th Congress. In the amendments of 1945 and 1946, these provisions were re-emphasized.)

[11] J. Karl Lee, "Irrigation policy for arid lands," Jour. Farm Econ., Vol. 32, No. 5, 1952, pp. 751-55.

[12] Policy implications are said to be these: "(1) the liberalization of existing policy with respect to repayment requirements, (2) the elimination of alternative opportunity or cost in the consideration of benefits, (3) repayment would become a secondary consideration, (4) acreage limitation would be continued, and (5) anti-speculation would be continued."

[13] In the Act of 1937 authorizing the Central Valley Project of California, power is designated as "a means of financially aiding and assisting other functions." This role of power goes back to the Reclamation Act of 1906.

[14] For examples in the area of the Southwest Power Administration, see Allocation Report, op. cit., pp. 15-26. For examples of the Missouri Basin see Missouri Basin Survey Commission, Missouri, Land and Water, U.S. Govt. Print. Off., 1953, p. 92.

[15] The name "benefit method" is applied mainly to two methods of cost allocation. The first allocates the total costs of a project among the purposes "in proportion to their estimated benefits." The second allocates to each purpose its "direct cost plus a share of the joint costs in direct proportion to the estimated net benefits." U.S. Congress, Allocation Report, op. cit., p. 4.

[16] The quotation marks are used because the quantitative definition of acreage limitation is, to a large extent, left to the discretion of the Secretary of the Interior. By statute "160

acres" is mentioned as a maximum. It can be — and has been — reduced by the Secretary of the Interior to as low as 40 acres for some projects. On the other hand, the limitation has been interpreted in such a way that man and wife may operate 320 acres. According to another interpretation, this figure can be increased even further by transferring land to other members of the family.

Sometimes the pressure of economic and political change forces a change in the rulings of the Secretary. For example the Orland Reclamation Project in California was operated under a 40-acre limitation from 1916-1953 (from 1907-1916 a limitation of 160 acres was in force). In 1953 a uniform limitation of 160 acres was decreed.

[17] Ciriacy-Wantrup, Resource Conservation, Economics and Policies, *op. cit.*

[18] 50 St. 731. Section 7 reads in part: "Rate schedules shall be based upon an allocation of costs made by the Federal Power Commission. In computing the cost of electric energy developed from water created as an incident to and a byproduct of the construction of the Bonneville Project, the Federal Power Commission may allocate to the costs of electric facilities such a share of the cost of facilities having joint value for the production of electric energy and other purposes as the power development may fairly bear as compared with such other purposes."

[19] U.S. Congress, Allocation Report, *op. cit.*, p. 9.

[20] *Ibid.*, p. 9.

[21] *Ibid.*, p. 10.

[22] The techniques and their difficulties and limitations are similar to those involved in determining the optimum state of conservation in social economics. For details see Ciriacy-Wantrup, Resource Conservation, Economics and Policies, *op. cit.*, Chaps. 16 and 17.

[23] In this connection a statement by R. I. Mittelstaedt, President, California Public Utilities Commission, before the California Farm Bureau is of some interest. See *California Farm Bureau Monthly*, Vol. 34, No. 4, 1953.

[24] Harold Hotelling, "The general welfare in relation to problems of taxation and of railway and utility rates," *Econometrica*, Vol. 11, No. 3, 1938, pp. 242-69.

Donald Wallace, "Kinds of public control to replace or supplement antitrust laws," *Amer. Econ. Rev.*, Vol. 30, No. 1, 1940, supplement, pp. 194-212.

Temporary National Economic Committee, Economic Standards of Government Price Control, U.S. Govt. Print. Off., 1941, 76th Cong., 3d Sess., Monograph No. 32, Senate Committee Print.

Emery Troxel, "Incremental cost determination of utility prices," *Jour. Land and Public Utility Econ.*, Vol. 18, No. 4, 1942.

Troxel, "Limitations of the incremental cost patterns of pricing," *Jour. Land and Public Utility Econ.*, Vol. 18, No. 1, 1943, pp. 28-39.

[25] With respect to public customers this preference is regulated by law. A public-preference clause in some form has been in the Reclamation Law since 1906. It was reaffirmed through Section 9 (c) of the Reclamation Act of 1939. A discussion of the economics and politics of public preference would lead us too far afield.

[26] According to the reclamation laws, nominal ownership of the main dams and reservoir sites remains with the federal government.

[27] Frequent criticism of 9 (e) contracts in California has led to an addition to the preamble reading as follows: "and such future contracts as may be made between the United States and the District."

[28] For a more detailed discussion of the effects of uncertainty upon resource use see Ciriacy-Wantrup, Resource Conservation, Economics and Policies, *op. cit.*, Chap. 8.

[29] Ciriacy-Wantrup, Resource Conservation, *op. cit.*, Chap. 21.

[30] Even the much criticized duplication of *federal* agencies in water resources development — for example of the Bureau of Reclamation and the Army Engineers — may be considered from the standpoint of the above paragraph. State and local governments may obtain consideration of their objectives by working with one of these agencies if they feel that their viewpoint is not sufficiently considered by the other. Differences are brought into the open. The much needed consolidation of the two agencies would be in accord with a system of countervailing economic powers only under the condition that state and local governments play a strong independent role in water resources development.

[31] U.S. Bureau of Reclamation, Central Valley Project Studies: Allocation of Costs, Problems 8 and 9, U.S. Govt. Print. Off., 1947, pp. 235-38. (Appendix J. Letters of Comment and Dissent Submitted by Committee Members.)

[32] Federal Reclamation Laws, Vol. 1-2, U.S. Govt. Print. Off., 1958-59, 2 v.

M. M. REGAN is Assistant to the Director, Resource Development Economics
Division, U.S. Department of Agriculture. He has actively participated in the application of economics concepts to federal water resource planning.

Chapter 13

MARK M. REGAN

Sharing Financial
Responsibility of
River Basin Development*

S HARING FINANCIAL RESPONSIBILITY of river-basin developments involves division of project and program costs among purposes, interests, groups and individuals. All costs of establishing
and maintaining resource programs must be borne by someone. Costs
not assigned to specific individuals or groups must be borne by the local, area or national public. Expected to share these costs are: (1) the
primary beneficiaries who receive immediate project services, (2) secondary beneficiaries, (3) states or provinces and local agencies or districts and (4) the national public.

Arrangements for cost sharing are many and varied. They include
the use of charges and assessments to recover all or part of the initial
capital outlays and meet annual costs; and various forms of cost-sharing
agreements among participants covering direct responsibility for segments of projects or providing specified types of resources, materials,
services or other contributions.

*A revision from *Jour. Farm Econ.*, Vol. 40, No. 5, 1958; and the *Canadian Agr. Econ.
Society*, Vol. 6, No. 2, 1958.

The opinions expressed in this article are those of the author and do not necessarily
represent the view of the Resource Development Economics Division, ERS [Farm Economics Research Division, ARS] or the USDA. The author is indebted to E. W. Weber, N. A.
Back, A. R. Johnson and John V. Krutilla for helpful suggestions.

The difference in emphasis between evaluation and cost sharing is sufficient to warrant a reasonably sharp distinction between the two. Whereas evaluation is concerned primarily with benefit-cost relationships in production, cost sharing centers attention on the distribution or incidence aspects of project effects. Efficiency in producing services is the controlling consideration in evaluation; in cost sharing, emphasis is on equitable distribution arrangements.

A divergence in viewpoints leads to certain differences in approaches appropriate for each. For evaluation purposes, for example, secondary benefits often represent a transfer effect. To the extent that such benefits can be identified, however, they provide as valid a basis for the distribution of costs as do direct benefits. The ability of a particular group of beneficiaries to bear project costs is independent of whether their benefits represent a net social gain or merely constitute a transfer from another group. The amounts of secondary benefits that merit consideration in cost sharing and reimbursement may exceed those available for the economic justification of a project from a national or social viewpoint. In evaluation, the cost of uncompensated damages is clearly a project cost — although usually it is not included in the costs that are shared.

The standards for reimbursement and evaluation may differ also. Reimbursement usually involves contractual obligations that require dollar payments, and possible price fluctuations become more significant than in evaluation, with its greater emphasis on purchasing power or real values. Also, the dollar costs that must be paid by an individual or group may vary from the social cost of utilizing resources. From the viewpoint of individuals or local groups the cost is the money outlay necessary to acquire resources or services; from the viewpoint of the public the cost is the productivity of the resources in alternatives that are foregone.

Despite the differences indicated, the reimbursement and evaluation considerations cannot be completely separated. Assessment and reimbursement requirements often provide an effective check on the reliability of the evaluation estimates. The willingness of individuals to pay for services received is substantial evidence of the existence of benefits. Further, when charges are likely to influence the utilization of project services, their relationship to the realization of project benefits must be considered. Although these interrelationships must be recognized, it is believed that most aspects of the cost-sharing problem may be treated more systematically if considered as distinct rather than as integral parts of the evaluation problem.

Although some attention has been given to cost sharing as either an aspect of resource policy or an incidental phase of evaluation,[1] a systematic analysis centering on cost sharing comparable to recent texts on evaluation is yet to be developed.[2] Logically the broad field of financial responsibility distribution covers all aspects of the incidence of project effects. It includes consideration of project impacts on regions, areas and individuals; the compensation required to make those adversely affected at least as well off with as without the project; the ways in which cost-sharing requirements may be used to adjust incidence; and the possibilities and limitations of alternative means of controlling incidence. This chapter attempts to deal with only a part of the broader field indicated. Attention centers primarily on the approaches, guides and problems involved in the division of project costs among interests and participants.

The economic, institutional and policy considerations that have a bearing on cost sharing are so numerous and so intertwined that neither a single nor a simple formula would appear to be appropriate for all situations. The chief types of considerations that warrant attention in devising arrangements for sharing financial responsibility are: (1) the objectives to be served, and (2) the merits and limitations of alternative basic approaches for apportioning charges or assessments. Attention also must be given to the adjustments and modifications necessitated by problems of practical application and acceptability.

PURPOSES AND OBJECTIVES

What purposes and objectives should cost-sharing requirements be designed to serve? Their general purpose, of course, is to distribute costs in such a way as to best serve the public interest. To accomplish this, cost-sharing requirements should be regarded as a positive means of maximizing the net social benefits from the use and distribution of project resources and services. These requirements have two main purposes or objectives: (1) contributing to the efficient use of resources and (2) promoting incidence and distribution policies. The desired arrangements are those under which conflicts between these two objectives are minimized.

The contribution toward efficiency goals stems from the effect that assessments and charges have on the use of project services. The absence of any charges might well induce a waste of services by beneficiaries, increase the pressure for unjustified projects by local interests and provide insufficient incentives for participation.[3] Excessive charges could result in underutilization of project services and failure to realize project potentials.

Promoting the attainment of other objectives of public policy also merits consideration in establishing cost-sharing requirements. These objectives include stimulating area and regional economic development, encouraging owner operation of family-sized farms, minimizing windfall gains, maintaining adequate levels of living, promoting increased economic stability through the reduction of risk and providing flexibility in repayment arrangements.

Little question arises concerning the desirability of taking account of these objectives in cost-sharing requirements. The chief issues relate to the impact of such provisions on efficient resource use and the effectiveness of alternative means for their accomplishment. Optimum development and use may be obtained under a range of charges and assessments, and other means are available for controlling the distribution and use of project services. Frequently both distribution and efficiency goals can be served if a reasonably close association is maintained between the incidence of benefits and costs. Benefit recipients are usually in a position to bear charges, while charges geared either to costs or to the value of services are likely to promote efficient use.

Desired distribution patterns for such attributes as land use and ownership might also be obtained by direct regulations. The 160-acre limitation and associated antispeculation provisions under reclamation law illustrate types of such regulations. Only farms of the permitted size are eligible for participation; all others are excluded. Differential charges could accomplish many of the desired distribution effects and perhaps be less likely to conflict with efficiency objectives. To the extent that differential charges absorb windfall gains, they would reduce the need for antispeculation restrictions. Thus family-sized farms might receive preference in the form of lower assessments and deferred repayment periods that would not be available to larger units. Or higher or graduated charges or assessments might be placed on acreages above a given size.

The need for considering the ultimate rather than the immediate aspects of incidence is often overlooked. If a wide distribution of benefits is emphasized, provision needs to be made for benefits reaching direct users of project services throughout the life of the project. When services are provided at less than their value, the advantage may be largely absorbed before reaching the intended beneficiaries. For example, if flood control or irrigation is provided for a charge substantially less than its value, present landowners would be in position to appropriate the capitalized value of the net benefit in case of sale. Succeeding owners would bear land costs approximating the value of the benefits and would receive no net advantage from the project. Any part of the value not absorbed as a project charge would go to a previous owner. In case benefits are subject to appropriation, either project charges should be sufficient to limit windfall gains or provision should be made to return the gains to the public. Otherwise the possibility of accomplishing long-term redistribution objectives through low project charges would be limited.

BASES FOR THE DIVISION
OF FINANCIAL RESPONSIBILITY

Bases for apportioning financial responsibility may be grouped into two main categories: (1) charges and assessments based on project costs and (2) charges and assessments based on the value of project services. Each category has several variants and cost-sharing requirements could incorporate various combinations of the two.

Cost Basis for Charges and Assessments

Under the cost approach, the sharing of financial responsibility among interests is geared to and limited by project costs. The main variants consist of: (1) sharing costs in proportion to benefits and (2) assigning the full cost of specified purposes to particular users or classes of beneficiaries.

The costs to be shared consist of those for initial installations and the recurring costs for operation, maintenance and replacement. All such costs may be expressed in either present value or annual terms. In annual terms, initial investment costs take the form of amortization allowances needed to retire the investment with interest over the life of the project.

For single-purpose projects, the necessary base is directly available, distributing total costs among the participating interests. In the case of multiple-purpose projects, an appropriate share of any joint or common costs must be added to the separable cost of each purpose to derive the total cost. Thus an initial step in the division of financial responsibility based on costs is the allocation of any joint costs among purposes.

Cost allocation. Many different cost-allocation procedures have been proposed and several are used in prevailing practice.[4] Their purpose is to provide a rational basis for apportioning costs of jointly used facilities among the purposes served. The range in results obtained from different methods is often wide, and the implications for cost sharing are substantial.

An appropriate cost-allocation method should allow each purpose to share proportionately in the advantages that result from the use of common facilities. The allocation should be consistent with proper economic formulation in that the total costs allocated to any purpose should be at least sufficient to cover the separable costs of its inclusion, but not in excess of the lesser benefits or alternative costs. The procedure is not an integral part of project formulation and hence should not preclude any purpose that produces benefits sufficient to cover its separable costs.

A method that meets the principal tests for an acceptable procedure is the Separable Costs-Remaining Benefits Method proposed by the Subcommittee on Evaluation Standards of the Inter-Agency Committee on Water Resources.[5] Under the method they recommend, each purpose is first charged with its separable costs. This cost is the difference in the total project cost resulting from the inclusion or deletion of any purpose. The difference between the sum of the separable purpose costs and the total project cost constitutes the common costs chargeable to all purposes served. This residual is distributed among purposes in accordance with the excess of its benefits over its separable costs. Alternative costs take the place of benefits when they are less.

The method has gained rather widespread acceptance both in agency practices and in recommendations made by various commissions and study groups. The chief modifications in application arise from the absence of adequate data on separable costs. This often necessitates the substitution of specific for separable costs in the formula.

Despite its general acceptance, certain unresolved questions arise in the application of the method to cost sharing. One issue centers around the stage in the cost-distribution process at which account should be taken of secondary benefits. If cost allocation is regarded as a method of imputing responsibility for project costs among purposes from a public viewpoint, then it would appear to be appropriate to disregard the transfer type of secondary benefits in the initial allocation. Any secondary benefits above those considered net project benefits would be needed to balance secondary benefits foregone from alternatives. Hence they would not be available to justify an increase in project costs assigned a particular purpose. Each purpose would share in joint costs in accordance with its contribution toward the net social benefits of the project.

Under this reasoning, the more appropriate stage for taking account of local secondary benefits would be in the division of allocated purpose costs among the benefited interests. Emphasis at this stage centers more on questions of individual and group incidence, with no need for distinguishing between transfer and net-project types of benefits. Only net-purpose benefits would be used in the allocation among purposes, with account taken of local and area viewpoints in the distribution of allocated purpose costs among groups and interests.

Another group of issues on cost-allocation procedures relates to the treatment of alternatives. These include questions as to whether alternatives should be used as a limit on the allocation or as a measure of benefits; whether the alternative should be based on public or private cost standards; and the extent to which a multiple-purpose site may be used in computing the cost of a series of single-purpose alternatives.

Under the standard Separable Costs-Remaining Benefits Method of allocation, alternatives are treated, in effect, as a measure of benefits. However, no essential characteristic of the basic method would be lost if alternatives were used as a limitation on the allocations. The primary distribution of joint costs could be based on benefits, with allocations permitted to approach alternative costs. Although this modification would increase the allocation to purposes with low-cost alternatives in relation to benefits, the net allocation might well be more in accord with their capacity to carry costs.

When both public and private standards are involved in evaluation, the question of which is appropriate for determining alternative costs in cost allocation becomes pertinent. Because only alternatives that are real in terms of those likely to develop in the absence of the project are significant, the use of costs applicable to such expected alternatives would appear to be appropriate. With benefits based on the costs of the most likely alternative source, the alternative cost-and-benefit base for the allocation of project costs to such purposes as power would often be the same.

Under prevailing practice, a multiple-purpose site is frequently used as a basis for computing the alternative single-purpose cost of each of several alternatives. As alternatives should represent a source of comparable service expected to develop in the absence of the project, they must be independent of the particular project under consideration. Assuming that a multiple-purpose project provides optimum use of a given site, such a site would no longer be available for developing alternatives that could be realized for the various separate purposes. Project development would preclude any other uses of the site, and it would be inaccessible for any single-purpose development.

Allocation of costs among purposes is only the first step in the process. More controversial issues arise in the distribution of the purpose allocations among and between the interests and groups that benefit.

Costs shared in proportion to benefits. This approach involves the distribution of project costs in accordance with benefits. The costs assigned to any interest or group would depend on the relative amount of the project benefits they received.

Although the method has considerable appeal as a reasonable and equitable approach, in application it has certain rather serious limitations. Both measurement and conceptual problems arise in attempting to appraise and compare benefits that accrue to interests with differing viewpoints. The main difficulty comes from attempts to classify and measure benefits that accrue to local compared with national interests.

For classification purposes, general public benefits could be defined to cover contributions to such activities as defense, maintenance of high employment levels, conservation of resources and attainment of other objectives considered to be national responsibilities. In addition, benefits that were widely dispersed among individuals and areas might also be considered as general public benefits. Many of the benefits indicated would be difficult to measure in quantitative terms, and their consideration in cost sharing would often need to be largely qualitative.

Conceptual problems also arise in dealing with effects that are benefits from a local or area viewpoint, but not necessarily from a national viewpoint. Most secondary benefits fall into this category. Logically, national benefits should be net of transfers, while local benefits are any that are expected to accrue in the zone of project influence.

Thus the difficulties of measuring public benefits in terms comparable to those of local participants often limit the extent to which a rigid proportional-benefits base could be used in apportioning costs between the two interests. The further distribution of costs assigned to local interests in accordance with benefits would involve fewer complications, as the benefits of those participating could be measured from a similar viewpoint and in reasonably comparable terms. The primary contribution of the approach lies in the distribution of costs among local and area beneficiaries after the initial assignment to local interests had been made. The approach also would be applicable to the division of responsibility between two countries if the viewpoints involved were reasonably comparable.

Assignment to users of all costs of specified purposes. The full costs of such vendible services as power and municipal water are frequently assigned to users. Irrigation represents a modification in which costs assigned to users are partially reimbursable. In the case of power and municipal water the costs assigned for repayment through charges or assessments usually include interest and an allocated share of the joint costs. Interest is excluded from the required irrigation repayments, and various parts of the initial allocation to irrigation are often reassigned to power or other reimbursable purposes for repayment. In order to establish total costs, an allocation of joint costs to the various purposes is required for multiple-purpose projects.

Requirements for the full reimbursement of costs assigned to designated purposes have led to the use of cost-allocation methods designed to minimize the cost-sharing requirements of the financially weaker purposes. These include assignment of costs approximating benefits to nonreimbursable purposes and the deferral and reassignment of irrigation costs to power and municipal water. The interest-free status of irrigation costs permits their accounting repayment from power revenues that accrue after the payout period for power. The St. Lawrence Seaway provides another example of an extreme shift in allocations. All the joint costs of the project have been assigned to power.[6]

Although full reimbursement is a typical requirement for the vendible type of services, the procedures often used in establishing costs have been neither rigorous nor realistic. The approach appears to be inflexible to serve as a general basis for cost sharing, as all costs of each of the purposes provided would need to be assigned to identifiable groups of beneficiaries.

Among the difficulties is that of developing an entirely satisfactory basis for deciding which purposes should be fully reimbursable and which should not. Full reimbursement requirements are likely to be most effective in the case of vendible services for which a direct charge can be made readily. Logically, cost-sharing policy should be determined by the nature and extent of the public interest involved rather than solely by the ease of collection. Also, partial reimbursement would appear to be feasible for some purposes that would escape assessment under a policy of either collecting all costs or none.

Despite the limitations indicated, the approach has a place in cost-sharing policy. The approach provides a basis for sharing the costs of purposes and activities undertaken wholly for local or area interests and possibly for types of services that enter into direct competition with private alternatives.

Charges and Assessments Based on Value of Services

If charges and assessments were geared to the value of the benefits, their determination could be largely independent of project and purpose costs. The division of financial responsibility for project costs would then consist of the assignment of charges to identifiable beneficiaries up to the value of their benefits. If returns did not equal or exceed costs, the residual would be borne by the general public. The magnitude of the benefits accruing to specially benefited groups would be the significant consideration rather than the relative amounts received by various interests.

If incentives are to be provided for individual and local group participation, the charges and assessments would need to be less than the full value of the benefits received. The charges would also need to be consistent with the cost of available alternatives, and further adjustments could be made to bring charges into line with the ability of beneficiaries to pay.

The main obstacles to acceptance of the approach as the primary basis for the division of financial responsibility include objections to a departure from the cost basis for determining charges, the latitude permitted for judgment or discretion in fixing the level of charges and difficulties in establishing the justification for having the residual costs borne by the public. [7]

The main advantages would include avoidance of controversial problems of cost allocation and difficulties in making precise estimates of national public benefits of the type needed for comparison with benefits accruing to local and area groups. The approach would provide sufficient flexibility to permit charges to be used to stimulate optimum development and use. Necessary adjustments could be made for particular purposes and conditions. The approach would obviate the practice of reassigning repayment obligations and the net costs borne by the public could be clearly identified. It would also provide a means of basing charges on the real or purchasing power value of benefits and thus allow recovery of real rather than financial costs.

With assessments for each proposal geared to the ability of identifiable beneficiaries to bear charges, the actual collections realized would probably increase.

Components in a Combined Approach

Various combinations of the approaches indicated are possible. Charges for some purposes could rest primarily on the value of service, with charges for others based on costs. Although prevailing practice emphasizes costs as a basis for charges for vendible services, values are frequently the real base. The reliance placed on values is sometimes obscured by a confusing and often unnecessary cost-determining process. The allocation procedure is such that assigned costs are actually often determined by benefits.

When payments by identifiable beneficiaries are expected to equal or exceed purpose costs, either the cost-of-service or the value-of-service approach would afford an appropriate base for the assignment of financial responsibility. The charges under either could be sufficient to insure reasonably efficient use of project services. Preference for the value-of-service base would depend on the weight given the desirability of recapturing any windfall gains that might accrue from charges that were lower than the value of services. But objections to government profits accruing from resource developments would be avoided by a cost basis for charges. The types of purposes to which either would be applicable would include power, municipal water and perhaps navigation and other types of vendible services.

When the payments by identifiable beneficiaries are expected to be short of purpose costs, the value-of-service base would appear to be effective for recovering any charges that could reasonably be paid. This is likely to be the case for such purposes as irrigation, drainage, flood control, watershed programs and recreation. Either direct charges for services or assessments on primary or secondary beneficiaries could be based on value. For some purposes, payments might come partly from service charges and partly from assessments.

The sharing of costs in proportion to benefits would provide a basis for sharing responsibility between countries and states and could be used in the distribution of assigned costs among individuals and groups. Neither it nor the assignment of full specified-purpose costs would appear to be appropriate as the primary base for a comprehensive national river-basin program.

The feasibility of making reasonably reliable assessments and difficulties of collecting them become a primary concern in considering the practical application of cost-sharing requirements. Groups of expected beneficiaries need to be clearly identifiable; an acceptable basis for determining charges should be established and a mechanism needs to be provided for the assessment and collection of charges or assessments.

The assessment of direct and indirect beneficiaries of many major purposes would probably require the establishment of conservancy or other special-purpose districts having taxing authority. Agreements also might be worked out for assigning a share of the financial responsibility to states and existing local governmental organizations. To the extent consistent with program objectives and purposes, the participation of such groups and interests in planning and formulation should be geared to the financial responsibility they are willing to assume.

COST SHARING IN INTERNATIONAL RIVERS

The considerations that affect the division of financial responsibility for national rivers would appear to be generally applicable to international rivers. Although more complications might be expected to arise, the main differences between national and international river problems are largely of degree rather than of kind.

In national rivers, cost sharing attempts to make an adjustment for any disassociation of benefits and costs between individuals, groups, areas and the nation. In international rivers its objective becomes that of devising arrangements to compensate for disassociations that occur between the participating countries.

When greater net benefits would result, it would appear possible to establish cost-sharing arrangements for joint development whereby each participating country would share equitably in its advantages. As a minimum, the net benefits accruing to each country under joint development should at least equal those obtainable under available independent alternative programs. Any gains over such a minimum could be distributed in a way that would allow each country to realize a comparable advantage.

Adequate consideration of each country's independent alternatives would appear to be a major requirement for establishing an equitable and acceptable basis for sharing financial responsibility. A more comprehensive treatment of project costs would be required than is commonly applied in the analysis of national rivers, where no direct allowance is made for site and water resource values. In effect, the net benefits over project costs become attributable to such resources as residual claimants. Allowance for the value of such resources supplied by countries would appear to be a proper component of the total costs of a joint project and creditable as a real cost contributed by participants. Under the assumption that the benefits accruing to each should at least be sufficient to cover the costs incurred, the inclusion of alternative opportunity costs would insure each country of being at least as well off under joint as under independent development.

The value of the site and water resource contributions may be measured by their expected productivity in available independent alternatives that are precluded or foregone as a result of the joint project. More precisely it would be the value of the net benefits expected to accrue within the country from the most advantageous independent alternative likely to be developed in the absence of the joint project. The foregone benefits would be the net of required development costs and their value adjusted for time and certainty of occurrence on the basis of standards comparable to those used for the joint project.

The alternatives used must be real in the sense that they are likely to be realized in the absence of the joint project. Also they should be consistent with the existing state of river-basin development, any governing treaties and acceptable principles of international law. The restraints imposed by the adoption of such principles of international law as those recommended by the International Law Association at its meeting at Dubrovink, Yugoslavia, in August 1956 would restrict alternatives to those that did not change the existing regime of a river to the detriment of other countries.[8]

The costs of a joint development project would thus include two components: (1) The outlays necessary for establishing and operating the project and (2) the opportunity costs reflected in the net benefits foregone from available independent alternatives.

The project benefits would need to be sufficient to cover both components of costs, with any excess indicative of the mutual advantage of joint development. The methods appropriate for computing the benefits of national rivers would appear to be generally applicable to international rivers. Some problems of differences in standards might arise, but perhaps much of this could be resolved by applying the standards considered appropriate for the optimum available uses of project services. To the extent that project services were mobile, they would be appraised in terms of their highest available market value.

The primary basis for determining benefits from development of a particular site might well be its expected contribution to the planned eventual development program or system. This would involve an estimate of the incremental benefits to the system expected to result from addition of a particular project. Benefits resulting from any of several segments of a planned program would be common to the system and hence not creditable to a specific segment merely because of its priority in scheduled development.[9]

Division of financial responsibility could take any of several forms. The costs of joint development could be shared in accordance with the incidence of benefits; benefits could be distributed to correspond to costs incurred by participating countries; various compensatory arrangements might be worked out to achieve a balanced distribution of benefits and costs; or primary responsibility for particular segments could be assigned.

The pattern of assignments, adjustments and compensation payments could be designed to provide each participating country with the same rate of return on investment or the same ratio of benefits to costs as for the project as a whole. The amount of the costs or the responsibility for segments to be assumed by each country would be subject to negotiation within such a framework.

CONCLUSIONS

The many water policy commission and study group reports prepared during the 1950's have emphasized the desirability of a thorough revision of cost-sharing requirements for water-development projects. They cite the variations that exist in prevailing practices between both agencies and major purposes and stress the need for establishing a more consistent national policy that will increase substantially the share of the costs to be borne by states and local identifiable beneficiaries.

A reduction in the federal share of the costs of water resource projects should not be regarded necessarily as a desirable end in itself. Rather, requirements should be established to serve more specific objectives as achieving optimum resource development and use and promoting desired incidence, distribution and stabilization policies.

Various basic approaches are available for assigning financial responsibility among participating interests. No single method appears to be adequate as a general basis for all purposes, although each has a possible place in a suitable pattern of cost-sharing requirements. In establishing requirements for most project purposes, greater emphasis should be placed on charges and assessments based on the value of services and less on the computed cost of providing services.

With modifications to allow for the full value of available alternatives, considerations involved in the division of financial responsibility for national rivers would appear to be generally applicable to international rivers. Cost-sharing agreements for both national and international rivers depend considerably more on policy considerations and negotiations than does the determination of economic justification. This difference is reflected in the frequent characterization of evaluation as mainly a "matter of principle," and cost sharing as mainly a "matter of public policy."

FOOTNOTES

[1] Typical are Missouri Basin Survey Commission, "Missouri land and water," 1953; the President's Water Resources Policy Commission, "A water policy for the American people," Vol. I, 1950; and The Presidential Advisory Committee on Water Resources Policy, "Water resources policy," 1955.

[2] Three major texts on evaluation were released in 1958: John V. Krutilla and Otto Eckstein, Multiple Purpose River Basin Development, Johns Hopkins University Press; Otto Eckstein, Economics of Water Resource Development, The Economics of Project Evaluation, Harvard University Press; and Ronald N. McKean, Efficiency in Government Through Systems Analysis, With Emphasis on Water Resource Development, Wiley and Sons.

[3] Whether the charges are fixed or variable has a direct bearing on use. For a discussion of various aspects of this problem see Michael F. Brewer, *Water Pricing by Small Groups*, California Agriculture, April, 1958; and S. V. Ciriacy-Wantrup, "Cost allocation in relation to western water policies," *Jour. Farm Econ.*, Vol. 36, No. 1, 1954. (Chap. 12 of this volume.)

[4] For a comprehensive discussion of various cost-allocation methods see J. S. Ransmeier, The Tennessee Valley Authority, Vanderbilt University Press, 1942.

[5] Proposed Practices for Economic Analysis of River Basin Projects, May, 1958.

[6] Martin Glaeser, "The St. Lawrence Seaway and power project," *Land Econ.*, Nov., 1954.

[7] Ciriacy-Wantrup suggests construction of a demand and supply function that might be independent of project costs as basis for establishing charges. *Op. cit.*, p. 120.

[8] Report by a Panel of Experts, "Integrated river basin development," United Nations, Department of Economic and Social Affairs, New York, 1958.

[9] A prior project under the planned development program could be credited with any increase in system benefits accruing before similar benefits were provided by other planned additions to the system.

M. F. BREWER is Assistant Professor of Agricultural Economics at the University of California, Berkeley. He has given particular attention to questions of water pricing and he has served on the staff of the President's Council of Economic Advisors.

Chapter 14

MICHAEL F. BREWER

Economics of Public Water Pricing: The California Case*

A SUBSTANTIAL CHAPTER of economic theory focuses on the pricing of publicly produced goods and services. Its empirical counterpart, manifest in public utility rate rulings, enabling legislation of governmental agencies and administrative dicta originating within other public groups, includes a wide variety of pricing methods. Several federal agencies, among them the U.S. Bureau of Reclamation, have well-established policies governing their pricing practices. Other public agencies are in the process of formulating such policies, and the propriety of particular pricing methods has been the subject of considerable argument. The development of relevant criteria and their application in the evaluation of specific pricing alternatives constitute the main theme of this chapter.

Several quite different "publics" often participate in water development. Federal agencies, federations of public districts, counties and local water districts all may be involved in the impoundment of water, its transportation and its distribution to eventual consumers. Water

*The study on which this report was written was financed in part by the Water Resources Center of the University of California. An earlier version of this paper has been published by the Calif. Agr. Exp. Sta. and Giannini Foundation of Agricultural Economics as Research Rept. No. 244, May, 1961.

rights and/or water service commitments are transferred through this chain of organizations. Five pricing methods are analyzed in this study which may be used in the transfer of water from a regional agency's distribution system to local groups. These latter, in turn, provide the necessary physical facilities and the administrative organization for subsequent distribution to individual users. "Regional agency" thus may be regarded as a water wholesaling body and "local groups" as retailing entities.

Proposals of the state of California to construct, finance and administer a statewide water development plan[1] are used for illustrative purposes. This plan includes a series of dams and reservoirs on northern California streams and a system of aqueducts and pumping stations, known as the California Aqueduct System, to distribute the regulated flow throughout the state. Completion of the first project of the California Water Plan — the Feather River Project — will produce 4.0 million acre-feet for annual distribution through the California Aquaduct System. It has been estimated that the predominantly agricultural southern San Joaquin Valley area will receive 44 percent of the total annual delivery from the system, and that 54 percent will be pumped over the Tehachapi Mountains, the southern terminus of the interior Central Valley, for southern California. Delivery contracts executed to date account for 1.18 and 1.91 million acre-feet for the two service areas respectively.

These proposals envisage the contracted delivery of this water from the state's aqueduct system to local organizations, of which the California irrigation district may be considered the prototype. These local districts in turn will serve their members contract water through their own distribution facilities.

A state water pricing method explicitly defines the conditions for water exchange between the state and the water districts. Although this exchange represents a "wholesale" transaction, the conditions which are established influence the financial position of local districts, which in turn bears upon the "retail" pricing methods they employ and thus affects the utilization of the water by eventual consumers. An understanding of the functions of price throughout this process of water transfer is basic to the identification of relevant criteria whereby the adequacy of alternative methods may be assessed.

Section I of this chapter describes the structure of the California water "market" and analyzes the role of price therein. Several different pricing methods are evaluated in Section II. This functional evaluation is extended to embrace broader policy considerations in the final section.

THE WATER MARKET AND WATER PAYMENTS

The Water Industry and Market

By economic convention the term water industry refers to firms which produce water. When a heterogeneous resource is involved, however, the term raises a number of problems. Water presents a broad qualitative spectrum — from sewer effluent to a chemical distillate — and its classification for purposes of transaction embodies broad criteria. Class I and II water are specified by the Bureau of Reclamation on the basis of probability of annual delivery, whereas some districts differentiate "treated" from "untreated" water, and others make a distinction on the basis of elevation at points of delivery. The availability of water from a particular source for given uses and users is partially determined by such institutions as water rights law and water organizations. Demand elasticity and cross elasticity also are affected by these institutions.

The *producing firm* within this industry also presents conceptual difficulties. The water industry is concerned with the development of a regulated flow of usable water. Here again, significant institutional qualifications exist, for such development must not illegally violate existing rights to water use.[3] Water production means making available for export or *in situ* use water otherwise unavailable within the existing institutional context. An organization, law, or administrative procedure facilitating such use thus "produces" water. The production function thus explicitly includes institutional parameters.

The water industry thus emerges as a much qualified concept, useful for exposition but hardly susceptible to relevant analysis by the definitions and hypothetical relationships of conventional industrial analysis.[4]

A "market" is defined with respect to the interaction among buyers and sellers. Properly described, it identifies the process of tenure transactions from producer to consumer, the institutions facilitating this process and the conditions of exchange — or the exchange ratios — prevailing at each stage.

Qualifications to conventional usage of this term are immediately apparent. Producers and sellers of water are not numerically equivalent. Some producers exclusively wholesale water, as does the U.S. Bureau of Reclamation through the Central Valley Project. Others are both wholesalers and retailers, as are local irrigation districts. The dominant qualification of the California water market is its size relative to the industry. Approximately 60 percent of California's irrigation water supply is consumed by producers without direct recourse to any form of water market. Most of this is pumped groundwater and is supplemental to other available sources. The aggregate of this joint production-consumption is, therefore, partially determined by the prices prevailing for water transactions occurring within the market. Actions of the producer-consumer also affect this price through demand cross elasticity and thus are a major extramarket influence that must be reckoned with for an understanding of water price behavior. All of these admitted difficulties notwithstanding, the term "water market" retains expository value.

Price and the Water Market

The meaning of "water price," or more properly "water payments," may be examined within this context. This term is used to introduce the possibility of periodicity of payments and a variety of forms which they may assume. Payment transactions between local agencies and their members likewise may vary in time and form.

Direct water sale receipts[6] made in connection with these transactions comprise only a part of the total revenue that may accrue to the local agency or state. For local districts, assessment and the transfer of funds representing payment for services other than water supply are additional revenues.[7] The size of these fund transfers frequently is related immediately to the direct water payments required of district members. At the state level in California, legislation provides for a similar transfer of funds — in the form of Tideland Oil fund monies[8] — and the possibility of employing general tax revenues at this level has not been ruled out. Thus, total revenues to both the district and state may take the form of: (1) receipts from water sales as specified in contracts or by a district board of directors, (2) assessment receipts and (3) fund transfers from other activities of the distributing unit.

From these revenue categories a distinction may be made among three substantive problem areas: (1) price, (2) payments and (3) financing. Price problems refer to the processes behind the accumulation of sales receipts. Payment refers both to the sales receipts and assessment receipts accounts and the processes they involve. Financing is most general, referring to all three categories of revenue. Although, in the interest of brevity, the problem of financing at the state level is not directly considered, the relationship between state pricing and financing at the local retailing level must be made explicit.

Evaluative criteria are needed to assess the several pricing methods considered. These criteria must permit preference ordering of a set of alternatives. They may be specified on the basis of *a priori* value assertions or from a pragmatic approach to the pricing process itself.[9] Public pricing policy is manifest through legal and administrative institutions which can be appraised relevantly by examination of their functions with the aid of appropriate criteria. The plural functions of water payments imply separate criteria for each level at which the costs or revenues inherent in payment procedures are incident. Three levels are suggested by the water market — regional, local and the consumer.

Payments at the Regional Level

The basic economic purpose of a regional plan of water development is to facilitate continuous enlargement of the real income of the respective region.[10] Attempts to substitute static, cross-sectional income optimization have been abortive.[11] A number of conditions and constraints surrounding this basic objective are important. Three of these have been enunciated in general terms for the Feather River Project: (1) no reduction in the state's credit position, (2) payment by beneficiaries and (3) a prevention of "unjust enrichment." The role of payments is discussed in connection with each.

Early proponents for state water development emphasized the desirability of a self-liquidating financing program,[12] and this initial emphasis has been accepted as an official position by the state.[13] Two interpretations of the phrase appear possible: that the state's water budget should remain in a solvent position and that the state, as a bond debtor, should not assume a major part of the risk that a position of solvency may not be attained.[14]

The first interpretation implies that economic criteria used in the conventional test of financial feasibility are relevant. Construed generally, they require that revenues to the project authority must be adequate to permit payment of interest and principal of those project costs termed "reimbursable," as well as payment of current expenses without resort to general taxation[15] or funds secured therefrom. Although the project's broad public benefits have been emphasized, no policy defining specific nonreimbursable costs yet has emerged. Presumably costs so classified could be met from general tax revenues without violating this condition.

The second interpretation requires keeping acceptably low the probability that risks of unfavorable future economic conditions[16] incident upon the regional authority will cause a drain on public funds. This becomes especially important in light of the long period of indebtedness that reasonably might be anticipated in connection with regional water development programs.

From the outset of discussion on the California Water Plan the principle that beneficiaries pay has been consistently espoused, although it too has been subject to various interpretations. One group of advocates holds that the payment be designated to maximize the return to the state. This has been suggested for project power sales but has been held relevant also for water sales to irrigation and other user groups.[17] A second interpretation advocates payments proportional to benefits received with total payments by beneficiaries being equal to, but not in excess of, total project costs, including interest on bonded debt.[18] One argument used in connection with this proposition has been the avoidance of "unjust enrichment." The relationship between these two arguments is considered on following pages. A third version of beneficiary payment considers only reimbursable benefits.[19] For present purposes the magnitude of aggregate size is more directly appraised by criteria pertaining to the protection of state credit. The general principle of beneficiary payment, on the other hand, may be measured by or compared with a standard in which payment is proportional to benefits received.

Private benefits in excess of costs are considered as a form of enrichment resulting from the project. General concern has been expressed over the incidence and magnitude of such private benefits. Avoidance of "unjust enrichment" has been a widely accepted condition for pricing and other aspects of project administration.

Two basic ways in which regional water development may affect the private benefits realized by individuals within the agricultural sector of the region's economy are important in this connection: (1) through the returns from production and (2) land values. Since these benefits may assume numerous forms, enrichment from participation in regional water development may be considered as positive changes in the net worth of individuals. The "justness" of individual enrichment is subject to various interpretations,[20] but its determination is not essential for purposes of evaluating alternative pricing methods. On the other hand, the extent to which a particular method permits the adjustment of enrichment, in terms of incidence and/or over-all magnitude, is of direct relevance.

Payments and the Local District

The ability of local districts to change the size and composition of member payments provides them with a tool for achieving water allocation objectives as well as a source of revenue. The composition of member payments has direct bearing on the district's financial position as the certainty of income streams from different forms of payment varies.

The various functions of payment and the relatively wide degree of latitude afforded public water districts under California law in this respect have been noted.[21] Although specific payment decisions will depend on particular attributes of individual districts, general criteria may be ascertained.

The provision of water at least cost to members is a prime constituent interest. In this regard, the nonprofit nature of the districts, their power to issue bonds and the technical economies of large-scale development and distribution facilities are advantages of this form of organization. When districts are so constituted that physical interrelationships among different water sources used by its members entail joint costs, district pricing practices, although directly related to district water deliveries alone, may also affect the costs of obtaining water from other sources.[22] Under such circumstances district pricing must be evaluated in terms of the entire water system available to members.

Retail pricing practices may result in different charges to individual members for similar amounts of water. Being unable to disassociate from the organization at will may give rise to factions or dissension groups. These may be sufficiently numerous and powerful in terms of member voting blocs that district administration becomes unwieldy and difficult. In several situations the development of such factions within California irrigation districts has resulted in the replacement of

district-wide development programs by smaller, localized units organized and financed through individual improvement districts[23] within
the same parent irrigation district. The extent to which different pricing practices avoid equity problems may thus be posited as a relevant
internal evaluative criterion.

Additional criteria relate to the effects of pricing on district solvency and to the security of a district's water rights. Under California
law, both the extent and type of water use by members of a district may
affect the tenure uncertainty of these rights, principally in terms of
their jeopardy to prescriptive capture.

Payments and the Water Consumer

The type of payment adopted by a district for its members shapes
their water-use decisions.[24] The district assessment may be considered a fixed cost for annual production decisions as it customarily is
based upon an unimproved property valuation. The water toll, on the
other hand, is a variable production cost. So long as member demand
elasticity is less than infinity, tolls of different sizes will induce use of
different quantities of the district supply. Thus the form and size of
payments set by a local district will partially determine the length and
direction of the water input vector[25] for irrigation production within the
boundaries of that district.

Often additional noncost allocating devices are used. Rotational delivery, necessitated by the limited capacity of distribution systems, effectively imposes an upper volume limit on individual deliveries. Pro-
rating methods of water rationing for those years in which effective
water demands exceed supply have been adopted by most water districts.
In spite of these provisions the direct consideration of water costs in
production decisions renders the payment schedule an effective tool for
allocating local water supplies.

The irrigating member of a local district that is a potential con-
tractee for regionally developed water judges regional pricing on the
basis of payment schedules adopted by his district. A regional pricing
method is deemed acceptable if it permits use of the enlarged district
water supply at a profit. This may result from an expansion of irrigated acreage, from a shift to more intensive irrigation practices or
from a substitution of a lower cost water source for a higher cost
source.

ECONOMIC ANALYSIS OF PRICING METHODS

A pricing method is considered to be a general formulation of price.
The methods discussed do not establish a numerical price by themselves; however, they do identify the major variables in a price function
and are susceptible to comparative evaluation.

Although one can conceive of innumerable major variables about which a price function may be defined — and indeed actual pricing methods demonstrate remarkable variety — a basic classification is nevertheless suggested. Three factors stand out as having been dominant variables to public water pricing decisions: location of delivery (in relation to the head of a surface distribution system), the type of use to which water is put and time.

Price may be systematically related to any or all of these variables or it may be functionally unrelated. It is not necessary to analyze each of the possible combinations. Five specific pricing methods are considered:

1. Postage-stamp pricing.
2. Differentiation by types of water use.
3. Zonal price differentiation.
4. Price variations over time.
5. Benefit pricing.

Of these the first four have been discussed widely in connection with public water development projects.

As defined, these methods are not necessarily mutually exclusive. Several may be used conjunctively; however, use of certain ones will preclude the simultaneous adoption of others. For instance, postage-stamp pricing is inconsistent with zonal price differentiation, whereas it might be used jointly with price variability over time.

Each of the methods discussed is appraised by reference to the functional criteria developed in the preceding section as well as by more formal criteria of economic efficiency.

Postage-Stamp Pricing

This pricing method is characterized by an identical price for given water uses throughout the service area. The principal exponent of postage-stamp pricing for water is the U.S. Bureau of Reclamation. Within a reclamation project, the same price is charged recipients (either districts or individuals) of water for agricultural purposes from any point on the distribution system.[26] Similar practices have been considered for a state water pricing policy. This pricing method may be evaluated both from formal and functional standpoints.

Establishing a single price for a public service raises the problem of how the charge is to be determined. Federal reclamation projects determine a cost designed to generate sufficient water sales revenues over the project's life to cover that part of allocated project costs termed "reimbursable." Federal accounting procedures frequently entail a write-off of certain reimbursable costs by fund transfer in multiple-purpose projects and by using interest-free capital. In the instance of the Feather River Project, more traditional agruments of marginal and average cost pricing appear pertinent as any write-off of project costs presumably will be minimal. This problem is parallel to that of public electric utility rate structures, and the not inconsiderable literature on this subject is relevant. A fundamental theoretical controversy covered in this literature is between incremental cost (or marginal cost) and average cost pricing.

Under certain conditions, economic theory demonstrates that marginal cost pricing will result in an efficient allocation of goods so priced. Whether or not a similar case can be made for the price of water has been subject to question in the literature.[27] The implied welfare criteria are those of a competitive market economy. This invokes assumptions of perfect foresight on the part of entrepreneurs and a long-run equilibrium such that for a given income distribution no subsequent transfer could increase the satisfactions of one water user without reducing those of another. These conditions require a long-run production situation such that marginal cost equals average cost and both equal price. Certainly the instantaneous, competitive economic model has desirable analytical attributes. But is it applicable to water? Water development units are hardly competitive in the way required, nor are the factors used perfectly divisible, permitting a situation in which no price would be possible such that it equals simultaneously marginal cost and average cost.

The central shortcoming of this pricing argument is that situations characterized by discrete change are represented in marginal terms. Marginal pricing distinguishes the dates of particular costs. Once factor opportunity costs have been paid, the argument runs, the producer need take no further account of them in deciding a current price. Thus, so long as a single factor is not perfectly divisible over time, losses occur under a marginal cost price. As has been pointed out by Wiseman,[28] the consequent water development must be a common multiple of the length of life of all productive factors. Any interval of different length would involve an arbitrary decision that the interval selected is one particularly relevant to the calculation of marginal cost and a value judgment that income should be redistributed over time in favor of the consumers of goods produced by factors of a given relative durability.

This charge has been parried by the adoption of the so-called investment principle.[29] This principle argues that marginal cost pricing be used to decide selling prices of goods or services in existence but that the investment necessary to create them initially may be considered justified only if a perfectly discriminating monopolist could recover his cost by perfect price discrimination, that is, if community benefits are in excess of community costs. The investment principle really begs the question. The problem of whether a particular decision is one of marginal pricing or of investment remains to be resolved on an arbitrary basis.

Average cost pricing has been another single price argument. It suggests a price which recovers all money outlays that could have been avoided if a product had not been produced. Its proponents have stressed the necessity of a price that induces investment in the perpetuation and expansion of existing plant and capacity. An incremental cost price would entail total sales receipts less than total production costs over rates of production characterized by decreasing average costs.

This argument has been questioned[30] on the basis that some of the factors included in average cost pricing are fixed costs and that their inclusion prevents optimum welfare conditions. These conditions call for additional consumption at a price not greater than additional costs necessarily incurred in providing for that consumption. Average cost pricing, therefore, would curtail use before the optimum consumption rate was reached under conditions of decreasing average cost or would stimulate excessive investment in additional capacity under rates of production characterized by increasing average cost.

Other attributes of postage-stamp pricing are important for a functional evaluation. These may be illustrated by reference again to the California Water Plan. Due to geographic dimensions, the total cost of water delivery increases as it is brought farther south in the state.

If water is purchased or contracts are signed at a single designated and fixed cost, the marginal value product presumably exceeds this magnitude. If postage-stamp pricing is employed and related to total aqueduct costs, there is no indication when the marginal cost of the distribution facility is in excess of the marginal value product at southerly locations in the state and thus there is no safeguard against overexpansion of the facility.

A related objection is seen with regard to the unjust enrichment criterion. Under postage-stamp pricing, a northern irrigator (assuming less favorable site and climatic conditions and thus a lower net return per acre) may have his consumer's surplus confiscated in greater degree than his more southerly counterpart. The northern irrigator, in fact, actually may be paying in excess of the marginal cost of providing water to his region; while southern farmers may experience a marginal value product less than the marginal cost of water supply. Under these circumstances efficient production would require an expansion of northern production and a contraction of more southerly irrigated acreages. Motivation for this adjustment may be removed by the use of a single price based on total costs.

From an operational standpoint a postage-stamp pricing method offers few problems. Requirements for its application are delivery data and water-use categories represented by contracting districts.

Differentiation by Type of Use

There is broad precedent for pricing water by type of use. The U.S. Bureau of Reclamation differentiates between municipal and industrial water and irrigation water sold from the Central Valley Project. Many irrigation districts employ domestic water rates different from those covering irrigation water service. Public utility commissions repeatedly have upheld rate differentiations on the basis of various costs of serving different uses.

From a regional standpoint a differentiation of price among types of water use appears to enhance real income through optimal allocation if the difference factor is made proportional to the respective marginal value products of water in each use. If reliance can be placed on profit maximization motives of individual water users, this pricing tool would make higher charges incident on those most able to meet them. This would strengthen the credit position of the state to a greater extent than would be true were postage-stamp pricing adopted.

If various types of water use are envisaged as taking place within a typical Marshallian "firm," a price differentiated by productivity factors would satisfy the unjust enrichment criterion. Under these circumstances consumers' surplus would be captured proportionately to the marginal value product of each use. Clearly the assumption is inconsistent with the actual diversity of units within each type of use. However, differential pricing by use requires a basic classification of uses. It may also be possible to classify users within each type depending upon available data.

In discussing the relevancy of this pricing tool to the California Water Plan, two positions have been advanced regarding the area over which such a differentiated price might be applied. One maintains that a given differential be made applicable for the entire state; the other argues for differentiation among uses by differing regions.

Because charges for agricultural water traditionally have been less than those for either domestic or municipal and industrial use, selection of the area within which such differentiation is effected has important cost incidence consequences.   For example, ordinarily a locally established differential would favor local agriculture if either or both of the following conditions obtain: the proportion of agricultural to industrial-domestic water use is relatively low or the land-use pattern is characterized by high value nonagricultural land uses, such as industrial use or domestic subdivision. This stems from two relationships. The larger the relative quantity of higher priced water for nonagricultural purposes, the lower the price of agricultural water for a given regional revenue target.[31] A related corollary lies in the economic shock-absorbing effect of the higher priced water uses. The price for agricultural water would tend to be less sensitive to changes of a regional revenue target.

The second regional advantage attaches to use of the property assessment component of the retail water payment complex. Differences in property valuation systems for California irrigation districts have been used effectively to change the incidence of total district costs (which may be considered total water costs) toward urban areas. So long as local contracting agencies have member assessment powers,[32] the favorable tax base of areas such as southern California may be used to reduce the portion of total cost per acre-foot of delivered water paid by agriculture. This regional advantage becomes especially apparent when total regional payments to the state are tied to designated costs. However, if price differentials among use designated on a state-wide basis, the resulting price ratios would be equal for all regions, and agriculture in areas with relatively low municipal and industrial use would gain the cost-sharing advantage of the state average.

Contractual stipulations are required to assure effective compliance at the retail level with water payment differentiation designated by a regional authority. Two difficulties immediately present themselves at this point: the reduction in district pricing flexibility entailed and the substitution of water from different sources within districts as a way of avoiding such resale stipulations.

Local irrigation districts have many factors to consider in determining a retail payments schedule. One such consideration relates to the management of the system of water available to the area served by a district. The payment complex may be used in a manner designed to induce use of a particular combination of water sources within the district consistent with the criterion of lowest total cost water over relatively long periods of time. Frequently such water management programs entail the integration of groundwater pumping with surface water use. In California and other states not having general regulatory jurisdiction over the operation of privately owned pumping plants, the payment complex affords the public water district a useful tool for water management programs. As both the assessment and water toll components are administratively determined by the district, the variable unit cost of district water may be "set" in any desired relationship to the comparable cost for pumped groundwater. In this manner, groundwater may be rendered either a prime source or one supplemental to district-delivered surface water. Thus, through the district organization, an entire area may be able to pursue water management activities generating benefits either so broad in their incidence or so future in their anticipated realization that individuals on their own initiative would not undertake them.[33] Use of contractual resale stipulations would diminish the flexibility of district pricing and its ability to pursue such programs.

A second operational difficulty stems from the substitutability of district supplies. Were a district to receive only water from the California Water Plan, such contract stipulations could be made binding. When other water sources are available, not thus encumbered by contract, a substitution of sources for particular uses could render this pricing method ineffective.

To these considerations should be added the fact that districts are public bodies. The efficiency with which a district operates — establishes mechanisms for decision making, assembles a competent staff, obtains the degree of member concensus to permit the implementation of management programs, etc. — is related to the stability of the organization and its executive body. This stability has been the major consequence of the evolved equilibrium between the political and economic forces internal to these organizations.[34]

The effects of different tools for state water price policy on a district's future organizational viability merit substantial consideration. A frequent basis for the separation of district members into factions is the type of water-use activity in which they are engaged. Many districts found that the expansion of initially small urban centers within their boundaries required major readjustments in the operations of their water systems, pricing arrangements and, in some instances, precinct redistricting for election purposes. The problems encountered and solutions pursued are unique to each individual district. A program of water price differentiation by type of use to the extent that contract stipulations require the adoption of new internal arrangements within the district, undoubtedly would meet with district opposition and would place in jeopardy the political equilibrium they have evolved. Thus, although partial analysis indicates an increase in economic efficiency by such practices, its overassiduous implementation might disrupt local districts at substantial social and economic cost.

Zonal Price Differentiation

Proposals for a zonal differentiation of state water price for the California Water Plan have been made under the general heading of the "delta pool concept."[35] This concept differentiates between the production and distribution phases of the regional water plan. It entails the designation of an average acre-foot charge for water at the delta of the Sacramento and San Joaquin rivers which subsequently is transported farther south by the California Aqueduct System. Zones are to be established along the southern course of this distribution system within which a single water price would prevail for contracting entities.[36] The zonal acre-foot cost will consist of a charge based upon the cost of facilities required to deliver water to each zone in addition to the designated delta charge.

Aqueduct costs are to be allocated to each such zone on the basis of proportional use of facilities. Other methods of cost allocation may be employed in connection with this pricing method, administration protestations notwithstanding.[37] For an aqueduct system entailing scale economies the problem becomes one of allocating negative joint costs — or joint benefits — among aqueduct reaches. If scale economies exist, the sum of the separable costs will be less than total aqueduct cost. The separable-cost-remaining-benefits method, generally adopted by federal agencies for cost allocation among different project functions, holds distinct advantages.[38] Its use in connection with zonal pricing appears relevant, as intrazonal deliveries may be considered different purposes of the entire "multi-purpose" aqueduct system.[39]

Absence of published data on the California Aqueduct System prevents a direct comparison between the two methods of cost allocation. It is possible, however, to infer the major difference. Use of the separable-cost-remaining-benefits method would allocate larger portions of joint benefits to southern California than to the San Joaquin River Valley area. This is due to two attributes of the regions. First, the temporal bunching of irrigation demand requires a larger capacity structure per acre-foot delivered annually than the constant demand of municipal and industrial water which comprises a high proportion of anticipated southern California demand.[40] Second, the relatively larger share of total benefits accruing to southern California does not tend to decrease the portion of total joint benefits accruing to southern California under the proportionate use of facilities method.

If zonal price differentiation is combined with preconstruction contract guarantees,[41] the incremental costs of southern water diversion will be covered by revenues from water sales, eliminating the possibility for facility overexpansion. A number of technical problems, however, accompany this proposal. If a zone north of the most southerly zone served indicates an unwillingness to contract for amounts of water adequate to assure receipts to the regional authority equivalent to costs, does this influence the size of contract payments to the more southerly zone? Will their costs be adjusted to cover the delinquent zones' excess costs? Are these excess costs to be amortized over all other potentially "solvent" zones along the distribution system?

This eventuality appears distinctly possible, especially if a differentiation of price among different uses is made by local agencies. The Metropolitan Water District of Southern California already has existing mechanisms for such a differentiation, effectively shifting cost incidence to urban or industrial areas by *ad valorem* property assessment. Although individual irrigation districts also have this power, their limited size probably would require a federated organization for effective intrazonal price differentiation by use. The southern California coastal plain would be able to shift a larger portion of the zone's cost to urban and industrial uses than would the Central Valley areas, as previously noted. Such a reduction of agricultural water costs might disrupt the current interregional patterns of agricultural competition within the state.

Conceivably, such a change in regional production may be economically efficient. This would be the case if the marginal value product of agricultural water were greater in southern California than in the San Joaquin Valley. If the urban center-agricultural hinterland thesis[42] is accepted, the intraregional shift of water cost incidence from agriculture to municipal and industrial water users would not impair the efficiency of agricultural production, as the urban area (comprising mainly municipal and industrial water users) is considered an integral part of regional agricultural production. If this thesis does not hold, the postulated agricultural production shift would represent a net loss of regional real income. Whether this thesis is appropriate for southern California is open to question. If the industrial-urban concentration of the southern coastal plain represents a self-contained economic unit whose functions are independent of an agricultural hinterland, the postulated shift in agricultural production would not satisfy optimal production conditions.

This admittedly is a static interpretation of efficiency. The willingness of southern California municipal and industrial water users to bear part of the cost of agricultural water doubtless reflects their desire to establish current use of this water. It will be available to the entire region at some point in future time when a substitution of expanded municipal and industrial water uses for former irrigation use is anticipated.

In this sense the marginal value product to this part of the state would be adequate to warrant the current underwriting of agricultural costs by municipal and industrial water users. This still does not assure a situation of economic efficiency for the state's total economy. The organization of water agencies through the Metropolitan Water District permits a longer time horizon for the conception and estimation of a marginal value product of water than is afforded the Central Valley organizations. Such assurance would require comparable planning horizons on the part of organizations in both parts of the state.

Price Variations Over Time

The initial financing proposals for the California Water Plan envisage the issuance of 50-year, general obligation bonds. The length of delivery contracts is 75 years. A variable acre-foot charge for contracted water during this period has been proposed. This proposal reflects the desire to receive payment commitments adequate to assure project solvency prior to state construction, on the one hand, and uncertainty with respect to the actual construction cost and immediate effective demand for state water on the other.

To the extent that a variation of contract price is passed on by a district to its members through the payment complex, contract water assumes cost attributes for the eventual consumer similar to those of pumped groundwater. A basic difference would be that cost changes of pumped groundwater are associated with physical conditions of the groundwater aquifer and power costs. As the latter are relatively stable by virtue of public utility rate regulations, future cost changes may be estimated by the analysis of past and current groundwater conditions. Variations in the price for state water would have different, and not necessarily as predictable, determinants with the possible consequence of higher on-farm costs of sudden adjustments to price changes. This could be minimized, however, by announcing cost estimates for future periods of delivery or stipulating maximum and minimum limits to such future cost changes.

From the standpoint of contracting districts, some guarantee is needed to assure that solvency can be maintained under a flexible price contract; some effective ceiling would have to be specified. The inability to project the eventual level of a district's future payment to the state renders the schedule of payments adopted for its members subject to future change. Prior to contracting for water from a regional water development program, a district's future water demand must be predicted. Districts anticipating an expansion of current demand — as the result of either members' substituting additional surface water for presently pumped groundwater or the expansion of irrigated acreage within the district — will attempt to contract for a quantity consistent with estimated future demand.

If the average acre-foot payment of the district to the regional authority increases to a point at which the associated internal payment complex removes the inducement to expand internal irrigation, the district would have overcontracted in terms of effective member demand. Under such conditions it would have to sell whatever possible of its excess water to nondistrict entities. Although there are at present no restrictions on such extradistrict sales, nondistrict demand for such water generally would tend to be lowest during those times when the largest surpluses would accrue.[43] Failing to dispose of its excess water by nondistrict sales, the additional revenue to the district needed for contract payments would have to be exacted from members by increasing either the water toll or assessment, or both. Thus, such a pricing device conceivably could result in a higher cost for water to individual water users than would be the case under a fixed contract payment.

From the standpoint of the regional authority, flexibility of price over time constitutes protection against the impairment of its credit by project financing arrangements. This follows from uncertainty surrounding structure and facility cost estimates and the uncertainty of future effective demand by districts as well as the size of future fund transfers. Should these costs substantially exceed present estimates or should current estimates of general obligation bond interest be incorrect,[44] the regional authority might have to repay bondholders from general fund monies or resort to general taxation. Both lines of recourse would impair its credit position as well as violate beneficiary payment criteria.

In the absence of price flexibility, the risk of increasing costs is effectively incident upon the regional authority. This is not necessarily consistent with the enhancement of regional income. Absence of this risk at the district or the consumer level precludes an effective stimulant to agricultural adjustment in connection with factor cost change and thus may freeze existing water use in patterns rendered inefficient by such change. Variation of price over time would, however, provide the regional authority with a means whereby adjustment of individual enrichment from public water development could be achieved continuously. Such enrichment may be expected to change over time with technological change and shifts in the relative prices of associated inputs.

A more significant aspect of price variation over time relates to the stimulation of water use in particular areas that is consistent with overall economic planning of a region. For example if, after the California Water Plan is constructed, an industrial or urban expansion is desirable in a particular area, flexible pricing would permit a payment change to be used as an inducement of such expansion.

Benefit Pricing

The final pricing method to be examined is one based upon benefits received. Conceptually it requires knowledge about the demand function for water; and in application it entails prices resembling those of a perfectly discriminating monopolist. So long as the demand functions of separate local districts are not equally elastic with respect to price, sales receipts are maximized by this pricing method. This elementary

theorem of economics refutes the widely held position that only a price
related to allocated costs can assure project solvency.[45] This latter
formulation in no way guarantees solvency, whereas actual financial
solvency of the state is increased by such a benefit-pricing system.
This derives from the fact that offers to contract will be conditional
upon the relationship between established price and value attributed. A
cost established in excess of this value will have no bidders and hence
no sales receipts regardless of whether its formulation is by a cost
base or any other type of base. Thus the solvency position of the state
depends on the cost-based price being not greater than the value of water in all instances of actual delivery. Where this is not so, repayment
by sales receipts would be incomplete.

Frequent attempts are made to analyze water-use activities within
potential service areas so as to guarantee such a favorable relationship
of cost-based price to benefits. However, the magnitude of benefits is
difficult to estimate and is subject to change with variations in the expectation of future events as well as with changes of factor price and
technical conditions of production. Regardless of the fact that the estimating procedures used by regional agencies appear to be somewhat
lacking, the susceptibility of benefits to change demonstrates forcefully
the need for price to reflect value changes — not merely the performance
of certain water accounts or cost allocations. Benefit pricing requires
such changes as future events and behavior show them to be necessary.
On the other hand, the tendency toward inflexibility of prices tied to
other computational bases works against such change in pricing conditions.

This method also would localize charges on beneficiaries. They
would be progressive and therefore tend toward an equalization of net
benefits received. This generally is consistent with the prevention of
unjust enrichment.[46]

At the local level this method may result in limiting the flexibility
of internal district pricing arrangements. This certainly would be the
case if resale stipulations were introduced into water delivery contracts
or if benefit pricing were imposed by regional authority directly upon
consumers. Such extreme interpretation of benefit pricing also entails
associated problems relating to the regional authority's ability to assess
the value of water to individual district members or internal groups.

A more moderate interpretation considers each district to be a production unit to which a unit water benefit may be imputed. This appears
the most feasible manner in which the method can be applied. It would
provide the basis for contract payments from individual districts and
would leave them their present flexibility in using the payment complex
for internal pricing arrangements. The availability of approximate benefit measures argues in favor of using the district as the unit for analysis as well as administration of such a pricing method. The cost to
particular organizations of already developed water supplies and of alternative but as yet undeveloped supplies may be used as confining limits to these benefits.

The value of benefits may be taken as a weighted average of benefits or marginal value product to individual water uses and users occurring within its boundaries. Technically each district would have a different average benefit but, in practice, ranges could be established into which recipient organizations could be grouped. The geographical configuration of actual payments resulting from this price tool would parallel that derived from a zonal price differentiation. For example, in the case of the Feather River Project, each of these pricing methods would result in average acre-foot payments increasing to the south. In one case this results from the allocation of aqueduct system cost; in the other case it results from the increasing limitation on alternative water supplies in that direction.

From the standpoint of water tenure uncertainty, value pricing appears to have positive attributes. This is particularly true for those contracting districts with appropriative water rights. If the quantity of water contracted, in addition to that from other district sources, exceeds effective demand, the possibility of prescriptive capture because of nonuse presents itself. Under benefit pricing arrangements, the price charged presumably will assure a ready local market and reduce the tenure uncertainty of district water from sources other than by contract.

A further advantage from the district standpoint of such a pricing method is that the direct link with benefits implies an automatic price adjustment geared to the particular phase of the business cycle prevailing at a given time. It would provide protection against the wholesale foreclosing experienced in many districts during the national depression when water payments were not adjusted accordingly.

PRICING METHODS AND WATER POLICY

The close relationship between water pricing and a number of important water policy issues may be made explicit by considering the three major areas of water policy issues: project evaluation and selection, financing and repayment, and water law and organization.[47] Water pricing is but one aspect of the second category, yet is closely interrelated with the other two. Forms of payment and conditions of proprietary transfer are partly determined by water organization and law. If a payment method is adopted that precludes a specific type of previously existing use, the calculation of benefits and costs needed to reach decisions of project selection must be recomputed. This in turn may alter the priority ranking of alternative water projects. Pricing thus is not an isolated matter to be resolved after other policy decisions have been made. Relevant economic analyses of public water development projects must consider methods of product payment and the form of organization that will be adopted.

Public investment activities[48] can be justified by the failure of private investment actions to satisfy social criteria. The composition of the private investment, its aggregate size or its timing may be inconsistent with these criteria. Of the several causes for this failure that have been indicated,[49] two are of immediate relevance to water pricing methods. These are price signal failures due to indivisible proprietorship and differences between private and public time preference rates.

Proprietary Indivisibilities

Indivisibilities in water "ownership" may be of two types: indivisibilities in quantity and over time. Both exist in most nonnegotiable contracts. Reduction of these indivisibilities facilitates proprietary transfer and thus potentially enhances the efficiency of the resulting water allocation. Reduction of quantitative indivisibilities tends to deter the development of a noncompetitive market environment wherein such transfer may occur. Reducing temporal indivisibilities increases the frequency of opportunities for water reallocation. Although in itself not sufficient, the ability to redefine proprietary interest is a necessary condition to such a reallocation.

A reduction of these two types of indivisibilities at the wholesale level may be considered to be an increase in the negotiability of water delivery contracts. Such negotiability bears directly upon the problem of water transfer in connection with secular economic adjustments of agriculture. It would permit water delivery contracts between the regional authority and a local district to be sold. Obviously, concurrence by both entities would be required to allow the transition to be incorporated into the delivery schedule of the former and avoid overcapacity demands on the aqueduct system.

Similarly, a legal transfer of liability for payments to the state during the remaining life of the contract would require agreement of all parties. Under these provisions, however, use of negotiable contracts would contribute to the economic efficiency of the operation of a regional program of water development and distribution. Particular advantage is seen from the standpoint of facilitating adjustment among water-using activities on the one hand and water supply organization on the other. That is, the proprietary interest may be shifted as different forms of local distributive organizations appear more suitable in light of future changes in the pattern of water use. Different forms of local distribution organization may be desired as a result of such a change in the use pattern, or they may be adopted specifically to induce those changes that are deemed desirable. Avoidance of lags in these shifts, resulting from a relatively fixed allocation of water supply, would be facilitated by this tool, permitting the more immediate realization of the increments in real income implied by the shift in the pattern of water use.

The negotiable contract *per se* would not tend toward equity problems. Linked with provisions for a centrally imposed assessment upon a new contract recipient, the cost to local organizations could be varied effectively so that a portion of consumers' surplus could be captured. Indeed, if the transfer implied no major change in the use pattern of the eventual consumption of that water, no assessment would be indicated. However, if a basic change in type of use was involved, the assessment would provide one mechanism to confiscate a larger portion of the marginal value product of that water assumed to exceed that of the previous water-use pattern. Thus such negotiability would be a deterrent to unjust enrichment problems if coupled with a centrally imposed contract transfer assessment.

An increase in negotiability also would tend to strengthen the credit position of the regional authority. It would facilitate the transfer of active contracts from organizations financially insolvent to others with a stronger financial position and thus considerably strengthen the collateral for future contracted payments to the authority. If the organization petitioning as transferee had an inadequate financial position, state approval could be withheld and the transfer prevented.

Such a provision would induce a market for contracts and thereby provide data enabling a more precise estimate of the value of its assets than would be the case if such a value were imputed. If price adjustments are to be made at some point during the life of the contract, as accurate information as possible on the asset value of outstanding contracts would assist materially in determining the magnitude and direction of such changes consistent with the over-all solvency position of the regional program.

The 50 years' liability and service commitment assumed by districts contracting from the California Water Plan may be commuted by sale of the contract. This is particularly important in light of the anticipated population expansion of California during the next 50 years and the attendant adjustments in water use that will accompany this growth.

Two aspects of this adjustment are significant: (1) the adoption of new forms of organization and (2) the changes in the financial base of local districts. Past experience of California irrigation districts evidences the difficulties of using this form of organization to construct, finance and administer extensive systems of domestic water supply. Most of these districts had assumed an initial function of providing irrigation water service. With the subdivision of previously agricultural land within their boundaries, many districts were faced with the need to provide domestic service in substantial quantity. Public health regulations requiring either a sanitation treatment of all district water or the construction of entirely separate domestic systems caused financial difficulties in a number of districts, especially during the early phases of such transitions in water use. In many instances new urban areas within irrigation districts established their own domestic water supply agencies, frequently purchasing water at wholesale from the district. Contract negotiability would facilitate the use of more adequate forms of organization dictated by the evolving conditions. It would not freeze the incidence of risk and uncertainty of meeting state payments on the older district and would simultaneously reduce price uncertainty of that water to the newer organization.

The changing financial base of local water districts likewise makes the negotiable contract desirable. Should this base become restricted, as occurred throughout the western United States during the depression of the 1930's, the district may attempt to alter its operations in response. The fixity of delivery quotas and the cost incidence of a nonnegotiable contract curtail the ability of the district to so adjust.

Differences Between Private and Public Time Preference

Time preference rates conceptually express the ratio of marginal monetary utility at the present time with some point in the future. Such utilities are summary expression of a host of real and illusory variables. No attempt is made to summarize the research into the specific functional relationships involved. Two generalizations are accepted and related to water pricing. First, the aggregate nature of a region, defined as consistent with the regional authority, may be characterized by time preference rates that differ from those of the largest private investment agents within the region or to the weighted average of such rates of all private investment agents therein. It further is accepted that changes in public time preference differ in magnitude, timing and possible direction from private rates. Plausibility of these assumptions derives from the influence of custom and habit patterned on what is generally considered "private" as opposed to "public" investment responsibilities.

Without the means to specify the character of these differences — and they must be so specified as must the changes in external influences on prices for optimization of the public-private investment mix — one may point to the need for project flexibility. This flexibility may be included through physical project design as well as through administrative and operative practices. Although such flexibility almost certainly will involve costs, failure to adapt to future conditions and changed objectives may incur substantially greater costs. Identifying the economic margin of buying program flexibility is an interesting analytical problem to which little professional attention has been devoted. In the absence of formal criteria to indicate the optimal degree of flexibility, one merely may stress the importance of the condition and consider the extent to which various pricing tools are conducive to such flexibility.

Physical flexibility relates to the adaptive capacity of the physical system of the plan to future changes in physical proportions. Variation in the initially proposed delivery schedule may require change in the capacity of designated portions of the southern California Aqueduct System. The extent to which such changes can be made in the future and their cost provide an index of the plan's physical flexibility.

Administrative flexibility is desirable for obvious reasons. Inaccuracy of future cost estimates, changing structures of local organizations or changing water-use patterns may make changes in cost and water tenure conditions desirable. Equally obvious is the fact that provisions for administrative flexibility must make allowance for certain guarantees to contractees. The incidence of risk among the various agents involved in the pricing procedure is a basic determinant of their time preference and planning horizon. If proposals for administrative flexibility entail subjecting individual districts or their consumers to a large uncertainty with respect to their future net returns from water-using activities, the time preference of those agents will be increased and their planning horizon decreased accordingly.

The extent to which any area-wide agency can shift the risk incidence to more local agents depends, of course, on its relative political strength and the number of alternatives available to the potential contractees. The optimal incidence of cost uncertainty cannot be specified on any *a priori* grounds. The capability of a local agency to absorb uncertainty depends upon its organization and its financial foundation — its recourse to bonds, other forms of credit and liability to obligations undertaken.

California has a relatively advanced organization of local water districts with the power of assessment and the recourse to receivership by a special state agency designed purposively as a way of avoiding bankruptcy proceedings.[50] More cost uncertainty can be tolerated there than in a state where the ability to hedge and the degrees of financial protection are not afforded.

CONCLUSIONS

A final remark relates to the status of state pricing policy at the end of the 75-year contract. What provisions for recontract, price and quantity variations are to be made? Consideration of this problem accepts a premise pertaining to the relationship between public water development and the broader concept of economic planning.

As discussed on preceding pages, the economic rationale of the California Water Plan is inferred as the increase of net productivity of the state. Although water development is considered relatively in isolation from other aspects of the California economy, frequently public resource development programs are integrated with general economic planning.

It is submitted that, although there is little public attempt to relate such development to economic planning, the future will see this relationship growing in political and economic importance. The purposeful use of water — or other resource development activities — to induce particular patterns of population and economic activity reasonably may be expected to become a more prominent issue for research and practical implementation.

If such a future trend is anticipated, proposals for state pricing policy must be made as accommodating as possible to future changes that will permit the integration of the administration of the California Water Plan into the broader scope of economic planning.

In light of this, proposals[51] to grant perpetuity contracts appear to be an inappropriate public pricing tool. The continued service by the state under conditions essentially similar to the initial contract would appear consistent with the enhancement of state income. If contract receipts exceed total costs of the California Water Plan, these receipts appropriately would be paid into the general fund of the state and thus be available for public reinvestment. Furthermore, additional outlays undoubtedly will have to be made in connection with the plan.

FOOTNOTES

[1]Calif. Dept. of Water Resources, "The California water plan," Water Resources Bul. No. 3, Sacramento, 1957, 246 pp.

[2]Charles T. Main, General Evaluation of the Proposed Program for Financing and Constructing the State Water Resources Development System of the State of California Department of Water Resources (final report; Boston: Chas. T. Main, Inc., 1960), pp. 7-8. These data were supplemented by more recent figures from the files of the California Department of Water Resources, Sacramento.

[3]Under California water rights law, appropriative, riparian and correlative rights may be violated legally by open, continuous, adverse use. Such use over a designated period of time may establish prescriptive rights to the adverse user. See Wells A. Hutchins, The California Law of Water Rights, State Printing Office, Sacramento, 1956, pp. 284-343.

[4]This term connotes the methodology based upon Stackelberg's approach to market analysis. See Heinrich Stackelberg, The Theory of the Market Economy, translated from the German with an introduction by Alan T. Peacock (1st German ed., 1943; Oxford University Press, New York, 1952).

[5]U.S. Bureau of the Census, United States Census of Agriculture: 1950 Irrigation of Agricultural Lands, the United States, 1952, Vol. 3, p. 3.

[6]Technically, this is the receipt of payments for water service, or water rental receipts, as there is no transference of a water right.

[7]The California irrigation district and most other forms of public water districts have the power of member assessment. Those that engage in functions that produce other vendible goods or services, notably electrical power, often transfer any surplus incurred to their water accounts in a manner comparable to the basin account procedure of the U.S. Bureau of Reclamation.

[8]California Assembly Bill No. 1062, signed by the Governor on April 18, 1959, as Chapter 140 of the California Water Code.

[9]For a discussion of these two approaches see Frederic O. Sargent, "A methodological schism in agricultural economics," Canad. Jour. Agr. Econ., Vol. 7, No. 2, 1960, pp. 45-52.

[10]A general economic objective of the California Water Plan has been stated as "securing the maximum benefit to all areas and peoples of the State," Calif. Dept. of Water Resources, op. cit., p. xxv. This statement needs to be modified if it is to serve as an operational economic criterion for public investment. The real income of the state is suggested as such a relevant concept. Although not explicitly stated, the enhancement of state income underlies the reasoning invoked by the California Department of Water Resources in meeting future "requirements." See Calif. Water Resources Board, "A preliminary projection of California crop patterns for estimating ultimate water requirements," Water Utilization and Requirements of California, Appendix A, Sacramento, 1955.

The original statement implies a first-order homogeneous function of state income, the validity of which has been subject to considerable discussion. See Karl Brandt, "Problems in planning for future demand of water," Economics of California's Water Development, edited by S. V. Ciriacy-Wantrup and Stephen C. Smith, Univ. of Calif., Committee on Research in Water Resources, Berkeley, 1958, pp. 7-21.

[11]An optimization criterion has been shown to have substantial shortcomings. See S. V. Ciriacy-Wantrup, "Concepts used as economic criteria for a system of water rights," Land Econ., Vol. 32, No. 4, 1956, pp. 295-312. Furthermore, the practical desirability of a highly refined formulation of an economic optimum has been questioned. See G. S. Tolley, "McKean on government efficiency," Rev. Econ. and Stat., Vol. 41, 1959, pp. 446-48.

[12]Calif. Dept. of Water Resources, op. cit., p. 226.

[13]Calif. Dept. of Water Resources, "Preliminary summary report on investigation of alternative aqueduct systems to serve southern California," Water Resources Bul. No. 78, Sacramento, Feb., 1959, p. VII-5.

¹⁴See statement of the Public Utility Commission of the City and County of San Francisco presented before the Calif. Senate Water Fact-Finding Committee by James H. Thurber, General Manager and Chief Engineer, San Francisco Water Department, and Harvey E. Lloyd, Manager and Chief Engineer of Hetch Hetchy Water Supply, Power, and Utilities Engineering Bureau, Oct. 9, 1959, Sacramento.

¹⁵This relates to taxes of statewide incidence such as income or excise tax receipts. It should be noted that express provision has been made for local taxation imposed by agencies contracting for deliveries from the California Water Plan. See Calif. Dept. of Water Resources, Contracting Principles for Water Service Contracts Under the California Water Resources Development System (Sacramento, 1960), item no. 13.

¹⁶This includes all future eventualities that weaken the ability to pay or increase the costs of the entire plan.

¹⁷See statement presented before the Calif. Senate Water Fact-Finding Committee by the Riverside County Water Authority, Oct. 8, 1959, Sacramento.

¹⁸See statement presented before the Calif. Senate Water Fact-Finding Committee by William R. Seeger, General Manager and Chief Engineer of the Marin Municipal Water District, San Rafael, Oct. 9, 1959, Sacramento.

¹⁹See statement presented before the Calif. Senate Water Fact-Finding Committee by James F. Wright, Chief Deputy Director of the Calif. Dept. of Water Resources, Nov. 20, 1959, Los Angeles.

²⁰Any of the following would serve as criteria for such determination: (1) A broad distribution of benefits in terms of some *a priori* standards. (2) Project costs (either total or some designated portion thereof) are repaid by beneficiaries (direct or indirect). (3) The capture of the increment in individual net worth of beneficiaries in excess of absolute amount. (4) The capture of a designated portion (percentage) of the increment to individual net worth. This is comparable to capturing enhancement per acre in excess of an absolute amount.

²¹Michael F. Brewer, Water Pricing and Allocation with Particular Reference to California Irrigation Districts, Univ. of Calif., Giannini Foundation Mimeographed Rept. No. 235, Berkeley, October, 1960. See particularly Chap. III, pp. 34-77.

²²When district surface water deliveries are used jointly with individually pumped groundwater, changing the proportion of a member's assessment to his total payment alters the "fixed cost" of his water supply. As the complementary variable cost is less than (or exceeds) the variable cost of pumping groundwater, surface water becomes a primary (or supplementary) supply.

²³Improvement district enabling legislation originally was enacted to supplement the activities of irrigation districts. Although generally such districts provide services in addition to those of the parent district, they have also been used to fraction district-wide programs due to equity problems stemming from district pricing.

²⁴Michael F. Brewer, "Repayment and product pricing in small watershed development," Water Resources and Economic Development of the West: Small Watershed Development, Rehabilitation and Reorganization of Irrigation Projects, Conf. Proceed., Comm. on the Econ. of Water Resources Development, Univ. of Calif., Rept. No. 6, Berkeley, 1958, pp. 45-60.

²⁵For a pioneering study that applied this term to economic analysis see Ciriacy-Wantrup, "Economics of joint costs in agriculture," *Jour. Farm Econ.*, Vol. 23, No. 4, 1941, pp. 771-818. Considerations of water quality are particularly important additional determinants of the factor input vector. The general problem of quality has been abstracted from this discussion in the interest of brevity.

²⁶There is a differentiation in price between Class I and Class II agricultural water. The first classification relates to a "firm" supply, the latter to a supply more susceptible to annual quantitative change. For the Friant-Kern and Madera units of the Central Valley Project, Class I water is delivered canalside for $3.50 an acre-foot and Class II for $1.50.

²⁷W. K. McPherson, "Can water be allocated by competitive prices?" *Jour. Farm Econ.*, Vol. 38, No. 5, 1956, pp. 1259-68 and discussion by R. Barlowe, pp. 1279-82.

²⁸J. Wiseman, "The theory of public utility prices," *Oxford Economic Papers*, Vol. 9, No. 1, 1957, pp. 56-74.

²⁹B. P. Beckwith, Marginal Cost Price-Output Control, Columbia University Press, New York, 1955, esp. Chaps. VII and VIII.

³⁰James C. Bonbright, "Two partly conflicting standards of reasonable public utility rates," *Amer. Econ. Rev.*, Vol. 47, No. 2, 1957, pp. 386-93.

[31] This assumes that the ratio of unit price for nonagricultural water to that for agricultural use exceeds unity and the ratio of average variable unit cost of "producing" nonagricultural water service to that for agricultural service. If regionally allocated fixed cost per time period were A, the quantities of water used for agricultural and nonagricultural purposes, q_a and q_n respectively, and unit prices, p_a and p_n, then:

$$p_a = \frac{q_n}{q_a}(\frac{A}{q_n} - p_n), \text{ with } \frac{p_n}{p_a} = \text{a constant for each region.}$$

[32] Conceivably the state could require, through its water contracts, that recipient organizations retail this water according to rate schedules and without recourse to assessment. On the other hand, the entire structure of local distributive organizations, such as public water districts, have traditionally had the power of member assessment. Furthermore, the flexibility afforded these local agencies by this price tool would be surrendered only reluctantly. The inequities arising from using this tool would have to be great indeed to warrant the loss of flexibility entailed by their abandonment.

[33] The Lower Tule River Irrigation District in California is pursuing such a program of ground-surface water-use integration through the payment complex. See W. A. Alexander, Lower Tule River Irrigation District: History and Operational Report, 1950-1957, Woodville, Calif., 1957.

[34] For a case study of such an evaluation see S. C. Smith, "The public district in integrating ground and surface water management: a case study in Santa Clara County," unpublished manuscript, 177 pp.

[35] This concept was initially presented in Calif. Dept. of Water Resources, Preliminary Summary Report..., Chap. VII. It has been more specifically defined in Calif. Dept. of Water Resources, Contracting Principles....

[36] This abstracts from policy which would differentiate between the average unit cost of irrigation water used on large as opposed to small farms by a factor equal to the net power revenues averaged on the basis of an acre-foot of delivered water. This measure, purported to eliminate "unjust enrichment," contains ambiguities that make determination of the actual difference impossible.

[37] The separable-cost-remaining-benefits method has been termed not applicable to the California Aqueduct System. See William R. Gianelli, "Statement of the California Department of Water Resources before the Senate Fact-Finding Committee on Water," Contracts, Financing, Cost Allocations...for State Water Development, Partial Report of the Senate Fact-Finding Committee on Water (Sacramento: Senate of the State of California, March, 1960), p. 32.

[38] Separable-cost-remaining-benefits method of cost allocation can never allocate more cost to a purpose than the benefits of the purpose nor less than its separable cost and, therefore, can never exclude a purpose whose benefits exceed separable cost. Moreover, it does not change the rank order of the benefit-cost ratios of the several purposes given by the more ideal ratio of benefits to separable costs. If benefits are computed so that they equal market values, the method insures that economically justified increments will be financially feasible. See Richard Albin, The Problem of Cost Allocation in Multiple Purpose Water Use Projects, University of Chicago, Office of Agricultural Economics Research Paper No. 5605, Natural Resources Paper No. 11 (Illinois, January, 1956).

[39] Whereas the separable-cost-remaining-benefits method allocates positive joint costs in proportion to the ratio of remaining benefits of each project purpose to total remaining benefits, joint benefits would be distributed in proportion to one less this ratio. These two methods of cost allocation are illustrated as follows:

b_i = estimated benefit of each of the n reaches of the aqueduct.
C = total cost of aqueduct.
ϕ = separable cost of reach i $(C - C_a \ldots h, j, \ldots n)$, or difference between total cost of entire aqueduct less its cost of delivery to reach i is excluded.
a_i = cost of aqueduct to serve only reach i.
$Y_i = b_i - \phi_i \mid b_i < a_i$, or $a_i - \phi_i \mid b_i > a_i$.
U_i = degree of use of total facility occurring in reach i (annual acre-feet delivery to reach i).

Ω = remaining benefit (assuming economies of scale exist) = $\sum_{i=i}^{n} \phi_i - C_i$.

Cost allocated to reach i by separable-cost-remaining-benefits method =

$$\phi_i - (1 - \frac{Y_i}{\sum\limits_{i=1}^{n} Y_i}) \, \Omega \, .$$

Cost allocated to reach i by proportionate-use-of-facilities method =

$$\phi_i - (1 - \frac{U_i}{\sum\limits_{i=1}^{n} U_i}) \, \Omega \, .$$

[40] It is estimated that the southern California coastal plain and coastal San Diego County would receive 63 percent of the total present worth of primary benefits of each of the three alternative routes of the southern California aqueduct. See Calif. Dept. of Water Resources, Preliminary Summary Report..., Tables 27, 28 and 29.

[41] The California Department of Water Resources announced the following policy: "Construction of any transportation facility financed wholly or in part through the sale of bonds, will not be started unless water service contracts have been executed which will insure recovery of at least 75 percent of the cost of such facility." See Calif. Dept. of Water Resources, "Contract principles," Contracts, Financing, Cost Allocations...for State Water Development, Partial Report of the Senate Fact-Finding Committee on Water (Sacramento: Senate of the State of California, March, 1960), p. 53.

[42] This thesis maintains the organic unity of urban centers and the agricultural area immediately adjacent thereto as units of social organization. Although primarily employed for purposes of sociological analysis, economic derivatives of the thesis have been used in the analysis of communities in the San Joaquin Valley of California. See W. R. Goldschmidt, Social Structure of a California Rural Community, unpublished Ph.D. dissertation, Dept. of Anthropology, Univ. of Calif., 1942.

[43] Due to the planned capacity use of facilities to each service area, such nondistrict sales would be limited to the same general service area in which the selling district was situated. Presumably, fluctuations in the demand for irrigation water would be similar throughout the general service area, rendering the selling district at a relative disadvantage. To the extent that interservice area sales of excess deliveries are possible (prior to full over-all project delivery), this relative disadvantage might be mitigated.

[44] As bond issues within the total authorization would be sold as the principal becomes required for capital outlay, the interest rate for particular issues will vary.

[45] Assembly Interim Committee, Economic and Financial Policies for State Water Projects, Assembly Interim Committee Reports for 1959-1961 (Sacramento: State Print. Off., Feb., 1960), Vol. 26, No. 1, Chap. II, p. 14.

[46] Benefit pricing would be consistent with interpretation 4 of unjust enrichment (see footnote 20), neutral with respect to 1 and 2 and inconsistent with interpretation 3 if the absolute amount of enrichment to be retained is constant for all uses and users.

[47] Implicit recognition of these policy categories is evident through the standard "tests" used by federal agencies. Economic justification and financial feasibility relate to the first two categories. More pragmatic tests in the form of local organization eligibility standards include the third.

[48] Public investment activity refers to more than the substitution of decision agents; it also embraces the determination of the physical dimensions of the capital good to be created and relevant administrative decisions such as pricing methods.

[49] Ciriacy-Wantrup has identified six forms of price breakdown particularly relevant for natural resource development. Ciriacy-Wantrup, "Social objectives of conservation of natural resources with particular reference to taxation of forests," Taxation and Conservation of Privately Owned Timber, Conference Proceedings, Bureau of Business Research, Univ. of Oreg., Jan. 27 and 28, 1959, Eugene, 1959, pp. 1-70.

[50] The Calif. Districts Securities Commission.

[51] Calif. Farm Bureau Fed., California Farm Bureau Monthly, Resolution No. 45, Vol. 41, No. 1, 1960, p. 24.

PART IV

Economics and Water Law

S. V. CIRIACY-WANTRUP is Professor of Agricultural Economics at the University of California, Berkeley. His significant contributions to the field of natural resource economics have earned him a national and international reputation.

Chapter 15

S. V. CIRIACY-WANTRUP

Concepts Used as Economic Criteria for a System of Water Rights*

ECONOMIC CRITERIA "IN" AND "FOR" WATER LAW

ECONOMIC CRITERIA are frequently implied in statutes concerned with water law, in judicial creation of water law through decisions in individual cases of controversy and in administrative regulations by executive agencies — criteria "in" water law.[1] Well-known examples are such concepts as "reasonable" and "beneficial" use, "waste," "surplus" of water, "maximum development," and "adequate compensation." A semantic analysis from the economic point of view of these and similar concepts would be interesting and useful. But an analysis of criteria "in" water law appears to cover only one aspect.

Economic criteria are common in semipopular and technical discussions, both in law and economics, when a system of water rights is considered as a whole — criteria "for" water law. Three systems prevail in the United States. First, in the eastern states water rights are based on the riparian doctrine — with modifications in some states such as North Carolina. Second, in the Great Basin and Mountain states water rights are based on appropriation. Third, around the fringes of this

*Reprinted from *Land Economics*, Vol. 32, No. 4, 1956. Prepared for the Symposium, "The Law of Water Allocation in the Eastern United States," Ronald Press, New York, 1958, pp. 531-63. (David Haber and Stephen W. Berger, eds.) The author wishes to acknowledge helpful comments by Wells A. Hutchins and Stephen C. Smith.

251

heartland of the appropriation doctrine, the prevailing system of water rights is a blend exhibiting features of both doctrines, although in secular perspective the appropriation doctrine appears in the ascendency. This blend is dominant in the Pacific Coast and the High Plains states.

In appraising these systems of water rights, a dichotomy of criteria is used. One criterion is exemplified by a set of concepts such as "security," "protection," and "rigidity" of water rights. The other criterion is represented by concepts like "flexibility," "adaptability," and "insecurity." Anyone familiar with the literature cannot fail to become impressed by the vagueness, plasticity and contradiction which characterize the use of these concepts. An examination of their economic meaning is needed.

This dichotomy of criteria is applied jointly. In examining its application we must explore the gradations on the logical axis between the two poles and the resulting compromise in institutional arrangements. But we also must examine to what extent the two criteria can be applied together without such a compromise.

The consequences of institutional arrangements, if viewed over time, are complex. Applying a logical polarity to relations in reality does not always give a perfect "fit." Although it frequently is true (examples will be given below) that a change in institutional arrangements results in an increase in terms of one criterion and a decrease in terms of the other, this does not always happen. In other words, that the two criteria are poles apart logically does not necessarily mean that a change in institutional arrangements cannot be considered which results in increases in terms of one criterion without changes in terms of the other or that results in increases (decreases) in terms of both. In this, and in other aspects, our dichotomy is similar to that of "order" and "freedom" which has occupied students of jurisprudence for a long time and is not being neglected by economists of quite different "schools." [2]

The two criteria imply a problem area which is one of the most important and difficult, both for economic theory and policy. This is the problem area of "economic change" and of "dynamics" versus "statics" in economic discourse. This area also contains the most acute and baffling issues. [3] Thus, focusing of these two criteria brings us to the core of the main theme.

Focusing on economic criteria used "for" water law does not mean that economic criteria used "in" water law are to be neglected. Both can be regarded as means of serving a common end — the "public interest". The public interest is the concept that connects criteria "for" with those "in" water law. Examining the economic meaning and implications of the former is not without relevance for the latter.

In examining concepts as criteria this chapter emphasizes functional relations in economics, not legal history or normative meanings in law. The significance of the case law in the United States is impressive — especially to the author, who grew up in the legal climate of the Code

Napoleon and its successors. But tracing historically the interpretation of economic concepts through the maze of case law is more a task for a student of law than for an economist. Likewise, it would be presumptuous for an economist to suggest how economic concepts should be interpreted in law.

A great deal has been written on the "integration" of law and economics. If this term means that students in the two disciplines need greater understanding for each other's problems, tools and limitations, we can wholeheartedly agree. If the term suggests that concepts and processes of concept formation employed by economists should be transplanted to law (and vice versa), the prospective benefits would seem dubious. On the other hand, emphasis on the functional relations of concepts used as economic criteria "for" and "in" law may help to clarify areas of common interest between two social science disciplines.

The functional relations to be studied in this chapter may be indicated by two closely connected questions. First, what are the economic implications — in the sense of logical and probable factual consequences — if concepts used as criteria "for" and "in" water law are interpreted and applied in certain ways? Second, how far and why are these implications helpful or obstructive if certain economic objectives are sought? The economic interpretations and objectives selected should have relevance, of course, for actual problems of public water policy.

Although indicated by these questions, it may be well to point out explicitly that the problem at hand will be viewed as one of positive rather than normative economics.[4] The consequences of this approach for the relations between economics and law will become apparent later.

INTERPRETATION OF "SECURITY" OF WATER RIGHTS

To the economist, "security" of water rights means something different and much broader than their "protection" means to the student of law. The latter concept is simply defined as protection against *unlawful* acts by others as such acts are construed by the law. Such protection is always subject to the two major categories of legal uncertainty: "rule uncertainty" and "fact uncertainty."[5] Legal uncertainty in this sense is a characteristic of judicial decisions. Like other types of uncertainty it also affects economic decisions.

Economists are inclined to disregard or underestimate the significance of legal uncertainty. Security of a water right connotes to them (1) protection against what I propose to call "physical uncertainty," that is, against variability over time of the quantity of water usable under the right due to seasonal or annual variability of "natural" runoff and groundwater recharge, and (2) protection against what I shall call "uncertainty of water tenure"[6] or, for short, "tenure uncertainty"; that is, protection against variability over time of the quantity of water usable under the right due to *lawful* acts of other individuals or groups, private or public.

We are concerned here with the relative degree of security resulting from different types of rights. Absolute security (transformation of
probabilities into single-valued expectations) cannot be obtained through
water law. Furthermore, we are not concerned with the many other
types of uncertainty which affect economic decisions — for instance, uncertainties connected with variability over time of wants, technology,
prices and incomes. A few examples may illustrate differences between water rights if "security" is interpreted in the way just indicated. [7]

Under natural conditions a senior appropriative right is more secure than a junior appropriative right against physical uncertainty but
not necessarily against tenure uncertainty. A water right in a high-
preference class is more secure than one in a low-preference class
against tenure uncertainty but not necessarily against physical uncertainty. A water right restricted by reservations in favor of other users
is less secure than these other rights against tenure uncertainty but not
against physical uncertainty. An appropriative right is more secure
against tenure uncertainty than a riparian right or a groundwater right
under the correlative rights doctrine, assuming that only one system of
rights applies to a water resource. Against physical uncertainty, however, an appropriative right is not necessarily more secure than a riparian or correlative right; this holds especially (but not solely) for a
junior appropriative right.

In all these examples the two main categories of legal uncertainty
are also present. The degree of legal uncertainty may be quite different for different water right systems and individual water rights. For
purposes of this chapter, however, it is meaningful to proceed as if the
degree of legal uncertainty were approximately the same.

If one speaks of quantity of water usable under a water right, one
implies certain characteristics of water quality. Over time, water
quality is also subject to legal, physical and tenure uncertainties. When
water rights are defined in quantitative terms — as under appropriation
and through adjudication under the riparian and correlative rights doctrines — reference should always be made to water quality.

Interrelation of Quality and Quantity

So we see the importance of quality. Security of water rights in
terms of water quality is no less significant economically than security
in terms of water quantity. Frequently the higher water uses in terms
of value product require a higher quality of water than the lower uses.
Furthermore, quality and quantity are directly interrelated: water of
high quality in terms of low mineral content, especially sodium and sul-
phates, can be reused, sometimes for more than one cycle. Such water
can also upgrade surface and groundwater of lower quality which could
otherwise be utilized only for lower uses or not at all. These interrelations of quality and quantity are especially significant when water
must be transported over great distances. Such transport may be economically feasible only for water of high quality. From the

interrelations of quantity and quality just explained, it follows that in setting minimum standards for water quality, problems of reuse of the same water and upgrading of other waters need to be considered. Minimum standards based on suitability for one cycle of direct ("unmixed") use alone may be too lenient, economically speaking.

Sometimes the only security of water rights in terms of quality is their protection against unlawful acts of water pollution (including, as defined in this chapter, contamination and nuisance). In many states, antipollution laws are being strengthened. More federal action is also being considered.[8] Dealing specifically with these attempts would require a separate discussion.

Problems of physical uncertainty can be significantly reduced mainly through the physical means of storing water above *and* below ground for season to season, from year to year and over a period of years. A reduction of physical uncertainty in this sense produces benefits for water users and others. Whether these benefits are "net" depends on the costs of constructing, maintaining and managing storage.

A system of water rights may impede construction of storage facilities by limiting development to a vaguely defined "safe yield" of a water resource and by making cyclical management of storage capacity and coordination of surface and subsurface storage more difficult.

The appropriation doctrine can easily be employed to limit water development. In several western states this doctrine has actually been utilized with this objective and result in the case of groundwater. With respect to surface water the actual facts are somewhat different. Most western surface waters are overappropriated. Sometimes appropriation covers a multiple of the average flow during the season of use.

After storage capacity has been provided and is managed with a view to reducing physical uncertainty, the relative economic status of appropriative rights alters without changes in their relative legal status. Priority in time, in conjunction with the quantitative definition of appropriative rights, limits the number of rights that can be served with the regulated flow. The better the flow is regulated, the less meaningful, economically speaking, become the rights exceeding this flow. For rights that can be served with the regulated flow, the new situation is not greatly different, in terms of economics, from that prevailing under a water delivery contract where a limited number of users are equal in rights although the quantities to which their contract entitles them may differ.

Thus the differentiation of water rights, so characteristic for the appropriation doctrine, has undergone a shift in its economic implications: within limits a junior right is no longer less secure against physical uncertainty than a senior right. Increasingly, storage is provided by large public or semipublic projects and managed by government agencies — public districts, state water departments and boards and federal bureaus.

In contrast to appropriation, riparian rights are coequal in law.[9]
An economic implication of this equality suggests that their legal status
is not a cause for differentiation in their security against physical uncertainty. This holds both for the riparian right to surface waters, as
generally applied in the eastern states, and for the application of the
riparian right to groundwater through the correlative rights doctrine
as, for example, in California.

This lack of differentiation on the basis of legal status does not necessarily mean that no differences exist between individual riparian or
correlative rights in security against physical uncertainty. Applying
legal equality through adjudication to a given stream system or groundwater basin is a time-consuming and costly process. For a while, at
least, individual riparian and correlative rights may differ in security
against physical uncertainty. Such differences are caused not by legal
but by physical facts such as relative location of diversions along a
surface stream and the location of wells with respect to the source of
recharge and the geologic characteristics of a groundwater basin.

Differences between individual water rights (and between water-
right systems existing side by side in the same general area) in security against physical uncertainty may obstruct or retard construction
and coordinated cyclical management of storage. Individuals and groups
who "have" greater security may be reluctant to join those who "have
not" if a portion of the costs of reducing physical uncertainty is incident
on the former.

In solving this problem, one notes a number of institutional approaches to this problem. One approach is based on a type of public
district which acquires or acts as agent to utilize water rights for coordinated cyclical management of surface and groundwater. This approach has been investigated in groundwater studies[10] for Santa Clara
County, California. In many parts of the West, water demand has increased so rapidly that the group of "haves" (in terms of security of
water rights against physical uncertainty) has become smaller absolutely and, of course, even more so relative to the number of "have
nots." The formation of public districts and of other institutional arrangements for coordinated water management is thereby facilitated.

Tenure Uncertainty

Turning now to security of water rights against tenure uncertainty,
it was mentioned earlier that appropriative rights are more secure in
this respect than riparian rights or groundwater rights under the correlative rights doctrine. The former are clearly defined in priority,
quantity, period of use, points of diversion, and in other ways. The
latter are coequal, and quantitative definition depends on adjudication,
which is in terms of shares and subject to the restriction that there
shall be reapportionment if the conditions upon which the original
apportionment was made change sufficiently to justify it. Such a
comparison at first seems easy. Several factors, however, modify
such a general comparison of water-right systems. The first

factor is prescription which operates under all water-right systems, with some differences in economic significance. The second factor is differentiation of preference classes based on purpose (kind, type) of water use. This factor also operates under all water-right systems but under appropriation only *before* rights are vested and under emergencies. Customary preference classes are "natural" and "artificial" under the riparian doctrine and "domestic," "municipal," "industrial," "agricultural," and "recreational" under appropriation.

The third factor is a restriction (reservation) on water rights to yield to future water demands by others. This factor operates only under appropriation and affects future (not already vested) rights. Water reservations are frequently used in favor of certain preference classes. But the connection with preference classes is not a necessary one. In California, water reservations in favor of whole regions are in force regardless of preference class.

There can be little argument on economic or any other grounds that domestic and municipal uses deserve special consideration as far as security against tenure uncertainty is concerned. This type of use can frequently prevail over other uses by eminent domain proceedings. Still, the highest preference ranking and water reservations in favor of this use are desirable because other uses, such as agricultural, may also be organized under public districts. By adequate requirements for the treatment of sewage, domestic and municipal use can be made largely nonconsumptive. Agricultural use, on the other hand, is largely consumptive.

An economic argument can be made in favor of abolishing the usually [11] lower preference rating of industrial uses relative to agricultural. The average [12] value product of consumptive use is higher in industry than in agriculture. Furthermore, in the western states, total consumptive use in industry, although increasing, is still relatively small as compared with that in agriculture.

In ascertaining the value product of recreational uses — which are largely noncomsumptive — we face the difficult problem of extramarket values. There are cases, however, in which the economic argument suggests a change in the preference ranking of recreational uses. Generally this ranking is the lowest. Under some statutes, recreational uses are not even recognized as reasonable and beneficial.

In spite of the existence of a favorable economic argument for abolishing the usual statutory ranking of industrial and agricultural uses and for other changes in preference classifications, inferences with respect to public policy would be premature without considering the criterion of flexibility jointly with that of security. The economic implications of water reservations likewise cannot be fully appraised without considering the criterion of flexibility. Before this can be done our interpretation of security of water rights must be related to protection of investment in water resources development.

SECURITY OF WATER RIGHTS
AND PROTECTION OF INVESTMENT

The relations between security of water rights and investment in
water resources development are generally the main point of emphasis
when the economic implications of differences in individual water rights
and whole water-right systems are discussed. This emphasis is justified. Most economic implications of security which were mentioned in
the preceding section are in this area. The objective of the present
section is to state some of these relations more explicitly and to consider them in the light of the concept, "protection of investment."

In economic theory, "investment" and its corollary "disinvestment"
refer to value changes in total capital of individuals or whole social
groups as a result of differences between income and consumption. This
is not what is meant here. In the present context, investment refers to
what the economist would call the value of particular durable physical
"assets."[13] The value of durable physical assets depends on the flow of
net income which the assets are expected to "yield" over time.[14] Assets
themselves, however, refer to the present; and the income flow which
determines their value is subject to a time discount and an allowance
for uncertainty. Thus we are concerned with the protection against
physical and tenure uncertainties to which this income flow is subject.
The degree of such protection differs greatly for water rights with different security, as explained in the preceding section.

At first glance it might be expected that, other things being equal, a
greater or smaller security of water rights will result in an increase
or decrease of investment in water resources development. This inference needs some scrutiny.

Frequently a greater degree of security for some water rights necessarily entails a smaller degree of security for other rights. For example, dividing appropriative rights on a given surface stream into
senior and junior rights increases security against physical uncertainty
for the former but decreases it for the latter. If a municipal use receives a higher preference ranking than an agricultural use, or if the
rights of the latter are restricted by water reservations in favor of the
former, security against tenure uncertainty is increased for water
rights held by the municipality but decreased for rights held by the agricultural users. This situation does not make the above inference in-
valid in terms of investment by individuals. But it should not be applied
to aggregate investment in water resources development of a given surface stream, groundwater basin, or region. Such aggregates of investment are important from the standpoint of public water policy.

The statement was made in the preceding section that generally
(that is, without taking account of modification through prescription,
preferences, reservations and physical factors) appropriative rights
give greater security against tenure uncertainty than riparian and correlative rights. This comparison refers to all water rights on a surface
stream, in a groundwater basin or in a region. In this case, therefore,

the inference with respect to investment is valid for aggregates of investment. For this reason the conclusion is justified that the appropriation doctrine favors investment in water resources development, if compared with the riparian and correlative rights doctrines. One should keep in mind, however, that only protection against tenure uncertainty (in the defined sense) is involved.

Adequate Compensation

When comparing different water rights and water-right systems in terms of implications for investment, we touch on aspects of the concept "adequate compensation." This occurs, for example, if the degree of protection against tenure uncertainty is affected by prescription, preferences and reservations. Prescription does not involve compensation according to law. Preferences and reservations involve compensation under some laws but not under others.[15] Regardless of the legal aspects, we may raise the question of whether and under what conditions compensation might be considered in public policy as a problem of economics.

Let us assume that a reservation exists on the flow of a surface stream and that a municipality holds the reservation and will not need the water for 20 years. During this period the water is available for temporary appropriation by other users. Let us assume that the only alternative use is agricultural. Let us assume further that such use involves considerable expenditure for diversion and storage dams, main canals, a distribution system, land leveling and other durable improvements. A private user will make these expenditures only if they seem warranted by the income stream that the durable assets are expected to yield. To the private user the duration of the income stream is uncertain because of his water tenure. Under these conditions the expenditure may not be forthcoming, and the water may go unutilized for 20 years.

In such a situation a guarantee of compensation for nonrecovery of expenditures because of termination of water tenure plus a sufficient profit margin would offset the deterrent to a private user to develop the available water on a temporary basis. Whether "protection of investment" in this sense would be economically warranted from the standpoint of public water policy is not self-evident but can be ascertained by benefit-cost analysis.[16]

In such an analysis some benefits are considered which the private user must leave out of account. Such benefits may, for example, result from flood control or groundwater recharge. Benefits yielded after 20 years are also considered. For instance, dams and other facilities may be usable by the municipality, although it may not be legally required to pay for them. Further, some costs of construction which the private user must consider appear smaller in benefit-cost analysis. One example could be labor costs of construction in a period of unemployment under sticky wage rates.

The foregoing argument in favor of protection of investment in water resources development is based on two necessary conditions: (1) that expenditures for durable assets are in the public interest although they may not be economical for private water users and (2) that the most economical alternative for public policy to develop water resources is a guarantee just sufficient to induce private development. There is no implication in this argument that protection of investment per se is in the public interest.

INTERPRETATION OF FLEXIBILITY
OF WATER RIGHTS

In interpreting flexibility of water rights we think first of all of "legal flexibility." This is a corollary to "legal uncertainty." Legal uncertainty may be regarded as the price that must be paid for obtaining legal flexibility. There has been considerable discussion within the legal profession on whether or not the product — a law responsive to the needs of the community — stands in fair relation to its price. During the twentieth century the trend in legal thinking has been to answer this question in the affirmative. To be sure, prominent legal thinkers hold differing opinions about the desirable degree of flexibility in particular areas of law, such as in property rights; but all agree (including non-American jurists) that flexibility is necessary. They also concur that the American development of the Anglo-Saxon common law is better suited than other legal systems for approaching the most desirable degree of flexibility through trial and error and step by step. Within jurisprudence this degree at a given time and place will remain the subject of perpetual discussion, reappraisal, shifting of emphasis and ambivalent attitudes. Far from being a weakness, such a condition would appear normal or even necessary for an effective contribution by the law to "social engineering" — to use a term popular with Roscoe Pound[17] and other students of law.

Within economics we are concerned not so much with legal flexibility as with the needs themselves to which the law responds. In economics, therefore, the interpretation of flexibility of water rights differs from that of flexibility of water law as discussed in jurisprudence, and an increase in flexibility of water rights is not necessarily incompatible with an increase in their security — as stated at the beginning of this chapter. The needs of particular interests in connection with flexibility of water rights are created by economic change.

The impact of economic change upon water use may be divided conceptually into two parts which are not independent in reality, and for water policy: (1) a change in aggregate development of water resources within a region (country, state, watershed, groundwater basin) and (2) a change in allocation of water resources between regions, uses (municipal, agricultural, industrial, recreational) and users (individuals, firms, public districts, government agencies). The criterion "security of water rights" (discussed in the preceding sections) is significant for the former change. The criterion "flexibility of water rights," as interpreted here, focuses on those aspects of water rights which facilitate or obstruct changes over time in the allocation of water resources between regions, uses and users. Several such aspects must be considered.

There is, in the first place, the transferability of water rights. Water rights, like other property rights, can be transferred in various ways. Voluntary transfer of water rights occurs through buying and selling — with land if rights are appurtenant or without land if they are not. Appropriative rights are better suited for such transfer than riparian rights because the former are clearly defined in quantity, priority, points of diversion and other ways. Transfer of riparian and correlative rights generally requires also transfer of land.[18] Furthermore they are not clearly defined quantitatively and are insecure against physical and tenure uncertainties. With respect to transferability, therefore, the appropriation doctrine favors flexibility of water rights in the course of economic change.

The market for water rights, and especially its "imperfections," is an interesting topic for the economist. This chapter, however, is more concerned with flexibility of water rights as a whole. Transfer of water rights through the market mechanism is only one aspect. Involuntary transfer of water rights is probably more important in number of transactions and quantity of water involved than transfers through the market.

Involuntary transfer first of all may be accomplished through condemnation for public use. This process, by constitutional provision, involves compensation. Appropriative rights are better suited for this process than riparian and correlative rights for the same reasons mentioned in connection with voluntary transfer. Furthermore it is usually sufficient to condemn only a few appropriative rights with high priority. Under the riparian doctrine it is frequently necessary to condemn *all* riparian rights. In this comparison we assume, of course, that only one system of rights applies to a water resource.

In the second place, involuntary transfer can be accomplished through prescription. This process of transfer does not involve compensation. As we have shown in the section starting on page 253, prescription operates under all water-right systems; but there are differences in its economic significance under various systems.[19] Prescription takes time — from 3 to 20 years (5 years in California), depending on the statute of limitation — to ripen into a vested prescriptive right. Adverse and open beneficial use, the condition for prescription, is more likely to persist without objection for such a period against downstream riparian rights and correlative rights than against appropriative rights. A prescriptive right can in turn be lost through prescription by others. Prescription, therefore, is not irreversible but is a potentially always present and economically interesting process of transfer.

Abandonment and forfeiture of water rights — operating only under appropriation — may also be regarded as processes of transfer. Their over-all significance for flexibility of water rights is minor. However, through defining conditions of forfeiture (legislative, judicial and executive defining and redefining of "beneficial" use), the economic significance of this process could be increased.

Voluntary and involuntary transfer of water rights is only one aspect of flexibility. There is fairly general agreement that, aside from the aspect of transferability, a water-rights system based on the riparian and correlative rights doctrines contains elements of greater flexibility than a system based on appropriation. Under the riparian doctrine, new uses created by economic change compete on an equal legal basis with older uses and obtain rights that are no less secure against physical uncertainty than older rights. This is a corollary to the tenure uncertainty so characteristic for riparian and correlative rights. Under the appropriation doctrine, on the other hand, new uses can obtain only inferior rights in terms of security against physical uncertainty. As just noted, however, the economic significance of such flexibility, inherent in riparian and correlative rights, is reduced over time for a given region through prescription.

Preferences and Reservations

Flexibility has other aspects. Preferences and reservations are important for flexibility because of their obstructive influence. They tend to continue into the future the favorable treatment of certain uses or users on the basis of present economic conditions. Preferences and reservations do not obstruct growth itself. Quite to the contrary, they are designed to facilitate growth. They facilitate, however, only the growth of that use which is deemed to deserve preferential treatment on the basis of past or present economic conditions. They obstruct the growth of other uses. Economic change may well require a change in the ranking of uses. As already suggested, preferential treatment is unobjectionable for domestic and municipal uses. On the other hand, extension of preferences to agricultural over industrial uses or extension of reservations in favor of counties and watersheds of "origin" against those of "destination"[20] obstructs changes over time in the allocation of water resources.

The aspects of flexibility discussed so far relate to statutory water law. It would be a serious mistake to overlook the great significance of the case law for flexibility. As already stated, concepts are used as criteria "in" water law that imply an economic appraisal. These rather plastic concepts give considerable scope to the judicial development of water law through decisions in individual cases of controversy. Concepts like reasonable and beneficial use, waste, surplus of water and maximum utilization are interpreted and reinterpreted by the courts continuously in the light of changing economic conditions. Over time, the result frequently has been a change in the allocation of water resources between uses and, through it, between users.

In legal cases, besides taking economic change into account in deciding controversies, the courts are directly concerned with the transfer of water rights through eminent domain. Condemnation of water rights for public use is well established in all states. Going much further than that, the State of Washington permits any person to condemn a lower water use for a higher use.[21] For this purpose any beneficial use is declared to be a public use. The courts determine which use is the higher one.

Under the American form of government the contribution of flexibility by the executive branch of government is probably smaller than that of the legislative and the judiciary because of the constitutional issue of delegation of power. In some states, however, the executive agency charged with the administration of appropriation statutes is given considerable discretion in granting and conditioning appropriation permits. Such discretion has been upheld by the courts.[22]

This section has considered the economic meaning of flexibility of water rights and the institutional possibilities through which flexibility may become operative in reality. There remains the task of considering flexibility jointly with security as economic criteria in public water policy.

WELFARE ECONOMICS AND WATER ALLOCATION

In an attempt to develop criteria for public policy, economists have developed a branch of normative economics called "welfare economics." This branch has become known as the "new" welfare economics to emphasize its development in England and the United States since the 1930's. Its essential problems were recognized and its relevant theorems developed in the 1890's by Pareto.[23]

In formulating policy criteria, welfare economics takes explicit account of differences in individual preferences and incomes and of the resulting problems in aggregating individual utilities. It is an economic axiom that the marginal utility of individual income decreases with increasing income. There is no agreement among economists on whether and in what sense — ordinally or cardinally — individual utilities can be compared, but welfare criteria that avoid interpersonal comparisons are generally preferred.

Classical and neoclassical economists were well aware of these problems.[24] They, however, focused on an increase of real aggregate national income as the main criterion of economic welfare.[25] Pareto's views were not in conflict with this emphasis because he believed — supported by historical experience as he saw it — that an increase of national income and greater equality of income distribution tended to be associated. In this case an increase of national income means also an increase of economic welfare according to Pareto's criterion, at least under some generally accepted assumptions.

The Pareto Criterion

The positive correlation between changes of national income and of equality of income distribution — sometimes called "Pareto's law" — was challenged by Pigou[26] and others; but Pareto's welfare criterion is independent of his law. This does not imply that the correlation noted by Pareto does not exist nor that Pareto's criterion is of greater significance for economic theory than his law. Quite the contrary, one may wonder whether the great intellectual effort which has been invested since the 1930's in developing Pareto's criterion might not have yielded greater dividends in knowledge and welfare if it had been employed for further investigation of Pareto's law and of the problems associated with the increase of national income.

The Pareto criterion says that a change that makes at least one individual better off and leaves no individual worse off represents an increase of welfare. This criterion is usually interpreted to mean that welfare is increased by a change rendering it possible to make at least one individual better off and leave no individual worse off by compensating the losers. Most of the discussion in the new welfare economics deals with this compensation principle.

The Pareto criterion "without" compensation is so restrictive that it has little relevance for an appraisal of public policies, even if it could be practically applied. There are scarcely any policies which make nobody worse off. Furthermore, if there were such policies, the criterion would be ineffective for choosing between more than one alternative to the status quo. The Pareto criterion "with" compensation is not so restrictive but its application is even less practical.

The Pareto "with" criterion is conceptually not identical with the criterion "increase of national income." But the latter criterion may be regarded as a practical, first approximation to the former, provided that the policy under consideration does not appreciably increase inequality of income distribution, and provided further that other policies operate independently and continually in the direction of greater equality of income distribution. Such policies include progression in income and property taxes, high inheritance taxes and social welfare legislation in the narrower sense (relating to old age, invalidity, unemployment, minimum wages, public health, education, and so on). In some practically important cases these two conditions can be regarded as fulfilled when considering resource policies in modern western societies.

Accepting an increase of national income as an economic criterion for public water policy does not imply that application of this criterion faces no theoretical and practical difficulties or that it is the most useful criterion under conditions where economic change and uncertainty are the central problems. We shall return to these problems in the concluding section.

Operational Application of Welfare Economics

Welfare economics has contributed a clarification of the theoretical meaning (or absence of it) of a social welfare function and social indifference curves and of the difficulties (or impossibility) of applying the Pareto criterion in actuality.[27] The disservice of welfare economics has been that its terminology is used by economists and others without pointing out these theoretical and practical difficulties. The false impression is created that a simple criterion is available for legislation, court decisions, administrative regulation and social planning in general. In the field of water allocation policy such application of welfare economics can best be shown by an example.

Optimum water allocation in social planning has been analyzed by superimposing smoothly convex social satisfaction indifference curves on a single production possibilities curve equidistant from the point of origin.[28] Anyone with a little knowledge of high school geometry has no difficulty in locating accurately a point of maximum social satisfaction in water allocation between two users.

No information is given as to how the social satisfaction indifference curves can be determined theoretically and computed in actuality. A higher indifference curve does not become "Pareto-better" by word magic. The suggestion that such curves could be used for water allocation in legislating and planning must be regarded as not warranted by the state of welfare economics.

For some time, cost and revenue indifference systems have been in use to analyze decision making in firm economics.[29] But applying a single equidistant possibilities curve to policy decisions raises questions no less serious than the use of social satisfaction indifference curves.

The ancestry of a single production possibilities curve, the apparent simplicity of which has made it rather popular, can be traced to two basic assumptions of programming.[30] These assumptions are: (1) existence of limitational factors, especially capital; and (2) independence of decisions regarding the intensity of each process and decisions regarding the combination of processes. No information is given as to what limitational factors are assumed. From the standpoint of policy, capital and other factors are limitational only under narrowly defined short-run static assumptions. Under such assumptions, water allocation through legislation, court decisions and administrative regulation has little meaning.

Under long-run static and under dynamic assumptions, policy decisions in water allocation are not independent of policy decisions in water development. A single production possibilities curve assumes away the essential problem of the meaning and the determination of marginal costs of water development. Water allocation policy deals with a whole system of cost indifference curves. Which one is relevant can be ascertained only *after* comparing them with a system of revenue indifference curves. The optimum point of water allocation then becomes a curve of "optimum direction," to use the terminology of vector analysis. This curve is not monotonic and under assumptions approaching reality it is a space curve.

The equidistant feature of the single possibilities curve implies that changes in the water use vector have no influence upon production possibilities. By this implication we assume away another essential problem of water allocation created by great differences in water quality requirements between water uses. This problem presents itself in economic terms through important relations between quality, quantity and costs. Some of these relations were indicated earlier in this chapter.

We must conclude, therefore, that a single equidistant production possibilities curve has no meaning for water allocation policy, whatever its use may be in firm economics.

The foregoing example is of some interest because it combines the approaches and techniques of the two most important branches of normative economics — welfare economics and firm economics — and attempts to derive from such a combination criteria for public water policy. The questions raised so far with respect to this attempt are overshadowed in their implications for water policy by another: Is it conceptually useful to make the maximization principle the basis of economic criteria for pursuing the public interest?[31]

ECONOMIC CRITERIA AND THE PUBLIC INTEREST

The maximization principle is applied in normative economics, first as an efficiency criterion for limited operations under restrictive assumptions and second as the assumed over-all objective of individuals and groups.

As efficiency criterion, the maximization principle is used, for instance, to find the optimum output under given cost and revenue functions and also to determine minimum costs for each output under given production functions and given price schedules of productive factors, i.e., in determining a cost function. For these and similar purposes the maximization principle is necessary. There can be no disagreement on the usefulness of such operations. We may call this application of the maximization principle "efficiency economics" or, more appropriately in some cases, "efficiency engineering."

If applied as the assumed over-all objective of individuals and groups, on the other hand, the maximization principle is a construct, a scientific fiction.[32] It is useful in economics, especially in modern Western culture, if employed in connection with the "firm," another construct. Frequent references to maxima of individual and social satisfaction in economic literature indicate that the maximization principle is more and more applied as a fiction.

A fiction is permissible in science if its character is clearly understood. A fiction is a deliberate, conscious deviation from reality. A fiction, however, is not a hypothesis or theory. By itself a fiction is not intended to be validated by testing with empirical evidence. But a scientific fiction should be useful as a stimulus for or as a part of hypotheses and theories which can be tested. This means that the test of a scientific fiction is its conceptual usefulness — its expediency in understanding, explaining and predicting reality. A fiction becomes mere dogma and therefore unscientific if its two characteristics — consciousness of its fictional nature and conceptual usefulness — are obliterated. There are many examples in the history of science of fictions changing into dogma.

One may wonder whether or not the maximization principle has sometimes become dogma in economics. There is increasing emphasis on techniques which facilitate greater numerical accuracy in the determination of optima for the firm. These same techniques are then used for maximizing social satisfaction of whole groups with no conceptual gain and at the expense of assuming away essential economic relations.

We have suggested in this chapter that, under certain conditions, an increase of national income may be accepted as a criterion for resource policies. The Pareto criterion, likewise, is suited only for ascertaining whether or not an increase of social welfare has occurred but not for determining a maximum.

The criterion "increase of national income" can be employed to effectively appraise water policies of more limited scope, for example in appraising an individual water development project or in deciding a particular case of controversy in water allocation. This is the approach of benefit-cost analysis referred to in Chapter 2. Limitations on the applicability of this criterion are imposed by a number of theoretical and practical difficulties, some of which can be overcome only by restrictive assumptions.

The quantities of goods and services making up the national income must be evaluated (weighted) in order to be aggregated. The weights used — market prices and unit values derived indirectly from prices and in other ways — are affected by income distribution and by the host of institutions which influence this distribution. Both value weights and quantities are affected by market form. Policies to be appraised may change income distribution and market form. Such an appraisal deals with the future. Over time, individual preferences and technology (both affecting value weights and quantities of national income) change, and these changes are uncertain. Again, policies to be appraised affect these changes.

Besides such structural changes there are changes connected with economic fluctuations of various amplitude and duration. These, likewise, are related to the policies to be appraised. All these problems are of interest for benefit-cost analysis, input-output studies of the Leontief type and other systematic attempts at a quantitative economic appraisal of policy.

Practical Approximations

Practical approximations to a solution of some of these difficulties are possible but only under restrictive assumptions with respect to institutions, preferences, technology and time periods. Frequently these assumptions are not made explicit when public water development projects are appraised through benefit-cost analysis and when judicial decisions and arguments before the courts involve equity of water allocation and the interpretation of reasonable and beneficial water use.

The restrictive assumptions needed for benefit-cost analysis become too burdensome for policies of broader scope. In appraising such policies the useful criteria evaluate their effects upon significant conditions which facilitate or impede an increase of national income rather than focus on such an increase itself. This approach to policy criteria relies heavily on economic theory but less on maximization; it is greatly interested in economic history and in relating one time period to another but not necessarily through increasing the number of variables and equations in mathematical models. It is especially suited for natural resources policies and has been discussed in detail elsewhere.[33]

The emphasis of this approach is on minimum standards in resource use rather than on the optimum use; on establishing base levels rather than on locating peaks; on avoiding dead-end streets and on keeping direction rather than on computing the shortest distance; on mobility and adaptability of productive factors rather than on their optimum combination; on reducing institutional obstacles to water development rather than on maximum development; and on provisions in water law that facilitate changes over time in water allocation rather than on an optimum water allocation at particular times and places.

This approach does not pretend to establish criteria for maximizing social satisfaction. But it offers effective direction signals for pursuing the public interest turn by turn.

It becomes apparent now in what sense security and flexibility of water rights can be regarded as economic criteria and why so much attention was given to these concepts earlier in the chapter. Both relate to significant conditions which facilitate or impede an increase of national income in a world of persistent but uncertain change. We saw that the security criterion is as significant for water development as flexibility is for water allocation. We also saw that the logical polarity of these criteria does not necessarily imply that they are competitive if applied in an economically meaningful way. This is a corollary of the economic interdependence of policies concerned with water development and those concerned with water allocation.

CONCLUSIONS

What are the conclusions for the relations between economics and law — taken as two important social science disciplines? Economics cannot define social optima which the law, as "social engineering," should aim to realize. What economics can do, however, is to explain why and how far certain conditions decisively influenced by the law facilitate or impede an increase of national income. Economics can point out the essential features of conflict situations and the probable consequences of changes in statutory provisions, judicial decisions and administrative regulations. Sometimes these consequences can be shown in quantitative terms under restrictive assumptions. More often the consequences can be indicated merely in terms of direction and in terms of relative magnitudes and rates of change.

Economics need not be passive in fulfilling this function. Frequently a conflict situation can be identified in economic terms before it has arisen in law as a controversy. After it has arisen as a controversy the essential economic features may not be clear to the contestants themselves.

A first, but necessary, step toward implementing such a relation between economics and law is mutual understanding with respect to the interpretation and application of key concepts used as economic criteria. In the area of water law, such concepts are security and flexibility of water rights.

Both normative and positive economics can make a contribution to such an understanding. If a value judgment is permitted, we may add that the contribution by positive economics has been far greater, and that this will probably hold also in the future. The law, on the other hand, is essentially a normative discipline. For this reason, doubt was expressed at the outset that the integration of law and economics is possible or desirable. But in spite of — or possibly because of — differences in basic orientation, positive economics and law have many complementary relations. To explore and to strengthen these relations will benefit both social science disciplines.

FOOTNOTES

[1] "Water law" will be interpreted broadly here to include contributions by the legislative, judicial and executive branches of government.

[2] John R. Commons, Institutional Economics, Macmillan, 1934; F. H. Knight, The Economic Organization, A. M. Kelley, New York, 1951, and Freedom and Reform, Harpers, 1947. Lionel Robbins, "Freedom and order," Economics and Public Policy, Washington, D.C., Brookings Institution, 1955. (Brookings Lectures, 1954.)

[3] See S. V. Ciriacy-Wantrup, "Some economic issues in water rights," Jour. Farm Econ., Dec. 1955, pp. 875-85.

[4] For a discussion of this differentiation see Milton Friedman, Essays in Positive Economics, University of Chicago Press, 1953.

[5] This terminology has been popularized by Frank. See Jerome Frank, The Law and the Modern Mind, 6th ed., Coward McCann, New York, 1948.

[6] Tenure uncertainty is not confined to water — and other "fugitive" resources — but is one of the most important economic forces affecting resource use. See Ciriacy-Wantrup, "Capital returns from soil-conservation practices," Jour. Farm Econ., pt.2, Nov. 1947, pp. 1181-96.

[7] For these examples we assume, of course, "other things being equal," that in this case physical conditions and legal features other than those under consideration are the same.

[8] The federal government is no newcomer in this field. See the legislation known as the Caminetti Act, 27 U.S. Stat. at L. (1893), 507, as amended by 30 U.S. Stat. at L. (1898), 631; 30 U.S. Stat. at L. (1899), 1148; 31 U.S. Stat. at L. (1900), 631; 34 U.S. Stat. at L. (1907), 1001; 48 U.S. Stat. at L. (1934), 1118; 52 U.S. Stat. at L. (1938), 1040.

[9] They are coequal within the two traditional preference classes of "natural" and "artificial" uses — except that an upstream user need not share with downstream users if the flow of the stream is only sufficient to satisfy his own natural uses.

[10] Stephen C. Smith, "Problems in using the public district for ground-water management," Land Econ., Vol. 32, No. 3, 1956. For other studies in this series see Patricia McBride Bartz, with a foreword by S. V. Ciriacy-Wantrup, Ground Water in California, The Present State of Our Knowledge, Univ. of Calif., Div. of Agr. Sci., Agr. Exp. Sta., Sept. 1949, 67 pp. (Giannini Foundation Ground Water Studies No. 1.) Processed; Herbert J. Snyder, with a foreword by S. V. Ciriacy-Wantrup, Ground Water in California, The Experience of Antelope Valley, Univ. of Calif., Div. of Agr. Sci., Agr. Exp. Sta., Feb. 1955, 171 pp. (Giannini Foundation Ground Water Studies No. 2.) Processed.

[11] Significant exceptions occur for example, in Texas.

[12] We are using the word "average" because each of the two preference classes covers water development by different users for different products in different time intervals. In the present context we refer, of course, to future additional water development. A change in preference classification does not affect already vested appropriative rights. Under the riparian doctrine, industrial and agricultural uses are both "artificial" and, therefore, coequal.

[13] We may differentiate between three forms of assets: (1) physical (natural resources, improvements, equipment, inventories); (2) money (securities, loans, cash); and (3) personal (labor, skills and good will of the individuals or groups who hold assets).

[14] The resale or scrap value of durable physical assets at the time they are sold or scrapped may be formally included in this flow.

[15] The constitutions of Idaho and Nebraska grant preferences in time of scarcity of water first to domestic uses, second to agriculture, but make exercise of the right contingent on payment of compensation. The Colorado constitution grants similar preferences without mention of compensation; but the Colorado Supreme Court has held that, despite that provision, full compensation is required. Statutes of Oregon and Utah give similar preferences in time of scarcity without mention of compensation. In Texas, reservation does not involve compensation, although there is a difference of opinion as to the validity of the statute granting blanket reservations to municipalities. In California, a municipality holding a reservation must compensate the temporary appropriator. For these and other differences in state laws, see Wells A. Hutchins, Selected Problems in the Law of Water Rights in the West, 1942, esp. pp. 337-58 (USDA Misc. Publ. No. 418).

[16] Ciriacy-Wantrup, "Benefit-cost analysis and public resources development," Chapter 2 of this volume, pp. 9-21.

[17] Roscoe Pound, The Spirit of the Common Law, Marshall Jones Co., Francestown, N.H., 1921.

[18] Riparian rights may be waived by a grant to nonriparians. Such a grant is not effective against other riparians and is not really a transfer of the riparian right. But from the economic standpoint it is just as effective. It frequently happens that riparian rights are bought up or condemned.

[19] The differences suggested here do not involve the legal problem of whether or not a prescriptive title "good against the world" can be established without the necessity of valid statutory appropriation. For different conclusions on this point see Russell R. Kletzing, "Prescriptive water rights in California: is application a prerequisite?" Calif. Law Rev., Sept. 1951, pp. 369-76; Delger Trowbridge, "Prescriptive water rights in California: an Addendum," Calif. Law Rev., Dec. 1951, pp. 525-27; Gavin M. Craig, "Prescriptive water rights in California and the necessity for a valid statutory appropriation," Calif. Law Rev., May 1954, pp. 219-42.

[20] State of California, Water Code, 1953 (Sacramento: California Printing Division), Section 10505, p. 195; ibid., Section 11460, p. 205; see also Ciriacy-Wantrup, "Some economic issues in water rights," op. cit.

[21] Rev. Code Wash., Sec. 90.04.030.

[22] Sections 1253 and 1254 of the California Water Code provide that the Department of Public Works shall allow appropriations under terms and conditions which "in its judgment" will best serve the public interest in water conservation. However, in acting upon applications the Department shall be guided by the policy that domestic use of water is highest and

irrigation next highest. The California Supreme Court, in East Bay Municipal Utility Dist. v. State Department of Public Works, 1 Calif. (2d) 476, 479-81, 35 Pac. (2d) 1027 (1934), upheld the action of the state agency in inserting into a permit, pursuant to these statutory provisions, the following condition: "The right to store and use water for power purposes under this permit shall not interfere with future appropriations of said water for agricultural or municipal purposes." In another decision, in Temescal Water Co. v. State Department of Public Works, 44 Calif. (2d) 90, 99-101, 280 Pac. (2d) 1 (1955), the court held that the cumulative effect of statutory changes had been to create a type of proceeding greatly different from that considered in some earlier decisions. In carrying out its present duty, held the court, the Department of Public Works exercises a broad discretion in determining whether the issuance of a permit will best serve the public interest. That determination requires an administrative adjudication. If issuance of the permit is protested as the statute authorizes, the administrative decision may be made only after a hearing of the protest. The decision is subject to judicial review by way of writ of mandate. These two decisions were called to the author's attention by Wells A. Hutchins.

[23] Vilfredo Pareto, Cours d'Economique Politique, F. Rouge, Librarire-Editeur, Lausanne, 1897.

[24] The first edition of Alfred Marshall's Principles of Economics appeared in 1890, seven years before publication of Pareto's main work in French. Marshall mentions Pareto only in passing and in a different connection.

[25] When comparing national income at different points of time and for different countries, per capita figures are used. In appraising alternative policies, it is more useful to focus on aggregate income.

[26] A. C. Pigou, The Economics of Welfare, Macmillan and Co., Ltd., London, 1938.

[27] For the last (but probably not final) word in this clarification see Paul A. Samuelson, "Social indifference curves," Quart. Jour. Econ., Vol. 70, Feb. 1956, pp. 1-22. This article cites the significant previous literature.

[28] Earl O. Heady and John F. Timmons, "Economic framework for planning and legislating efficient use of water resources," presented at the Seminar on Iowa's Water Resources, sponsored by the Agricultural Law Center, College of Law, State University of Iowa, and the College of Agriculture, Iowa State Univ., Ames, March 26, 1956, 22 pp. Processed.

[29] Ciriacy-Wantrup, "Economics of joint costs in agriculture," Jour. Farm Econ., Dec. 1941.

[30] The origin of formal programming — as *linear* programming — is generally dated with the unpublished papers by Jerome Cornfield (1941) and G. B. Dantzig (1947). The latter paper was published as "Maximization of a Linear Function of Variables Subject to Linear Inequalities" in T. C. Koopman's (Ed.) Activity Analysis of Production and Allocation (Wiley, New York, 1951). The title of the Dantzig paper can serve as a definition of linear programming.

[31] Since 1956, when this analysis was first published, it has been amended and amplified. See: Ciriacy-Wantrup, "Philosophy and Objectives of Watershed Policy," pp. 1-3 in Economics of Watershed Planning, G. S. Tolley and F. E. Riggs, (Eds.), Iowa State Univ. Press, Ames, 1960. Idem, "Projections of Water Requirements in the Economics of Water Policy," Jour. Farm Econ., Vol. 43, No. 2, 1961, pp. 197-214. Idem, "Conservation and Resource Programming," Land Econ., Vol. 37, No. 2, 1961, pp. 105-11.

[32] Next to mathematics and law, economics is the discipline in which scientific fictions are most common. But the natural sciences, especially modern physics, frequently employ fictions.

[33] Ciriacy-Wantrup, Resource Conservation: Economics and Policies, rev. ed., University of California Div. Agr. Sci., Berkeley, 1963. See especially Chap. 18.

FRANK J. TRELEASE is Dean of the School of Law at the University of Wyoming. He is widely recognized for his contributions to the field of water law and has been on the staffs of the University of Wisconsin and the University of Chicago.

Chapter. 16

FRANK J. TRELEASE

The Concept of Reasonable Beneficial Use in the Law Of Surface Streams

IN THE WESTERN LAW of water use and allocation much emphasis has been placed on concepts of "reasonable use" or "beneficial use." Economists interested in the best utilization of our water resources necessarily must have an interest in the meaning of these concepts, for a legal concept may conflict with an economic concept. In such a case, what might appear to an economist as an ideal allocation of water to certain uses might conceivably be foreclosed if the proposed allocation conflicts with the law under which it might be made. If it can be assumed that the economist has arrived at an allocation pattern better than the one permitted by existing law, he may play an important part in the growth of the law, keeping it a living thing in tune with the times. His work may persuade the people to change the law by legislative processes or convince a judge to accept the new pattern, modifying or overruling precedent.

The purpose of this chapter is, therefore, to give the economist some idea of the law on this subject. From the economist's point of view the law may be relevant in several ways. It may be a datum to consider in forming economic premises, a tool to use in accomplishing a desirable result or an obstacle to progress that must somehow be removed.

272

It is doubtful if much of the law that follows will come as a surprise to those economists interested in water development, but perhaps some of the details offered may be of assistance to him. The chapter will cover the various uses the law has approved both under the doctrine of riparian rights and the law of prior appropriation, and it will attempt to define the limits of those uses. It will then consider the situations in which the law has ascribed relative values to competing uses or classes of uses.

REASONABLE USE IN RIPARIAN LAW

The riparian law evolved for England and the eastern United States still has some validity in the West Coast states and in that tier of Great Plains states stretching from North Dakota to Texas on the border between the semiarid and the subhumid parts of the country.[1] Under riparian law it has always been said that the owners of lands bordering upon or crossed by a stream have correlative rights to use the water, but the exact nature of those rights has undergone a change. According to some early authorities, the fundamental right of a riparian proprietor was to have the stream flow as it was accustomed to flow in nature, unimpaired in quality and undiminished in quantity.[2] Of course the enforcement of such a theory to the ultimate extreme would have prevented almost all uses of the waters, so that even in its strictest form it has been modified to permit some use by riparian proprietors, although nonriparian uses of any nature were forbidden under this theory.

But these are words from a dead age. Everywhere in the West such riparian rights as are recognized at all are based upon the theory that the fundamental right of the riparian proprietor is to the reasonable use of the water of the stream and to be free from unreasonable interference with this use. Under this "reasonable use" theory the interest of the riparian that receives protection is not in the natural state of the stream but in the use of water actually enjoyed. Between riparians the western courts have always applied the rule of reasonable use, recognizing that each riparian owner has a right to diminish the stream for his own purposes and that the lower proprietor must show actual damage to his existing uses in order to get an injunction against an upper riparian diverter.[3] Even in controversies between appropriators and riparians, a riparian can complain only of nonriparian appropriations that cause an actual loss or injury to his use of water under reasonable methods of use and diversion.[4] With the ghost of the natural flow theory thus laid, let us look at the uses of water which the courts have held might receive protection when made by a riparian owner.

Natural and Artificial Uses

In a famous Illinois case, Evans v. Merriweather,[5] the court divided the wants of man in regard to water into two classifications; natural and artificial. Natural wants were those absolutely necessary for man's survival; artificial wants increase his comfort and prosperity. The importance of this classification was that the upper riparian on a small stream might consume all the water for his natural wants, and a lower proprietor who so needed the water might insist that upper proprietors curtail their artificial uses so as to let water down to him. Each proprietor in turn might, if necessary, consume all the water for his natural uses.[6] As for artificial wants, each owner had a right to participate in the common benefit. The basis of this rule is apparently the theory that it is better for a few to have water sufficient for their health and well-being, even at the expense of driving others to making their homes elsewhere, than that many should suffer from only a partial supply of water.[7]

Natural uses were stated to be those for domestic and stock-watering purposes, and irrigation and manufacturing uses were classified as artificial. The Illinois court also suggested that irrigation might be a natural want in drier climes. If this theory had been adopted in states where water was scarce, it would have given a material advantage to the upper riparian owners; but such is not the rule in any western state.[8]

Several western states have adopted this classification of uses, sometimes using "ordinary" and "extraordinary" as synonymous with "natural" and "artificial."[9] Others have doubted its validity as involving somewhat fanciful distinctions[10] or have expressly repudiated it.[11] The principles of reasonable use would seem adequate to decide most conflicts between domestic users and irrigators or manufacturers in favor of the householder. However, some vitality seems to remain in the rule, for while the nomenclature of the old classification may not be used, a number of jurisdictions give preference to the domestic and stock-water demands of riparians over the use of the water for other purposes.[12]

Domestic Use. Although it is quite generally held that a riparian proprietor may, if necessary, exhaust the stream for his domestic purposes, there are few cases that clearly define the exact limits of domestic use. Obviously it includes water for drinking,[13] cooking,[14] laundry and sanitation,[15] and the courts frequently add a catch-all classification such as "other household purposes,"[16] "for the maintenance and sustenance of the proprietor and his family."[17] In Oregon it has been held that domestic use includes the watering of such garden and other produce reasonably necessary for the riparian's domestic consumption,[18] and it is frequently stated that it also includes water for stock and other domestic animals.[19] But the use of water for swimming, boating and for ornamental pools is not classed as domestic.[20]

The use for domestic purposes is often thought to involve small quantities requiring no considerable diversion of water,[21] but there are situations in which a large number of people are entitled to such use and the quantity needed may be substantial. The fact that human beings are the occupants of hotels, apartment houses, motels or resorts does not exclude them from the preferential class of domestic users.[22] State institutions such as penitentiaries and mental hospitals have been the subject of conflicting holdings. Some courts say that they may[23] and others that they may not[24] take water for the use of large numbers of inmates. Although generally municipalities are not entitled to riparian rights for the domestic purposes of their inhabitants,[25] it has been held in Texas that a city has such a right and that it is superior to the rights of riparian owners for irrigation.[26] The United States, as the proprietor of a military establishment housing up to 50,000 men, has been likened to a hotel or resort owner and has been decreed water for the domestic needs of the men stationed at the camp.[27]

Stock Water. It cannot be denied that the use of a stream for the watering of all types of livestock is a reasonable riparian use, but there is some question as to the extent to which a preference exists for this purpose over other uses of the water. Stock watering is frequently listed as a "natural" use or a preferential use for which the stream may be exhausted without reference to the needs of others, or else it is included in the definition of domestic uses. Usually no limitation is put upon the number of cattle or other animals that may be watered, and 15 head of cattle and 200 chickens have been held to be included in domestic use.[28] But in Oregon the court has restricted the definition of domestic animals to those necessary for the proper sustenance and maintenance of the proprietor and his family.[29] In California the court has questioned whether the exhaustion of a stream by large herds of cattle ought to be permitted.[30] Since the consumption of water by cattle may be very substantial in relation to the supply of a small intermittent stream,[31] restricting the preferential right to the quantity of water needed for an average number of barnyard animals kept for family use would seem wise. Otherwise the upstream riparian stockgrower or dairyman would be in a favored position over those downstream who desired water for the same purposes. In such circumstances the application of the rule of reasonable use and an apportionment of the stream between them would seem more fair.

Irrigation. As has been said, in the arid and semiarid West where irrigation is necessary to the successful cultivation of the soil, the doctrine of riparian rights was necessarily modified or enlarged so as to permit the reasonable use of water for irrigation, although such use may appreciably diminish the flow of the stream. It is now well settled that between riparian irrigators all are entitled, without precedence, to a fair and reasonable share of the stream[32] and that no proprietor may take all of the stream so as to exclude other riparian owners from the use of the water for irrigating purposes.[33] It has been held in Nebraska that irrigation is not necessarily a reasonable use under all circumstances and that a riparian seeking such use of the stream must plead and prove that his land is arid and that irrigation is essential.[34]

Power. One of the earliest uses of streams was for the generation of water power for the operation of mills and factories. Today the most important application of water power is its conversion into electricity by means of turbines and dynamos, and the reasonable use of waters of the streams and rivers for this purpose is recognized as an exercise of riparian rights.[35] However, certain limitations placed by the courts upon riparian power operations make sole reliance upon riparian rights as a source of water undesirable. It has been held that a definite quantity of water for power purposes cannot be decreed in advance,[36] and some states prohibit the storage of water for this purpose,[37] thus making a firm supply uncertain. There are holdings that it is an unreasonable use to discharge water from a dam in unusual quantities, preventing its use by lower riparian irrigators,[38] or even to restrain the flow during the day and release it at night to the inconvenience of riparian irrigators,[39] rulings which make it difficult to time releases of water to meet demands for power.

Soil Conservation. Many small detention dams, gully plugs, dikes, levees and stock-water reservoirs have been constructed in order to check runoff, create natural subirrigation, aid in flood protection and conserve the soil. Where these are built upon watercourses they raise problems of riparian rights. An important Kansas case recognized the value of these soil and water conservation measures and ruled it a reasonable use to erect small dams, averaging less than one acre-foot in capacity, to hold the water of a small intermittent stream for the use of cattle and the spreading of water through subirrigation to alfalfa fields if the flow of the stream was not materially reduced.[40]

Other Uses. There is no fixed category of riparian uses; almost any application of water that fulfills a need or desire of man can be considered a proper use so long as it is reasonably exercised with due regard to the equal rights of other riparian proprietors. The courts have upheld many uses of water that serve some commercial or industrial need; the harvesting of ice is a use that has been recognized since early times,[41] and a railway company owning riparian lands may make reasonable use of the stream for the purpose of supplying its engines and running its railroad so long as the rule of fairness and equality is observed and the quantity taken causes no injury.[42] A municipal light and power plant may use substantial quantities of water for cooling its engines,[43] and water may be abstracted from a stream for use in oil drilling operations.[44]

This does not mean that a commercial or industrial application is a necessary attribute to a proper riparian use; the water may be used merely to satisfy a desire for pleasure or esthetic enjoyment. It may fill a swimming pool[45] or maintain a park and fishing resort.[46] Broad rights of boating, bathing and fishing have been upheld.[47] In regard to lakes where the chief value of the surrounding lands is for resort purposes and summer homes, the lake level may not be lowered to the point where the lake is turned into a mud flat.[48]

BENEFICIAL USE IN APPROPRIATION LAW

The concept of beneficial use — that water appropriated must be put to useful and beneficial purposes — is fundamental in western water law. A nonuseful appropriation is of no effect,[49] and the application of water to useful and beneficial purposes is the *sine qua non* of a water right under the doctrine of prior appropriation. This concept is frequently expressed in the maxim that beneficial use is the basis, the measure and the limit of the right to use water, and the concept has been enacted into the statutory law of many western states[50] and incorporated into the federal reclamation law.[51]

Although it is sometimes said that what is a beneficial use is a question to be decided upon considering the facts of each case,[52] a number of uses have received general approval as useful and beneficial, and these will be discussed first.

Statutory Definitions

No state statute defines beneficial use in general terms, but in three states the legislatures have listed the purposes for which water can be appropriated. For instance, in Arizona these uses are domestic, municipal, irrigation, stock-watering, water power, wildlife (including fish) and mining purposes, for direct use by the appropriator or for delivery to consumers.[53] South Dakota and Texas have similar provisions.[54]

On the face of these statutes, the lists or definitions of beneficial use seem to be conclusive and to exclude other uses that do not come within the classifications set forth. If this construction should be adopted by the courts, new uses which an advancing civilization demands, such as air conditioning and the dilution of wastes to prevent stream pollution, might be prohibited unless the listed purposes can be stretched to include them. It is arguable that the statutes only insure that the listed uses are beneficial and that other uses are permissible if they fall within the common-law concept of beneficial use. No cases have been found which discuss this problem.

Many other state and federal statutes merely identify certain uses of water as beneficial and clearly do not exclude all other uses as nonbeneficial. So the lists of preferences among uses also may be construed as legislative declarations that each purpose listed is beneficial. A few states have laws defining particular beneficial uses. These statutes will be discussed in connection with those uses.

Domestic Purposes. All statutory definitions of beneficial use include domestic uses.[55] Practically every statute giving preference to certain uses of water places these uses at the top of the preferred list.[56] In California, domestic use is described as the highest function of water.[57] These laws are simply recognitions of the elemental fact that water is necessary to sustain the life and health of man and that no other demand for water can transcend its purpose to that end.

Most of the cases and statutes dealing with the scope of domestic use relate to the extent of the preference granted by such statutes. It is said that an appropriation for domestic purposes is limited to such uses as the riparian owner has at common law to take water for himself, his family, his stock and the like.[58] Drinking and cooking are of course covered,[59] as are general household purposes[60] and home and farm use.[61]

There are three other problems concerning the limits of domestic use. One is the question of whether it includes any right to irrigate plants. The Kansas statutes define the term as including "the irrigation of lawns and gardens";[62] Washington permits domestic water to be used for the irrigation of a "family garden";[63] and in Arizona the irrigation of gardens not exceeding one-half acre to each family is allowed.[64] On the other hand, an Idaho statute construes domestic use as not including any manner of land irrigation,[65] and in Colorado it is a criminal offense to employ water appropriated for domestic purposes for irrigation or for application to land or plants in any manner or to any extent.[66]

Another problem is whether domestic water may be used to water stock. The preferential right given to the riparian is limited to the watering of domestic and barnyard animals kept with and for the use of the household. In view of the separate recognition of stock watering as a beneficial use, a similar construction would probably be applied to the domestic preferences given by appropriation statutes. An Idaho law so limits the use of domestic water by animals,[67] but in Kansas the preference perhaps may be extended to all uses for stock, even for large herds. In that state the statutes include as domestic the use of water for livestock and poultry, in addition to specifying farm and domestic animals.[68]

The final area of dispute has questioned whether the domestic needs of the inhabitants of a community can be lumped together into a municipal appropriation for "domestic use." It has been uniformly held that such municipal demands cannot have the preference granted to the individual domestic user.[69] But in several instances it can be determined from the context that statutory references to "domestic use" probably include the use of water for what is more commonly called municipal use.[70]

Stock Water. The watering of herds of stock and of all types of domestic animals is a beneficial use. Stock watering is included in the statutes of all of the states that list the specific purposes for which water may be appropriated,[71] and is recognized as a useful and beneficial purpose by the statutes and decisions of all other states.

Municipal Purposes. Appropriations to supply cities and towns are authorized in all of the western states, whether made directly by the community or by a private water company given a franchise to supply the municipality and its inhabitants.

Municipal uses actually encompass a large number of different applications of water for different beneficial purposes. Some of these are direct uses by the town or city itself as a consumer, such as water for fire fighting,[72] for use in public buildings, for flushing sewers,[73] for watering parks[74] and supplying fountains[75] and lakes.[76] But most of the so-called municipal purposes are in fact uses by the inhabitants of the community and the resident industrial enterprises. The bulk of water use in cities consists of domestic uses,[77] irrigation of lawns and gardens,[78] sanitary purposes,[79] the use in shops and business establishments and for the manufacture of goods,[80] the production of steam,[81] cooling and condensing,[82] refrigeration,[83] air conditioning and for laundries[84] and railroads.[85] The municipality or company appropriating the water is in reality appropriating for purposes of sale to the ultimate consumer.

Although illustrations of these uses may be found in the statutes and reports, there are few cases directly dealing with the problem of how far a municipality may go in using or distributing water for specific purposes. Technological advances have outmoded some older cases approving the use of water for horse troughs[86] and street sprinkling.[87] Most of the more recent decisions have considered the power of a city to supply water to areas outside the city limits. The validity of such acts will more often turn on the existence and construction of statutes concerning municipal powers than on the proper interpretation to be given to the phrase "municipal purposes."

Irrigation. The use of water for the irrigation of land in order to supply the deficiencies of natural rainfall is so widespread in the western United States that "water law" and "irrigation law" have come to be substantially synonymous terms. It has never been questioned that irrigation, in general, is a beneficial use.

Irrigation has been defined as a sprinkling or watering, the causing of water to flow over lands for nourishing plants, and in its special sense in irrigation statutes, as the application of water to lands for the raising of crops and other products of the soil.[88] But it is not strictly limited to agricultural purposes because it has also been held to include watering trees and grass in cities and cemeteries.[89] While ordinarily the word implies the use of artificial means, as distinguished from sub-irrigation, the method of application — by flooding, channeling or sprinkling — is immaterial.[90]

Generally the law makes no distinction between the various crops that may be grown by irrigation. The use of water to grow native hay and other forage for livestock is on an equal footing with its use for crops of greater immediate value.[91] Where the irrigation of pasture land causes a great increase in the amount of grass produced, the use has been held a useful and beneficial one. Compared with the irrigation of hay land, the difference lies only in the manner in which the grass is fed to stock.[92] If the irrigation produces only slight plant growth of very little value, it is possible that consideration of reasonableness of the particular use compared with other uses might lead a court to hold that such a use was not reasonably beneficial.

Mining. The doctrine of prior appropriation originated when the miners of the California Gold Rush days washed the gold from the gravel in the waters of the streams on the public domain. The use of water in placer mining and its use in milling gold ore to run the crushing machinery and separate the gold from the tailings were thus the earliest beneficial uses that justified the appropriation of water.

The extent of the permissible use in connection with mining

operations has never been judicially defined. Early cases recognized that an appropriation for mining gave the miner the privilege of encumbering the stream with debris from placer operations, but it has been held that the Idaho preference for mining and milling does not permit the obstruction of the stream with debris and its pollution with poisonous wastes from mills.[93] The use of water in drilling for oil and gas has been permitted in Texas and Oklahoma as a proper riparian use[94] and by analogy may be considered a beneficial appropriative use. The Texas statutes allow appropriations for mining and the recovery of minerals and provide for temporary permits of three months' duration,[95] which would seem to provide adequately for such drilling uses.

Manufacturing. The use of water to furnish power to run sawmills was the second beneficial use to receive judicial recognition as a basis for the appropriation of water.[96] Statutory authority to appropriate for manufacturing purposes has been expressly granted by the federal and some state governments[97] and is to be implied from statutes of other states permitting the use of water for power or milling purposes.[98]

Of course, water may be utilized in connection with the manufacture of goods in many ways other than for the production of power to run machinery. An Oklahoma statute gives preferential status to uses of water in the processes of manufacture, for the production of steam and for refrigeration, cooling and condensing.[99] The Texas legislature has given a like preference in processes designed to convert materials of a lower order of value into forms having greater usability and commercial value, including the production of steam power.[100] These uses are undoubtedly beneficial under the laws of any state. The dearth of cases on the exact boundaries of "manufacturing purposes" is probably due to the commonly accepted practice of manufacturers in obtaining their water from municipal supplies so that not many direct appropriations are made for manufacturing uses other than power.

Power. Direct use of the power of falling water to run sawmills, flour mills and machinery was one of the earliest uses for which appropriations were made.[101] Of course the principal function of water power is for the production of electricity to furnish light, heat and power to the public, and such use is everywhere recognized as useful and beneficial.[102]

Recreation. It is undoubtedly beneficial to use water for beautifying parks and resorts where people may rest and enjoy themselves, and for forming pools and lakes for swimming, boating, fishing and hunting, but the limits of appropriations for these purposes have not been fully explored or stated by the courts.

The statutes of Kansas and Oklahoma name recreation as a beneficial use without further description; South Dakota lists "public recreation"; and the Arizona law mentions the use of water for wildlife, including fish.[103] Texas legislation is the most explicit, listing "public parks, game preserves, recreation and pleasure resorts."[104] The Montana court has indicated that the use of water for a swimming pool and fish pond is beneficial;[105] in New Mexico it has been said that recreation and fishing are included in the beneficial uses for public waters;[106] and in Colorado the irrigation of parks and the filling of lakes and reservoirs within a city have been held to be beneficial.[107]

The leading court case involved the owner of a mountain resort who sought to enjoin a power company from diverting a stream that flowed through the resort and formed a beautiful waterfall. The court held that public health, rest and recreation constitute a beneficial use and said:

Places such as that described here, favored by climatic conditions, improved by the work of man, and designed to promote health by affording rest and relaxation are assuredly beneficial. They are relatively as important as sanitariums and hospitals, and should not be dismissed by calling them mere resorts for idleness. They are a recognized feature of the times, are important in their influence upon health, and multitudes of people avail thèmselves of them from necessity.[108]

The resort owner lost the case, however, for he sought to preserve the cascade in its natural state. The court held that no appropriation had been made by means that were not unnecessarily wasteful or excessive, although it regretted that natural objects of great beauty such as these falls had not been preserved by the legislature.

In Oregon this suggestion of the court has been acted upon, and many streams that form beautiful falls or that are famous fishing waters have been reserved from appropriation.[109] In Idaho the governor is authorized to appropriate the water of certain lakes in trust for the people, and the preservation of the lakes for scenic beauty, health and recreation purposes is declared to be a beneficial use of the water.[110] Although in reality not an appropriation, like the Oregon laws, a reservation of the water prevents its being appropriated for more mundane purposes. In the absence of such a special statute, a private person cannot make an appropriation of a lake or stream in its natural state for such purposes.

Appropriations for fish and wildlife purposes ordinarily take the form of reservoirs that provide a habitat for game fish and waterfowl. It is common practice today to include these purposes in the list of beneficial uses to be served by reservoir projects. To the extent that these recreational features are incidental concomitants of the storage of water for irrigation, power and other well-accepted uses, questions do not arise as to the validity of the storage of water for these purposes.

When it is sought to take water solely for these purposes, however, several problems may crop up. In general it has been said that public waters may be impounded for recreation, fishing and hunting purposes.[111] Whether this may be done for private or only public recreation has never been squarely decided. Water for a fish pond, apparently private, was approved without discussion in Montana.[112] A Texas court has said in *dicta* that water appropriated for game preserves and pleasure resorts may be diverted to private lands and there used to the exclusion of the public.[113] But when a private club in Utah sought an appropriation for filling duck ponds and for growing vegetation attractive to wildfowl, it ran afoul of the Utah rule that an appropriator must have the exclusive benefit and control over the appropriation. The application was denied since the land to be flooded was public domain open to all for hunting.[114]

In California two cases have denied gun clubs the right to use well water to flood lands in order to create duck marshes. Regulations forbidding the use of underground water except for certain named purposes were upheld on the basis that California underground water law requires the water to be reasonably used in connection with the land from which it is taken.[115] It was said that while the maintenance of such duck ponds would contribute greatly to the enjoyment of those owning the hunting privileges, it was not a use which was beneficial to the land.

Hunting, fishing and other recreational activities connected with streams and lakes constitute major attractions of many parts of the western states, and millions of dollars are spent by tourists from less attractive areas. Public recreational facilities, when sponsored by public agencies, are beneficial in a broad sense to a large segment of the population and when operated for profit are an important source of wealth. Appropriations of water for such facilities would in most cases be nonconsumptive — except for evaporation, once reservoirs are filled — and should receive the recognition and protection of law. Private facilities for the benefit of individuals or of clubs with restricted membership may constitute property of great value to their owners. No dogmatic rule should be adopted allowing or forbidding the taking of water for such private recreation, but each such attempted appropriation should be scrutinized, and the effect of its allowance upon foreseeable demands for water for other purposes should be considered.

Miscellaneous Uses. Water has been put to many other uses that have received legislative or judicial sanction as beneficial or useful. An early Idaho case held that the use of water for railway necessities was unquestionably for a beneficial purpose,[116] and the statutes of Oregon and Wyoming so declare.[117] Other statutes permit water to be taken for the production of steam[118] for refrigeration, cooling and the manufacture of ice[119] and for maintaining sanitary conditions of streamflow by the dilution of sewage and wastes.[120] In California the storage of water underground is a beneficial use if the recharged groundwater is later put to beneficial use.[121]

The use of water is indispensable to the operation of fish hatcheries, of course, and it is self-evident that the water so diverted is devoted to beneficial use.[122] Such a use has been likened to irrigation in that its result is to increase the food supply of the population.[123]

Not all uses to which man can apply water for some immediate benefit are classified as beneficial in the legal sense. The drowning of gophers will not justify an appropriation.[124] Although the use of water to carry debris from a reservoir to keep it out of turbines would be useful and beneficial to the owner, it will not be allowed when it would interfere with use of the water for irrigation, where other means to control the debris could be devised.[125]

COMPARATIVE REASONABLENESS OF USE

Up to this point this chapter has dealt with whether a particular type of use *as such* has received court or legislative approval as a "reasonable use" or "beneficial use" and has attempted to point out the limits of the legal definition of such use. It may seem a sterile approach to an economist to consider each use in the abstract and to tag it as reasonable or unreasonable, beneficial or not beneficial; yet, by and large, that has been the method of the courts and legislatures until quite recently. This seemingly one-sided approach has resulted in this list of uses characterized as reasonable or beneficial in general, and apparently the courts have merely approved of a particular use that has come in question if it falls within one of these categories.

But actually there are few absolutes on this list. In fact, this one-sidedness is more apparent than real, at least in the litigated cases. Each case was actually a dispute between two people fighting for water insufficient for the needs of both. When one urged that the other's use was not beneficial, he was usually relying upon the often inarticulate premise that it was not beneficial because his use was *more* beneficial. Therefore most of the cases did actually amount to a choice by the courts between one use over another, but analysis of the cases in these terms is generally impossible because that is not the way the courts discussed them.

But new concepts evolved as competition for the supply grew fiercer and as the realization grew upon the courts and legislatures that the allocation of water involved a problem in the conservation of natural resources. Each use must not only be beneficial in the abstract sense but must also be a reasonable and economic use in the light of other demands for the little water remaining to be allocated.

Reasonableness of Riparian Use

It has always been the law that a riparian's use of the water must be reasonable in the light of the equal rights of all other riparians on the stream. What is reasonable will vary with the circumstances of each case.[126] In each case the quantity permitted a particular riparian will vary from year to year and from season to season,[127] not only from the varying water volume at different times of one or of different years but also from the amount of settled land and the extent of the use of the waters by others for irrigation and for the so-called natural purposes.[128] A riparian owner who has been accustomed to use a certain amount of water on his land may increase the quantity if it is reasonably required for extended irrigation.[129] On the other hand, what might be a reasonable use of water giving no grounds for complaint in good years may become highly unreasonable in time of drouth.[130] This flexibility of the riparian right is regarded by some economists as undesirable since it produces an instability in the water right. Conversely, it has been praised as providing a flexibility guaranteeing that a particular use pattern will not become frozen and prevent changes that progress demands.

The use of water by one riparian proprietor that causes substantial harm to another has been said to be unreasonable unless the utility of the use outweighs the gravity of the harm.[131] Reasonableness is not to be determined solely by reference to the needs of the user nor solely from the standpoint of the person harmed. If there is no injury to the rights of the lower proprietor, of course there is no liability under the rule of reasonable use.[132] But the mere fact of damage and substantial inconvenience to other riparians does not itself make the use unreasonable.[133]

For example, it has been held that where a small quantity of water is far insufficient to meet the needs of all riparians, a use may be reasonable even though it consumes so much water that lower riparians may be put to some expense in order to utilize the remainder.[134] On the other hand, the mere fact of benefit to the user does not establish its reasonableness. The full flow of the stream cannot be demanded to the detriment of other irrigators merely because some slight benefits result from the overflow, such as the depositing of beneficial silt upon lands or the washing of salt from marshes, or the replenishing of groundwaters.[135] And although the use for electric power may be proper,[136] to alternately restrain and release the flow of water stored for that purpose so as seriously to inconvenience irrigators has been held unreasonable.[137]

Reasonableness of Beneficial Use

The courts early laid down the rule that no appropriation of water was valid where the water simply went to waste, and the courts held that the appropriator who diverted more than was needed for his actual requirements and allowed the excess to go to waste acquired no right to the excess.[138] Also, they have always exercised the power to declare that some uses were not beneficial or that certain applications of water did not fall within accepted classifications of beneficial uses.[139]

These concepts have been merged into a new rule: that a particular use must not only be embraced within the general class of beneficial uses, or must not only be of benefit to the appropriator, but it must also be a reasonable and economic use of the water in view of other present and future demands upon the source of supply. Thus in the Oregon case of In re Deschutes River,[140] the use of 40 second-feet of water during the irrigation season to clean debris from a reservoir and keep it out of electric turbines was denied, although the benefit to the appropriator was admitted. The court pointed out that that quantity of water could otherwise be utilized to irrigate 1,600 acres of land, and the appropriation was denied as wasteful. The difference between absolute waste and economical use was said to be one of degree only.

Similarly, the validity of local regulations which permit the use of underground water only for irrigation, domestic and fish propagation purposes has been upheld in denying an appropriation of such water for flooding land to make duck marshes for private gun clubs, although the benefit to the members of the clubs was recognized.[141]

An amendment to the California constitution expresses the concept in this fashion:

It is hereby declared that because of the conditions prevailing in this state the general welfare requires that the water resources of the state be put to beneficial use to the fullest extent of which they are capable, and that the waste or unreasonable use or unreasonable method of use of water be prevented, and that the conservation of such waters is to be exercised with a view to the reasonable and beneficial use thereof in the interest of the people and for the public welfare.[142]

Construing this section, the California court has said that what may be a reasonable beneficial use where water is present in excess of all needs would not be a reasonable beneficial use in an area of great scarcity and need, and that what is beneficial use at one time may, because of changed conditions, become a waste of water at a later time.[143]

Preferences. In addition to litigation between users in which the relative value of their beneficial purposes are weighed, other statutes give preference to certain classes of uses. These are legislative determinations that one type of use is of relatively greater value than another.

The subject of preferences is too broad to cover exhaustively in this short space,[144] but we can mention three major types here. The most common gives the preferred user the right to condemn a nonpreferred water right upon the payment of compensation.[145] Exercising such preference will result in permanently transferring the water right to the new owner, who succeeds to the right of the former owner. The most common example of such a preference is the familiar picture of a city condemning an irrigation water right.

The second type is called a "true" preference, which gives the preferred user a superior right over other users and in effect places him at the top of the priority list. Stated another way, a true preference exists when the preferred use may be initiated without regard to the fact that the supply is already fully appropriated for other purposes, and the preferred user may take water without paying compensation to persons whose uses are thereby impaired.

There are several examples of this second class of preference on interstate streams. The Colorado River Compact lays down the rule that the impounding and use of waters for power shall be subservient to the use and consumption of water for agricultural and domestic purposes and shall never interfere with or prevent the use of water for these dominant purposes.[146] A desire to safeguard further development caused the Montana legislature to qualify a grant of permission to flood Montana land by a dam to be built in Idaho by giving a preference to future irrigation and domestic appropriations over the use of generating power at the dam.[147] When plans were made for the almost complete development of the Missouri River, the upstream states, fearing that the maintenance of a navigation channel in the downstream reaches of the river might some day curtail consumptive uses, forced the insertion of the O'Mahoney-Millikin amendment into the 1944 Flood Control Act that authorized the project. By that amendment water can be used only for navigation if it does not conflict with present or future beneficial uses for domestic, municipal, stock water, irrigation, mining or industrial purposes.[148] This principle is not limited to the Missouri River but has been extended to all waters arising in the 17 western states. There are few true preferences in state law, but in Texas all appropriations made since 1931 are granted subject to future appropriations for municipal purposes.[149]

The third type of preference encompasses the state statutes regulating appropriations by requiring permits from state water officials. Several states expressly empower their water administrators to choose among several applicants who seek to appropriate the same supply when the available waters are insufficient for all. Statutes listing the order in which application should be considered exist in California, Arizona and Texas.[150]

In many states, water officials are given the power to choose among applicants or deny permits on broad grounds involving the exercise of discretion instead of the application of a fixed list of preferences. In Utah the state engineer is directed to prefer "the more beneficial use,"[151] and there the state engineer has subordinated to a multi-purpose project a power appropriation that would have cut the heart out of the project.[152] In Oregon due regard is to be accorded for conserving water and for its maximum economic development,[153] while the Texas water engineers are to give preference to those applications which will effect maximum utilization and prevent the escape of water without contribution to beneficial public service.[154]

There is little agreement about the order in which these uses should be preferred. In all of the western states, cities and towns are empowered to condemn water rights for municipal supplies and hence have a preferred right in this sense, although most of the statutes conferring the power are found in the laws relating generally to municipal government and not in the water codes.[155] In the earlier preference statutes the typical order set out is domestic over all other uses and irrigation over manufacturing,[156] although in Idaho mining districts mining uses are preferred over irrigation.[157] Wyoming's preference statute perhaps shows the importance of railroading in the state's economy, for "domestic and transportation" purposes are preferred over all others.[158] Other statutes have expanded the lists and changed the order somewhat.

Preferences in permission to appropriate Texas waters are listed in this order: (1) domestic and municipal uses; (2) water used in the process of converting materials into forms having greater usability and commercial value, including stream generation of power; (3) irrigation; (4) mining and recovery of minerals; (5) hydroelectric power; (6) navigation; and (7) recreation and pleasure.[159] Oklahoma conservancy districts are to give preference among applications first for domestic and municipal water supply; second to water for processes of manufacture, production of steam, refrigerating, cooling and condensing and for maintaining sanitary conditions of streamflow; and third for irrigation, power development, recreation, fisheries and other uses.[160] Where appropriations of Kansas water conflict, uses take precedence in the following order: domestic, municipal, irrigation, industrial, recreational and water power uses.[161]

CONCLUSION

The economist will first note from this mass of law that the legal concepts of reasonable riparian use and beneficial purpose of appropriation act as only a slight check on water users. It should be remembered that most of this law was evolved in the 1800's, in a period of water resources development in a pioneer economy when laissez-faire principles dominated the thoughts of entrepreneurs, legislators and judges. In pioneer times any use of a resource could be said to be an economic gain. In riparian law the emphasis on the right of the individual to do as he pleased so long as he did not damage his neighbor too greatly stemmed from that same philosophy.

In the rather new concept of reasonable beneficial use, the courts have just begun to show an awareness of the economic relativity of specific uses and the comparative benefits to be realized from different, competing uses. But it should be noted that the courts have hesitated to set themselves up as economic planners and have used this power very sparingly, although it may become very important in future decisions as the amount of available water diminishes. Laissez-faire economics has determined the relative desirability of projects and decided which should be built. Every project precludes some future project by the very nature of the doctrine of priority. Developments sufficiently feasible and economical to justify the immediate expenditure of the capital necessary to put them into effect have always received the better right to the water by being built first. This is still true to a large extent, although such decisions are subject to check by administrative officials who may choose between applications of projects either on broad public interests grounds or in accordance with a set list of preferences.

The preference statutes seem to be in great need of overhauling. There is a wide variation as to what shall be preferred and how the preference is to operate. There is general agreement only in that man's personal needs come first, so that domestic and municipal purposes head every list, and there seems to be a fairly uniform resolve not to let waters run unused into the seas, with the consequence that power and navigation operations are generally found near the bottom. But irrigation, manufacturing, mining and railroad transportation jockey with each other for preferment in the middle ground. There is no uniform effect given to preferences even for one particular purpose; for instance domestic users are given an absolute preference in some states, a right to condemn in others and only a better chance to receive a permit elsewhere. Many states have not consciously chosen any order of preference other than giving communities the right to condemn a municipal supply.

A reappraisal of these laws and the policies behind them on both state and national levels would not be out of place. Archaic laws may shape ultimate development in an undesirable fashion or may provide stumbling blocks that retard or discourage progress.

In selecting the values on which a modern system of preferences should be based, obviously priority should be accorded the uses directly necessary to human life and health. Second, uses for irrigation and industrial consumption, where there is no substitute for water, must take precedence over other uses for which substitutes can be found, such as power and water transportation.[162] New uses may demand a place on the preference list. Recognition has been given to the importance of maintaining a streamflow adequate to dilute municipal and industrial wastes and to prevent downstream health problems. Anyone who has spent a summer in Oklahoma might urge that air conditioning be included in the preference there given to "refrigeration, cooling and condensing." The industrialization of the West may cause some states to review their present policies of preferring irrigation over manufacturing. In states where catering to tourists and sportsmen has become a major industry, the protection of recreational, fish and wildlife value takes on a commercial as well as an esthetic importance. Lastly, care should be taken that the hands of future generations should not be too tightly bound.

In such an appraisal of preferences, the extent of the preferment should be considered and its ultimate effects understood. Whenever water is taken from one beneficial use and put to another, an economic loss occurs, whether it is taken under a true preference or by means of eminent domain. The type of preference merely determines whether the loss falls on the first user or on the taker. But the total loss may be smaller if a true preference is used instead of condemnation: a city is likely to condemn an early right and put valuable land out of production, but a city whose new uses head the priority list will squeeze out the marginal land at the bottom. If policy demands that compensation be paid, the latter solution may present insuperable obstacles in the computation of damages, since different appropriators will be affected as streamflow varies.

A factor that weighs against the true preference, however, is that its potential exercise may prevent development because investors may refuse to put their money into enterprises dependent upon legally unstable water rights. Where water uses already approach the maximum level, establishing a system of preferences between future appropriations may accomplish little. The power to choose the more desirable of pending applications may be of little effect unless application for major projects happens to coincide.

Actually the future is more in the hands of economists, engineers and administrators than in the hands of lawyers and judges. Sometimes the law acts as a brake upon new ideas and new schemes, but usually this occurs when their application will be injurious to an individual. In such cases the courts will try to strike a balance between progress and protection of rights. Legislators may be slow to accept new ideas. But by and large, western water law has been the handmaiden of progress, and we can be confident that it will not impede development.

FOOTNOTES

[1] Frank J. Trelease, "Coordination of riparian and appropriative rights to the use of water," *Texas Law Rev.*, Vol. 33, No. 1, 1954, pp. 24-69 (Univ. of Texas); Wells A. Hutchins, "History of the conflict between riparian and appropriative rights in the western states," *Proc., Water Law Conference* (Univ. of Texas, 1954) p. 106.

[2] Webb v. Portland Manufacturing Co. (1938) 3 Scam. 189, 29 F. Cas. 506.

[3] Lux v. Haggin (1884) 69 Cal. 255, 4 P. 919 (1886) 10 P. 674; San Joaquin & Kings River Canal & Irrigation Co. v. Fresno Flume and Irrigation Co. (1910) 158 Cal. 626, 112 P. 182.

[4] Gin S. Chow v. Santa Barbara (1933) 217 Cal. 673, 22 P2d 5; Peabody v. Vallejo (1935) 2 Cal. 2d. 351, 40 P2d 486; Clark v. Allaman (1905) 71 Kans. 206, 80 P. 571; Crawford Co. v. Hathaway (1903) 67 Neb. 325, 93 NW. 781; McDonough v. Russell-Miller Milling Co. (1917) 38 ND. 465, 165 NW. 504; Smith v. Stanolind Oil & Gas Co. (1946) 197 Okla. 499, 172 P2d 1002; Jones v. Conn (1901) 39 Ore. 30, 64 p. 855, 65 p. 1068; Redwater Land & Canal Co. v. Jones (1911) 27 SD. 194, 130 NW. 85; Watkins Land Co. v. Clements (1905) 98 Tex. 578, 86 SW. 733, 70 LRA 964, 107 ASR 653; Brown v. Chase (1923) 125 Wash. 542, 217 p. 23.

[5] (1842) 3 Scam. (Ill) 492, 18 AD 106.

[6] Evans v. Merriweather (1842) 3 Scam. (Ill) 492, 18 A.D. 106; Lone Tree Ditch Co. v. Cyclone Ditch Co. (1902) 15 S.D. 519, 91 N.W. 352 (1910) 26 S.D. 307, 128 N.W. 596.

[7] Lone Tree Ditch Co. v. Cyclone Ditch Co. (1902) 15 S.D. 519, 91 N.W. 352 (1910) 26 S.D. 307, 128 N.W. 596.

[8] Watkins Land Co. v. Clements (1905) 98 Tex. 578, 86 S.W. 733, 70 L.R.S. 964, 107 A.S.R. 653; Meng v. Coffey (1903) 67 Neb. 500, 93 N.W. 713.

[9] Watkins Land Co. v. Clements (1905) 98 Tex. 578, 86 S.W. 733, 70 L.R.S. 964, 107 A.S.R. 653; Lone Tree Ditch Co. v. Cyclone Ditch Co. (1902) 15 S.D. 519, 91 N.W. 352 (1910) 26 S.D. 307, 128 N.W. 596.

[10] Lux v. Haggin (1884) 69 Cal. 255, 4 P. 919 (1886) 10 P. 674.

[11] Meng v. Coffey (1903) 67 Neb. 500, 93 N.W. 713.

[12] Emporia v. Soden (1881) 25 Kans. 588, 37 A.R. 265; Frizell v. Bindley (1936) 144 Kans. 84, 58 P 2d 95; Crawford Co. v. Hathaway (1903) 67 Neb. 325, 93 N.W. 781; Prather v. Hoberg (1944) 24 Cal. 2d 549, 150 P 2d 405; Hough v. Porter (1909) 51 Ore. 318, 98 P. 1083.

[13] Meng v. Coffey (1903) 67 Neb. 500, 93 N.W. 713.

[14] Crawford Co. v. Hathaway (1903) 67 Neb. 325, 93 N.W. 781.

[15] Salem Flouring Mills v. Lord (1902) 42 Ore. 82, 69 P. 1033, 70 P. 832.

[16] Meng v. Coffey (1903) 67 Neb. 500, 93 N.W. 713.

[17] Hough v. Porter (1909) 51 Ore. 318, 98 P. 1083.

[18] *Ibid.*

[19] Martin v. Burr (1921) 111 Tex. 57, 228 S.W. 543; Hough v. Porter (1909) 51 Ore. 318, 98 P. 1083; Crawford Co. v. Hathaway (1903) 67 Neb. 325, 93 N.W. 781.

[20] Prather v. Hoberg (1944) 24 Cal. 2d 549, 150 P 2d 405.

[21] Crawford Co. v. Hathaway (1903) 67 Neb. 325, 93 N.W. 781; Emporia v. Soden (1881) 25 Kans. 588, 37 A.R. 265.

[22] Prather v. Hoberg (1944) 24 Cal. 2d 549, 150 P 2d 405.

[23] Filbert v. Dechert (1903) 22 Pa. Super 362.

[24] Salem Flouring Mills v. Lord (1902) 42 Ore. 82, 69 P. 1033, 70 P. 832.

[25] Emporia v. Soden (1881) 25 Kans. 588, 37 A.R. 265.

[26] Grogan v. Brownwood (Tex. Civ. App. 1919) 214 S.W. 532.

[27] United States v. Fallbrook Public Utility District (S.D. Cal. 1951) 101 F. Supp. 298 (1952) 108 F. Supp. 722, 109 F. Supp. 28.

[28] Church v. Barnes (1933) 175 Wash. 327, 27 P 2d 690.

[29] Hough v. Porter (1909) 51 Ore. 318, 98 P. 1083.

[30] Lux v. Haggin (1884) 69 Cal. 255, 4 P. 919 (1886) 10 P. 674.

[31] USDA, Better Feeding of Livestock, U.S. Govt. Print. Off., Aug. 1952, p. 16. Farmers' Bul. No. 2052 states that up to 10 gallons per day should be allowed for beef cattle and up to 25 for dairy cows. With some allowance for evaporation and seepage, this could amount to as much as one acre-foot of water every three weeks for 500 cows.

[32] Frizell v. Bindley (1936) 144 Kans. 84, 58 P 2d 95.

[33] Harris v. Harrison (1892) 93 Cal. 676, 29 P. 325.

[34] Slattery v. Harley (1899) 58 Neb. 575, 79 N.W. 151.

[35] Mentone Irrigation Co. v. Redlands Electric Light & Power Co. (1909) 155 Cal. 323, 100 P. 1082, 22 L.R.A. N.S. 382, 17 Ann. Cas. 1222; Southern Nebraska Power Co. v. Taylor (1923) 109 Neb. 683, 192 N.W. 317; *In re* Hood River (1924) 114 Ore. 112, 227 P. 1065; Lone Tree Ditch Co. v. Rapid City Electric Co. (1903) 16 S.D. 451, 93 N.W. 650.

[36] *In re* Hood River (1924) 114 Ore. 112, 227 P. 1065.

[37] Herminghaus v. Southern California Edison Co. (1926) 200 Cal. 81, 252 P. 607.

[38] Moore v. California Oregon Power Co. (1943) 22 Cal. 2d 725, 140 P 2d 798.

[39] Lone Tree Ditch Co. v. Rapid City Electric Co. (1903) 16 S.D. 451, 93 N.W. 650.

[40] Heise v. Schultz (1949) 167 Kans. 34, 204 P 2d 706.

[41] McDonough v. Russell-Miller Milling Co. (1917) 38 N.D. 465, 165 N.W. 504.

[42] Atchison, Topeka & Santa Fe Ry. Co. v. Shriver (1917) 101 Kans. 257, 166 P. 519.

[43] Fairbury v. Fairbury Mill & Elevator Co. (1932) 123 Neb. 558, 243 N.W. 774.

[44] Smith v. Stanolind Oil & Gas Co. (1946) 197 Okla. 499, 172 P 2d 1002.

[45] Sayles v. Mitchell (1932) 60 S.D. 592, 245 N.W. 390.

[46] Broady v. Furray (1933) 163 Okla. 204, 21 P 2d 770.

[47] *In re* Clinton Water District (1950) 136 Wash. 284, 218 P 2d 209.

[48] Martha Lake Water Co. v. Nelson (1929) 152 Wash. 53, 277 Pac. 382; Los Angeles v. Aitken (1935) 10 Cal. App. 460, 52 P 2d 585.

[49] Ide v. United States (1924) 263 U.S. 497.

[50] For example, Nev. Comp. Laws No. 7892 (1929); Wyo. Comp. Stats. No. 71-401 (1945); N.M. Stats. No. 77-102.

[51] Reclamation Act of 1903, No. 8.

[52] Denver v. Sheriff (1939) 105 Colo. 193 96 P 2d 836.

[53] Ariz. Code No. 75-102 (1939).

[54] S. Dak. Code No. 61.0102; Tex. Civ. Stats. Art. 7470 as amended Tex. Laws 1953 c. 354.

[55] *Supra* notes 51 and 52.

[56] See *infra* notes 152 to 158.

[57] Cal., No. 105.

[58] Montrose Canal Co. v. Loutsenhizer Ditch Co. (1896) 23 Colo. 233, 48 P. 532; Crawford Co. v. Hathaway (1903) 67 Neb. 325, 93 N.W. 781.

[59] Crawford Co. v. Hathaway (1903) 67 Neb. 325, 93 N.W. 781.

[60] Idaho Code No. 42-111 (1948).

[61] Okla. Stats. Tit. 82 No. 577.

[62] Kans. Gen. Stats. No. 82a-701(c) (1949).

[63] Wash. Rev. Stat. (Rev. 1929) No. 7399.

[64] Ariz. Code No. 75-106 (1939).

[65] Idaho Code No. 42-914 (1948).

[66] Colo. Rev. Stat. No. 147-2-6 (1953).

[67] Idaho Code No. 42-111 (1948).

[68] Kans. Gen. Stat. No. 82a-701(c) (1949).

[69] Montrose Canal Co. v. Loutsenhizer Ditch Co. (1896) 23 Colo. 233, 48 P. 532.

[70] For example, S. Dak. Code No. 61.0102 (Supp. 1952); Cal. Water Code No. 1460 (1954).

[71] *Supra* notes 51 and 52.

[72] Holt v. Cheyenne (1913) 22 Wyo. 212, 137 P. 876.

[73] Crawford Co. v. Hathaway (1903) 67 Neb. 325, 93 N.W. 781.

[74] Denver v. Brown (1913) 56 Colo. 216, 138 P. 44.

[75] Water Supply Co. v. Albuquerque (1912) 17 N.M. 326, 128 P. 77, 43 LRANS 439.

[76] Denver v. Brown (1913) 56 Colo. 216, 138 P. 44.

[77] Cal. Water Code No. 1460 (1954).

[78] Denver v. Sheriff (1939) 105 Colo. 193, 96 P 2d 836.

[79] Crawford Co. v. Hathaway (1903) 67 Neb. 325, 93 N.W. 781.

[80] Wyo. Comp. Stat. No. 71-402 (1945); Okla. Stats. Tit. 82 No. 577 (1953).

[81] *Ibid.*
[82] Okla. Stats. Tit. 82 No. 577 (1953).
[83] Wyo. Comp. Stat. No. 71-402 (1945).
[84] *Ibid.*
[85] *Ibid.*
[86] Water Supply Co. v. Albuquerque (1912) 17 N.M. 326, 128 P. 77, 43 LRANS 439.
[87] Crawford Co. v. Hathaway (1903) 67 Neb. 325, 93 N.W. 781.
[88] Platte Water Co. v. Northern Colorado Irrigation Co. (1889) 12 Colo. 525, 21 P. 711.
[89] Denver v. Brown (1913) 56 Colo. 216, 138 P. 44.
[90] Morrow v. Farmers' Irrigation District (1928) 117 Neb. 424, 220 N.W. 680.
[91] Wyoming v. Colorado (1922) 259 U.S. 419,42 SCt 552, 66 LEd 999.
[92] Sayre v. Johnson (1905) 33 Mont. 15, 81 P. 389.
[93] Hill v. Standard Mining Co. (1906) 12 Idaho 223, 85 P. 907.
[94] Texas Co. v. Burkett (1927) 117 Tex. 16, 296 S.W. 273, 54 ALR 1397; Smith v. Stanolind Oil & Gas Co. (1946) 197 Okla. 499, 172 P 2d 1002.
[95] Tex. Civ. Stats. Art. 7471 (1948); Tex. Laws 1953 c. 355.
[96] Tartar v. Spring Creek Water and Mining Co. (1885) 5 Cal. 395.
[97] 14 Stat. 253 Sec. 9 (1866); see also notes 51 and 52 *supra.*
[98] Lamborn v. Bell (1893) 18 Colo. 346, 32 P. 989, 20 LRA 241.
[99] Okla. Stats. Tit. 82 No. 577 (1953).
[100] Tex. Civ. Stat. Art. 7471 (1948).
[101] Tartar v. Spring Creek Water & Mining Co. (1885) 5 Cal. 395.
[102] For example, Lodi v. East Bay Municipal Utility District 7 Cal. 2d 316, 60 P. 2 439 (1936); Salt Lake City v. Salt Lake City Water & Electrical Power Co. (1902) 24 Utah 249, 67 P. 672 (1903) 25 Utah 456, 71 P. 1069; *In re* Deschutes River (1930) 134 Ore. 623, 286 P. 563, 294 P. 1049.
[103] *Supra* notes 51 and 52.
[104] Tex. Civ. Stat. Art. 7470 as amended.
[105] Osnes Livestock Co. v. Warren (1935) 103 Mont. 284, 62 P 2d 206.
[106] State v. Red River Valley Co. (1945) 51 N.M. 207, 182 P 2d 421.
[107] Denver v. Brown (1913) 56 Colo. 216, 138 P. 44.
[108] Cascade Town Co. v. Empire Water & Power Co. (d Colo. 1910) 181 Fed. 1011, rev'd on other grounds, (9 Cir. 1913) 205 Fed. 123.
[109] Ore. Rev. Stat. Nos. 538. 110 to 538. 300 (1953).
[110] Idaho Code Nos. 67-4301, 67-4304 (1948).
[111] State v. Red River Valley Co. (1945) 51 N.M. 207, 182 P 2d 421.
[112] Osnes Livestock Co. v. Warren (1935) 103 Mont. 284, 62 P 2d 206.
[113] Diversion Lake Club v. Heath (1935) 126 Tex. 129, 86 S.W. 2d 441.
[114] Lake Shore Duck Club v. Lake View Duck Club (1917) 50 Utah 76, 166 P. 309, LRA 1918B 620.
[115] *Ex parte* Elam (1907) 6 Cal. App. 233, 91 P. 811; *ex parte* Mass. (1933) 219 Cal. 422, 27 P. 2d 373.
[116] Drake v. Earhart (1890) 2 Idaho 750, 23 P. 541.
[117] Ore. Rev. Stat. No. 537. 310 (1953); Wyo. Comp. Stat. No. 71-402 (1945).
[118] Okla. Stat. Tit. 82 No. 531 (1953); Wyo. Comp. Stat. No. 71-402 (1945).
[119] *Ibid.*
[120] Okla. Stats. Tit. 82 No. 531 (1953).
[121] Cal. Water Code No. 1242 (1954).
[122] Faden v. Hubbell (1933) 93 Colo. 358, 28 P 2d 247.
[123] *Ex parte* Elam (1907) 6 Cal. App. 233, 91 P. 811.
[124] Tulare Irrigation District v. Lindsay-Strathmore Irrigation District (1935) 3 Cal. 2d 489, 45 P 2d 972.
[125] *In re* Deschutes River (1930) 134 Ore. 623, 286 P. 563, 294 P. 1049.
[126] Meng v. Coffey (1903) 67 Neb. 500, 93 N.W. 713; Jones v. Conn (1901) 39 Ore. 30, 64 P. 855, 65 P. 1068.
[127] Prather v. Hoberg (1944) 24 Cal. 2d 549, 150 P 2d 405.
[128] Lone Tree Ditch Co. v. Cyclone Ditch Co. (1902) 15 S.D. 519, 91 N.W. 352, (1910) 26 S.D. 307, 128 N.W. 596.
[129] Redwater Land and Canal Co. v. Reed (1910) 26 S.D. 466, 128 N.W. 702.
[130] Meng v. Coffey (1903) 67 Neb. 500, 93 N.W. 713.
[131] Restatement of Torts, Nos. 851-854.

[132] Fairbury v. Fairbury Mill & Elevator Co. (1932) 123 Neb. 558, 243 N.W. 774.

[133] Turner v. James Canal Co. (1909) 155 Cal. 82, 99 P. 520, 22 LRA 401, 132 ASR 59.

[134] Rancho Santa Margarita v. Vail (1938) 11 Cal. 2d 501, 81 P. 2d 533.

[135] Peabody v. Vallejo (1935) 2 Cal. 2d 351, 42 Pad 486.

[136] Lone Tree Ditch Co. v. Rapid City Electric Co. (1903) 16 S.D. 451, 93 N.W. 650.

[137] Broady v. Furray (1933) 163 Okla. 204, 21 P 2d 770.

[138] Power v. Switzer·(1898) 21 Mont. 523, 55 P. 32.

[139] In re Deschutes River (1930) 134 Ore. 623, 286 P. 563, 294 P. 1049.

[140] Ibid.

[141] Ex parte Elam (1907) 6 Cal. App. 233, 91 P. 811; Ex parte Mass. (1933) 219 Cal. 422, 27 P 2d 373.

[142] Cal. Const. Art. 14, No. 3.

[143] Tulare Irrigation District v. Lindsay-Strathmore Irrigation District (1935) 3 Cal. 2d 489, 45 P 2d 972.

[144] See Frank J. Trelease, "Preferences to the use of water," Rocky Mountain Law Rev., Vol. 27, 1955, pp. 133-60, Univ. of Colo.

[145] Colo. Const. Art. 16, No. 6; Idaho Const. Art. 15, No. 3; Neb. Const. Art. 15, No. 6; Wyo. Comp. Stat. No. 71-402 (1945).

[146] 45 Stat. 1057 Art. 4(b) (1928).

[147] Mont. Rev. Stat. 89-895 (1953).

[148] 33 U.S.C. 701-1b (1944).

[149] Tex. Civ. Stat. Art. 7472.

[150] Cal. Water Code No. 1254 (1954); Ariz. Code No. 75-106 (1939); Tex. Civ. Stat., Art. 7471 (1948).

[151] Utah Code No. 100-3-8 (1943).

[152] Tanner v. Bacon (1943) 103 Utah 494, 136 P 2d 957.

[153] Ore. Comp. Laws No. 116-601 (1940).

[154] Tex. Civ. Stat., Art. 7472c (1948).

[155] F. J. Trelease, op. cit.

[156] See note 143 supra, Utah Code 100-3-21.

[157] Idaho Const., Art. 15, No. 3.

[158] Wyo. Comp. Stat. No. 71-402 (1945).

[159] Tex. Civ. Stat., Art. 7471 (1948).

[160] Okla. Stat. Tit. 82 No. 577.

[161] Kans. Gen. Stat. No. 82a-707 (1949).

[162] Missouri Basin Survey Commission, Missouri: Land and Water, U.S. Govt. Print. Off., 1953, p. 64.

WELLS A. HUTCHINS is a leading authority on western water rights law. His reputation has been developed while serving for over fifty years on the staff of the U.S. Department of Agriculture. He is attached to the Resource Development Economics Division, Economic Research Service, U.S. Department of Agriculture.

Chapter 17

WELLS A. HUTCHINS

*Groundwater Legislation**

G ROUNDWATER in common parlance is all water in the ground. However, in dealing with water rights laws, we need not consider some subsurface water. For the purpose of this chapter, groundwater may be taken to be all water in the ground that is free to move by gravity and to enter wells, capable of being extracted from the ground and susceptible to practicable legal control.

PERCOLATING WATERS
AND DEFINITE UNDERGROUND STREAMS

Throughout the history of groundwater law a legal distinction between waters of definite underground streams and percolating waters has run through various texts, statutes and court decisions.[1] According to this distinction, a definite underground stream has the characteristics

---
*The author wishes to acknowledge the helpful comments of Harold E. Thomas, United States Geological Survey, and Dean C. Muckel, Soil and Water Conservation Division, Agricultural Research Service.

Reprinted with permission of the *Rocky Mountain Law Rev.*, Vol. 30, No. 4, 1958, pp. 1-25. Since 1958 important statues have been enacted or amended, and important court decisions rendered respecting groundwater rights — which are not included in this reprinting of the original *Rocky Mountain Law Review* article.

of a watercourse on the surface — definite channel with bed and banks, definite stream of water and definite source or sources of supply — whereas percolating waters comprise all groundwaters that do not conform to the classification of a definite stream.

This classification has been criticized by groundwater hydrologists as having no scientific basis or satisfactory applicability.[2] It has been eliminated from the water rights statutes of some western states.[3] In some other statutes it has been minimized by the device of so broadening the applicability of the legal procedures therein provided as to encompass most occurrences of groundwater over which neighboring landowners might quarrel.[4] Nevertheless the groundwater laws of some states — including both California and Texas, with their great developments of groundwater for various purposes and their millions of acres of irrigated land — still adhere to the historical distinction. Obviously, in a general discussion of groundwater laws, continued acceptance of the distinction in some jurisdictions must be noted. Also, it is necessary to point out that by far the largest number of appellate court decisions handed down concerning groundwater rights have pertained to cases in which the water was not proved to be part of any defined subterranean stream.

Groundwater Doctrines: Definite Streams

The definite underground stream, being a counterpart of a surface watercourse, is governed by the same legal doctrines related to the latter[5] — a practice that has a sound hydrologic basis. Therefore, in states that recognize the riparian doctrine of rights in surface streams, lands that overlie or are contiguous to definite underground streams have riparian rights in their waters. Likewise, appropriative rights may attach to underground streams in those jurisdictions in which the appropriation doctrine is recognized. And on some major western streams both doctrines are applicable.[6]

The presumption is that groundwaters are percolating. Hence one who asserts that a definite underground stream exists has the burden of proving it.[7]

The underflow of a surface stream is a facet of a common watercourse, part of which is above the ground and part within it. Rights that attach to one portion of the watercourse extend to the other as well.[8]

Groundwater Doctrines: Percolating Waters[9]

Percolating waters "belong" to the owners of overlying lands in some jurisdictions, but are subject to appropriation in others.

Of these doctrines of groundwater rights that are inherent in overlying landownership, the English rule of absolute ownership — sometimes termed the common law doctrine — is the earliest in American jurisprudence. In some jurisdictions it still persists.[10] Some courts,

however, have imposed qualifications upon the exercise of rights incident to absolute ownership to the extent that the water be used without
malice, negligence or unnecessary waste.

Unfavorable experience with the English rule in some localities led
to adoption by some courts of the American rule of reasonable use.
This rule recognizes the landowner's right to capture and use the water
that exists in his land but limits him to such quantity of water as is
necessary for some useful purpose in connection with the land from
which the water is extracted. The chief limitations are that waste of
the water, or export of the water for distant use, are not reasonable if
the result deprives other overlying landowners of the opportunity to
make reasonable use of the common supply on their own lands.

An outgrowth of the American rule which has found its greatest expression in California is known as the California doctrine of correlative
rights. As developed in a series of court decisions extending over a
period of 55 years, the chief features of this doctrine are: (1) owners
of all lands that overlie a common supply of percolating water have coequal rights of reasonable use on or in connection with their overlying
lands, (2) any surplus above reasonable requirements of landowners
may be appropriated for nonoverlying use and (3) in the event of a water
shortage, the common supply may be apportioned by court order among
the overlying owners in proportion to their reasonable needs.[11]

In many western states percolating waters have been subjected to
prior appropriation under principles first developed with respect to
surface watercourses and, as pumping developments increased, adapted
to conditions that pertain to waters in the ground. This chapter chiefly
relates to legislation in this field.

DEVELOPMENT OF THE STATUTORY FIELD[12]

An enactment by the Territory of Dakota in 1866 was probably the
first groundwater legislation in the West. It purported to apply common law principles by declaring that the landowner owned the water
standing on or flowing over or under the surface but not forming a definite stream, and that he might use the water of a definite natural surface or subterranean stream while on his land but might not prevent its
natural flow. This statute was incorporated into the laws of the states
of North Dakota and South Dakota, which were formed out of the original
territory, and it was later enacted in Oklahoma as well.[13] In 1891 and
1911 Kansas enacted rather unclear statutes pertaining to subterranean
waters but without influencing noticeably the development of the state's
water laws. From 1899 to 1919 various acts relating to the appropria-
bility of groundwaters, either generally or within physical classifications, were passed in Idaho, Utah, Nevada, California and Arizona.

About the turn of the century there appeared the beginning of a trend toward specifically including groundwaters within state administrative procedures for acquiring and administering appropriative rights. Then, shortly after 1925 a series of more and more comprehensive groundwater enactments began — a movement still active — in which a large majority of western jurisdictions have participated. The first two of these laws were passed in New Mexico and Oregon in 1927.

In the 1930's outmoded groundwater laws were replaced in Utah and Nevada. Then from the close of the war to 1958 each biennium brought forth in the West at least one major groundwater enactment. States concerned in this progressive lawmaking (aside from amendments designed to make needed changes and improvements but without amounting to large-scale overhauling or the changing of fundamental principles) were Kansas and Washington in 1945; Wyoming, 1947; Arizona, 1948; Oklahoma and Texas, 1949; Idaho, 1951 and 1953; Colorado, 1953; North Dakota, South Dakota and Oregon, 1955; and Colorado, Kansas and Wyoming in 1957.[14]

Statutes in 11 of the 17 western states authorize the appropriation of percolating water. These are Idaho, Kansas, Nevada, New Mexico, North Dakota, Oklahoma, Oregon, South Dakota, Utah, Washington and Wyoming. In three states — Arizona, Colorado, Texas — statutory restrictions are not based on priority of appropriation. The three remaining states — California, Montana and Nebraska — have made small beginnings in the field of groundwater legislation.

REPLACEMENT OF LANDOWNERSHIP DOCTRINES
BY APPROPRIATION STATUTES

In most western states in which the appropriative principle has been applied to rights of use of percolating waters, enabling legislation has preceded court decisions. Several exceptions, however, may be noted: The California Supreme Court, without prestatutory approval, declared that percolating waters in excess of the reasonable requirements of overlying lands may be appropriated for nonoverlying use; i.e., use of the water outside the area or under public utility service within it.[15] Indeed, the California statutes that provide for the appropriation of water have never applied to percolating groundwater.[16] The Utah Supreme Court, after having acknowledged and adopted landownership doctrines, broke away from this philosophy in 1935 in favor of the appropriation doctrine, and its decisions were followed within a few months by legislative action.[17] In New Mexico the legislature, it is true, spoke first. Then the supreme court held the groundwater statute unconstitutional on technical grounds but went to considerable lengths in laying the basis for passage of an act free from the objectionable features. The court concluded that the faulty act, while objectionable in form, was declaratory of existing law and in harmony with the appropriative principle that had been consistently applied in that jurisdiction to surface waters.[18]

Coverage of Appropriation Statutes [19]

A statute that makes adequate provision for the appropriation of
groundwater must contain, among other things, such features as designation of waters affected, designation of public administrative agency,
recordation of claims of pre-existing water rights, procedure for acquiring new rights, determination or adjudication of groundwater rights,
supervision of extractions of groundwater, changes in exercise of
groundwater rights, loss of rights.

Several original groundwater laws, in specifying waters subject to
appropriation, set up rather elaborate classifications of groundwaters
having reasonably ascertainable boundaries. The trend has been away
from elaborate classifications and toward complete coverage of all
groundwaters subject to practicable administration. For example, the
Washington law relates to all water under the surface if its existence
and boundaries may be reasonably established or ascertained; and the
1955 Oregon law applies to all water in the ground except capillary
moisture.[20]

The Wyoming statute of 1957 purports to be all-inclusive.[21] The
Wyoming law applies to "underground water," which includes all water
under the surface of the land or under the bed of any body of surface
water. However, although the Utah statute also purports to relate to all
water in the ground, the Utah Supreme Court has held that it cannot apply to small occurrences of shallow water that produce plant life but
that cannot be traced to lands other than that in which the water is
found.[22]

The administrative agent charged with administration of the groundwater statute is the state engineer or other comparable state official or
agency. Provision is made for registering in the administrator's office
all claims of rights to the use of groundwater initiated before the statute was enacted, based upon previous actual application of water to beneficial use. These recorded verified claims are *prima facie* evidence
of the rights so described.

The excess water in the source of supply above the quantities to
which holders of pre-existing rights are entitled is available for appropriation under the specific procedure prescribed in the statute. These
procedures parallel those provided for appropriations of surface waters,
with variations caused by differences in character of water supplies
and in methods of withdrawal.

The trend is toward including in the appropriation statutes procedures for administrative determinations of water rights followed by
court adjudications. In some cases the procedures in the general water
appropriation statutes are made applicable; in others they are separately
provided in the groundwater statutes.

Supervision over withdrawals of water requires determinations of
availability of the water supply for rights that attach to it and imposition
of controls in the event of water shortage. It has the same object as
administration of surface water rights, but the techniques necessarily

differ. Under some statutes when it appears that a groundwater supply is in danger from standpoints of quantity or quality, such an area is to be designated as "critical" and, if investigations and hearings show that controls are needed, authorized controls are to be enforced. The area is closed to further development of groundwater while the critical condition persists. Several statutes authorize apportionment of withdrawals of water in accordance with respective priorities.[23]

Other matters that are found in various groundwater appropriation statutes comprise exemptions from compliance with the act, chiefly in the case of small domestic, stock-watering and other uses; authorization to change the location of wells, place and purpose of use; forfeiture of rights for failure to exercise them for prescribed periods of years; licensing of well drillers; restriction on the right to have the water level maintained at any particular depth from the surface; and provision for recharge and recapture of artificially stored groundwater.

Statutes Not Based on Prior Appropriation

Many years of effort to obtain legislation in Arizona for the control of groundwater finally resulted in a 1948 enactment that applies to percolating water only.[24] It provides for the designation by the state land commissioner of "critical groundwater areas" in which the supply has been overdrawn. In such areas permits are required for installation of irrigation wells in excess of 100-gallons-per-minute capacity. No permit will be issued for the irrigation of new land. The last-named provision of this act definitely restricts the right of a landowner in an overdrawn area — not to pump water but to extend his irrigated acreage. The constitutionality of the act was sustained by the Arizona Supreme Court.[25] (See section on constitutional problems, page 305.)

The Texas restrictive laws operate within groundwater conservation districts, which include areas coterminous with subterranean reservoirs designated by the State Board of Water Engineers and which are created by vote of the property tax-paying residents.[26] They may issue bonds and levy *ad valorem* taxes. Their purposes are the conservation, preservation, protection and recharging, and the prevention of waste of groundwaters of subterranean reservoirs. Subject to the rules and regulations of the district for the purpose of preventing waste, the ownership and rights of the landowner in groundwater are recognized,[27] and priorities and provisions of the surface water laws do not apply.

The Colorado statute applies to all groundwater — "any water not visible on the surface of the ground under natural conditions."[28] It provides for the designation, alteration and abolishment by a groundwater commission of "tentatively critical groundwater districts" in which further development of groundwater may be suspended or curtailed while the designation remains in effect. To cooperate with the commission and the state engineer in regulating groundwater diversion and use in such a critical area, a district advisory board is locally elected. Permits to use groundwater must be obtained from the state engineer before drilling new wells or increasing withdrawals of water from existing wells. Except for the provisions of the statute relating to well drilling, exemptions include wells used solely for stock watering and domestic and artesian wells having small discharge pipes.

In addition, several statutes that relate to groundwater withdrawals have been enacted in California, Montana and Nebraska. Three California statutes enacted in 1951, 1953 and 1955 apply only to specified southern counties in which important groundwater supplies are seriously overdrawn, and they do not purport to restrict the exercise of any groundwater right.[29] The use of an alternate supply of water from a nontributary source will be deemed equivalent to a reasonable beneficial use of groundwater not extracted because of the substitute supply. Preliminary injunctions for the protection of groundwater basins may be issued while rights therein are being determined. The water user must make annual reports of information essential to determinations of groundwater rights to the state water rights board, and failure to file the reports may prevent the accrual of prescriptive rights in his favor.

The Montana legislature in 1957 passed an act providing for filing with every county clerk logs of all wells drilled,[30] in order to perpetuate the records of priorities for use in future adjudications of rights relating to particular aquifers.[31]

Three acts were passed by the Nebraska legislature in 1957.[32] Irrigation wells must be registered with the state department of water resources, minimum spacing between irrigation wells is provided for and closer spacing requires special permits. Preferential uses of groundwater are prescribed, with domestic use having first preference and agriculture second.

HUMAN AND LEGISLATIVE PROBLEMS

Opposition From the Public

Opposition from persons who want no legal restrictions on well drilling or on individual pumping has effectively blocked enactment of proposed legislation in many jurisdictions and has delayed "tightening up" of mild restrictions. One phenomenon sometimes noted in connection with this public attitude is the hostility of many farmers even at times when water levels are dangerously receding.

A sample of this was reduced to statistics in an article giving results of a survey made in 1956 in the Bijou Basin, Morgan County, Colorado.[33] The survey area depends entirely on wells for irrigation water. Each well has been drilled to its maximum depth. The water table has been lowered considerably by pumping, and the water supply is overdrawn. Seventy-four irrigation farmers were interviewed. Thirty-one of these were owners and 43 were tenants.

Significant results of the Bijou Basin survey were these: Of the interviewed who answered, 76 percent opposed restrictions on replacement or new wells on irrigated land, but 46 percent favored restricting development of new irrigated cropland (as against 40 percent opposed), and 62 percent favored restrictions on spacing of future wells; 66 percent opposed taxation of water use, but 58 percent favored a property tax or use tax for importing water; opposition was expressed to rationing water, to sharing equally in reducing pumped water and to curtailing irrigation. Lack of support for a statute based on priority of appropriation is indicated by *opposition* to curtailment of pumping in reverse order of drilling (82 percent), restricting use by newcomers after a set date in the future (61 percent), limiting of pumping to certain days only (73 percent), and holding a junior well owner liable if he lowers the water level of his neighbor's wells (57 percent); and by *approval* of proposals that unrestricted use of groundwater be allowed to continue (59 percent) and that a farmer be allowed the legal right to do anything with groundwater (70 percent).

If controls are administered, 66 percent recommended that the agency be local people only, 12 percent local people and the government together, and 5 percent the state engineer or other state administrator. Factors contributing to the strong bias toward negative answers, say the authors, are the short-run prosperity resulting from unrestricted use of groundwater, which would have been lessened by controls in the most seriously affected areas, and a natural opposition to any interference with their farming operations. Yet the researchers report that the survey findings indicate a general gradual decline in the productivity of irrigated land if water levels continue to decline.

Opposition from the public has been effective at some of the legislative sessions in the past, and in some jurisdictions it still persists. For example, in 1955 groundwater proposals were defeated in Colorado, Montana, Oklahoma and Wyoming. But the trend toward overcoming the opposition has continued, for in 1957 Colorado and Wyoming (two of the states just named) enacted statutes vesting public control in state administrative agencies. The Colorado act — which, it will be noted, was passed in the year following the Bijou Basin survey — replaces a statute that had been passed in 1953; and the Wyoming law replaces one enacted in 1947 which, although based on appropriation, had made the state engineer's office one of public record rather than effective public control.[34]

And in Kansas, although the opposition was considerable, the 1957 legislature extensively revised the 1945 appropriation statute (relating to both surface and groundwater) in order to clear up uncertainties and to make it more workable and more effective in administering water rights insofar as possible on an appropriative basis.[35]

Feasibility of Administrative Control

From the first, the feasibility of public control of groundwater rights under appropriation statutes has been seriously disputed.[36] Opposition to enactments still comes from some who may not be personally concerned but who consider public control unnecessary, undesirable, impracticable or even unconstitutional — the last-named objection, invalidity, being a "time-honored" one.[37]

Nevertheless, such legislation continues to be enacted and administered, and the administrators continue to gain much valuable experience. No western state that had adopted this policy has abandoned it. On the contrary, some of the original brief statutes have been replaced by longer ones with broader coverage and more detailed procedure. The constitutionality of only a few statutes has been resolved by appellate courts, as noted in the section on Constitutional Problems (page 305), but in many states concern over the possibility of adverse decisions appears to be lessening as time goes on.

Relation to Surface Water Statutes

A question that has arisen in the East in connection with proposals for new water legislation is whether the proposed law should apply to both surface and groundwaters or should be restricted to watercourses on the surface. In view of the physical interdependence of waters on the surface and those in the ground, discussed later in this chapter, it is realized that the better policy is to have a statute that applies to all these interconnected waters, with such separate provisions as required for surface streams and for groundwaters. However, in a state that has no water rights legislation, enactment of any water law is a long step to take. Furthermore, opposition to legal control of groundwater may be enough greater than opposition to a surface water proposal so that a combined bill is defeated. For such practical reasons, in order to get a water control program under way, sometimes it has been deemed expedient to concentrate on a surface stream law and to progress from there to groundwater when the time seems more propitious.[38]

In the West, where for many decades each of the 17 westernmost states has had statutory laws governing the appropriation of surface stream waters, introduction of groundwater features began with brief amendments of the general water statutes. In a few states there is now a single procedure that applies to all waters, surface and subterranean, with some sections specially pertaining to groundwaters. But in the large majority of the western states that have placed groundwater rights on an appropriative basis, a separate statute governs the latter, with references to applicable sections of the general water appropriation statute in order to avoid repetition of duplicate features. The effect of this is to apply the same procedures to surface and groundwaters so far as practicable and at the same time to consolidate provisions dealing with groundwater control only — features that have been developed by the legislatures more and more comprehensively.[39] The difference between the two methods is a matter of arrangement of statutory sections; certainly, if carefully worded, there need be no difference in legal effect.[40]

Correlation of Rights in Interconnected Surface and Groundwaters

Essential to the completeness of a groundwater administrative system is correlation of rights to the use of common water supplies (interconnected surface and groundwaters) with respect to their administration, adjudication and supervision of diversions and withdrawals. The degree of correlation effected by statutes or court decisions, or both, varies from one state to another, but in the West on the whole it has been increasing. Harold Thomas points out that although it is still possible in many states to administer water laws as if surface water and groundwater were separate and independent resources, complex problems inevitably arise as water utilization increases. These problems can be settled only by complete integration of all water rights in the light of sound knowledge of hydrologic principles and their application.[41]

The fact that surface streams "lose" water into the ground at some times and places and "gain" water at others long has been recognized not only by groundwater hydrologists and engineers but also by attorneys, judges and legislators as well. Nevertheless, integration of surface and groundwater doctrines and rights of use has not always kept pace with comprehension of physical conditions. Rival claimants to waters of surface streams have usually litigated their relative rights — between themselves, without intervention of owners of wells which depend on groundwater feeding the stream or escaping from it, and the reverse holds true with respect to most adjudications of groundwater rights. Lack of correlation has more serious results in such cases than where separate adjudications are made of rights on a surface stream and on its main tributaries, because the character of the surface water rights is the same — appropriative, or appropriative and riparian, depending on the jurisdiction. But in some states surface stream rights may be solely appropriative and groundwater rights may be based on landownership — even the rule of absolute ownership in overlying land. Repeated court decisions may have welded this rule into a rule of property, which may be difficult to overturn when many more rights become vested and more knowledge about physical interrelationships is available.

What opportunity is there for correlation of rights in a stream and in the groundwater reservoir that supplies it or that is supplied by it, or both, in a state in which watercourse rights are exclusively appropriative and rights in percolating groundwaters are based on absolute ownership? Yet that is the situation in Montana,[42] and it was the case in Wyoming prior to enactment of the groundwater appropriation statutes.[43] It was also the case in Arizona until 1953,[44] when the supreme court departed from its earlier decisions to the extent of holding that the landowner's right is that of reasonable use, not absolute ownership.[45]

On the other hand, both surface and subterranean stream and tributary waters in Colorado are correlated on a basis of prior appropriation;[46] in California, appropriative and riparian rights in watercourses and correlative and appropriative rights in interconnected percolating waters have been coordinated as the result of court decisions over many years, the leading factor being reasonable beneficial use.[47] But it should be noted that although rights to the use of both surface and subterranean waters, whether in streams or percolating, may be adjudicated in California in a private suit either under the court reference procedure or otherwise, percolating water rights may not be adjudicated under the complete statutory adjudication procedure.[48] The New Mexico Supreme Court has held that a statutory suit to adjudicate water rights in a stream system includes rights of appropriators from an artesian basin who claim that the stream waters contribute to the recharge of the artesian supply, the suit being all-embracing.[49]

Some of the groundwater statutes contemplate the determination of both surface water rights and groundwater rights in the same proceeding,[50] whereas certain others relate specifically only to groundwater rights, which are to be determined, so far as applicable, under the same procedure as that provided for surface waters.[51] Although the Wyoming law of 1957 provides for adjudications of groundwater rights within districts and subdistricts that overlie water-bearing formations, without reference to rights in streams that cross these areas, another section (Sec. 18) states in part:

Where underground waters in different aquifers are so interconnected as to constitute in fact one source of supply, or where underground waters and the waters of surface streams are so interconnected as to constitute in fact one source of supply, priorities of rights to the use of all such interconnected waters shall be correlated and such single schedule of priorities shall relate to the whole common water supply.[52]

It may be reasonably inferred from the broad language of Paragraph 2, Section 15, of the 1957 groundwater act that the Wyoming procedure for correlating adjudication decrees issued separately with respect to a stream and its tributaries is applicable to this surface and groundwater relationship. Thus the state engineer will have a sound basis for administering Section 18. Where groundwaters and surface stream waters are physically connected (as was claimed in the New Mexico case cited above), the equities of the case would seem to demand integration of all water rights, and statutory procedure for harmonizing them is indicated whether or not some of the rights have been previously adjudicated.[53]

Problems in Administering the Statute

A major problem in enacting any legislation imposing public control upon groundwater rights is that of making the law workable. As with laws in other fields, it may be so burdened with details which hamper the administrator unnecessarily or, on the other hand, so sketchy that he is left without adequate guidance in performing important functions. The administrator needs a reasonable measure of flexibility and opportunity for the exercise of sound discretion to perform his duties, but his authority is no more than the legislature has granted either expressly or by necessary implication; and of course an administrative officer is not the final judge of the necessity for a legislative implication. Recommendations in reports of state engineers for clarifying amendments have been not uncommon, and the legislative trend has been toward adding functions and details, not toward restricting or eliminating them.

The author once had occasion to correspond with several state engineers with respect to their groundwater administrative problems.[54] There had been little opportunity for problems to arise in some states owing to the short period of time the statute had been in force or to the small measure of authority vested in the administrator. But even here, local opposition to enforcement plus claims of unconstitutionality were noted. Need for more complete legislation, including authority and specific procedure for adjudicating and administering groundwater rights, was indicated in several replies. Necessarily, where statutory procedures are not provided, adjudications are limited to suits begun by private parties which may or may not include all claimants. Most of the groundwater appropriation statutes include such procedures.

In the field of administering rights to withdraw groundwater and supervising withdrawals, cooperation between the state administrator and representative groups, which is provided in several states, tends to inject a statewide viewpoint and to offset possible local bias when supervision is left wholly to local persons. For example, in Idaho administrative determinations of adverse claims (not adjudications of rights, which are provided for elsewhere) are made by temporary groundwater boards comprised of the state reclamation engineer, a private engineer or geologist and a resident irrigation farmer. The board is dissolved when the claims the members were appointed to hear are finally resolved.[55]

The 1957 laws of both Colorado and Wyoming provide for broad representative groups. In Colorado, the appointive members of a commission are chosen from the irrigation divisions; in Wyoming provision is made for a separate committee for each water division as well as for local advisory boards for "critical" groundwater districts to work with the state water administrators in administering the statute.[56] Likewise, in New Mexico artesian conservancy districts have concurrent authority with the state engineer to regulate artesian waters;[57] in Nevada the state engineer at his discretion may avail himself of the services of water conservation boards or water districts.[58] Both the Oregon and Wyoming statutes encourage the execution of voluntary agreements among users of water from a common groundwater supply.[59]

Coverage of a groundwater statute with respect to appropriable waters has been involved in some controversies. For example, although the New Mexico statute of 1931 did not specifically so provide, the supreme court of that state held that it included shallow groundwater areas overlying artesian areas,[60] and the legislature has since declared that all groundwaters are public waters, subject to appropriation, but that permits to appropriate them are required only in groundwater areas designated by the state engineer.[61] The communications of several state engineers stressed the importance of public relations and stated that educational programs were proving valuable in implementing controls in areas in which wells had been previously drilled and water used without thought of legal restriction. Reliable information about geologic and hydrologic conditions is an obvious prerequisite to successful administration, and the western state engineers and the United States Geological Survey have been and are cooperating in this field.

Operation of laws regulating the drilling of water wells and providing for the licensing of well drillers is an important phase of administration. In states that do not require such licensing and the obtaining of permits to drill wells, lack of control over their drilling is a problem. Wells constructed therein may be and in some cases have been so located as to interfere with existing installations, or they may be improperly constructed or may tap confined aquifers without being properly sealed. State administrators have been called upon to assist owners of illegal wells in solving their problems. The Idaho groundwater law was passed with the cooperation of the well drillers association, as well as other statewide organizations. Also reported are the facts that the New Mexico well drillers' law has been of immeasurable value in curbing illegal drilling and that Utah drillers have become an important link in administration of the groundwater law.

CONSTITUTIONAL PROBLEMS

Only a few of the western groundwater control statutes have been taken to the high courts for determination of their validity. This is true despite the fact that so many of the appropriation statutes supplanted groundwater doctrines based on landownership the existence of which had been either held or acknowledged by the courts. The constitutionality of legislation purporting to subordinate unused rights or claims of right to new appropriations would be particularly vulnerable if in a given jurisdiction enough court decisions had previously declared that rights to the use of groundwaters were inherent in the ownership of the overlying land and, in reliance thereon, enough action had been taken by landowners and water users to make out a *prima facie* case for establishment of a rule of property.

However, in various instances such few court decisions as existed had been rendered long before, and of course the statutes made provision for recognizing vested rights in those who had made actual use of groundwater prior to the enactments, for ascertaining and recording claims of vested rights and for honoring those that could be substantiated. In most cases, therefore, there was no rush to the courts on the ground that due process was being denied. There may be further attacks in some jurisdictions. Nevertheless, with the passage of time, with the growth of groundwater installations and uses and of property values resulting therefrom and with widespread acceptance of the statutes and their administration by the public, the soundness of the basic principles seems to be generally taken for granted.

The first of the separate statutes to be enacted — and to be declared unconstitutional — was the New Mexico law of 1927.[62] However, the declaration of invalidity was based on the purely technical ground that extending provisions of existing law therein violated a provision of the state constitution which reads that no law should be revised or amended, or its provisions extended, by reference to its title only, but that each section as revised, amended or extended should be set out in full.[63] The New Mexico Supreme Court approved the doctrine of appropriation, which from time immemorial had been the exclusive doctrine that governed uses of water of watercourses in that jurisdiction and believed that the same principles should be applied to definite bodies of artesian water. The 1927 statute, said the court, was declaratory of existing law and was fundamentally sound even though technically void; the waters of an artesian basin with established boundaries were held subject to appropriation even without the aid of the statute. A new statute free from the faulty features was enacted in 1931.[64] This act was actively administered for many years before its validity was contested by defendants in suits brought by the state for the purposes of enjoining unlawful uses of groundwater. Both the supreme court of New Mexico and the United States Supreme Court held that the statute is constitutionally unobjectionable.[65]

The Utah groundwater legislation was enacted after the supreme court of that state had held that artesian waters are subject to appropriation.[66] Previously the decisions of the court had passed through the stages of (1) recognizing the rule of absolute ownership of percolating water as against appropriations initiated after the water-bearing lands had passed to private ownership, but holding that water taken from land on the public domain is subject to appropriation whether it is percolating or stream water and (2) later holding that the rule of correlative rights obtains between owners of land overlying a common artesian basin.[67]

In moving on to the doctrine of appropriation, the supreme court was sharply divided on the issue, with dissents by two of the five justices indicating their conviction that rights in groundwaters that had vested by reason of landownership should not and could not be disturbed. The court has not since had occasion to pass on the constitutionality of the legislation that promptly followed the 1935 decisions, but controlling sections of the act have been construed as governing all appropriations of groundwater made after their enactment other than small isolated occurrences of diffused water close to the surface.[68] After a quarter century of administration of the groundwater law, with neither expressed nor implied disapproval of its validity in the few groundwater cases that have been before the court, it is a safe assumption that the underlying principle is sound.

Kansas passed an act in 1945 to establish the effectiveness of the appropriation doctrine as against common law claimants of both surface and groundwater rights.[69] This was done in the year following a decision by the Kansas Supreme Court that strongly reaffirmed the landowner's right to both running water and groundwater on his property against an attempted appropriation.[70] In 1949 this legislation was approved unqualifiedly by the state supreme court on all points raised and considered.[71] The court took an entirely new approach to the solution of water rights questions. Previously individual interest had been the sole basis; now, in harmony with the statutory declaration that all water was dedicated to the use of the people, subject to state regulation, the subject was approached on the basis of public interest but without losing sight of the beneficial use the individual was making or had the right to make. "Unused or unusable rights predicated alone upon theory become of little if any importance." Later attacks in the federal courts against the legality of the 1945 act likewise were unsuccessful.[72]

In 1955 the constitutionality of the Arizona groundwater code of 1948[73] — not an appropriation act, but one that provides controls in overdrawn or "critical" groundwater areas, the effect of which prohibits placing new lands under irrigation — was sustained by the Arizona Supreme Court.[74] This was done notwithstanding previous decisions of the same court which held that percolating water rights are based on ownership of the overlying land.[75] In the instant case the court took the position that where the public interest is significantly involved, the preferment of that interest over the property interest of an individual even to the extent of its destruction is a distinguishing characteristic of the exercise of the police power; that there is a predominant public concern in the preservation of lands presently in cultivation as against lands potentially reclaimable; and that, under the circumstances presented by a critically overdrawn water supply, the court could not say that invocation of the police power in carrying out the provisions of the groundwater act involved a denial of due process.

The Orange County Water District in southern California — created in 1933 by special act of the legislature — was authorized by amendment in 1953 to levy, in any year in which an overdraft could be found to exist, in addition to any general assessment, a "replenishment assessment" against all persons who would produce groundwater in the ensuing water year.[76] Operation of a water-producing facility could be enjoined for failure to register it or for failure to pay a delinquent replenishment assessment. The replenishment charge was fixed at a uniform rate per acre-foot of water production. In the event of a basin-wide adjudication, this charge was limited to the excess above adjudicated rights. Its purpose was to raise funds to purchase water from the Metropolitan Water District in order to replenish the district's groundwater supplies. The constitutionality of the 1953 act was sustained under attack on numerous grounds. We need note only the following.[77] The act was passed to enable the district to meet a vital need which affected, directly or indirectly, all persons living therein, and it did not discriminate unlawfully between groundwater pumpers and users of canal water. The charge was held to be not a land tax but more in the nature of an excise tax levied upon the activity of producing groundwater by pumping operations.

While recognizing the somewhat newness of the situation with respect
to legal precedents, the court expressed its appreciation of the growing
importance of the problems faced by the district.

Protection of Individual Groundwater Rights

Protection is afforded by the courts to an individual's groundwater
right for the essential purposes of preventing interference with pumping
operations, safeguarding the water supply against impairment or destruction and preventing the ripening of prescriptive titles against the
paramount or prior right. Remedies lie in damages, injunctions or
both. [78]

The question of one's right of protection in his means of diversion
has given some difficulty. Courts have generally upheld the right of an
appropriator of surface water to a reasonable means of diversion, and
in several significant decisions they have applied the same line of reasoning to appropriative groundwater diversions. [79] But does this hold
true under appropriative groundwater statutes that have no express
provisions on the subject? Justice Wade of the Utah Supreme Court
stated — although it was not necessary to the decision — that it is the
Utah legislative policy that later appropriators under the statute shall
stand all the expense that their appropriations cause to prior appropriators. [80] Several other justices, while concurring in the result, disagreed with his reasoning on this point. The groundwater statutes of
Kansas, Nevada and Wyoming contain provisions that the appropriator's
water right does "not" include the right to have the water level maintained at the point at which he first encounters it. [81]

No appellate court decisions between overlying owners only have
come to the author's attention in which the right to maintenance of the
water level was squarely involved. It is the author's belief that under
none of the groundwater doctrines based on landownership — absolute
ownership, reasonable use or correlative rights as developed in California — does the landowner have a sound basis for claiming damages from
other owners whose pumping for use on their overlying lands causes the
water level in his own land to recede. [82]

SOME COMMUNITY AND PUBLIC WELFARE PROBLEMS

Although problems in the early phase of development in a groundwater area have largely concerned individuals, later they inevitably involve community or even statewide interest. With threatened dangers
to groundwater reservoirs, the resources of the individual are not adequate to meet these formidable problems or even to appraise them accurately. The fact must be faced that with the advent of great increases
in development, it has become increasingly necessary to utilize the resources of group organizations and public agencies.

Safe Yield and Overdraft

The so-called "safe yield" of a groundwater reservoir is the quantity of water that can be extracted annually from the reservoir without significantly impairing the continued usefulness of the water supply. But difficult complications ensue in proceeding from that broad generalization to a specific determination of safe yield for a given reservoir. This is because such determination may depend upon many assumed criteria — hydrologic, quality of water,[83] character of means of diversion and their location, uses of the water, land subsidence[84] and other physical and economic factors. "Overdraft" is the quantity of water pumped in excess of the safe yield.

In view of changing physical and economic conditions, a determination of safe yield and of resulting overdraft, if any, must depend on conditions that exist or that are forecast at a specific time, and so, to be valid, the determinations necessarily are subject to change.[85] It is the province of the legislature in enacting a control statute to direct that such determinations be made and that in the process certain factors, among others, be taken into consideration. It is the province of administrators and courts to make the authorized determinations. But experience indicates the wisdom of providing for revisions whenever necessary, particularly as concepts change concerning the economic or physical limits of the safe yield. Safe yield or overdraft determined on the basis of data available at one time may require substantial revision in the light of subsequent data and analysis.

Overdraft is not bad *per se*. Great values have been built up in some areas in which individual pumping has been unrestricted; some such communities can now afford to pay for imported water supplies with which to sustain the economy thus attained. And in planned utilization of groundwater reservoirs, referred to in a following section, overdrafts will be a part of the program. But protracted overdraft conditions in many areas have had adverse effects. These include continued depletion of the reservoir, with increasing pumping costs and threatened destruction of the water supply, contamination of the water, salt water intrusion and land subsidence.[86]

Groundwater Mining

The "mining" of groundwater results when withdrawals considerably exceed replenishment, or when, as in various western areas, replenishment is negligible. Pumping may continue at current or even greater rates for many years, but obviously not permanently.[87]

Inasmuch as the groundwater resource is not inexhaustible, the time comes when the unrestricted mining economy must give way to something else. In one such area in New Mexico the theoretical life of the groundwater supply for reasonable use of prior appropriators was computed as 60 years, but because of the impossibility of dewatering the reservoir completely, this indicates a practical life of about 40 years.[88]

With reference to Antelope Valley, California, where long-term over-draft at an increasing rate is a feature of the groundwater economy, Snyder discusses various action programs for combatting it which, he says, have led to only slight gains.[89] In California, where the doctrine of correlative rights is so firm, legislative controls must take account of the landowner's well-established rights of property in the water that occurs in his land.

Planned Utilization of Groundwater Resources

The planned utilization of groundwater resources for the purpose of achieving full conservation of available water supplies at reasonable cost[90] is a wide departure from the laissez-faire philosophy of the early common-law doctrine of absolute ownership. It has become an integral part of master planning in California,[91] where the landowner's unused correlative right may be protected against loss by prescription and can-not be taken or impaired without due process of law and where the leg-islature has repeatedly recognized the serious impact of overdrawn groundwater supplies in parts of the state and the urgent need for cor-rection.[92] The California Water Plan contemplates not only full devel-opment of groundwater resources but also conjunctive operation of sur-face and underground storage under integrated management.[93]

Planned utilization is predicated on the availability of substitute water supplies that may be imported for correcting deficiencies, for replenishing depleted reservoirs and for terminal underground storage. Difficult legal problems may be forecast. The California state report[94] points out that among prerequisites to executing such a program are comprehensive studies, widespread adjudications of groundwater rights and authority to set up procedures for planning utilization of groundwa-ter basins and to adjust conflicts with existing rights, within the scope of due process, by payment of compensation either in cash or in kind.

Group and Public Agencies

Assuming that extensive collective action for protecting in court, controlling and supplementing private developments of groundwater is inevitable, what forms of organization are suitable?

Some matters can be handled by mutual companies in which the wa-ter users hold shares of the capital stock. Others require exercise of the power of eminent domain, the power to tax and availability of large financial markets. Certainly the planned utilization of groundwater res-ervoirs will necessitate (1) public district organizations or water au-thorities with broad powers, or (2) participation of governmental agen-cies — state or federal or both or (3) concerted action by governmental agencies and public group organizations.

Experience with groundwater management by public districts is not lacking. In California, water replenishment activities have been carried out since the 1930's.[95] The Orange County Water District, California —

mentioned in the section "Constitutional Problems" — was organized to protect the water rights of the area and to import water in order to replace local overdrawn supplies.[96] The district has purchased Colorado River water imported by the Metropolitan Water District, and it levies "replenishment" or "extraction" taxes on pumpers to pay the cost of replenishing the groundwater supplies.[97] In Texas, where the courts have recognized the common-law rule of absolute ownership of percolating water, "underground water conservation districts" may be formed for groundwater management purposes with the consent of the property tax-paying residents (see section starting on page 298). Districts have been formed and are operating under this act.[98] On the whole, although the public district's experience in the fields of groundwater and integrated surface and groundwater management has been limited in comparison with what will eventually be required, enough has been gained to indicate that it can play a useful role.

INDIVIDUAL RIGHTS AND THE PUBLIC INTEREST

Public concern in the conservation of groundwater is exemplified not only by the remarkable interest and activity in obtaining legislation in most western states since the 1930's, but by observations of courts that have passed on the legality of statutes, discussed in the preceding section "Constitutional Problems." Thus we have the frank statement of the Kansas court that it must now look to the interest of the whole people, not merely that of the individual; the Arizona court's holding that a significant public interest takes precedence over the property interest of an individual; and the recognition by the California court that the public welfare may be so profoundly affected by a falling water table as to justify taxing the water pumper to pay for its replenishment.

Protection of private property rights is unquestionably a matter of public concern; constitutional guarantees are invoked in securing the individual's right. For example, the California landowner has a property right in the use of the water in his land whether or not he exercises the right; his *unused* right stands as high as his *used* right, and if its loss is threatened, it may be protected by a declaratory judgment and decree.[99] Since 1902 the courts of California in repeated decisions have built and solidified this philosophy of the relation between landownership and the use of underlying percolating water. Landowners, water users, tax assessors and the public generally have long considered it established and have acted upon it. These correlative rights may be taken by condemnation or acquired by voluntary agreement, and doubtless they are subject to regulation under the police power; but under the California law, that is as far as the public may go. However, in other western jurisdictions in which landownership doctrines have had judicial sanction, the foundation of a rule of property is not nearly so strong. There, the outlook for widespread public control over private uses of groundwater without having to acquire or extinguish the rights by recognized legal means is more favorable.

Many times legislatures and courts have stated, in effect, that the conservation and efficient utilization of both surface and subterranean water supplies is in the public interest. Owing to physical differences between surface and subterranean conditions, management problems differ. Continued heavy overdrafts and mining of groundwater resources have no counterpart in the use of surface-water supplies, even where the use of surface storage is so heavy as to allow no carry over. The public interest is affected more adversely by the former. Extensive groundwater developments and their inevitable association with surface-water resources have brought new problems to solve, justifying a new look at the relation between individual rights and the public welfare. Substantial private rights will be and should be protected. This is in the public interest. On the other hand, the perpetuation of unsubstantial, unused and ill-used rights in an overdrawn groundwater reservoir is not in the public interest. High court decisions, few though they are, have indicated a growing awareness of this.

FOOTNOTES

[1] 2 Wiel, Water Rights in the Western States Secs. 1039-1175 (3rd ed. 1911); 2 Kinney, A Treatise on the Law of Irrigation and Water Rights, Secs. 1148-1211 (2nd ed. 1912); Hutchins, Selected Problems in the Law of Water Rights in the West 146-265 (1942) (hereafter cited as Selected Problems); National Resources Planning Board, Subcommittee on State Water Law, State Water Law in the Development of the West, 69-85, 118-27 (1943).

[2] Thompson and Fiedler, "Some problems relating to legal control of use of ground waters," 30 *Jour. Amer. Water Works Assn.* 1049-91, particularly 1055-61 (1938); Thomas, The Conservation of Ground Water 247-50, 1951.

[3] See Idaho Code Ann. Secs. 42-226 to 42-239 (Suppl. 1953); Kans. Gen. Stat. Ann. Secs. 82a-701 to 82a-722 (1949); Nev. Rev. Stat. Secs. 534.010 to 534.190 (1957); Ore. Laws 1955, c. 708; N.D. Rev. Code Sec. 61-0101 (1943), as amended, Laws 1955, c. 345; and Laws 1957, c. 372; S.D. Laws 1955, c. 431; Utah Code Ann. Sec. 73-1-1 (1953); Wyo. Comp. Stat. Ann. Secs. 71-420 (Suppl. 1949).

[4] See N.M. Stat. Ann. Secs. 75-11-1 to -12 (1953); Wash. Rev. Code Secs. 90.44.010 to 90.44.240 (1951).

[5] See 2 Wiel, *op. cit. supra* note 1, Sec. 1077; 2 Kinney, *op. cit.* footnote 1, Sec. 1157; Hutchins, Selected Problems, *op. cit. supra* note 1, at 151-52; National Resources Planning Board, *op. cit. supra* note 1, at 70-71, 76, 118-27.

[6] See Hutchins, "Trends in the statutory law of ground water in the western states," 34 *Tex. Law Rev.*, 157, 158 (1955).

[7] *Id.* at 159-60.

[8] *Id.* at 160.

[9] *Id.* at 160-65.

[10] See the Hawaiian Supreme Court's criticism of the styling of an absolute ownership rule as the common law rule in City Mill Co. v. Honolulu Sewer & Water Commission, 30 Hawaii 912, 938-43 (1929).

[11] For a study of California doctrines relating to groundwater rights see Hutchins, The California Law of Water Rights, State Print. Off., Sacramento, 418-514, 1956.

[12] For a more detailed statement of groundwater enactments in the western states to 1955, inclusive, see Hutchins, *supra* note 6, at 166-72.

[13] In Redwater Land & Canal Co. v. Reed, 26 S.D. 466, 474, 128 N.W. 702, 707 (1910), the South Dakota Supreme Court stated that this statute, which then was Sec. 278 of the Revised Civil Code of South Dakota — and which had been taken from Sec. 255 of the Civil Code of the Territory of Dakota — was the same as Sec. 256 of the New York Civil Code as proposed by the Code Commissioners of that state. "There is no suggestion in the report of the commissioners of an intention to change the common law respecting riparian rights.

Therefore section 278 of our Civil Code should be regarded as merely declaratory of the common law as understood by the commissioners when their report was prepared."

[14] The major 1957 enactments were: Colo. Laws 1957, c. 289, Colo. Rev. Stat. Ann. Secs. 147-19-1 to -18 (1953); Kans. Laws 1957, c. 539; Wyo. Laws 1957, c. 169.

[15] Pasadena v. Alhambra, 33 Calif. 2d 908, 925-27, 207 P. 2d 17 (1949); Burr v. Maclay Rancho Water Co., 154 Calif. 428, 434-37, 98 Pac. 260 (1908).

[16] Calif. Water Code Sec. 1200 (West 1956).

[17] Hutchins, Selected Problems, *op. cit. supra* note 1, at 255-59.

[18] *Id.* at 234-36.

[19] For more detail see Hutchins, "Trends in the statutory law of ground water in the western states," 34. *Tex. Law Rev.* 157, 172-79 (1955).

[20] Wash. Rev. Code Sec. 90.44.010 (1951); Ore. Laws 1955, c. 708.

[21] Wyo. Laws 1957, v. 169, Sec. 27.

[22] Utah Code Ann. Sec. 73-1-1 (1953), Riordan v. Westwood, 115 Utah 215, 229-31, 203 P. 2d 922 (1949).

[23] Ore. Laws 1955, c. 708, 27 (3) (b); Utah Code Ann. Sec. 73-5-1 (1953); Wyo. Laws 1957, c. 169, Sec. 17 (2) (3). Compare Idaho Code Ann. Sec. 42-237a (Suppl. 1953). For some additional controls, see Ore. Laws 1955, c. 708, Sec. 27; Wyo. Laws 1957, c. 169, Sec. 17.

[24] Ariz. Laws 1948, 6th Spec. Sess., c. 5; Ariz. Rev. Stat. Ann. Secs. 45-301 to -324 (1956).

[25] Southwest Engineering Co. v. Ernst, 79 Ariz. 403, 291 P. 2d 764 (1955).

[26] Tex. Rev. Civ. Stat., Art. 7880-3c (Suppl. 1950).

[27] The courts of Texas recognize the rule of absolute ownership of percolating water: Corpus Christi v. Pleasanton, 154 Tex. 289, 292-94, 276 S. W. 2d 798 (1955); Houston & Texas Cent. Ry. v. East, 98 Tex. 146, 149-50, 81 S. W. 279 (1904); Cantwell v. Zinser, 208 S. W. 2d 577, 579 (Tex. Civ. Appl. 1948).

[28] Colo. Laws 1957, c. 289, Colo. Rev. Stat. Ann. Secs. 147-19-1 to -18 (1953).

[29] These statutes are in Calif. Water Code Secs. 1005.1, 1005.2 (1951); Secs. 2020, 2021 (1953); Secs. 4999 to 5008 (1955).

[30] Mont. Laws 1957, c. 58.

[31] Letter to the author from Fred E. Buck, State Engineer of Montana, dated September 24, 1957.

[32] The three acts are codified, respectively, in Neb. Rev. Stat. Secs. 46-601 to -607 (L. B. 109), 46-608 to -612 (L. B. 110), and 46-613 (L. B. 598) (Suppl. 1957).

[33] Davis and Farmer, "Surveys point up ground water problem," 7 *Colo. Farm and Home Res.* 6, 8-10 (1957).

[34] Colo. Laws 1957, c. 289, 15, Colo. Rev. Stat. Ann. Sec. 147-19-15 (1953), repealing Colo. Laws 1953, c. 246; Wyo. Laws 1957, c. 169, Sec. 28, repealing Wyo. Laws 1947, c. 107.

[35] Kans. Laws 1957, c. 539.

[36] An interesting parallel is found in Katz v. Walkinshaw, 141 Calif. 136, 70 Pac. 663 (1902), 74 Pac. 766 (1903), in which the objection was made that adoption of the correlative rights rule in place of that of absolute ownership would throw upon the court a duty impossible to perform — that of apportioning an insufficient supply of water among a large number of users. The California Supreme Court conceded the difficulty but concluded that was not a sufficient reason for abandoning the rule and leaving property without any legal protection. Nearly a half-century later this first case involving an apportionment among most of the large water users from a groundwater basin was decided by the California Supreme Court: Pasadena v. Alhambra, 33 Calif. 2d 908, 207 P. 2d 17 (1949). The difficulty was resolved by holding that uses initiated after the beginning of overdraft became prescriptive against prior uses but that the latter, in continuing to pump, either retained part of their original rights or acquired new rights to do so, and by reducing all uses proportionately to conform to the safe yield.

[37] Concerning statutory adjudication of water rights, "every forward-looking piece of legislation meets the old and time-honored objection — unconstitutional." Bray v. Superior Court, 92 Calif. App. 428, 441, 268 Pac. 374, 379 (1928). A hearing was denied by the California Supreme Court in 1928. And on the same subject: "If a statute radically different from anything to which we have been accustomed is enacted, the average lawyer becomes alarmed and at once brands it as unconstitutional." Vineyard Land & Stock Co. v. District Court, 42 Nev. 1, 26, 27, 171 Pac. 166, 173 (1918).

[38] The water conservation measure enacted in 1957 in Arkansas — Ark. Laws 1957, Act 81 — after many attempts at water legislation related to surface waters only.

[39] For an example, see the comprehensive Oregon "Ground Water Act of 1955": Ore. Laws 1955, c. 708.

[40]Note that the first New Mexico groundwater appropriation statute was held void as contravening a constitutional provision to the effect that no law should be revised or amended or the provisions extended by reference to title only, but that each revised, amended or extended section should be set out in full. Yeo v. Tweedy, 34 N.M. 611, 627-29, 286 Pac. 970 (1929).

[41]Thomas, The Conservation of Ground Water 250 (1951).

[42]Hutchins, "Summaries of the water-law doctrines of the seventeen western states," 3 Report of the President's Water Resources Policy Commission, Water Resources Law 734-38 (1950).

[43]Id. at 774-77.

[44]Id. at 711-15.

[45]Bristor v. Cheatham, 75 Ariz. 227, 235-38, 255 P. 2d 173 (1953).

[46]National Resources Planning Board, op. cit. supra note 1, at 119-20.

[47]Id. at 118-19; Hutchins, The California Law of Water Rights 507-19 (1956).

[48]Calif. Water Code, Secs. 2000, 2001, 2500 (West 1956).

[49]El Paso & R. I. Ry. v. District Court, 36 N.M. 94, 95, 8 P. 2d 1064 (1931).

[50]See, e.g., Utah Code Ann. Sec. 73-4-3 (1953); Wash. Rev. Code Sec. 90.44.220 (1951). In the general determination of water rights in the Esaclante Valley Drainage Area, Utah, the interlocutory decree dated July 12, 1957, includes both lands irrigated from surface streams and those irrigated from wells, limits water users to three acre-feet per acre, and retains jurisdiction of the question of duty of water for three years.

[51]See (e.g.) Ore. Laws 1955, c. 708, Secs. 15-21; Wyo. Laws 1957, c. 169, Sec. 15.

[52]Wyo. Laws 1957, c. 169, Secs. 15, 18.

[53]In a letter to the author dated October 22, 1957, E. J. DeRicco, Assistant State Engineer of Nevada, advises that to the knowledge of the state engineer's office there are no court decrees in Nevada that correlate surface and groundwater rights, and that their office policy on this matter requires any applicant to appropriate groundwater who drills a well near a surface water source to case the well without perforations to the first impervious stratum.

[54]Some of their observations are summarized by Hutchins, "Development of ground water laws," 26 Proc. Assn. Western State Engineers 123-30 (1953), and Hutchins, "Legal ground water problems in the West," 22 Proc. National Reclamation Assn. 81-91 (1953). See also Bliss, "Administration of the ground water law of New Mexico," 43 Jour. Amer. Water Works Assn. 435-40 (1951).

[55]Idaho. Code Ann. Secs. 42-237b to 42-237e (Suppl. 1953).

[56]Colo. Laws 1957, c. 289, Secs. 3, 4, Colo. Rev. Stat. Ann. Secs. 147-19-3, 4 (1953); Wyo. Laws 1957, c. 169, Secs. 3-6.

[57]N.M. Stat. Ann. Secs. 75-12-1 to -21 (1953).

[58]Nev. Rev. Stat. Secs. 534.030 (1957), as amended by Stat. 1957, c. 383.

[59]Ore. Laws 1955, c. 708, Sec. 31; Wyo. Laws 1957, c. 169, Sec. 17 (b).

[60]State ex rel. Bliss v. Dority, 55 N.M. 12, 15, 30-31, 225 P. 2d 1007 (1950), appeal dismissed, 341 U.S. 924 (1951).

[61]N.M. Stat. Ann. Secs. 75-11-19 to -22 (1953).

[62]N.M. Laws 1927, c. 182.

[63]Yeo v. Tweedy, 34 N.M. 611, 615-17, 619-21, 286 Pac. 970 (1929).

[64]With amendments and additions this is N.M. Stat. Ann. Secs. 75-11-1 to -12 and 75-11-19- to -22 (1953).

[65]State ex rel. Bliss v. Dority, 55 N.M. 12, 225 P. 2d 1007 (1950), appeal dismissed, 341 U.S. 924 (1951).

[66]Utah Laws 1935, c. 105, Utah Code Ann. Secs. 73-1-1 to -19 (1953). Jutesen v. Olsen, 86 Utah 158, 40 P. 2d 802 (1935); see Wrathall v. Johnson, 86 Utah 50, 40 P. 2d 755 (1935).

[67]For citations see Hutchins, "Summaries of the water-law doctrines of the seventeen western states," 3 Report of the President's Water Resources Policy Commission, Water Resources Law 768 (1950).

[68]See Riordan v. Westwood, 115 Utah 215, 219-29, 203 P. 2d 922 (1949); Hanson v. Salt Lake City, 115 Utah 404, 408-17, 205 P. 2d 255 (1949).

[69]Kans. Laws 1945, c. 390, Kans. Gen. Stat. Ann. Secs. 82a-701 to -722 (1949). Extensive amendments were made in 1957: Kans. Laws 1957, c. 539.

[70]State ex rel. Peterson v. State Bd. of Agriculture, 158 Kans. 603, 610-14, 149 P. 2d 604 (1944).

[71]State ex rel. Emery v. Knapp, 167 Kans. 546, 555, 207 P. 2d 440 (1949).

[72]Baumann v. Smrha, 145 F. Suppl. 617 (D. Kans. 1956), aff'd per curiam, 352 U.S. 863 (1956). See Note, 5 Kans. L. Rev. 470 (1957). See also Williams v. Wichita, Civ. Action No. W-756 (D. Kans. 1955), modified and aff'd mem., 230 F. 2d 959 (10th Cir. 1956).

[73] Ariz. Rev. Stat. Ann. Sec. 45-301 to -324 (1956).

[74] Southwest Engineering Co. v. Ernst, 79 Ariz. 403, 291 P. 2d 764 (1955).

[75] See Bristor v. Cheatham, 75 Ariz. 227, 235-38, 255 P. 2d 173 (1953). See also Hutchins, Selected Problems, *op. cit. supra* note 1, at 182-87.

[76] Cal. Stat. 1933, c. 924, as amended by Stat. 1953, c. 770. Replenishment assessments are provided for in amended Secs. 23 to 35.

[77] Orange County Water Dist. v. Farnsworth, 138 Cal. App. 518, 528-31, 292 P. 2d 927 (1956). A hearing was denied by the California Supreme Court in 1956.

[78] Protection of groundwater rights as worked out in many California cases — including burden of proof, remedies, reverse or inverse condemnation, physical solutions, declaratory decrees and reservation of continuing jurisdiction — is discussed in Hutchins, The California Law of Water Rights 476-94 (1956).

[79] Hutchins, Selected Problems, *op. cit. supra* note 1, at 168-79: Hutchins, "Protection in means of diversion of ground-water supplies," 29 *Calif. Law Rev.* 1 (1940).

[80] Hanson v. Salt Lake City, 115 Utah 404, 417-22, 205 P. 2d 255 (1949). Justice Wade disagreed with the present author's suggestion in Hutchins, Selected Problems, *op. cit. supra* note 1, at 176-79, that in order to obtain the greatest development of a groundwater resource, one who appropriates groundwater under the Utah law (or administrative law of another state) should be held to submit to some lowering of the water level caused by later appropriations so long as there remains an adequate water supply of equivalent quality at lower depths from which it is feasible for the prior appropriator to pump. He based his disagreement on the section of the Utah law granting the right of replacement to a junior appropriator whose appropriation diminishes the quantity or impairs the quality of appropriated groundwater, at the junior's sole expense. This, he stated, clearly indicated the legislative policy that later appropriators shall stand all the expense they cause to prior appropriators. However, this section relates to quantity and quality only. It says nothing about a situation in which there is no diminution in quantity or impairment of quality — only a lowering of the static water level. See Utah Code Ann. Sec. 73-3-23 (1953).

[81] Kans. Laws 1957, c. 539, Kans. Gen. Stat. Ann. Secs. 82a-711a (Supp. 1957); Nev. Rev. Stat. Sec. 534.110 (1957); Wyo. Laws 1957, c. 169, Sec. 10.

[82] See Hutchins, Selected Problems, *op. cit. supra* note 1, at 180-82.

[83] See papers by L. V. Wilcox, Erman A. Pearson, Lloyd L. Doneen and Gerald T. Orlob at the session on "Quality considerations in ground water utilization," *Proc. Conference on the California Ground Water Situation*, Berkeley, Calif. 121-56 (1956).

[84] See Poland, "Land subsidence and ground water development in California," *Proc., Conference on the California Ground Water Situation*, Berkeley, Calif., 106-19 (1956); Cal. State Dept. Water Resources, Bul. No. 3, "The California Water Plan" 35 (1957).

[85] See Thomas, The Conservation of Ground Water 261-64 (1951); Richter, "Overdraft conditions in California ground water reservoirs and effect," *Proc., Conference on the California Ground Water Situation*, Berkeley, Calif., 22-28 (1956).

[86] See Richter, *supra* note 84, and ensuing discussions at 22-48.

[87] Thomas, The Conservation of Ground Water 36-42, 93-95, 263 (1951).

[88] Letter to the author from John H. Bliss, State Engineer of New Mexico, dated August 3, 1953.

[89] Snyder, "Ground water in California," "The experience of Antelope Valley," 2 Univ. Calif. Giannini Foundation Ground Water Studies 129-56 (1955). See also Snyder, "Economics of ground-water mining," 36 *Jour. Farm Econ.*, 600-610 (1954).

[90] Banks, "Problems involved in the utilization of ground water basins as storage reservoirs," 26 *Proc., Assn. Western State Engineers*, 91-105, p. 92 (1953). Banks is Director of Water Resources, California State Department of Water Resources, which is charged with responsibility for investigations relating to the California Water Plan (see note 91 *infra*). See also Robert O. Thomas, "General aspects of planned ground water utilization," 81 *Proc., Amer. Soc. Civil Engineers*, 706 (1955): Harold E. Thomas, The Conservation of Ground Water, pp. 213-43, 258-76 (1951).

[91] Calif. State Dept. Water Resources Bul. 3, "The California Water Plan" (1957). See Calif. Water Code Secs. 10000 to 12875 (Div. 6, The State Water Plan, Authorities, and Boards).

[92] See the legislative declarations in Calif. Water Code Secs. 1005.1, note (1951), 2020, note (1953), 4999 (1955), and 60047 (1955).

[93] Calif. State Dept. Water Resources, *op. cit. supra* note 91, at 219-21. See Holsinger, "Some legal aspects of ground water and the California water plan," 47 *Jour. Amer. Water*

Works Assn. 374 (1955). Holsinger, formerly Principal Attorney of the State Division of Water Resources became the first chairman of the state water rights board and is now deceased.

[94] *Ibid.*

[95] Smith, "Problems in the use of the public district for ground-water management," 32 *Land Econ.* 259 (1956); Smith, "The role of the public district in the integrated management of ground and surface water," *Proc., Conference on Ground Water Economics and the Law,* Berkeley, Calif., 81 (1956). See Calif. Water Code Secs. 60000 to 60449 (Div. 18, Water Replenishment Districts, specified counties only). For authorizations in other California general district laws, see Calif. Stat. 1931, c. 1020, 2 (water conservation districts); Calif. Water Code Sec. 22078 (irrigation districts); Calif. Water Code Sec. 31047 (county water districts).

[96] See Cooper, "Imposition of pumping tax to finance replenishment of ground water supplies with imported water," *Minutes of Convention, Irrigation Districts Assn. of Calif.,* San Francisco 18 (March 1954).

[97] For an engineering report on the status of the district's ground water supplies and operations, see Bailey, "Engineer's report on ground water conditions in the Orange County water district," March 13, 1957.

[98] See Duggan, "Texas ground water law," *Proc., Water Law Conferences,* Austin, Tex., 11 (1952, 1954); Duggan, "Rights in ground water in Texas," *Proc., Water Law Conference,* Austin, Tex., 72 (1955).

[99] Peabody v. Vallejo, 2 Calif. 2d 351, 274-75, 40 P. 2d 486 (1935); Burr v. Maclay Rancho Water Co., 154 Calif. 428, 435-39, 98 Pac. 260 (1908); San Bernardino v. Riverside, 186 Calif. 7, 15, 16, 198 Pac. 784 (1921).

SHO SATO is Professor of Law at the University of California, Berkeley, where
he teaches a course on water resources law and has compiled cases and materials entitled Water Resources Allocation.

Chapter 18

SHO SATO

Water Resources: Comments Upon the Federal-State Relationship*

W HEN THE SUPREME COURT of the United States rendered its
decision in FPC v. Oregon,[1] popularly known as the Pelton Dam
Case, the hue and cry of states' rights was loudly voiced in a
new setting. That case signalled the start of much speculation and controversy and even raised doubts about the security of our water rights
which we had cherished as vested property.[2] To some people it has
created the spectre of unlimited control by the federal government over
water resources. To people in California who may be embarking upon a
1 3/4 billion-dollar venture it is especially important to know whether
any control or latent right inconsistent with the project can be asserted
by the federal government in the future. The Pelton Dam Case has
compelled us to turn our attention to the complex problems of federalism as applied to water resources, and demands are being made upon
Congress to resolve the difficulties by legislation.

It is the purpose of this chapter to review and to explore briefly two
delegated powers of Congress that have served as the principal basis of
its jurisdiction over water resources: (1) the power to regulate

---

*Following presentation to the Committee on the Economics of Water Resources Devel-
opment, Report No. 8, this chapter was published in the *Calif. Law Rev.*, Vol. 48, p. 43,
1960, and is reprinted with their permission.

interstate commerce[3] and (2) the authority to regulate and dispose of the property of the United States.[4] The exercise of the treaty, war and appropriation powers of the federal government has had a significant impact on the development of water resources, and although they present interesting problems, only the existence of such constitutional bases can be mentioned at this time.

The second objective is to discuss the various proposals[5] to resolve these problems.

THE COMMERCE CLAUSE

The Constitution provides that Congress shall have the power "... to regulate Commerce...among the several States ...."[6] These few words, abstract in meaning and elastic in application, have been the justification for economic and social legislation by Congress. Federal controls over labor practices,[7] farm production[8] and gambling,[9] to name a few, have received judicial blessings when such activities affect interstate commerce.

From a very early period it had been determined that the power to regulate commerce included control over navigation.[10] While it would be interesting to trace the modest beginnings of "navigation," as a springboard to congressional action, to the present scope of the commerce power over water resources, it is enough to indicate that the earlier exercises of this power dealt with the use and preservation of navigable waters for navigation purposes.[11] And the classic definition of navigable waters was that which was navigable in fact.[12] In 1899, however, in United States v. Rio Grande Dam & Irrigation Company,[13] federal jurisdiction over nonnavigable waters in order to protect navigability downstream was sustained. This was an extension of jurisdiction to nonnavigable portions, but the older concept of navigability was still in order and the preservation of that navigability was still the theme.

Another significant development occurred in 1940 when United States v. Appalachian Electric Power Company[14] indicated a marked change in attitude as to what constitutes a navigable stream. The court stated: "To appraise the evidence of navigability on the natural condition only of waterway is erroneous. Its availability for navigation must also be considered."[15] It then proceeded to hold that navigability may be determined by the improvements which can make the watercourse navigable in fact, even though no improvement might be contemplated by Congress.[16] It would appear from this that if any portion of a river system can be made navigable by reasonable improvements, federal jurisdiction attaches to that portion, and not only to that portion but also to upper stretches and tributaries, under the Rio Grande doctrine, even though they cannot be made navigable.[17]

Another point of importance in the Appalachian case is the court's conclusion that federal jurisdiction over navigable waters is not limited to control for purposes of navigation only. Rather, federal authority "is as broad as the needs of commerce."[18] Thus, licensing power projects requiring compliance with terms unrelated to preservation of the river for navigation was deemed valid.[19] Subsequently, a lower court has held that the Federal Power Commission may deny a license to construct a dam on a navigable river in order to preserve its recreational use.[20]

Logically the ultimate extension of these principles would result in the authority of Congress to regulate the use of waters in nonnavigable streams, although such control may be unrelated to navigation, so long as such nonnavigable streams flow into watercourses which can be made navigable by improvement. Whether this logical extreme will be reached remains to be seen.

Hitherto, the expanse of the power granted under the commerce clause has been discussed only in terms of congressional power to regulate navigation as such. There is, however, one very important corollary of this regulatory power over navigation which directly affects existing uses of water and needs to be particularly underlined to give full meaning to the problems discussed. This corollary may be introduced in the form of the issue it presents: whether the "plenary power of Congress" over navigable streams permits interference and even destruction of existing water uses with respect to watercourses within the scope of that power *without compensation.*

Navigation Servitude

Congress may provide for a system of national highways under the commerce power, but undoubtedly in establishing such a system, Congress must condemn and pay just conpensation in the absence of purchase or gift whenever private land is to be used for the project.[21] When Congress exerts its power over navigable streams, however, a significant contrast is to be noted. As an original proposition it might have been argued that even though Congress has regulatory power over navigable bodies of water, such authority must be exercised with due regard to and consistent with private usufructuary rights attaching to such water. Thus, while such private rights might be restricted in their enjoyment under proper police power regulation, there should be compensation where such rights are "taken" for positive public benefit. At an early date, however, a contrary approach was taken. The commerce power was deemed to include control over navigation; that control is complete, and the people and the state alike are subject to the Constitution which has granted such complete dominion to the federal government. Therefore, any private usufructuary rights are acquired subject to such control.[22] This dominant federal control has found a shorthand expression: it is the "navigation servitude" or "easement."

This is not to say that there is no confine on the breadth of this servitude, but the limitation is not presently subject to precise definition.

It has been held that a riparian owner is not entitled to compensation when his access to the navigable water is impeded by piers constructed in the river;[23] that a riparian owner may not be compensated

for the loss of water power in the navigable stream;[24] and that the destruction of an oyster bed when the channel of a navigable body was
deepened was a loss to be borne by the private party.[25] It is to be noted
that these cases are concerned with the use in or the right to the navigable water or bed thereunder. It would seem clear that, in the absence
of any statute, water diversion from a navigable stream for beneficial
uses by a riparian or an appropriator would suffer the same fate, that
is, the water use would be subject to the servitude, and thus interference would not be a compensable taking.

Greater difficulty is encountered when rights in nonnavigable
streams are affected or when the value of the fast lands are dependent
upon their proximity to navigable waters.

Initially the navigation servitude was restricted to interference operating upon and within the ordinary and natural condition of the stream.
Therefore, the mill owner was allowed compensation where a mill run
by water power on a nonnavigable tributary could no longer be operated
because the federal government had constructed a dam on the navigable
main stream which raised the level of the nonnavigable tributary.[26]
Subsequently, the servitude was said to exist up to the ordinary high-
water mark so that, despite a dam which altered the natural condition
of streamflow, no compensation was allowed for injury to the embankment of a navigable river up to the ordinary high-water mark.[27] Likewise, a claim for compensation for the loss of power head when the
level of the river was raised was rejected.[28] This test was later qualified so as to restrict the servitude upon the bed of the stream, the high-
water mark designating the bed for servitude purposes. Thus compensation was required for an injury to the land abutting a nonnavigable
tributary when the water plane was raised by a dam in the navigable
mainstream.[29] Finally, it has been held that compensation need not include the value of the condemned land attributable to its suitability for
a dam site.[30]

One may wonder whether the navigation servitude underlies water
withdrawals for beneficial uses from nonnavigable tributaries of a navigable mainstream. The conclusion that the servitude does extend so
far upstream can be rationally supported by the argument that the servitude is coextensive with the commerce power.[31] If this argument is
correct, a servitude would exist with respect to consumptive uses of
nonnavigable tributaries flowing into navigable bodies of water.

THE PROPERTY CLAUSE

The second major constitutional basis for congressional control
over water resources stems from Article IV, Section 3 of the Constitution which provides that Congress shall have power to dispose of and
make all needful rules and regulations respecting territory or other
property belonging to the United States. The exercise of this power is
easily defined when applied to parcels of real property. Nor is there

difficulty when the federal government seeks to dispose of surplus power generated at its plants. These situations invite the application of traditional concepts of ownership. When the realm of public domain with its streams, rivers and tidewaters is entered, a fog enshrouds the congressional dispositive power.

Availability of water was critical to economic development and progress in the vast territory acquired by the United States from France, Mexico and other nations.[32] So long as the public domain and the settlers remained under the sole political guidance of Congress, it mattered little whether the central government was vested only with regulatory powers as a sovereign or more broadly with ownership interests in the water resources of the public domain. It was a matter of indifference that Congress dictates the conditions under which the land and water may be used by individuals pursuant to one theoretical basis or the other — the control is effective in either case. As soon as additional political organs intruded, the symmetry was destroyed.

After the western states were admitted into the Union, did the sovereign control of water resources in the public domain pass to the states? Of course, even after admission the states cannot exercise dispositive power over lands remaining in the public domain unless Congress has acquiesced, because the Constitution expressly vests such control in Congress. But the question remains whether water resources fall within a like category — more specifically, whether any water rights are appurtenant to land within the public domain, and if they are, the nature of such water rights. That such a fundamental and important question can go unresolved can be understood only in the light of the fascinating history of the development of the West and the judicial and congressional response from time to time to the then existing conditions.[33]

Early History of the West

The early history of the West reveals an influx of miners dependent upon water for hydraulic mining, trespassing upon federal land with no rights of ownership and relying on mere possessory title to protect their interests against other intruders. With them came the custom which recognized priority in time as superiority in right.[34] Rather than evicting these squatters, Congress encouraged their presence in the development of the West and enacted three statutes which gave recognition to the alleged claims of the squatters. Section 9 of the Act of July 26, 1866,[35] recognized the custom of priority just mentioned, effecting promotion of the rights of the squatters to a greater dignity. Section 17 of the Act of July 9, 1870,[36] provided that patents should be subject to vested water rights. Finally the mandate of the Desert Land Act of 1877[37] was that the right to use water shall depend upon prior appropriation and that surplus waters of nonnavigable waters shall remain free for appropriation.

With the possible exception of the Act of 1866, there is no indication on the face of the statutes that Congress had intended to transfer to the states the responsibility of defining the acquisition of water rights. To the contrary, it would appear from the then current conditions that Congress, pursuant to its dispositive power, had adopted the appropriation system for public lands. At any rate, the states that adopted the appropriation system as part of their common law and believed in their own sovereign authority over water resources were unaffected by these statutes.[38]

But in California, which had embraced the riparian law, a curious development occurred. Implicit in the decisions of the California Supreme Court was the notion that lands within the public domain were vested with riparian rights so that a patentee succeeded to such rights as the federal government possessed in the land.[39] The outcome was a recognition of appropriative rights from public domain only when acquired after 1866 and before the patent of riparian lands to individuals.[40] On the other hand, Oregon decided that the Desert Land Act of 1877 resulted in the severance of water rights from the public land so that riparian rights did not inhere in a patent of riparian land.[41]

These theories are poles apart. When the United States Supreme Court was faced with the resolution of this conflict in California-Oregon Power Co. v. Beaver Portland Cement Co.[42] the court maintained a neutral position by concluding:

What we hold is that following the Act of 1877, if not before, all nonnavigable waters then a part of the public domain became publici juris, subject to the plenary control of the designated states, including those since created out of the territories named, with the right in each to determine for itself to what extent the rule of appropriation or the common-law rule in respect of riparian rights should obtain.

Although this case confirmed the existing state practices and thus maintained a status quo with respect to private water rights derived from ownership of what were previously public lands, there have been expressions in *dicta* that the lands in public domain, prior to being patented to private parties, were vested with water rights. In United States v. Rio Grande Dam & Irr. Co.[43] the court stated:

Although this power of changing the common-law rule as to streams within its dominion undoubtedly belongs to each State, yet two limitations must be recognized: First, that in the absence of specific authority from Congress a State cannot by its legislation destroy a right of the United States, as the owner of lands bordering on a stream, to the continued flow of its waters; so far at least as may be necessary for the beneficial uses of the Government property.

And in California-Oregon Power Co. v. Beaver Portland Cement Co.[44] are these remarks:

The Desert Land Act does not bind or purport to bind the states to any policy. It simply recognizes and gives sanction, insofar as the United States and its future grantees are concerned, to the State and local doctrine of appropriation, and seeks to remove what otherwise might be an impediment to its full and successful operation.

Pelton Dam Case

Such was the inconclusive situation of the law in 1955 when the case was decided which caused the battle flags of the western states to be unfurled and the call to arms for preservation of states' rights to be sounded. The case was FPC v. Oregon (349 U.S. 435, 1955), alluded to at the outset of this chapter. The issue in that case, simply stated, was whether the Federal Power Commission could license the construction of a power project on reserved lands of the United States, which would use water of a nonnavigable river flowing past without regard to the requirements imposed by the State of Oregon. (Reserved lands are those lands owned by the United States but withheld from private appropriation under the public land laws. In the principal case, the bed and one bank of the river were owned by the United States; the opposite bank was within an Indian reservation, consent having been given to the power project.)

The court found ample constitutional authority in Article IV, Section 3 of the Constitution (the property clause) for Congress to regulate the use of the reserved land and the river in question under the Federal Power Act.[45] Having cleared the constitutional hurdle, the court construed the Federal Power Act as prohibiting dual regulatory control. It was asserted on behalf of Oregon, however, that the Act of 1866, Act of 1870 and Desert Land Act of 1877 were "delegation or conveyance to the State of the power to regulate the use of nonnavigable waters." The response of the court was that those acts applied only to public lands subject to private appropriation and did not apply to reserved lands — lands withdrawn from disposition or sale.

Justice William O. Douglas dissented on the ground that the Federal Power Act relates to use of public lands and reservations and does not provide for water rights; consequently, use of water for the power projects must be obtained pursuant to state law.

Many evils have been conjured from this case. It has been suggested that implicit in the decision is the recognition of riparian rights in federal lands.[46] From this premise it is argued that appropriative rights on a stream system where reserved lands are located might be subject to the latent riparian rights of the reserved land.[47] And the extreme was bound to be fancied. So if the federal government should condemn any riparian land in a state exclusively following the appropriation doctrine, the assertion is made that riparian rights to surplus waters would suddenly come into being in the condemned land.[48] Another difficulty foreseen arising from the decision is the administrative problem of apportioning the water among the federal licensees and those claiming by virtue of state laws.[49]

Evaluation of Pelton Dam Case

Does the Pelton Dam Case open the floodgates to all these results? First of all let us analyze the actual holding of the case. This was a case in which two sovereigns, each subject to the respective constitutional limitations, were asserting conflicting authority to regulate the use of nonnavigable waters. It would be difficult to hold as a matter of constitutional law that Congress lacked the authority to license power projects on its land and the use of nonnavigable waters flowing past. This is especially so where the lands owned by the federal government were part of the original public domain.

The question then reduces itself to a construction of various congressional acts to determine whether Congress has in fact relinquished its conceded supremacy. The Supreme Court was not without reason for its conclusion in the Pelton Dam Case that the acts of 1866, 1870 and 1877 were addressed to individuals locating on public domain or receiving patents to public property. In short, there is nothing to indicate a complete abandonment of federal authority in favor of state control.

Although these acts do represent a congressional policy that the state system of water law should suffer as little dislocation as possible by imposing conformity with state laws upon individuals seeking the acquisition of public property,[50] Congress can change that policy in favor of one where, despite conflict with state law, certain activity relating to watercourses within its constitutional grant of control should be subject to a national policy. In essence this is what the Supreme Court has said Congress has done with respect to power projects on the reserved lands by the enactment of the Federal Power Act. So far as the fundamental question of state control is concerned, the breach in the congressional policy of conformity had already been declared in First Iowa Coop. v. FPC.[51] Does the decision really extend further than this? Are present appropriative rights subject to latent riparian rights of reserved lands? The Pelton Dam Case certainly does not so hold.

The case of Nevada v. United States[52] might be interpreted as so holding. In that case Nevada claimed that the United States must secure a state permit in order to withdraw underground percolating waters by wells dug on federal property. To assert freedom for the United States from any state supervision with respect to such use[53] the federal district court relied upon the property clause fortified by the decision in the Pelton Dam Case, and also upon the fact that national defense activity was involved. But here again the issue is one of regulation; there was no interference by the United States with any prior water users.

The cases, and in particular the Pelton Dam Case, the subject of this chapter, which have created the consternation in this complex relationship between the states and the federal government, are not too alarming when confined to precisely what was decided in each. The cases do, however, leave unanswered the very vital question of the kind of water right which may be secured in the future under state law in waters where there is an existing federal, or federally licensed, project. Thus in the Pelton Dam Case the question remains whether Oregon might issue permits to appropriate water which would interfere with the power project. And in Nevada v. United States one wonders what will happen when private appropriations are made from the same basin under the state law and the naval installation faces expanded need in the future.

These and further forebodings stemming from these cases and contentions now being asserted on behalf of the executive branch of the United States, such as alleged federal ownership of unappropriated waters in nonnavigable waters,[54] or claim of riparian rights upon purchase or condemnation of riparian lands,[55] prove to be discomforting.

THE DEMAND FOR NEW LEGISLATION

This then is the history behind the clamor for new legislation by Congress. In response to this fervent demand, several bills have been under consideration. But before a discussion of these bills is launched, the picture must be completed by alluding to the instances in which Congress has expressly directed the officers and agencies of the federal government to comply with state water law.[56] Most notable, of course, is Section 8 of the Reclamation Act of 1902.[57] And under Section 1 of the Flood Control Act of 1944[58] Congress has expressly given preference to beneficial uses existing on navigable waters of the western states over navigation. Section 27 of the Federal Power Act provides that the act is not to affect the state law controlling the distribution of water for irrigation, municipal or other uses.[59] Moreover, licensees under the Federal Power Act have not been permitted to rely upon the navigation servitude to cause injury to existing rights without compensation.[60]

In the light of this background the next logical inquiry encompasses the action required in the present instance. In any consideration of the problems it is necessary to divorce the issue relating to the proper political organ to develop water resources and the issue regarding the desirability of giving security to water users.

The bills before Congress deal with problems discussed herein and may be classified into four groups, each with difficult constructional questions involved.

Within the first group is a bill[61] under which all western waters, navigable or not, would be freed for appropriation and would be subject to state control for all beneficial uses.[62] The federal government would be required to proceed in conformity with state laws in the appropriation and use of the water.[63] The provisions of the bill are so broad in their terms, at least with respect to unappropriated waters, that there would be, if enacted, little federal control over any western water resources.[64] The Federal Power Commission would no longer be able to license power projects without previous approval of the state with respect to the use of water. But the broad provisions might be construed as relating only to acquisition of water rights and not applicable to the operation of federal projects. Thus such provisions as the "160-acre limitation" found in the Reclamation Act of 1902[65] might be unaffected.

The bills [66] within the second group embody a comprehensive provision whereby recognition is afforded state control over water resources, including water on public lands of the United States.[67] These bills would require the federal government and its licensees to appropriate and use water in compliance with state laws.[68] An exception, however, to these requirements is provided "where water is available for acquisition upon proper application to a State for a right to water to be used for any purpose when certified as necessary to the conduct of an authorized federal program." [69] The effect of this exception is not clear.

The third group includes a bill [70] which appears self-contradictory. On the one hand it requires the federal government to act in accordance with the "same procedures as provided by the laws of the several states for the control, appropriation, use, and distribution of water by private persons," and on the other hand it refers to acquisition of water by the federal government "pursuant to federal law." [71] Perhaps the bill is to be harmonized by interpreting the first clause as requiring compliance with the state laws in the acquisition of unappropriated waters, but state law is not to be controlling when water rights are condemned. The unique feature of this bill in comparison to others is the provision waiving sovereign immunity from jurisdiction in state judicial and administrative agencies concerning the "acquisition, determination and exercise of rights to the use of water or the administration of such rights." [72]

The bills [73] in the fourth group appear to be less pervasive than the others. First, they provide that withdrawal or reservation of public lands shall not affect any right to use of water acquired pursuant to state law either before or after the establishment of such withdrawal or reservation.[74] These provisions undoubtedly are intended to quiet the fears that arose after the Pelton Dam Case about the possible existence of latent riparian rights appurtenant to lands from the date of reservation. The other bills contain a similar provision or would have the same effect by protecting rights acquired under state laws.

Second, the bills in the fourth group provide that the withdrawal or reservation of public land is not to affect state jurisdiction over water rights as conferred by the act admitting such state into the Union or such state's constitution.[75] This is ambiguous at best. If this is an implicit recognition of the doctrine that sovereign powers over water reside in the states, the United States may have no jurisdiction over non-navigable streams except as embraced by the commerce power and except as the United States might acquire ownership of water rights by condemnation.[76] Aside from the above vague provision, there is nothing in these bills which would require the federal government to comply with state laws in acquiring unappropriated water. Finally there is a provision which appears to give security to water rights acquired under state law, even from navigable streams. [77]

All the bills, except that in the third group, contain clauses safeguarding rights existing under interstate compacts and judicial decrees, rights of Indians and provisions of international treaties.

The Case for National Control

With respect to the basic policies it appears unwise to repose the development of water resources in the states exclusively. Congress has been delegated certain powers in order that it may legislate on behalf of all the states in the national interest. To deny the necessity of the federal government's exercising its judgment in the conduct of foreign affairs or in the preparation of national defense is to deny the existence of a Union. A denial of the necessity of a national policy might have a similar effect in this area. The broad powers of the United States might be the only effective method of dealing with river-basin developments that transcend state boundaries. Perhaps there may come a time when extensive federal powers to reallocate our water resources among states must be relied on — when sea-water conversion becomes economically feasible.

On the other hand, states are realizing that water allocation can no longer rest on a laissez-faire basis. California, for example, has contemplated a multi-billion dollar project pursuant to a preconceived water plan. [78] There will be need for a state master plan under which land-use patterns, communications, transportation and water use may be coordinated. But projections and plans, in turn, rest upon a dependable future water supply. [79]

To coordinate the conflicting demands upon a limited resource is not easy. It does seem, however, that the solution does not lie in an uncompromising grant to either the state or the federal government for the development of water resources. Each can serve a very needed and useful task within its respective jurisdiction. Maximum utilization of water resources is neither a static nor a local concept, and a constant re-examination of our policies is necessary. It should be recognized that the primary administration of water resources has been developed within the context of state laws, and therefore that the dislocation of state law, with its resultant disruption of the security of existing or future water rights, should be avoided wherever possible.

In order to accomplish this objective and to give recognition to congressional execution of a national policy or program, the federal government should be permitted to appropriate unappropriated waters when within its scope of constitutional power. But because of the impact upon state plans, such action should be taken only when Congress has authorized or expressly delegated such action after due consideration has been given to any established state water plan or other state interest. [80] Congress should, however, even when claiming unappropriated water, recognize the necessity of state interest in proper supervision and consequently should report the quantity claimed and the use therefor to the state administrator. [81] Where future projects are contemplated, Congress should be permitted to reserve in a clear and unambiguous manner the quantity of water required but to allow temporary uses under state control. [82] This would mean that navigation servitude or any latent riparian right of federal land should be subordinated to existing use.

The development of the economy based upon water resources can occur only when the users can be secure in the future availability of water. Thus the federal government should be required to compensate for injury caused to any existing private rights recognized, under state law in navigable or nonnavigable waters. Moreover, even when temporary uses for reserved waters are allowed, consideration should be given to some scheme of compensation that would not give any value to the water right as such but would reimburse the user for obsolescence of unamortized capital improvements constructed in dependence upon the temporary use.[83] This latter suggestion requires further refinement of course.

The proposals in this chapter are offered not as definitive solutions but as suggestions which may warrant further examination.

ADDENDUM

Since the writing of the original chapter several significant cases have been decided by the Supreme Court of the United States, and unabated activity continues in Congress to enact a statute defining the extent of federal subservience to state laws in water resources control. The purpose of this supplement is to discuss these developments.

RECENT SUPREME COURT DECISIONS

The "navigation servitude" was put to a severe test in United States v. Virginia Electric Power Co.[84] The United States, in order to build a dam and a reservoir in a navigable river system, condemned a flowage easement over certain lands riparian thereto.[85] The power company, a condemnee in the action, owned a flowage easement, previously purchased by its predecessor in interest, over most of the land involved.[86] The issue was whether there was any compensable value in the flowage easement of the power company. Both parties agreed that, under the authority of United States v. Twin City Power Co.,[87] the power company was not entitled to compensation for value derived from the availability of the land for water power purposes. But the government argued that the Twin City Power Co. case also denies any compensable interest in the power company because its flowage easement could be exercised only in conjunction with water power development; that is, with the use of the navigable waters subject to the navigation servitude.

The circuit court sustained the district court's ruling that the measure of damage sustained by the power company was the difference in the value of the land with and without the flowage rights acquired by the United States plus any severance damages.[88] Although recognizing that the flowage easement of the power company could be exercised only with the consent of the United States, the circuit court reasoned that no one could have used the land in question for power purposes without the acquisition of the flowage easement owned by the power company, and the fair market value of such an easement would in effect be the value of the fee because the fee for nonriparian uses such as agriculture or grazing was made valueless by the easement. The amount attributable to severance damages was upheld because the easement holder, by a prior agreement with the owner of the fee, had been relieved of any damage by the exercise of the easement to the remainder of the land owned by the fee owner and this release added value to the easement. In short, the circuit court sustained a measure of the value by the amount one would have to pay to acquire the flowage easement from the fee owner.

The Supreme Court also rejected the government's contention on the ground that the easement was destructive of the use of the land for agriculture, timbering and grazing and its marketability was roughly equivalent to the marketability of the subservient fee. The Supreme Court, however, held that it was an error to measure the value of the easement as if the fee were being taken; that such a measure would fix the maximum amount which can be awarded but would not necessarily measure the value of the easement itself since the probability of the exercise of the easement must be taken into consideration. [89]

The dissent[90] argued that there was no value to the flowage easement because the exercise of the easement was dependent upon the issuance of a federal license, and at the time the government took the easement there was no possibility of the power company's acquiring such license. The dissent also reasoned that the exercise of the easement by the power company was dependent upon the use of the river in which a navigation servitude existed.

In appraising this case we should remember that the Supreme Court, in United States v. Twin City Power Co., [91] had held that the owner of land riparian to a navigable stream was not entitled, upon condemnation of such land by the United States, to any recovery for the value arising from the suitability of the land for power development because power development was dependent upon the use of the navigable river in which a federal servitude existed. It would appear that, if the premise established in the Twin City Power Co. case, namely, that the value which is dependent upon use of the navigable river is noncompensable, is accepted, the position of the majority is untenable and the dissent has the better of the argument.

Although the United States was able to acquire the interest of the fee owner at a value of one dollar because of the agreement of the owner, the owner in the absence of the agreement should have been entitled to the value of the land considered for its nonriparian uses and depreciated by the probability of the exercise of the flowage easement by the power company.[92] To the extent that the value of the subservient fee has been depreciated by the existence of the flowage easement in the power company, the fee owner already has been compensated by the previous sale of such interest. The power company, however, is left uncompensated for its investment in the flowage easement if it is denied any recovery in the condemnation action.

But this result is no different from that in the Twin City Power Co. case in which an owner of a riparian land, who might have had to pay the value inherent in the land for use as a power site when the land was purchased from a private party,[93] would be left uncompensated for such value when the land is condemned by the United States. The dramatic feature of the result which should follow from a logical application of the Twin City Power Co. doctrine is that the total award for the divided interests is less than the award which would have been required had there been no flowage easement in the power company.

That the government may acquire an interest in the land at a lesser amount simply because of the accident by which the interests in the land condemned are divided is abrasive to one's sense of equity. But the fault lies not in the reasoning of the dissenting opinion but in the premise established by the court in the Twin City Power Co. case. The fact that the value of the land riparian to a navigable stream might be greater because of its suitability for power purposes should not make that element noncompensable based on navigation servitude. Although power development cannot be accomplished without the use of the navigable river, neither can the development occur without the use of the riparian fast land. The fact that a land suitable for industrial purposes requires the construction of an industrial plant before the land can be actually used for that purpose does not deprive the land of its value for that purpose. Moreover, a commercial property in close proximity to office buildings owned and operated by the United States might be more valuable because of its strategic location, but a condemnation of such property would require a compensation based on the market value considering its location value.[94] The Virginia Electric Power Co. case marks a retreat from the harsh, if not erroneous, principle of the Twin City Power Co. case.

The second case of significance is United States v. Grand River Dam Authority.[95] In that case the Grand River Dam Authority, an agency created by the State of Oklahoma to develop hydroelectric power, owned land riparian to a nonnavigable tributary which flowed into a navigable river. When the United States condemned the land to build its own project, the Authority demanded compensation for the loss of water power rights. This assertion was sustained by the Court of Claims.[96] It was the position of the government that "the navigational servitude of the United States extends also to nonnavigable waters, pre-empting state-created property rights in such waters, at least when asserted against the government."[97] The Supreme Court felt that it was unnecessary to decide the contention of the government. The Authority was refused compensation for the loss of water power rights because the federal project was deemed related to flood control and navigation and "when the United States appropriates the flow either of a navigable or a nonnavigable stream pursuant to its superior power under the Commerce Clause, it is exercising established prerogatives and is beholden to no one."[98] According to the court, there was no taking of property but merely a frustration of an enterprise.

The Authority argued that it had vested rights to the water, seeking to trace its title through Oklahoma under a statute.[99] But the statute in question was held to give Oklahoma mere regulatory powers and not title to the water rights involved. The Court then made the statement:

Yet the Federal Government was the initial proprietor in these western lands and any claim by a State or by others must derive from this federal title.... Congress has made various grants or conveyances or by statute recognized certain appropriations of lands or waters in the public domain made through machinery of the States.[100]

But the Authority could not base its rights under any grant or statute.

Although the court refused to answer the contention that the navigation servitude is coextensive with the power under the Commerce Clause, has the court in fact decided the question? Or is the opinion more narrowly construed to mean only that the United States had the right to regulate the construction of dams on nonnavigable tributaries of a navigable river and the United States is merely exercising such power under the Commerce Clause by disallowing the Authority to build a dam by constructing one itself? Is the decision a mere reiteration of United States v. Rio Grande Dam & Irrigation Co.,[101] in which the court upheld the power of the federal government to regulate the construction of dams on nonnavigable headwaters of a navigable river? Would the result have been different had a private party, who had a storage right for use of water for irrigation purposes under the state law, been frustrated in the accomplishment of that purpose? Would such a right recognized under the Act of 1866, Act of 1870 or the Desert Land Act be a compensable right?

In the most restricted reading of the opinion the court has advanced the problem of federal-state jurisdictional conflict no more than the Rio Grande Dam & Irrigation Co. case. If read a little more broadly, perhaps the court is saying that the state or its agency cannot have title to the water, that any attempt by it to use the water for beneficial purpose is an exercise of a regulatory power, as opposed to a proprietary power, and that when a conflict in regulation arises, the state must bow to the superior federal power under the Commerce Clause.[102] Whether the opinion stands for any broader proposition remains to be seen. At least this much appears to be clear: the court has said that the federal government had proprietary interests in the western lands and waters and has relinquished its interests only by grants or by statute. The United States, then, has proprietary interest in any waters in the original public domain to the extent rights have not already been conveyed or recognized, and Congress is free to repeal any statute that permits acquisition of rights in such waters under the state law in order to reserve the water for federal control or disposition.

THE DRIVE FOR CONGRESSIONAL ACTION

Ever since the Pelton Dam case,[103] which was the focus of the discussion in the original chapter, bills have been introduced in Congress seeking to make the United States comply with state laws in varying degrees and to protect existing private water rights secured under the state law from any latent riparian rights of the federal government. Although none of these bills has met any success, the Eighty-eighth Congress has proved no exception. Two bills related to this problem have been introduced in the Senate and referred to the Senate Committee on Interior and Insular Affairs.

The first, S.101,[104] commences with the declaration that the withdrawal or reservation of public lands shall not affect state-created water rights acquired before or after withdrawal or reservation. Moreover, the withdrawal or reservation is not to affect state jurisdiction over water rights as conferred by the act admitting the state into the Union or by the state constitution as accepted by the act of admission. These provisions have appeared in earlier bills and their significance has been discussed before.[105]

Compensation is required for the taking of water rights acquired before the enactment of a statute authorizing a federal project for storage, diversion or development. This provision would mean that rights even in navigable waters would be protected against the servitude but would put persons on notice after the authorizing act is enacted that water rights obtained thereafter would not be protected under the provisions of the bill under discussion.

When the federal project is for the beneficial and consumptive use of persons who would be subject to state laws relating to appropriation, use and distribution if they were undertaking the project, the United States must proceed in conformity with the state laws "insofar as they are not in conflict with the laws of the United States." It would appear that any water project for a military base or other strictly governmental purposes would be excused from conformity, but the water from projects such as reclamation projects would have to be distributed in compliance with state laws unless there is an express federal provision.[106] Similar conformity provisions appear with respect to federal loans or grants for the construction of a water project.

Finally, the bill contains the usual exceptions relating to interstate compacts and international treaties.

The second bill, S.1275,[107] contains the protection against withdrawal or reservation of public lands appearing in the first bill. A unique feature of the second bill is that which makes Section 1(b) of the Flood Control Act of 1944[108] applicable to all federal projects. In effect, the use of water for navigation is subordinated to consumptive or withdrawal uses in the western states. Finally, rights in navigable waters which cannot be taken without compensation under a state law, if a state were to condemn such rights, receive similar protection against federal taking. Again, exceptions are provided.

These bills are considerably more modest in that total federal sub-ordination is not the objective; the second bill does little more than protect the prior state-created water rights and does nothing to settle the question of federal or state development of water resources.

Perhaps the more promising approach to the problem left unre-solved in S. 1275 is that embodied in S. 1111[109] and its counterpart, H.R. 3620,[110] which seek to establish river basin commissions with federal and state representation to coordinate federal, state, interstate and local water development plans and to recommend a schedule of pri-orities for the planning and construction of projects. The plans are to be reviewed by a council composed of the Secretaries of the Interior, Agriculture, Army and Health, Education and Welfare. The plans are then submitted to the President for his review and transmittal to Con-gress.

A cooperative arrangement among interested political entities in formulating plans for river basin development is preferable to any scheme whereby the federal government is inflexibly required to com-ply with state laws. Each river basin will have its own unique prob-lems; each river basin plan must be formulated based upon factors rel-evant to that basin. Under the proposed scheme a forum is provided for the conflicting interests and the final determination to exercise the pervasive federal power rests with Congress in those instances where authorization is necessary.[111] An improvement in this approach would be to require licensing agencies, such as the Federal Power Commis-sion, to act generally in accordance with any approved coordinated plan.

FOOTNOTES

[1] 349 U.S. 435 (1955).

[2] Corker, "Water rights and federalism — The Western Water Rights Settlement Bill of 1957," *Calif. Law Rev.*, Vol. 45, p. 604, 1957; J. Munro, "The Pelton Decision: a new ripar-ianism?", *Ore. Law Rev.*, Vol. 36, p. 221, 1957; Address, "State v. federal control of water" by Prof. Frank J. Trelease, Conference of Western Law Schools, Seattle, Wash. For a gen-eral discussion of these problems, see King, "Federal-state relations in the control of water resources," *Univ. Detroit Law Jour.*, Vol. 37, p. 1, 1959.

[3] U.S. Const. Art. I, Sec. 8.

[4] U.S. Const. Art. IV, Sec. 3.

[5] See notes 61, 66, 70 and 73, *infra*.

[6] U.S. Const. Art. I, Sec. 8.

[7] E.g., NLRB v. Jones & Laughlin Steel Corp., 301 U.S. 1 (1937).

[8] E.g., Wickard v. Filburn, 317 U.S. 111 (1942).

[9] E.g., Lottery Case (Champion v. Ames), 188 U.S. 321 (1903).

[10] Gibbons v. Ogden, 22 U.S. (9 Wheat.) 1 (1824).

[11] See Starr, "Navigable waters of the United States — state and national control," *Harvard Law Rev.*, Vol. 35, pp. 154, 169-73, 1921; Comment, *Michigan Law Rev.*, Vol. 39, pp. 976, 977, 1941.

[12] The Montello, 87 U.S. (20 Wall.) 430 (1874); The Daniel Ball, 77 U.S. (10 Wall.) 557 (1870). In reviewing the test which has been applied, the court in Economy Light & Power Co. v. United States, 256 U.S. 113, 121-22 (1921) states: "The test (is) whether the river, in its natural state, is used, or capable of being used as a highway for commerce, over which trade and travel is or may be conducted in the customary modes of trade and travel on water. Navigability, in the sense of the law, is not destroyed because the water-course is

interrupted by occasional natural obstructions or portages; nor need the navigation be open at all seasons of the year, or at all stages of the water."

[13] 174 U.S. 690 (1899). For a later case see Oklahoma v. Guy F. Atkinson Co., 313 U.S. 508 (1941).

[14] 311 U.S. 377 (1940).

[15] *Id.* at 407.

[16] *Id.* at 407-408. In Montana Power Co. v. FPC, 185 F. 2d 491 (D.C. Cir. 1950) it was held that Congress does not lose jurisdiction over streams that were once navigable even though later artificial obstructions make them nonnavigable.

[17] Georgia Power Co. v. FPC, 152 F. 2d 908 (5th Cir. 1946) seems to sustain jurisdiction of the FPC on nonnavigable portions of a stream where downstream can be made navigable by reasonable improvement.

[18] United States v. Appalachian Elec. Power Co., 311 U.S. 377, 426 (1940).

[19] *Id.* at 426-27. The Supreme Court, however, has not completely broken away from navigation as the basis for jurisdiction over a nonnavigable tributary. See Oklahoma v. Guy F. Atkinson Co., 313 U.S. 508, 522-25 (1941).

[20] Namekagon Hydro Co. v. FPC, 216 F. 2d 509 (7th Cir. 1954).

[21] Cf. Phelps v. United States, 274 U.S. 341 (1927).

[22] United States v. Chandler-Dunbar Co., 229 U.S. 53 (1913). Scranton v. Wheeler, 179 U.S. 141 (1900).

[23] Scranton v. Wheeler, note 22 *supra.* See also United States v. Commodore Park, Inc., 324 U.S. 386 (1945).

[24] United States v. Chandler-Dunbar Co., 229 U.S. 53 (1913).

[25] Lewis Blue Point Oyster Co. v. Briggs, 229 U.S. 82 (1913).

[26] United States v. Cress, 243 U.S. 316 (1917).

[27] United States v. Chicago, M., St. P. & P.R.R., 312 U.S. 592 (1941).

[2F] United States v. Willow River Power Co., 324 U.S. 499 (1945).

[29] United States v. Kansas City Life Ins. Co., 339 U.S. 799 (1950).

[30] United States v. Twin City Power Co., 350 U.S. 222 (1956). *But* cf. United States v. River Rouge Improvement Co., 269 U.S. 411 (1926) (in computing severance damages in eminent domain, benefit accruing to riparian owner, despite navigation servitude, held not to be negligible).

[31] The contention that the navigation servitude does not extend to nonnavigable portions was advanced in United States v. Gerlach Livestock Co., 339 U.S. 725, 736-39 (1950), but the court thus sidestepped the issue by declaring the project to be controlled by the Reclamation Act of 1902, Sec. 7 of which, 32 Stat. 389, 43 U.S.C., Sec. 421 (1958), requires compensation for "taking" of private rights.

The court in United States v. Kansas City Life Ins. Co., 339 U.S. 799, 806 (1950), was careful in referring to the servitude as being limited to the "bed of the navigable river." There is also found the statement: "It is not the broad constitutional power to regulate commerce, but rather the servitude derived from that power and narrower in scope, that frees the Government from liability in these cases." *Id.* at 808. See also Grand River Dam Authority v. United States, 175 F. Suppl. 153 (Ct. Cl. 1959) *cert. granted,* 80 Sup. Ct. 292 (1960) (No. 503). (United States, acting under the commerce power, was required to compensate a state agency for the latter's water rights in a nonnavigable stream flowing into a navigable river.)

[32] U.S. President's Water Resources Policy Commission Rept., Vol. 3, *Water Resources Law,* 33 (1950).

[33] See Bannister, "The question of federal disposition of state waters in the priority states," *Harvard Law Rev.,* Vol. 28, p. 270, 1915.

[34] Broder v. Water Co., 101 U.S. 274(1879); Jennison v. Kirk, 98 U.S. 453 (1878); Cave v. Tyler, 133 Cal. 566, 65 Pac. 1089 (1901); Irwin v. Phillips, 5 Cal. 140 (1855).

[35] Rev. Stat., Sec. 2339 (1875), 30 U.S.C., Sec. 51 (1958).

[36] Rev. Stat., Sec. 2340 (1875), 43 U.S.C., Sec. 661 (1958).

[37] Sec. 1, 19 Stat. 377, as amended, 43 U.S.C., Sec. 321 (1958).

[38] Coffin v. Left Hand Ditch Co., 6 Colo. 443 (1882).

[39] E.g., Lux v. Haggin, 69 Cal. 255, 4 Pac. 919 (1884), 10 Pac. 674 (1886).

[40] E.g., Cave v. Tyler, 133 Cal. 566, 65 Pac. 1089 (1901); San Joaquin & Kings River Canal & Irr. Co. v. Worswick, 187 Cal. 674, 203 Pac. 999 (1922); Cory v. Smith, 206 Cal. 508, 274 Pac. 969 (1929).

[41] Hough v. Porter, 51 Ore. 318, 388, 399, 95 Pac. 732 (1908), 98 Pac. 1083, 1095 (1909).

[42] 295 U.S. 142, 163-64 (1935).

[43] 174 U.S. 690, 703 (1899).

[44] 295 U.S. 142, 164 (1935).

[45] Federal Power Act secs. 4(e), 23(b), as amended, 49 Stat. 840, 846 (1935), 16 U.S.C. secs. 797(e), 817 (1958). The constitutional issue in FPC v. Oregon is discussed in 349 U.S. at 441-46.

[46] Corker, "Water rights and federalism — The Western Water Rights Settlement Bill of 1957," *Calif. Law Rev.*, Vol. 45, p. 604, 1957; Address, "State v. federal control of water," Trelease, Conference of Western Law Schools, Seattle, Wash., Apr. 3, 1959.

[47] Corker, *supra* note 46, p. 609. But see Munro, "The Pelton Decision: A New Riparianism?," *Ore. Law Rev.*, Vol. 36, p. 221, 1957, who argues that water has been dedicated to the public, and the federal government can secure water rights only as a proprietor under state law.

[48] Corker, *supra* note 46, at 612.

[49] Munro, *supra* note 47, at 250-51.

[50] See California-Oregon Power Co. v. Beaver Portland Cement Co., 295 U.S. 142, 164-65 (1935), wherein the court states: "The Desert Land Act does not bind or purport to bind the states to any policy. It simply recognizes and gives sanction, in so far as the United States and its future grantees are concerned, to the State and local doctrine of appropriation, and seeks to remove what otherwise might be an impediment to its full and successful operation. ... The public interest in such State control in the arid-land states is definite and substantial."

[51] 328 U.S. 152 (1946) (where licensee under the Federal Power Act was permitted to divert nearly all the water of Cedar River, which was navigable, to the Mississippi River although prohibited by Iowa law).

[52] 165 F. Suppl. 600 (D. Nev. 1958).

[53] But see United States v. Fallbrook Pub. Util. Dist., 165 F. Suppl. 806 (S.D. Cal. 1958).

[54] See Nebraska v. Wyoming, 325 U.S. 589, 611 (1945).

[55] See note 48 *supra*.

[56] See Corker, *supra* note 46 n. 27, for a list of federal acts which have given recognition to state water laws.

[57] 32 Stat. 390, 43 U.S.C., Secs. 372, 383 (1958).

[58] 58 Stat. 887, 33 U.S.C. Sec. 701-1 (1958).

[59] 41 Stat. 1077 (1920) 16 U.S.C., Sec. 821 (1958). See First Iowa Coop. v. FPC, 328 U.S. 152 (1946), on the effect of this section.

[60] Henry Ford & Sons, Inc. v. Little Falls Fibre Co., 280 U.S. 369 (1930); and FPC v. Niagara Mohawk Power Corp. 347 U.S. 239 (1954).

[61] H. R. 2363, 86th Cong., 1st Sess. (1959). An identical earlier bill was S. 863, 85th Cong., 1st Sess. (1957). See Hearings on S. 863 Before the Subcommittee on Irrigation and Reclamation of the Senate Committee on Interior and Insular Affairs, 84th Cong., 2d Sess. (1956); See also Hearings on H. R. 4567, H. R. 4604, H. R. 4607, H. R. 6140, H. R. 5555, H. R. 5587, H. R. 5618, H. R. 5718, H. R. 5748, H. R. 1234, H. R. 2363, Before the Subcommittee on Irrigation and Reclamation of the House Committee on Interior and Insular Affairs, 86th Cong., 1st Sess. (1959).

[62] H. R. 2363, *supra* note 61, Sec. 6.

[63] *Ibid.* Exceptions are provided for flood control and for storage and diversion in national parks and monuments.

[64] "Federal agencies and permittees, licensees, and employees of the Government, in the use of water for any purpose in connection with federal programs, projects, activities, licenses, or permits, shall acquire rights to the use thereof in conformity with State laws and procedures relating to the control, appropriation, use or distribution of such water: ...*Provided further*, That the United States may acquire such rights, when authorized under federal law, by purchase, exchange, gift, or eminent domain." *Ibid.* It is not clear whether rights acquired by purchase or condemnation would be subject in their use to state law.

[65] 32 Stat. 389, 43, U.S.C., Sec. 431 (1958); 44 Stat. 649, as amended, 70 Stat. 524, 43 U.S.C., Sec. 423e (1958); see Ivanhoe Irrigation District v. McCracken, 357 U.S. 275 (1958).

[66] The following bills are identical: S. 1416, H. R. 5748, H. R. 5718, H. R. 5618, H. R. 5587, H. R. 5555, 86th Cong., 1st Sess. (1959).

[67] E.g., H. R. 5555, *supra* note 66, Sec. 1.

[68] E.g., H. R. 5555, *supra* note 66, Sec. 2.

[69] E.g., H. R. 5555, *supra* note 66, Sec. 2.

[70] H. R. 1234, 86th Cong., 1st Sess. (1959).

[71] H. R. 1234, *supra* note 70, Sec. 1.

[72] H. R. 1234, *supra* note 70, Secs. 2, 3.

[73] These bills are identical: S. 851, H. R. 6140, H. R. 4607, H. R. 4604, H. R. 4567, 86th Cong., 1st Sess. (1959).

[74] E.g., H. R. 4567, *supra* note 73, Sec. 1.

[75] E.g., *ibid.*

[76] Trelease; *supra* note 46.

[77] E.g., H. R. 4567, *supra* note 73, Sec. 2 (3).

[78] See Calif. Stat. 1959, ch. 1762 (Calif. Water Code, Sec. 12930).

[79] See statement of Harvey O. Banks, then California State Engineer, in Hearings on S. 863 Before the Subcommittee on Irrigation and Reclamation of the Senate Committee on Interior and Insular Affairs, 84th Cong., 2d Sess. 218 (1956).

[80] See the Flood Control Act of 1944, Sec. 1, 58 Stat. 887, 33 U.S.C., Sec. 701-1 (1958), which provides for notice to and consultation with state officials in the planning of navigation and flood control projects in the western states.

[81] In this connection consideration should be given to a more liberal joinder of the United States in water rights adjudication or litigation. See the "McCarran Amendment," 66 Stat. 560 (1952), 43 U.S.C., Sec. 666 (1958).

[82] Cf. Calif. Water Code Secs. 1460-64.

[83] *Ibid.*

[84] 365 U.S. 624 (1961).

[85] Although the Supreme Court states that the United States was condemning a flowage easement, 365 U.S. at 625, the lower court opinion indicates that the subservient fee was being condemned as well. United States v. 2979.72 Acres, 270 F. 2d 707, 709 (4th Cir., 1959).

[86] The owner of the subservient fee had agreed to transfer his interest for one dollar under an agreement with the United States. The agreement is irrelevant to the discussion here.

[87] 350 U.S. 222 (1956). See text accompanying footnote 30 for a discussion of this case.

[88] United States v. 2979.72 Acres; *supra* note 85.

[89] The court stated that "the value of the easement is the nonriparian value of the servient land discounted by the improbability of the easement's exercise." 365 U.S., p. 635. What the court means by this ambiguous statement is that the value of the flowage easement of the power company is the difference between fee value of nonriparian use of land and the fee value depreciated by the probability of the exercise of the easement. If the probability of the exercise of the easement is extremely remote, the value of the servient fee might be affected very little. The probability of the exercise is to be determined by a consideration of such factors as the difficulty of assemblage of necessary land, the market for power, the advantage of steam over hydroelectric plants, etc. 365 U.S., p. 634.

[90] Three justices dissented.

[91] *Supra* note 87.

[92] See *supra* note 89.

[93] See dissenting opinion in United States v. Twin City Power Co., 350 U.S. 222, 237 (1956).

[94] "If a distinct tract is condemned, in whole or in part, other lands in the neighborhood may increase in market value due to the proximity of the public improvement erected on the land taken. Should the Government, at a later date, determine to take these other lands, it must pay their market value as enhanced by this factor of proximity." United States v. Miller, 317 U.S. 369, 376 (1943).

[95] 363 U.S. 229 (1960).

[96] Grand River Dam Authority v. United States, 175 F. Suppl. 153 (Ct. Cl. 1959). The majority of the Court of Claims reasoned that the State of Oklahoma owns the waters of a nonnavigable stream, that the Authority acquired an appropriative right from the state, that the navigation servitude does not extend to nonnavigable tributaries although flowing into navigable rivers and that, therefore, compensation for taking of property was required.

[97] 363 U.S., p. 232.

[98] 363 U.S., p. 233.

[99] 363 U.S., p. 233.

[100] 363 U.S. at 235.

[101] 174 U.S. 690 (1899).

[102] This was the reasoning of the dissenting opinion in Grand River Dam Authority v. United States, 175 F. Suppl. 153 (Ct. Cl. 1959).

[103] FPC v. Oregon, 349 U.S. 435 (1955).

[104] S. 101, 88th Cong., 1st. Sess. (1963).

[105] See text accompanying notes 74 and 75.

[106] Ivanhoe Irrigation District v. McCracken, 357 U.S. 275 (1958), held that Section 8 of the Reclamation Act of 1902, 32 Stat. 390, 43 U.S.C., Sec. 383 (1958), required the United States to comply with state laws when it becomes necessary for it to acquire water rights or vested interests therein. But in City of Fresno v. State of California, 372 U.S. 627 (1963), in rejecting the applicability of the state areas-of-origin preferences, the court held that Section 8 merely refers to the state law to define the property interests for which compensation must be made and does not mean that state law can prevent the United States from acquiring water rights by condemnation. Whether the provisions of S. 101 would be similarly construed remains to be seen.

[107] S. 1275, 88th Cong., 1st Sess. (1963).

[108] 58 Stat. 889; 33 U.S.C. 701-1 (1958).

[109] S. 1111, 88th Cong., 1st Sess. (1963).

[110] H. R. 3620, 88th Cong., 1st Sess. (1963).

[111] See 109 Cong. Rec. 6104 (daily ed., Apr. 11, 1963, reprint of a speech by Banks).

PART V

Organization

STEPHEN C. SMITH is Professor of Economics at Colorado State University. He has been on the staff of Civil Functions, Office of the Secretary of the Army; the University of California, Berkeley; and the Tennessee Valley Authority. His research and writing in natural resource economics have dealt mainly with questions of organization.

Chapter 19

STEPHEN C. SMITH

The Role of the Public District in the Integrated Management of Ground and Surface Water*

T HE PUBLIC DISTRICT is one of several public agencies which may play a role in the integrated management of ground and surface water. How widely the district will be used for this purpose is not yet certain as the western states are in the process of adopting and adjusting their procedures for dealing with this problem. Some state legislatures have granted rather broad powers to state executive branches of the government and have made them responsible for operating a system of groundwater appropriations and for initiating use of a variety of techniques to accomplish basin-wide management. In other states the courts have played a more dominant role in defining limits within which water management may proceed without violating a system of private water rights vested in the overlying owners. The public district may act as an agency for integrating management of ground and surface water in both instances, but it has been more highly developed for this purpose in the nonappropriation states.

The role which the district performs could be examined from many

*Prepared while the author was on the staff of the University of California, Berkeley. Presented to the Committee on the Economics of Water Resources Development, 1956, Report No. 5. The comments of S. V. Ciriacy-Wantrup, Wells A. Hutchins and J. H. Snyder. are appreciated.

points of view. For purposes of this discussion I shall view it as a
public agency which is used in organizing integrated management of
ground and surface water. It is through this process of organization
that integration takes place. Through the district, holders of property
rights to groundwater and other parties interested in the management
of the local waters may organize to take collective action to overcome
uncertainties inadequately protected against in water law. The district
provides an organizational structure for representing these interests.
Integration is achieved through representation of these interests internally within the district. But internal representation is frequently not
enough. These interests must in turn be integrated with external interests. And the district may have the legal, political and economic responsibility to perform this function. For example, water importation
may be required for recharge purposes in order to overcome uncertainties associated with a particular basin.

ECONOMIC VALUE OF WATER RIGHTS, INTEGRATED MANAGEMENT AND THE PUBLIC DISTRICT

An important contribution of a water-right system is that it defines
the legal privileges of water use in terms of a property right and pre-
scribes legal remedies for infringement of these privileges. These legal definitions not only have significant economic import, but their
meaning is shaped, in part, by the demands of economic existence.[1]
Thus the principle of mutual prescription was enunciated in an economic
situation which had encouraged groundwater draft and permitted utilization of an imported surface-water source. On the other hand, the public
district has been called into use to give economic meaning to existent
rights. As an agency for integrated management it counteracts such
factors as an increasing depth to water, salt-water intrusion, compaction and excessively high water tables. In this way forces tending to
destroy the economic value of water rights are combated.

California's correlative rights doctrine grants a coequal right to
overlying landowners to use groundwater. The effect of this system
has been the rapid but uncoordinated development of a large number of
California's groundwater reservoirs.[2] This development has had the
economic value of contributing to the build-up of the economy which
utilizes this water[3] and of permitting each user to economically relate
his use of groundwater to other available sources of water with minimum legal restriction.

As a result of this use, a wide variety of problems have ensued
which cannot be solved in terms of legal privileges and remedies. For
example, in northern Santa Clara Valley[4] the depth to water increased
109 feet from 1915-16 to 1933-34;[5] from 1933-34 to 1942-43 the water
table rose 85 feet; from 1942-43 to 1950-51 the depth to water increased
110 feet; and from 1950-51 to 1954-55 the water table rose 21 feet.[6]
This rise continued until 1959[7] with a decline following in 1960 and

1961.[8] The State Department of Water Resources classified this as a
reservoir with overdraft.[9] Santa Clara Valley groundwater users were
troubled with the physical uncertainty due to cyclic fluctuations in recharge and from the effects of secular overdraft.

A portion of this uncertainty comes from the cyclic nature of the
rainfall which supplies water for groundwater recharge. During the
dry portion of the cycle the depth to water increases with added water
costs and with no knowledge of how much nor for how long the water
table will decline. In such a situation the correlative rights doctrine
spreads the uncertainty equally among all reservoir users. The responsibility is not placed with a state agency for limiting draft.

From the point of view of the local area, overdraft may not be cyclic in nature. Secular overdraft is prevalent in many parts of the
West with overdraft continuing throughout all phases of the cycle.[10]
The groundwater stock is being mined. In this situation the correlative
rights doctrine with the court-reference procedure has been applied to
define individual water rights and to restrict the draft permitted under
the right. These rights are determined upon a historical base, and restriction of draft is defined as a percentage of the approved base. The
court may vary the volume of the draft by changing the percentage,
thereby integrating draft with importations.[11] But provision is not made
for a more complete integration of management.

The correlative rights system does not furnish protection against
the physical uncertainties of water supply, nor does this system place
responsibility upon a state agency. However, this economically important element of security may be sought through actions of a local public
district. Through such action of integrating the management of surface
and groundwater, the physical uncertainty of overdraft may be allevi-
ated by such means as water importations and artificial recharge.

The public district's role is somewhat similar under the Texas application of the English rule. This rule does not provide the coequal
status of the correlative rights doctrine.[12] Each holder of a right can
extract as much water as he needs without the restraints usually given
to the terms "reasonable" and "beneficial" use. To overcome some of
the problems involved in this type of procedure, the Texas legislature
passed an enabling act to permit districts to recharge, to control waste,
to regulate spacing of wells, to limit the amount of water which can be
produced from a well and to carry on educational and planning functions.[13] Again the district contributes the organizational framework
through which the interests in the groundwater basin can function.

For example, one policy adopted by the High Plains Underground
Water Conservation District No. 1 establishes minimum distances for
spacing of wells.[14] In other words, well owners gain security from the
adverse effects of pump drawn down from neighboring wells, and thus
the value of their water right is protected. Security of this sort was
not provided under the English rule, but such protection may be given
by the district in performing its role as an agency for collective action.
This is accomplished through the power of the district as a body politic

to carry out the provision of the state constitution regarding "preservation and conservation of all such natural resources of the State since they are each and all hereby declared public rights and duties." Therefore, through the local approval of district ordinances the district is granted a public welfare right to control use of a private-property right. In this way certain techniques of groundwater management may be executed.

States with the appropriative system of groundwater law rely upon local organizations to a varying degree. Colorado and Oregon are examples of states which authorize the use of local organizations. However, these powers of administration and control are generally vested in some office such as the state engineer. In these states the main attempt has been to rely upon administration of property rights to give adequate groundwater management through regulation of draft. Rights may be granted up to the administratively determined "full" appropriation of the groundwater reservoir. If a reduction in draft is called for, reduction would proceed in reverse order from that of appropriation. Accordingly, the impact of cyclic fluctuations would fall upon the junior appropriators and would affect their security of investment. As their groundwater problems become more acute with increased reservoir development, it may become necessary to adopt other management techniques such as artificial recharge, disposal and reuse of return flows and other such measures.[15] These activities could be executed by a state agency in conjunction with administration of the appropriative system.

On the other hand, the district form of organization could also be used within the same framework. Hutchins indicates that the trend in the West is apparently toward statutory authorization of local associations and districts in both appropriative and nonappropriative states.[16] Whichever form of organization might be chosen, it is evident that the appropriative system may provide some techniques for an integrated management program. But supplementary action may be required, and this may be provided through a state or a local organization.

This review of groundwater law reveals that states generally have procedures which establish private-property rights to use groundwater or at least legislative or judicial recognition that such rights exist. As these rights are used and developed, problems frequently emerge which require a program of integrated management of ground and surface water. The systems of groundwater law may not supply the organizational framework for taking the collective action necessary for program execution, although they may be particularly important in controlling draft. The responsibility of the district is to make an organizational framework available.

Integration Through Internal Interest Representation

A second aspect of the role of the public district is to provide for integrated management of ground and surface water through creation of an organization which will represent the interests internal to the management plan. These internal interests are associated with various parts of the plan; however, they are not necessarily in agreement with each other. In fact, conflicts of interest generally exist, and a principal duty of the public district is to furnish an internal organizational structure for reaching a common interest among the conflicting interests.

One of the important features of this structure is the electoral procedure which may determine whether a statutorily favorable common interest [17] exists among the internal interests of the groundwater reservoir. In this fashion the physical as well as the economic necessity of having control over the whole basin may be achieved without requiring unanimity of interest. The entire area benefited may be included, even though some opposition exists. Generally this area is considered to be all of the overlying land irrespective of groundwater use.[18] In addition, individuals with a primary economic interest in reservoir management, but not the holders of a water right, may find a means for representation in district affairs. This may be accomplished by designating who may possess the voting privilege. Property requirements and voting in proportion to assessed property valuation are not uncommon.

On the other hand, if groundwater is widely used throughout the district, permitting all registered voters to participate in district elections seems reasonable.

A step toward integrated management is achieved if all relevant interests have an opportunity to be heard. Of course, for this to be effective the issues must be presented to the voters so that a decision can be reached concerning problems of interrelating groundwater and surface water rather than considering them as separable, independent resources. In this way the district can play an important role in determining voter preferences in questions of integrated management. The neutral, competitive and complementary aspects of management need internal representation for the district to operate in this fashion. For example, a water-conservation reservoir may be used for recreational purposes; or these same detention dams may hold some floodwater; or floodwaters may be diverted to settling ponds and then to infiltration ponds for recharge purposes. The district may ask the interests associated with water conservation, flood control and recreation to take part in policy formation as internal participants.

The problem which is involved may be illustrated from the experience in Santa Clara County. In this case internal representation has not existed for all interests. Each of these interests has been represented by its own organization. The oldest governmentally organized interest is associated with water conservation for purposes of artificial recharge;[19] the second oldest is the flood-control and storm-water drainage interest,[20] while the youngest is the recreational interest.[21] Each of these interests is represented by a public agency; and each organization carries on or has potential to carry on activities which are of little concern to the other organizations.

One of the major issues in recreational policy is whether

conservation reservoirs should be developed for recreational purposes due to extreme fluctuations of the reservoir level.[22] Of course a recreational program could be developed upon the basis of the commonly accepted standards of operation if uncertainties of fluctuations were properly evaluated in estimating the recreational potential. Integration could take place in this fashion.

On the other hand, public agencies could bargain among each other and arrive at a solution which might require adjustment of the reservoir operating policy. In terms of economic analysis this would require operating studies of each proposal. These studies could be used in the bargaining process in order to assist in achieving agreement. However, since neither party has the other interest internally represented, it is quite conceivable that initial bargaining positions would be poles apart even if each had made his individual studies, and there might be no pressure to accept the values of the other party unless there has been a considerable build-up of third-party interest. This third-party pressure could come from special-interest groups or from public sentiment expressed in other ways. Existence of such pressure is frequently associated with major decisions but would be relatively inactive in the "minor" decisions. On a cumulative basis these small decisions often prove to be of major importance.

A third possibility would be for the recreational interests to be represented within the water conservation district.[23] This might be done in at least two ways. One alternative would be for the district to operate the recreational facilities and to develop the reservoirs. This line of action has been rejected in favor of signing development contracts upon a demand basis. Each proposal was considered as an individual item of business, and little over-all policy existed except for maintenance of public access points. The result of this course of action has been what might be termed an erratic development with the district never accepting this as an essential element of its responsibility. However, the district board always has maintained that the public should be allowed to use the facilities.

Internal representation could be supplied by the recreational commission or the planning commission. In other words, the internal operating and developmental plans could be reviewed by recreational specialists on these staffs. Integration of this type might be particularly important for achievement of efficient use of small staffs and budgets. But such an inter-agency approach certainly has greater opportunities for rift and has no built-in system of securing integration. Such a "built-in" would be available if both the recreational and the water agency reported to the same board. Pressure from such a board could be usefully applied to bring integration.

Another major interest in the integrated management of ground and surface water in northern Santa Clara Valley is exemplified in use of conservation dams for downstream flood protection.[24] To briefly summarize the complexities of this situation, there are again two public agencies — the Santa Clara Valley Water Conservation District and the

Santa Clara County Flood Control and Water Conservation District. The activities of these two districts are complementary in such operations as capturing floodwater in the forepart of the rainy season and at other times when reservoir levels are lowered. The general policy is to drop these levels as soon as percolation conditions are favorable.

This element of complementarity was graphically demonstrated during the historic flood of December 1955. Between December 21 and December 25 Lexington Dam held back 13,400 acre-feet of water, and Coyote Dam and Anderson Dam stored 30,250 acre-feet of water. Existence of this storage capacity made it possible to "avert a disaster of major proportions in the town of Los Gatos and in part of the city of San Jose."[25]

Competition exists, however, for reservoir use. Water with a high silt and debris content cannot be diverted into percolation ponds since clogging is a danger.[26] Consequently, storm water must be held in storage until conditions will permit its release. In addition, the rate of discharging water from reservoirs for percolation purposes would be slower than if the reservoirs were used solely for flood-control purposes. Conservation water may be held into the irrigation season to aid in combating seasonal overdraft or to be used for recreational purposes. Thus, less storage space is available to capture succeeding rainfall for flood protection.

The extent of mutual interest in diverting and utilizing water originating on the valley floor is still undecided. Reservoirs do not give full flood protection. Disposal of storm waters from rapidly growing areas of urban land use has created many major difficulties. And integration of floodwater disposal with protection from tidal action also has created a problem. Levees constructed to keep out the tide hold back flood flows and flood low-lying land. Can these waters be economically utilized for other purposes?

These interrelationships are among those which have given rise to problems of integrating the activities of the water conservation district and the flood control district. These difficulties appeared in the formation process of the flood control district, and they have continued to the present time. The problem was clear when both districts desired to ask voters for approval of new projects. The water conservation district included dams with claimed flood-control benefits which were not supported in the flood control district's proposal.[27] The water conservation district has been restudying these plans.

In another section of the county the water conservation district proposed construction of two detention dams. The flood control district stated that construction of these works would eliminate approximately $795,000 in channel construction. On the basis of its estimates the flood control district asked voters in the zone of benefit to approve a bond issue for $795,000. These funds would then be used to reimburse the water conservation district if its dams were constructed. In the event these dams were not constructed, the monies would be expended by the flood control district on the same streams.

Voters in this zone of benefit defeated the flood control district's proposal.[28] Now the possibility exists that construction of the same dams will be proposed to voters of the water conservation district. In this case sanction will rest with voters residing in almost all portions of the northern valley floor rather than in the confines of a zone of benefit defined by the watershed of a small stream. If such approval is forthcoming, the incidence of cost will be spread over the larger area with the area benefiting from flood control paying at the same rate as all artificial recharge interests. Of course the possibility exists that a special assessment could be placed upon the flood-control interests through organization of a subdivision within the water conservation district.

From this experience the fact that these two interests were represented by separate organizations has not resulted in integrated management of ground and surface water. It must be recognized, however, that one reason for restudying the water conservation district plan was because of lack of support for some of its stated flood-control benefits. In this situation external representation forced some integration. Also, a strong third-party pressure urged that integrated management be organized. This strong pressure came from west-side cities which would benefit both from water conservation in terms of their water supply and from flood control. It might be suggested that if these interests were represented internally within one organization, major elements of the conflict could have been settled through staff study and debate. Such integration would not eliminate conflicts nor the benefits from a strong third-party pressure in major decisions. But it could add continued management pressure for integration in all small decisions. In addition, integration would not present voters with the alternative of voting *no* in order to spread their costs more widely. Such a solution implies that control and responsibility would be attached with internal representation, making it possible to achieve integration within one agency.

Another aspect of internal representation within the public district is that through district procedures a reasonable relationship can be worked out between the provision of a service for benefit and charging for this benefit. This may not be an easy task, but by use of the district form of organization a wide variety of procedures is available if adequate enabling provisions are enacted. A tax upon land exclusive of improvements, a tax upon land and improvements, a charge for surface-water delivery and a charge upon water pumped into the owner's well have been in use in California.

This aspect of integrating the management of ground and surface water is important, and use of the public district as the agency for integration permits a wide range of action. In this connection use of zones of benefit needs further exploration. Such an analysis implies a study of possible pricing plans, but these can be studied better in the specific context of a particular integrated management plan. For our purposes it is sufficient to note that the public district is quite flexible on this point.

Integration Through External Interest Representation

A third feature of the role which the public district plays is to represent internal interests so they may be integrated with external interests. By being able to perform this function the district may relate itself to sources of water far beyond the bounds of local watersheds. Of course, this has evolved as a cornerstone to much western water development. The long-distance transport of water is no longer unusual. Consequently, an integrated management program may use surface water which originated several hundreds of miles away from the groundwater basin. The district represents perferences of internal interests in the bargain for acquisition of imported water and of managing the acquired water according to the agreed-upon plan. For example, the Orange County Water District purchases water for spreading, which is transported from the Colorado River, and taxes the draft from individual wells to pay the charges. The Los Angeles County Flood Control District purchases Colorado River water and stores it in groundwater reservoirs to give security from cyclic variations in rainfall, to combat salt-water intrusion and to give an element of security to the area's defense.

But plans for integrating the management of ground and surface water are on an even grander scale. In California the recurrent water plans have discussed the use of groundwater reservoirs for temporary storage in transporting water from north to south. These reservoirs are subject to the long-standing proprietary interests of overlying users, but the assertion of a broader state interest is being heard. This state interest is not in the water within the reservoir but in the storage capacity of the reservoir.

Many difficulties beset the execution of such a plan. Detailed physical information is lacking. Operation should not be attempted prior to the obtaining of this knowledge. But there are also many problems of interest to the social scientist. These reservoir areas are not starting with an "institutional" clean slate. Irrigation districts overlie the underground reservoirs, and these district boundaries are inconsistent with groundwater flow and with the necessities of management techniques. However, existing irrigation districts do not seem to be appropriate agencies for organizing this management activity. In addition, proprietary rights under the correlative rights doctrine are of long standing and are quite firm. It would not be unreasonable for holders of these rights to have an interest in basin management different from that of a regional operating agency. One possible source of difference might be in the proposed management variations in the depth to water. For example, in the southern San Joaquin Valley storage would take place in aquifers lying from 10 to 200 feet below the surface.[29] Intentional variability in depth to water within this range might well cause an operating agency to be confronted with legal demands for compensation. In addition, basin management might require rather stringent control of draft to insure maintenance of a desired storage volume. This in turn would affect requirements for delivering surface water. For large groundwater basins, complicating factors of the type previously mentioned would be numerous and complex, involving the reaching of an operating agreement among the many interests.

One method for reaching agreement might be for the state to operate these basins in the interests of region-wide planning. The ability to exercise eminent domain and the police power might be sufficient if proper legislation authorized such action. The interests in the groundwater basin could be met on an individual basis by the operating agency by condemnation and other means.

Another possibility might be for the interests internal to basin operation to organize a new district which would represent their internal interests with respect to broader interests. In fact, precedent for such action exists. We have already noted that districts do have experience in integrating the management of a local groundwater reservoir with imported water supplied by another agency. In addition, districts have been used to "protect" the interests of groundwater users. A stated purpose of the Kings County Water District was "to protect the underground supplies of the area from excessive pumping and to guard against transportation of underground water to areas outside the district."[30] Thus the integrated management would be dependent, in large part, upon the ability of the district to represent the external interests — such as the operating agency, the existing irrigation districts and others — to the internal interests.

Requirements for organizing the use of underground reservoirs in the interregional transport of water need more investigation. Many procedures of action need to be studied. These would involve the state's right of condemnation, a district's use of reverse condemnation, a system of exchange contracts or compensatory payment and a procedure of scheduling recharge and discharge. Problems of this type will require serious scrutiny.

CONCLUSIONS

The public district is an agency for collective action. The role of the district is to provide an organization for the integrated management of ground and surface water. The performance of this role has been encouraged in California and Texas where state statutory administration of water rights is lacking. And in some appropriative states use of the district or other local organization is authorized to integrate local interests with state interests, even though state statutory administration exists. The district may function under both legal systems to carry out programs such as combating physical uncertainties due to cyclic fluctuations, salt-water intrusion or compaction.

Many management practices may be executed by the district without affecting the legal status of water rights. On the other hand, the district as a governmental organization may perform certain acts which will restrict application of these property rights in the interests of general welfare.

The district may also integrate management of ground and surface water through internal representation of conflicting interests associated with the management plan. Conflicts that might exist between interests such as recreation, water conservation and flood control could be settled internally within the organization. In addition, the district can perform the internal financial role of relating repayment of a current investment in water-utilization facilities to economic benefits which accrue to the area over an extended period of time. This role has been a prominent feature in the use of the district as a water-management agency since the late 1800's. The district may use a variety of taxing and pricing schemes to forward this objective, thus making it an adaptable form of organization.

Finally, the district can represent internal interests within the district on a common basis to external interests in water management. As a result, private property rights in a local groundwater reservoir may be related to the broader interests involved in a regional water plan. Contractual relationships may be established for such purposes as regulation of recharge, discharge and compensation. In this instance the agency representing the broader interest would have a responsible local agency with which to deal. And this local agency would be related to the local economic base.

FOOTNOTES

[1] For a thorough discussion of this point as it relates to systems of water rights see S. V. Ciriacy-Wantrup, "Economic criteria for a system of water rights," *Land Econ.*, Vol. 32, p. 4, 295-312.

[2] The following statement indicates the number of basins in which overdraft conditions exist. However, it does not indicate the relative economic importance of these basins. "A condition of overdraft is not unique to any one area of the State of California. Any tendency on the part of local areas or groups to consider that overdevelopment of ground water with attendant overdraft and adverse effects is unique to its area should be dispelled by the knowledge that as of 1954 overdraft existed in at least 33 ground-water basins, approximately 15 percent of the 223 ground-water basins so far identified within the State." Raymond C. Richter, "Overdraft conditions in California ground-water reservoirs and effects," a paper presented to the Conference on the California Ground-Water Situation, University of California, Berkeley, California, State Department of Water Resources, Sacramento, December 3, 1956, p. 12 and Appendix p. 8.

[3] S. V. Ciriacy-Wantrup, "Some economic issues in water rights," *Jour. Farm Econ.*, Vol. 37, p. 5, 1955, p. 879.

[4] Northern Santa Clara Valley lies at the southern tip of San Francisco Bay.

[5] Unpublished data collected by Patricia Bartz for the Univ. of Calif. from the files of the Santa Clara Valley Water Conservation District, San Jose, Calif.

[6] The average depth to groundwater from 1933-55 was compiled by the staff of the Santa Clara Valley Water Conservation District. These figures are for the month of October.

[7] Stephen C. Smith, "The public district in integrating ground and surface water management: a case study in Santa Clara County." Univ. of Calif., Agr. Exp. Sta., Berkeley, Giannini Foundation Research Rept. No. 252, April, 1962, 135p.

[8] Santa Clara Valley Water Conservation District, "Report of activities and data," May, 1963 (San Jose, Calif.).

[9] Richter, *op. cit.*

[10] J. Herbert Snyder, with a foreword by Ciriacy-Wantrup, "Ground water in California: the experience of Antelope Valley," (Univ. of Calif., Div. of Agr. Sci., Agr. Exp. Sta., Berkeley, Feb., 1955) pp. 81-86. (Giannini Foundation Ground Water Studies No. 2.)

[11] J. H. Snyder, "Economic implications and appraisal of the court reference procedure for allocating ground water," Rept. No. 5, Committee on the Economics of Water Resources Development, Berkeley, Calif., Dec. 20-21, 1956, pp. 37-65.

[12] Wells A. Hutchins, "Trends in the statutory law of ground water in the western states," Tex. Law Rev., Dec. 1955, pp. 157-91.

[13] Arthur P. Duggan, "Texas ground water law," Proc., Water Law Conferences, Univ. of Tex., School of Law, Austin, Nov. 20-21, 1952, and June 10-11, 1954, pp. 11-29. Texas, Board of Water Engineers, "Rules, regulations, and modes of procedure," 1955 Revision, Austin, 1955, Act. 7880-3c., pp. 46-54.

[14] High Plains Underground Water Conservation District No. 1, Rules of High Plains Underground Water Conservation District No. 1, Lubbock, Tex.

[15] Oregon's appropriative groundwater law permits the state engineer to exercise a wider range of management techniques than many appropriative laws. Ore. Stat. (1955), Chap. 708.

[16] Hutchins, op. cit.

[17] This is not the place to discuss the interesting implications of a statutory common interest, although the problem is ever present in many attempts to define the public interest. Suffice it to say that a statutory common interest is achieved at election time if a predetermined precentage of the electorate approves a proposed action. This percentage is usually stated in the enabling legislation.

[18] For a case on this point, see Atchison, Topeka, and Santa Fe Railway Company v. Kings County Water District, Advance California Reports, San Francisco, Oct. 23, 1956, 47 A.C. No. 9, pp. 134-41, L.A. No. 24184.

[19] The Santa Clara Valley Water Conservation District was organized in 1929.

[20] The Santa Clara County Flood Control and Water Conservation District was organized in 1952.

[21] The Santa Clara County Parks and Recreation Commission was established in 1955.

[22] San Jose Mercury-Herald, June 16, 1956.

[23] Personnel of the water conservation district took an active interest in the recreational problems, and recreational interests were continually making representations before the district's board of directors. However, no recreational specialist was attached to the district's operations.

[24] The extent to which flood protection has been provided has been the subject of engineering review. However, the subsequent discussion indicates the extent they were used for this purpose, especially in December 1955.

[25] Calif. Dept. of Public Works, Division of Water Resources, Floods of December 1955, State Print. Off., Sacramento, Jan. 1956, pp. 3-11, A-4.

[26] The reservoirs act as settling basins; however, downstream flows may need clearing prior to percolation.

[27] Robert Roll, Report to the Honorable Board of Directors of the Santa Clara Valley Water Conservation District on 1956 Waste Water Salvage Projects, Santa Clara Valley Water Conservation District, San Jose, Mar. 8, 1956 .

Santa Clara County Flood Control and Water Conservation District, Engineer's Report on Proposed Improvement for Zone E-1, Zone NC-1 and Zone NW-1, San Jose, Calif., Aug. 1956.

[28] San Jose Mercury-Herald, Oct. 2, 1956.

[29] Calif. Dept. of Water Resources, Division of Resources Planning, The California Water Plan, State Print. Off., Sacramento, May 1957.

This range of depth is applicable for the south San Joaquin-Tulare Lake area. Use of other groundwater reservoirs is discussed in other portions of this three-volume report.

[30] Op. cit., footnote 18. See also Coachella Valley County Water District v. Stevens, 206 Cal 400 (274 P. 538).

STEPHEN C. SMITH is Professor of Economics at Colorado State University. He has been on the staff of Civil Functions, Office of the Secretary of the Army; the University of California, Berkeley; and the Tennessee Valley Authority. His research and writing in natural resource economics have dealt mainly with questions of organization.

Organizations and Water Rights In the Rural-Urban Transfer of Water*

T HE ECONOMICS OF WATER ALLOCATION has a fundamental concern with institutions whether they are legal or organizational. The rural-urban competition for water expresses itself *through* laws and organizations and *over* the acceptance or rejection of particular ways of doing things. This role of institutions *in* water economics will be developed in Section I.

"Institutional machinery" will be delineated in Section II. As a point of view this machinery is not considered as fixed. It is subject to change and has changed since California's earliest days. On the other hand, changes are generally not made capriciously or lightly. They evolve and grow as the result of a continual state of conflict which surrounds their creation.

The concept of a water right has an important economic content.

*This chapter is a combination of two earlier articles: "Legal and institutional controls in water allocation," *Jour. Farm Econ.*, Vol. 42, No. 5, pp. 1345-58, 1960, and "The rural-urban transfer of water in California," *Natural Resources Jour.*, Vol. 1, No. 1, pp. 64-75, 1961.

The comments of S. V. Ciriacy-Wantrup, Michael F. Brewer and Wells Hutchins on an earlier draft are appreciatively acknowledged. Also, discussions with J. C. Spencer, Leland Hill and Leslie C. Jopson of the California State Water Rights Board and Gleason Renound of the U.S. Bureau of Reclamation were helpful.

For 100 years western litigation has been struggling to define rights to water to be consonant with our economic precepts. This definition as it relates to economic change from rural to urban water use will be examined in Section III.

Economic values and interests are expressed through institutions other than the market. In the western United States, public agencies have performed a major task in organizing water resource development and management — with the private public utility and the mutual company having a foot on both sides. The way in which the economic competition of farm and city is expressed internally within the organization and externally between organizations will be the concern in Section IV.

Great diversity exists when one speaks about water rights and organizations. The diversity comes from, first, the variety in the physical and economic context in which water is used throughout the nation. Second, and in partial response to the first, the legal and organizational context differs from state to state and from region to region. Because of this diversity, overgeneralization can be very hazardous unless the details are thoroughly in mind. For these reasons my illustrative material will come from California. By staying within a particular frame of reference, comparison with other situations is facilitated.

I. ECONOMICS IN WATER POLICY

Why should a discussion of the economics of allocating water between rural and urban uses concern itself with laws and institutions? Why not leave these problems to the lawyer, the political scientist and the sociologist? Clearly, the content of each of these disciplines has an important contribution to make; yet this does not diminish the significance of law and institutions for economics. The economist must study and understand them because they form both a base for economic decisions as well as constitute the decision-making machinery itself.

The economics of water allocation directly involves questions of public policy or of public action rather than just questions of the market. In saying this, no sharp dichotomy is implied between centralized versus private decision making or between private property and the market versus administrative and judicial judgment. Such an argument is misleading when applied to the real world of affairs. Private and public decisions are highly interdependent. In fact the public character of many water decisions is recognized whether they are made by a private individual or an individual acting as an officer of a public organization.

Water rights have been particularly important in the allocation of water. They define property relationships which are basic to both private and public action. But by its very nature the definition of the types of property rights is a public matter. Also, creation of organizations to make public investments in water resources is public policy as well as the actions which the agencies take. Public policy is central to water resource economics, whether it relates to investment, water rights, organizations or to one of the many other aspects.

This fact raises a very interesting question with respect to a portion of economics which has proven useful in areas such as benefit-cost analysis: Is it appropriate to reason via the application of maximization techniques from given ends, objectives and goals as the whole criteria of policy analysis?[1] The use of the means-ends scheme in a puzzle-solving fashion for optimization is hardly adequate[2] when the essence of policy is the determination of ends, not having them given. Consequently the focus is upon deciding these ends. For this purpose an interest in institutions such as laws and organizations is fundamental. Of course, ends may not be decided explicitly in themselves; frequently the issues for decision are a means with the ends just forthcoming.

Before the decision, there is no one objective but a host of conflicting and competing objectives each put forward by a group or special interest. Public water policy results from this conflict — this lack of harmony. The policy is not given. It is determined by action. Nor are the laws and institutions specified restraints to attain a given objective. They are variables which may be controlled and in turn they exercise strong force to control. They are born, grow and die with evolution very much in evidence and mutations always a possibility.

The problem immediately arises: How does one study these laws and institutions? What is their relationship to economics? In attacking this problem the observer economist is concerned with the sequence of action through time,[3] giving attention to both the formal and informal organization. Such an inquiry carefully attempts to expose the values imbedded within the laws and institutions and to judge their policy impact. Conflicts of values in the situation can be appraised as well as the complementarities. By such examination, the direction[4] of institutional change may be assessed in terms of impending or possible policies.

Of course the contrast to another type of analysis which allegedly appraises institutions is apparent. An alternate approach suggests that comparison of an economic optimization analysis, A, with one set of institutional assumptions, to optimizing solution, B, with another set of institutional assumptions, tests whether the institutional structure of A is better or worse than B. Well-conceived analyses of this type have produced insight. But they do not ascertain how the institutions worked — particularly how they worked over time. To answer this question the economist must examine institutions directly and not judge them as irrelevant assumptions.[5]

In saying this it is assumed that the type of organization does influence outcome; it does influence the values which are represented in the decision-making process. If this were not the case, struggles over organization would be of little point. Using this context for viewing organizations means that the ability to execute or carry out commands is not the most fundamental with respect to policy formation, although it may play one of the instrumental roles. The use of cross-sectional analysis often results in the essential binding element which relates one action to another action remaining undetected. The quality of "institutional leadership"[6] or of "leading ideas"[7] which often is omitted by the sharp demarcation of ends and means in the analysis of public policy decision should be captured by the analysis. This involves a fundamental question of handling values.[8]

A host of conflicting and complementary values have to be considered in the allocation of water between rural and urban uses. These values are partially incorporated in the laws and institutions which are used to make decisions. The laws and institutions are objects of value; they are used to represent values in the policy-making process; and they stand for the values which result from the policy decision. In such a situation a maximization model used as the criterion for judging policy is inappropriate.[9]

The suggestion is to look at the process of legal and institutional functioning over time. What is the sequence of decision making? What economic interests are in fact expressed in the operations of these institutions? Is the effect over time one of inhibiting the transfer of water from rural to urban uses?

II. INSTITUTIONS OF WATER TRANSFER

Part of the "institutional machinery" pertinent to the transfer process is California's system of water rights, public districts, municipalities, state government and the federal government. A large literature exists which details many facets of each of these;[10] consequently, only selected points will be noted for purposes of clarity.

An initial item is that water rights are real property, and appropriative rights are transferable either with or without the land. The concept of a water right has an important economic content. For over 100 years western statutes and litigation have been struggling to define rights to water to be consonant with our economic precepts. California's appropriative rights to surface water are "diversionary" rights developed within our property system. The courts have "uniformly . . . (held) . . . that the appropriative water right is real property."[11] The water tenure system they prescribe is usufructuary in character. The body of the water in the stream is not subject to private ownership, but "is the property of the people of the State."[12] After diversion and capture, the water may become private, real or personal property under California law, depending on whether contact of the water with land is maintained or is severed.[13]

Appropriative Rights

The appropriative right may be conveyed; its appurtenance to land may be separated. This conveyance must be in writing, as that of other

real property.[14] The old fundamental rule for distinguishing between
appropriators is to rank them with a time priority — "first in time,
first in right." Under this rule, in general, preferences as to use play
their important role on only a limited number of cases having equal
status in time. However, important exceptions to this rule are made
by statute. For example, the California Water Code states that application for a permit by a municipality for domestic purposes "shall be
considered first in right, irrespective of whether it is first in time."[15]

Riparian Rights

Riparian rights are also of interest and economic importance in
California. The stream-land relationship is familiar, as is the general
inability to separate the right from immediately riparian land. Consequently a land transfer is needed to accomplish conveyance of the riparian right. These rights in their classical form were not subject to
precise definition; however, the pressure of increased water use has
circumscribed these rights in application, thus giving greater definition.
Appropriators, would-be pre-emptors and other riparians keep a careful watch on each other; and these rights are stated in quantitative
terms following an adjudication.

Correlative Rights

The correlative rights doctrine is relevant to groundwater and has
an analogy to the riparian system. Overlying landowners have coequal
rights to pump and to use the water on the land. These rights are not
quantitatively defined except in the case of an adjudication or an injunction. Pumpers of water for use on nonoverlying land, and municipal or
other pumpers for public use either within or outside the groundwater
area, are technically appropriators. If their pumping interferes with
the ability of overlying landowners or prior appropriators to produce
water and if the interference can be proved in court, damages may be
obtained or injunctive action could limit the defendant's pumping rights
to specific volumes of water, or both.[16]

Beneficial Use

The last general water rights concept to be noted at this point is
that of beneficial use. In this connection only the California Water
Code's dictum will be stated: "water of the state, both surface and underground, should be developed for the greatest public benefit"[17] and
that these waters be "put to beneficial use to the fullest extent of which
they are capable ... in the interest of the people and for the public welfare...."[18]
    Water rights may be held by individuals or groups legally capable
of owning property. Individuals and mutual and private companies have
been important owners, particularly in early development, but the large

diversions in terms of acre-feet have been accomplished by municipalities, public districts and the federal government. For the future, particular attention needs to be given to both the reciprocal internal structure and the external relationships of these organizations. These agencies will have rights to large volumes of water. Of course these rights will be for specified major uses. But deciding which major uses to satisfy over time will be organizational decisions to a greater extent than at present.

For this reason the structure for making these decisions will be of paramount importance. Through this structure the various interests in water use will find representation. When questions of changing the structure are at issue, the conflicts will center over the form of structure to be approved. The formation of public districts or the authorization of a federal project are frequently such points.

State government has played a significant role in the past, but a projection of California's past trend does not shed light into all of the relevant areas of its operations during the coming decades. With the voters' approval of a $1,750,000,000 bond issue in November 1960 for a start in state financing of water facilities, the capacity of state government as a large-scale operating water development and management agency is yet to be tested.

As an operator of a water development system the state will be the owner of important water rights. Major state filings date back to 1927. The state's applications must be made in connection with

...a general or coordinated plan looking toward the development, utilization, or conservation of the water resources of the state.... Applications filed pursuant to this part shall have priority, as of the date of filing, over any application made and filed subsequent thereto...diligence shall not apply to applications filed under this part....[19]

According to current opinion such filings have precedence over Sec. 1460 previously noted.

III. WATER RIGHTS IN THE RURAL-URBAN TRANSFER OF WATER USE

Appropriative water rights, their administration and their status before the courts have been condemned as not conducive to the transfer of water from rural to urban uses. The argument singles out agriculture as having a favored legal position which blocks the more productive municipal uses. Aspects of this relationship will be examined.

The character of California's early economy was dominantly mining and agrarian. These interests readily observed that water was a key factor limiting economic development. In the turmoil and battles over water allocation, both the appropriative and the riparian doctrines were incorporated into California's law of surface water rights.[20] These battles as physical acts of violence and more enduringly legal and organizational struggles resulted in establishment of policy. Competition for water existed during the first 50 years of the state's development.

For the most part the early water contests pitted miner against miner, miner against farmer and farmer against farmer with only occasional rural-urban competition. Major rural-urban competition for water did not arise until after the turn of the century. At the center of these controversies were issues of transferring water rights. The contest behind the Sierra Nevada is familiar. The voters of Los Angeles in their quest to establish a firm economic base voted in 1905 a $1,500,000 bond issue to purchase water rights in the agricultural Owens Valley.[21] Areas of origin still hold the embers of resentment from this flaming controversy. Even so the rural-urban transfer was made at the source of the physical supply.[22]

Water Rights as Real Property

Cases such as these illustrate the basic nature of water rights as real property, with a legal definition which permits economic transfer. Direct water transfers from rural to urban are not common. Those that I have been able to discover are largely of a minor and incidental character.[23] The fact that this type of direct transfer is uncommon implies there has been no strong economic pressure to consummate such transactions. The alternative of developing "new," unappropriated water has been present in most situations and has been exercised rather than an attempt to buy water rights whose value has been capitalized into going concerns. Since the development cost of subsequently captured water has been higher, the pressure has been to create development and management organizations with larger financial resources.

Of course the transfer as well as abandonment of old mining water rights to more productive uses is more prevalent, but these are not of the nature which hold our prime attention. Both situations, however, make it clear that water rights can be and have been transferred from low to higher productive uses.

The transfer of water rights which has taken place in the supersession of one economic activity or organization by another is more important for this discussion. As one organization became inefficient and outmoded, a more productive system purchased the old organization. The succession of water rights transfer was from individual diverter of surface flow, to ditch company, to large district. This chain of succession generally did not involve major rural-urban transfers, but the transfers were in the direction of increased productivity. In a very real sense the early enterprises laid the foundation for later expansion — for the development of more expensive and more productive water.

The water rights purchase and exchange contract between the Miller and Lux interests and the Central Valley Project is not of the preceding type, but the transfer is of interest. The private interests were paid $2,450,000 plus a specified annual delivery of exchange water.[24] This transaction was instrumental to the construction of the Central Valley Project which forestalled the use of certain potential dam sites by the City of Fresno.[25] The main point in the present context is that the

transfer did take place, thus enabling the water to be used more pro-
ductively. The water was put to productive use in agriculture in the
absence of immediate urban development. Frequently urban growth
has taken advantage of water developed by agriculture, as will be noted.

Urban Expansion

Rural-urban competition for water may affect water rights in another way. In this case no transfer of right takes place, as stated in
the previous discussion. The process is different: Suburbia gradually
"floods" the agricultural plain and transforms the irrigation district
into a municipal water supply agency.[26] As far as water rights are concerned, the principal effect is to change the purpose of use. Little
change may be evidenced in terms of volume of water, with the exception that new standards of quality must prevail and the timing of demand
is somewhat modified. Quite certainly the management problems are
different, but they are not the main focus of this chapter. If anything,
"the average acre" of urban use, at present levels of prices and assessments, demands somewhat less volume of water than an acre devoted to
agriculture.[27] For purposes of planning, the term water requirement is
used frequently in this context with misleading results. Such requirements usually are defined in physical terms under assumed conditions
of usage. Among these assumptions are cost-price relationships and
social pressure as to acceptable standards of efficiency which should
prevail. As the scarcity of water increases, these relationships change,
thereby changing the so-called requirement.

So long as the "new" urban demand is basically a replacement involving only a change in land use, the appropriative right generally would
not inhibit the change. The shift, however, may call for examination of
the wording of the water right to amend the purpose of use. In fact,
more than one purpose may be stated on the license.[28] Since the rural-
urban shift is from a highly consumptive use to a less consumptive use,
problems have not frequently arisen. However, in terms of administrative processing, they are handled much as a new application.

Urban expansion may require "new" water and thus create competition if nonirrigated land is developed for urban use and if the supersession of irrigated agriculture by urban land use pushes agricultural demand to a different geographic location. In the first instance the urban
water supplier may seek to develop "new" water, while in the second
the location of competition has shifted. Also, the competitors themselves may have shifted. But in either case the appropriative right *per
se* is not an obstacle.

Mass rural-urban competition for surface water rights has not been
pressing, in part because of the relationship of the groundwater reservoir. Agriculture in many sections of the state has developed on this
base. As the city expands into the irrigated areas, farm wells are
abandoned and municipal service is supplied by a large utility district
or the city from surface sources. The groundwater reservoir may be

left to the remaining farmers or a program of integrated surface-ground water management may be initiated. Again water rights have not stood in the way of the transfer.

A reversal of this situation exists in other localities where the regime of water management is different. Irrigating farmers have developed surface sources as well as groundwater, while the urban population has depended upon municipal wells. Competition has centered upon groundwater reservoirs rather than focusing on surface water rights. The traditional solution has been to develop more distant water for importation. Quantitative restriction is not in accord with the correlative rights doctrine except by adjudication or injunction. Both have been used in only a limited way. Generally the more productive uses have not been denied access to water by the law.

Fear of a transfer from rural to urban uses also is imbedded in the county and watershed of origin laws. Casting this within the frame of reference of a rural-urban conflict is, in part, a matter of timing. Smaller urban and agricultural communities hope that, by limiting the physical transfer of water from their region, total growth within the state will continue unabated but will be directed to their locality because of the availability of water. The conflict is mainly over the expectations of future urban growth. Since uncertainty in these expectations exists, good judgment would argue that organizational procedures be developed to take it into account.[29]

The conclusion so far is that California's appropriative water rights system has performed the economic function of defining a transferable property right. Because of water availability it has not blocked the transfer of water from rural to urban use. Of course if public interest demands, municipalities have the power of eminent domain as the last resort.

Agency Conflict

But what of the future? The big shift will center the competition on inter-agency and intra-agency conflict. To a degree water rights will be involved, but the main focal point will be over the terms of organization.

Two items should be mentioned, however, in the emerging pattern of inter-agency conflict with a water rights component. The state can file and has filed for specified quantities of water, as can other corporate entities. This practice was begun on a large scale in 1927 in anticipation of a Central Valley Project.[30] But there is a great difference between these state filings and other filings: The state is not held to the requirement of due diligence in perfecting its right. These rights are kept until someone wants to use them in accordance with the overall plan.

At times the state takes the initiative in filing; at other times it may be done upon request and with consultation of local groups. When the rights are to be used, the state assigns the filing to the party in question.

For example, part of the rights held by the United States government has been assigned by the state and these rights are being developed by the federal government. In other cases the rights are released in favor of filings of others who propose a development at variance with the state application but which would nevertheless serve the general purpose of the state filing. With an assignment, priority runs from the date of state filing; with a release, priority runs from the date of the developer's application. The state merely agrees not to assert its earlier priority against it. Thus the state can be in an important controlling position in water project development by use of this power.

One important rural-urban conflict has resulted from this process. The California Water Code says that applications of municipalities for domestic purposes shall be "first in right, irrespective of whether they are first in time."[31] However, in 1959 the State Water Rights Board denied the 1930-31 application of the city of Fresno in favor of an assignment to the Bureau of Reclamation of a 1927 state filing.[32] The basis for this action was the priority of the state filing, Section 10500 of the Water Code.[33] This position was reinforced by a concept of public interest.[34] So we conclude that maintenance of the large, predominantly agricultural Central Valley Project which had priority of right and in furtherance of which $145 million had been expended for dams or conveyance works was to the greater public interest than granting a permit to the city of Fresno which had spent or obligated nothing for works.[35] Yet the city retains the ability to obtain water necessary for its future growth, as will be shown. This case has not run the gauntlet of courts, but its force appears to give a responsibility for providing water to those agencies with a capacity for such service and a willingness to initiate contracts for service within a reasonable time.

IV. ORGANIZATIONS AND RURAL-URBAN TRANSFER

During the next several decades the importance of organizations in making major water allocation decisions will be heightened. This will be true as the water supply function moves increasingly into the province of large-scale operations carrying out complex engineering and economic activities.

The allocation of water to rural and urban uses will be inter- and intra-organizational. Rural and urban forces will compete within this frame of reference. Two points of conflict will be given special attention. One focuses upon the plan for action with the other centering on the terms of organization.[36] These conflicts may arise during the formal act of organization or through the continual process of organizational adaptation which is necessary for viability over time. In either case, basic decisions concerning who will acquire water are made during these periods of organization rather than in a market context.

Most obviously, rural-urban competition takes place in planning the services to be supplied by the physical system. As a result, elements of allocation are built into the system. To what extent shall both rural and urban interests be serviced by the same organization? Competition concentrates upon inclusion or exclusion of facilities as well as inclusion or exclusion of territory within the boundary. As previously noted, plans for exporting water from areas of origin (frequently rural) to other areas (frequently urban) have been major issues and still are of importance. Elements in the 1960 California water bond campaign may be interpreted in this light.

Preparation of Plans

Where a common interest is being sought on a plan and boundary, experience from districts and municipalities is instructive. Usual practice is to prepare for discussion a plan with boundary. If the constituents find it unacceptable, incremental changes are made in the plan and boundary, followed by another try. The choice is one at a time, over time. At any given time each decision is made on a nothing or all basis. But if one attempt fails, all is not lost; otherwise many projects never would have been built. The plan is changed and considered again at a later time.

The constituent voters, however, do not consider alternative plans. An important observation should be made concerning this process. The heavy responsibility of examining alternatives falls upon the project leaders. In other words it is important that the various interests in water planning be heard early in the planning process.

Effective competition for water also is evidenced *over* the terms of organization. These terms are familiar. They specify relationships of one internal constituent to another, internal to external interests, as well as the relationship of the constituent to the service rendered. To the extent that rural and urban interests are competitive, disagreements often arise over the nature of the repayment plan, method and level of service charges, the procedures through which the project is controlled and the ability to incorporate new values into the organizational structure over time. These are all terms which have been points of conflict in the past and will remain in the future.

All of these issues cannot be examined within the present limitations of space, but the way in which the competitive process takes place can be illustrated. In the late 1920's the urban residents of Santa Clara County refused to accept an assessment upon buildings to help pay for a groundwater recharge program which benefited both city and farm. The terms finally reached provided for assessment of land exclusive of improvements.

The "cooperative" nature of most public water development programs dictates that water charges should be based upon costs. In such situations competition centers upon methods of allocating costs. Each of the major methods, for example separable costs remaining benefits, proportional use of facilities or proportional increments of design capacity, distributes the costs — and thus the charges — differently between rural and urban users. We should recognize that the method selected is often the result of a bargaining process over the equity of the incidence of cost. Economically the argument over this term of organization is an argument over the pricing complex for water. The issues would be faced in a clearer fashion if the price were discussed directly.

The dynamic character of California's economy has been previously noted. The demands of an organization's constituents often change over time. Districts supplying irrigation water in 1948 may find subdivisions "lining" their canals and demanding service. In this situation organizational conflicts may arise over control of the board of directors. Such a transition may be orderly or heated as farm businessmen are replaced by urban businessmen. New interests become evident or a necessity. Public health standards of water quality are not the same for children as for alfalfa. Water acceptable in a factory may be quite different from water usable on the land. In addition, the spreading of housing developments over the valley floors frequently creates serious flood and drainage problems. These new interests may attempt to find representation through a new or different organization with the result of interorganizational conflict often involving the same assessment base.

Internal Policy

As large interregional transfer agencies become more predominant, the pertinent questions become ones of internal policy. In the conflict between the city of Fresno and the United States government the municipal uses of the city of Fresno were subordinated to the priority of the predominantly agricultural interest of the Central Valley Project. Since the primary mission of the Bureau, as stated in the 1939 Act and elsewhere, has been to promote an irrigated agriculture,[37] one could argue that such a ruling by the State Water Rights Board might be standing in the way of the transfer of water to a use with a greater productivity.

But the Board did not leave the city without an alternative; it will not become dry. Rather, the allocation was "internalized" within the Central Valley Project. The water right which it would prefer[38] was denied, but the way was opened for a contract which was signed between the city and the Bureau.[39] This action seems to recognize the public responsibility of those large-scale programs which are conveying water from one region of the state to another. Likewise, in other localities circumstances may require organizations which are developing water to accept a broader public interest in supplying water.

The Central Valley Project assumed responsibility to transport municipal and industrial water since its inception, with the first water being delivered through the Contra Costa Canal in 1940. Pressures to expand this type of service may well increase so that greater recognition will have to be given to this role in all Bureau of Reclamation activities. This same role was taken when the Feather River Project was proposed, with municipal and industrial service receiving major attention in all considerations — from design to financing.

A greater shift in this direction will have significant impact upon the organizational structure used to represent these new interests. For example, as California develops an action program, the roles of the governor and the legislature will be greatly different than in the past. The water right will be held by large organizations,[40] with the service contract being a point of prime interest. These water service contracts are basic to investment programs by water users. Contracts and investment programs become interdependent, since the asset markets are characterized with numerous imperfections. Our interest at the moment is not upon this aspect but upon structural impediments to changing these contractual relationships. Economic conditions change. "Revolutions" of many kinds may take place within the span of four decades. Towns grow; technology changes; economics is dynamic. These and other factors may affect the demand for water.

In view of this dynamic character of the economy, should not such practices as subcontracting or purchasing of contracts be explored as avenues to maintain elements of flexibility within the organization as well as the ability to renegotiate specific terms? Such flexibility may result in developmental economies due to better asset utilization.

The use of organizations to "produce" water raises a question of integrity and competence of management. It is an ever-present problem but is handled differently when dealing with property relationships rather than with organizations. Of course these elements are important to subjects other than the rural-urban transfer of water; but their impact here is significant. Does the planning and development process insure that all facets of the problem are considered — not only the immediate partisan interests which have the power to be heard in any event, but the public whose voice is less articulate? An insistence upon professional standards may assist in this process. Of course, granting a responsibility to act with a clear line of public accountability can be helpful to maintain integrity.

For the future, rural-urban competition will be expressed through and over the institutions of water organization. Ingenuity and insight based upon research will be required to provide avenues for water interests to express themselves in water organizations.

FOOTNOTES

[1] S. V. Ciriacy-Wantrup, "Concepts used as economic criteria for a system of water rights," *Land Econ.*, Vol. 22, No. 4, pp. 295-312, 1956.

[2] Paul Streeten, "Introduction," in Gunnar Myrdal, Value of Social Theory, Harpers, 1958, pp. ix-xiv; Kenneth Parsons, "The problem-solution basis of forward pricing," *Land Econ.*, Vol. 25, No. 4, pp. 423-27, 1949; Kenneth Parsons, "The value problem in agricultural policy," Agricultural Adjustment Problems in the Growing Economy, Earl O. Heady *et al.*, eds., Iowa State University Press, Ames, 1958, pp. 285-99.

[3] Leonard A. Salter, "Cross-sectional and case grouping procedures in research analysis," *Jour. Farm Econ.*, Vol. 24, No. 4, pp. 792-805, 1942.

[4] S. V. Ciriacy-Wantrup, Resource Conservation, Economics, and Policies, University of California Press, Berkeley, 1952.

[5] Eugene Rotwein, "The methodology of positive economics," *Quart. Jour. Econ.*, Vol. 73, No. 4, pp. 554-75, 1959. Rotwein argues that assumptions are important.

[6] Philip Selznick, Leadership in Administration, Row, Peterson, and Co., Evanston, Ill., 1957, p. 81.

[7] Stephen C. Smith, "The process of county planning: a case study of Henry County, Indiana," *Land Econ.*, Vol. 26, No. 2, pp. 162-70, 1950.

[8] Gunnar Myrdal, Value in Social Theory, Harpers, 1958.

[9] Charles E. Lindblom, "Handling of norms in policy analysis," The Allocation of Economic Resources, Moses Abramovitz et al., eds, Stanford University Press, Stanford, 1959, pp. 160-79; Streeten, *op. cit;* Ciriacy-Wantrup, "Concepts used...."

[10] The following illustrate some of this literature: Wells A. Hutchins, The California Law of Water Rights, State Print. Off., Sacramento, 1956; Michael F. Brewer, Water Pricing and Allocation with Particular Reference to California Irrigation Districts, Univ. of Calif., Giannini Foundation Mimeo. Rept. No. 235, Berkeley, 1960; S. V. Ciriacy-Wantrup, "Concepts used...."; Stephen C. Smith, "Problems in the use of the public district for ground water management," *Land Econ.*, Vol. 32, No. 3, pp. 259-69, 1956; Stephen C. Smith, "The role of the public district in the integrated management of ground and surface water," *Water Resources and Economic Development of the West: Ground Water Economics and the Law*, Rept. No. 5, Committee on the Economics of Water Resources Development, Berkeley, 1956, pp. 81-91.

[11] Hutchins, *op. cit.,* p. 121.

[12] State of California, Water Code, Div. 1, C. 1, Sec. 102.

[13] Hutchins, *op. cit.*, pp. 38-40.

[14] *Ibid.*, pp. 126-30.

[15] State of California, Water Code, Div. 2, C. 7, Art. 3, Sec. 1460.

[16] Hutchins, *op. cit.*, pp. 488-502 (includes a long discussion on correlative rights with adjudication and injunction).

[17] State of California, Water Code, Sec. 105.

[18] *Ibid.*, Sec. 100.

[19] *Ibid.*, Sec. 10500.

[20] Many fascinating stories focus on the development of western water. For example, the struggle for water played an important role in the life of Henry Miller (Miller and Lux). See Edward F. Treadwell, The Cattle King, rev. ed., Christopher Publishing House, Boston, 1950. It was in Lux v. Haggin that the appropriative doctrine became imbedded in California law of water rights.

[21] Vincent Ostrom, Water and Politics, The Haynes Foundation, Los Angeles, 1953, p. 54.

[22] The term rural refers to the general rural economy. Thus merchants in a rural economy would be classed as a rural interest.

[23] Minor cases do exist. For example, California State Water Rights Board Application No. 10011, Permit 5685, License 2581, Gaston and Urrutia, City of Portola; Application No. 8496, Graeagle Land and Water Company.

[24] Clair Engle, Central Valley Project Documents: Part 2, Operating Documents, U.S. Govt. Print. Off., 1959, p. 577.

[25] California State Water Rights Board, Decision No. D935 (1959), p. 21. "Applications... of the City of Fresno as filed in 1930 and 1931, envisioned a 490,000 acre-foot capacity storage dam on the San Joaquin River in the approximate, if not the exact, location of the present Friant Dam...." It should be pointed out that the city of Fresno did not utilize these dam sites following its 1930-31 applications.

[26] Harry Griffen, C. G. Watters, Jr., Byron M. Miller and W. H. Jennings, "Conversion of an irrigation district from an irrigation system to a metropolitan supplier of domestic water," Minutes of the Fall Convention of the Fiftieth Year, Irrigation Districts Association of California, San Francisco, 1960, pp. 38-48.

[27] For example, in the Santa Ana River area south of Los Angeles, urban consumptive use ranges from 1.31 to 1.75 acre-feet in the valley and .14 to .72 in the hills while agriculture in the same area ranged from 1.85 to 2.77 and .89 to 1.61 acre-feet per acre per year. See Calif. Dept. of Water Resources, *Santa Ana River Investigation*, Bul. No. 15, Sacramento, 1959, p. 60. Similar reports for other areas show comparable results.

[28] For example, in Decision No. D935, previously cited, the purpose of use was amended to read, "irrigation, domestic, municipal and recreational," p. 108. The California State Water Rights Board, Rules, Regulations, and Information in California, p. 39, state that major uses may not be consumptive and nonconsumptive in one application.

[29]The settlement of the East Bay Municipal Utility District (EBMUD) with Calaveras and Amador Counties, counties of origin, is a case in point. EBMUD received a release from the right of these counties to exercise a priority with respect to specified state filings. The counties received $2,000,000 each plus 27,000 acre-feet of water for Calaveras County and 20,000 acre-feet for Amador County. See Francis B. Blanchard, "Municipal and domestic use in the competition for water quantity," paper presented at Water Resources Center Conference, Univ. of Calif., Davis, Jan. 11-13, 1960, unpublished.

[30]Now in the State of California, Water Code, ad Div. 6, Part 2, Sec. 10500-10507.

[31]State of California, Water Code, Sec. 1460.

[32]California State Water Rights Board, Decision D935, op. cit.

[33]State of California, Water Code, Sec. 10500, "Applications filed pursuant to this part shall have priority, as of the date of filing, over any application made and filed subsequent thereto."

[34]California State Water Rights Board, Decision D935, op. cit., p. 56, "We are not constrained to resolve the issues before us on the narrow basis provided by a comparative construction of Section 1460, 10500, and 10505. The rule that conflicting applications shall be determined on the sole basis of statutory priority has been modified and in large part superseded by an entirely different concept, that of public interest, which is next discussed," and p. 62, "We therefore conclude that in the public interest Application 234, 1465, and 5638 of the United States should be approved in order that the project may function as now envisioned by the United States...."

[35]Ibid., p. 62, "The narrowest interpretation of the Board's discretion in the public interest would require that commanding consideration be given to these expenditures. (Previous paragraph cites expenditures of the federal government and local water development agencies.) Any action that might substantially impair the investments thus represented should be avoided, if reasonably possible."

[36]Stephen C. Smith, The public district in integrating ground and surface water management: a case study in Santa Clara County, unpublished.

[37]U.S. Department of Interior, Federal Reclamation Laws Annotated, Vol. 1, p. 598.

[38]California State Water Rights Board, Decision D935, op. cit., pp. 401-6.

[39]San Francisco Chronicle, Jan. 8, 1961, p. 3.

[40]Smaller projects in the same Bureau of Reclamation region in California also provide municipal service; for example the Cachuma Project will service Santa Barbara.

JAMES W. FESLER is Alfred Cowles Professor of Government at Yale University. In the resources field he has served as a staff member or consultant with the National Resources Planning Board, the U.S. Departments of Agriculture and of the Interior, and the National Security Resources Board. In the War Production Board he was executive secretary of the Planning Committee and the Resources Protection Board.

Chapter 21

JAMES W. FESLER

*National Water Resources Administration**

T HE FEDERAL GOVERNMENT'S relation to water resources is perplexingly complex. So commonplace has such an observation become that the truth it expresses may require revitalization by example. Take Monday, February 4, 1957, an ordinary day of proceedings in the United States Senate and House of Representatives.

Senator Ives introduced and explained a bill for construction of a hydroelectric power project at Niagara Falls by the New York State Power Authority.[1] Senator Neuberger, from across the continent, introduced and spoke for a resolution proposing a Columbia River basin account through which federal power revenues would help finance irrigation and reclamation projects.[2] Senator Beall obtained unanimous consent to publish in the *Congressional Record*'s appendix an editorial on pollution problems of the upper Potomac River.[3] Senator Symington protested alleged neglect of Missouri in the administration of drought relief by Secretary of Agriculture Benson.[4] The Senate adopted Senator Murray's joint resolution for a National Conservation Anniversary

*A revision from a symposium, "Water resources," Summer, 1957, by permission from Law and Contemporary Problems, published by the Duke University School of Law, Durham, North Carolina, copyright, 1957, by Duke University.

Commission to celebrate the fiftieth anniversary of the 1908 conservation conference of state governors called by President Theodore Roosevelt.[5] Senator Carlson seized this opportunity to urge Senator Murray and his Committee on Interior and Insular Affairs to give favorable consideration to Senator Carlson's bill to establish a commission on the conservation, development and use of renewable natural resources and particularly "problems of drought, decreasing water supply, and the wind erosion of our soil."[6]

In the other wing of the Capitol, Representative Cooley explained for his Committee on Agriculture why the drought relief bill was delayed by objections of the Department of Agriculture,[7] and Representatives Poage, Rogers, Hoffman, Fisher, Hays and Christopher expressed sharply their disappointment at the delay.[8] Representative Perkins addressed the House on the flood disaster in eastern Kentucky (and West Virginia, Virginia and Tennessee).[9] The Board of Commissioners of the District of Columbia submitted draft legislation authorizing it to construct two bridges over the Potomac River.[10] The House Committee on Interior and Insular Affairs submitted a report on a bill to amend the Small Reclamation Projects Act of 1956.[11] Bills were introduced for a fish hatchery, for return of certain lands to their former owners at the Buford Dam and Reservoir in Georgia, for appropriations for continued construction of the Calumet-Sag Channel in Illinois, for "certain works of improvement" in the Niagara River, for inclusion of "additional works of improvement" in the Watershed Protection and Flood Prevention Act, for congressional approval of a Great Lakes Basin Compact, and for preventing certain lake levels from dropping excessively because of the use of hydroelectric generators.[12]

Variety and complexity are at the heart of the problem of organizing for water resources administration. The observer feels as if he were looking into a steadily rotating kaleidoscope in which each mosaic pattern yields to another before the first can be fully registered on the consciousness. Partly for simplicity's sake, two possible ways of halting the rotation will be excluded from consideration here. One effort to weld variety into a patterned unity is the valley authority. Another is the proposal to devise a truly joint regional instrument of the states and the federal government. These will be assumed, without prejudice, to be unavailable as solutions on a nationwide basis. Our concern, on this assumption, will be the organization of the federal government for its water resources responsibilities.

I. THE SEARCH FOR THE ORGANIZING IDEA

Many official inquiries attest that the federal government is poorly organized for the development and execution of water resources programs. There is less agreement on what should be done. This is largely because there is no consensus on a definition of the problem, and so none on the starting point for organizational analysis. For organization is rational only as it relates to problems expressible in nonadministrative terms. Such problems, for example, might include agricultural production, government printing, children, labor, the South. Because so many problems clamor for governmental attention, only a few can be recognized as "organizing ideas" at the higher levels of organization. We cannot indefinitely multiply executive departments or even "independent establishments."

Selection of the most important organizing ideas is, therefore, mandatory. Such a selection is high policy, and so properly political. It may be done well or ill, by conscious choice or by indifferent acceptance of historical patterns. It will never be wholly satisfactory, for the concerns of government are too numerous and interrelated to fit neatly into ten or twenty or thirty tidy compartments. The organizational pattern may fail to settle which agency should have power finally to determine the contents and format of a government pamphlet on the children of migratory agricultural laborers in the South. But some problems, such as how much money the federal government should spend where on construction of what kinds of dams, may be so important to the public that these problems thrust themselves up into the level of important organizing ideas. Where we are in history helps to determine this agenda of major public concerns. Water resources, it is said, has now emerged as among the critical concerns of our time.

Whether "water resources" is the true organizing idea for the kinds of functions that should be grouped together administratively is not so clear as many assume. We need to have a clear statement of the problem to which administrative organization is meant to be responsive. There is no agreement on what that statement should be.

There are three principal ways of visualizing the nature of the problem. The first sees a single "whole" — water, for example — as the focus. The assumption is that if all executive agencies' functions related to this whole were brought together or otherwise harmonized, the problem would be solved. The second sees a process with distinct, and so separable, stages; planning, construction, operation would be illustrative in the water resources field. If each stage is unified, one need not worry so much about administrative unification of the whole process. The third sees legislative policy as the principal unifying or divisive element. The assumption is that if Congress would bring its policies, as embedded in statutes, into a consistent whole, we could abandon the emphasis upon administrative realignments.

Those who see a "whole" to which administration might be attuned do not agree on what that whole is. Yet, this needs to be settled, for it is the clue to determination of which functions and agencies need to be brought together organizationally.

One starting point might be *water*. At its simplest, this means water in the channel, with an emphasis on navigation, flood control and fishing. But from this starting point, one quickly moves to recognition of the flow of the water *to* the land for irrigation and for water supply; and then proceeds to the flow of water *from* the land, which raises questions of on-land measures to purify the flow by pollution control and to reduce the rate of flow and of siltation by forestation and other water-holding practices. This may all be considered an approach based on water-in-the-channel, although already land as it relates to water has come so clearly within the limits of the concept that what has been embraced has potentially startling administrative implications.

The shift to *natural resources* as a starting point for thinking about administration seems almost imperceptible. But water is no longer the touchstone for assertions of relevancy. Now water and land are seen so married by nature that "land-and-water" can be the focus. Subsoil mineral resources expand the focus further.

To move from either water or natural resources to the idea of a whole *drainage basin* introduces two new ways of visualizing the problem around which organization might be designed. First, it is an advanced step in the historical process marked by successive shifts from the single-purpose, single-dam approach, to the multiple-purpose designing of single dams by a single agency, and then to the multiple-purpose designing of single dams by collaboration among several agencies. We are, it appears, moving past the point when each dam, even if multiple-purpose in design, can be treated as an isolated project unrelated to upstream and downstream dams. But this interrelating of channel works is not the full realization of the basin concept. For the basin approach tends to absorb the land-and-water unity concept and to move on to the general resource base of the basin's economy.

Second, the basin concept introduces a new kind of "whole" into organizational thinking. The basin is an areal whole, as distinguished from "water" or "natural resources," which would be termed functional wholes. To attempt to organize around the idea of a series of areas such as basins introduces new problems of definition, for basins vary in size, have interrelations with neighboring basins,[13] and are contributors to and beneficiaries of national and international policies and events.

Economic Development

Water, natural resources and the basin concept may all be brought into a new focus — that of *economic development*. This, too, is a point that can be reached by so natural a progression that it hardly seems a distinctly different basis for administrative organization. Water, partly because of its fluid gold quality for agricultural development in the arid West, and partly because of its white coal quality as a yielder of hydro-electric power for industrial development in underdeveloped regions, acquires a strategic significance as a convenient lever with which to plan and effect economic growth. Yet, it is but one lever, and such other bases of economic development as thermal power, transportation facilities, mineral deposits, labor force, and research and education are factors demanding consideration in their own right.

Water seems a convenient taking-off point for analysis, policy-making and administrative action pointed toward economic development.

But there are alternatives that seem equally plausible. Water may carry one logically to hydroelectric power; hydroelectric power may carry one to some thermal power for "firming up" the hydroelectric power on those occasions during the year when the water flow cannot deliver energy at the peak level; from this, especially if hydroelectric power sites are exhausted and demand continues to increase, one may be carried to thermal power as the dominant energy source. The Tennessee Valley Authority has traversed this road leading away from the river. In 1950, hydroelectric plants produced 90 per cent of the system's power requirements; in 1956, steam plants produced 72 percent of those requirements.[14] Perhaps, then, energy sources, rather than water, are the key to economic development and, hence, the idea around which organization should be built.[15]

Economic development is sometimes equated with regional development. Yet, regional development has a specifically areal focus, while economic development (or economic planning) does not. Observe, for instance, the possibility that so much emphasis on regional development of underdeveloped regions like the South and the West may lead to neglect of the relatively long-developed industrial East and Middle West. Here, the problems of out-migration of certain industries, in-migration of new elements for the labor force, accelerated urbanization, water supply, water pollution, shortage of recreational areas and floods may call less for stimulation of economic development than for delicate adjustment of competing interests in an already well-developed economic and social complex. National considerations may well come to the fore, not excluding the national concern with the *relative* development or decline of the several regions of the country and, so far as national funds and energies are called upon, with the optimal disposition of these investments for promotion of the national interest. In such considerations, national defense may loom as large as will equitable balance in the development of regions. To organize for the making and execution of these major strategic decisions that impinge on regional development may then be thought the principal challenge to our administrative capacity.

Public Works

Water, natural resources, the drainage basin, economic development — each is a possible focus for administrative organization. But *public works* is yet another alternative. The construction of dams, irrigation works, water-purification plants and electric-transmission lines seems the most obvious manifestation of governmental efforts to bring water into the service of the people. The construction of thermal power plants, highways, post offices, federal office buildings, hospitals and other public buildings has potential significance for the economic condition of each region and of the nation at large. So much is this true that since early New Deal days (and even earlier), there has been recurrent effort to accumulate in good times a shelf of public works projects that can be quickly undertaken when a depression threatens. Note

how swiftly the ground has shifted, though. For now public works of all
sorts are thought to warrant unified handling through central planning
and activation. Add to this the appealing thought that if all the engineering talents of the government were in one department or bureau, there
would be economies and a high *esprit de corps,* and one is well on the
way to organizing around an idea that is wholly distinct from the other
"organizing ideas" that have been reviewed.

Recapitulating, one way of visualizing the nature of the problem that
we confront organizationally is to see a single whole that can serve as
the focus for organization. Which whole we see matters a great deal,
for a rational administrative structure must start from some premise
about the nature of the substantive problem with which government is
attempting to deal. Without seeking to develop any merely speculative
hypotheses about the definition of the substantive problem, we have
seen that, in fact, reasonable men define the problem quite differently.
Some see water per se; some see land-and-water or natural resources
as a kind of seamless web; some see economic development or planning
(and that in such various guises as basin-based, regional, interregional
and national); and some see government as a great builder of physical
structures — some on drainage systems, but others on land and unrelated to water or other resources.

It is common to assume that all functions related to a particular
substantive problem of government should be brought together in a single agency. This has been implicit in what has been said to this point.
But there are other ways of looking at organization than in this all-or-
nothing way. One of the other ways, if we are thinking of water resources development, rests on a sharp distinction among planning, constructing and operating the projects. Planning may be thought of as involving the selection of projects to be built (or recommending them to
higher bodies for authorization and financing). This may turn on economic feasibility, engineering feasibility, relation to other developments on the river system and on land, indirect social benefits and
costs, relative importance of other regions' proposals, and so on. It
may also require a consideration of the multiple purposes of the project
and an assurance that the project design serves these purposes in the
proportions believed sound. It may as well be said immediately that
"planning" so described becomes a rather mixed pot of technical research, highest-level economic and social planning, politics and engineering design. This accounts for some confusion over how to organize for the planning function in the water resources field. But, despite this confusion, planning — all of which precedes the turning of a
spadeful of earth — can be distinguished from construction.

Construction could be conceived of as simply an engineering task
of building to specifications provided by the planners. Perhaps it becomes immaterial where the construction responsibility lies organizationally, so long as the specifications provided by the planning group
are accepted as controlling.

Operation of completed projects can be regarded as what happens after the construction engineers have "delivered" the completed project. Under present conceptions of the relations among projects on the same drainage system, it can be argued that a single operating agency must control all dams on a particular drainage system, for the release of water upstream affects the flow of water into reservoirs downstream. The nature of this operating agency will be affected by the fact that operation is no merely mechanical routine task, but involves a nice balancing of the competing claims of the multiple purposes for which the dam or system of dams was built. The volume and timing of water flow that is ideal for hydroelectric power production may not be ideal for navigation, flood control, irrigation or other purposes. A single water master is needed, and his role will be more than a merely technical one. Yet, this is no argument for unification of land and water operations. As Charles McKinley has persuasively indicated, what needs to be treated as a unity for planning purposes need not be treated as a unity for operating purposes.[16]

The main point to be made is that planning-construction-operation can be thought of as a chain with weak links. So regarded, the argument that all three stages of water-related activities must be organizationally united loses its *prima facie* validity. Instead, a wholly new way of looking at the organizational problem has been developed.

The Role of Congress

The third principal way of defining the problem is to see it as really a congressional problem. A recurrent theme in much of the official and professional literature of water resources administration is that the policies of Congress, as set forth in statutes, are inconsistent; that Congress has so organized its committee structure as to abet organizational confusion in the executive branch of the government; and that Congress encourages the project-by-project approach at the expense of comprehensive basinwide or nationwide programming. It is doubtful that any responsible student of the subject would care to question the factual accuracy of this theme, which a congressional subcommittee has put in these terms:[17]

Your subcommittee is convinced that, for the maximum economic return from Federal water resource developments, a single integrated plan must be developed and provided for each stream. It is of the opinion that the processing of unintegrated segments through different committees and the ultimate enactment of conflicting projects can lead only to waste and a chaotic situation. It believes that no segment of a plan should be approved by any committee or enacted by Congress so long as major conflicts exist between such segment and the parts properly under jurisdiction of some other element of the executive branch. The insistence of Congress upon coordination through its refusal to authorize conflicting elements would probably bring about the necessary coordination more quickly than any amount of reorganization. The agencies of the executive branch must be shown that they cannot attain their conflicting ends by playing one committee of Congress against another.

*   *   *   *   *   *   *

On the question of organization, then, the subcommittee is of the opinion that present problems would not be solved in any marked degree by simple reorganization or by the establishment of a special board of review.

No serious student would fail to support efforts by Congress to improve its own relation to water resources problems. But what is in doubt is whether without remedial congressional action an attempt should be made to improve administrative organization.

To be sure, separate administrative agencies are allied with separate congressional committees, separate interest groups and separate policies. But to think of these agencies as wholly passive elements in this pattern may be naïve; indeed, the subcommittee itself recognizes this.[18] If, of the four elements in alliance, the executive agencies are the element most readily altered, then there is a probability that significant organizational changes among the agencies would break up the prior alliances, induce a reforming of congressional committee structure and sharpen awareness of policy inconsistencies.

II. OFFICIAL PROPOSALS, 1949-53

Review of the official recommendations that have streamed from the U.S. Government Printing Office presses since the 1950's is the most efficient way of perceiving the alternative organizational solutions that have appealed to thoughtful men who are not insensitive to the tension between the "one best way" (though they differ on what it is) and the political limits of tolerance. A convenient watershed for such a review is the inauguration of President Eisenhower in January, 1953. In the Truman period, water resources organization was examined by the first Hoover Commission, the President's Water Resources Policy Commission, and the Missouri Basin Survey Commission, reporting, respectively, in 1949, 1950, and early 1953. In the Eisenhower period, there were the Temple University Survey, the second Hoover Commission, and the Presidential Advisory Committee on Water Resources Policy. The first reported in 1953 and the last two in 1955. We shall follow this review by an examination of the confused efforts in the Kennedy period to precipitate a clear substance from the very mixed pot of available solutions.

First Hoover Commission

The first Commission on Organization of the Executive Branch of the Government, chaired by former President Herbert Hoover, proposed that the Department of the Interior have a clear mission of "development of subsoil and water resources" and, arguing from the fact that such development required large public works, concluded that the department should manage other public works as well.[19] This would bring together, in a water development and use service in the Interior Department, the rivers and harbors and the flood-control functions hitherto performed by the Army Corps of Engineers alongside the reclamation and power activities already in the department.[20] The other principal "services" in the department would concern themselves with building construction, mineral resources and recreation.[21] The land-management work of the department would be transferred to the Department of Agriculture; certain other transfers would remove units incompatible with the new concept of the department.[22]

The commission recognized that the Department of Agriculture would have an interest in the selection of irrigation projects, that the Department of State would appropriately handle international negotiations, and that the Federal Power Commission would continue to have concerns tangential to the water development and use functions of the Interior Department.[23] These interdepartmental concerns are hardly the reason, though, for the commission's recommending that there be in the President's office a Board of Impartial Analysis for Engineering and Architectural Projects, composed of "five members of outstanding abilities in this field." The board would "review and report to the President and the Congress on the public and economic value of project proposals by the Department" and "periodically review authorized projects and advise as to progress or discontinuance."[24] Finally, the commission proposed that each major drainage area have a drainage area advisory commission consisting of representatives of the Department of the Interior, the Department of Agriculture and each state.[25]

This sets the stage well for much that was to emerge from the deliberations of subsequent official study commissions. Note the several elements here displayed. First, the commission proposed to bring the civil work of the Corps of Engineers into the Interior Department, thus simultaneously bringing to a focus, within a single department, both the principal water or river activities of the government and the principal dam-construction work of the government. These are related, of course, but it is of some organizational significance to clarify which is the conceptual basis for thus joining what history and politics have thrust asunder. Second, it proposed to bring other major construction work into the Interior Department — particularly public buildings construction — on the premise that as long as engineers for construction of dams and irrigation systems were being gathered together in the department, the government's engineers working on dry land might as well come along too.

Third, the commission proposed a board of review at the presidential level. The most clear-cut rationale for the recommendation was that "there is no adequate check in the Government upon the validity or timing of development projects and their relation to the economy of the country."[26] Elsewhere, one of the jobs of the board is described as that of assuring that the Department of Agriculture gets a chance to examine Interior Department proposals for irrigation and reclamation projects.[27] These are distinct, even if not inconsistent, concepts of the board's role, and it is useful to keep them clear. The board was proposed even though, as a result of interdepartmental transfers of functions, most project proposals would be initiated by the Interior Department. A question left unanswered is why the Interior Department should not be expected to do the assessment job instead of having to pass the projects on up for a second going-over at the President's level. It is quite a different thing to work from the assumption of scattered and competing points in the federal bureaucracy for initiation of project proposals, with no hierarchical superior to these initiating points save the President. On that assumption (characteristic of some of the later survey commissions), a case can be made for a review board to do much of the President's project-review work for him. A further feature of the commission's proposed board of review needs to be noted. The board members were not to be representatives of the several concerned federal departments, but rather, if the commission's Task Force on Public Works were to have its way, of "the seagreen incorruptibles of the engineering profession." [28]

Fourth, the commission recognized the drainage-basin concept of water development and the desirability of in-the-basin organization for collaboration among interested agencies and governments. Indeed, one of the more interesting passages in the report reads, "A further reason for unified organization of water development agencies [in the Department at Washington] is to permit the determination of policies upon a watershed basis." [29] The commission quotes with approval the advocacy by its Task Force on Natural Resources of "regional decentralization of the Water Development Service ... by river basins where practicable, to facilitate 'grass roots' decisions, interservice cooperation, and local participation in planning. ..." [30] But then, in recommending a series of drainage area advisory commissions, the Hoover Commission makes clear that their purpose "should be coordinating and advisory, not administrative." [31]

Pegs for much of the subsequent thinking about water resources administration are these four ideas — the consolidation of water resources activities in one department (which would also have mineral resources, but not public lands), the consolidation of construction engineering in one department, the review of water resources project proposals at the presidential level by a special board, and the drainage basin as a unit for planning, cooperation and advice (if not for administration).

Minority Proposal

What is missing from this agenda is the idea expressed in the dissenting report of a distinguished minority of the first Hoover Commission. Commissioners Dean Acheson, James K. Pollock (a leading political scientist), and James Rowe (a former Assistant to the President) recommended establishment of a Department of Natural Resources. In their eloquent statement, the three dissenters argue from a conviction that "the conservation, development, and use of [all] our public resources is a single indivisible problem," and that forests, water, public lands, minerals, wildlife, fisheries, recreation and power are but parts of that single problem. The department they propose would include approximately the same functions as those favored by the commission majority for the Department of the Interior, with two principal differences: (1) a forest and range service would be created to include the Forest Service and forest insects and disease research (by transfer from the Department of Agriculture), and the Interior Department's

Bureau of Land Management (which the majority had proposed to shift to Agriculture); and (2) public building construction work would not be brought into the department. The dissenters concur substantially with the majority on the need for a board of review in the President's office and go beyond the majority in welcoming the regional authority device for "some river basins." [32]

Some of the points made in the minority report require examination, for they add to the dimensions in which we may think about the organizational problem. It is already clear that two key propositions of the minority are, first, that land-*and*-water (and minerals) is the problem, and second, that government should be administratively organized to give strength to "major purposes." Both propositions lead to the proposal of a department that encompasses all natural resources and emphasizes resources *development* in the public interest as the major departmental purpose. The second proposition explains why the minority prefer that construction unrelated to resources development be left to other departments having other major purposes. A curiosity in the minority's logic, however, is that they wind up not really meaning what they certainly appear to say. What they do mean is that *public* lands should be under the aegis of the department that has water resource development functions. Private lands, they grant, belong with the Department of Agriculture, which might well "focus its responsibility on harmonizing the producer interest in private lands with the need for conservation of . . . soil resources."[33] So, oddly, what we have is a division of jurisdiction in terms of public and private ownership of land — not in terms of the unity of land and water. Furthermore, because almost all of the public lands are located west of the one hundredth meridian, the minority are implying unity of western land and water, but disunity of eastern land and water — a point that was never made explicit.

President's Water Resources Policy Commission

The President's Water Resources Policy Commission, chaired by Morris L. Cooke, reported in December 1950. Although requested by President Truman to steer clear of questions of administrative organization and focus on policy matters, the commission could not escape the interrelations of policy and administration. It allied itself with the Acheson-Rowe-Pollock minority of the Hoover Commission, in favor of a department of natural resources, with a decentralized water development service through which basin development programs would be planned and managed.[34] But as the Hoover Commission's reports had been before the President and Congress for a year and a half without any action to unify water resources activities, the Cooke Commission considered what might be done in absence of such action. It chose to advocate congressional approval of inter-agency drainage basin commissions, each to include equal representation from all federal agencies with functions included in water resources programs, and each to be presided over by an independent chairman appointed by and

responsible to the President. A federal board of review would be created in the executive branch, composed of members "with a broad understanding of the economic and social as well as the technical aspects
of regional development." [35] The commission recognized, as an alternative to the basin commissions, the creation of regional or valley administrations to manage the water and related land resources of the
several basins.

More than most investigating groups, the Cooke Commission derived its organizational conclusions from immersion in the substantive
problems of water resources and from an analysis of how the planning
and development processes should be designed. It was not the first or
the last group to find that gross inconsistencies in congressional policies and standards applicable to different types of projects and agencies
were at the root of much of the difficulty. This being the case, mere
organizational shufflings are not likely to be effective remedies. And
yet, using existing organizational units as building blocks, it may be
possible to introduce combinations and juxtapositions that will introduce
more order than that of a jumbled pile. And it may be possible to design processes by which questions will be posed to Congress for decision that preclude Congress's escaping the responsibility for effecting
reconciliation of its own several policies.

The heart of the matter, as the Cooke Commission saw it, was a
basin program of a comprehensive, multiple-purpose type that would
be related to the prospective economic and social development of the
region, as a factor in the growth of the nation. The tool for destroying
separatistic approaches by the several national agencies was to be appropriations. "At each step in the planning, authorization, and appropriation process," the commission said, [36]

... the basin program should be treated as a single program for all purposes
rather than as an aggregate of plans for separate purposes to be individually approved. This procedure should replace the diverse authorization process now
followed by the Federal agencies. Appropriations should therefore be made to
the basin programs as a whole, on the basis of budgets showing the approximate
amounts to be allocated to the specific projects and participating agencies, rather
than to specific functions.

All projects and programs recommended by the basin commissions
would be analyzed and reviewed by the proposed board of review with
an eye to economic feasibility, the broad national interest and possible
modifications in the public interest. [37]

Were the procedures to be adopted along with the commission's organizational proposals, a substantial shift in administrative power
would be probable. The projection of the President into the basin commission, through the independent chairman, together with the principle
of equal representation of all agencies with functions included in water
resources programs, might lead to more fully integrated basin programs than emerge from, say, inter-agency committees chaired by the
Corps of Engineers and operating on the absolute veto principle. The
independent chairman and the minor-interest representatives (from the

Forest Service, National Park Service, Fish and Wildlife Service and Public Health Service, among others) might be expected to reject such self-serving propositions as the primary combatants — the Corps of Engineers and Bureau of Reclamation[38] — might advance. The fact that agencies would be able to approach Congress for planning and survey money, for authorization of projects and for appropriations for projects only through each basin commission would reduce the mutual reenforcement of fragmentation typical of relations between agencies and congressional committees. The system would probably occasion a recasting of the congressional committee system in the water resources field, although the Cooke Commission was careful to avoid saying so.

The recommended board of review appears to be patterned after the Hoover Commission proposal, but has, in fact, a rather different role. It would review basin programs primarily to assure their compatibility with the larger concerns of the nation, which necessarily includes a consideration of the relations among programs of the several basins. In other words, its role would be less that of achieving coordination among the national agencies concerned with water resources than that of seeing to it that regionally-oriented basin commissions did not let their local enthusiasms blind them to the larger national interest in defense, maintenance of a national and world market and balanced development of the national economy.

Missouri Basin Survey Commission

Early in 1952, President Truman established the Missouri Basin Survey Commission, under James E. Lawrence's chairmanship, to "study the land and water resources of the Missouri River Basin and ... related matters ... and ... prepare recommendations with respect to an integrated and comprehensive program of development, use, and protection of said resources."[39] Just before the expiration of President Truman's term in January, 1953, the commission submitted its report, *Missouri: Land and Water.* The 11-member Survey Commission, with three members dissenting, proposed that Congress establish a Missouri Basin Commission of five full-time members, to be appointed by the President with the consent of the Senate, from basin residents belonging to both political parties.[40] There are ambiguities in the statement of the commission's purposes and powers, but the terms used are as follows. The general purpose is:[41]

... to prepare and direct the development of a land and water resource program for the Missouri Basin. It will be the Commission's task to harmonize and reconcile the interrelated features and purposes of such a program *by directing and coordinating the activities of all Federal agencies relating to resource development.* [italics added]

The proposed commission would review all uncompleted investigations, plans, programs and projects of each federal agency, even if they were approved or authorized by Congress prior to establishment of the commission; and all future investigations, examinations and surveys would be directed by the commission, which sometimes would ask agencies to conduct joint studies of these types. Requests from agencies for authorization of completed project plans would have to be submitted to the commission for analysis of engineering and economic feasibility and relation to the basin programs; and the request, accompanied by the commission's report and recommendations, would then go to Congress "through the established channels of review in the Executive Office of the President."[42] The Federal Power Commission would be unable to issue any permit or license if the Missouri Basin Commission, to which the application would have to be referred, held it inconsistent with the basin program.

Annually, the commission would prepare "a consolidated Basin Resource Budget for land and water resource development, in consultation with the operating agencies," including budgets for basic data, planning, construction and operation, and indicating three alternate levels of expenditure "for the guidance of Congress in appropriating funds for resource development."[43]

The difficulty in defining the role of the commission lies in the fact that, in contrast to the situation of the Tennessee Valley in 1933, the Missouri Valley has already been in process of resources development through construction programs of federal agencies. Rejecting the "authority" idea, the Lawrence Commission sought to devise "a basin agency responsible for directing and coordinating the special skills and competences of the existing Federal agencies in a unified program of resource development" — that is, "an organization which would not replace the Federal agencies, but would direct and coordinate their activities."[44] Yet, a line is attempted between the construction activities, which are left to individual agencies (under the commission's guidance), and the operation of the completed structures. In the latter phase, the commission "is given the responsibility for integrated operation of the main stem and tributary reservoirs for water control and power generation and dispatching."[45]

Missouri: Land and Water contains a perceptive and enlightening review of the organization problem as it existed in the basin at the time. Specific experiences are described, and the existing coordination devices are carefully appraised.[46] But, even though inadequate existing arrangements prove sufficiently that anything else will be better, the rationale for the commission's proposed organization is nowhere clearly stated. It is difficult to visualize the Missouri Basin Commission, with its principal offices in the basin, coordinating, advising, guiding, directing and establishing "operational goals and administrative policy"[47] for the field officials of the national functional agencies. As Hubert Marshall has pointed out, the role proposed for the new commission[48]

... would create a schizophrenic situation in which operating officials recruited by and responsible to bureau chiefs in Washington, would at the same time be working under the immediate supervision of the commission. . . . There is every reason to suppose that the operating bureaus, if allowed to remain in the basin, would not readily abdicate their control of policy and program to a new commission.

Yet, in its very failure to face such problems, the Lawrence Commission accents the difficulty and, hopefully, forces a clarification. How can an area-based agency be related to national function-based agencies?

III. OFFICIAL PROPOSALS, 1953-55

In late 1952, preparatory to the inauguration of Dwight D. Eisenhower as President, a study was undertaken "in order to bring the Hoover Report up to date and prepare guidelines for continued reorganization in the new Administration."[49] While not an official study in the usual sense, it was designed to facilitate the work of the incoming administration, and, in fact, it fed directly into the President's Advisory Committee on Government Organization established under Nelson A. Rockefeller immediately after the inauguration.[50] This, the *Temple University Survey of Federal Reorganization*, proposed that the Interior Department have a water development service that would include "the civil functions of the Army Corps of Engineers; the functions of the Bureau of Reclamation; all flood-control functions of the Department of Agriculture which consist of actual engineering as distinct from counseling in farming practices"; and certain other responsibilities.[51] The Interior Department would also contain a power service comprised of the Bonneville, Southwestern and Southeastern Power Administrations and certain planning authorities vested in the Federal Power Commission. A minerals service would complete the principal large blocks of the Interior Department's structure, but the National Park Service and Fish and Wildlife Service would also continue. The Bureau of Land Management would be transferred to the Department of Agriculture. Finally, the planning of water resources development would be decentralized through establishment of "State-Federal inter-agency regional committees operating under the leadership of field representatives of the Division of Water Resources Programming."[52]

Curiously, these recommendations do not flow naturally from the analysis the study group set on paper. The *non sequitur* is simply that from the premise that "all our natural resources are inextricably interrelated,"[53] the group concludes that the Interior Department should have water and mineral resources and parks, and the Department of Agriculture should have land resources, including public lands, soil and forests. Note this statement of the problem of the Department of the Interior:[54]

The main effort of this Department is addressed to the development and conservation of the nation's water, land and forest resources. Yet, for all its size, Interior presently encompasses a comparatively small portion of federal activities in these areas. And that, with respect to the Department of the Interior — and the nation — is the problem.

Or the following passages:[55]

Careful study... shows that the leadership and impetus required to administer federal resources activities with due regard for their importance to the national welfare requires that a *single* Cabinet Department be devoted to the main purpose of wise conservation and development of the nation's resources. [italics added]
*   *   *   *   *   *
Reorganization of the federal natural resources functions should provide a means for achieving a proper balance among the various Federally-supported resources programs which, in the past, have been weighted heavily in favor of river development.

Yet, the burden of the recommendations made is that land resources and water resources should be in different departments! The explanation (inconsistent, of course, with earlier expressions) is that the most important use of land (including the public domain) is the production of food and fiber crops. This is already the concern of the Department of Agriculture, as are also forestry, soil conservation and grazing.[56]

The recommendation for absorption of the civil functions of the Army Corps of Engineers by the Interior Department rests on familiar grounds: that "there cannot logically be two plans for one river," and that "every effort at voluntary cooperation has failed."[57] Which way the consolidation tide should run seems clear, for logic cannot support the conduct of large-scale operations of a purely civilian nature by any branch of the armed services.

The Temple University study, however, was the last official study to recommend a transfer of the civil functions of the Army Corps of Engineers. From 1953 on, the Corps was to be treated as an immovable object against which no irresistible force could be effectively mobilized. Politics makes strange river-bedfellows.

Second Hoover Commission

The second Hoover Commission, reporting in 1955, had given particular attention to problems of water resources and power. According to Commissioner Chet Holifield, $430,000 was spent on the commission's inquiry into these problems;[58] this was almost a sixth of total commission expenditures. Eschewing the first Hoover Commission's strong advocacy of a shift to the Interior Department of the civil functions of the Corps of Engineers, the second commission simply recommended (a) strengthening of the Bureau of the Budget's staff to "enable it to fully perform the function of evaluation of the merits of water development projects presented to it for appropriations,"[59] and (b) creation of a water resources board in the Executive Office of the President. This board would include some Cabinet members, five public members and "a non-Government chairman." The board's public members were to be chosen from "engineers, economists, and others of recognized abilities." The board would have two functions: (1) "to determine the broad policies for recommendation to the President, and, with his approval, to the Congress," and (2) "to devise methods of coordination of plans and actions of the agencies both at the Washington level and in the field."[60]

This, it would appear, is an abdication of the commission's responsibility to find an answer to the administrative evils it describes. A content analysis of the commission's report would reveal its awareness of these evils: "overlaps and conflicts between Federal agencies"; "when the control of reservoirs in the same river is under different agencies with different responsibilities and motivations there is inevitable conflict in point of view"; "the diffusion of authority among the agencies on water development, and the need for clarification and coordination";[61] "flood control is not an isolated administrative segment of our water development. It involves great problems of coordination between Federal agencies engaged in water development."[62]

The commission's report does devote attention to river basin coordination, although this yielded no formal commission recommendation. "With some exceptions," the report reads, "the critical place for coordination of water development projects is at the river-basin level." It then harks back to a 1926 speech by then Secretary of Commerce Hoover proposing that each river basin have a commission to coordinate development which would consist of representatives from each state and major federal agency concerned, and from "the private development agencies."[63] After tracing this idea through the reports of intervening study commissions and legislation, the Hoover Commission declares that the proposed federal water resources board "would set up such basin commissions to represent fairly the Federal, State, and private interests." They would not be administrative bodies, nor would they necessarily include all streams in a particular drainage area; further, "they should be varied in scope and purpose with changing economic, social, or political conditions" (a welcome thought thirty years after the Secretary of Commerce set forth the model). In distinctive prose, the commission states, "Their function would be limited to plans, coordination of projects in each particular basin, and to coordinate between basins where such interests overlap."[64]

This vague proposal for basin commissions must somehow be reconciled with the clear-cut recommendation for incorporating as public enterprises the Columbia River basin system, the Hoover-Parker-Davis Dams Administration, the Central Valley Project of California, the Missouri River basin project, the Southwestern Power Administration and the Southeastern Power Administration.[65] This is coupled with recommendation that these would-be-corporations and the Tennessee Valley Authority be required to secure their capital for future improvements, when authorized by Congress, by issuing their own securities to the public. The joint purpose of the two recommendations is "to release the Federal Government of further call upon the taxpayers to finance the seven major Federal power organizations."[66] A plausible reconciliation would be that the basin-commission proposal is pointed toward the planning of projects and the incorporation proposal toward the operation of power production and sale from the constructed projects.

But this fails to square with the expectation that the incorporated enterprises would be proposing "future improvements" to Congress.

The treatment of the civil functions of the Corps of Engineers is one of the more curious aspects of the Hoover Commission's report. It is worth examining, for it marks abandonment of the consolidation emphasis of previous reports. The commission cites chapter and verse of errors in cost estimates by the Bureau of Reclamation, Tennessee Valley Authority, Soil Conservation Service and Corps of Engineers.[67] This exposure of the agencies' miscalculations is followed by a handsome disclaimer:[68]

The defects cited here are not intended to cast doubt upon the competence of the Federal agencies concerned with water development. Their integrity and the engineering qualifications of their personnel are not in question. Federal agencies have an enviable record for safe engineering design, and for successfully carrying out large engineering projects. They have been signally free of the taint of dishonesty in administering construction programs. Most of the blame must be placed on the lack of consistent national policies, and the absence of adequate provisions for review, inspection, and coordination of projects at Washington and basin levels.

Oddly enough, virtually this whole statement is repeated with specific respect to the Corps of Engineers when the commission deals gingerly with flood-control activities. Lest there be any doubt, the commission adds, "The Commission wishes no sentence in the report to be construed as a reflection upon the Corps."[69] In "deadpan" fashion, the commission describes the organization of the Corps, noting without further comment that in late 1954 the Corps had 116 army engineers and 25,445 civilians assigned to the civil works program. The commission thus refuses to draw the obvious conclusions from this ratio that were drawn both by the first Hoover Commission and by Albert L. Sturm in his impressive study of the Corps's case for retention of civil works activities — a study prepared for the second Hoover Commission's own task force.[70]

Proceeding to consider critically the Soil Conservation Service's headwater dam construction program, which "has raised many questions of conflict and overlap with the Corps of Engineers," the commission formally recommends "that the construction of headwater dams in the flood control program of the Soil Conservation Service be transferred to the Corps of Engineers." This recommendation is arrived at "in view of the engineering competence of the Corps of Engineers and because its staff is operating in all streams of the country, and because another large engineering organization is undesirable in the Federal Government."[71] So the net result of the commission's consideration of the civil works role of the Corps is a recommendation for its enhancement.

Presidential Advisory Committee

We turn finally to the December, 1955, report by the Presidential Advisory Committee on Water Resources Policy.[72] The committee consisted of Secretary of the Interior Douglas McKay (chairman), Secretary of Agriculture Ezra Taft Benson and Secretary of Defense Charles E. Wilson. The President established the committee on May 26, 1954, well aware that he already had the Bureau of the Budget, the President's Advisory Committee on Government Organization and the second Hoover Commission available as potential alternative sources of at least organizational advice in the water resources field. However, he chose to set up the Cabinet committee, with the Bureau and the Advisory Committee in cooperating roles, and with the relation to the Hoover Commission defined as a committee prepared to assist in executive branch consideration and review of the Hoover Commission's recommendations, when submitted. As the Hoover Commission's report on water resources and power was submitted to Congress in June, 1955, the Cabinet Committee could have drawn on it and its related three-volume, 1800-page task force report for information, points of view and specific proposals. However, the Cabinet made no mention of any of its sources. The degree of its acceptance and rejection of Hoover Commission recommendations is, therefore, left for determination by those patient enough to compare the two reports.

The McKay Committee proposes four organizational creations: a coordinator of water resources, a board of review for water resources projects, a federal inter-agency committee on water resources, and, at the regional or basin level, a series of water resources committees.

The coordinator of water resources, located in the Executive Office of the President, would "provide Presidential direction to agency coordination and . . . establish principles, standards, and procedures for planning and development of water resources projects."[73] He would be permanent chairman of the federal inter-agency committee on water resources, would cooperate with the Bureau of the Budget and the Council of Economic Advisors in evaluating departmental requests for appropriations, work with the Coordinator of Public Works Planning in relation to water resources developments and assist in reconciling water resources policy with other federal policies.[74] However, he would not assume the budgetary, fiscal policy review or legislative clearance functions of the Bureau of the Budget.

The board of review for water resources projects would also be in the Executive Office of the President. It would consist of three individuals, serving full-time, appointed by the President for terms corresponding to his own and serving at his pleasure, and, in now familiar terms, "should be chosen from qualified engineers, economists, or others of recognized abilities and judgment in the resources field."[75] The reason for proposing creation of the board is that "the President, before making final decision on water resources projects, should have the benefit of advice" of such a board. In operation, the board would "report to the President through the Coordinator of Water Resources" and, in fact, address its recommendations, for the most part, to the coordinator directly. The board would have its own chairman, and the coordinator would not be a member.[76] Its terms of reference are variously phrased.

It is "to analyze the engineering and economic feasibility of projects,"[77] to "evaluate, in the light of policy established by the Congress and criteria established by the Coordinator of Water Resources, all reports on water resources projects . . . ," to recommend any modifications "considered desirable from a comprehensive national viewpoint," and to recommend changes it deems advisable in the criteria for water resources projects.[78]

The inter-agency committee on water resources would be permanent, advisory in role and chaired by the coordinator already described. Its members would be the head or an assistant-secretary-rank official of the departments of Agriculture, Army, Commerce, Health Education and Welfare, and Interior, and the Federal Power Commission. Advisory to the President, the committee would be "the medium for coordination of the interrelated functions of the several agencies" and would "have authority by unanimous action to determine finally inter-agency relationships." It would be "the channel for advice between the President and Federal representatives on the water resources committees"[79] — to which we now turn.

Each water resources committee at the regional or basin level would consist of a permanent nonvoting chairman appointed by the President and one representative from each federal department having water resources responsibilities and one representative from each affected state, to be appointed by the governor. All members would be equal, but "the total number of either Federal or State representatives is regarded as immaterial, since the conflicts should be resolved by cooperation and not by voting strength."[80] However, unresolved disagreements would be referred to the coordinator of water resources. Each committee chairman would be responsible to the coordinator and would have "a small independent staff and funds for independent use."[81]

An inconspicuous footnote in the Cabinet committee's report suggests that consideration might be given to broadening the scope of these committees to include all natural resources. Even under the name, "water resources committees," each is to prepare "a comprehensive plan which will best serve the region and the Nation in the development of water and related land resources."[82] The committee would recommend an annual work schedule to be reflected in the budget requests of each cooperating agency and would report annually on progress.

A careful reading of the Cabinet committee's description of these water resources committees leaves an impression of care to maintain the separate responsibility and vigor of the several national agencies with water resource interests. Every sentence in the following brief paragraph contributes to the full flavor:[83]

The water resources committees should be the principal and continuing medium through which the various departments, State and Federal, coordinate resources planning and development activities. The committees should serve as the mechanism through which the several agencies would prepare and publish joint plans for water resources development. Action on specific projects of joint plans, however, would be taken by the appropriate agency or agencies. The committee may foster studies of water resource problems not otherwise sponsored by any agency.

The concise report (a mere 35 pages) of the Cabinet committee makes selection and summary almost impossible. Yet, the report itself is such a discriminating distillation of much of the thinking that has taken place about water resources administration that some characterization of the reasoning behind the recommendations must be attempted. The facts that the word "power" does not appear until page 14, and that one looks in vain for a mention of power development in the list of six objectives of "a sound water policy"[84] need not deter one from seeking the report's wisdom on other matters. What may be thought of as the summary findings or conclusions of the committee include two points of importance for administration. "The greatest single weakness in the Federal Government's activities in the field of water resources development," says the committee, "is the lack of cooperation and coordination of the Federal agencies with each other and with the States and local interests."[85] Largely to blame for this is the fact of "different laws empowering different agencies to pursue particular programs for different purposes."[86] Second, the committee believes that although planning the coordinated development of water resources *by river basins* is generally sound, it can be unduly emphasized, and the appropriate planning area, in some instances, may be the region, rather than the basin.[87]

Elsewhere, the committee provides further foundation stones for the construction of effective water resources planning and development. Note the scope of the statement, "The objective of planning should be the best utilization of all water resources from the time precipitation falls upon the land until the water again finds its way into the sea,"[88] — clearly a far cry from emphasis on water simply in the channel. A subtle point of some administrative moment is made in the recognition that most of the planning to date has been with respect to flood control, navigation, irrigation, soil conservation, watershed control and hydroelectric power, at the expense of due concern for drainage, fish and wildlife preservation, recreation, scenic values, pollution control and water supplies.[89]

The committee finds that mere circulation for comment among interested agencies of the plans prepared by one agency is no answer to the need for coordination. A plan so prepared is "frequently lacking in the over-all viewpoint that should be controlling,"[90] and other agencies do not sufficiently contribute the missing viewpoint in their rather hurried efforts to consider the proposal. Nor would an effective solution lie in consolidation of "all Federal agencies engaged in natural resources development, including water ... into a single Federal agency," even apart from the question whether it would be adopted by Congress without a long delay.[91] The problem is inconsistencies in policies, and a single agency responsible for all water resources development could not effectively operate until that problem was resolved.

The committee's administrative proposals depend heavily upon the rigor with which its procedural views could be implemented. No agency would initiate an investigation of a major project without specific approval of Congress. No agency would have authority to proceed with any major project or program unless Congress had authorized it "by specific act of Congress for each such project." No agency would seek such authorization until its proposal had been reviewed for a reasonable time by the various federal departments, the board of review, the states and local interests directly affected, nor until it had been cleared by the coordinator of water resources. No agency would seek appropriations for an authorized project without re-examining the economics and engineering in a report that would be submitted through the Bureau of the Budget to the appropriations committees; if significant economic or engineering changes had been made since the date of authorization, a report would have to be submitted to the board of review and then to the appropriate legislative (i.e., nonappropriations) committees of Congress for approval or modification of the project. If five years should elapse after a project had been authorized, with no funds appropriated for construction, the full review process would need to be fully repeated. [92]

IV. OFFICIAL PROPOSALS, 1961-62

The final days of the Eisenhower administration afforded the opportunity for both a serious proposal and, in political terms, a frivolous proposal to be included in the January 16, 1961, budget message for fiscal 1962. The politically frivolous one, not heard since the administration's own first days, read:

...Action should be taken to consolidate the civil water resources functions of the Corps of Engineers of the Department of the Army, the Department of the Interior, and the responsibilities of the Federal Power Commission for river basin surveys, in order to bring about long needed improvements in the coordination of the increasingly important Federal civil water resources activities. [93]

The serious proposal, destined to be revived by the Kennedy administration, was that Congress "authorize the President to establish water resources planning commissions as needed in the various river basins or regions," their members to be presidentially appointed from the various federal agencies and the states; their task would be to "prepare" and keep current comprehensive, integrated river basin plans." [94] Under the circumstances, however, this proposal received no serious consideration in the early days of the new Congress.

In the course of his election campaign and his first six months in office President Kennedy took three different positions on organization for water resources planning and development. At the time of his inauguration he was plausibly understood to favor a definition of the problem and an organizational arrangement that had been expressed in a bill introduced by Senator Murray in the preceding Congress,[95] the

Democratic Party Platform of 1960, the October 10th report of the Democratic Advisory Council's Committee on Natural Resources, his own pledges in campaign addresses (the last on November 3 before his election), and the January 17, 1961, report of the President-Elect's Natural Resources Advisory Committee.[96] The problem, and so the organizing idea, was to be "natural resources," rather than a single resource such as water. The organizational mechanism was to be a council of resources and conservation advisers in the Executive Office of the President "which will engage in over-all resource planning and policy, which will assess our national needs, and recommend national programs to meet them."[97] The Council of Economic Advisers was the model in mind, which means that the new council would report directly to the President and would consist of presidential appointees for the purpose rather than of agency representatives. On January 9, 1961, Senator Engle, on behalf of 30 senators and himself, introduced S. 239, the "Resources and Conservation Act of 1961," which embodied these proposals and was substantially the same as Senator Murray's bill in the last Congress.

But all of this was quickly scuttled. The President's special message on natural resources on February 23 stated his intention to take executive action (a) redefining natural resources responsibilities within the Executive Office of the President and authorizing a strengthened Council of Economic Advisers to report on the status of natural resources programs in relation to national needs; (b) "establishing under the Council of Economic Advisers, a Presidential Advisory Committee on Natural Resources, representing the Federal agencies concerned in this area and seeking the advice of experts outside of Government," and (c) "instructing the Budget Director, in consultation with the departments and agencies concerned, to formulate within the next 90 days general principles for the application of . . . user charges at all types of Federal natural resource projects or areas; and to reevaluate current standards for appraising the feasibility of water resource projects." The President added that he had already asked the budget director, working with appropriate department and agency heads, to schedule a progressive, orderly program of starting new projects to meet accumulated demands.[98]

Although this sufficed to doom S. 239, confronted at the April hearings by a unanimous agency front against the bill in view of the President's stated intentions, those intentions did not become operative. As early as January 23 the President increased the staff strength of the Bureau of the Budget and the Council of Economic Advisers for public works and resources planning. An executive order was drafted by the Bureau of the Budget on April 7 to assign resource planning responsibilities to the Council of Economic Advisers and establish under it an inter-agency Presidential Advisory Committee on Natural Resources. But the draft order also attempted to set forth the Bureau of the Budget's responsibilities in the resources and public works areas, and this aroused members of Congress who had long complained of the Bureau's restrictive approach to project evaluation. Agreement by White House staff and the budget director to delete all mention of the Bureau seems not to have cleared the way for the order; it was never issued.[99] And the President's intent to have the budget director re-evaluate by May 23 the standards for appraising the feasibility of water resources projects was unfulfilled; only a year after the deadline were new standards announced and they were the product not of the Budget Bureau, but of an *ad hoc* interdepartmental committee chaired by the Secretary of the Interior.[100]

Proposed Water Resources Council

A third and final Kennedy administration position was reached in July, 1961. It was developing in May and June, for Senate committee requests of April and early May for agency views on bills providing grants-in-aid to the states for water resources planning were not answered until mid-July when the administration's new formula had been determined.[101] The organizing idea had by then changed from natural resources to water resources, and the organizational mechanism from the Council of Economic Advisers aided by an interdepartmental advisory committee to a free-floating Water Resources Council composed of four department heads and not specifically placed in the Executive Office of the President. That the administration had come full circle is suggested by the fact that on March 9 the President had terminated the Presidential Advisory Committee on Water Resources, consisting of three department heads (the McKay Committee described above).

The Water Resources Planning Act (S. 2246), proposed by Senator Anderson on July 14, 1961, as drafted by the administration, combined the already pending grants-in-aid program for the states with provision for basin and regional planning of "water and related land resources." The water resources council would consist of the secretaries of the Interior, Agriculture, the Army, and Health, Education and Welfare, with the chairman designated by the President. The council would study "the adequacy of supplies of good quality water in each water resource region" as against regional and national requirements, "appraise the adequacy of existing policies and programs to meet such requirements, and make recommendations to the President" on these matters. It would also "establish, with the approval of the President, principles, standards, and procedures for the formulation and evaluation of Federal water resources projects."

The President would have authority "to create a river basin water resources commission for any region, major river basin, or group of related river basins." Each commission would comprise a chairman, appointed by the President and holding no other federal position, representatives of federal agencies, one or more members from each substantially interested state (but appointed by the President, preferably but not necessarily by acceptance of gubernatorial nominees), and perhaps representatives of geographically related interstate compact commissions and international commissions. Each river basin commission would report to the water resources council, and would submit to it, after canvassing reactions of federal agencies, state governments, and interstate and international commissions, "a comprehensive, integrated, joint plan for Federal, State, and local development of water and related land resources in its geographic area." The water resources council would review each basin commission's plan, "make such modifications in such plan ... as are desirable in the national interest," and transmit the plan with the modifications and with the comments by others on the plan to the President "for his review and transmittal to the Congress." In addition, the Council would administer grants-in-aid to the states for comprehensive water resources planning.

Finally, S. 2246 disclaims "superseding, modifying, or repealing existing laws applicable to the various Federal agencies which are authorized to develop or participate in the development of water and related land resources, or to exercise licensing or regulatory functions with respect thereto.... "

What is curious is the lack of novelty and promise in these arrangements. The bill, said Senator Anderson, is almost exactly the same bill that President Eisenhower proposed just before his term expired.[102] An inter-agency committee has been commonplace as an institutional device for water resources coordination. Indeed, some testimony at the Senate committee hearings indicated a belief that provision for the water resources council would simply give statutory authority to the existing Inter-Agency Committee on Water Resources, or was deficient because the council would include only four of the six agencies represented on that committee or because the council's powers would be no greater than those of the committee. The bill specifically eschews a disturbance of federal agencies' existing statutory authorizations for development of water and related land resources, assigns the council no direct authority to review individual agency-sponsored projects, and builds agencies' jurisdictional sensitivities into the council membership itself. It offers an opportunity for a supra-agency point of view only at the basin-commission level, where the chairman and perhaps some state representatives might question agency biases. Nonetheless, this continued to be the Administration's bill. In his special message on conservation, of March 1, 1962,[103] President Kennedy again urged passage of the bill. By mid-1962 thought was once again being given to the possibility of establishing the organizational mechanisms (in this case, a water resources council and river basin planning commissions) by executive action.

V. CONCLUSION

The very fact that the choice of water resources projects is of political moment both complicates and simplifies our task. It complicates the task because a due respect for what is possible or impossible

politically should lead one to modify his preferences for ideal administrative solutions. What Congress will accept then becomes the key
question. If Congress will clarify its water resources policy, then administrative consolidation of water resources agencies becomes less
necessary — such, at least, is one position. If Congress will interpose
no objection to a presidential reorganization order that consolidates
water resources agencies, then consolidation may be a tactical move
directed toward eventually persuading Congress to reconcile its con-
tradictory policies. If Congress will neither clarify its policies nor
permit consolidation of agencies, then the immediately practical step
is to strengthen coordination among water resources agencies in planning and in final processing of project proposals. These are all reasonable efforts to adapt administration to "the facts of life" on Capitol
Hill.

Congress, however, will accept none of these solutions. It has
shown no disposition to clarify its policies, or, for that matter, to simplify its structure of committees concerned with water resources.[104] It
has even been distrustful of administration efforts to standardize the
methods by which the several agencies estimate economic and engineering feasibility of projects, lest congressional freedom of choice be
thereby constricted.[105] It has opposed consolidation of water resources
agencies, and no recent President has dared to send to Congress a reorganization plan for this purpose. It has opposed the strengthening of
coordinative and review machinery in the Executive Office of the President.[106]

The retreat before congressional obduracy may halt with the discovery of the drainage basin committee formula for peace. Members
of Congress are notably area-oriented and might find it easier to establish a kind of suzerainty over the committee for the basin from which
they are elected[107] than to work out a rewarding relation to a nationally-
integrated water resources program developed in the Executive Office
of the President. But no organizational formula has been evolved for
drainage basin committees that will satisfy the area orientation of congressmen, the national orientation of the President, and the functional
orientation of the several water resources agencies.

Earlier confidence in inter-agency committees at the national and
basin levels has evaporated. The second Hoover Commission's task
force on water resources and power spoke in wholly disenchanted terms
about the inter-agency committee device. Typically, each agency has
an absolute veto; each representative on a committee is subject to reversal by higher officials in his own agency; each agency avoids criticism of a fellow agency lest the compliment be returned; the chairmanship is either held by one of the agencies or it rotates among the agencies (and either method is bad); the committee staff work is either
farmed out to the agencies or is performed by an *ad hoc* staff assembled
by detailing of personnel from the agencies (and again, either method is
bad); and there is "the massive defect" of "the absence of formal, external control, and the fact that . . . the agencies will be sitting in judgment on their own plans and actions."[108]

To be sure, there are ways of correcting many of these defects.
But the corrections destroy the reasons for hope that Congress might
accept basin committees, even if it will accept no other administrative
solution. Any improvements in the inter-agency water resources committee must strengthen presidential control — through a chairman appointed by the President and affiliated with none of the represented
agencies, through the independent chairman's possession of determina-
tive power in cases of disagreement within the committee (or power to
refer disputes to the President's office), through provision of a staff
and budget for the chairman, and through the vesting of final power to
formulate the basin program in the President's office so that merely
additive agreements among agencies may not come to take the place of
truly integrated programs. Once this much is conceded, it seems impossible for the presidency to avoid adding a national viewpoint that
may relate each basin committee's program to those coming from
other basin committees and so introduce a comprehensive national policy approach that will inevitably modify the results of the basin-
oriented work.[109]

There seems no reason to expect that Congress would welcome
such an arrangement, for the President would again be forcing Congress to think of water resources development as a national program
rather than as a disparate assemblage of specific projects in the districts of the individual congressmen.

The indications that Congress cannot be appeased by any administrative arrangement so far devised simplifies our immediate task of
drawing conclusions about national water resources administration.
Until further political analyses disclose a way in which Congress might
accommodate the patent need for more reasonable arrangements for
consideration of water resources programs, we can revert to relatively
apolitical modes of analysis. In doing so, we may reopen questions that
have been closed for several years in deference to the limits of what
seemed possible.

The bulk of the planning, construction and operation of water resources programs and projects should be in a single major national
department. The civil functions of the Army Corps of Engineers, the
headwater dams work of the Soil Conservation Service, and the irrigation and reclamation work of the Bureau of Reclamation should be consolidated in this department. Included in the department — presumably
a reconstituted Department of the Interior — might well be certain other
resource bases of economic development, particularly such energy
sources as coal, oil and gas. Nonetheless, even if the department embraces minerals and public lands, it cannot be a truly comprehensive
department of natural resources, and the exclusion of atomic energy
stands in the way of its achieving a total view of energy resources.

The emphasis upon water and upon construction of dams has obscured the fact that these are means, not ends. It follows that the planning of water resources projects must be oriented to policy judgments
about ends to which water and construction projects can contribute.

Because water and physical structures are strategic levers, control of which carries substantial influence on human welfare, the uses to which the levers shall be put must not be left to determination by staffs of construction engineers. Ultimately, the broad decisions must be made by Congress. But the decisions will be more rational if programs are formulated in the first instance in the executive branch.[110]

Water resource program formulation should be primarily the task of the secretarial level of the contemplated department, and something comparable to the Interior Department's program staff of the pre-1953 period should aid the secretary in this responsibility.[111] Both the secretary and the program staff will do a better-rounded job if the department includes several resources (and even resource uses, such as recreation and commercial fishing). The programmers need constantly to be reminded within their own department that the planning problem is not water, but the relation of water to other resources and to human needs.

To build up the department secretary's role would proportionately relieve the pressure on the presidency, and so reduce the tendency to multiply various coordinative and "objective" boards and committees in the Executive Office. The latter tendency has been prominent in official reports and suggests a too easy dumping of problems into the President's office.

A distinction needs to be drawn between water resources development and economic development. The latter, it has been suggested earlier, is a far broader concept and involves a much greater variety of elements than does water resources development. Administratively, this warrants recognition by different organizational levels. Responsibility for economic planning might be placed in the Executive Office of the President, while responsibility for water resources planning might rest with the secretary of the proposed department. This does not mean that water resources programs formulated in the department should not be reviewed in the President's office before transmittal to Congress. It does mean that the review should be broad in nature.

Decentralization of initial drafting of water resources programs to the drainage basin level should be easier to manage within a single department than would be an attempt to vest a presidential basin representative with authority to direct field agents of several national agencies. And it would certainly be more effective than would be loose-jointed cooperation through interdepartmental committees.[112] Decentralization of initial preparation of economic development programs, on the other hand, might well follow regional, rather than basin, lines and might need to draw on a number of agencies through interdepartmental committees, temporary assemblage of joint staffs and assignment of individual research projects. Our experience has indicated that reports on regional economic development are likely to be informative and suggestive, but are not firm plans or programs that will be formally adopted by the President or Congress. "Hard" planning of water resources programs and "soft" planning of economic development are, therefore, likely to raise different administrative questions, or at least to raise the same questions with different intensities.

These reflections do not resolve the problems of administrative organization raised in the early pages of this chapter. The neat categories of administrative logic are seldom exactly reproduced in the untidy world of administrative reality. But certain marginal gains may be anticipated from action along the simple lines suggested. The reconstituted Department of the Interior would be oriented nationally, instead of westerly. This is in part because absorption of the Corps of Engineers' civil functions would bring into this department the rivers and harbors-dredging and the flood-control activities of the East and South. It is in part, too, because a clearly-identified administrative center for water resources programming would predictably concern itself with the increasingly urgent water problems of heavily-populated and industrialized sections of the country. If the department were oriented in this fashion, certain other pieces of the puzzle would fall into place.

A nationally-oriented department, with a well-integrated objective whose accomplishment is substantially compatible with the public interest, may, with some luck, become a worthy possessor of responsibilities that otherwise would have to be retained in the President's office. That is, a department that is concerned solely with a particular section of the country, or a particular resource or a particular use of a resource (e.g., irrigation, power) is in the role of a biased advocate, and its proposals must be carefully evaluated at a higher level where a broader perspective prevails; but if these identifications of interest can be expanded, a broad perspective may be hoped for at the departmental level. This, it is true, will not follow unless the programming responsibility is kept at the secretary's level. If it is shifted to the bureau level, there may follow a segmentation of interests, a narrowed perspective on the public interest, a tendency to find satisfaction in energetic pursuit of limited objectives. The building of dams is more likely to become an end in itself, and engineers are more likely to be making policy judgments beyond their ken.

Within this framework, there would appear to be room for two other developments. One is resolution of the conflict between areal and functional bases of organization, which underlies much of the difficulty surrounding the idea of basin committees or basin staffs. The other is the encouragement of congressional attitudes that may lead to a programmatic approach to authorization and appropriation for water resources projects, a development of consistent policies and a reconsideration of the present jurisdictional divisions among the Public Works, Agriculture, and Interior and Insular Affairs committees. Both developments would be advanced by a redesigned Interior Department.

To go beyond this point of reflection and prediction one has need of "An eye that like a diver to the depth / Of dark perplexity can pass and see, / Undizzied, unconfused." [113] He who possesses such an eye might cast his gaze on the political obstacles to improvement of water resources administration. [114]

FOOTNOTES

[1]103 *Congressional Record* 1290-91 (daily ed. Feb. 4, 1957).

[2]*Id.* at 1294-95.

[3]*Id.* at 1295.

[4]*Id.* at 1301-2.

[5]*Id.* at 1310-11.

[6]*Id.* at 1310.

[7]*Id.* at 1335.

[8]*Id.* at 1335-39, 1353-54.

[9]*Id.* at 1348-53.

[10]*Id.* at 1357.

[11]*Ibid.*

[12]*Id.* at 1358-59.

[13]Even the Tennessee Valley, so long an areal focus for resources development, does not stand alone. A former chairman of the board of the Tennessee Valley Authority writes: "The stream flow of the Tennessee accounts for some 25 per cent of the Ohio's discharge into the Mississippi....On the lower Ohio and Mississippi rivers this [TVA] system can reduce flood crests by $2\frac{1}{2}$-3 feet, depending on the origin of the flood....

"...Half of its [TVA's] flood-control benefits accrue outside the Valley on the lower Ohio and lower Mississippi as far south as the mouth of the Red River." Gordon R. Clapp, The TVA, An Approach to the Development of a Region, University of Chicago Press, 1955, pp. 17, 86.

[14]TVA Ann. Rep. 3 (1956).

[15]The Report of the President's Materials Policy Commission chose energy resources as a coordinative focus:

"The Commission is strongly of the opinion that the Nation's energy problem must be viewed in its entirety and not as a loose collection of independent pieces involving different sources and forms of energy....

"Ideally, the Nation should have a comprehensive energy policy and program which embraces all the narrower and more specific policies and programs relating to each type of energy and which welds these pieces together into a consistent and mutually supporting pattern with unified direction.... The multiple departments, bureaus, agencies and commissions which deal with separate energy problems must be less compartmentalized — more aware of the problems of coal *vis-à-vis* oil and gas; of waterpower as compared with lignite as a source of electricity; of the effects of pipeline regulation, for example, on oil imports from Venezuela....

"...[A] comprehensive understanding can be achieved only if one central agency of the Government has clear responsibility for assaying trends and policies throughout the entire energy field. The scrutiny will be effective only to the extent that the same agency carries out the broad analysis required to appraise the various specific energy policies and programs for which today responsibility is scattered among a score of agencies." 1 President's Materials Policy Commn., Resources for Freedom 129, 130 (1952). Elsewhere, the same Commission starts from water, instead of energy resources, and urges "integrated action in each major drainage basin" and endorses the proposal of a board of review to appraise costs and benefits of proposed basin development projects. *Id.* at 55.

[16]Charles McKinley, "The Valley Authority and Its Alternatives," *Amer. Polit. Sci. Rev.*, Vol. 44, p. 618 (1950).

[17]Subcommittee To Study Civil Works of the House Committee on Public Works, The Civil Functions Program of the Corps of Engineers, United States Army, 82d Cong., 2d Sess. 38, 39 (1952).

[18]The subcommittee added its opinion that "if Congress were to establish clearly four elements of policy, much of the apparent need for reorganization and for establishment of a review board would cease to exist. These four elements are (1) phases in water-resource development for which the Federal Government should assume some responsibility and some measure of the degree of that responsibility, (2) the place of local and State interests in the Federal development of water resources, (3) uniform standards for use by the executive branch for the measurement of the economic justification of water resource development projects, and (4) uniform standards for the allocation of costs in multiple-purpose projects and uniform criteria for the establishment of rates for the sale of products to recover such costs." *Id.* at 39.

Admirable as it would be to have these policy elements clarified, it seems most doubtful that such clarification would make the need for reorganization vanish.

[19] U.S. Comm. on Organization of the Executive Branch of the Government, Reorganization of the Department of the Interior 1 (1949).

[20] Sen. John C. McClellan and Rep. Carter Manasco, members of the commission, dissented and filed a spirited defense of the Corps of Engineers. *Id.* at 81-89.

[21] *Id.* at 15 *et seq.*

[22] *Id.* at 7 *et seq.*

[23] *Id.* at 38. The report was not entirely clear concerning the Federal Power Commission, but proposed "a study as to separation of certain general survey activities from the Federal Power Commission and their inclusion in this Department." *Id.* at 15.

[24] *Id.* at 2-4.

[25] *Id.* at 38.

[26] *Id.* at 2.

[27] *Id.* at 39.

[28] *Id.* at 6.

[29] *Id.* at 36.

[30] *Id.* at 37.

[31] *Id.* at 38.

[32] *Id.* at 54, 68.

[33] *Id.* at 79.

[34] 1 President's Water Resources Policy Commn., Report 49 (1950).

[35] *Ibid.*

[36] 1 *id.* at 52.

[37] 1 *id.* at 53.

[38] The Soil Conservation Service seems too newly active to be a "primary combatant," but too ambitiously involved in watershed projects to loom as merely a minor interest.

[39] Quoted in Missouri Basin Survey Comm., Missouri: Land and Water 25 (1953).

[40] *Id.* at 264. The commission split on exactly how the states should be related to the new organization. The majority proposed an advisory committee of governors.

[41] *Id.* at 8. See also *id.* at 265.

[42] *Id.* at 265.

[43] *Ibid.*

[44] *Id.* at 9, 11.

[45] *Id.* at 11-12.

[46] *Id.* at 213-46.

[47] *Id.* at 266.

[48] Hubert Marshall, "Organizing for river basin development," *Pub. Admin. Rev.,* Vol. 13, p. 273, 1953.

[49] 1 Temple Univ. Survey of Federal Reorganization, preface (1953).

[50] Exec. Order No. 10432, 18 Fed. Reg. 617 (1953), 5 U.S.C. §133z (Supp. III, 1956).

[51] 2 Temple Univ., *op. cit. supra* note 492, at 34.

[52] 2 *id.* at 35.

[53] 2 *id.* at 31.

[54] 2 *id.* at 29.

[55] 2 *id.* at 30.

[56] 2 *id.* at 36.

[57] 2 *id.* at 35.

[58] 2 U.S. Comm. on Organization of the Executive Branch of the Government, Water Resources and Power 10 (1955).

[59] 1 *id.* at 39.

[60] 1 *id.* at 38.

[61] 1 *id.* at 11-13.

[62] 1 *id.* at 66.

[63] 1 *id.* at 30.

[64] 1 *id.* at 31.

[65] 1 *id.* at 121.

[66] 1 *id.* at 120.

[67] 1 *id.* at 20-25. But see Commissioner Holifield's criticism, in his dissent to the commission's report. 2 *id.* at 10, 46-51.

[68] 1 *id.* at 25.

[69] 1 *id.* at 67.

[70] Albert L. Sturm, "Civil Functions of the Corps of Engineers — Relation to Military Mission," 3 U.S. Comm. on Organization of the Executive Branch of the Government, Task

Force Report on Water Resources and Power, 1473-1578 (1955). For the Task Force's own conclusions, see 1 *id.* at 190 *et seq.*

[71] 1 U.S. Comm. on Organization of the Executive Branch of the Government, *op. cit. supra* note 58, at 70-71.

[72] Presidential Advisory Comm. on Water Resources Policy, Water Resources Policy (1955).

[73] *Id.* at xi.

[74] *Id.* at 18.

[75] *Id.* at 19.

[76] *Ibid.*

[77] *Id.* at xi.

[78] *Id.* at 19.

[79] *Id.* at 18.

[80] *Id.* at 17.

[81] *Id.* at 18.

[82] *Id.* at 17.

[83] *Ibid.*

[84] *Id.* at xi, I. For a somewhat different list, also omitting power, see *id.* at 13.

[85] *Id.* at 2.

[86] *Ibid.*

[87] *Id.* at 3 *et seq.*

[88] *Id.* at 13.

[89] *Id.* at 13 *et seq.*

[90] *Id.* at 14.

[91] *Ibid.*

[92] *Id.* at 28 *et seq.*

[93] The Budget of the United States Government for the Fiscal Year Ending June 30, 1962 (1961), M 18.

[94] *Id.* at 65.

[95] S. 2549, introduced August 20, 1959, by Senator Murray and 30 co-sponsors. See Hearings before the Senate Committee on Interior and Insular Affairs on S. 2549, Proposed Resources and Conservation Act of 1960, 86th Cong., 2d Sess. (January 25, 26, 28 and 29, 1960). Senator Murray cited two sources for the bill's provisions: the recommendations of the President's Materials Policy Commission (Resources for Freedom, June 1952) and the Employment Act's delineation of the functions of the Council of Economic Advisers and the Joint Economic Committee (*id.* at 9 and 11). The executive branch opposed the bill, holding the proposed Council of Resources and Conservation Advisers unnecessary in view of the success of coordination through inter-agency machinery and through the Bureau of the Budget and Council of Economic Advisers (*id.* at 175-89). The provision for another joint congressional committee fell afoul of House Speaker Rayburn's prejudice against such committees; Senator Anderson calls this "the stumbling block on which [the] legislation failed." In Hearing cited *infra,* footnote 96, at 31.

[96] The 1960 and early 1961 commitments are quoted in Hearing before the Senate Committee on Interior and Insular Affairs on S. 239 and S. 1415, Resources and Conservation Act of 1961, 87th Cong., 1st Sess. (April 13, 1961), 17-19. Only the Democratic Advisory Council's Committee called for a joint congressional committee as well as a Council of Resources and Conservation Advisers in the Executive Office. S. 239 called for a joint committee; S. 1415, otherwise identical, omitted that provision.

[97] Quoted from Senator Kennedy's addresses of June 25 and 27, 1960. *Id.* at 18.

[98] 107 *Congressional Record* (daily ed.) 2414.

[99] The January 23 transfer of staff positions from the President's Special Assistant for Public Works Planning, located in the White House Office, to the Bureau of the Budget and Council for Economic Advisers "as an interim step toward" "developing the capabilities of the Bureau of the Budget and the Council of Economic Advisers in public works and resources matters" was tardily and indignantly discovered by members of Congress only on May 9, when the President requested supplemental appropriations for the Bureau of the Budget's "added public works and resources planning responsibilities" consequent on the transfer. The May 9th date of the request appeared to some on Capitol Hill to mean that the April 27th agreement to delete statement of resources and public works functions of the Bureau of the Budget from the proposed Executive Order was being evaded by. the administration. Hearings before a Subcommittee of the House Committee on Appropriations, General Government Matters, Department of Commerce, and Related Agencies Appropriations for 1962, Part 2, 87th Cong., 1st Sess., 516-44 (May 17, 1961); and Hearings before the Sub-

WATER RESOURCE DEVELOPMENT

committee of the Senate Committee on Appropriations on H.R. 7577, General Government
Matters, Department of Commerce, and Related Agencies Appropriations for 1962, 87th
Cong., 1st Sess., 730-47 (May 22, 1961). In the latter is reproduced the draft of the pro-
posed Executive Order, 731-35.

[100]Policies, Standards, and Procedures in the Formulation, Evaluation, and Review of
Plans for Use and Development of Water and Related Land Resources: prepared under the
direction of the President's Water Resources Council [sic], 87th Cong., 2d Sess., Senate
Document No. 97 (1962). The report and the President's approval of it "for application by
each of your Departments and by the Bureau of the Budget in its review of your proposed
programs and projects" are dated May 15, 1962. The President had assigned the task of
preparing such a report on October 6, 1961, to "the Secretaries who would comprise the
Water Resources Council under [the] proposed Water Resources Planning Act" (quoted from
the Secretaries' transmittal letter of May 15, 1962), i.e. the secretaries of the Interior
(chairman), the Army, Agriculture, and Health, Education and Welfare. The secretaries
proposed in their 1962 report, and the President agreed, that pending creation of the Water
Resources Council, the secretaries should proceed to joint consideration of "policies, standards, and procedures relating to cost allocation, reimbursement, and cost sharing, [topics
"not generally included" in the present report], and other subjects of mutual concern...."

[101]Joint Hearings of the Senate Committee on Interior and Insular Affairs and the Committee on Public Works on S. 2246, S. 1629, and S. 1778, Water Resources Planning Act of
1961, 87th Cong., 1st Sess. (July 26 and August 16, 1961) (with which is bound Hearing of
the Senate Committee on Interior and Insular Affairs on S. 1629, July 10, 1961), 27-29, 155f.
S. 1629, Water Resources Planning Act of 1961, was confined to a grants-in-aid program, to
be administered by the Secretary of the Interior. S. 1778, the Public Works Planning Act of
1961, was similarly confined, but called for administration by a water resources planning
board composed of agency representatives. Their introducers were respectively Senator
Anderson, chairman of the Interior and Insular Affairs Committee, and Senator Kerr, chairman of the Public Works Committee.

Although the administration's new position was developing in May and June, the ap-
proach by executive order was still alive as late as May 22 when Chairman Heller of the
Council of Economic Advisers testified, "We are to establish an advisory committee on
natural resources," and Budget Director Bell testified that whether the Council of Economic
Advisers or a separate natural resources unit in the Executive Office should advise the
President on issues of long-range resources development policy was an issue on which the
President "will find it necessary to reach a final conclusion before issuing the Executive
Order." Hearings, cited supra in footnote 99, of House Committee, 682, and of Senate
Committee, 740.

[102] Joint Hearings cited supra in footnote 101, at 141. Secretary of the Interior Udall described the bill as "really an outgrowth of the main recommendations of the Select Committee on Water Resources headed by Senator Kerr...." Hearings before a Subcommittee of
the Senate Committee on Public Works on S. 856, Delaware River Basin Compact, 87th
Cong., 1st Sess. (August 24, 1961), 40. The Kerr Committee's report, Senate Report No.
29, 87th Cong., 1st Sess. (January 30, 1961), advocated river basin planning and grants-in-
aid to the states for water resources planning. It made no recommendations on administrative and congressional organization, concluding against efforts to establish a joint congressional committee, and against any merger of water resource agencies; it sanguinely "believes
that the existing agencies are and will be able to accommodate themselves to carrying out the
improvements in the areas suggested herein and should do so." Id. at 69-71.

[103] 108 Congressional Record (daily ed.) 2828-31.

[104]One example of awkward committee arrangements is the Watershed Protection and
Flood Prevention Act of 1954, as amended in 1956. The Secretary of Agriculture is authorized to assist a local organization in constructing "works of improvement" having a total
capacity not exceeding 2500 acre-feet and involving a federal contribution of not over
$250,000. But "no appropriation shall be made for any plan" exceeding the acre-feet or dol-
lar figures cited "unless such plan has been approved by resolutions adopted by the appropriate committees of the Senate and House of Representatives: Provided, That in the case
of any plan involving no single structure providing more than 4000 acre-feet of total capacity the appropriate committees shall be the Committee on Agriculture and Forestry of the
Senate and the Committee on Agriculture of the House of Representatives and in the case of
any plan involving any single structure of more than 4000 acre-feet of total capacity the appropriate committees shall be the Committee on Public Works of the Senate and the Committee on Public Works of the House of Representatives, respectively." 68 Stat. 666 (1954),

as amended, 70 Stat. 1088, 16 U.S.C. §1002 (Supp. III, 1956). Undoubtedly, the introduction of the Committees on Public Works was designed not only to protect their jurisdictional claims, but to protect the Corps of Engineers against undue trespass on its claimed jurisdiction by the Department of Agriculture. See Hearings before a Subcommittee of the Senate Committee on Public Works on H.R. 8750, Amending the Watershed Protection and Flood Prevention Act, 84th Cong., 2d Sess. (1956). See also *supra* footnotes 95 and 102.

[105] Bureau of the Budget, Circ. No. A-47, Reports and Budget Estimates Relating to Federal Programs and Projects for Conservation, Development, or Use of Water and Related Land Resources (1952) and the proposed revision of Nov. 29, 1954, were attacked in S. Res. 281, 84th Cong., (1956), S. Res. 148, 85th Cong., (1957), and related hearings. Joint Hearings of the Senate Committees on Interior and Insular Affairs and on Public Works on S. Res. 281, Conservation and Development of Water Resources, 84th Cong., 2d Sess. (*passim* 1956). The project-evaluation standards agreed on by the *ad hoc* Cabinet committee and approved by the President May 15, 1962, replaced Budget Bureau Circ. A-47 and, according to Senator Anderson "conform in an important degree with those set forth in Senate Resolution 148." 108 *Congressional Record* (daily ed.), 7967.

[106] Robert E. Merriam, Assistant to the Director of the Budget, testified to the impasse on implementation of recommendations of the Presidential Advisory Committee on Water Resources Policy: "Then, too, I must say, Mr. Chairman, in all candor, that we discovered ourselves in this position: that as far as organizational matters are concerned, which is where the President's Advisory Committee thought it ought to start in its analysis of legislative proposals, we are faced with a situation, in which the chairmen of the two pertinent committees of the Senate ... have already indicated opposition to, as I understand it, at least 2 of the 3 specific organizational proposals that would require legislation, namely, that of a coordinator and a board of review." *Id*. at 64. Senator Murray earlier had commented on the President's Committee proposals: "It is manifest that the repetitive review which these processes would entail could succeed in bringing Federal participation in land and water-resources conservation and development to a complete standstill." *Id*. at 5.

[107] The proposal of a Missouri Basin Commission emerged from the Missouri Basin Survey Commission, in which six of the eleven commissioners were members of Congress. The persistent efforts of Sen. Kenneth McKellar, of Tennessee, to establish patronage rights over the Tennessee Valley Authority, even though successfully resisted, are suggestive of congressional expectations about "their" constituency areas.

[108] 1 U.S. Comm. on Organization of the Executive Branch of the Government, *op. cit. supra* note 70, at 74. See also 3 *id*. at 1395-1472, for the excellent article, Vawter, "Case study of the Arkansas-White-Red River Basin Inter-Agency Committee." A later treatment is Fox and Picken, The Upstream-Downstream Controversy in the Arkansas-White-Red Basins Survey, University of Alabama Press, 1960.

[109] Basin committees and commissions have been multiplying, but on a case-to-case basis, with varying organizational designs and without satisfactory relations to Washington. Several older inter-agency committees have continued (e.g., for the Columbia Basin, Pacific Southwest, Arkansas-White-Red Basins, the Missouri Basin and New England) and are related at the national level to the Inter-Agency Committee on Water Resources. In 1958 Congress established temporary river basin study commissions for Texas and the Southeast, each with six federal agency representatives, a presidentially appointed chairman from the area and eight (Texas) or four (Southeast) area residents normally nominated by the governor(s) and appointed by the President. The Delaware River Basin Compact, signed November 2, 1961, creates a commission on which one federal representative speaks for all federal agencies, and four governors represent their states; the Delaware Commission has extensive powers, ranging from planning, coordination and control to the design, construction and operation of water resource projects. Shortly before his term ended, President Eisenhower approved a "Guide for Federal Representatives on Interstate Compact Commissions" (transmitted to agencies by the Budget Bureau on January 6, 1961), instructing such representatives to report annually to the Budget Bureau, which was also made their channel for advice on policy and legal matters and for processing of compact amendments. Problems of basin organization are discerningly explored in Roscoe C. Martin *et al*., River Basin Administration and the Delaware, Syracuse University Press, 1960.

[110] The ideal conception of the relation between formulation by the executive branch and decision by Congress calls for the formulation of, say, three alternative programs costing different amounts; thereby Congress would actually choose, instead of merely ratify.

[111] See Wengert and Honey, "Program planning in the U.S. Department of the Interior, 1946-53," *Pub. Admin. Rev*., Vol. 14, p. 193, 1954.

[112]Growth of joint federal-state river basin commissions under federal statute (as in Texas and the Southeast) or under interstate compacts (as in the Delaware Basin and, awaiting congressional approval, in the Northeast) increase the need for a single spokesman for the federal government at the basin level, even though this further complicates the question of distribution of voting power on such joint commissions.

[113]Aeschylus, "The Suppliants," in 1 Whitney J. Oates and Eugene O'Neill, Jr., eds., 1 *The Complete Greek Drama*, Random House, 1938, p. 22.

[114]The focus should perhaps be stated somewhat differently. We now have a number of admirable descriptive accounts of political obstacles. See Arthur Maass, *Muddy Waters: The Army Engineers and the Nation's Rivers*, Harvard University Press, 1951; Norman Wengert, *Natural Resources and the Political Struggle*, Doubleday, 1955; Vincent Ostrom, *Water and Politics*, Haynes Foundation (Los Angeles), 1953. What we lack is a discerning analysis of ways to emerge from the long-standing political impasse.

HUBERT MARSHALL is Associate Professor of Political Science at Stanford University. He served on the Program Staff, Office of the Secretary, U.S. Department of the Interior, and his research has contributed to the field of natural resource administration.

Chapter 22

HUBERT MARSHALL

Rational Choice in
Water Resources Planning

IN EXAMINING THE LITERATURE of public administration we find two distinctive models of the decision-making process.[1] The first, an idealized description of how decisions ought to be made, emphasizes the rational capacities of man and the need for behavior realistically adapted to its ends.[2] Thus a decision is rational if the alternative chosen is an appropriate means for reaching a desired goal or maximizing a desired value. However we phrase it, the task of rational decision involves (1) identification of the value or values to be maximized, (2) ranking of values in terms of relative importance when values conflict or when more than one value is to be maximized, (3) identification of alternative possible courses of action, (4) determination of the consequences that follow from each alternative and (5) comparative evaluation of the consequences of the alternatives in terms of the value or values to be maximized. This is the orthodox concept of rationality. It minimizes costs, maximizes gains and is, of course, closely related to the concept of economic man.

The second model emphasizes decision making as it occurs in the real world of administrative practice.[3] Its proponents argue that values are difficult, if not impossible, to rank or even to identify with clarity and that ends and means are never quite so distinct as presupposed in

403

the orthodox model. It emphasizes the limitations of man's intellectual capacities and the inevitable inadequacy of information available to the decision-maker. In real life many alternatives are precluded by law or cannot be considered because of the opposition of powerful interests. Lack of time and resources makes it impossible to explore the consequences of alternative courses of action; in fact, important affected values, important policy alternatives and important outcomes are all neglected.

How, then, are decisions actually made? They are made by what Lindblom calls successive limited comparisons. That is, policy decisions normally differ only incrementally from earlier policies and are made by comparing alternative courses of action that differ only at the margin. It is assumed that a whole series of constraints ordinarily limits freedom of choice and that, within the area of freedom remaining, values and decision alternatives are not weighed so much as alternative decisions are "tried on" to see which "fits" best. As Lindblom says:

Somewhat paradoxically, the only practicable way to disclose one's relevant marginal values even to oneself is to describe the policy one chooses to achieve them. Except roughly and vaguely, I know of no way to describe — or even to understand — what my relative evaluations are for, say, freedom and security, speed and accuracy in governmental decisions, or low taxes and better schools than to describe my preferences among specific policy choices that might be made between the alternatives in each of the pairs.[4]

Despite the realism of the second model, the unattainable ideal of the orthodox model of rational choice is still of value. It stands as a warning against failure to explore relevant values and the consequences of decision alternatives. It cautions against too slavish an attention to alternatives that differ only marginally when a clean break with past policy may constitute the only truly viable course of action. Finally, it underscores the fact that knowledge — the product of research and investigation — reduces the area of uncertainty and hence, at least up to the point of psychological jamming, contributes to the likelihood of viable decision.

It is precisely here that economic analysis has so much to contribute to the decision-making process. In public policy formation, economic consequences rank high among the considerations that must be taken into account in appraising the consequences of decision alternatives. No matter which model one prefers, unbiased economic information, by rolling back the area of uncertainty, lends rationality and hence viability to the process of choice. In analyzing public investment decisions, for example, economic analysis can tell us much about the distribution of benefits and costs between regions and the nation and between income and other economic groups. It can tell us much about both the absolute and relative contributions of projects to real national income. It can cast useful light on conflicts over competing and mutually exclusive uses and on the economic motives of interest groups that play such an important role in the decision-making process. And it can tell us much about the true cost to the nation of raising funds through borrowing and taxation and about the consequences of various repayment policies. In short, we have much to gain in knowledge from market-oriented analyses of public expenditure and public revenue.

In real life, as we know, many decisions will not be based on market criteria at all. A variety of extramarket values may emerge as decisive criteria. Bargaining within and between organizations and interests may be substituted for the criteria of the market. Often the government may serve as little more than broker between competing interests. Political situations at times become so structured as to permit little recognition of economic consequences. Yet economic analysis is important precisely because it tells us something of the economic consequences of letting other criteria dominate the decision-making process. Thus when economic costs of choosing on the basis of noneconomic criteria become too great, the conflict between market-based criteria, on the one hand, and extramarket values and institutional factors affecting choice, on the other, will be highlighted with the consequence that economic considerations may be given greater weight in the final decision. Economic analysis thus contributes to the rationality of the decision-making process. For this reason the development, perfection and unbiased use of optimizing criteria are essential.

It has been argued so far that knowledge contributes to rational choice quite irrespective of our preference for decision-making models, whether we are concerned with ends or means or whether our responsibility involves minor administrative matters or policy at the highest levels. Moreover, it remains true whether we are committed in water resources development to criteria such as the maximization of real national income, to the regional redistribution of income implicit in notions such as the desirability of the development of the West or to such wholly noneconomic considerations as "the psychological value society derives from the development of a region."[5] This being the case, a key issue in the study of water resources decision making is the adequacy and reliability of the economic information available to those men in the executive and legislative branches of government who bear the ultimate responsibility for decision.

ADEQUACY OF THE DECISION-MAKER'S KNOWLEDGE

The history of the economic evaluation of federal water development projects goes back for a considerable period of time,[6] but is was not until after enactment of the Flood Control Act of 1936[7] that benefit-cost analysis came into common use. Today it is the standard means for evaluating federal water projects and is used (although with differences in procedure) by the Corps of Engineers, the Bureau of Reclamation and the Soil Conservation Service. Given congressional and public captivation by the symbols of the business world, it is difficult to exaggerate the importance of benefit-cost analysis in the decision-making process.

Reliability of Estimates of Direct Benefits

In light of the many accusations directed at rivers and harbors bills over the years, it is surprising that no congressional committee or central staff agency of the federal government, such as the Bureau of the Budget, has ever investigated the soundness of the field estimates of benefits which find their way into benefit-cost ratios. Two such investigations, however, have been undertaken by official, but independent, commissions of the federal government.

One check on the use to which benefit-cost analysis is being put was undertaken by the second Hoover Commission's Task Force on Water Resources and Power.

The Task Force investigation, conducted by F. A. Clarenbach, was directed principally to securing an answer to the question: "Are the estimates of agricultural flood damage and of land enhancement from flood reduction [made by the Corps of Engineers and the Soil Conservation Service] reasonable and dependable?"[8] The inquiry included an examination of the work sheets of the two agencies and interviews with agricultural economists, independent appraisers, bankers, farmers and others intimately acquainted with the productivity and value of agricultural land in a small number of basins in Kansas, Oklahoma and Texas on which the agencies had recently completed economic evaluations.

One area investigated comprised 10,430 acres of cultivated land along the Verdigris River, valued by the Corps at $94 per acre — a figure confirmed by Clarenbach. The Corps claimed many benefits had arisen from construction of a dam to protect this area. The most easily verified were direct crop damages and other direct damages to agriculture (including supplies, stock, equipment, land and improvements) which the Corps claimed would be averted if floods were checked by construction of the dam. Corps data, based on 1949 prices, indicated that in flood-free years the net earning power per acre of cultivated land was $8.28. For the same area, the Corps estimated average annual crop damages due to floods at $6.87 per cultivated acre. Other estimated annual (noncrop) losses to agriculture came to $0.97 per cultivated acre, making a total average annual loss of $7.84 per acre. If the Corps figures are accurate, these flood losses leave a residual net return to cultivated land of only $0.44 per acre. At a capitalization rate of 5 percent, this annual return would justify a land value of only $9 per acre. Nevertheless, actual land values, as noted, were approximately $94 per acre. The most reasonable explanation for the evident inconsistency in the Corps' appraisal results would seem to be that direct flood damages were significantly overestimated.

In his investigation of Soil Conservation Service projects Clarenbach found an even greater inflation of direct benefits. In one of these projects he found that net residual return to flood-free bottom land averaged less than the average annual direct flood damages to crops and pasture claimed by the SCS. What the SCS was saying was that farmers in this area annually lose more from flood damages than their land can produce even in a flood-free year! This is simply not believable.

Another field check of the validity of the estimates of benefits accruing from a federal water development project was made when the Missouri Basin Survey Commission investigated the Corps of Engineers' navigation program for the Missouri River. The Commission's report, published in 1953, gives no hint of the methodology used in checking the Corps' estimates. But where the Corps of Engineers claimed $11,795,000 annually as benefits from erosion control along the Missouri, the Commission estimated these benefits at $964,000.[9] The Corps estimated annual savings due to the navigation project at $6,699,000, while the Commission estimated them at $2,050,000. For erosion control, the Corps' estimates were 12 times larger than those of the Commission; for navigation the Corps' estimates were more than three times those of the Commission. For the navigation project as a whole the Corps calculated a benefit-cost ratio of 1.9 to 1; the Commission arrived at a ratio of 0.8 to 1. Hence it is clear why Clarenbach refers to the economic evaluation now conducted by the agencies as a "considerable accumulation of absurdities,"[10] why the Jones Subcommittee holds that benefit-cost analysis serves "only an expedient self-deception"[11] and why Ciriacy-Wantrup says that "benefit-cost analysis can be and has been distorted and abused."[12]

Obviously economic evaluation is not an exact science, and reasonable men may differ on the assumptions and estimates that find their way into benefit-cost ratios. But differences of the magnitudes cited here are not dictated by the inexactitude of engineering and economic science.[13] The result, of course, is to misinform high-level decision makers in both the executive and legislative branches, and the public at large.

An Appropriate Interest Rate

Use of an appropriate interest rate in economic evaluation is, of course, crucial. A rate that is too low may result in waste of resources on a project yielding less satisfaction to the community than would alternative uses. An excessively high rate, on the other hand, may leave water resources undeveloped as compared to other aspects of the nation's economy. In the past, federal construction agencies have used an interest rate approximating the cost of borrowing to the government.

Krutilla and Eckstein challenge this practice, holding that the true social cost of federal financing is not the rate at which individuals voluntarily lend to the government, but rather the interest rate that reflects the value of money to those from whom the necessary taxes are collected.[14] In their view, when government imposes taxes in order to finance public investment, it levies a compulsory loan or forced saving on the community, which releases resources for the public undertaking. The taxes inevitably lead to a reduction of consumption by households, to a decline in investment, or both.

The social cost of capital raised from foregone investment is clear:

it is equal to the foregone rate of return on private investment. On the consumption side, they argue that individuals borrow at rates ranging from 12 percent on automobile loans down to 5 percent (in the year in which they made their analysis) for home mortgages, and that these interest rates reflect the value of consumption to these individuals. Taxation reduces consumption, and hence the cost of this part of federal financing is equal to the interest rates that individuals face in borrowing. Without going into the elaborate analysis made by Krutilla and Eckstein, suffice it to say that they arrive at a social cost of federal financing of about 5.5 percent, a figure considerably in excess of the rate of interest currently used in economic evaluation.

Krutilla and Eckstein thus define social cost in terms of the opportunities foregone in the private sector of the economy, either because of curtailed investment or of curtailed consumption. Defining social cost in this way is surely open to criticism because it attaches greater weight to consumer sovereignty — to the private judgments of individuals — than it does to the collective wisdom of the community. It may lead to inadequate amounts of saving and investment for society as a whole. But these are value-laden arguments and of no concern here. What is pertinent is that the economists of neither the construction agencies, nor the Bureau of the Budget, nor the staffs of congressional committees have seen fit to raise the matter of interest rates for the explicit consideration of decision makers. The matter is not beyond the comprehension of intelligent laymen and it is an important issue of policy. To fail to call it to the attention of decision makers is to make rational choice impossible.

The Consideration of Relevant Alternatives

One of the requirements of rational choice is that decision makers have the opportunity to consider alternative proposals that may better accomplish specified goals or may accomplish them at less real cost. Unfortunately, the jurisdictional jealousies of the several construction agencies make dispassionate consideration of alternatives all but impossible. A few examples will illustrate the point.

On January 11, 1960, the Chief of Army Engineers recommended the construction of flood control and hydroelectric power projects on the Columbia River, estimated to cost well in excess of $1 billion.[15] Although the Columbia loops for a considerable distance into Canada, all projects recommended by the Chief of Engineers were located in the United States. John Krutilla has spent a considerable period of time in the Northwest studying the Corps' program and checking with Canadian authorities on a number of sites along the Columbia in Canadian territory. He agrees with the Corps that projects providing approximately 195 million acre-feet of additional usable storage are needed on the Columbia main stem.[16] But he feels that the most economic sites are located in Canada. Water storage in Canada would, of course, greatly increase flood protection and power output in the United States. A joint international commission, consisting of representatives of Canada and the United States, has proposed a plan for the cooperative development of the Columbia; but the Corps shows no evidence of seriously considering the Krutilla proposal that Canadian storage be developed first.

Other agencies are no more anxious than the Corps to have their objectives met by activities performed by others outside their areal jurisdictions. Thus the Bureau of Reclamation argues that there is no justification for comparing the relative merits of a proposed federal irrigation development with some other reclamation possibility, such as draining a swamp.[17] In any event, the moral must again be the same. Congress in its wisdom may wish to locate dams in the United States rather than in Canada or to irrigate arid land in the West rather than drain swamp land in the Southeast; but rational decision making requires that the costs of doing these things be made explicit. They cannot be made explicit if alternatives are not investigated.

Finally, a study by Gilbert White again underlines the urgent necessity for considering alternatives.[18] No doubt most Americans who give the matter any thought have been under the impression that the Corps of Engineers' flood control program has resulted in some net progress in protecting the nation from floods. In the 20 years following 1936, some $4 billion was spent on this program. Yet if White's data are correct, "mean annual flood losses increased over the period of record and at a rate that has not declined notably since 1936."[19] Even when we discount the rise in damage resulting from increases in the price level and from a rise in the frequency of disastrous storms, the record is one of rising damage. Apparently the Corps' failure to reduce the nation's flood hazard arises from the continuing invasion of floodplains by industry, commercial enterprises and residential housing. In one sense the Corps has become one of the nation's major real estate developers; even as engineering plans are announced to provide an incremental degree of protection, developers invade the floodplain and begin raising new structures that require an ever greater degree of protection.

It may be true that construction costs on sloping ground are so greatly in excess of those on the floodplain that economic efficiency dictates a national system of flood protection, perhaps even involving outlays in excess of those currently being made. But it is conceivable, also, that the costs of public flood protection are in excess of the extra cost involved in locating structures outside the floodplain or in making private adjustments to reduce flood losses, in which case economic efficiency would dictate a flood warning system or floodplain zoning, or both. But over the years the Corps has shown little interest in these alternatives.

There is much evidence to show that the President and Congress, generally speaking, have not been as uninformed on other issues of public policy as they have been on water resources development. On a host of issues (such as tariff and labor policies) well-organized interest groups make certain that decision makers hear arguments on both sides. On foreign and fiscal policy issues the tradition has developed for congressional committees to seek out testimony from disinterested university experts. Indeed, recent congressional inquiries on economic growth and the adequacy of our decision-making apparatus for foreign and military policy have actually assumed a scholarly cast.[20] The government may act wisely or unwisely on these issues, but at least it has the means of becoming informed.

No doubt Congress could become as well informed on water resources issues as on other great issues of public policy if it wished to. Surely there is nothing in the nature of the issues to make water resources more difficult to understand than monetary policy. But there is much evidence that Congress prefers to remain uninformed, to leave serious issues of water policy unexplored. Here a variety of circumstances, mainly in the form of institutional arrangements, conspire to aid those who favor water projects and make it difficult for their opponents to secure the necessary information or to mobilize for effective opposition. The result, of course, is inadequate exploration of water issues, false information, little awareness of alternatives and hence a lack of that knowledge which is essential to rational choice.

We turn now to an examination of some of the institutional arrangements that make rational decision difficult in the water development field.

THE BALANCE OF INTERESTS

John Adams once wrote: "The nation which will not adopt an equilibrium of power must adopt a despotism. There is no other alternative."[21] This was the prevailing doctrine of our constitutional period, and its hold on our minds has continued undiminished. We conceive government to be an automatic machine, regulated by the balancing of competing interests. This image of politics, of course, is closely related to the official image of the economy; in both an equilibrium is achieved by the pulling and hauling of many interests, no one of which is powerful enough to dominate the scene. In politics the fragmentation of power necessary to achieve balance is secured by separation of powers which divides authority between legislative, executive and judicial branches, by federalism which divides power geographically and by seeing to it that no sector of the economy — business, labor or agriculture — has sufficient power to dominate the government. With power thus divided, liberty prevails.

The essential concept behind the theory of balance is that action cannot take place until something approaching a consensus has been reached. No transitory majority will have the sustained strength to control the several branches of government whose assent is necessary before a proposal becomes policy. In the 1900's many writers have dwelt on an additional advantage of balance; its contribution to rational choice. The role of political parties in this respect has long been recognized. Issues are raised, arguments are put forth, the opposition's contentions are analyzed and criticized, fallacious arguments are exposed, fact-finding is encouraged — and in the end the nation is better informed. We now recognize that interest groups, including the three branches of government, participate in the political process and contribute perhaps more than the parties themselves. So much has this idea appealed to political scientists, and so powerful do the groups seem in actual case studies of decision making, that group studies of one kind or another have all but dominated postwar scholarship in the field of politics.

The contribution of group conflict to rational choice seems very real indeed. The Farm Bureau and National Farmers Union dissect each others' proposals. Labor unions and the National Association of Manufacturers debate the right to work. The United Steelworkers of America and the steel industry provide data in support of their positions on wage increases, fringe benefits and work rules. Organized small business, importers, exporters, independent retailers, the chain stores, the National Association for the Advancement of Colored People and a thousand other organizations and interests contribute to the process. No one believes this great debate is carried on solely for our edification, nor need one believe that the information presented is unbiased. But there is considerable evidence that the public is at least partially enlightened by the process of mutual criticism, and congressmen report that they gain much information and insight available in no other way.

But where is there evidence of countervailing power in the field of water resources? Where are the organized groups supported by effective staff research who stand ready to criticize, point out and defend alternatives or argue for no program at all? Opposition exists, to be sure, to public power and river navigation programs. But even here the opposition is based largely on generalities, since the construction agencies provide no opportunity for scrutiny of the manner in which benefit-cost ratios are calculated. One may oppose public power on principle, but there is little chance to criticize water projects on a strictly economic basis. As Senator Paul Douglas once lamented, "Any member who tries to buck the system is only confronted with an impossible amount of work in trying to ascertain the relative merits of a given project."

Thus we have the comparatively unusual situation in which the absence of countervailing power places great power in the hands of the executive agencies and congressmen who, as we shall see, have so much to gain by serving local interests. Nor does the balancing power of the President have much effect. In his first six years and eight months in office, President Eisenhower vetoed 145 acts of Congress, and his veto in each case was amazingly sustained. His 146th veto was of a public works appropriation bill, and this veto was overridden with almost no debate.[22] No president will lightly challenge Congress on a water resources measure.

Moreover, presidents have had difficulty in developing independent information on water projects. When the National Resources Planning Board was abolished by Congress in 1943, the President was forbidden to transfer its function of reviewing water projects to any other executive agency.[23] Thus we face a situation in which the absence of countervailing power outside the government and the weakness of executive authority make it difficult for anyone outside the construction agencies to form an independent appraisal of the merits of individual projects.

THE REPRESENTATIVE'S ROLE

Why is it that Congress evidences so little desire for information that would make objective rationality possible? Perhaps a good way to begin is with Burke's famous Speech to the Electors of Bristol (1774). Parliament, he said:

... is not a *congress* of ambassadors from different and hostile interests; which interests each must maintain, as an agent and advocate, against other agents and advocates; but parliament is a *deliberative* assembly of *one* nation, with *one* interest, that of the whole; where, not local purposes, not local prejudices ought to guide but the general good, resulting from the general reason of the whole.[24]

In this statement Burke was speaking of two analytically separable roles that the legislator may play. The first, which we can call his style of representation, deals with the how of his representation. Does he come to the legislative body as an ambassador, carrying instructions from the represented that dictate his every move? Or does he come empowered to use his own judgment in a deliberative assembly? These are respectively the roles of "delegate" and "trustee."

The second analytically separable role, which we can call his focus, deals with whom or what he represents. Does he come to serve the interests of his district, or the general good of the entire nation?

Professor Eulau and a group of associates published in 1959 the results of a series of interviews with state legislators which are of interest in this connection.[25] Asking state legislators what they conceived their roles to be, he found that trustees outnumbered delegates in the ratio of about 4 to 1. This is not surprising in view of the ethically higher role of the trustee. But the large number of trustees was attributable to another factor as well: many citizens lack the information to give intelligent instructions; the representative is unable to discover what his constituents want; preferences remain unexpressed; or interest groups are so nearly equal in power that the representative perforce must use his own judgment.

Turning to the focus of representation, he found that district-oriented representatives outnumbered state-oriented representatives in the ratio of 2 to 1. Interestingly enough a great many trustees were district oriented; but no delegate was state oriented.

While Professor Eulau was not concerned with public works legislation, it is possible to surmise the impact of such legislation on the role orientation of the representative. As indicated, all of Eulau's delegates were district oriented, and it takes no great effort to imagine how such a representative, in Congress, would vote on public works legislation. His trustees were about equally divided between district orientation and statewide orientation. But many of his trustees had a statewide orientation only because they had no instructions from constituents, because legislative matters were so complex that constituents could not make up their own minds or because important interest groups were approximately balanced in power. But a public works bill gives the trustee no such freedom.

The issue here is clear. Increased local economic activity and other advantages flow directly from the construction of veterans hospitals, military installations or flood control or irrigation works, while the tax burden is distributed throughout the nation and is largely masked in the public mind by taxation for defense and other items that loom large in the annual budget. While the taxes are largely masked, the project is conspicuous. Finally, organized local interests will not ordinarily divide on a public works bill and cancel each other's effective power. The district will ordinarily be united, and the trustee of statewide orientation will of necessity become a delegate on this issue. And, of course, all delegates are district oriented. Only the representative who plays the trustee role out of ethical conviction will use his own judgment on a matter of this sort; and he, like Burke, may pay for it by retirement from office.[26]

Necessity for Delegate Role

The legislator's need to remain district oriented on matters of direct concern to his constituents is insured by the nature of the American party system. A realistic examination of Congress reveals that its members, *vis-à-vis* the national parties, constitute separate islands of power. Each member is in fact responsible not through his party but directly to his constituency. He is nominated by securing a modest number of signatures on a petition and winning a primary election in which he raises his own campaign funds. Having won the primary, he enters the general election under the banner of his party no matter how widely his views diverge from those of the party leadership or how much independence he will show in Congress if elected. In the general election he must again raise campaign funds, ordinarily with only nominal assistance from the party's national committee or congressional campaign committees. The general election won, he enters Congress beholden to no one but the electorate of his constituency and the local interests which financed his campaign or otherwise delivered the vote. No national party organ or leadership group in Congress commands his allegiance or has the power to control his vote. No mechanism exists to compel or even to direct his attention to the national interest. Power is fragmented, party cohesion is minimal and party responsibility all but nonexistent.

Indeed, no single group speaks continuously for the party or can claim to represent it; our parties, in fact, are an odd confederation of state and local parties onto which have been grafted such weak or transient institutions as the national party committee and the quadrennial convention. Accordingly, political scientists characterize American parties variously as weak, decentralized or irresponsible. But however the parties may be characterized, the result is a Congress from which the emerging legislation represents not a coherent party view of the national interest but a summation of the parochial views of a large number of constituency interests.

Whatever the defects of our party arrangements, there is much to suggest that they mirror rather accurately the diversity of our national economic and social structure, our sectional differences and the federal nature of our governmental system. This being the case, it seems likely that reforms will be slow in coming. Nevertheless, the literature of political science is filled with speculation as to how our party system might be modified in order to make the parties more effective instruments of our national purposes and needs.

Feasibility of National Party Control

Many of the reforms suggested would affect minor institutional arrangements and, except in concert, would not likely have a dramatic impact on the parochial outlook of senators and representatives. Short of adoption of the British parliamentary system (which is no longer seriously proposed), reforms which seem adequate to the task are national party control of the nominating process and of campaign finance. In Great Britain, candidates are nominated by local party associations, but before the candidate's name is placed on the ballot he must be approved by the central organ of the party. In this way the candidate's loyalty is ensured and he is made subject to party discipline in the House of Commons.

A similar arrangement in the United States might require the candidate to secure approval of the party national committee before he entered the party primary. Without doubt such a reform would weaken the primary system by restricting the range of choice available to the voter, but the primary is already under some attack. The fact must be faced that one cannot have simultaneously the advantages of party centralization and unmitigated local control.

The second reform — national party control of campaign finance — could come in several forms. In its more extreme form, Congress might simply require that all campaign contributions for Senate and House contests be sent to the national committees of the respective parties to be reallocated by them at their discretion to the parties' candidates throughout the country. Such a reform would have a revolutionary effect on American politics, releasing the congressman from bondage to local interests by placing him under heavy obligation to the central organ of his party. True, neither the congressman nor his

national committee could ignore his constituency interests since the
voters could always turn to the opposition party, but the shift in power
relationships would be substantial. A more moderate step in the same
direction might be achieved by the provision of federal appropriations
to the national committees to be used at their discretion (with strict
accounting) in supporting congressional campaigns or by offering federal income tax credits to those who contribute to the national committees. Either plan would again greatly strengthen the national party organization and in some degree compel the congressman to balance
national interests and needs against those of local interests.[27]

Even to discuss reforms of this sort is to indicate the unlikelihood
of their adoption. Social change comes slowly, and the American people
must evidence considerably more awareness of the weaknesses of their
party system before change will be supported. Over a considerable
period of time, the decline of sectionalism, the nationalization of many
political issues such as welfare, housing and education, and the growing
importance of foreign policy may slowly wreak changes in our party
structure. In the meantime we must look elsewhere for the means of
introducing more rationality into the decision-making process.

ORGANIZATIONAL LOYALTY

To the constituency orientation of the legislature and the absence of
countervailing power in militating against rational decision, we must
add the phenomenon of organizational loyalty. It is a commonplace in
the study of the natural history of organizations to note that members
of a group tend to identify with that group. Usually in business and
government organizations the values of the group are initially imposed
on the individual through the exercise of authority; but in time the values become internalized and are incorporated into the psyche of the individual. He acquires a loyalty to the organization that automatically
guarantees decisions consistent with the values and goals of the group.
Indeed we may say that, through internalization of organization values,
the participant in an organization in time acquires an "organization
personality" distinct from his personality as an individual.

This loyalty to the organization has two analytically distinct facets:
it may involve an attachment to the service goals of the organization,
that is, the goals the organization was created to serve; or it may involve an attachment to the organization itself, to its survival and growth
and hence to the power, prestige, income and status of its members.
Both forms of loyalty exist in all organizations and at least in some degree in all their members; but it is no great task to identify organizations or even individuals in whom one form of loyalty predominates
over the other. Examples of the commitment to substantive objectives
are seen in the Trotskyite movement, the Prohibitionist Party, and in a
number of minor religious sects which have preferred to remain "pure"
at the expense of organizational growth. Yet in far more numerous

instances — our major political parties are examples — we find individuals behaving as though the organization's welfare were the primary goal to be served.[28] This, rather than the conflict of service goals, is the principal cause of the inter-unit competition and wrangling which characterizes so much of organizational life.

Viewed in one fashion, there is little conflict between service goals and organization welfare in the water resources field. The larger the agency and its program, the more it is likely to accomplish. On the other hand, if efficiency is an aspect of service goals (as clearly required by the Flood Control Act of 1936), the conflict is real indeed. We are forced to conclude from our earlier examination of agency behavior that the organizations have in part become ends in themselves. As we have seen, benefit-cost ratios are unreliable, and alternative means of achieving agency goals remain unexplored if they conflict with organizational growth and survival. What we have here is administrative behavior conditioned heavily by loyalty to the organization. It has the desirable effect of imbuing agency personnel with enthusiasm and commitment; but its cost is opportunistic behavior at the expense of the public purpose the agency was created to serve.

THE PROSPECTS FOR RATIONAL CHOICE

It has been argued in the preceding sections that rationality in water development decision making in the federal government is hampered by (1) the near absence of countervailing pressures, (2) the constituency rather than national orientation of Congress and (3) the commitment to bureaucratic ends which are an inevitable accompaniment of organizational life. It has been argued further that little can be accomplished by way of reform through the conscious manipulation of institutions to create countervailing pressures or to alter the constituency orientation of congressmen. However, the gradual nationalization of life in the United States may ultimately strengthen our central party organizations to the point where local concerns are to an increasing degree subordinated to the national interest. In this final section, attention will be focused on two developments which, if they occur, could do much to undercut organizational loyalty and mitigate its undesirable effects. The first deals with the professional identifications and loyalties of economists and engineers in the government service; the second concerns possible shifts in the location of decision-making authority in the national government.

Professionalization

In the preceding section we saw how loyalty to the organization limits the perspective of the employee, making it possible for him to reach decisions essentially opportunistic in nature without a sense of personal conflict. Barnard[29] and Simon[30] have developed the concept of the "zone of acceptance" within which the employee will permit the organization to dictate his behavior. The breadth of the zone depends, of course, upon a variety of factors including salary, status, opportunity for promotion and psychological identification both with the organization and its goals. The greater these inducements, the greater the zone of acceptance. But there are limits to the zone of acceptance beyond which the individual will not behave organizationally. At this point competing values and identifications assert themselves, the individual resists authority and the existing equilibrium between employee and organization is disturbed. In the adjustments which follow, the organization may alter its demands upon the individual, adjusting to his values, or the individual may withdraw from the organization.

An important competing identification which may limit the zone of acceptance is the employee's commitment to the professional standards that are relevant to his activities. To the extent that they exist, the employee will desire to adhere to the standards of craftsmanship and technical knowledge pertinent to his profession, and in doing so he may be motivated by the powerful compulsion of professional group opinion. To ignore this compulsion may entail loss of professional status or self-respect, or both. One corrective, then, for the abuse of economic analysis or the unwillingness to consider project alternatives which are not organizationally desired is to so strengthen the professional identification of agency economists and engineers that efforts to impose organizational values at the expense of professional standards will fall outside the individual's zone of acceptance. Obviously much will depend upon the strength of the employee's professional commitment; and this in turn will depend upon (1) the degree of professional consensus regarding technical standards and (2) success of the profession in communicating this consensus to practitioners as well as generalist decision makers.[31]

If this line of reasoning is correct, the obvious need in strengthening rational decision making in the water field is to counterbalance organizational loyalty with professional loyalty. Progress, of course, has been made in reaching professional agreement on principles of economic evaluation. Publication of the Green Book[32] was a milestone in the development of professional standards, and in the brief decade after its appearance there was a greater contribution to the theory of economic evaluation than in any comparable period. While this outpouring of comment is not indicative of complete consensus on matters of theory, still it is certain to have great influence in strengthening the professional identification of agency economists. If the attention to project evaluation continues, as now seems certain, there can be little question but that it will ultimately have an influence on agency practice.

But the slow osmotic process by which a developing professional consensus penetrates agency practice may take needlessly long. Since economic analysis is relevant to human affairs only as it becomes a basis for social action, it becomes an obligation of the profession to do what it can to see that agency practices keep pace with developing theory.

But on what matters could economists, operating through professional associations, agree in sufficient degree to justify making statements on acceptable theory and practice? Given the economists' commitment to formal optimization, there should be no difficulty in insisting upon (1) full development of relevant information, (2) full consideration of alternative means of achieving project goals, (3) objectivity and reliability in estimation of benefits and costs and (4) planning of projects with the objective of maximizing their contribution to national income except where clearly stated goals involving income distribution or extra-market values dictate the contrary. Perhaps, also, agreement could be reached on more specific matters such as appropriateness of counting secondary benefits during periods of full employment and a defensible interest rate and period of analysis. A variety of other matters suggest themselves upon a few moments' reflection.

Precedent for professional society activity of this sort exists, of course, in a number of fields. Some professional associations in the natural sciences prescribe specifications for materials, and some have adopted resolutions on matters which affect them but range far from their fields of professional competence. The cost accountants have been active in urging their preferred systems on the Internal Revenue Service; and the American Statistical Association has played an important role in advising several government agencies on appropriate professional practice.[33]

In 1949 the Engineers Joint Council, representing five national engineering societies,[34] appointed a National Water Policy Panel and charged it with developing an official position on water policy for the engineering profession. When President Truman appointed the President's Water Resources Policy Commission in 1950, the Engineers Joint Council authorized its National Water Policy Panel to cooperate with the new commission and "to present to it, on behalf of Engineers Joint Council, specific proposals for a desirable revision of National Water Policy."[35] The panel went about its work with the assistance of 10 committees composed of some 78 experts representing mainly the engineering profession, as well as geology, agricultural economics and wildlife. Some months later the panel submitted its report to the President's commission and subsequently published it for general distribution under the title Principles of a Sound National Water Policy.

Whatever one thinks of the generally conservative cast of the panel's recommendations, the fact remains that five engineering associations played a responsible role in formulating and seeking adoption of what they conceived to be appropriate standards for the planning and operation of federal water development projects. In their endorsement of value-impregnated policies, the engineers went far beyond the suggestions made in the paragraphs above and perhaps in doing so undermined the effectiveness of their presentation. Whatever one thinks of the substance of the Engineers Joint Council recommendations, it can hardly be denied that professional agreement on the few relatively value-free matters listed above would be hard for Congress and professional personnel in the public service to ignore.

Strengthening the Executive Office of the President

We have seen in the sections above that the institutionalized individual develops a personal interest in organizational success and so identifies with organizational goals that in making decisions he takes into account only a limited set of values. As Simon put it, "... it is unsound to entrust to the administrator responsible for a function the responsibility for weighing the importance of that function against the importance of other functions."[36] Clearly the only person who can approach competently the task of weighing the relative importance of two functions is one who is responsible for both or for neither. Thus no agency is psychologically free to balance objectively its financial needs against the financial needs of other agencies. And the need is therefore universally recognized for a centrally located budget agency free of the biases certain to afflict an operating agency. More specifically, and in terms of water development programs, final authority in the executive branch over program and budget should be located in the Executive Office of the President where (1) there is no vested interest in organizational survival or growth and (2) the need for water development can be weighed objectively against the need for all other federal programs with some degree of freedom from the localized constituency pressures found in Congress.

Yet in practice economic evaluations are made by the construction agencies and are reviewed by the Budget Bureau only for conformance to loosely prescribed procedure. The consequence is that the expenditure of billions of dollars for water projects is being justified by economic evaluations that receive no effective review whatsoever, despite the evidence of bias in their calculation. Importance of the benefit-cost ratio in securing congressional authorizations cannot be overestimated. Projects with unfavorable ratios are never authorized by Congress, and those with favorable ratios generally receive favorable consideration unless — as rarely happens — local interests are opposed. Given our commitment to the symbols of the market economy and the concept of investment and return, it is simply a fact that a favorable benefit-cost ratio has a soporific effect upon Congress and the public which all but transfers final authority over decision making to the construction agencies. Considering the importance of the benefit-cost ratio in the decision-making process, one would think that the Bureau of the Budget would check on reliability of agency estimates of direct benefits and costs and would prohibit the very considerable dependence upon secondary benefits that has developed in the Bureau of Reclamation.

But Congress prohibited the Bureau of the Budget from assuming the functions of the defunct National Resources Planning Board, and in the ensuing years the Bureau has not found the means or presidential support for checking on the validity of the estimates of benefits and costs initially made in the field. It is an interesting sidelight indeed on our attitudes toward government that neither the President nor Congress has permitted expenditure of money by an executive agency without pre-audit and post-audit of the integrity and legality of the expenditure. Yet the President and Congress have allowed themselves to remain wholly at the mercy of the economic calculations of agencies with an obvious interest in the outcome.

But, it may be argued, the Budget Bureau controls the appropriations requests sent to Congress, and the President can veto both authorization or appropriations bills. Yet these are slender reeds upon which to lean. First, the President himself is at the mercy of the economic evaluations of the agencies and hence may have little objective basis for opposing authorizations or appropriations. Second, Congress often increases water resources appropriations over the President's requests.[37] And third, Congress shows no hesitation in overriding presidential vetoes of authorization and appropriation bills.

Benefit-cost analysis thus assumes a crucial nature. Congress will pit its judgment against the President's on matters of authorization or appropriation so long as it can argue that the return will exceed the investment. But given the symbolic importance of the investment-return concept, Congress will not lightly challenge the President over projects with unfavorable ratios. Therefore the benefit-cost ratio, which has been a powerful instrument in the hands of the construction agencies, can be turned into a powerful instrument for rationality in decision if only the President can control its use and insist upon its reliability.

Over the years many proposals have been made to reorganize federal water agencies to improve the quality of decision making. The most frequent proposal has been to consolidate the Corps of Engineers with the Bureau of Reclamation and place the unified agency in the Department of the Interior or a new department of natural resources (or conservation). Others would blanket part or all of the nation with valley authorities.[38] Either proposal would constitute an advance toward true multiple-purpose planning because all present agencies emphasize one or at most two functions at the expense of others, and either probably would promote in some degree the consideration of relevant alternatives since inter-agency competition would be reduced.

But neither proposal would eliminate organizational loyalty nor promote the full consideration of alternatives, especially where the latter might lead to floodplain zoning, or a flood warning system, or otherwise obviate the need for construction. Moreover, for all its desirability, Congress has seemed unwilling to approve wholesale reorganization of executive agencies barring the accidental concurrence of an extremely influential President and a catastrophic flood. We may get one or the other in the years ahead, but statistically the chances of acquiring them simultaneously are not great.

This leads us to return to the need for strengthening the Executive Office of the President in its control over the several water development agencies. The advantage of this approach is that it can be accomplished gradually and without the fanfare certain to attend any effort at wholesale reorganization. Through gradual strengthening of the Bureau of the Budget and the concomitant imposition of regulations governing the calculation of benefit-cost ratios, presidential control would be increased. Field checks on the reliability of estimates of benefits and costs could be instituted, and the construction agencies could be forced to consider alternative means of achieving project goals. A determined President could insist upon a loyal Chief of Engineers, he could forbid the Corps to transmit to Congress reports not in accord with his program and he could impound appropriations in excess of his budget requests.

No President will lightly embark on such a program. After all, if he opposes subsidy, he will find it in larger amounts and more conspicuously visible in the agricultural price-support program and in the Post Office. In light of the amounts of money involved, a President may elect to trade water resources projects for congressional support of his major foreign and domestic policies.

But this only recognizes the normal difficulties besetting any attempt at governmental reform. Given a determined President, the advantage of strengthening the Executive Office lies in the fact that it cannot be thwarted so readily by Congress. In this reform and in the development and expression of professional consensus on economic evaluation lie the major hopes for improving the rationality of water resource decisions.

FOOTNOTES

[1] Since administrators often make policy or advise on policy, and since legislators often decide matters of procedure, no attempt is made here to distinguish between policy making and decision making.

[2] For an extended discussion of rational choice in administrative situations see Herbert A. Simon, Administrative Behavior, Macmillan, 1951, pp. 45-78.

[3] Charles E. Lindblom, "The science of 'muddling through,'" Public Admin. Rev., Vol. 19, No. 2, pp. 79-88, 1959; John M. Pfiffner, "Administrative rationality," Public Admin. Rev., Vol. 20, No. 3, pp. 125-32, 1960.

[4] Lindblom, op. cit., p. 82.

[5] William E. Folz, discussion of papers included in Water Resources and Economic Development of the West: Benefit-Cost Analysis, reproduced by the Committee on the Economics of Water Resources Development of the Western Agricultural Economics Research Council, p. 30.

[6] R. J. Hammond, Benefit-Cost Analysis and Water-Pollution Control, Food Research Institute, Stanford Univ., 1960, pp. 3-16.

[7] The act provided that "...the Federal Government should improve or participate in the improvement of navigable waters or their tributaries, including the watersheds thereof, for flood-control purposes if the benefits to whomsoever they may accrue are in excess of the estimated costs...." 49 Stat. 1570, 33 U.S.C. Sec. 701a (1952).

[8] Fred A. Clarenbach, "Reliability of estimates of agricultural damages from floods" in U.S. Commission on Organization of the Executive Branch of the Government, Task Force Report on Water Resources and Power, U.S. Govt. Print. Off., 1955, Vol. 3, p. 1278.

[9] U.S. Missouri Basin Survey Commission, Missouri: Land and Water, U.S. Govt. Print. Off., 1953, p. 122.

[10] Clarenbach, op. cit., p. 1298.

[11] U.S. Congress, House, Committee on Public Works, Economic Evaluation of Federal Water Resource Development Projects, U.S. Govt. Print. Off., 1952, p. 51, (82d Cong., 2d Sess. House Committee Print No. 24).

[12] S. V. Ciriacy-Wantrup, "Benefit-cost analysis and public resource development," Jour. Farm Econ., Vol. 37, No. 4, p. 676, 1955.

[13] The writer is aware of no truly independent investigation which supports the validity of

the estimates of direct benefits made by the Corps of Engineers, the Bureau of Reclamation or the Soil Conservation Service for any project in the United States. For an example of the inflation of direct benefits secured through the overestimation of the frequency of serious floods see Ray K. Linsley, "Engineering and economics in project planning," in Water Resources and Economic Development of the West, Conference Proceedings of the Committee on the Economics of Water Resources Development of the Western Agricultural Economics Research Council, Berkeley, 1960, p. 75. (Chap. 7, this volume.)

[14] John V. Krutilla and Otto Eckstein, Multiple Purpose River Development, Johns Hopkins Press, Baltimore, 1958, pp. 78-130.

[15] New York Times, Jan. 12, 1960, p. 17.

[16] John V. Krutilla, Sequence and Timing in River Basin Development, Resources for the Future, Inc., Washington, 1960.

[17] "Comments and Recommendations for Revision of Bureau of the Budget Circular No. A-47," a memorandum attached to a letter from Ralph A. Tudor, Acting Secretary of the Interior, to Joseph M. Dodge, Director, Bureau of the Budget, Jan. 14, 1954.

[18] Gilbert F. White, et al., Changes in Urban Occupance of Flood Plains in the United States, Univ. of Chicago, 1958 (Department of Geography Research Paper No. 57).

[19] Ibid., p. 3.

[20] U.S. Congress, Joint Economic Committee, Federal Expenditures Policy for Economic Growth and Stability, papers submitted by panelists appearing before the Subcommittee on Fiscal Policy and Hearings before the Subcommittee on Fiscal Policy, 85th Cong., 1st Sess., 1957 (U.S. Govt. Print. Off., 1957 and 1958) and U.S. Congress, Senate, Committee on Government Operations, Organizing for National Security, Hearings before the Subcommittee on National Policy Machinery, 86th Cong., 2d Sess. (U.S. Govt. Print. Off., 1960), parts 1-7, pp. 1-1001.

[21] John Adams, Discourses on Davila, Russell and Cutler, Boston, 1805, p. 92.

[22] New York Herald Tribune (Paris ed.), Sept. 11, 1959, p. 1.

[23] 57 Stat. 170 (1943).

[24] The Works of Edmund Burke, C. C. Little and J. Brown, Boston, 1839, Vol. II, pp. 12-13.

[25] Heinz Eulau, et al., "The role of the representative: some empirical observations on the theory of Edmund Burke," Amer. Polit. Sci. Rev., Vol. 53, No. 3, pp. 742-56, 1959.

[26] Lord Bryce said of American legislators: "They are like the Eastern slave who says 'I hear and obey.'" The American Commonwealth, Macmillan, 1918, Vol. II, p. 272.

[27] It would be an illusion to suppose that a greatly strengthened national leadership for our parties would be immune to local pressures. But politicians with an essentially national constituency are able to balance interest against interest and in doing so gain a measure of freedom to play the role of trustee with a nationwide orientation. Surely this is true of the American presidency and most political scientists would agree that it has been a consequence of central party control in Great Britain.

[28] For the development of this idea as applied to the business firm see Robert A. Gordon, Business Leadership in the Large Corporation, The Brookings Institution, Washington, 1945. At page 306 he says: "Power thus secured increases with the size of the firm. Here lies an important explanation of the tendency of many large firms to become larger, even if sometimes the profitability of such expansion is open to serious question. The working of the power urge in this respect is reinforced by the tendency of businessmen to identify themselves with their enterprises. Expansion is desired for the enhancement of personal power and also because of the satisfaction of being associated with a powerful organization."

[29] Chester I. Barnard, The Functions of the Executive, Harvard University Press, Cambridge, 1938, pp. 167-70. Barnard uses the term "zone of indifference."

[30] Herbert A. Simon, Administrative Behavior, Macmillan, 1951, pp. 131-33, 204.

[31] For two case studies illustrating the conflict for economists between organizational and professional loyalty see "Indonesian Assignment" in Harold Stein, ed., Public Administration and Policy Development, Harcourt, Brace and Co., 1952, pp. 53-61; and Corinne Silverman, The President's Economic Advisers, University of Ala. Press, 1959, 18 p.

[32] Subcommittee on Benefits and Costs, Federal Inter-Agency River Basin Committee, Proposed Practices for Economic Analysis of River Basin Projects, U.S. Govt. Print. Off., 1950.

[33] See, for example, "The attack on the cost of living index" in Stein, op. cit., pp. 773-853.

[34] American Society of Civil Engineers, American Society of Mining and Metallurgical Engineers, The American Society of Mechanical Engineers, American Institute of Electrical Engineers and American Institute of Chemical Engineers.

³⁵National Water Policy Panel of Engineers Joint Council, Principles of a Sound National Water Policy, New York, 1951, p. 5. The panel was quite certain of the propriety of making recommendations to the government, holding that "many members of the engineering profession are technically skilled in the field of water projects, and — in the aggregate — professional engineers represent the group which has the primary knowledge and economic perspective in the field of water resources. Moreover, they are by no means without sociological instinct and experience. It is natural, therefore, that the organized engineering profession should be extremely sensitive to any matter of confusion, waste, or conflicting policy in this field, and that others should turn to that profession for assistance in the analysis of our water problem as a whole and for recommendations for the creation of a comprehensive national water policy to govern future operation." *Ibid.*, p. 1.

³⁶Simon, *op. cit.*, p. 215.

³⁷This is easily done in the case of the Corps of Engineers since the Corps publishes annually in November or December (a month before the President's budget is released) "a detailed statement of the amount that can be profitably expended in the next succeeding fiscal year for new work on all projects." This estimate may be several times the size of the President's budget request, so it is an easy matter for Congress to appropriate more than the President desires. See Arthur Maass, Muddy Waters: The Army Engineers and the Nation's Rivers, Harvard University Press, Cambridge, 1951, pp. 57-58. Further, the Corps shows no hesitation in sending to Congress authorization requests not in accord with the President's program.

³⁸For a brief account of early reorganization proposals see Maass, *ibid.*, pp. 61-68; and for an account of more recent proposals and an incisive discussion of the dilemmas of organizational theory see James W. Fesler, "National water resources administration," *Law and Contemporary Problems*, Vol. 22, No. 3, pp. 444-71, 1957.

JOHN GALLUP LAYLIN, partner, and BRICE McADOO CLAGETT, associate, Covington & Burling, Washington, D.C., are well known for their work in the law of international watercourses. Mr. Laylin has been legal advisor to a number of governments, and served in 1933-35 as a special assistant on international questions to the Undersecretary to the Treasury. Mr. Clagett assisted Mr. Laylin in representing Pakistan in drafting the Indus Water Treaty in 1960. Also, Mr. Clagett was a lawyer for Cambodia in the case concerning the Temple of Preah Vihear (Cambodia vs. Thailand) in the International Court of Justice.

Chapter 23

JOHN G. LAYLIN
BRICE M. CLAGETT

The Allocation of Water
On International Streams

ALLOCATION OF WATERS on international streams has been a problem from earliest times,[1] but the pervasiveness, the seriousness and the immediacy of the problem have increased immensely in recent years.[2] As long as the means of controlling and utilizing waters common to more than one state were relatively limited, it was often possible for each state to develop its part of an international watercourse without noticeable effect on other reparian states. The same was true of provinces or states of federated nations. As opportunities for the control and fuller exploitation of waters have increased since the mid-nineteenth century, and particularly since the beginning of this century, severe competition has arisen in the apportionment of the not unlimited supplies.

Problems of allocation have increased as demands upon available supplies have multiplied with the upsurge in population and with growth of industry and agriculture. Villages that have become cities along interstate and international watercourses make growing demands on water for municipal purposes and create problems related to disposal of sewage. Scientific and technical gains have created new uses and have made expansion of old ones possible. But while technology has vastly increased the demand for water, it has not as yet found (though it may be on the threshold of finding) practical ways of substantially increasing the supplies.

This competition for limited supplies, intensified by increased demands for water and by the new technology for exploitation of natural supplies, has been encountered by federated states as well as by fully sovereign states.[3] The problems in each case have been similar, but because common enforcing agencies exist among federated states, a richer body of judicial precedents has arisen there.[4] Federal courts have recognized the similarity in the problems of federated states to those of fully sovereign states and have been guided in reaching their decisions by principles applicable by analogy to fully sovereign states.[5]

In the international field, controversies over the allocation of water supplies have been further multiplied by the division of states, such as occurred with the breakup of the Austro-Hungarian and Ottoman empires and later of the great colonial areas of Asia and Africa.[6]

Problems involved in the allocation of waters of international streams, while having much in common with those involved in the allocation of waters among states of a federation, are rendered more difficult because independent nations frequently lack a sense of community adequate to make them willing to give proper consideration to the interests of one another. This is true of older states largely because they are likely to consist of integrated economic and cultural as well as juridical and political units, and of the newer states because of the exaggerated sense of nationality that usually accompanies recently won independence.[7] Also among sovereign states, lacking as they do a common enforcing agency, confidence that a system of interdependent works or water controls will not be abused is unfortunately not always encouraged by past experiences; and a legitimate desire for self-sufficiency is closely related to the sense of need for military security.

It must be recognized, however, that an international stream is a resource moving from one country to another, to which the literal application of strictly territorial concepts of sovereignty is inappropriate. The law governing allocation of the benefits of this common resource is derived from basic concepts of international law.[8] Each state in the drainage basin of an international river system is entitled to a just and reasonable share of the benefits. What is just and equitable depends upon all the relevant factors in each particular case. These concepts as applied to the allocation of the benefits of international (and interstate) waters are collectively referred to, with increasing frequency, as the principle of equitable apportionment.[9]

I. EQUITABLE APPORTIONMENT

When conflicts have arisen between sovereign states over the allocation of the waters of international streams, it has sometimes regrettably happened that attempts were made to obtain or impose a solution with little reference to law or indeed to any general standard or principle other than "might makes right." In the case of uses which involve a change in quantity, quality or rate of flow of water, an upstream state has, other factors being equal, a critical advantage over its downstream coriparian through its physical capacity to take within its own territory what water it pleases. Conversely, the lowest riparian on a navigable stream has a like advantage of physical control within its territory over passage to the sea of the ships of other riparians.

Other advantages possessed by one riparian, such as disparate bargaining power arising from greater economic and military strength, or the capacity to trade or withhold other benefits, may often lead to an accommodation which is *sui generis*, related to and indicative of no generally applicable standard of justice. Let us assume, however, that the states in question seek to apply the principle of equitable apportionment without reference to extraneous issues or, having failed to reach agreement, have accepted the jurisdiction of an international tribunal for resolution of their differences on the basis of customary international law. What criteria are to be employed in applying the doctrine of equitable apportionment?

In determining the just and reasonable shares of riparian states, the guiding principle is to apportion the benefits according to whatever agreements, judicial decisions, awards and customs are binding upon the parties, and, as to any supplies not controlled by these factors, in the light of the relative needs of the riparian states.[10]   It is seldom that the result can be reached with simplicity; but, as with many complicated problems, the solution is found in beginning with the simplest case and making progressive adjustments to deal successively with the complexities.

Criteria for Consideration

Let us begin, then, with only two states, with a single River Y forming their common boundary. Their populations, cultivable acreage irrigable from the river, and other water resources are equal; their climate is the same. The past and probable future development of each is parallel. Aside from water for domestic uses, their interest in the river supplies is solely in water for irrigation. One cubic foot of water per second ("cusec") yields the same results in each country. For each, agriculture has the same relative importance. Farmers in each country use the supplies with equal efficiency. The soil on each side of the river absorbs no more and no less water, and from each a like amount of water returns to the river after application on the fields. At the time of apportionment each has appropriated, without objection by the other, the same amount of supplies, which are devoted to equally

beneficial uses. Say that out of 10,000 cusecs of dependable supplies of
the River Y, 1,000 cusecs remain unappropriated. The equitable apportionment of the entire supply consists clearly in allocation to each of
one half — that which it is using and 500 cusecs more.[11]

Now let us consider the effect of a series of variants.

Of the total supply of 10,000 cusecs, State A has already dedicated
to existing uses 5,000 cusecs; B, 4,000. Everything else remains equal.
Equitable apportionment of the remaining 1,000 cusecs would be heavily
weighted in favor of B up to the full amount.

Now, with the existing uses at the rate of 5 to 4, suppose that the
population and cultivable acreage of B, instead of being equal to that of
A, are only two-thirds that of A — i.e., the population and acreage ratio
of A to B is 6 to 4. An equitable apportionment of the total 10,000 cusecs would be weighted heavily in favor of A up to allocating to it the entire unappropriated supply, resulting in 6,000 cusecs to A and 4,000 to B.

In practice there will be many more variations from equality, but
each can be dealt with progressively, always with reference to the basic
criterion of relative need. Say, for example, that the situation is as
stated in the last example, except that A has other water supplies of
2,500 cusecs on the River Z. With the 5,000 cusecs it has appropriated
from the River Y, A enjoys a total of 7,500 cusecs. If B were to be allocated all of the 1,000 cusecs left on the River Y, then A would have
7,500 cusecs and B would have 5,000. This ratio of 6 to 4 would reflect
their relative needs.

In few cases in reality do the facts fit so neatly, and in the apportionment of river supplies between sovereign nations there are many
further variants. Take for example the situation, not at all uncommon,
in which the population and development of one country has reached a
stage of relative maturity. The less-developed coriparian state with a
rapidly growing population will maintain with good cause that in the apportionment of unappropriated supplies account should be taken of its
relatively greater future needs.

The Egyptian-Sudanese negotiations over apportionment of the supplies to be made available from storage at the Aswan High Dam had this
factor to consider. It was resolved by allocating supplies on the basis
of assumed future development in the Sudan with a temporary "lending"
back to Egypt of a portion of those supplies.[12] A similar problem found
a similar solution in the 1961 treaty between the United States and Canada regarding development and apportionment of the water resources
of the Columbia River basin.[13]

So far we have had in mind the allocation of water for the same or
similar consumptive uses, such as withdrawals for irrigation. The
complexities multiply in cases where competing uses are as different
as irrigation and navigation, domestic uses and a use which results in
pollution, fishing and industrial use.

A thermal power company in State A desires to use river water to
condense steam. All the water withdrawn is returned to the river.
There is no change in rate of flow, but the temperature is raised to

such an extent as to impair fishing in State B. It is the task of those applying the principle of equitable apportionment to weigh the relative benefits. Here one use is such that it cannot be divided with the other. One must give way. Among the questions presented by this example is how much weight can be accorded to the fact that one of the competing uses is already established and the other is only proposed.

This brings us to the competition between new or proposed beneficial uses and old, lawfully established[14] beneficial uses. As between such uses we know of no instance in which a state, under the principle of equitable apportionment, has been required to relinquish, without full replacement from other sources, a lawfully established beneficial use in order to enable a coriparian state to develop a new use or uses of the same kind.

Protection of Existing Uses as Vested Rights

Such is the respect accorded to rights acquired through lawfully established beneficial uses that they are classified in a category with rights arising out of agreements, judgments and arbitral awards. Recognition of "vested" rights stemming from possession and use is well known in international law, as, for instance, in determination of territorial rights.[15]

One formulation of the principles governing uses of international rivers, after stating the principle of equitable apportionment that "competing uses or their benefits must be shared on a just and reasonable basis," continues:

In determining what is just and reasonable, account is to be taken of rights arising from agreements, judgments and awards, and from lawfully established beneficial uses, and of such considerations as the potential development of the system, the relative dependence of each riparian upon the waters of the system, and the comparative social and economic gains accruing from the various possible uses of the waters, to each riparian and to the entire community dependent upon the waters.[16]

Another formulation states that in apportioning the benefits there shall be taken "as the basis the right of each state to the maintenance of the status of its existing beneficial uses and to enjoy, according to the relative needs of the respective states, the benefits of future developments."[17] Other formulations do not attempt to single out those rights that are to be preserved in allocation of waters under the principle of equitable apportionment, but rely on the undisputed rule that, for an allocation to be just and reasonable, effect must be given to rights and obligations binding upon the parties whether arising from treaties or judgments or awards or from such customs as the practice of respecting lawfully established beneficial uses.[18] Thus, the resolution of the Institut de Droit International refrains from mentioning vested rights which should be taken into account, on the ground, as stated by the rapporteur in his preliminary report, that "the whole body of rules of the proposed resolution has taken vested rights into account without mentioning them, and that a special provision on this subject is superfluous."[19]

In his comments the rapporteur lists among the rights that must be respected, "rights acquired by virtue of an agreement between the riparian states" and "vested rights" "existing through appropriation." He adds, "the members of the Commission are in general of the opinion that these [latter] must be respected, but not in an absolute manner."[20]

This leads us to ask what if any exceptions are to be made, in applying the principle of equitable apportionment, to preservation of rights arising out of treaties, judgments or arbitral awards or lawfully established beneficial uses.

Exceptions to the Protection of Existing Uses

In most formulations of the law governing international rivers this question is left for determination in accordance with the general principles of international law. The maxim *pacta sunt servanda* applies to treaties establishing servitudes over streams with a force at least equal to that of its application to other types of agreements.[21] The only grounds, if any, on which rights created by a rivers treaty could be considered terminated would be those which would justify termination of any other type of servitude. The same would be true where the right is founded on a judgment, an arbitral award or on a lawfully established beneficial use instead of on a treaty.

It should be emphasized that it is the benefit of the use rather than the precise manner thereof which is entitled to protection and preservation. Thus, substitution for one source of supply of an established use of another source which provides equal benefits has sometimes been effected in the course of allocation of waters. The arbitral tribunal in the Lake Lanoux case[22] upheld the right of France to divert waters on its territory from a river flowing into Spain as long as France substituted at its own expense an equal flow farther downstream but still above the border. The tribunal stressed that the flow was to be in every respect equal, and suggested that a different result might have followed if there were so much of a change as an alteration in the temperature of the water.[23]

In the Indus Basin, before Partition between India and Pakistan, a commission appointed to resolve a dispute between two provinces dealt with another situation which is likely to occur in allocation of international, as well as interstate, waters.[24] The Province of the Punjab proposed to store flood waters used by the Province of Sind for its inundation canals. The canals were not deep enough to take off water at the lower levels to which the river would be reduced, but the supplies would be adequate and usable if diversion dams were constructed just below the intake of the canals. The commission expressly applied the principle of equitable apportionment when it determined that the Punjab would be acting within its rights in storing certain flood supplies upstream. However, it provided that the Punjab should reimburse Sind for that portion of the cost of building diversion dams necessary to effect replacement of the flood supplies previously relied upon to raise the river level. If the diversion dams would also serve to provide additional supplies, the portion of the total cost attributable to the new benefits was to be borne by Sind.

One can conceive of instances in which one type of use might become relatively so wasteful or unimportant as to warrant action in the nature of international eminent domain in order to make greater benefits possible. Such a taking, like any expropriation of a vested right, would of course require adequate and prompt compensation.

Let us examine the case of a river originally providing the only means of transporting heavy freight. A railroad is built parallel to it which provides for most freight a more economical means of carriage. With changing circumstances, the greatest usefulness of the river has shifted from supplying navigation to the production of hydroelectric power. Nationals of State A have a small fleet of barges, the last to survive the competition of the railroad. It would not be economical to invest in a new fleet, but with the surviving one the owners can eke out a precarious livelihood for a few more years. Their use of the river was lawfully established and is still beneficial, yet the benefit has become trivial compared to that of the hydroelectric power which would be made possible by a series of dams proposed by State B, which would obstruct navigation in State A. Clearly the barge owners, or State A on their behalf, are entitled to just compensation for the loss of their use, but with such reparation clearly the use itself must give way to the greater good of the international community.

Protection of Existing Uses as a Corollary of Equitable Apportionment

Moving from this extreme case to one where the benefits are less disproportionate, one encounters situations such as the following: all the factors except one which are relevant to the application of the principle of equitable apportionment lead to an equal division of the waters of the River Y between State A and State B. The exception is that State A has already established a beneficial use of six-tenths of the water supply, and State B of the remaining four-tenths. Let us suppose that State A has agreed with State B to accept a reallocation of the water supplies on the basis of their present relative needs without regard to vested rights as such. Prior appropriation and existing use are evidence of such importance as to the needs of the two states, and the economy of State A is so dependent on the already established uses, that in weighing all the relevant factors (including the fact of prior and existing use) an arbitral tribunal would in the ordinary course hold that the established ratio of six to four constitutes equitable apportionment.

Thus, entirely apart from their status as vested rights, existing uses are so crucial a factor in determining what apportionment is equitable that rarely if ever would they fail to receive full recognition and protection.

There are compelling reasons for such a conclusion. Water is a prime necessity on which whole populations and economies depend. A use of water which has become an integral part of the economy of a region, and which if long established probably has had a profound influence on the very distribution of population, is entitled to a degree of protection which for most purposes must be decisive. A use of water, moreover, involves a very substantial capital investment, the value of which is predicated entirely on the prospect of long-term benefits. Some of the most conspicuous and costly works by which man has altered his natural environment are works designed to harness and exploit water. If the law did not clearly recognize the decisiveness of existing beneficial uses to an equitable apportionment, these investments would be perpetually insecure. It would be very difficult to induce states to enter upon large-scale exploitation of waters or upon expansion dependent on the use of waters if there were no guarantee that such development would not be cut off at a later time on the ground of new needs or demands elsewhere.

The inviolability of existing beneficial uses has been recognized in each of the known international arbitral awards dealing with the point,[25] and has been conceded by a number of governments in situations where the concession severely limited the amount of water which they might otherwise claim or take.[26] A survey of some 100 water treaties prepared in 1942 by the United States Section of the International Boundary Commission, United States and Mexico, showed that more than three-fourths of those treaties made reference to existing uses, and that in each of these cases the existing uses were accorded full protection.[27]

Special respect can appropriately be given, as relevant by analogy,[28] to the decisions in interstate cases of the United States Supreme Court, which has had more experience than any other judicial body in applying the doctrine of equitable apportionment. A survey of these decisions demonstrates that protection of lawfully established existing uses has invariably been accorded first priority, overriding every other consideration.[29] Reasons given by the court for this consistent practice are equally convincing on the international level. They include those already indicated.

Priorities Among Classes of Uses

Textbooks discuss the relative priority to be accorded different classes of uses. In former times and in areas where navigation was the most important use, first priority after domestic use was often given to navigation.[30] It is now generally recognized that no rule of thumb of general application of priorities should be adopted or applied.[31] The principle of allocation among states on the basis of their relative needs connotes distribution among the different uses according to their relative importance to the states entitled to share in the benefits of the watercourse. In the delta of the Ganges and Brahmaputra, navigation is the only practicable means of surface transport. Irrigation is also important. In evaluating the significance of these two important uses account must also be taken of the necessity for control of the disastrous floods which are a salient feature of these rivers.[32]

Navigation on the Great Lakes has an importance that cannot be disregarded by the United States when regulating the supplies which may be withdrawn by Chicago for disposal of sewage.[33] In contrast, on the upper reaches of the Tigris and Euphrates navigation is of little importance compared with irrigation. On other international rivers — e.g., the Columbia — hydroelectric power development has an importance beyond navigation; on others logging comes first; on others the supply for municipal purposes overshadows every other use; on still others fishing is of prime interest to the states concerned. In some areas recreational uses must be considered. Fortunately some uses are noncompetitive or are even complementary and enhance the benefits to be derived through other uses; but where one use competes with another a delicate balancing, allowing for the greater weight to be given to the uses of greater benefit, is required in making allocations under the principle of equitable apportionment.

It is not to be overlooked that a river is not only a source of supplying water but a means of drainage and disposal. State A may have a servitude over the river while flowing in State B for its share of the river supplies, but State B has a servitude over the river while it continues its course through State A to the sea for the drainage of its outflow. Conflicting uses arise if State B wishes to use its right of drainage to convey noxious industrial or other waste. Often the harm to State A is disproportionately great. In an extreme case, such as the dumping of atomic waste in, for instance, Lake Champlain on the United States side of the border, Canada could invoke the doctrine of the Trail Smelter case[34] to collect damages and require cessation of the harmful practice.

Cases of less harmful pollution present practical difficulties as we move toward a closer balance between the benefit derived by the upper riparian and the harm suffered by the lower riparian, particularly when the pollution has been practiced without protest over a long period. The problems caused by pollution are among the most difficult in allocating water (and the benefits of water) on international streams. The eventual solution will involve recognition of the fact that a system of international waters is an integrated whole and that for each riparian to reap the maximum benefits the system should be developed and operated as a unit.[35]

Need for Integrated Development

The inadequacy of a piecemeal approach is particularly apparent in dealing with situations where the potentiality for storage is in one state and the potentiality for use is in another. This has come to be appreciated on the Columbia River system, where for the most part the undeveloped natural storage sites are in Canada and the natural hydroelectric power sites are in the United States. Little progress was possible so long as the negotiators for each party insisted on the maximum benefits to be derived by developing only on their side. But once the parties became willing to share in the costs and benefits of both storage reservoirs in Canada and power plants in the United States, a constructive solution of great benefit to both countries was achieved.[36]

To give a few other examples, Egypt and the Sudan reached an agreement in 1959 under which each side recognized the need for a cooperative approach. The Aswan High Dam in Egypt backs up the waters of the Nile on Sudanese as well as Egyptian territory; and the unappropriated supplies, including those which this storage makes available, are divided 65.9 percent to the Sudan and 34.1 percent to Egypt.[37] We have already noted the provision for "lending" to Egypt part of the Sudanese share for a period until development in the Sudan catches up with the new supply.

The Falcon Dam on the Rio Grande is a striking example of collaboration which makes possible benefits that neither side could achieve alone. Half of the multipurpose dam is on American territory and the other half is in Mexico. Each side benefits from increased power and irrigation supplies and from better flood control. [38]

Argentina and Uruguay agreed in 1958 on the joint exploitation of their boundary River Uruguay for hydroelectric power to be used by both states.[39] In 1963 Brazil proposed a special inter-American conference on the question of the regulation and cooperative development of the international waters of the Western Hemisphere.[40]

Among the many water treaties adopted by European states since the end of World War II are several between Yugoslavia and Austria, which provide for the regulation of power plants on common rivers in both states to achieve maximum benefit on both sides of the border.[41]

As is well known, the states in the drainage basin of the Mekong have agreed to a cooperative development of that river system with assistance of the United Nations.[42]

India and Pakistan have recognized the need for cooperation in development of the Ganges River to provide increased irrigation supplies without injury to navigation.[43] Their Indus Waters Treaty, 1960, demonstrated that with persistence and good will the most bitter of water disputes can be resolved to the benefit of both sides.[44]

Seven of the nine states which share the Niger River system — Niger, Guinea, Chad, Dahomey, Ivory Coast, Nigeria and Upper Volta — met at Niamey, Niger, in February 1963 and gave tentative approval to a treaty providing for freedom of navigation on and joint utilization of the waters of that river.[45]

Many other examples of successful cooperation in developing the benefits of international rivers could be cited. Among the major existing situations in which need for cooperation has been demonstrated are the Tigris-Euphrates (Turkey, Syria, Iraq and Iran),[46] the Helmand (Afghanistan and Iran),[47] the Jordan system (Lebanon, Syria, Israel and Jordan)[48] and the Blue Nile (Ethiopia, Egypt and the Sudan).[49]

Procedures for allocating the supplies of international streams are in the opinion of many students at least as important as the substantive rules in effecting equitable apportionment. We shall now turn to this aspect of the problem.

II. PROCEDURES FOR ALLOCATION OF WATERS

Means of Facilitating Agreement

The most frequent and satisfactory means of allocating waters of international watercourses is, of course, agreement.[50] This being the case, when one state protests against a projected development by another or a dispute arises in any other way, it is so essential that the states in question should seek to reach a solution by negotiating in good faith that it is often said they are under a duty to do so.[51] When countries desire aid from more prosperous states or from international agencies, procedures to this end have been encouraged by the aid-giving body's following the practice of withholding aid from a projected waters development so long as an unresolved dispute exists between the riparian states.[52]

A full and honest exchange of information between the interested states concerning the physical regime of a river and, in particular, concerning development projects under consideration or construction is, in the opinion of those who have participated in settling water disputes, a fundamental necessity.[53] It is usually desirable to have a joint inspection of the sites or works in question by representatives of the interested states and perhaps also of impartial engineers or international agencies.[54] An entirely unnecessary element of bitterness and suspicion can easily be introduced into a dispute if either party acts on information available only to it and refuses to submit the data to scrutiny by disinterested experts or those of the other side.

Advance notice of contemplated projects is likewise necessary, so that a state or states that might be affected will have the opportunity to assess the magnitude of the project in question and its effect. Informed negotiations can thus be undertaken before the project becomes a *fait accompli* and before attitudes have hardened. Objectionable features of the project can often be removed without lessening its value to the proposing state.[55] Opportunities for accommodation are always better while the project is in the formative stage. So necessary is advance notice to the satisfactory resolution of waters disputes, by agreement or otherwise, that it is becoming generally recognized that the party contemplating a new project is under a legal duty to give all other interested states sufficient information to enable them to assess its magnitude and effect.[56]

Other procedures often useful in facilitating agreement are to procure the advice of technical experts or agencies, either in eliciting the facts or in recommending a scheme of development adjusted to the needs of both parties; to constitute bilateral or multilateral commissions or agencies to study the problems presented in developing the common waters; and, if agreement proves difficult, to resort to an impartial mediator or good officer.[57]

Types of Agreements

It has been pointed out that maximum development of an international river is usually best furthered by adoption by the interested states of complementary plans which jointly provide for optimum exploitation of the common resource.[58] Formation of such a scheme can — but need not always — result in a high degree of interdependence between the states in question, with works in one state supplying uses in another, with joint construction of works and with the proper functioning of the whole depending on regulation and operation of works in the general interest.[59] Such interdependent development, which is sometimes essential for boundary streams, and can also be highly successful on successive watercourses, involves coordination through a bilateral or multilateral commission with administrative and sometimes judicial powers.[60] An interdependent arrangement presupposes a history warranting trust between the states. Such a history, unfortunately, is not always present. The absence of such trust may require that the coordinated plans ensure a substantial degree of independence for the works and supplies of each country. This may fail to achieve maximum development and may make it more costly.

There are many stages between these two extremes. Even in a scheme involving no joint works or projects, many potential conflicts between uses can often be eliminated or mitigated if each side will accept obligations to operate its works, as far as is consistent with their purposes, for the benefit of the other party — such as an upstream state's scheduling releases from multipurpose storages to accommodate irrigation or navigation downstream. Similarly, one state may refrain from developing hydroelectric power sites in return for a share of the power produced by a coriparian state from competing sites. [61] For such arrangements as these to be feasible, relations between the two states must be such that the state which accepts a dependent status has grounds for relying on the other to perform its obligations so that it is willing to construct its own works on the assumption that such performance will continue. Such a relationship can, moreover, involve very complex financial questions.

Alternatives on Failure of Agreement

Now let us suppose that agreement has not been possible. Three alternatives have been advanced. The first is that each state may proceed on its own view of its rights over the objections of affected coriparian states. Those espousing this alternative recognize (except, of course, for the few who deny the doctrine of equitable apportionment altogether) that a state may have to respond in damages and remove works by which more than its equitable share is appropriated.[62] The second alternative is that no state may proceed with any development of the waters so long as any state which might be adversely affected objects and persists in its objections. [63]

In each of these alternatives there are critical defects. The third alternative is embodied in a rule that has come to be recognized as comporting with proper application of the principle of equitable apportionment. This rule is that each state is free to proceed on its own view of its rights over the objections of an affected coriparian state if — but only if — the latter state declines to submit the validity of its objections to resolution by peaceful procedures including reference to adjudication or arbitration. This rule has found expression in various forms. The United States State Department has expressed it this way:

3(a) A riparian which proposes to make, or allow, a change in the existing regime of a system of international waters which could interfere with the realization by a coriparian of its right to share on a just and reasonable basis in the use and benefits of the system, is under a duty to give the coriparian an opportunity to object.

(b) If the coriparian, in good faith, objects and demonstrates its willingness to reach a prompt and just solution by the pacific means envisaged in article 33(1) of the Charter of the United Nations, a riparian is under a duty to refrain from making, or allowing, such change, pending agreement or other solution. [64]

The Institut de Droit International has expressed the rule as follows:

Article 4

No State can undertake works or utilizations of the waters of a watercourse or hydrographic basin which seriously affect the possibility of utilization of the same waters by other States except on condition of assuring them the enjoyment of the advantages to which they are entitled under article 3, as well as adequate compensation for any loss or damage.

Article 5

Works or utilizations referred to in the preceding article may not be undertaken except after previous notice to interested States.

Article 6

In case objection is made, the States will enter into negotiations with a view to reaching an agreement within a reasonable time.

For this purpose, it is desirable that the States in disagreement should have recourse to technical experts and, should occasion arise, to commissions and appropriate agencies in order to arrive at solutions assuring the greatest advantages to all concerned.

Article 7

During the negotiations, every State must, in conformity with the principle of good faith, refrain from undertaking the works or utilizations which are the object of the dispute or from taking any other measures which might aggravate the dispute or render agreement more difficult.

Article 8

If the interested States fail to reach agreement within a reasonable time, it is recommended that they submit to judicial settlement or arbitration the question whether the project is contrary to the above rules.

If the State objecting to the works or utilizations projected refuses to submit the judicial settlement or arbitration, the other State is free, subject to its responsibility, to go ahead while remaining bound by its obligations arising from the provisions of articles 2 to 4.[65]

This rule avoids the critical defects of the first and second alternatives stated above. The first alternative is defective because it overlooks the fact that the interests of states in the continuation and development of their share of the common water supplies are of great importance. For another state to act on its unilateral view of its share, therefore, is likely to endanger the peace or lead to a situation tantamount to a use of force in violation of the undertakings under the United Nations Charter[66] or, at the least, to cause injuries for which the payment of damages will not afford adequate reparation. The second alternative is defective in disregarding the irreparable injury likely to be caused to states proposing changes through the exercise by coriparian states of what amounts to a veto. The solution is provided by the rule that requires the objecting state, if it wishes protection from unilateral determination by the proposing state of its rights, to afford that state protection also from unilateral determination by the objecting state of the validity of its objections.

To support this rule it is not necessary to assume that international law contains any commitment, apart from special treaty, to resolve differences by adjudication or arbitration. Unilateral action, over protest, which affects the physical regime of waters flowing in the protesting state would infringe the prohibition of the United Nations Charter against the use, or threat of use, of force to resolve conflicts between states except in self-defense.[67] If, therefore, an offer to arbitrate has no legal effect, then a law-abiding state proposing new works is stymied so long as the objecting state refuses to agree. But under the rule we have described the proposing state is not without a remedy. If the objecting state — though, by hypothesis, not obligated to adjudicate or arbitrate the validity of its objection — nevertheless refuses to volunteer or agree to do so, then it is not in a position to complain if the proposing state proceeds with the course of action to which objection has been taken. If the objecting state is to have the benefit of a restraint against the proposing state from acting on its unilateral view of its rights, the rule requires the former to accept the concomitant duty to subject to impartial scrutiny its own unilateral views as to the validity of its objection.

States having treaties committing them to submit waters disputes to adjudication or arbitration have, in effect, accepted this rule. Most of the major international rivers of the world are governed by such commitments. At least 66 sovereign states have made agreements of this type with one or more of their neighbors,[68] and only some 15 states riparian to international rivers appear to have made none.[69] In 1954, when the International Law Association first took up the question of the law governing international rivers, the major existing international waters disputes concerned apportionment of the benefits of the waters of the Columbia, the Indus, the Jordan, the Helmand and the Nile. Not surprisingly, the coriparian states involved are among those which did not then have effective compulsory arbitration agreements with each other.

The treaties requiring submission of disputes to adjudication or arbitration often spell out that, pending resolution by such means, neither party will take any action to aggravate the dispute or to make its resolution more difficult.[70] Even when not stated explicitly, this obligation is implicit in the very undertaking to submit the dispute in good faith to impartial resolution.[71]

The rule we have described has a significant bearing on the protection to be accorded existing uses. As far as we are concerned with uses affecting civilized communities, established since a consciousness of international law became prevalent among states, or with practically any use established in the future, there is a fully adequate remedy for a state which fears that the faster and earlier development of a coriparian state may unfairly restrict its own long-term development.[72] That remedy is to protest before the use in question is put into effect, and to offer to work towards a solution by negotiation, and if that fails, by the other peaceful means of settlement including adjudication or arbitration. If such a protest and offer were made within a reasonable time after the protesting state received notice of the proposed use and were rejected by the state establishing the use, it would be given crucial importance by a tribunal subsequently determining what protection an existing use should be accorded. Conversely, a state will not be heard to argue that an existing beneficial use should be destroyed if, having had notice of the proposed use, it did not enter a timely objection or protest or if its objection was not accompanied by the demonstration of a willingness to submit the dispute to impartial determination.

It has occasionally been suggested that the availability of resolution by arbitration or adjudication will discourage settlement by agreement.[73] Actual case histories indicate that recognition of a duty not to act unilaterally over protest has been in fact a powerful incentive to reaching agreement.[74] The reasons are not difficult to find. If the alternative to agreement is that one state may go it alone, that attitude of mutual accommodation essential to the reaching of agreement will inevitably be discouraged, at least on the part of the state that has the physical power to put its plans into effect. If, in contrast, the alternative to agreement is a solution objectively determined, the intransigence which prevents agreement is discouraged. With a commitment in advance to accept the determination of an impartial tribunal, neither side is likely to prefer the risks of such a determination to the concessions involved in a reasonable adjustment of conflicting views.

Thus the mere availability to either party of resolution by a tribunal made up of lawyers, or lawyers and engineers, applying customary international law, will promote agreement and make resort to the tribunal unnecessary in many if not in most cases. But let us assume a situation in which the parties have found that they could not agree. Let us suppose — to take the hardest case — that they could agree on nothing beyond the desirability of reaching agreement. There are those who, faced with such a situation, nevertheless maintain that arbitration or adjudication is not appropriate. Such procedures are not suitable, they argue, for resolving the intricate problems of a water dispute.

Our answer is that a tribunal to which the dispute is referred will itself be aware of the desirability of resolving the question by agreement. Furthermore, the parties will not fail to bring home to the tribunal its own limitations. They will also disclose the fundamental causes of their inability to agree. The tribunal — as tribunals have done — can lay down principles for a master or a commission to follow in assembling relevant facts and in making recommendations to the tribunal and the parties.[75] Little by little, areas of agreement and lines of disagreement will be isolated until the issues on which agreement cannot be reached will be narrowed to the point where accommodation or decision will be possible.[76] A water dispute can be so complicated or involve interests so intangible and speculative as to appear at the outset to be beyond the powers of a tribunal to resolve. But unlike a nonjusticiable political dispute, it is susceptible or judicial resolution by the application of recognized criteria. And let it be recalled that so long as both sides are faced with the prospect of an impartial determination they are encouraged at every stage to renew their quest for a solution by the universally recognized superior method of agreement on a cooperative and constructive basis.

It might further be argued that waters disputes are not susceptible to arbitration or adjudication because it is impossible for a tribunal sufficiently to foresee future needs and conditions to be able to apportion large quantities of surplus water for which no immediate exploitation is projected. Such a plenary allocation, however, will rarely be necessary. When the procedural framework outlined above is followed, then a dispute will typically arise in relation to a specific new use which one riparian state proposes to make and against which a coriparian state has protested. The issue before the tribunal will be the legality of that use, and an apportionment of other unused waters need be made only if all parties so request or if at the petition of any party the tribunal concludes that in the circumstances such an apportionment on the basis of law is possible and desirable.[77]

III. CONCLUSION

Allocation of water on international streams is a subject of increasing importance to the prosperity and peace of nations. The governing principle is simple: each co-riparian state is entitled to a just and equitable share. Determination of such shares is a difficult problem, which seldom fails to present baffling complexities. The guiding rule to equitable apportionment of the benefits of an international watercourse allocates the benefits according to relative needs. These can be determined only by weighing all relevant factors. Among these are agreements, judgments, awards and established rights to the extent that they are binding on the parties. These rights are subject to re-examination, as are all vested rights in a changing world, subject to the duty to provide just compensation for rights that are taken away for the common good.

In applying the principle of equitable apportionment, the procedure is as important as the substantive rules. Fundamental to the question of procedure is the recognition that water is so essential that no state should act on its views of its rights over the objection of coriparian states that demonstrate their willingness to subject the validity of their objections to impartial scrutiny. Neither may any state unwilling to accept an independent judgment as to the validity of its objection exercise a veto over the development of a river by those prepared to accept an adjudication as to the equitable share of the coriparians.

As a general proposition all states stand to benefit most by a cooperative development and operation of an international river system. For this reason they have an interest in such a development, but each state possesses an economic, juridical and political unity which must also be taken into account. Ideally each national plan of development will be dovetailed into eventual integrated development of an international river system. While this goal is being achieved each state owes a duty to every coriparian state to respect that state's right to an equitable share of the total benefits of the river system and its right to participate fairly in the determination of what that share is.

FOOTNOTES

[1] A Buddhist legend regarding the Buddha as peacemaker begins: "It is recorded that two princes were once about to engage in a terrible battle in a quarrel that took place about a certain embankment constructed to keep in water...." Humphreys, Buddhism 38 (1951).

The twelve ancient Greek states which founded the Amphictiony made a treaty by swearing at Delphi: "I promise never to destroy any of the cities of the Amphictiony and not to destroy the bed or interfere with the use of their flowing waters in time either of war or of peace." De la Pradelle, "Les Rapports de Voisinage et l'Amenagement Industriel des Eaux Frontières," Revue de Droit International 1057 (1927).

A description has survived of water administration, distribution and practices in China under the Chou dynasty (c. 300 B.C.). See Caponera, Principi di Diritto delle Acque nel Sistema Giuridico Cinese 13 (1959).

The earliest European treaties dealing with navigation concern the river Po (1177) and the Rhine (1255). See Cano, "The Juridical Status of International (Non-Maritime) Waters in the Western Hemisphere," in Principles of Law Governing the Uses of International Rivers and Lakes; Resolution Adopted by the Inter-American Bar Association at its Tenth Conference Held in November, 1957, at Buenos Aires, Argentina, together with Papers Submitted to the Association (1958) (Lib. Cong. Cat. Card No. 58-12112) (hereinafter referred to as Principles...Buenos Aires), at 75.

[2] The literature describing recent international waters disputes is very extensive. For general surveys and bibliography, see Smith, The Economic Uses of International Rivers (1931); Olmstead (ed.), Research Project on the Law and Uses of International Rivers (1959). For a summary of United Nations activity in the field of water development, see UN, Water Resources Development Centre, First Biennial Report (1960), UN Doc. E/3319.

[3] The many compacts and adjudications between states of the United States are collected in Witmer (ed.), Documents on the Use and Control of the Waters of Interstate and International Streams (1956); see also Univ. Mich. Law School, Water Resources and the Law, p. 353-422 (1958). Twenty compacts were in force in 1956. For a discussion of inter-provincial agreements in Argentina, see Cano, op. cit. supra n. 1 at 83. Australia and India also furnish examples of interstate compacts; see U.N. Economic Commission for Asia and the Far East, Proceedings of the Regional Technical Conference on Water Resources in Asia and the Far East 316 (Flood Control Series, No. 9) (1956); Cano, op. cit. supra n. 1 at 85; The River Boards Act, 1956 (India), No. 49 of 1956. The treaty signed in 1841 between the Swiss cantons of Zürich and Schwyz probably constitutes the earliest such precedent. See Schulthess, Das Internationale Wasserrecht 26, 41 (1916). Germany has provided at least one judicial precedent, Württemberg and Prussia v. Baden (1926), 116 Deutsches Staatsgerichtshof, Entscheidungen des Reichsgerichts in Zivilsachen, Suppl., at 18.

[4] United States: The United States Supreme Court has original jurisdiction of actions between states. Its opinions in waters disputes up to 1956 are set out in Witmer, op. cit. supra n. 4 at 457-733. Cases before the Supreme Court at the beginning of the October 1962 term were Wisconsin, Minnesota, Ohio and Pennsylvania v. Illinois (Original No. 1), Michigan v. Illinois (Original No. 2) and New York v. Illinois (Original No. 3), proceedings to compel the City of Chicago to return to Lake Michigan water withdrawn for sanitary purposes; Illinois v. Michigan, Ohio, Pennsylvania, Minnesota, New York and Wisconsin (Original No. 11), relating to other withdrawals by Illinois from Lake Michigan; and Arizona v. California (Original No. 8), relating to the apportionment of the waters of the Colorado River system. 31 U.S. Law Week 3004. The last-named case was decided on June 3, 1963. 373 U.S. 546.

Switzerland: Among the intercantonal waters disputes decided by the Federal Supreme Court are Schwyz v. Zürich, BGE 52 I 170 (1926); Aargau v. Zürich, BGE 4, 34 (1878); Aargau v. Solothurn, BGE 18, 689 (1892); Fribourg v. Vaud, BGE 78 I 14 (1952).

Germany: Württemberg and Prussia v. Baden, op. cit. supra n. 3.

India (pre-Partition): Sind v. Punjab, 1 Rept. of the Indus (Rau) Commission, 1942 (reprinted 1950); arbitration between Madras and Mysore (1914), mentioned in Qadir, "The Uses of the Waters of International Rivers," in Resolution Adopted by the International Law Association at Its Conference Held in August, 1956 at Dubrovnik, Yugoslavia, together with Reports and Commentaries Submitted to the Association (Lib. Cong. Cat. Card No. 57-10830) (hereinafter referred to as Principles...Dubrovnik), at 6. The Sind-Punjab dispute was subjected to analysis on the basis of law by the Commission in an advisory capacity to the Government of India. Post-Partition India has provided for special tribunals "for the adjudication of disputes relating to waters of inter-State rivers and river valleys." Inter-State Water Disputes Act, 1956, No. 33 of 1956.

Some of the Argentine interstate compacts provide for resolution of disputes by the Federal Supreme Court. Olmstead, op. cit. supra n. 2 at 25-26.

[5] The United States Supreme Court has said in an interstate waters case, Kansas v. Colorado, 185 U.S. 125, 146-47 (1902): "Sitting, as it were, as an international as well as a domestic tribunal, we apply Federal law, state law, and international law, as the exigencies of the particular case may demand...." In Württemberg and Prussia v. Baden, op. cit. supra n. 3, the German Staatsgerichtshof expressly based its decision (that a German state is under a duty not to damage another through interference with common waters) on the application by analogy of the same doctrine in international law.

The process was reversed, and interstate decisions used to formulate international law by analogy, in the decision of the Trail Smelter Arbitral Tribunal, 35 Amer. Jour. Intl. Law 684 (1941). In a case between the United States and Canada involving pollution of the air, the tribunal held that decisions of the United States Supreme Court on both water and air pollution "may legitimately be taken as a guide in this field of international law, for it is reasonable to follow by analogy, in international cases, precedents established by that court in dealing with controversies between States of the Union or with other controversies concerning the quasi-sovereign rights of such States, where no contrary rule prevails in international law and no reason for rejecting such precedents can be adduced from the limitations of sovereignty inherent in the Constitution of the United States."

For scholarly opinions that interstate decisions are relevant in the formulation of international law by analogy, see Olmstead (ed.), *op. cit. supra* n. 2 at 199; Lauterpacht, "Decisions of Municipal Courts as a Source of International Law," X Brit. Yearbook Intl. Law 65 (1929); Cowles, "International Law as Applied Between Subdivisions of Federations," 74 Recueil des Cours 659 (Hague Academy, 1949, I). But see Berber, Rivers in International Law 171 ff. (1959); see also the discussion of Dr. Berber's views in Principles ... Buenos Aires, *op. cit. supra* n. 1 at 32.

[6]In 1900 there were about 55 sovereign or semi-sovereign entities in the world. After the First World War this number increased to about 70. By 1962 the United Nations alone consisted of 104 members, 1961-1962 ICJ Yearbook 17. There were in addition more than 10 nonmember states possessing at least *de facto* independence. The creation of new states, principally in Africa, has continued at a rate faster than ever before. It is notable that the creation of new states has been largely concentrated in the arid areas of northern Africa and southern Asia.

[7]Cf. Olmstead (ed.), *op. cit. supra* n. 2 at 7.

[8]The resolution on the utilization of non-maritime waters adopted by the Institut de Droit International at its Salzburg meeting in September, 1961, introduces its formulation of the law with the statement that "the obligation not to cause unlawful harm to others is one of the basic general principles governing international neighborly relations ... [and] this principle is also applicable to relations arising from different utilizations of waters." This resolution (hereinafter referred to as IDI Resolution) which is probably the most comprehensive and scholarly formulation of the law in this field which has yet appeared, was adopted by the Institut without a dissenting vote and with only one abstention. The resolution was the outcome of years of study and discussion by the Institut's Ninth Commission, with Professor Juraj Andrassy of Yugoslavia as rapporteur. See Institut de Droit International, Neuvième Commission, Utilisation des eaux internationales non maritimes (en dehors de la navigation), Rapport definitif présenté par M. Juraj Andrassy (1960) (hereinafter referred to as IDI Final Report). Since this resolution is not readily available in published form, the complete text follows:

I.   Utilization of Non-maritime International Waters
(except for navigation)

(Ninth Commission)

The Institute of International Law,

Considering that the economic importance of the use of waters is transformed by modern technology and that the application of modern technology to the waters of a hydrographic basin which includes the territory of several States affects in general all these States, and renders necessary its restatement in juridical terms,

Considering that the maximum utilization of available natural resources is a matter of common interest,

Considering that the obligation not to cause unlawful harm to others is one of the basic general principles governing neighborly relations,

Considering that this principle is also applicable to relations arising from different utilizations of waters,

Considering that in the utilization of waters of interest to several States, each of them can obtain, by consultation, by plans established in common and by reciprocal concessions, the advantages of a more rational exploitation of a natural resource,

Recognizes the existence in international law of the following rules, and formulates the following recommendations:

Article 1

The present rules and recommendations are applicable to the utilization of waters which form part of a watercourse or hydrographic basin which extends over the territory of two or more States.

Article 2

Every State has the right to utilize waters which traverse or border its territory, subject to the limits imposed by international law and, in particular, those resulting from the provisions which follow.

This right is limited by the right of utilization of other States interested in the same watercourse or hydrographic basin.

Article 3

If the States are in disagreement over the scope of their rights of utilization, settlement will take place on the basis of equity, taking particular account of their respective needs, as well as of other pertinent circumstances.

Articles 4-8

[See pages 436-437, *supra*]

Article 9

It is recommended that States interested in particular hydrographic basins investigate the desirability of creating common organs for establishing plans of utilization designed to facilitate their economic development as well as to prevent and settle disputes which might arise.

Text adopted by a vote of 50 to 0, with one abstention.

(11 September 1961)

For the views of the Swiss government on the basic principles of neighbor-relations law, as applied to a problem similar to the use of international rivers, see XIV Annuaire Suisse de Droit International 158-172 (1957). See also I Oppenheim, International Law 345-47 (8th ed. Lauterpacht 1955), who deduces the law of rivers, as do other scholars, from the maxim *sic utere tuo ut alienum non laedas.*

[9] The overwhelming majority of governments, scholars and associations today express agreement with these rules, whether or not called by the name "equitable apportionment." For opinions of governmental bodies see, e.g., the opinion of the Swiss government, *op. cit. supra* n. 8; U.S. Department of State (prepared by William L. Griffin), Legal Aspects of the Use of Systems of International Waters, S. Doc. No. 118, 85th Cong., 2d Sess. 89-90 (1958) (hereinafter referred to as State Department Memorandum); Württemberg and Prussia v. Baden, *op. cit. supra* n. 3; I Report of the Indus (Rau) Commission, 1942, pp. 10-11 (reprinted 1950).

For opinions of representative individual scholars see, e.g., Qadir, "The Uses of the Waters of International Rivers," in Principles...Dubrovnik 6; Olmstead (ed.), *op. cit. supra* n. 2 at 197; opinions of scholars summarized in Economic Commission for Europe (Sevette), Legal Aspects of the Hydro-Electric Development of Rivers and Lakes of Common Interest 51-68 (1952) (U.N. Doc. E/ECE.136); Eagleton, "The Use of the Waters of International Rivers," 33 Canadian Bar Review 1018, 1023 (1955); Bourne, "The Columbia River Controversy," 37 Canadian Bar Review 444, 457-461 (1959); Arechaga, "International Legal Rules Governing Uses of Waters from International Watercourses," Inter-American Law Review 329, 330 (1960).

Formulations by leading associations which have considered the subject in recent years include Principles III, IV, and V adopted by the International Law Association in 1956, in Principles...Dubrovnik 1-2; Principle 2 adopted by the International Law Association in 1958, in International Law Association, Report of the Forty-Eighth Conference, New York 100 (1958); Articles 2, 3 and 4 of the IDI Resolution; Principle II adopted by the American Branch of the International Law Association in 1958, in Proceedings and Committee Reports of the American Branch of the International Law Association 1957-1958, at 101-102; Paragraph I(2) of the Resolution adopted by the Tenth Conference of the Inter-American Bar Association (1957), in Principles...Buenos Aires 4.

One still occasionally encounters two views in conflict with the principle of equitable apportionment. One is that no riparian state may, without the consent of every other affected riparian state, make any substantial modification in the natural flow of the river. This seems to be the literal meaning of Article II(3) of the declaration adopted at Madrid in 1911 by the Institut de Droit International: "No establishment...may take so much water that the constitution, otherwise called the utilisable or essential character of the stream, shall, when it reaches the territory downstream, be seriously modified...." Quoted in Principles...Buenos Aires 45. F. J. Berber, in his Rivers in International Law (1959) (reviewed at 53 Amer. Jour. Intl. Law 729 (1959)), deduces from treaties a purely regional rule of customary international law, limited to Europe, to the effect of "requiring the consent of the other riparian state for works likely to affect materially the flow of water in that state" (pp. 155-56). This rule seems unduly weighted in favor of downstream states in that it permits them freedom of action while giving them a veto power on development in upstream states. As Dr. Berber shows, treaties incorporating this rule are numerous in Europe, where the more heavily consumptive uses, such as irrigation, are rare and projects can usually be adjusted so as not to have a substantially adverse effect in another country. For a critical discussion of Dr. Berber's apparent contention that customary international law of general application contains no judicially enforceable rules regarding the uses of international rivers, see review by Fortuin, 4 Netherlands Intl. Law Rev. 414 (1957).

The other view sometimes encountered is that there is no rule of law restricting the freedom of action of states regarding waters within their own boundaries, even if such action would appropriate, for instance, all the waters of an international river and leave another riparian state high and dry. The most quoted exposition of this view is the opinion of U.S. Attorney-General Judson Harmon given in 1895 in the course of negotiations with Mexico regarding the waters of the Rio Grande. 21 Ops. Atty. Gen. 278 (1895). The United States nevertheless in 1906 entered into a treaty with Mexico undertaking obligations on the Rio Grande, 34 Stat. 2953. In the course of Senate committee hearings in 1945 regarding a subsequent treaty with Mexico, 59 Stat. 1219, Frank Clayton, counsel for the United States section of the International Boundary Commission, testified that "Attorney General Harmon's opinion has never been followed either by the United States or by any other country of which I am aware." Hearings before Senate Committee on Foreign Relations on Treaty with Mexico Relating to Utilization of Waters of Certain Rivers, 79th Cong. 1st Sess., pt. 1, at 97-98 (1945). Dean Acheson, then Assistant Secretary of State, testified that the Harmon Doctrine "is hardly the kind of legal doctrine that can be seriously urged in these times." Hearings, *supra*, pt. 6, at 1762; see also Arechaga, *loc. cit. supra* n. 9.

The Harmon opinion has been definitively repudiated by the United States Department of State, see State Department Memorandum, *supra*. A survey made in 1952 revealed that of some 30 scholars who had written on the subject all but four (possibly three) rejected this view. Sevette, *loc. cit. supra*. For a study of the fortunes of the Harmon opinion, see Austin, "Canadian-United States Practice and Theory Respecting the International Law of International Rivers: A Study of the Influence of the Harmon Doctrine," 37 Canadian Bar Review 393 (1959).

[10] See, e.g., Principle V of the Resolution adopted by the International Law Association in 1956 at Dubrovnik, in Principles...Dubrovnik 2; Principle II proposed by a committee of the American Branch of the ILA in 1958, in Proceedings and Committee Reports of the American Branch of the International Law Association 1957-1958, at 101; Institut de Droit International, Neuvième Commission, Utilisation des eaux internationales non maritimes (en dehors de la navigation), Rapport provisoire présenté par M. Juraj Andrassy (1959) (hereinafter referred to as IDI Preliminary Report), at 58-65, 81.

[11] In an actual situation, even the degree of equality of circumstances which has been outlined may not rule out all factors making for variation. For example, we have stipulated that there are 10,000 cusecs of dependable supplies. Some of these supplies, however, will be lost by evaporation and seepage, and the amounts of losses will be related to how far upstream or downstream the withdrawals are made. Adjustments must be made, therefore, to apportion these losses if the two states are to receive an equal amount of net usable supplies.

Moreover, even after a quantitative apportionment has been worked out, the schedules of withdrawals must be determined to correspond with the needs of the dependent uses. *When* water is withdrawn can be even more important than *how much* water is withdrawn.

Such factors as these would have to be taken into account by experts in any actual allocation. Since they cannot be reduced to conclusions with which laymen can deal, they have not been introduced into the examples given in the text.

[12] "Full Text of Nile Accord," The Egyptian Gazette, Nov. 9, 1959; Badr, "The Nile Waters Question" 23 reprinted from Revue Egyptienne de Droit International No. 15-1959; Andrassy, "Accord sur les eaux du Nil," 2 Jugoslovenska Revija Za Medunaroono Pravo 244 (1960). There are many excellent background materials on the history of the utilization of the Nile and disputes relative thereto; see especially Batstone, "The Utilisation of the Nile Waters," 8 Intl. and Comparative Law Quart. 523-58 (1959), which includes, at 540-57, a thoughtful discussion of the criteria relevant to an apportionment. Although Batstone is of the opinion, id. at 558, that "equitable apportionment" under that name is not a doctrine of international law, he also concludes, ibid., that "riparian States possess no right of disposing freely of the waters of international rivers traversing their territory irrespective of the effect on other States."

[13] Treaty between Canada and the United States Relating to Cooperative Development of the Water Resources of the Columbia River Basin. Signed at Washington, January 17, 1961. For the issues involved in the protracted negotiations leading up to the conclusion of this treaty, see The Diversion of Columbia River Waters, Institute of International Affairs, Univ. of Wash., Bul. No. 12, Part 4, 1956; Cohen, "Some Legal and Policy Aspects of the Columbia River Dispute," 36 Canadian Bar Review 25 (1958); Bourne, op. cit. supra n. 9; Vallance, The Settlement of International Boundary Waters Questions in North America 279 (1959); Martin, "The Diversion of Columbia River Waters," Proceedings of the American Society of International Law at Its Fifty-First Annual Meeting, Washington, D.C., April 25-27, 1957 (1958), at 2; Department of State Press Release No. 885, Dec. 30, 1959, to which a copy of the 1959 report of the International Joint Commission is attached. The treaty has been ratified by the United States, but not yet, as of this writing, by Canada.

[14] As used in this article, a beneficial use, to be "lawfully established," (1) must not infringe any binding treaty, judicial decision or arbitral award; (2) must not encroach upon a beneficial use already lawfully established by a co-riparian state which has not given its consent to the encroachment; and (3) must not have been established over the timely protest of a co-riparian state which offered to resolve by peaceful means — including, if necessary, arbitration or adjudication — the question whether the use comes within the equitable share of the state proposing it. The first of these qualifications is required by general principles of international law; the second is inherent in the concept of the acquisition of rights by lawful use. The third is discussed at pages 428-31, infra.

[15] See, e.g., The Island of Palmas Case (United States v. The Netherlands), Permanent Court of Arbitration, 1928, Scott, Hague Court Reports 83 (2d ser. 1952), 2 Repts. Intl. Arbitral Awards 829. See also Bishop, International Law 271-81 (1953), and authorities there cited.

[16] Principle II of the statement adopted by the American Branch of the ILA, in Proceedings and Committee Reports of the American Branch of the International Law Association 1957-1958, at 101.

[17] Paragraph I (2) of the resolution adopted by the Inter-American Bar Association, Principles ... Buenos Aires at 4. The State Department Memorandum, in Paragraph 2(b) of its conclusions (at 90), stated the principle as follows:

"In determining what is just and reasonable account is to be taken of rights arising out of —
   (1) Agreements.
   (2) Judgments and awards, and
   (3) Established lawful and beneficial uses; and of other considerations such as —
   (4) The development of the system that has already taken place and the possible future development, in the light of what is a reasonable use of the water by each riparian;
   (5) The extent of the dependence of each riparian upon the waters in question; and
   (6) Comparison of the economic and social gains accruing from the various possible uses of the waters in question, to each riparian and to the entire area dependent upon the waters in question."

[18] E.g., the resolution adopted by the ILA at New York in 1958. Principle 2 reads: "Except as otherwise provided by treaty or other instruments or customs binding upon the parties, each co-riparian state is entitled to a reasonable and equitable share in the beneficial uses of the waters of the drainage basin. What amounts to a reasonable and equitable share is a question to be determined in the light of all the relevant factors in each particu-

lar case." International Law Association, Report of the Forty-Eighth Conference, New York 100 (1958).

[19] IDI Preliminary Report at 64.

[20] *Id.* at 62-63. This observation suggests a qualification that must be made to the protection of existing uses as to any other principle. One can conceive by way of hypothesis of extreme situations where the principle might not be fully applicable; for example, where one riparian state had appropriated *all* the water of a great river and converted the co-riparian into a desert.

[21] When by formal agreement, custom or otherwise, one state acquires a right or interest in specific territory of another, the resulting rights and obligations are often termed a "servitude" and are considered to be not merely contractual arrangements between states, but vested rights inhering in the territory itself. Rights and obligations relating to the apportionment of the benefits of an international river are classic examples of servitudes. Servitudes are regarded by most authorities as a very high order of international obligation, so that, for example, they survive the denunciation of the instrument which created them and survive a change of sovereignty over the areas affected. See McNair, The Law of Treaties 469 (3d ed., 1938); Schwarzenberger, A Manual of International Law 41 (3d ed., 1952); O'Connell, "A Re-consideration of the Doctrine of International Servitude," 30 Canadian Bar Review 807 (1952); Fenwick, International Law 151 *et seq.* (3d ed. 1948); Jones, "State Succession in the Matter of Treaties," 24 Brit. Yearbook Intl. Law 360 (1947).

[22] Affaire du Lac Lanoux, Sentence du Tribunal Arbitral (1957). The award also appears in 29 Revue Gén. de Droit Int. Pub. 79-119 (1958).

[23] Affaire du Lac Lanoux, Sentence du Tribunal Arbitral 38 (1957).

[24] The report of the Commission was reprinted by the Superintendent, Government Printing, Lahore (Punjab) in 1950, under the title Report of the Indus (Rau) Commission, 1942. The principle of equitable apportionment is stated to be the governing rule, I Report 10-11. For the Commission's conclusions, see 52-54. For a description of the Commission's work, see Laylin, "Principles of Law Governing the Uses of International Rivers: Contributions from the Indus Basin," in Am. Soc. Intl. Law Proceedings (1957) at 24-26.

[25] When the lower basin of the Helmand River was divided between Iran and Afghanistan in 1872, the award of Sir Frederick Goldsmid provided that "no works are to be carried out on either side calculated to interfere with the requisite supply of water for irrigation on the banks of the Helmand." I St. John, Lovett and Smith, Eastern Persia: An Account of the Journeys of the Persian Boundary Commission, 1870-71-72, Appendix B (1876).

The chancellery of Brazil arbitrated a dispute between Ecuador and Peru regarding the waters of the Zarumilla River. The award (1945), accepted by the two governments, stated in part: "Peru undertakes, within three years, to divert a part of the Zarumilla River so that it may run in the old bed, so as to guarantee the necessary aid for the subsistence of the Ecuadorian populations located along its banks, thus ensuring Ecuador the co-dominion over the waters in accordance with international practice" (our transl.). Informe del Ministro de las Relaciones Exteriores a la Nación 623 (Ecuador) (1946).

In 1929 the President of the United States, acting as good officer in the Tacna-Arica dispute between Chile and Peru, proposed a settlement which would award to Chile sovereignty over territory containing canals on which uses in Peru depended. The President included in the terms of settlement the provision that "the canals... shall remain the property of Peru, with the understanding, however, that wherever the canals pass through Chilean territory they shall enjoy the most complete servitude in perpetuity in favor of Peru. This servitude includes the right to widen the actual canals, change their course, and appropriate all waters that may be collectible in their passage through Chilean territory." 23 Amer. Jour. Intl. Law 183 (Suppl. 1929). These terms were accepted by the two governments.

When the great irrigation system of the Punjab province was divided between India and Pakistan in 1947, the bodies established to determine questions related to the Partition assumed as a matter of course that the existing uses on both sides of the border would be respected. The report of Reconstituted Committee "B" on the Division of Physical Assets of the Punjab included the statement: "The Committee is agreed that there is no question of varying the authorised shares of water to which the two Zones and the various canals are entitled." Report of Reconstituted Committee "B", Paragraph 15 (1947). The Arbitral Tribunal proceeded to apportion the assets of the united province, assessing the various canals and headworks at their value as part of an operating irrigation system, that is, a system with water in it. The assumption by the tribunal that water would continue to be supplied to existing uses as previously was acknowledged by Sir Patrick Spens, chairman of the tribunal, at a joint meeting in London of the East-India Association and the Overseas League, in 1955: "Our awards were published at the end of March, 1948....I was very much upset that almost within a day or two there was a grave interference with the flow of water on the basis of which our awards had been made." The interference referred to, which initiated the Indus Waters Dispute, was India's action in cutting off the supplies to Pakistan in a number of major canals shared by both countries.

The Arbitral Tribunal in the Lake Lanoux Case, while drawing mainly on existing treaty obligations to ensure full protection for Spain's existing uses, relied also on customary international law. See Affaire du Lac Lanoux, Sentence du Tribunal Arbitral 47 (1957); Laylin and Bianchi, "The Role of Adjudication in International River Disputes: The Lake Lanoux Case," 53 Amer. Jour. Intl. Law 45-47 (1959).

[26] A number of such concessions relative to the Nile and other rivers are summarized in Principles... Buenos Aires at 63-69.

[27] Hearings before Senate Committee on Foreign Relations on Treaty with Mexico Relating to Utilization of the Waters of Certain Rivers, 79th Cong., 1st Sess., pt. 1, 97-98 (1945). For a discussion of the value of treaties as evidencing rules of customary international law see, e.g., Starke, "Treaties as a 'Source' of International Law," 23 Brit. Yearbook Intl. Law 346 (1946); Principles of Law and Recommendations on the Use of International Rivers, Statement of Principles of Law and Recommendations with a Commentary and Supporting Authorities' Submitted to the International Committee of the International Law Association by the Committee on the Uses of Waters of International Rivers of the American Branch (1958) (Lib. Cong. Cat. Card No. 58-12111) (Hereinafter referred to as Principles... American Branch Committee), at 24-25.

[28] See n. 5.

[29] See Kansas v. Colorado, 206 U.S. 46, 109, 113 (1906); Wyoming v. Colorado, 259 U.S. 419, 469, 485, 495 (1922); Connecticut v. Massachusetts, 282 U.S. 660, 667, 669, 672, 674 (1930); New Jersey v. New York, 283 U.S. 336, 342-343, 347 (1930); Washington v. Oregon, 297 U.S. 517, 522, 526-529 (1936); Colorado v. Kansas, 320 U.S. 383, 393-394 (1943); Nebraska v. Wyoming, 325 U.S. 589, 618-622, 644 (1945).

The case of Wisconsin v. Illinois, 278 U.S. 367 (1929) and 281 U.S. 179 (1930), in which the Court required Chicago to reduce its diversions from Lake Michigan for sewage-disposal purposes to a volume considerably less than that of prior years, is sometimes cited as a case in which the Court permitted destruction of existing uses. The Court found in effect, however, that the Chicago diversion was not "lawfully established" because it resulted in damage to prior uses: "to navigation and commercial interests, to structures, to the convenience of summer resorts, to fishing and hunting grounds, to public parks and other enterprises, and to riparian property generally." 278 U.S. at 408. The Chicago litigation is therefore not only fully consistent with, but positive support for, the principle that lawfully established beneficial uses will be protected.

Also occasionally cited as inconsistent with the protection of existing uses is Hinderlider v. La Plata River & Cherry Creek Ditch Co., 304 U.S. 92 (1938), in which the Court denied a claim by a Colorado appropriator of water that its vested rights (which had previously been confirmed by a Colorado decree) had been impaired by a compact between Colorado and New Mexico which resulted in a reduction in the volume of water it received in some periods, though an increase in others. The Court's holding, however, was based on (1) the fact that upholding the claim would mean destroying appropriations in New Mexico which were senior, that is, that plaintiff's use was not lawfully established; and (2) the view that a compact between the co-riparian sovereigns, fairly and honestly agreed upon, is an appropriate means of making an equitable apportionment with which the Court will not interfere. The holding is not inconsistent with the position that, between sovereigns which have not agreed on any different result, lawfully established beneficial uses are entitled to protection.

In Arizona v. California, 373 U.S. 546 (1963), the Court held that "perfected rights" as of the passage of the Boulder Canyon Project Act by Congress in 1928 were entitled to absolute priority. It further held that, by providing in the Act that the waters of a navigable stream shall be harnessed, conserved, stored, and distributed through a government agency under a statutory scheme, Congress had vested authority in the Secretary of the Interior to make allotments which included the power, in periods of shortages, to reduce proportionally, instead of on a basis of priority, uses which had grown up since 1928. The Court recognized that the principles of equitable apportionment and prior appropriation would require a different result, but held that in this instance, with water made available through the federal project, Congress had authorized the Secretary to depart from these principles.

[30] E.g., Article VIII, Boundary Waters Treaty of 1909 between the United States and Canada, 36 Stat. 2448; Article 1, Agreement and Additional Protocol Relative to the Utilization of the Rapids of the Uruguay River in the Zone of Salto Grande, 1946, Pan America 61 (1947). Such a priority for navigation has occasionally been said to be a rule of customary international law. See, e.g., I Report of the Indus (Rau) Commission, 1942, at 11 (1950), and the opinion of two members of the Ninth Commission of the Institut de Droit International, summarized in IDI Preliminary Report 64.

[31] IDI Preliminary Report 64-65; State Department Memorandum at 90.

[32] See Olmstead (ed.), op. cit. supra n. 2 at 46-50.

[33] For the history of the Chicago diversion controversy, which has been an active issue between states of the United States for more than 60 years and has been the subject of negotiations between the United States and Canada, see Adams, "Diversion of Lake Michigan Waters," 37 U. Detroit L.J. 149 (1959); Vallance, The Settlement of International Boundary Waters Questions in North America 284 ff. (1959); Report of the A.B.A. Committee on Uses of International Inland Waters, American Bar Association, Section of International and Comparative Law, Proceedings 1959, at 127 (1960); Hearings before a Subcommittee of the Committee on Public Works, U.S. Senate, on H.R. 1 and S. 308, 86th Cong., 1st Sess., July 13, 14, 27 and August 7, 1959.

[34] See footnote 5. The Arbitral Tribunal enjoined Canada from permitting "the use of its territory in such a manner as to cause injury by fumes in or to the territory of another or the properties of persons therein...." 35 Amer. Jour. Intl. Law 684, 716 (1941).

[35] For a study of a number of technical aspects of this subject, see "Water Supply and Pollution Problems," pp. 97-130 of IV Proceedings, United Nations Scientific Conference on the Conservation and Utilization of Resources, E/Conf. 7/7 (1951); Wisdom, The Law on the Pollution of Waters (1956). The associations which have studied the law of international rivers have recognized the problems related to pollution. See, e.g., Recommendation 8 of the ILA's New York resolution, International Law Association, Report of the Forty-Eighth Conference, New York 101 (1958).

A question has arisen between the United States and Mexico regarding increased salinity in the Colorado River resulting from deep-well pumping of a highly saline aquifer underlying the Wellton-Mohawk project on the Gila River, a Colorado tributary in Arizona. See Piper, "A Justiciable Controversy Concerning Water Rights," 56 Amer. Jour. Intl. Law 1019 (1962). At issue is the question of the quality of water to be delivered by the United States to Mexico under the Water Utilization Treaty of 1944, 59 Stat. 1219, and perhaps under customary international law as well.

[36] See n. 13 supra.

[37] "Full Text of Nile Accord," The Egyptian Gazette, Nov. 9, 1959. The agreement recognizes existing uses to be 48 billion cubic meters for Egypt and 4 billion for the Sudan. As yet unappropriated supplies assigned to Egypt and the Sudan are 7.5 and 14.5 billion cubic meters respectively. For an analysis of this and other provisions of the treaty in the light of principles of customary international law, see Badr, "The Nile Waters Question," reprinted from Revue Egyptienne de Droit International No. 15-1959.

[38] See Rio Grande International Storage Dams Project: Proposed Amistad Dam and Reservoir, S. Doc. No. 65, 86th Cong., 1st Sess. 9-10 (1959). The dam was jointly constructed in accordance with the provisions of the 1944 treaty between the United States and Mexico, 59 Stat. 1219. Other joint works are in operation, under construction and under consideration.

[39] Agreement and Additional Protocol between Argentina and Uruguay Relative to the Utilization of the Rapids of the Uruguay River in the Zone of Salto Grande (1946), Pan America 61 (1947). The treaty came into force when ratified by Uruguay in 1958.

[40] Letter of the Brazilian Ambassador to the Organization of American States, H. E. Ilmar Penna Marinho, to the Secretary-General of that organization, March 27, 1963. In 1962 the Juridical Committee of the OAS adopted a resolution calling for a study of the law and practice concerning the uses of international rivers for industrial and agricultural purposes. Such a study was carried out under the supervision of Vetilio A. Matos, of the Dominican Republic, as rapporteur.

[41] E.g., Convention between Yugoslavia and Austria Concerning Water Economy Questions Relating to the Drava (1954), 227 U.N. Treaty Series 128; Treaty Between Austria and Yugoslavia concerning Hydro-Economic Questions Relating to the Frontier and the Frontier Waters on the Mur (1954), Austrian Federal Law Gazette No. 119/1956. These and other Austro-Yugoslav treaties are analyzed in Paunovic, "The Uses of the Waters of International Rivers," Principles... Dubrovnik 5-6.

[42] Convention Regulating Maritime and Inland Navigation on the Mekong and Inland Navigation on the Approach to the Port of Saigon, between Cambodia, Laos, and Vietnam (1954), Doc. of France, Jan. 25, 1955, No. 1.973, p. 7. See UN (ECAFE), Development of Water Resources in the Lower Mekong Basin (1957), Flood Control Series No. 12, E/CN.11/457.

[43] "... The Government of India would appreciate cooperative development by India and Pakistan of the water resources of the Ganga...." Note No. F.6(8)-Pa. III/51, dated May 22, 1953, from the Ministry of External Affairs, Government of India, to the High Commission for Pakistan in India.

"The Government of Pakistan note with satisfaction that the Government of India appreciate the desirability of co-operative development by India and Pakistan of the water resources of the Ganges. The Government of Pakistan agree that such co-operation must be on a reciprocal basis." Note No. F.62(20) P/54.2944, dated Sept. 14, 1954, from the High Commission for Pakistan in India to the Ministry of External Affairs, Government of India.

In 1956 the two states initiated a program for cooperation in communicating flood warnings. See Olmstead (ed.), op. cit. supra n. 2 at 49-50.

[44] Indus Waters Treaty, 1960, signed at Karachi, Pakistan, September 19, 1960. 55 Amer. Jour. Intl. Law 797 (1961).

[45] The Secretary-General of the United Nations was represented by Mr. Marc Schreiber of the United Nations Legal Department. This is an interesting example of the constructive role which can be played by international organizations in facilitating cooperative development of international rivers.

[46] See Sevian, "Economic Utilization and Development of the Water Resources of the Euphrates and Tigris," IV Proceedings, United Nations Conference on the Conservation and Utilization of Resources, E/Conf. 7/7 (1951), at 148-56; The Economic Development of Iraq, Report of a Mission Organized by the International Bank for Reconstruction and Development at the Request of the Government of Iraq (1952). By a treaty of 1946 Turkey and Iraq agreed on exchange of information about their common waters and Turkey accepted in principle the construction of works on its territory for the benefit of Iraq, to be built at Iraq's expense. Treaty of Friendship and Neighbourly Relations Between Iraq and Turkey, Protocol No. 1 Relative to the Regulation of the Waters of the Tigris and Euphrates and Their Tributaries, 1946, 37 U.N. Treaty Series 281. Aside from this agreement, the Tigris and Euphrates present generally a picture of unilateral developments by the several riparian states which sooner or later are bound to come into conflict unless a comprehensive plan is agreed upon.

[47] See Principles... American Branch Committee 92-95; Hirsch, "From the Indus to the Jordan: Characteristics of Middle East International River Disputes," 71 Polit. Sci. Quart. 203 (1956). In 1951 an international commission, acting as good officer, recommended a settlement based on protection of existing uses in both countries. Differences still exist as to the extent of such uses and the quantities of water necessary to supply them. The history of the Helmand negotiations, in which perhaps the chief obstacle to agreement has been the inadequacy of mutually accepted factual data, is an excellent illustration of the need for impartial technical studies which would remove this obstacle.

[48] See Hirsch, "Utilization of International Rivers in the Middle East: A Study of Conventional International Law," 50 Amer. Jour. Intl. Law 81 (1956); Smith, "The Waters of the Jordan: A Problem of International Water Control," 25 International Affairs 415 (1949). The history of the running dispute between Israel and the Arab states, and particularly their acrimonious exchanges in the United Nations, demonstrate the extreme difficulty of finding a solution to waters problems once the issues have become confused by the intrusion of extraneous political factors.

[49] See Batstone, op. cit. supra n. 12 at 551; Olmstead, op. cit. supra n. 2 at 167, 172-73, 175, 180-82. More than 70 percent of the total flow of the Nile (6/7, according to Ethiopia; 5/7, according to Egypt) originates in Ethiopia, which has not as yet undertaken any developments but has intimated its intention to do so in the future. The 1959 Sudan-Egypt treaty

provides that the two parties will form a common front in the event of a claim by another riparian state to a share of the waters. See Badr, *op. cit. supra* n. 37 at 22.

[50]See, e.g., I Report of the Indus (Rau) Commission, 1942, at 10 (1950).

[51]"International practice reflects the conviction that States must strive to reach... agreements [on waters questions]; there would thus be an obligation to accept in good faith all the negotiations and contacts which must, by a wide comparison of interests and by reciprocal good will, put them in the best position to conclude agreements." Affaire du Lac Lanoux, Sentence du Tribunal Arbitral (1957) (unofficial transl.).

Principle VI adopted by the ILA at Dubrovnik reads: "A state, which proposes new work (construction, diversion, etc.) or change of previously existing use of the water which might affect utilization of the water by another state must first consult with the other state. In case agreement is not reached through such consultation, the states concerned should seek the advice of a technical commission; and if this does not lead to agreement, resort should be had to arbitration." Principles... Dubrovnik 2.

The IDI Resolution provides: "In case objection is made, the States will enter into negotiations with a view to reaching an agreement within a reasonable time" (Article 6).

Recommendation 1 of the ILA New York resolution reads in part: "In the eventuality of a failure of... consultation to produce agreement within a reasonable time, the parties should seek a solution in accordance with the principles and procedures (other than consultation) set out in the Charter of the United Nations and the procedures envisaged in Article 33 thereof." The most important of the procedures envisaged in Article 33 are mediation (conciliation) and arbitration or adjudication. The Hamburg resolution (1960) of the ILA, adopted "in furtherance of" New York recommendation 1, begins with a recognition of "the importance of resolving by peaceful means differences between co-riparian States as regards their rights in respect of the waters of a drainage basin." It goes on to set out detailed provisions for consultation, conciliation and arbitration, and recommends that the parties avail themselves of these procedures until a solution is reached.

[52]This policy has been adopted by the United States and by the International Bank for Reconstruction and Development. (The United States Export-Import Bank loan to Afghanistan for a storage and diversion project on the Helmand was made before the adoption of this policy.) The desire to refrain from subsidizing one side in a waters controversy was at least one of the reasons for the United States' withdrawal in 1956 of its offer to finance the Aswan High Dam. Batstone, *op. cit. supra* n. 12 at 523; Dougherty, "The Aswan Decision in Perspective," Polit. Sci. Quart. 21, 24-25 (1959).

[53]See, e.g., Affaire du Lac Lanoux, Sentence du Tribunal Arbitral 59 (1957): "The State exposed to the repercussions of works undertaken by a neighboring State is the sole judge of its own interests, and if the latter has not taken the initiative, the right of the former to exact notification of works or concessions which are the object of a project could not be denied" (unofficial transl.). Most waters treaties contain provisions requiring, either explicitly or by necessary implication, the exchange of data. See, e.g., the Austro-Yugoslav treaties discussed in n. 41 *supra;* the Indus Waters Treaty of 1960, n. 44 *supra;* and the Columbia River Basin agreement, n. 13 *supra*. The exchange-of-information provisions are analyzed by Paunovic, "The Uses of International Rivers," in Principles... Dubrovnik 1, 4-5.

[54]See n. 47 *supra*. Among the treaties providing for joint inspection by representatives of the parties, or by representatives of one party on the territory of another, are the Convention of Geneva Relating to the Development of Hydraulic Power Affecting More than One State, 1923, 36 League of Nations Treaty Series 77 (Art. 2); Boundary Treaty of Clèves between Prussia and the Netherlands, 1816, 3 Martens, Nouveau Receuil des Traités 45 (Arts. 29, 33); Treaty Concerning the Administration of Frontier Waterways between Germany and Lithuania, 1928, 89 League of Nations Treaty Series 353 (Arts. 14, 18); Nile Waters Agreement between Great Britain and Egypt, 1929, 21 Martens, Nouveau Receuil des Traités (3d Ser.) 97 (Para. 4); Treaty between Iraq and Turkey, Protocol No. 1 Relative to the Regulation of the Waters of the Tigris and Euphrates and of Their Tributaries, 1946, 37 U.N. Treaty Series 281; the Indus Waters Treaty of 1960, see footnote 44. See also Kenworthy, "Joint Development of International Waters," 54 Amer. Jour. Intl. Law 592, 593-96 (1960).

[55]For instance, in the Lake Lanoux negotiations between France and Spain, France made a series of proposals for modifying its project so as to ensure against any injury to Spanish interests. These proposals had greatly narrowed the scope of the dispute by the time it was

submitted to arbitration. See Laylin and Bianchi, "The Role of Adjudication in International River Disputes: The Lake Lanoux Case," 53 Amer. Jour. Intl. Law 30 at 37-39 (1959).

[56] Affaire du Lac Lanoux, n. 53 *supra*. The Declaration of Montevideo on the uses of international rivers, issued by the Seventh International Conference of American States in 1933, expressed in its fundamental principles the views of the signatory states as to customary international law apart from treaties. Article 7 of the Declaration reads: "The works which a State plans to perform in international waters shall be previously announced to the other riparian or co-jurisdictional States. The announcement shall be accompanied by the necessary technical documentation in order that the other interested States may judge the scope of such works, and by the name of the technical expert or experts who are to deal, if necessary, with the international side of the matter." Principles...Buenos Aires 54.

Article 5 of the IDI Resolution provides that: "works or utilizations referred to in the preceding article [that is, "works or utilizations... which seriously affect the possibilities of utilization of the same waters by other States"] may not be undertaken except after prior notice to interested States." This and similar formulations, such as Principle III of the American Branch (ILA) statement of 1958, Proceedings and Committee Reports of the American Branch of the International Law Association 1957-1958, at 101, necessarily imply that the data accompanying the notice shall be adequate to enable the party receiving it to assess the magnitude and effect of the project in question. See also State Department Memorandum at 90, Paragraph 3(a).

The American Branch statement goes further and requires exchange of information apart from new projects: "A riparian may not unreasonably withhold from a co-riparian, or refuse to give it access to, data relevant to the determination or observance of their respective rights and duties under the existing regime of the system of international waters, or data with respect to any proposed change in that regime." Principle V, Proceedings, *supra*, at 102. See also Recommendation 3 adopted by the International Law Association at New York in 1958, International Law Association, Report of the Forty-Eighth Conference, New York 100 (1958).

[57] An outstanding case of settlement of a waters dispute with the aid of a good officer is the Indus Basin Dispute. Mediation by the International Bank for Reconstruction and Development was accepted by India and Pakistan in 1951, and the Bank participated in all the subsequent negotiations leading up to the conclusion of the Indus Waters Treaty, 1960. Many of the treaties providing for arbitration or other third-party settlement of disputes visualize a prior reference to a conciliation commission. See, e.g., Treaty of Friendship, Conciliation and Judicial Settlement between Austria and Italy, 1930, 105 League of Nations Treaty Series 97.

[58] See United Nations, Department of Economic and Social Affairs, Integrated River Basin Development: Report by a Panel of Experts, E/3066 (1958); Kenworthy, "Joint Development of International Waters," 54 Amer. Jour. Intl. Law 592 (1960). Principle VIII of the resolution adopted by the ILA in 1956 states: "So far as possible, riparian states should join with each other to make full utilization of the waters of a river, both from the viewpoint of the river basin as an integrated whole, and from the viewpoint of the widest variety of uses of the water, so as to assure the greatest benefit to all." Principles... Dubrovnik 2.

[59] A very close cooperation sometimes involves the construction of works by one state on the territory of another. Agreements providing for such construction include a treaty of 1926 between Argentina and Paraguay, described in Olmstead, *op. cit. supra* n. 2 at 29; and the Nile Waters Agreement between Great Britain and Egypt, 1929, 21 Martens, Nouveau Receuil des Traités (3d ser.) 97. This type of agreement is visualized in Article 3 of the Geneva Convention, 36 League of Nations Treaty Series 77.

[60] There are a great many such commissions presently in existence on both the international and interstate or interprovincial levels. For a general discussion, see Smith, The Economic Uses of International Rivers (1931), Chapter V, "The Function of International Commissions," at 120-35. Contemporary waters treaties almost invariably provide for a joint commission to supervise their implementation. For a discussion of interstate and interprovincial commissions in the United States, Argentina, Australia and India, see Cano, *op. cit. supra* n. 1 at 73, 83-85. For a detailed history of the exercise of the judicial functions of the Canadian-United States commission, see Bloomfield and Fitzgerald, Boundary Waters Problems of Canada and the United States (1958).

[61] E.g., the Columbia River Basin agreement. See n. 13 *supra*.

WATER RESOURCE DEVELOPMENT

[62] This view was proposed as one of two alternatives by Herbert W. Briggs, one of the members of the Ninth Commission of the Institut de Droit International. See IDI Preliminary Report 149.

[63] This is the procedural equivalent of the substantive "veto power" discussed in the fourth paragraph of n. 9 *supra*. See also question IX proposed by Andrassy, IDI Preliminary Report at 138, and the answers thereto. See also Article I(3) of the Inter-American Bar Association resolution, in Principles . . . Buenos Aires 5.

[64] State Department Memorandum at 90-91.

[65] An implicit corollary of the last paragraph is, of course, that if the protesting state is willing to submit the question to arbitration or adjudication but the state proposing the works refuses, then the latter remains under an obligation *not* to proceed with the works in question.

For similar formulations see Proceedings and Committee Reports of the American Branch of the International Law Association 1957-1958, 101 (Principle III): International Law Association, Report of the Forty-Eighth Conference, New York 100 (1958) (Recommendation 1); Declaration of Montevideo, 1933, in Principles . . . Buenos Aires 53-54 (Paragraphs 2, 3, 7, 8, 9 and 10).

The American Bar Association's Section of International and Comparative Law has adopted the same principle with reference to the United States. ABA, Section of International and Comparative Law, 1959 Proceedings 127, 128. This resolution was adopted in connection with a bill proposed in Congress which would have authorized unilateral diversion of international waters over the protest of Canada, the co-riparian state. The ABA Section's resolution was made a part of the Senate hearings on the legislation, Hearings before a Subcommittee of the Committee on Public Works, U.S. Senate, 86th Cong., 1st Sess., on H.R. 1 and S. 308, at 317. (1959). The bill, though reported favorably by the Committee on Public Works, was referred by the Senate to its Committee on Foreign Relations. It was not passed. Similar proposed legislation was twice before vetoed by President Eisenhower on the ground, *inter alia*, of Canada's interest. See ABA, *op. cit. supra* at 129.

[66] Article 2(4) of the Charter provides that "All Members shall refrain in their international relations from the threat or use of force against the territorial integrity or political independence of any state, or in any other manner inconsistent with the Purposes of the United Nations."

Article 33(1) provides that "The parties to any dispute, the continuance of which is likely to endanger the maintenance of international peace and security, shall, first of all, seek a solution by negotiation, enquiry, mediation, conciliation, arbitration, judicial settlement, resort to regional agencies or arrangements, or other peaceful means of their own choice."

The Security Council affirmed in its resolution of July 19, 1960 on Cuba's complaint, adopted by a vote of 9 to 0 with two abstentions (Poland and the Soviet Union), "that it is the obligation of all Members of the United Nations to settle their international disputes by negotiation and other peaceful means in such a manner that international peace and security and justice are not endangered" (U.N. Doc. S/4395).

Unilateral action which is likely to endanger the peace is, of course, forbidden by Article 33. But in the case of international waters, such action, if a co-riparian state protests, is also an act of state force against the sovereign territorial rights of that state, and therefore violates Article 2(4). Professor Andrassy reaches the same conclusion; see IDI Preliminary Report, *op. cit. supra* n. 63 at 70-75.

In the United Nations discussions regarding the definition of agression, the Lebanese delegate criticized one proposed draft on the ground that it would not include a situation where one state altered the course of an international river "so that the neighboring country suffered hunger and thirst . . . . " Gen. Ass. 6th Sess. 6th Comm. 202 (1952); see also Kelsen, Collective Security Under International Law 64 (1957); United Nations, Report of the Secretary-General: Question of the Definition of Aggression, paras. 328-29, U.N. Doc. A/2211.

David Lilienthal, after visiting an area in Pakistan from which India had temporarily withheld irrigation supplies, wrote of the similarity between such action and military attack: "Pakistan includes some of the most productive food-growing lands in the world in Western Punjab (the Kipling country) and the Sind. But without *water for irrigation* this would be desert, 20,000,000 acres would dry up in a week, tens of millions would starve. No army, with bombs and shellfire, could devastate a land as thoroughly_as Pakistan could be devastated by the simple expedient of India's permanently shutting off the sources of water that keep the fields and the people of Pakistan alive." Lilienthal, "Another Korea in the Making?" *Collier's*, Aug. 4, 1951, at 58.

It is interesting to note that diversion of waters on which populations depend has been used as a means of military aggression, e.g., in the siege of Gloucester by royalist troops in 1643, Wedgwood, The King's War 1641-47, at 245 (1958), and in Cortes' assault on Mexico City in 1521, Castillo, The Discovery and Conquest of Mexico 398-99 (1956).

In the Lauca River controversy between Bolivia and Chile, involving diversions by Chile from a river which flows into Bolivia, the latter has contended that Chile's action constituted "aggression." Chile has not disagreed with any of the principles stated in this chapter, but rather contends that it has observed them. The dispute was debated at length in May, 1962, in the Council of the Organization of American States, which on May 24 adopted a resolution calling on the parties to attempt to resolve the dispute by the peaceful means enumerated in the Inter-American Treaty for Reciprocal Assistance of 1947. Bolivia chose mediation but Chile declined that means, arguing that the issues were legal and should be submitted to arbitration or to the International Court of Justice.

[67] See n. 60 *supra;* see also McDougal and Feliciano, "International Coercion and World Public Order: The General Principles of the Law of War," 67 Yale Law Jour. 771 (1958).

[68] These commitments are listed and described in Clagett, "Survey of Agreements Providing for Third-Party Resolution of International Waters Disputes," 55 Amer. Jour. Intl. Law 645 (1961).

The countries which are known to have made such commitments are: Afghanistan, Albania, Argentina, Australia, Austria, Belgium, Bolivia, Brazil, Bulgaria, Burma, Cambodia, Canada, Chile, Colombia, Costa Rica, Czechoslovakia, Denmark, Dominican Republic, Ecuador, Egypt, El Salvador, Ethiopia, Finland, France, Germany, Ghana, Great Britain, Greece, Guatemala, Haiti, Honduras, Hungary, India, Iran, Iraq, Italy, Jordan, Laos, Liechtenstein, Luxembourg, Mexico, Netherlands, Nicaragua, Norway, Pakistan, Panama, Paraguay, Peru, Poland, Portugal, Rumania, Saudi Arabia, Spain, Sweden, Switzerland, Syria, Thailand, Turkey, United States of America, Union of South Africa, Union of Soviet Socialist Republics, Uruguay, Venezuela, Viet Nam, Yemen, Yugoslavia. There are three common forms in which such commitments are made: (1) arbitration provisions in a waters treaty covering disputes arising under the treaty; (2) general arbitration treaties the terms of which would cover some or all waters disputes; and (3) reciprocal acceptances of the compulsory jurisdiction of the International Court of Justice. However, no state has been included in the above list solely on the basis of an acceptance of the jurisdiction of the ICJ which is limited by a self-judging ("Connally") reservation.

[69] Bhutan, China, Guinea, Indonesia, Ireland, Israel, Korea, Liberia, Libya, Malaya, Mongolia, Morocco, Nepal, Sudan. Most of these are relatively new states; some of them may be bound by commitments undertaken by their predecessor states; most of them are not riparian to any significant international watercourse. Liberia and the Sudan are committed, but subject to self-judging reservations, to submit waters disputes with Great Britain to the ICJ. See Clagett, *op. cit. supra* n. 68.

States which have come into existence since 1959 have not been included in the lists in this and the preceding footnote because of the still formulative character of their treaty arrangements.

[70] E.g., Treaty of Peace, Friendship and Arbitration between the Dominican Republic and Haiti, 1929, 105 League of Nations Treaty Series 215 (Article 9; waters provisions, Article 10).

[71]*Accord,* Simpson and Fox, International Arbitration: Law and Practice 162 (1959).

[72] For expressions of this fear, see Scott, "Kansas v. Colorado Revisited," 52 Amer. Jour. Intl. Law 432, 448 (1958); Cohen, "Some Legal and Policy Aspects of the Columbia River Dispute," 36 Canadian Bar Review 25 (1958).

[73] Scott, *op. cit. supra* n. 72 at 454. Berber, Rivers in International Law 262-66 (1959); "K.K.R.," "The Problem of the Indus and Its Tributaries: An Alternative View," The World Today, June 1958, at 266, 274-75.

[74] The deliberations of the United States Senate regarding ratification of the 1944 waters treaty with Mexico, settling the outstanding questions regarding the Rio Grande and Colorado, provide a beautiful illustration of how a commitment to arbitrate furnishes an inducement to agree. During the hearings a member of the State Department Legal Adviser's office was questioned closely as to whether, if the treaty were not ratified, Mexico could compel the United States to submit the question of reasonable and equitable shares to arbitration. The answer was in the affirmative, since the two states were parties to a general arbitra-

tion treaty, the Inter-American Arbitration Treaty of 1929, 49 Stat. 3153. It is clear that in the minds of at least some senators the existence of the obligation to arbitrate was a principal reason for consenting to ratify the treaty. See Hearings before the Senate Committee on Foreign Relations on Treaty with Mexico Relating to the Utilization of Waters of Certain Rivers, 79th Cong., 1st Sess., pt. 5, at 1738-52 (1945).

For a discussion of the part played by the existence of a commitment to arbitrate in bringing the parties closer together in the Lake Lanoux dispute between France and Spain, see Laylin and Bianchi, *op. cit. supra* n. 25 at 30 (1959).

Also relevant are certain aspects of the discussions between states and provinces of pre-Partition India regarding apportionment of the waters of the Indus system of rivers. The principles of law declared by the Indus (Rau) Commission in 1942 were accepted by all the parties in question and became the basis for negotiations. The resulting agreement, which by 1947 had been completed except for certain outstanding financial questions, failed to come into effect only because of the consequences of Partition of the Indian sub-continent. Principles... American Branch Committee 82-83. This is an example of a case in which knowledge of legal rights and the availability of an appeal to a tribunal helped the parties in reaching an agreement. For a suggestion that knowledge of legal rights hinders agreement, see Scott, *op. cit. supra* n. 72 at 454 (1958).

It is interesting to note the fortunes of arbitration and adjudication in the post-Partition Indus dispute between India and Pakistan. In a letter of August 23, 1950, Pakistan "request[ed] the Government of India to accept the jurisdiction of the International Court of Justice to decide on the application of either party any issue arising out of the dispute respecting the apportionment of the waters common to India and Pakistan" in the Indus Basin. India declined this proposal, but in a letter of Sept. 15, 1950, made a counter-proposal that the dispute be arbitrated by an *ad hoc* tribunal consisting of two judges appointed by each country. Pakistan indicated a willingness to accept this proposal if India would agree to provide for some form of third-party determination of questions on which the *ad hoc* tribunal might be deadlocked. In a note dated Nov. 24, 1950, India declined to commit itself to this. The original Pakistan offer was renewed on several occasions, e.g., by a letter dated August 29/30, 1958. The Indus Waters Treaty, 1960, incorporates provisions for impartial and binding resolution of all differences or disputes arising under the treaty.

[75] This is the usual practice of the United States Supreme Court.

[76] See n. 55 *supra*. *Accord*, Bourne, *op. cit. supra* n. 9 at 471 (1959).

[77] The United States Supreme Court has, so far, confined itself to enjoining new uses or works which would interfere with existing uses and to establishing priorities among existing uses. See, e.g., Kansas v. Colorado, 206 U.S. 46 (1906); New Jersey v. New York, 283 U.S. 336, 347 (1930); Colorado v. Kansas, 320 U.S. 383 (1943). The Court has expressly left open, however, the question whether a state can have present rights in unappropriated water which would warrant allocation or injunction against interference. The Court raised without deciding the question in Arizona v. California, 298 U.S. 558, 567 (1956): "A justiciable controversy is presented only if Arizona, as a sovereign state, or her citizens, whom she represents, have present rights in the unappropriated water of the river, or if the privilege to appropriate the water is capable of division and when partitioned may be judicially protected from appropriations by others pending its exercise."

Index

Economics and Public Policy in
Water Resource Development